U.S. MARINES IN VIETNAM

HIGH MOBILITY AND STANDDOWN

1969

by
Charles R. Smith

HISTORY AND MUSEUMS DIVISION
HEADQUARTERS, U.S. MARINE CORPS
WASHINGTON, D.C.

1988

COVER: *Men of the 1st Battalion, 9th Marines wait to board the amphibious transport* Paul Revere *at Da Nang, during the first phase of the withdrawal of American forces from Vietnam.*
Department of Defense Photo (USMC) A800469

HQMC
20 JUN 2002

ERRATUM
to
USMC MARINES IN VIETNAM

HIGH MOBILITY AND STANDDOWN 1969 (SFT)

1. Change the distribution PCN read 19000310300 "vice "19000310200.

DISTRIBUTION: PCN 19000310380

Volumes in the Marine Corps Vietnam Series

Operational Histories Series

U.S. Marines in Vietnam, 1954-1964, The Advisory and Combat Assistance Era, 1977

U.S. Marines in Vietnam, 1965, The Landing and the Buildup, 1978

U.S. Marines in Vietnam, 1966, An Expanding War, 1982

U.S. Marines in Vietnam, 1967, Fighting the North Vietnamese, 1984

U.S. Marines in Vietnam, 1970-1971, Vietnamization and Redeployment, 1986

In Preparation

U.S. Marines in Vietnam, 1968

U.S. Marines in Vietnam, 1971-1973

U.S. Marines in Vietnam, 1973-1975

Functional Histories Series

Chaplains with Marines in Vietnam, 1962-1971, 1985

Marines and Military Law in Vietnam: Trial By Fire, in preparation

Anthology and Bibliography

The Marines in Vietnam, 1954-1973, An Anthology and Annotated Bibliography, 1974, reprinted 1983; revised second edition, 1985

Library of Congress Card No. 77-604776
PCN 19000310300

Foreword

This is the sixth volume in a planned nine-volume operational and chronological series covering the Marine Corps' participation in the Vietnam War. A separate functional series will complement the operational histories. This volume details the change in United States policy for the Vietnam War. After a thorough review, President Richard M. Nixon adopted a policy of seeking to end United States military involvement in Vietnam either through negotiations or, failing that, turning the combat role over to the South Vietnamese. It was this decision that began the Vietnamization of the war in the summer of 1969 and which would soon greatly reduce and then end the Marine Corps' combat role in the war.

The Marines of III Marine Amphibious Force continued the full range of military and pacification activities within I Corps Tactical Zone during this period of transition. Until withdrawn, the 3d Marine Division, employing highly mobile tactics, successfully blunted North Vietnamese Army efforts to reintroduce troops and supplies into Quang Tri Province. The 1st Marine Division, concentrated in Quang Nam Province, continued both mobile offensive and pacification operations to protect the city of Da Nang and surrounding population centers. The 1st Marine Aircraft Wing provided air support to both divisions, as well as other allied units in I Corps, while Force Logistic Command served all major Marine commands.

Although written from the perspective of III MAF and the Marine ground war in I Corps, an attempt has been made to place the Marine role in relation to the overall American effort. The volume also treats the Marine Corps' participation in the advisory effort, the operations of the Seventh Fleet Special Landing Force, and, to a lesser extent, the activities of the 101st Airborne Division (Airmobile), 23d Infantry (Americal) Division, and 1st Brigade, 5th Infantry Division (Mechanized). There are separate chapters on Marine air, artillery, surveillance, and logistics.

The nature of the war facing III MAF during 1969 forced the author to concentrate on major operations. This focus in no way slights those Marines whose combat service involved innumerable patrols, wearying hours of perimeter defense, and long days of providing logistical and administrative support for those in the field. III MAF's combat successes in 1969 came from the combined efforts of all Americans in I Corps.

The author, Charles R. Smith, has been with the History and Museums Division since July 1971. He has published several articles on military history, and is the author of *Marines in the Revolution: A History of the Continental Marines in the American Revolution, 1775-1783* (Washington: Hist&MusDiv, HQMC, 1975). He is a graduate of the University of California, Santa Barbara, and received his master's degree in history from San Diego State University. He served in Vietnam with the 101st Airborne Division (Airmobile) in 1968 and 1969, first as an artilleryman and then as a historian.

E. H. SIMMONS
Brigadier General, U.S. Marine Corps (Ret.)
Director of Marine Corps History and Museums

Preface

U.S. Marines in Vietnam: High Mobility and Standdown, 1969, like its predecessors, is largely based on the holdings of the Marine Corps Historical Center. These holdings include the official unit monthly command chronologies, combat after-action reports, daily message and journal files, files and studies of HQMC staff agencies and those of the Office of the Commandant, and the Oral History, Personal Papers, and Reference Collections of the Center.

The author supplemented these above sources with research in the records of the other Services and pertinent published primary and secondary sources. Although none of the information in this history is classified, some of the documentation on which it is based still carries a restricted or classified designation. More than 200 reviewers, most of whom were participants in the events covered in this volume, read a comment edition of the manuscript. Their comments, where applicable, have been incorporated into the text. A list of those who made substantial comments is included in the appendices. All ranks used in the body of the text are those held by individuals in 1969.

Like the previous volumes in the series, the production of this volume has been a cooperative effort. Members of the Histories Section, History and Museums Division, past and present, have reviewed the draft manuscript. Mrs. Joyce Bonnett, head archivist, and her assistants, aided the author's access to the records of the division and Headquarters Marine Corps staff agencies. Miss Evelyn A. Englander, head librarian, and her assistant, Mrs. Patricia E. Morgan, were very helpful in obtaining needed reference materials, as were members of the Reference Section, headed by Mr. Danny J. Crawford. Mrs. Regina Strother, formerly with the Defense Audio-Visual Agency and now with the History and Museums Division, graciously assisted in the photographic research. Mr. Benis M. Frank, head of the Oral History Section, was equally helpful in not only making his tapes and transcripts available, but also in interviewing a number of key participants and reviewing a copy of the draft manuscript.

Mr. Robert E. Struder, head of the Publications Production Section, adeptly guided the manuscript through the various production phases and assisted the author in partially mastering the intricacies of computer publication. The typesetting of the manuscript was done by Corporal James W. Rodriguez II and Lance Corporal Javier Castro. Mrs. Catherine A. Kerns contributed significantly to the typesetting effort, developed the charts accompanying the text, and cheerfully and professionally provided considerable technical expertise on typesetting procedures. Mr. William S. Hill, the division's graphics specialist, expertly produced the maps and completed the design and layout of the volume. The index was prepared by the author and Mrs. Meredith P. Hartley with the guidance and assistance of Mr. Frank.

The author gives special thanks to Brigadier General Edwin H. Simmons, Director of Marine Corps History and Museums, whose policies guide the Vietnam series; to Deputy Directors for History, Colonel Oliver M. Whipple, Jr., Colonel John G. Miller, and their successor, Colonel James R. Williams, who provided continuing support and guidance; to Mr. Henry I. Shaw, Jr., Chief Historian, who aided the author by giving him the benefit of his considerable experience in writing Marine Corps history, encouragement, advice, prodding when needed, and general editorial direction; and to Mr. Jack Shulimson, Head, Histories Section and Senior Vietnam Historian, for providing advice and guidance, and for editing the final manuscript.

The author is also indebted to his colleagues in the historical offices of the Army, Navy, Air Force, and Joint Chiefs of Staff, who freely exchanged information and made pertinent documents available for examination. The author must express his gratitude also to all those who reviewed the comment edition and provided corrections, personal photographs, and the insights available only to those who took part in the events. To all these individuals and all others connected with this project, the author is indebted and truly grateful. In the end, however, it is the author alone who is responsible for the content of the text, including opinions expressed and any errors in fact.

CHARLES R. SMITH

Table of Contents

Foreword iii
Preface v
Table of Contents vii
Maps, Charts, and Tables xi

PART I THE CONTINUING WAR 1

Chapter 1 Planning the Campaign 2
   I Corps Order of Battle 2
   Strategy: A Reevaluation of Priorities 8
   I Corps Planning 12
Chapter 2 Mountain Warfare 15
   Northern I Corps 15
   Off Balance 16
   From the Cua Viet, South 24
Chapter 3 The Spring Offensive Preempted 27
   Strike into the Da Krong 27
   A Phased Operation 28
   Phase I 31
   Backyard Cleanup 33
Chapter 4 The Raid into Laos 38
   Across the Da Krong 38
   The NVA Retaliates 39
   Ambush Along 922 39
   Heavy Fighting 45
   Back Into Laos 47
   Persistent Problems 47
   Phased Retraction 48
   Laos: Repercussions 51
Chapter 5 The Quang Tri Border Areas 52
   No Change in Tactics 52
   The DMZ Front 52
   Brigade Mauls *27th* 58
   The 9th Battles the *36th* 61
   The Vietnam Salient 62
   Apache Snow 67
   Central DMZ Battles 72
   Eastern Quang Tri and Thua Thien 76

PART II SOUTHERN I CORPS BATTLEGROUND 79

Chapter 6 Destruction of Base Area 112 80
   Defense of Da Nang 80
   Attack into 112 82

    "A Little Urban Renewal"... 95
    Americal's TAOI... 101
Chapter 7 The Battle for Quang Nam Continues........................ 103
    Rockets Equal Operations.. 103
    Operation Oklahoma Hills... 103
    5th Marines and the Arizona... 116
    Securing the Southern and Northern Approaches...................... 121
    Americal Battleground... 125

PART III THE THIRD'S FINAL MONTHS............................. 127

Chapter 8 Redeployment: The First Phase............................. 128
    Keystone Eagle.. 128
    "A Turning Point"... 133
Chapter 9 "A Strange War Indeed"................................... 138
    Company Patrol Operations.. 138
    Idaho Canyon.. 138
    "A Significant Step".. 149
    Specter of Anarchy.. 154
Chapter 10 "A Difficult Phase"..................................... 159
    Maintaining a Protective Barrier.................................... 159
    "You Shouldered Us"... 165
    The Brigade Takes Over.. 170

PART IV QUANG NAM: THE YEAR'S FINAL BATTLES................... 173

Chapter 11 Go Noi and the Arizona.................................. 174
    Vital Area Security... 174
    Pipestone Canyon: The Destruction of Go Noi Island.................. 174
    1st Marines: Protecting the Southern Flank.......................... 187
    The Arizona... 190
Chapter 12 Da Nang and the Que Son Valley.......................... 201
    The 7th Marines... 201
    26th Marines: Protecting the Northern Flank......................... 212
    Quang Tin and Quang Ngai Battleground............................... 215
    Results... 216

PART V SUPPORTING THE TROOPS................................... 219

Chapter 13 Marine Air Operations................................... 220
    1st MAW Organization and Deployment................................. 220
    Single Management: Relations with the Seventh Air Force............. 223
    Upgrading of Aviation Assets.. 226
    I Corps Fixed-Wing Support.. 229
    The Interdiction Campaign... 231
    Air Control... 234
    Helicopter Operations... 236
    Improving Helicopter Support.. 239
    Air Defense... 241
    Accomplishments and Costs... 241
Chapter 14 Artillery and Surveillance.............................. 243

  Artillery Operations..243
  Surveillance and Reconnaissance Activities.......................251
Chapter 15 Supplying III MAF..260
  Force Logistic Command..260
  Naval Support Activity, Da Nang.................................264
  Engineer Support..267
  Motor Transport...270
  Medical Support...272
  Communications..274
  Logistics of Keystone Eagle and Keystone Cardinal...............275

PART VI UNIQUE CONTRIBUTIONS...279

Chapter 16 Pacification...280
  The National Perspective..280
  Pacification Planning In I Corps................................283
  Line Unit Pacification..285
  Civic Action..287
  The Grass Roots Campaign..288
  Results...294
Chapter 17 Special Landing Force Operations...........................297
  The Strategic Reserve...297
  Organization and Operations.....................................298
  The Fleet's Contingency Force...................................310
Chapter 18 The Advisory Effort and Other Activities...................311
  Marine Advisors and the Vietnamese Marine Corps.................311
  1st Air and Naval Gunfire Liaison Company (ANGLICO).............316
  U.S. Marines on the MACV Staff..................................317
  Embassy Guard Marines...318
Chapter 19 1969: An Overview..319

NOTES...323

APPENDICES
  A. Marine Command and Staff List, January-December 1969.........336
  B. Glossary of Terms and Abbreviations..........................349
  C. Chronology of Significant Events, January-December 1969......354
  D. Medal of Honor Citations, 1969...............................358
  E. List of Reviewers..374
  F. Distribution of Personnel, Fleet Marine Force Pacific (31 January 1969)....376
  G. Distribution of Personnel, Fleet Marine Force Pacific (8 December 1969)...381

INDEX...386

Maps, Charts, and Tables

Map, Reference Map, I Corps Tactical Zone..................................... xii
Map, Allied Commands in I Corps, January 1969........................... 4
Chart, III MAF Command Relationships..................................... 6
Map, Enemy Order of Battle, Northern ICTZ, January 1969.............. 16
Map, 3d Marine Division Outposts and Operational Areas, January 1969....... 21

Map, Assault into the Da Krong Valley, 22-25 January 1969.................. 32
Map, 9th Marines Movement into Base Area 611............................ 40
Map, Movements and Objectives of the 3d and 4th Marines, March-July 1969... 58
Map, Operation Maine Crag, 15 March-2 May 1969........................ 65
Map, Operations of the 9th Marines, May-August 1969...................... 73

Map, Enemy Order of Battle, Southern ICTZ, January 1969................. 82
Map, Assault on Base Area 112... 90
Map, Enemy Ground and Rocket Attacks Against Da Nang, February 1969..... 98
Map, 7th Marines' Operation Oklahoma Hills, 31 March-29 May 1969......... 109
Table, The MACV List: Composition of Keystone Eagle....................... 135

Map, Denial Operations of the 3d Marines, July-August 1969................ 140
Map, 3d Marine Division Operations, July-September 1969.................. 144
Table, The MACV List: Composition of Keystone Cardinal.................... 167
Map, Operation Pipestone Canyon: Attack on Go Noi......................... 180
Map, Cordon of Tay Bang An, 15-17 July 1969................................ 184

Map, Scheme of Maneuver, 5th and 7th Marines, July-December 1969........ 192
Map, Hiep Duc Valley Counterattack, 21-26 August 1969..................... 208
Map, Hiep Duc Valley Counterattack, 26-29 August 1969..................... 208
Map, 1st Marine Aircraft Wing Locations, 1969................................ 222
Chart, III MAF Logistic Command Relationships and Facilities, 31 March 1969... 261

Chart, Special Landing Force Command Relationships........................ 298
Chart, Strength, Arms, and Equipment of a Typical Special Landing Force...... 299
Map, Special Landing Force Operations, 1969.................................. 304
Chart, Marine Advisory Unit, 1969... 312

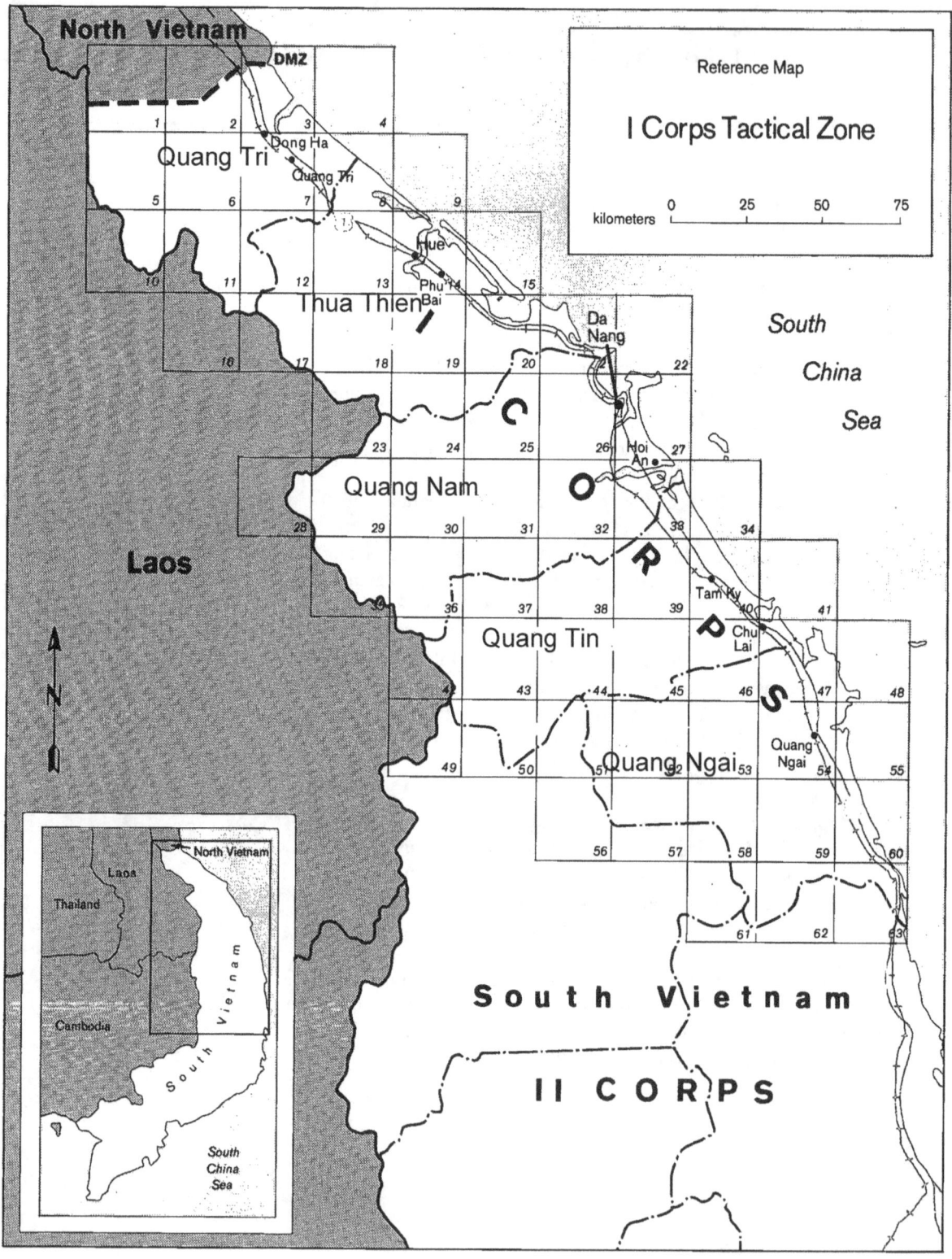

PART I
THE CONTINUING WAR

CHAPTER 1
Planning the Campaign

I Corps Order of Battle — Strategy: A Reevaluation of Priorities — I Corps Planning

I Corps Order of Battle

Responsibility for the defense of the Republic of Vietnam's five northernmost provinces of Quang Tri, Thua Thien, Quang Nam, Quang Tin, and Quang Ngai in January 1969 rested with III Marine Amphibious Force (III MAF). Commanded by Lieutenant General Robert E. Cushman, Jr., III MAF consisted of approximately 81,000 Marines situated at positions throughout the provinces which constituted I Corps Tactical Zone (ICTZ). Major General Charles J. Quilter's 15,500-man 1st Marine Aircraft Wing (1st MAW) controlled more than 500 fixed-wing and rotary aircraft from fields at Chu Lai, Da Nang, Phu Bai, and Quang Tri. Headquartered on Hill 327 southwest of Da Nang, Major General Ormond R. Simpson's 1st Marine Division, 24,000 strong, operated throughout Quang Nam Province. The 21,000-man 3d Marine Division, commanded by Major General Raymond G. Davis and controlled from Dong Ha Combat Base, was responsible for Quang Tri Province. At Da Nang, the 9,500 officers and men of Brigadier General James A. Feeley, Jr.'s Force Logistic Command (FLC) provided the wing and two Marine divisions with combat materiel and maintenance support. Scattered throughout the hundreds of villages and hamlets of the five provinces were the 1,900 officers and men of the Combined Action Program (CAP), under Colonel Edward F. Danowitz, who continued the Marines' ambitious experiment in local security, still hampered somewhat by the residual effects of the enemy's 1968 *Tet* Offensive.

In addition to Marines, III MAF controlled approximately 50,000 United States Army troops. Located in Quang Tri Province, 5,000 officers and men of the 1st Brigade, 5th Infantry Division (Mechanized), commanded by Colonel James M. Gibson, USA, aided in preventing enemy infiltration of the coastal plains. To the south, in Thua Thien Province, the 101st Airborne Division (Airmobile), under Major General Melvin Zais, USA, deployed three brigades totalling 20,000 men in an arc protecting the ancient imperial capital of Hue. These two Army units, which had been shifted to I Corps in 1968, together with the 3d Marine Division, constituted XXIV Corps, commanded by Army Lieutenant General Richard G. Stilwell.* Located at Phu Bai, Stilwell's organization was under the operational control of III MAF. Based at Chu Lai in southern I Corps, the 23,800 Army troops of Major General Charles M. Gettys' 23d Infantry (Americal) Division operated in Quang Tin and Quang Ngai Provinces under the direct control of III MAF. Also under the direct control of General Cushman, in his capacity as Senior U.S. Advisor in I Corps, were the 400 officers and men from all services of the United States Army Advisory Group (USAAG), who provided professional and technical assistance to South Vietnamese military units operating in I Corps Tactical Zone.

As a member of the III MAF staff, Mr. Charles T. Cross, the civilian deputy for Civil Operations and Revolutionary Development Support (CORDS), coordinated the pacification effort in I Corps through his U.S. civilian and military representatives at the province and district level. Directly controlled by MACV, CORDS was created to integrate and direct the country-wide pacification program.

Other U.S. and allied contingents that were neither attached to nor controlled by III MAF also operated within the boundaries of I Corps. Assigned to the U.S. Army Support Command, U.S. Naval Support Activity, 3d Naval Construction Brigade, 45th Army Engineer Group, Task Force Clearwater, and the Air Force's 366th Tactical Fighter Wing were approximately 31,000 U.S. Army, Navy, and Air Force personnel. While controlled by their respective services, these support units cooperated closely with III MAF. Like the other five major allied organizations, the 7,800-man 2d Republic of Korea Marine Brigade, commanded by Brigadier General Dong Ho Lee, which protected an enclave south of Da Nang centered on Hoi An, received operational guidance from III MAF, but was under the direct authority of the commanding general

---

*In order to provide operational direction for the expanded United States military effort in northern I Corps during *Tet*, MACV Forward was established at Phu Bai in early February 1968. On 10 March, the command unit was redesignated Provisional Corps, Vietnam, and on 15 August again redesignated as XXIV Corps.

LtGen Robert E. Cushman, Jr., right, is congratulated by Gen Creighton W. Abrams, Commander, U.S. Military Assistance Command, Vietnam, after being presented a Gold Star in lieu of a second Distinguished Service Medal. As Commanding General, III Marine Amphibious Force since June 1967, Cushman oversaw a doubling of III MAF's strength.

of Korean Forces in Vietnam, whose headquarters was in Saigon.

The Army of the Republic of Vietnam (ARVN) and its paramilitary forces gradually were assuming a much greater share of the fighting in I Corps by 1969. Lieutenant General Hoang Xuan Lam, commanding ICTZ, controlled a force of 34,000 ARVN regulars. Headquartered at Hue, the 17 battalions of Major General Ngo Quang Truong's 1st ARVN Infantry Division pursued enemy forces in Quang Tri and Thua Thien Provinces. In southern I Corps the 2d Division's 12 infantry battalions, commanded by Brigadier General Nguyen Van Toan, fought both enemy regulars and guerrillas throughout Quang Tin and Quang Ngai Provinces. Between the two ARVN infantry divisions, the 51st Infantry and Armored Cavalry Regiments operated in Quang Nam Province. The 1st Ranger Group, normally stationed at Da Nang, acted as corps reserve, while the Vietnamese Air Force's 41st Tactical Wing, also located at Da Nang, provided overall air support.

Reinforcing ARVN regulars were 49,800 troops of the Regional and Popular Forces (RF and PF), and 8,500 trained members of the part-time People's Self-

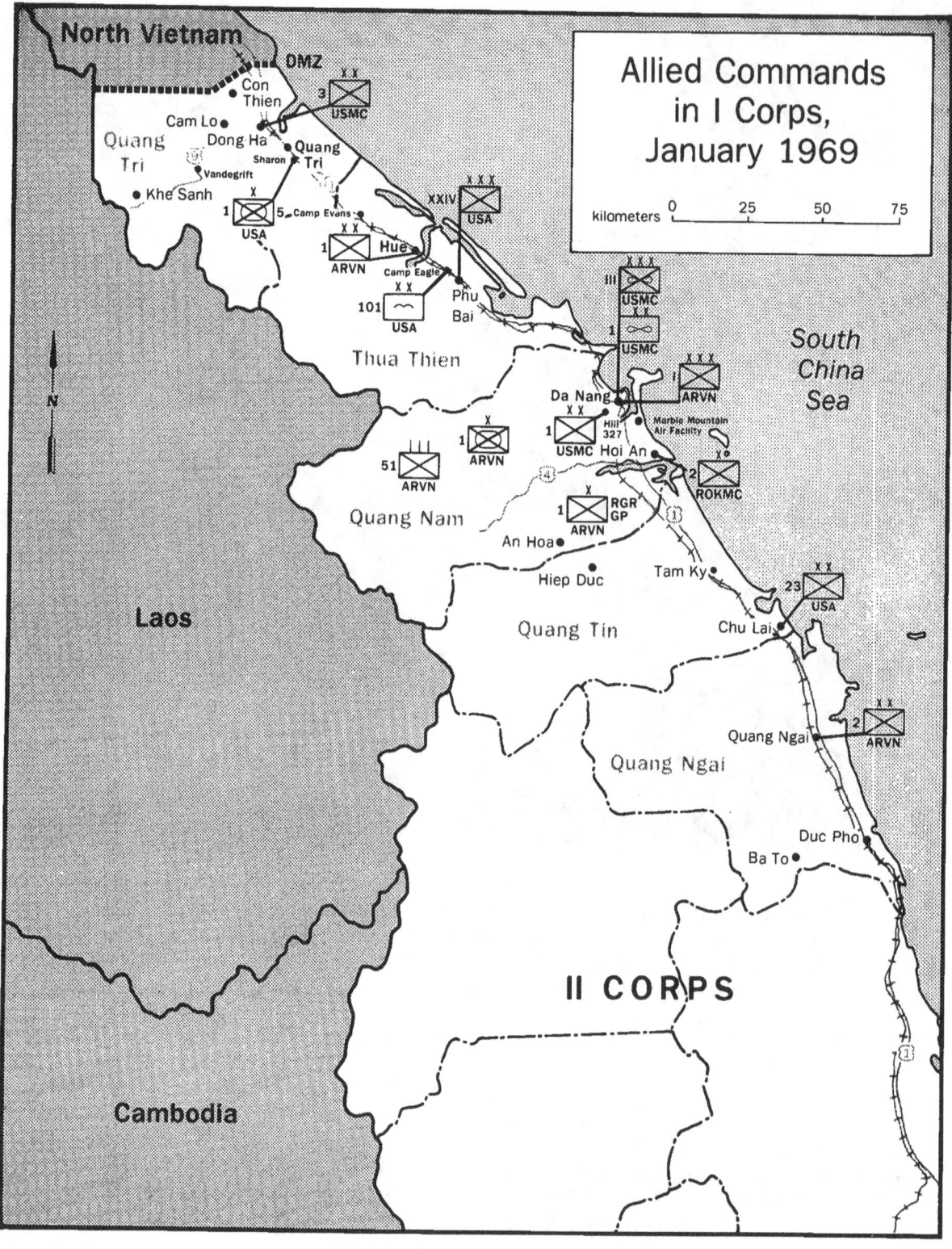

Defense Force (PSDF)—a paramilitary organization recruited, trained, and stationed in local areas. Among other Vietnamese units available to combat small groups of guerrilla infiltrators and root out members of the local Viet Cong Infrastructure (VCI), were the 9,000-man National Police, and the National Police Field Force with a strength of 2,500. In addition, there were 6,200 men of the Civilian Irregular Defense Group (CIDG), composed of Montagnard and Nung tribesmen, Cambodians, and Vietnamese, recruited and trained by the South Vietnamese Special Forces and advised by the U.S. Army's 5th Special Forces Group (Airborne), which occupied nine mountain camps rimming the lowlands. Their task was to collect intelligence on enemy activities and attempt to block enemy infiltration routes into the heavily populated coastal plains.[1]

From a modern complex of air-conditioned buildings on the banks of the Song Han at Da Nang, General Cushman coordinated the activities of this diverse group of forces. Like his predecessor, Lieutenant General Lewis W. Walt, he functioned within a complex chain of command. III Marine Amphibious Force was under the operational control of the Commander, U.S. Military Assistance Command, Vietnam, General Creighton W. Abrams; but with respect to administrative matters affecting his Marines, General Cushman reported directly to Lieutenant General Henry W. Buse, Jr., Commanding General, Fleet Marine Force, Pacific (FMFPac), in Hawaii. As commanding general of III MAF, General Cushman not only directed the operations of all United States combat units in I Corps, but also provided guidance to the commander of the Korean Marine Brigade and others as I Corps Coordinator for United States and Free World Military Assistance Forces and, as Senior U.S. Advisor for I Corps, coordinated the activities of Lieutenant General Lam's ARVN units with those of his own.

General Cushman was well prepared when he assumed the post of top Leatherneck in Vietnam. A graduate of the Naval Academy (Class of 1935) and recipient of the Navy Cross as a battalion commander during the recapture of Guam, Cushman served four years on Vice President Richard M. Nixon's staff as Assistant for National Security Affairs. In addition he commanded the 3d Marine Division in 1961, and later while serving as Commanding General, Marine Corps Base, Camp Pendleton, headed both the 4th Marine Division Headquarters nucleus, and the newly organized 5th Marine Division. In April 1967, he was appointed Deputy Commander, III Marine Amphibious Force. Three months later he assumed the duty of Commanding General, III MAF, replacing Lieutenant General Walt.

During his tenure, General Cushman managed III

LtGen Hoang Xuan Lam, left, Commanding General, I Corps; LtGen Richard G. Stilwell, USA, Commanding General, XXIV Corps; and MajGen Ngo Quang Truong, right, Commanding General, 1st ARVN Division, pose with Gen Cao Van Vien, center left, Chairman of the South Vietnamese Joint General Staff during the latter's visit to Phu Bai.

Department of Defense Photo (USA) SC649680

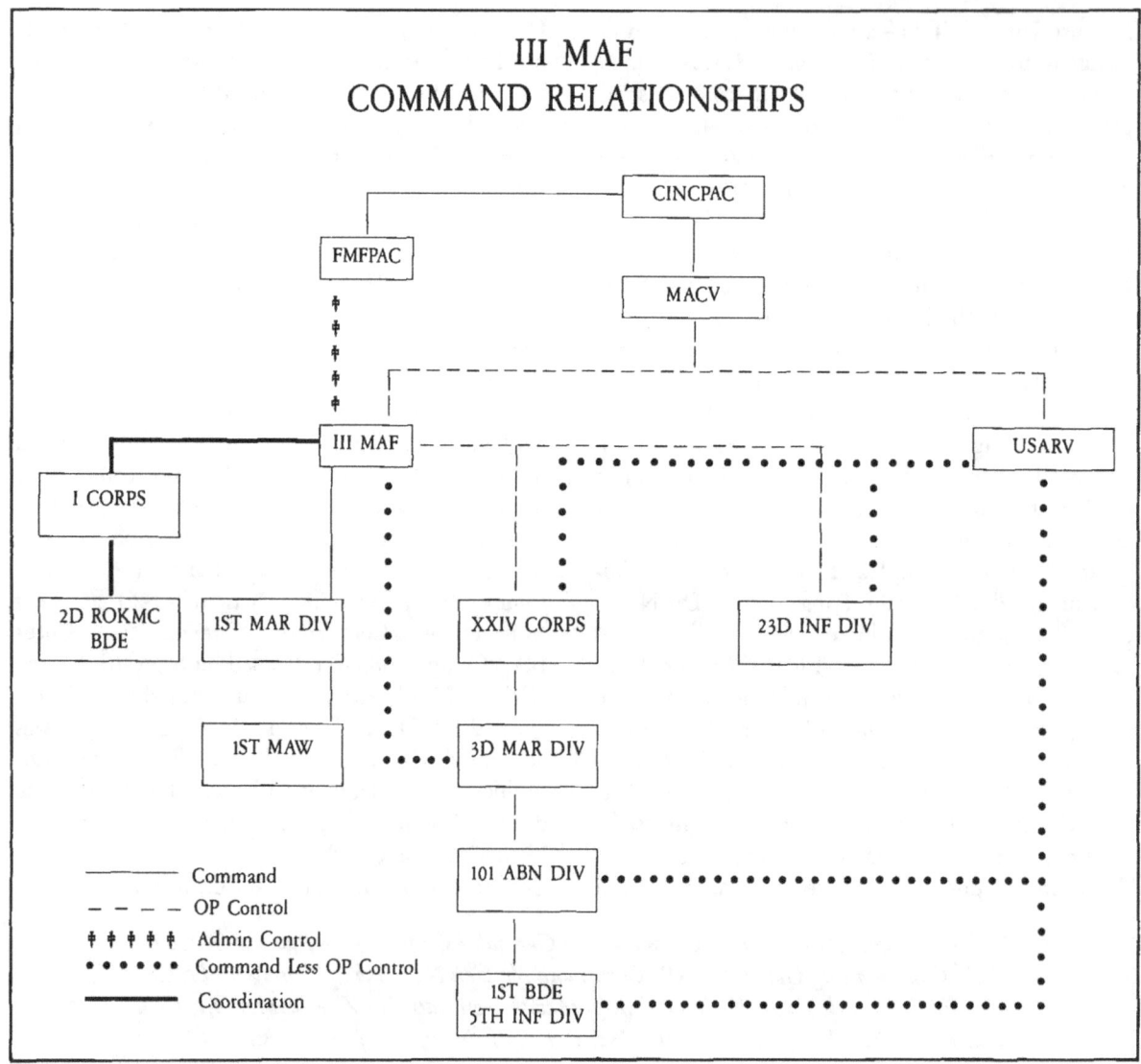

MAF's growth from a force of 97,000 Marine, Navy, and Army personnel to 172,000 by the beginning of 1969. His responsibilities, however, changed little. Like General Walt, Cushman was charged with the defense of I Corps Tactical Zone. Although the smallest in area and population, ICTZ was the most strategically located of the four South Vietnamese military regions due to its proximity to major enemy infiltration and supply routes, and base areas in Laos, the Demilitarized Zone (DMZ), and North Vietnam. Cushman would be replaced in March 1969 by Lieutenant General Herman Nickerson, Jr., a highly decorated veteran of World War II and Korea, and former commanding general of the 1st Marine Division in Vietnam from October 1966 to May 1967.

Opposing American, South Vietnamese, and Korean forces within the boundaries of I Corps, the Demilitarized Zone, and contiguous North Vietnamese and Laotian border regions, were 123 North Vietnamese Army (NVA) and 18 Viet Cong (VC) combat and support battalions composed of close to 89,000 enemy troops. According to allied intelligence estimates of early 1969, 42,700 were North Vietnamese Army regulars while 6,500 were Viet Cong main and local force unit members. In addition, there were approximately 23,500 guerrillas and 16,000 political and quasi-military cadre. Added to these known North Vietnamese and Viet Cong units were additional infantry and support battalions with an estimated strength of 30,000 troops located within striking distance of the corps tactical zone.

Five different headquarters directed enemy operations within the corps tactical zone to varying degrees: the *B-5 Front* which controlled troops along the DMZ;

PLANNING THE CAMPAIGN

Marine Corps Historical Collection

LtGen Herman Nickerson, Jr., right, relieves Gen Cushman as Commanding General, III Marine Amphibious Force in formal ceremonies at Da Nang on 26 March 1969. LtGen Nickerson previously served in Vietnam as Commanding General, 1st Marine Division and Deputy Commanding General, III MAF.

7th Front which directed units within Quang Tri Province; *Tri-Thien-Hue Military Region* which had charge of units in Quang Tri and Thua Thien Provinces; troops attached to the *4th Front* which operated in Quang Nam and Quang Tin Provinces, and the city of Da Nang; and units subordinate to *Military Region 5* which operated in Quang Ngai Province. The five political and military headquarters were thought to receive orders from the Central Office for South Vietnam (COSVN), which in turn was subject to the directives of the Reunification Department of the North Vietnamese Lao Dong Party.*

The dramatic and massive corps-wide attack, concentrated in the northern two provinces, and resultant severe losses during the *Tet* and post-*Tet* Offensives of 1968, forced the enemy to reevaluate his military position as the new year began. As a result, Viet Cong and North Vietnamese Army strategy and tactics shifted from an attempt to win an immediate victory to an attempt to win by prolonging the conflict. Large unit assaults were to be undertaken only if favorable opportunities presented themselves; small unit operations, particularly highly organized hit-and-run or sapper attacks, attacks by fire, harassment, terrorism, and sabotage would be used more extensively. The Communists hoped to inflict troop losses by cutting allied lines of communication, attacking base, rear service, and storage areas while conserving their military strength, defeating the pacification effort, and strengthening their negotiating position at Paris. Through such actions the enemy hoped to maintain an aura of strength and demonstrate to the South Vietnamese populace that its government was incapable of providing security for its people.

The differences in terrain and population north and south of Hai Van Pass, which essentially bisected the corps tactical zone, resulted in markedly different military situations by the end of 1968. In the north, with less than a third of the zone's population, the enemy tended to concentrate regular units in the uninhabited, jungle-covered mountain areas, close to border sanctuaries. The war in the north, then, was one fought between allied regular units and North Vietnamese Army regiments and divisions. It was, to draw an analogy, "like the Army fighting the Japanese in New Guinea—inhospitable jungle, mountainous terrain; the enemy being not little guys in black pajamas, but little guys in well-made uniforms and well-equipped and well-led, and certainly well-motivated."[2]

Faced with a smaller population base and a somewhat weaker infrastructure in the northern two provinces, and pursued at every turn by allied forces, enemy strength by year's end had dwindled to about 29 battalions from a high of 94 in mid-1968. The allied shift to a more mobile posture and the saturation of the remote mountain regions of western Quang Tri and Thua Thien Provinces with numerous patrols, sweeps, and ambushes resulted in the opening of vast areas of hitherto uncontested enemy strongholds, exposing havens and supply caches. Further, it allowed allied forces to exploit the advantages of the helicopter to the fullest, which permitted the massing of regimental or multi-regimental-size units anywhere within the provinces in a matter of hours. Allied operations north of the Hai Van Pass by the end of 1968 had produced a yearly total of almost 40,000 enemy casualties, forcing both North Vietnamese and Viet Cong units to withdraw in an attempt to regroup, reindoctrinate, refit, and prepare for the winter-spring

---

*COSVN, the North Vietnamese forward control headquarters, consisted of a few senior commanders and key staff officers organized as an extremely mobile command post. Thought to be located in Tay Ninh Province, III Corps, near the Cambodian border, COSVN, although targeted by numerous American and South Vietnamese operations, eluded capture throughout the war.

offensive scheduled to begin in the early months of 1969.

The three provinces which constituted southern I Corps posed a contrasting problem to that of the northern provinces. The large population base and stronger enemy infrastructure, built up over many years in the region south of Da Nang and around Quang Ngai, created a continuous threat to the large population centers and allied military complexes, which were, in spite of the best attempts, the targets of frequent enemy ground and rocket attacks. Population and territorial security was progressing, albeit slowly, and by the end of 1968, 69 percent of the civilian population, according to allied statistics, lived within secure villages and hamlets. As enemy strength in the north diminished and engagements became progressively rarer, the enemy was able not only to maintain current force levels in the south, but even to increase them slightly. The 42 enemy battalions in southern I Corps in mid-1968 were increased to about 54 by the end of the year.[3]

Taking advantage of favorable weather and the allied out-of-country bombing pause, which went into effect on 1 November, the enemy renewed efforts to build and repair strategic roads, greatly expanding resupply capabilities within the corps tactical zone and surrounding border areas. With the infusion of men and material from the north, tactical redisposition of forces, and increased determination to carry on the fight, the Communists began the new year as they had begun the previous year—seeking the overthrow of the South Vietnamese Government and the reunification of the two Vietnams under Communist domination. III MAF was ready to ensure that the enemy did not succeed.[4]

Strategy: A Reevaluation of Priorities

In 1969, the sixth year of direct United States combat operations in Southeast Asia, the basic issues of the war remained largely unchanged. The Viet Cong, supported by regular North Vietnamese troops, continued to seek control over South Vietnam by attempting to destroy the existing governmental structure and substituting in its place one of Communist domination. On the other hand, the Government of the Republic of South Vietnam, with allied assistance, sought to check the VC and NVA assaults by building a viable nation immune to Communist overthrow. To accomplish this, the South Vietnamese Government asked for and received United States economic and

Courtesy of Maj Charles D. Melson, USMC
Enemy troops assemble in preparation for battle. The Russian-designed 7.62mm automatic rifle each carries was the standard rifle of North Vietnamese Army soldiers and of guerrillas fighting in South Vietnam.

military support, particularly the manpower, mobility, and firepower of the United States Armed Forces.

In the four years prior to 1969, the United States presence grew rapidly as did its preoccupation with successful military operations. The protection and fortification of South Vietnam's political, economic, and social institutions had been, to a large extent, left to its own government, and improvement and modernization of its combat power had received little emphasis. The advisory effort of the 1950s and early 1960s had become United States direction and prosecution of the war. The realization, both in Washington and Saigon, that the enemy had the capability of launching a major offensive in 1968 led to greater emphasis on meaningful programs, leading to increased population security, a stable government, and a military strategy designed to seize the initiative. These goals, combat operations to defeat the enemy and promote security, increased effort to improve and modernize the Vietnamese Armed Forces, and emphasis on building a viable state, were to receive equal attention.[5] The transition, then, was to turn the course away from "Americanization of the war" toward "Vietnamization of the peace."

PLANNING THE CAMPAIGN

For the enemy, too, 1969 was a year of transition. From 1965, the main thrust of Viet Cong and North Vietnamese strategy was to match the United States troop buildup and endeavor to defeat the allied forces on the battlefield, a strategy that was followed until *Tet* of 1968. The failure of the *Tet* and post-*Tet* Offensives resulted in the reformulation of strategy and tactics. North and South Vietnamese Communist leaders set forth a new, pragmatic strategy that dismissed the possibility of a total victory on the field of battle over United States and South Vietnamese Forces, seeking instead to parlay limited military victories into withdrawal of U.S. troops, establishment of a coalition government, and ultimate Communist political victory in South Vietnam. It was a strategy designed to weaken and exhaust the allies. As a captured enemy document noted: "For each additional day [U.S. troops] stay, they must sustain more casualties. For each additional day they stay, they must spend more money and lose more equipment. Each additional day they stay, the American people will adopt a stronger anti-war attitude, as there is no hope to consolidate the puppet administration and Army."[6]

Tactics, like overall strategy, were to change. North and South Vietnamese Communist leaders championed the more frequent use of small unit tactics in the form of ground attacks or attacks by fire against population centers, economic areas, and allied bases, while still maintaining the option of large unit actions. They emphasized the importance of the political aspects of the war and moved to bolster their political appeal in the South by establishing a formal governmental structure. They prepared for either protracted warfare or a ceasefire, while trying to broaden their options in South Vietnam, and enunciating their major demands at the on-going peace negotiations in Paris. The basic enemy campaign plan for South Vietnam aimed to blunt the allied security program and to foil attempts to Vietnamize the war.

With the first large commitment of United States troops to the war in 1965, U.S. strategy focused on assisting the Government of South Vietnam and its armed forces in defeating Communist subversion and aggression. This strategy stressed military operations, and advisory and financial assistance to aid in creating a secure environment, necessary for the success of national development programs. Further, efforts were made to encourage and assist the South Vietnamese in assuming greater responsibility for the development and maintenance of a free and independent nation.

Various operational concepts to support this strategy were developed by the Joint Chiefs of Staff (JCS) and Commander-in-Chief, Pacific (CinCPac), with primary emphasis on maintaining maximum pressure against the enemy's disruptive and war-making capabilities through three interrelated undertakings. First were the destruction of the Viet Cong main and North Vietnamese Army forces in South Vietnam, forcing the NVA to withdraw, and the separation of the VC units from the population by providing a protective shield through ground, air, and naval offensive operations against the remaining enemy main force units. The second undertaking involved the establishment of a militarily secure environment within which the governmental apparatus of South Vietnam could be extended, consolidated, and sustained. This entailed accelerating offensive operations against Viet Cong guerrilla and main forces, with priority being given to the elimination or neutralization of the enemy's political and military infrastructure while simultaneously developing and improving the Republic's armed and security forces. Third was the improvement of the national development effort through a number of integrated security, political, economic, and social programs.

Although all three of these undertakings were conducted simultaneously well into 1968, priority was given to the first operational goal. Military operations designed to inflict unacceptable casualties on the enemy and thereby bring about a successful outcome to the war were stressed. A strategy of attrition, while never formally articulated, was adopted. As General William C. Westmoreland, Commander, United States Military Assistance Command, Vietnam, until July 1968, stated:

> Our strategy in Vietnam is to secure our bases which are essential if we are to fight troops and sustain combat; to control populated and productive areas, . . . to neutralize his [the enemy's] base areas which are in the main situated . . . along international borders, . . . to force the enemy back, particularly his main forces, back to peripheral areas and to contain him there. Next to interdict infiltration. And finally to inflict maximum attrition on his ranks.[7]

In short, until mid-1968, "it was to grind down the enemy using the combined forces available in South Vietnam."[8] The other two operational goals received relatively little in terms of effort and resources.

As allied losses declined and territorial security improved following the enemy's failed *Tet* and post-*Tet* Offensives, greater emphasis was placed on population security and improvement of South Vietnam's Armed Forces. Out of this change in operational emphasis evolved a balanced approach which was to become the guiding principle for all future allied operations. In September 1968, General Creighton W. Abrams, General Westmoreland's successor at MACV, advanced the "one war" concept which in essence recognized no such thing as a separate war of big units or of population and territorial security. Under this integrated strategic concept, allied forces were to carry the battle to the enemy simultaneously, in all areas of conflict, by strengthening cooperation between U.S. advisors and commanders and their South Vietnamese military and civilian counterparts. Major elements of the "one war" concept were population security, modernization and improvement of South Vietnam's Armed Forces, and combat operations, each to receive the highest priority, and each to be kept abreast of the other and moving forward with the ultimate aim of ensuring a strong and viable nation. No single element was to be allowed to overshadow the other two.

Under this concept, all allied forces were to be marshalled into a single integrated, all-out attack against the enemy's forces, organization, activities, and facilities. Working in close coordination with the Armed Forces of the Republic of Vietnam and other governmental agencies, each element within the overall effort was to be assigned a mission and related tasks most appropriate to its particular capabilities and limitations. Emphasis was to be placed on combined operations in which Free World Military Assistance Forces and Republic of Vietnam Armed Forces would join in an effort to increase the latter's experience and confidence. In all operations, mobility and flexibility were to be stressed; as the enemy situation changed, existing plans were to be rapidly modified to counter or capitalize on the changing situation. The strategy of attrition was dead. As General Abrams pointed out to his major field commanders in mid-October:

> The enemy's operational pattern is his understanding that this is just one, repeat one, war. He knows there's no such thing as a war of big battalions, a war of pacification or a war of territorial security. Friendly forces have got to recognize and understand the one war concept and carry the battle to the enemy, simultaneously, in all areas of conflict. In the employment of forces, all elements are to be brought together in a single plan—all assets brought to bear against the enemy in every area, in accordance with the way the enemy does his business . . . . All types of operations are to proceed simultaneously, aggressively, persistently and intelligently—plan solidly and execute vigorously, never letting the momentum subside.⁹

The "one war" concept embodied Abrams' long-held belief that both the multi-battalion and pacification wars were mutually supporting aspects of the same struggle.*

As a corollary to the "one war" concept, significant emphasis was to be given to the Accelerated Pacification Campaign (APC), initiated in November 1968. Recognizing that insurgency would fail if cut off from popular support, allied efforts were to be directed toward denying the enemy access to population and rice-growing centers, which in turn would deprive him of his mobility and force him to divert combat troops to logistical duties for which he would otherwise impress local laborers.

Guided by these principles, the South Vietnamese Joint General Staff (JGS), in coordination with General Abrams' MACV staff, issued two documents late in 1968 which set forth strategy for the conduct of the war in the coming year. The 1969 Pacification and Development Plan was the first attempt by the South Vietnamese Government to present in a single document the strategy, concepts, priorities, and objectives which were to guide the total pacification effort. Issued on 15 December by South Vietnamese Premier Tran Van Huong and members of the newly formed Central Pacification and Development Council (CPDC), it was to take effect with the termination of the Accelerated Pacification Campaign in February 1969. Although a unilateral plan, it was considered to be directive in nature for all allied forces. The primary objectives of the plan were to provide at least a measure of security for 90 percent of the South Vietnamese population by the end of 1969, and extend national sovereignty throughout the country by eliminating the Viet Cong Infrastructure, strengthening local government, increasing participation in self-defense forces, encouraging defection among enemy units and their supporters, assisting refugees, combating terrorism, and promoting rural economic development and rice production.

---

*In commenting on the "one war" concept, promulgated by General Abrams, General Westmoreland stated: "It was not Abrams that did it, it was the changed situation which he adapted to. The change was the situation, it was not the personality because, General Abrams was my deputy for over a year. He and I consulted about almost every tactical action. I considered his views in great depth because I had admiration for him and I'd known him for many years. And I do not remember a single instance where our views and the courses of action we thought were proper, differed in any way." Continuing, "there was no change in strategy. But there was a change in the situation, a profound change after the defeat of the *Tet* Offensive." (Gen William C. Westmoreland intvw, 4Apr83, pp. 7, 19 [OralHistColl, MCHC, Washington, D.C.])

Department of Defense Photo (USMC) A192540
A Marine infantryman scrambles down a steep mountain slope during a typical patrol in I Corps' rugged, jungle-covered mountainous terrain in search of North Vietnamese Army Forces, base camps, and cache sites.

The four corps and Capital Military District commanders were given primary responsibility for executing the pacification plan on the basis of province plans prepared under corps supervision and reviewed in Saigon. To focus and ensure success for the effort, intermediate goals were established. These goals, to be accomplished by 30 June 1969, were deliberately set high in order to exact maximum effort.

The second document issued was the Combined Campaign Plan (CCP) for 1969, which provided basic guidance for all Free World forces in the conduct of military operations in South Vietnam. The 1969 plan inaugurated a number of changes in annual campaign planning which strengthened the status of the South Vietnamese Joint General Staff. Unlike previous campaign plans, which were prepared by MACV, the 1969 plan was prepared by the JGS with assistance from MACV. In addition, U.S. forces were for the first time listed among Free World forces instead of separately, and more significantly, the plan, once drawn up, was signed by each of the national commanders.

The basic assumptions included in the plan remained unchanged from those of 1968, except for acknowledging the on-going Paris peace negotiations and assuring that allied force levels would remain stable throughout the year. Under the plan, United States and South Vietnamese troops were to continue mobile operations against enemy forces and bases, while screening population centers against attack and infiltration. The plan also directed continued extension of government control by securing major cities, towns, and military installations, and denying enemy access to important economic regions, rail and road links, and centers of government. Again emphasized were the need for population security, elimination of enemy infrastructure, development of local self-defense forces, and civic action programs, but to a much greater degree than similar programs had received in previous campaign plans.

Twelve major objectives and goals were enumerated for use in measuring progress. As compared with the 1968 plan, the 1969 campaign plan reduced and simplified the list, making it more meaningful and more reasonably attainable than were the percentile goals used in the past. The goals established for Free World forces varied: defeat Viet Cong and North Vietnamese armed forces; extend South Vietnamese Government control; modernize and raise the level of South Vietnam combat readiness; inflict maximum enemy casualties; increase the percentage of territory and population under South Vietnamese control through an expanded pacification effort; reduce the enemy's ability to conduct ground and fire attacks against military and civilian targets; destroy or neutralize enemy base areas; enhance the effectiveness of provincial security forces; secure vital lines of communication; neutralize the enemy's infrastructure; increase the number of Viet Cong and North Vietnamese Army deserters; and, maximize intelligence collection and counterintelligence activities. In order to make substantial progress in achieving these goals, allied military resources were to be applied to critical areas, with economy of force being practiced in less essential areas.

In ICTZ, allied forces were to be committed primarily to offensive operations in order to destroy enemy forces throughout the tactical zone and those which might cross the Demilitarized Zone and Laotian border. Operations were also to be conducted to destroy enemy base areas, and to protect the major population centers of Hue, Da Nang, Quang Ngai, and the main lines of communications, especially Routes 1 and 9. Pacification activities would be concentrated on the populated coastal areas surrounding the major cities and extended to other populated areas along Route 1.

In essence, the 1969 country-wide Combined Campaign Plan abandoned the earlier concept of a protective shield of containment, and both emphasized and implemented the concept of area security and control, while again stressing the spirit of the offensive and relentless attack against the enemy. It recognized both the enemy's political and military threats and advocated expanded spoiling and preemptive operations against all types of enemy organizations and facilities, with particular emphasis placed on eliminating the Viet Cong Infrastructure. Further, it recognized that there was just one war and the battle was to be carried to the enemy, simultaneously, in all areas of conflict. Friendly forces were to be brought together in a single plan against the enemy in accordance with the way he operated. "The key strategic thrust," as stated in the MACV Strategic Objectives Plan approved by General Abrams early in 1969, was "to provide meaningful, continuing security for the Vietnamese people in expanding areas of increasingly effective civil authority." As envisioned by MACV and the JGS, the "one war" concept was to be forcefully implemented on all fronts in 1969. As General Abrams stated to a gathering of his major field commanders early in January:

> Pacification is the "GUT" issue for the Vietnamese. This is why I think that we cannot let the momentum die down. I started off by saying that I think we have the cards. I believe that. But the artistry in this situation is going to be to play the cards at the proper time and in the proper place. We do not have so many extras that we can afford to blunder around and put forces where the enemy isn't and where the pacification effort doesn't need it. It is going to require the utmost in professional work and professional judgment during the next weeks to ensure that we play our cards in the most effective way. If we do not and we get sloppy, pacification is going to really suffer. You can't let the old steam roller get going and not feed it fuel and expect it to keep going.[10]

I Corps Planning

On 26 December 1968, South Vietnamese, Korean, and American commanders in I Corps Tactical Zone issued their Combined Campaign Plan for 1969. Designed to implement the objectives outlined in the nationwide campaign and pacification plans, this document was to provide basic guidance for the operations of Marines and allied forces in ICTZ throughout the coming year.

The drafters of the plan assumed that the North Vietnamese and Viet Cong in I Corps would continue to follow the strategy used during the campaigns of late 1968—that of concentrating men and materiel in attacks on population centers in order to inflict a defeat on the ARVN and incite a popular uprising that would culminate in either the overthrow of the South Vietnamese Government, or its replacement by a coalition government which would include representatives of the National Front for the Liberation of South Vietnam.

Due to a number of decisive tactical defeats, heavy casualties, and failure to gain popular support by 1969, allied planners noted:

> Realizing that he cannot win a military victory, the enemy is apparently resorting to a "fighting while negotiating" strategy. In adopting such a strategy, he now hopes to gain political advantage at the conference table through continued offensive action in RVN [Republic of Vietnam]. The enemy is expected to expand his efforts to control the rural areas and strengthen his infrastructure as a base for further action.[11]

In pursuit of this goal, the planners declared, the NVA and VC in I Corps would endeavor to "wear down and eliminate RVNAF [Republic of Vietnam Armed Forces] and Allied forces to the maximum extent possible and to draw friendly forces away from urban areas and thereby relieving pressure on those enemy forces attacking the urban areas."[12] In the attack on the urban population, Communists forces would continue to rely on such standard tactics as assassination, rocket and mortar attacks on vital areas and key installations, and direct assaults on isolated units, outposts, and towns. These actions were aimed, the planners noted, at demoralizing allied forces, discrediting the South Vietnamese Government, and disrupting its pacification effort.

To meet and eliminate the enemy threat, campaign planners divided the opposing force into two categories, the VC and NVA main force units often found in remote areas and local VC guerrilla units and their supporters, concentrated in and around urban population centers. They assigned a distinct yet overlapping function to each allied unit: Korean, American, and ARVN regulars were to focus on destruction of the enemy's main forces, neutralization of base and logistical areas, and prevention of infiltration of population centers. Regional and Popular, People's Self-Defense, and National Police forces were to weed out and eliminate Viet Cong local force units and infrastructure. These auxiliaries were to furnish "security for hamlets and villages and will defend the LOCs [lines of communication], political and economic centers and government installations. They will also participate in and coordinate with the ARVN regular

Abel Papers, Marine Corps Historical Center

LtGen Robert E. Cushman, left, Commanding General, III Marine Amphibious Force; LtGen Hoang Xuan Lam, Commanding General, I Corps; and BGen Dong Ho Lee, right, Commander, 2d Republic of Korea Marine Brigade, sign the I Corps Combined Campaign Plan for 1969, outlining allied coordination and assistance policies for I Corps.

forces in the protection of cities and provincial and district capitals."[13]

The major task assigned to the regular forces under the plan was to locate and "systematically neutralize" the enemy's base areas scattered throughout the tactical zone, predominantly in the mountains adjacent to the Laotian border. Allied troops were to concentrate on those enemy command, control, and logistical facilities which "directly affect the selected RD [Revolutionary Development] priority areas, key population and economic centers, and vital communications arteries."[14] Priority was given to those enemy base areas within striking distance of Dong Ha and Quang Tri City (Base Area 101), Da Nang (Base Area 112), and Quang Ngai City (Base Area 121).* For the more remote bases where complete neutralization and permanent denial was impossible, "repeated air strikes with random pattern ground operations" were to be used to "create insecurity, disrupt command channels, and deter stationing and movement of VC/NVA forces" within those areas.[15] The drafters of the campaign plan were convinced that:

> The destruction of the enemy's command, control, and logistics facilities will contribute to his eventual defeat. The neutralization of these bases will also require the enemy to place greater demands on the people for more manpower and resources. As these demands increase, the people will become more susceptible to friendly psychological operations. This will support the objective of assisting the GVN in expanding territorial control.[16]

"Territorial control" or territorial security was stressed by the authors as the primary objective of all allied activity in I Corps:

> The campaign to provide sustained territorial security in the countryside and concurrently to introduce political, economic and social reforms which will establish conditions favorable for further growth and stability, is just as important as anti-aggression operations. Operations to annihilate the enemy, while clearly essential to pacification, are by themselves inadequate. The people must be separated and won over from the enemy.[17]

---

*Each enemy base was assigned a three-digit number. The first digit represented the country in which it was located (1 for South Vietnam and 6 for Laos), while the last two digits indicated sequential position of discovery by allied troops.

Each allied unit was assigned a security function, in addition to its other allotted duties. American, Korean, and ARVN regulars, when not engaged in major operations against enemy base areas and main force units, were to "prevent enemy infiltration into the fringes of towns, cities, and areas adjacent to population" centers by constantly patrolling those areas.[18] They were to reinforce territorial units under attack, furnish air and artillery support, and assist them in their campaign to eliminate local Viet Cong. Regional and Popular Force units within the tactical zone were to carry out ambushes, cordons, and patrols near inhabited areas, while the National Police and People's Self-Defense Forces were to maintain public order and conduct operations aimed at eradicating the enemy's infrastructure.

I Corps planners also sought to delineate the often conflicting responsibilities for pacification by requiring each locality to be placed into one of five general security categories: uninhabited areas, North Vietnamese Army- or Viet Cong-controlled areas, contested areas, areas being secured, and those areas considered completely secure. Uninhabited areas encompassed that territory just inside the national frontiers which did not contain officially recognized hamlets. NVA- or VC-controlled areas were regions in which the enemy was present and able to exert military and political influence. In both of these areas, allied units were to conduct only transient operations, with no intention of gaining complete and permanent control.

Closer to the main population centers were the contested areas. Selected as targets for Revolutionary Development activities, these areas were to be cleared permanently of all organized enemy main force and guerrilla unit activity by regular forces. In areas in the process of being secured, all "organized resistance" was considered to have ceased and the government to be in the process of destroying what remained of the enemy's guerrilla network, thereby preventing its reemergence.

Secure areas, the final category, were densely populated regions where government control was complete, or where permanent New Life Hamlets (Ap Doi Moi) were being developed. Here the population could move freely without fear of organized enemy attacks, except for occasional individual acts of terrorism or sabotage, and indirect attacks by fire. In both secure areas and areas being secured, the responsibility for defense and maintenance of public order rested with local officials and their principal security forces, the RF and PF, the PSDF, and the National Police.

The purpose of this regional organization was not only to fix responsibility for pacification, but to integrate and unify all allied activity. Combat operations, population and teritorial security, and RVNAF improvement and modernization were to be equally emphasized in the "one war" concept as enumerated by the ICTZ/III MAF Combined Campaign Plan for 1969.

Against this background, the battlefields of I Corps Tactical Zone were relatively quiet during the early days of 1969. The Viet Cong's unilateral 72-hour New Year's truce ended on 2 January, but intermittent fighting took place as allied forces, who had refused to recognize the ceasefire, continued both large and small unit operations.

CHAPTER 2
Mountain Warfare

Northern I Corps — Off Balance — From the Cua Viet, South

Northern I Corps

Arrayed within the provinces of Quang Tri and Thua Thien as 1969 began were the following major United States headquarters and combat units: Headquarters XXIV Corps; 3d Marine Division; Task Force Hotel; 101st Airborne Division (Airmobile); 1st Brigade, 5th Infantry Division (Mechanized); XXIV Corps Artillery; and U.S. Navy Task Force Clearwater. Generally deployed along the Demilitarized Zone and Laotian border within Quang Tri Province was the 3d Marine Division, less two battalions of the 3d Marines, with the 1st Brigade, 5th Infantry Division (Mechanized) under its control, operating throughout the eastern portion of the province, primarily within the piedmont and coastal lowlands. Located at Vandegrift Combat Base in western Quang Tri was Task Force Hotel, which essentially functioned as 3d Marine Division Forward Headquarters. Deployed within Thua Thien Province were the three brigades of the 101st Airborne Division (Airmobile), headquartered at Camp Eagle, south of Hue and northwest of Phu Bai. Collocated with Headquarters, XXIV Corps, at Phu Bai Combat Base was XXIV Corps Artillery, while stationed at Dong Ha was the subordinate 108th Artillery Group. The Navy's Task Force Clearwater, with the mission of river and inland waterway security, operated from a base near the mouth of the Song Cua Viet in Quang Tri Province, with river patrol groups securing the Song Cua Viet and Song Huong (Perfume River), and patrol air cushion vehicle (PACV) elements patrolling inland waterways.

Enemy activity throughout northern I Corps was light and sporadic during the early days of January 1969. Along the Demilitarized Zone, units of the 3d Marine Division and 1st Brigade, 5th Infantry Division (Mechanized) faced elements of six North Vietnamese regiments, the *138th, 270th, 84th, 31st, 27th,* and the *126th Naval Sapper*, all independent regiments of the unlocated *B-5 Front Headquarters*. Three regiments of the veteran *320th NVA Division* had withdrawn from western and central Quang Tri Province for refitting in North Vietnam following their third defeat in late 1968.[1] What enemy activity there was, was generally limited to infrequent rocket and mortar attacks on allied positions, ground probes by squad- and platoon-size units, and attempts at interdicting the Song Cau Viet with mines. Artillery fire from within and north of the Demilitarized Zone had all but ceased in December.

Within the central portion of Quang Tri Province, units subordinate to the *7th Front*, including three battalions of the *812th Regiment*, were for the most part pulled back into jungle sanctuaries on the Quang Tri-Thua Thien provincial border for resupply and infusion of replacements. These three units were badly mauled during the 1968 *Tet* and post-*Tet* Offensives, and their forward base areas and cache sites destroyed by Marine and ARVN search and clear operations during the late summer and fall campaigns. Enemy strength at the end of January, within the Demilitarized Zone and Quang Tri Province, was estimated at 36,800, approximately 2,500 more than the December total. Of these, more than half were confirmed to be combat troops.

In Thua Thien Province the enemy situation was similar. North Vietnamese Army units, with the exception of small forward elements of the *4th* and *5th Regiments*, had been withdrawn into the A Shau Valley and Laos under constant U.S. and ARVN pressure during the previous year. These forward elements did conduct occasional attacks by fire, but were forced to confine much of their effort to attempts at rice gathering and survival in the foothills of the province. Viet Cong local force units and the Viet Cong Infrastructure remained under steady pressure from Army, ARVN, and provincial forces, and likewise devoted much of their energy toward survival and avoiding discovery. End-of-January estimates placed enemy strength within the province at 15,200, a 25-percent increase over December figures.

To the west, in the A Shau Valley and beyond, there were signs of increasing enemy activity. Roadwork was being conducted on Route 548 in the valley and on Route 922 in Laos. Vehicular traffic and troop movement was light at the beginning of the month, but soon picked up as January progressed, particularly in and around Route 922 and enemy Base Area 611 in Laos.

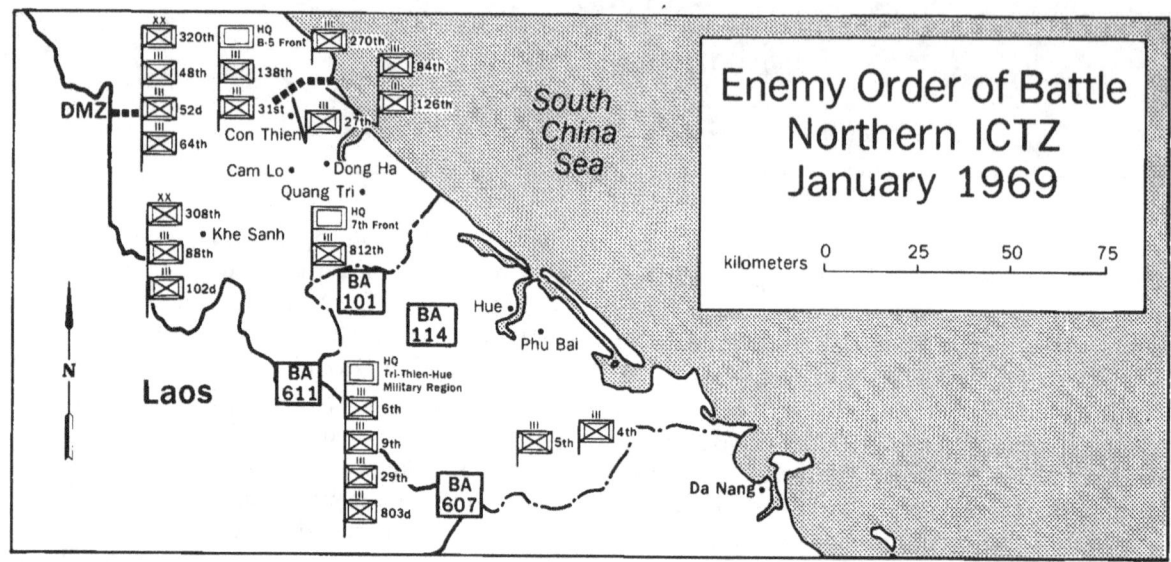

See Reference Map, Sections 1-27

Off Balance

While the enemy generally avoided contact in January, American and South Vietnamese forces in northern I Corps continued their efforts at keeping him off balance, striking at his traditional base areas and infiltration routes, and increasing security within populated areas. Driving deeper into the mountains and areas bordering the Demilitarized Zone, allied forces pushed and probed for evidence of infiltration and supply build-up, in order to determine the enemy's intentions in the months ahead and thwart them before they could be implemented.

Leading the effort in Quang Tri Province was the 3d Marine Division under the command of Major General Raymond G. Davis. A veteran of the Guadalcanal, Cape Gloucester, and Peleliu campaigns of World War II and Medal of Honor recipient for actions at the Chosin Reservoir during the Korean War, Davis assumed command of the division in May 1968, following a short tour as Deputy Commanding General, Provisional Corps, Vietnam.

Under Davis' leadership, the tactical disposition of the division would be turned around. No longer consigned to defensive positions, the 3d Marine Division, with helicopter support, now would assume a highly mobile posture, characteristic of Army air cavalry and airborne operations of 1968. As General Davis noted:

> We had something like two dozen battalions up there all tied down (with little exception) to these fixed positions, and the situation didn't demand it. So, when the Army moved into Pegasus to relieve the Khe Sanh operation [in April 1968] they applied forces directly responsive to the enemy's dispositions and forgot about real estate—forgetting about bases, going after the enemy in key areas—this punished the enemy most. Pegasus demonstrated the decisiveness of high mobility operations. The way to get it done was to get out of these fixed positions and get mobility, to go and destroy the enemy on our terms—not sit there and absorb the shot and shell and frequent penetrations that he was able to mount. So all this led me, as soon as I heard that I was going, it led me to do something I had never done before or since, and that is to move in prepared in the first hours to completely turn the command upside down. They were committed by battalion in fixed positions in such a way that they had very little mobility. The relief of CGs took place at eleven o'clock. At one o'clock I assembled the staff and commanders; before dark, battalion positions had become company positions. It happened just that fast.[2]

In addition to establishing a more mobile posture, Davis reinstituted unit integrity. For various reasons, the regiments of the division had slowly evolved into operational headquarters which might have any battalion of the division assigned. There was constant rotation; the 9th Marines, for example, might have a battalion of the 3d Marines, a battalion of 4th Marines, and only one of its own. Thus, as Colonel Robert H. Barrow, one of Davis' regimental commanders and later Commandant of the Marine Corps, noted, the individual battalions "felt . . . they were commanded by strangers. Every unit has a kind of personality of its own, often reflecting the personality of the commander, so you never got to know who did what best, or who would you give this mission to."[3] Davis changed that; each regiment, under normal operating circumstances, would now control its constituent battalions. As General Davis later commented, "it was the key to our success."[4]

As battalions of the division moved from defensive operations to more aggressive operations against elements of the *320th NVA Division* during the latter half of 1968, the need for helicopters grew. "I was very fortunate in this," Davis was later to state, "that the later model of the CH-46 was arriving in-country in large numbers. Whereas it would pick up a platoon, the old 46 would hardly pick up a squad."⁵ In addition, due to his close working relationship with Army Lieutenant General William B. Rosson, Provisional Corps commander, and Lieutenant General Richard G. Stilwell, his successor at XXIV Corps, Davis had the promise of Army helicopter support if needed. More important, however, was the creation of Provisional Marine Aircraft Group 39 and the subsequent assignment, initially on a temporary basis, of a Marine air commander for northern I Corps who, as General Davis stated, "had enough authority delegated to him from the wing, where he could execute things; he could order air units to do things."⁶* With helicopter transport assured, division Marines moved from relatively static positions south of the Demilitarized Zone and along north-south Route 1 and east-west Route 9, the main lines of communication, into the mountainous regions of Quang Tri Province in search of the enemy and his supplies.

Davis' concept of mobile operations depended not only on the helicopter, but on the extensive exploitation of intelligence, specifically that gathered by small reconnaissance patrols, which he continuously employed throughout the division's area of responsibility and which supplemented both electronic and human acquired intelligence. Operating within range of friendly artillery were the heavily armed "Stingray" patrols, whose mission was to find, fix, and destroy the enemy with all available supporting arms, and rapid reinforcement, if necessary. In the more remote areas, beyond artillery range, he used "Key Hole" patrols. Much smaller in size and armed with only essential small arms and ammunition, the function of these patrols was to observe.⁷ The 3d Marine Division, Davis noted, "never launched an operation without acquiring clear definition of the targets and objectives through intelligence confirmed by recon patrols. High

Department of Defense Photo (USMC) A192746
MajGen Raymond G. Davis led 3d Marine Division.

mobility operations [were] too difficult and complex to come up empty or in disaster."⁸

Armed with information on probable enemy troop and supply locations provided by reconnaissance patrols and other intelligence sources, such as radio intercepts, 3d Division Marines would advance rapidly into the proposed area of operations. Forward artillery positions, or fire support bases (FSBs), defended by a minimum of infantry personnel, would be established on key terrain features. These mutually supporting bases, constructed approximately 8,000 meters apart with a 3,000-meter overshoot in order to cover enemy mortars, provided ground troops operating under the fan with continuous, overlapping artillery support. Once inserted, Marine rifle companies, and even entire battalions, would move rapidly, although methodically, and largely on foot, throughout the area to be searched. Additional fire support bases would be constructed, permitting deeper penetration of the area of operations.

The purpose of the intelligence collection effort and subsequent combat operations, if required, was to prevent the enemy from sticking his "logistics nose in-country." "The [enemy's] first order of business," as Colonel Barrow later noted, was to "move all the things of war; all of their logistics forward from the sanctuaries of North Vietnam, just across the DMZ, or from Laos." This movement would take weeks, or possibly

---

*Assistant Wing Commander, Brigadier General Homer S. Hill, was temporarily assigned to 3d Marine Division Headquarters for "operations requiring more than routine air support and used his normal position within the Wing to coordinate air operations on the spot." The assignment of a Marine air commander to northern I Corps "did not involve any new command structure." (Col Edwin H. Finlayson, Comments on draft ms, 25Nov86 [Vietnam 69 Comment File, MCHC, Washington, D.C.])

months. At the appointed time, troops would quickly move in, marry up with the cached supplies, and then do battle. As General Davis believed and Barrow later stated:

> We must do everything we can to find that stuff, wherever its exists and obviously destroy it. And if we miss any of it, we must attempt by vigorous patrolling, radio intercept, signal intelligence, recon team inserts, and whatever else, to find out when any troops were moving in. Maybe we hadn't found their logistics, their caches, and we didn't want to have the surprise of not finding them until after they had married up and were about to engage us some place.[9]

Thoroughly indoctrinated in the mobile concept of operations, Marines of the 3d Division at the beginning of 1969 could be found from the Laotian border to the coastal lowlands. To the west, elements of Colonel Robert H. Barrow's 9th Marines continued searching north of the Khe Sanh plateau in operations begun the year before. In the center, the 4th Marines, under Colonel William F. Goggin, patrolled the mountainous areas north of Vandegrift Combat Base and south of the Demilitarized Zone. Further east, one battalion of Colonel Michael M. Spark's 3d Marines continued to search areas south of the DMZ and north of Route 9, while the remainder of the regiment assisted the 5th Marines in Operation Taylor Common in Quang Nam Province.

On 31 December 1968 and 1 January 1969, teams from the 3d Reconnaissance Battalion were inserted west of Khe Sanh along the Laotian border, initiating Operation Dawson River West. The teams immediately secured seven landing zones, eliminating the need for preassault artillery and air strikes. On the morning of the 2d, elements of Barrow's 9th Marines and supporting artillery made simultaneous helicopter landings into the secured zones north of Route 9. The initial assaults were made by Lieutenant Colonel George W. Smith's 1st Battalion, Lieutenant Colonel George C. Fox's 2d Battalion, and Company L, 3d Battalion under First Lieutenant Raymond C. Benfatti. A battalion of the 2d ARVN Regiment assaulted south of Route 9 to the right of the 2d Battalion, 9th Marines on the 4th. Fire Support Bases Geiger and Smith, occupied by batteries of Lieutenant Colonel Joseph Scoppa, Jr.'s 2d Battalion, 12th Marines, supported the 9th, while an ARVN artillery battery at Fire Support Base Snapper supported the South Vietnamese.

Throughout the three-week operation, Barrow's Marines experienced minimal enemy contact during the

Infantrymen of the 1st Battalion, 9th Marines move through waist-high elephant grass in search of enemy troops and supply areas around Khe Sanh during Dawson River West.

Department of Defense Photo (USMC) A800506

A solitary Marine moves up a small stream near the abandoned Khe Sanh base, carefully checking out both banks for hidden North Vietnamese Army supplies and harbor sites.

search. They uncovered numerous small weapons caches, of which a great majority contained U.S. equipment, rations, and ammunition lost during and after the sieges of Lang Vei and Khe Sanh in 1968. The South Vietnamese located more recent hoards of 122mm rockets, mortars, and artillery rounds along Route 9 in the vicinity of Lang Vei. The general pattern of search during the operation was from the Laotian border north of Route 9, in the vicinity of Fire Support Base Argonne, south and astride Route 9; a probe into the "Vietnam Salient," that portion of South Vietnam which protrudes into Laos, near Fire Support Base Passport; and finally back toward Vandegrift Combat Base. At the close of Dawson River West, the 3d Battalion, 9th Marines resecured Fire Support Bases Henderson, Tun Tavern, Cates, and Shiloh near the Ba Long Valley, southwest of Vandegrift.

While the 9th Marines accounted for few enemy casualties and limited equipment captured, Operation Dawson River West proved significant in ascertaining that no sizeable enemy concentrations or supplies existed in the Khe Sanh area or Vietnam Salient at the time. "If there was ever a piece of ground in the western part of Quang Tri that was searched out thoroughly," Barrow remembered, "that was that operation."[10] In addition, the 9th Marines created a number of landing zones and fire support bases, facilitating continued operations against the NVA in western and southwestern Quang Tri Province, and providing a springboard for the regiment's turn to the south and future push into the upper Song Da Krong Valley, southwest of Vandegrift.

East of the Dawson River area of operations, Colonel Goggin's 4th Marines continued search and clear operations in the Scotland II area, while elements of the 3d Marines' Task Force Bravo, in Operation Kentucky, conducted search and cordon operations in the vicinity of the outposts at Cam Lo, Con Thien, and Charlie-2, south of the DMZ. Scotland II, a continuation of operations initiated in November 1967 in and around Khe Sanh by the 26th Marines, was begun 15 April 1968 under the control of Task Force Glick, later redesignated Task Force Hotel and now under the command of Assistant 3d Division Commander, Brigadier General Frank E. Garretson. Employing various battalions of the division, led by the 4th Marines, and elements of the 2d ARVN Regiment in search and clear operations in an area generally bounded by Route 561, Route 9, the Demilitarized Zone, and the Laotian border, Marines of Task Force Hotel had, since April the previous year, accounted for nearly 4,000 enemy killed and 1,100 weapons captured.

Ground combat was light and scattered throughout January and into early February as Lieutenant Colonel George T. Sargent, Jr.'s 1st Battalion, 4th Marines conducted searches of the area surrounding Nui Tia Pong, west of Elliott Combat Base (Rockpile), and Lieutenant Colonel Joseph E. Hopkins' 2d Battalion continued extensive squad-size reconnaissance patrols along the Demilitarized Zone, north and west of Con Thien. The 3d Battalion, under Lieutenant Colonel William A. Donald, in cooperation with the Quang Tri Provisional Rifle Company, maintained patrols from Ca Lu and Vandegrift Combat Base. The searches and extensive patrolling did uncover several important enemy fighting positions and supply caches. On 10 January, two companies of Lieutenant Colonel Sargent's 1st Battalion discovered a large bunker complex northeast of Fire Support Base Neville, containing over 120 mortar rounds, miscellaneous small arms ammunition, and explosives. Company L, working in conjunction with the 2d Battalion, 2d ARVN Regiment, on 23 January uncovered nearly 500 mortar rounds in multiple dumps in the vicinity of bases Charlie-1, Charlie-2, and Alpha-1, northwest of Cam Lo. It appeared from the location of the caches that the NVA were prepositioning ammunition and supplies as far forward as possible along the Demilitarized Zone in order to support future offensive operations.

As a result of these and other discoveries within the Scotland area of operations, Colonel Goggin ordered Lieutenant Colonel Hopkins' 2d Battalion to conduct reconnaissance patrols within the southern half of the Demilitarized Zone, while maintaining search and clear operations immediately to the south. "Our operations north of the southern boundary of the DMZ," Hopkins noted, "were not search and destroy operations per se. There were certain political implications involved, obviously. It had to be a carefully controlled

Marines of Company B, 1st Battalion, 4th Marines pick their way among rocks as they cross one of the many streams which traversed the rugged mountainous terrain which characterized the Scotland II area of operations, south of the Demilitarized Zone.

Department of Defense Photo (USMC) A800539

MOUNTAIN WARFARE

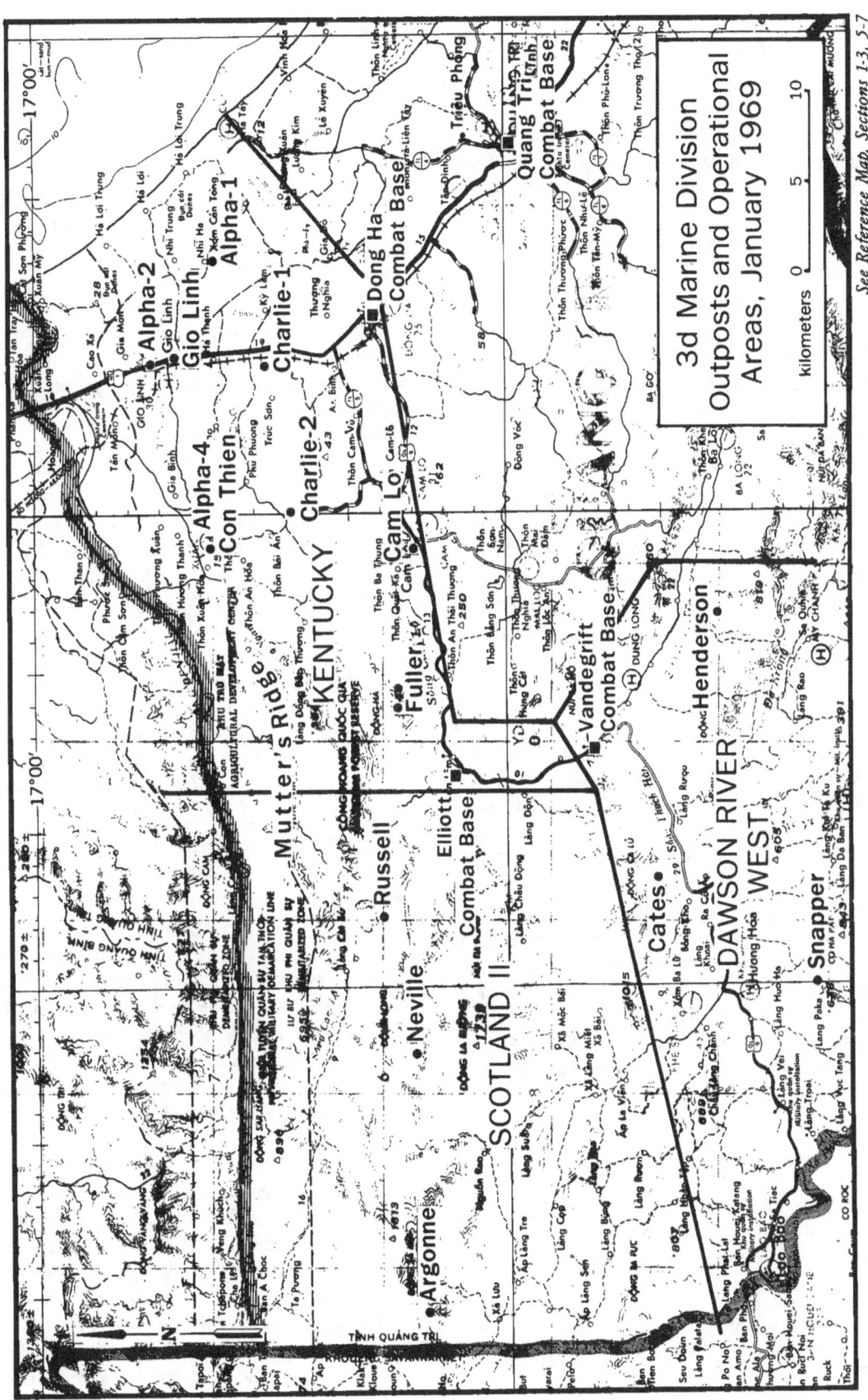

reconnaissance of the southern half of the DMZ under some specific rules of engagement which rather limited the number of personnel who might be in that area at any time."[11]* The reconnaissance effort was to involve teams from the division's 3d Reconnaissance Battalion and a rifle squad from Companies F, G, and H; a squad being the largest unit which could be introduced into the Demilitarized Zone for any purpose. Specific targets of the reconnaissance effort were enemy forces, fortifications, and supply caches.

Operations within the DMZ began on 1 February with the insertion of three division reconnaissance teams and an equal number of squads from the 2d Battalion. Generally, the teams covered less area and were involved in more fighting than Hopkins' squads during the two-week effort. As a result, the division reaction force, designated "Sparrow Hawk," was usually sent in to reinforce the reconnaissance teams. This technique, as Lieutenant Colonel Hopkins later reported, "offered an opportunity to put a larger force of Marines in, an additional platoon, and by walking them directly south, offered the opportunity to perform a good solid reconnaissance by a good-size unit of a portion of the area."[12]

Under the watchful eyes of North Vietnamese soldiers, some of whom stood in the open on the northern bank of the Ben Hai which bisected the DMZ, Hopkins' squads covered approximately 50 percent of the 36-square-kilometer reconnaissance zone assigned. Contact was sporadic, the actions involving either transients, local guides, cache guards, or screening and reconnaissance units of no more than a squad. Although the enemy's maneuverability was lessened and a number of his large cache sites discovered and destroyed, the reconnaissance effort was unable, according to the battalion's intelligence officer, First Lieutenant Larry L. Eastland, to discern "what their future plans are, what their future plan for a short period of time is to be."[13] Near the end of February, the enemy struck—first at Fire Support Base Neville and then at Russell, north of Vandegrift.

In the early morning hours of the 25th, Fire Support Base Neville, located northeast of the Elliott Combat Base, and defended by two platoons of Company H, 2d Battalion, 4th Marines and Battery G, 3d Battalion, 12th Marines, and protected by concertina wire, tanglefoot, listening posts, mines, and sensors, was assaulted by 200 highly trained and highly motivated sappers (raiders) from the *246th NVA Regiment*. "The night of the attack was pretty much of a typical night at Neville," reported Captain John E. Knight, Jr., Company H's commander, "very foggy; it looked like something right out of a horror movie with fog drifting through the trees; visibility almost nil. . . . The first indication we had that anything was out of the ordinary other than just normal movement was when a trip flare went off and evidently they were infiltrating at that point and one of their people had set off a trip flare. We H and I'd [harassing and interdiction fires] the area with the 60's and approximately a half an hour after that, at 0030 we were taken under attack by the sappers."[14] After infiltrating the concertina wire barrier on the west side of the perimeter, the attacking force systematically crisscrossed that portion of the fire base occupied by the 1st platoon and Battery G's number six gun pit, tossing satchel charges which forced the defenders into bunkers which the enemy then destroyed.

In the glow of flares and burning powder, the Marines rallied and with the assistance of 60mm mortar fire, drove the attacking force from the hill. "We beat these sappers, which are supposed to be the worst thing the North Vietnamese got," noted Gunnery Sergeant John E. Timmermeyer. "We beat these people not with air, not with arty, not with any supporting arms; we beat them and we beat them bad with weapons we had in our own company . . . . M-16s, or M-79s, or 60s, or frags, everything we had in the rifle company, this is what we used to beat these people with, we didn't have to have supporting arms. We did it without them."[15] At dawn, Captain Knight's Marines, who lost 11 killed and 29 wounded, found 36 enemy dead and wounded, several of whom still had satchel charges and other explosives strapped to their backs and quantities of opium in their pockets.

Ten kilometers east, Fire Support Base Russell, defended by platoons of Companies E, F, and K, Mortar and H Batteries of the 12th Marines, and a detachment from the 1st Searchlight Battery, came under attack the same evening. A sudden heavy mortar barrage followed by a 200-man sapper attack by troops of the *27th NVA Regiment*, swiftly breached the base's northeast perimeter. "In the first few minutes, the 81mm mortar section and the company CP, both located on the east and southeast side were decimated."[16]

---

*Then current rules of engagement prohibited U.S. ground forces from crossing the southern boundary of the DMZ without specific orders from COMUSMACV. Every local commander, however, retained the right and responsibility for the defense of his forces. (COMUSMACV msg to CGIIIMAF, et al., dtd 20Feb69, MACV HistDocColl, Reel 54)

Marine Corps Historical Collection

Fire Support Base Russell occupied a mountaintop within range of the Demilitarized Zone, and because of its location was often subjected to enemy mortar and ground attacks.

Fighting was hand-to-hand as the Marines, with the help of a heavy artillery cordon, coordinated by the battalion operations officer at Vandegrift Combat Base, drove the enemy back through the perimeter. At daybreak, Marine air came on station, and consolidation began with only two officers and one staff noncommissioned officer left out of the original complement. The Marines on Russell suffered 26 killed and 77 wounded, while accounting for 25 enemy troops, most of whom were cut down inside the wire. Marine patrols pursued the enemy north toward the DMZ at dawn, and reported finding bloody uniforms and bandages, as well as several fresh grave sites along trails the enemy used in their escape.

Both fire bases were reinforced the following day, but continued to report enemy probing activity. Fire Support Base Neville remained surrounded by enemy units employing mortars from several positions for several days despite heavy air concentrations, artillery and counter-mortar fires, and extensive patrols, and was eventually relieved of pressure by Company G which moved into the area by forced march over rugged terrain.[17]

The end of February found the 4th Marines engaged in base security and reaction force duties, and in patrolling the areas immediately around Fire Support Bases Neville and Russell in an attempt to severely punish the *27th* and *246th NVA Regiments*. On the 28th, Operation Scotland II ended with most regimental units remaining in place throughout the operational area.

Further east, two brigade-size operations were being conducted in support of the South Vietnamese Government's resettlement and pacification effort as the new year began. Centered in the Cam Lo and Con Thien areas, and along the Song Cua Viet, Operation Kentucky consisted of one Marine infantry battalion, one tank battalion, and elements of the 1st Amphibian Tractor (Amtrac) Battalion, under the control of the 3d Marines' Task Force Bravo. This search, clear, and cordon operation, begun in November 1967, had at one time included all three battalions of the 3d Marines and the 1st Brigade, 5th Infantry Division (Mechanized), following its arrival in northern I Corps in July 1968. In December, the 1st Brigade redeployed to an area south of the Cua Viet, and the 1st and 3d Battalions, 3d Marines moved to southern I Corps where they joined elements of the 1st Marine Division in Operation Taylor Common.

The new year found Lieutenant Colonel James J. McMonagle's 2d Battalion, 3d Marines conducting pacification operations in the Mai Loc area south of Route 9, securing friendly positions along the Con Thien-Cam Lo corridor, and assisting Regional Forces around Cam Lo. Lieutenant Colonel George E. Hayward's 3d Tank Battalion continued armored combat, security patrols, and road sweeps between Quang Tri and Dong Ha Combat Bases, and in the vicinity of Con Thien, while the 1st Amtrac Battalion, under Lieutenant Colonel Walter W. Damewood, Jr., continued motorized patrols near the Cua Viet, not far from Mai Loc. As the month progressed and the enemy became more furtive, the battalions began a series of short platoon- and company-size reconnaissance-in-force operations, designed to expose enemy positions, infiltration routes, and supply caches. Results were disappointing; most of the North Vietnamese and Viet Cong having been driven out by the intense artillery and air bombardments.

On occasion these small but frequent operations did initiate short skirmishes, and these skirmishes, combined with intelligence from captured enemy troops, pointed to Leatherneck Square as the only active area within the Kentucky area of operations.* As a result, on 18 January, the 2d ARVN Regiment, assisted by Lieutenant Colonel McMonagle's battalion and Lieutenant Colonel William A. Donald's 3d Battalion, 4th Marines, with tanks attached, began a cordon and search operation northeast of Cam Lo, the local district headquarters. The Marines maintained blocking positions along the square's northern boundary, while the ARVN force swept from Gio Linh to Cam Lo, hunting for enemy troops and resettling any displaced villagers in the Cam Vu Valley. As the cordon dissolved on the 26th, the 3d Battalion, 4th Marines, less Company M, rejoined its regiment, and a land-clearing operation, utilizing 20 to 30 tractors of the Army's 59th Engineer Battalion, was begun. The 2d Battalion, 3d Marines, assisted by Company M, 4th Marines; 1st Brigade, 5th Infantry's Troop A, 4th Squadron, 12th Cavalry; and later Troops B and C, 3d Squadron, 5th Cavalry, provided security for the engineers and conducted reinforced company-size search and destroy operations in the Con Thien, Cam Lo, and Mai Loc areas.

Task Force Bravo's control of the aggressive patrol operations within the Kentucky area continued until 18 February, when the remainder of the 3d Marines returned from southern I Corps and reassumed control of the task force, which was later deactivated. Following the return of the regiment, the 3d Battalion, 3d Marines began operations in the Cam Lo and Nhi Ha areas, replacing two companies of the 2d Battalion, helilifted west into Fire Support Bases Cunningham and Erskine, overlooking the Song Da Krong, to support the 9th Marines in Operation Dewey Canyon. With the westward shift of elements of the 2d Battalion and the transfer of control of the 1st Battalion to Task Force Hotel at Vandegrift, the 3d Marines ended Operation Kentucky.

From the Cua Viet, South

South of the Cua Viet, elements of the Army's 1st Brigade, 5th Infantry Division (Mechanized) and the 1st ARVN Regiment continued a combined search and clear and cordon operation (Marshall Mountain), begun on 10 December. The area of operation encompassed the political districts of Trieu Phong, Mai Linh, and Hai Lang, and Quang Tri City; and the area stretching from the coastal dunes west of Highway 1 to the jungle-canopied eastern portions of enemy Base Area 101 in southwestern Quang Tri Province. Approximately two-thirds of the province's population lived in the area, and consequently it was a key target for enemy infiltration and harassment efforts.

Friendly forces taking part in Operation Marshall Mountain were to interdict enemy movement by employing small-unit (squad and fire team) patrols and ambushes, known as "Hunter Killer" teams, and conduct detailed cordon and search operations in conjunction with the 1st ARVN Regiment, Regional and Popular Forces, Provincial Reconnaissance units, and National Police Field Forces. Capitalizing on the mobility of the 1st Brigade along the coastal plains and

---

*Leatherneck Square was a four-by-six-kilometer piece of cleared, flat piedmont about three kilometers east of the Vietnamese coast. Often characterized as a "parking lot" or "golf course," the area was bordered by Con Thien and Gio Linh on the north, and by Dong Ha and Cam Lo on the south.

Department of Defense Photo (USMC) A800470

Men of the 3d Marines on board tanks of the 3d Tank Battalion sweep the Con Thien Corridor within the Kentucky Area of Operations, north of Cam Lo District Headquarters.

in the piedmont, ready reaction forces were maintained to close rapidly in the event significant numbers of enemy troops were encountered.*

During the initial stages of the operation, elements of the 1st Brigade and 1st ARVN Regiment moved into the western portion of the area of operations to clear out remaining detachments of enemy main force units which had previously withdrawn to the mountainous regions of the province. These stay-behind enemy troops attempted to maintain rice collection points, not only posing a threat to the security of villages and hamlets throughout the area, but also hampering the government's pacification efforts. The forces involved simultaneously conducted combined search and cordon operations within the three districts, and by the end of the operation on 28 February, 37 such searches and cordons had been carried out. North of the Song Cua Viet, the 1st Amtrac Battalion supported the brigade with a search and clear operation along the beach from Ha Loi to the Demilitarized Zone.

Enemy action was generally defensive, with scattered attacks by fire and widely dispersed mines and other surprise firing devices. At the termination of the brigade operation, 568 enemy troops had been killed, 397 captured, and 307 civil defendants rounded up, many of whom were later identified as local infrastructure members. Four hundred ninety-six individual and 41 crew-served weapons were captured, along with miscellaneous arms and nearly 80 tons of rice.

In northern Thua Thien Province on 31 December, Operation Todd Forest began within the 101st Airborne Division's area of operation. In response to intelligence indicating a significant enemy presence in Base Area 101, the 1st Battalion, 501st Infantry and elements of the 1st ARVN Regiment conducted combat assaults into the Nam Hoa District highlands. Subsequent reconnaissance-in-force operations met light enemy resistance as NVA and VC troops again chose not to expose their forces, and Todd Forest ended within two weeks.

In the central portion of the province, around Hue, various elements of the 101st Airborne Division continued to conduct a large-scale division-level operation, initiated 17 May 1968, in support of the South Vietnamese Government's Accelerated Pacification Campaign. The initial goal of Operation Nevada Eagle had been to clear the provincial lowlands of NVA units following the *Tet* Offensive, and then to sever the link between NVA regular units and VC local forces

---

*The brigade and its subordinate units were configured into three task forces: the first, infantry with a tank company attached; the second, armor with an infantry company attached; and the third, mechanized infantry with tanks attached.

in the coastal plains. A series of combat operations were grouped under Nevada Eagle, all directed at the pacification of Thua Thien Province. During the summer of 1968, combat assaults in and around Base Area 114, coupled with rice denial operations, forced the *803d NVA Regiment* to withdraw its main elements from Thua Thien. A succession of cordon and sweeps were then carried out within the province to harass and destroy local-force VC units and the infrastructure, including highly successful Vinh Loc and Phu Vang security operations. This all-out offensive against the VC included night ambushes to intercept rice gathering parties, propaganda and proselytizing teams, and blocking attempts by the Viet Cong to regroup. Phu Vang IV, conducted during December and January, was a combined cordon and search of the Phu Vang, Huong Thuy, and Phu Thu Districts by the 1st Battalion, 501st Infantry; elements of the 54th ARVN Regiment; Regional Forces; and patrol units of Task Force Clearwater, which thwarted attempts by the VC to reenter the coastal area. Seventy-five of the enemy were killed and 35 infrastructure members were captured. Ambush operations in Phu Loc District, particularly in the vicinity of the Song Truoi, during January, severely restricted attempts by the *4th* and *5th NVA Regiments* and VC local forces to gain provisions, and to propagandize the area.

Just north of the Hai Van Pass, which separated northern and southern I Corps, elements of the 2d Battalion, 502d Infantry, and the 1st and 2d Battalions, 327th Infantry, initiated Platte Canyon on 6 January, a reconnaissance-in-force operation in the vicinity of the Ruong Ruong Valley. This portion of southern Thua Thien had long been considered the traditional location of the *4th NVA Regiment*. Rain and low-hanging clouds, typical of the northeast winter monsoon season, hampered initial operations, but the three battalions pushed on against moderate resistance as here too the enemy elected to disengage and avoid decisive combat. One large staging area was located and destroyed by reconnaissance elements, along with miscellaneous enemy equipment and ammunition.

Certain signs pointed to the likelihood that an offensive effort was brewing north of the Hai Van Pass as the Vietnamese Lunar New Year season approached. The evidence was strong that major elements of the *6th* and *9th NVA Regiments* were attempting to work their way eastward through the A Shau Valley. Enemy activity in Base Area 611, straddling the border between Laos and South Vietnam, had gradually increased through the end of 1968, and continued to provide evidence that the North Vietnamese were moving personnel and supplies toward the Vietnamese border in large numbers. Then, too, the NVA were active along the DMZ, although losing materiel nearly as fast as it could be positioned forward. Also, many of the supply and ammunition caches uncovered were arranged in temporary or makeshift facilities, which suggested ready accessibility for further transport in support of offensive operations. Finally, several caches were discovered in areas recently checked and found "clean," pointing to an intensification of efforts to push ammunition and supplies forward.

Even though the enemy's forward supply areas had been disrupted, the *4th* and *5th NVA Regiments* forced out of their traditional forward operating areas, and the VC local force and infrastructure restricted along the coastal lowlands, it seemed apparent that the NVA intended an offensive of some kind in the near future. A victory, even against one or more limited objectives of minor or temporary tactical value, could have significant impact upon the civilian population, and a more far-reaching effect upon bargaining positions at the ongoing Paris Peace Talks. The enemy's jungle logistics system therefore would have to be destroyed before it could be used.[18]

CHAPTER 3
The Spring Offensive Preempted

Strike into the Da Krong — A Phased Operation — Phase I — Backyard Cleanup

---

Strike into the Da Krong

With the beginning of the new year, Vietnamese border areas again became the focal point of allied concern about enemy activity in northern I Corps. From various intelligence sources it was learned that North Vietnamese Army engineer units, inactive for several months, had reopened a number of major infiltration routes, among them Route 922 which parallels the Laotian border and then enters Vietnam south of the Song Da Krong Valley, becoming Route 548. Reports also indicated a dramatic surge in vehicular traffic; the enemy again was attempting to stick his logistics nose into South Vietnam. The number of trucks traveling south along 922 and then east on 548 doubled in early January—Marine and Air Force reconnaissance and attack aircraft at times sighted more than 1,000 trucks a day. Allied air interdiction efforts successfully closed a number of choke points on both roads, but only for short periods as enemy engineers quickly repaired the damage.

North Vietnamese determination to maintain and defend Routes 922 and 548 also was evident as the volume of antiaircraft fire increased during the same period. Friendly aircraft on armed reconnaissance, interdiction, and direct support missions reported heavy 12.7mm, 25mm, and 37mm fire with airbursts as high as 16,000 feet.[1] The only reported loss was an A-6 "Intruder" from Marine All Weather Attack Squadron (VMA[AW]) 242, which was shot down by 37mm antiaircraft over the northern A Shau Valley on the night of 17 January. The squadron conducted both visual and electronic searches, but the plane and its pilot and navigator were not found.[2]

Main enemy forces in the area were tentatively identified as elements of the *6th NVA Regiment, 9th NVA Regiment, 65th Artillery Regiment*, and the *83d Engineer Regiment* — largely support and replacement troops. Intelligence reports also noted that these units, which recently had crossed over from Base Area 611 in Laos, were stockpiling materiel, and then attempting to work their way eastward through the Da Krong and A Shau Valleys to Base Area 101 southwest of Quang Tri and Base Area 114, west of Hue.[3]

These recent developments in enemy activity did not go unnoticed at Dong Ha where Major General Raymond G. Davis and his staff at Headquarters, 3d Marine Division, closely monitored all pertinent intelligence information as it became available. When it looked as if the potential enemy threat might become an eventuality, General Davis requested authority from XXIV Corps to conduct an operation in the upper Song Da Krong Valley to block the threat. On 14 January, General Davis ordered Brigadier General Frank E. Garretson, Commanding General, Task Force Hotel, to prepare plans for a regimental-size search and clear operation in the Da Krong, scheduled to take place "as soon as practicable after 22 January, on order."[4] The following day, the 9th and its supporting 2d Battalion, 12th Marines, then conducting a similar operation (Dawson River West) near the Laotian border west of Khe Sanh and north of Lang Vei, were put on alert by General Garretson, who requested that the regiment submit a detailed plan of operation for approval prior to D-Day.[5]

At this time, Colonel Barrow's 9th Marines was the division's "swing" regiment; it could be used at any time or place as the situation dictated. As such, it operated under the direct orders of General Davis even though the regiment was under the control of Task Force Hotel. "It was a strange sort of a relationship," Barrow remembered, "I was under his [Garretson's] OpCon [operational control], but most of what the relationship was, . . . was to support me with whatever Task Force Hotel and Vandegrift Combat Base could provide" in terms of supplies. "I got most of my orders, if you will, directly from General Davis."[6]

Except for information gleaned from agent reports and aerial reconnaissance photographs, little was known about the upper Song Da Krong Valley. Surrounded by high mountains broken by a number of sharp protruding ridgelines and bisected by the meandering Da Krong, the valley was located in the remote southwest corner of Quang Tri Province, 62 kilometers west of Hue and 48 kilometers southwest of Quang Tri. Several kilometers further south lay the A Shau Valley. Between the two, and dominating both, were two large hill masses: Tam Boi (Hill 1224) and Co A

Marine Corps Historical Collection
Aerial photograph of the Da Krong Valley with the Song Da Krong in the foreground, paralleling Route 922, one of the enemy's major supply routes from Laos into Vietnam.

Nong (Hill 1228), commonly known as Tiger Mountain. Co Ka Leuye, a razorback ridge 1,500 meters high and 3,500 meters long, sitting astride the Laotian border, formed the valley's western boundary. Vegetation in the area varied, consisting of head-high elephant grass mixed with brushwood west of the river, and rugged triple-canopied jungle in the eastern half of the valley. South of the river, which ran east to west and then abruptly turned north, the area was stripped of much of its natural ground cover by frequent allied air and artillery bombardment.

During the final months of the northwest winter monsoon, January to March, temperatures in the valley were generally chilly compared to the 100-degree temperatures of the lowlands, rarely rising above 71 degrees or falling below 51 degrees. Skies were overcast with light drizzle or occasional thunderstorms, but no significant rainfall was recorded. As a result, the mountains were continually shrouded in clouds while the valleys and numerous ravines were blanketed with heavy fog.

A Phased Operation

Planning for the Da Krong operation, codenamed Dawson River South, began in earnest even before the 9th Marines returned to Vandegrift Combat Base from Dawson River West. Colonel Barrow made several visual reconnaissance flights over the objective area with his battalion commanders, staff, and the direct support artillery battalion commander, Lieutenant Colonel Joseph Scoppa, in order to select appropriate sites for fire support bases.[7] In extensive discussions which followed there emerged a number of factors which would bear heavily upon the operation's concept, execution, and eventual success. Of primary importance was intelligence. The 3d Marine Division warning order stated simply: "Intelligence agencies indicate considerable enemy activity in the subject area." No concrete information was provided as to exact enemy strength, location, or composition, other than the existence of antiaircraft artillery, which Barrow noted, "was a tip-off that they were protecting something."[8] The effect was to urge prudence. Instead of simultaneous heliborne assaults over a wide area, a phased operation requiring strong fire support base defense, extensive infantry patrols, and a reliable intelligence system designed to locate enemy antiaircraft and artillery positions was decided upon.

A second factor was time. General Davis had expressed a desire to have maximum forces available in critical areas of Quang Tri Province during *Tet*, which was to begin 17 February. Since the operation, therefore, was limited to approximately 24 days, a mini-

Marine Corps Historical Collection

Col Robert H. Barrow, Commanding Officer, 9th Marines, led the regiment in the assault into the Da Krong Valley and enemy Base Area 611 beyond.

mum force of three infantry battalions and three 105mm howitzer batteries with 155mm support would be necessary; anything less would severely restrict the regiment's ability to conduct the operation and meet Davis' *Tet* deadline. Distance and weather were likewise viewed as limiting factors. Operating 50 kilometers from the nearest Marine combat base and logistical supply point, requests for resupply, reinforcements, medical evacuations, and air support would be delayed, 45 to 60 minutes for helicopters and 30 to 45 minutes for fixed-wing aircraft. Air operations would be hindered further by weather, at best unpredictable during the final months of the northwest monsoon.[9]

What emerged after five days of discussions, briefings, and frequent liaison with all participating or supporting echelons, including Headquarters, XXIV Corps, was a phased operation involving the step-by-step deployment of three infantry battalions protected by overlapping artillery fans, all requiring a minimum of helicopter support. The first phase was to consist of getting the regiment and its direct support artillery battalion into the area of operations and establishing fire bases within eight kilometers of each other to support the scheme of maneuver. The second phase was to include extensive patrolling around the fire support bases and the alignment of forces prior to launching into the target area. The final phase was visualized as a conventional three-battalion attack into the objective area. During this critical phase the regiment would depart from the highly mobile concept of operations, so successful in the past, and make the final move overland, securing ground and permitting helicopter resupply and support over an area already cleared of enemy forces, calming fears voiced by representatives of the 1st Wing. Aircraft and troop losses due to expected heavy antiaircraft defenses in the target area therefore would be reduced.[10] The 2d ARVN Regiment and the 101st Airborne Division (Airmobile) were to conduct supporting operations east and southeast of the Dawson River South area of operations. As in the past, a high degree of flexibility was built into the plan of operations so as to permit a refocusing of effort should either allied or enemy situations change.[11]

The entire concept of operations required the close coordination of Marine supporting arms. Fixed-wing aircraft based at Da Nang and Chu Lai were to provide landing zone preparations and close air support. Colonel Walter Sienko's Provisional Marine Aircraft Group 39 at Quang Tri, augmented by Marine Aircraft Group 36 at Phu Bai under Colonel Bruce J. Matheson, was to furnish helicopter support. The direct air support center (DASC), collocated with the 9th Marines' fire support coordination center (FSCC) at Vandegrift, was to control all aircraft. As the operation progressed, the FSCC and a DASC subunit were to move with the regiment into the operational area. The six firing batteries (three 105mm, two provisional 155mm, and one 4.2-inch mortar) of the 2d Battalion, 12th Marines (Reinforced), were to be deployed at eight kilometer intervals throughout the area of operations. A battery of Army 175mm guns from the 1st Battalion, 83d Artillery at Fire Support Base Jack, west of Hue, was to provide long-range support.[12]

The operational plan further provided that the logistic support area (LSA) at Vandegrift be designated the primary resupply point for all classes of equipment. Quang Tri Combat Base and the 3d Brigade,

101st Airborne's Camp Evans, north of Hue, were to be used as alternate or emergency resupply points in case of bad weather, and would be stocked with an additional 6,200 rounds of 105mm, 155mm, and 4.2-inch mortar shells.[13] Marines themselves were to carry an extra day's long-range patrol ration, plus twice the standard load of dry cell batteries and ammunition.[14]

Phase I

The first stage of the movement into the area of operations was to open three previously established fire support bases which stretched southward from Vandegrift. On 18 January units of Lieutenant Colonel Elliott R. Laine, Jr.'s 3d Battalion, 9th Marines resecured FSB Henderson, eight kilometers southwest of Ca Lu, in conjunction with a brief operation in the Ba Long Valley. This operation was a natural corollary to the base security mission picked up by the 9th Marines as it returned to Vandegrift from Dawson River West. On the 20th, Company L, 3d Battalion, 9th Marines reopened FSB Tun Tavern, unoccupied since early December 1968, after a team from the 3d Reconnaissance Battalion checked for mines and boobytraps.

Battery D, 2d Battalion, 12th Marines occupied reconstructed artillery positions later the same day, and began shelling FSB Shiloh, another eight kilometers south.

Shortly after Marine air prepped Shiloh on the 21st, Company A, 1st Battalion, 9th Marines occupied the fire base. Insertion of the artillery was delayed due to a fuze malfunction on one 750-pound bomb; the bomb detonated on impact instead of above ground, wiping out two previously constructed 105mm howitzer parapets, half of a third, and two ammunition berms. To repair the damage required seven hours of bulldozer work. With the reoccupation of Shiloh by two batteries of the 12th Marines, a forward LSA was established on the site and stocked with 5,000 rounds of artillery ammunition, and a 10-day supply of rations and batteries for an infantry battalion.

Shiloh turned out to be a "vacation land" for the Marines of Company A who were assigned the mission of providing security for the two artillery batteries. In addition to the normal patrols, as Lieutenant Colonel Wesley L. Fox, then a first lieutenant and com-

Infantrymen of the 2d Battalion, 9th Marines relax while waiting for helicopter transport at Vandegrift Combat Base prior to jumping off on operations in the Da Krong.

Department of Defense Photo (USMC) A192763-B

pany commander, later remembered, "a platoon a day went off of the hill to the small river at the foot . . . for swimming and fishing. Swimming and lying in the sun on the nice sand bar were great, but the real treat was the fish provided by the fishing expedition. The platoons would wind up their day at the river by throwing grenades in the deep holes and simply wading out and picking up the fish that floated to the top." Throughout the remaining days of the operation, during which the company would experience a number of heavy firefights, shortages of both water and rations, and exhaustive patrols, Fox continued, "Marines were heard to talk about the good old days back on Shiloh."[15]

With Henderson, Tun Tavern, and Shiloh reoccupied, the 9th Marines was now poised to launch attacks into the new area of operations. On the morning of 22 January, four companies of Lieutenant Colonel George C. Fox's 2d Battalion lifted off from Vandegrift with a two-fold mission: Companies E and H were to assault a 600-meter hilltop about eight kilometers south-southeast of Shiloh, while Companies F and G would secure a landing zone, Dallas, five kilometers beyond to the southwest. Except for scattered small arms fire the landings of Companies E and H went unopposed, and work on the fire support base, named Razor, began immediately.*

Razor was similar to other bases constructed by the 9th Marines' infantry, artillery, and engineer team during the previous eight months of mountain warfare, but technically more difficult. Trees measuring three to four feet in diameter—the largest encountered—had to be cleared, a job which posed major problems for the inexperienced Marines of Company H. According to Captain David F. Winecoff, commanding officer of the company:

> We went in with . . . enough power saws and axes to do the job if we had the experienced people to work these things. But, I found out that there are very few people in Hotel Company, and we were the ax swingers, that knew how to swing an ax properly, and we immediately proceeded to bust about 50 to 60 percent of our axes . . . . It was only through the cooperation of the engineers and all hands concerned in Hotel Company [that] with the power saws and the limited amount of axes that we got . . . Fire Support Base Razor opened up in time . . . . It was quite a feat.[16]

Winecoff's Marines cleared the trees, but the gentle slope on one side coupled with two hummocks on the flanks proved troublesome, and light bulldozers were brought in by helicopter to widen the landing zone and build gun pits and ammunition berms.

In the rapid buildup which followed, CH-46 "Sea Knight" helicopters, under the control of the wing DASC and the protective umbrella of gunships and observation aircraft, brought 1,544 Marines and 46 tons of cargo into the landing zone. By the evening of 23 January, a battery of 105mm howitzers was in place. The following day, the regimental command group displaced to Razor and occupied the gently sloping finger on the fire base's northwestern edge. The 2d Battalion, 12th Marines' command and fire control groups followed a short time later. Direction of the FDC and FSCC was then passed from Vandegrift to Razor without loss of continuity or centralized fire control. Six days after the introduction of Laine's 3d Battalion, the regiment was well into the zone of action.

On the morning of the 25th, after heavy air strikes, Laine's battalion assaulted three landing zones atop Ca Ka Va, a 1,100-meter-long razorback ridgeline, 6,000 meters south-southwest of FSB Razor. A short time later an artillery advance party and a team of engineers helilifted into the landing zones and began construction of what was to become FSB Cunningham, named for the first Marine aviator, Lieutenant Alfred A. Cunningham. From an artillery standpoint, Cunningham was ideal. Being at the center of the planned operational area and large enough to accommodate an integrated battalion position, it represented a simple solution to fire support requirements and coordination. As for the 9th Marines, its 11-kilometer artillery fan extended south and southwest almost to the limit of the area of operations.

Within the next four days the regimental command group and five artillery batteries moved into position on Cunningham. Mortar and D Batteries, the former from Vandegrift and the latter from Tun Tavern, displaced by sunset on the 25th. The 1st and 3d Provisional 155mm Howitzer Batteries helilifted in on 28 January from Ca Lu and Shiloh, respectively. When Battery E displaced from Shiloh to Cunningham the following day, the artillery movement into the Da Krong Valley was complete.

Soon after Cunningham opened, a small regimental forward logistical support area, capable of resupplying eight rifle companies with rations, water,

---

*The first fire support base established in the area of operations was named by Colonel Barrow in honor of General Davis. "Razor" was the nickname given Davis by Major General James M. Master, Sr., when both served on Okinawa in the early 60s: "the razor cuts to the root of problems." (Gen Raymond G. Davis, Comments on draft ms, Aug86 [Vietnam 69 Comment File, MCHC, Washington, D.C.])

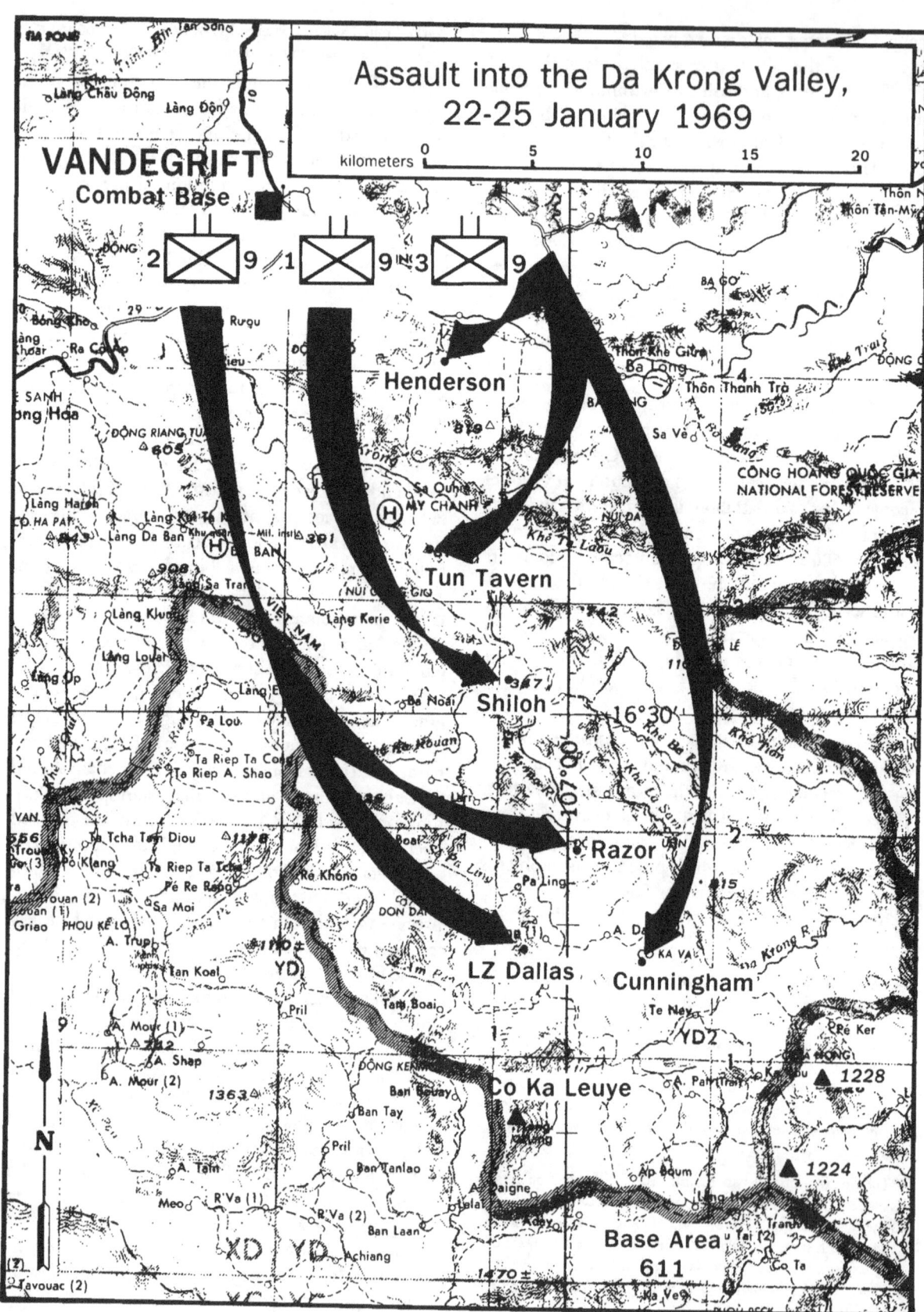

Department of Defense Photo (USMC) A193044

A CH-53 Sea Stallion lands supplies and ammunition at Fire Support Base Razor shortly after the mountaintop was secured by members of the 2d Battalion, 9th Marines.

batteries, and small arms ammunition on a daily basis, was established. A tactical logistical group (Tac Log), used primarily in amphibious operations, also was established, enabling the supply officer to work closely with the regimental commander, the operations officer, and the air liaison officer. As Major Charles G. Bryan, the regimental S-4, noted: "The procedure permitted the establishment of realistic priorities to minimize interference with tactical operations and also to ensure maximum utilization of available helicopter assets. And it further provided for a more effective control and coordination of resupply operations." The tactical logistical group was set up "with an administrative Tac Log net from each battalion with the logistics requirements being passed through the regiment; the regiment would then pass these logistic requirements to the personnel in the rear at Vandegrift who would ensure that these supplies were promptly staged on the LSA and lifted to the field."[17] This technique would prove invaluable as the regiment moved into the second phase of the operation, now called Dewey Canyon.*

Backyard Cleanup

Following the rapid movement of the regiment into the area of operations, companies of the 2d and 3d Battalions moved out from Razor and Cunningham on the 24th and 25th, initiating Phase II. Their mission was to clear the area around the two fire support bases, secure the flanks, and then gradually move into position along the Da Krong's east-west axis, designated Phase Line Red, for Phase III. This placed the 3d Battalion on the eastern flank and the 2d Battalion on the western flank near the Laotian border. The 1st Battalion, 9th Marines, under Lieutenant Colonel George W. Smith, would be introduced into the middle once the two battalions were in place. Among the critical second phase objectives were: the seizure of the Co Ka Leuye ridgeline, assigned to Company G; the construction of FSB Erskine, four kilometers southwest of Cunningham, by Company F; and the occupation of Landing Zones Lightning and Tornado, located four kilometers northeast of Cunningham, by Company K.

Patrolling 2,000 to 3,000 meters apart, the two battalions encountered screening forces of major enemy units thought to be operating further south. Engagements with single NVA soldiers or small bands of support troops were commonplace, and the ensuing firefights short. On 25 January, one such contact led to the discovery of a sophisticated four-strand communications wire by Company M. Running from Laos into Base Area 101 to the east, the line was strung between tree-mounted porcelain insulators and well concealed by overhead cover. A five-man special Marine and Army intelligence team, which had accompanied the Marines, tapped the wire and eventually broke the

---

*After a majority of the regiment was deployed, and the area of operations expanded, the operational codename was changed from Dawson River South to Dewey Canyon. However, Dawson River South remained in effect for those elements of the 9th Marines still at Fire Support Bases Tun Tavern and Henderson.

NVA code, but no information was provided the 3d Battalion as it was "presumed to be of strategic rather than tactical value," noted Lieutenant Colonel Laine.[18]

Another significant find during the first stage of Phase II was the *88th NVA Field Hospital*. Discovered by Company F, 2d Battalion, near the Song Da Krong, the complex consisted of eight large permanent buildings capable of accommodating 150 to 160 patients. A detailed search revealed large quantities of Russian-made stainless steel surgical instruments, antibiotics, foodstuffs, and evidence that the area had been evacuated the previous day.[19]

Company G, under Captain Daniel A. Hitzelberger, launched its attack on Co Ka Leuye (Hill 1175) the afternoon of 31 January from LZ Dallas. After a short skirmish with a small group of NVA soldiers who sought to draw it into an ambush at sunset, the company crossed a tributary of the Da Krong and advanced 500 meters up the mountain before settling in for the night. The following morning the Marines continued their climb, roping up sheer rock cliffs and traversing slopes with grades averaging 65 to 75 degrees. As the day progressed, the weather began to deteriorate, adding yet another obstacle. Heavy rains alternated with drizzle and dense fog, reducing the hard, red Vietnamese soil to mud, visibility to 25 meters, and the ceiling to zero. Despite weather and terrain problems, Company G continued the climb toward the objective.

As Hitzelberger's company moved up Co Ka Leuye, the two other regimental objectives were taken. Company F secured the ground for Erskine on 1 February, but was prevented from developing the fire support base by the same bad weather hampering Company G's movement. Four kilometers east of Cunningham, Company K secured a landing zone and began construction of FSB Lightning. Within hours of completion, the 1st and 2d Battalions, 2d ARVN Regiment, plus the 1st Battalion, 62d Artillery Regiment (ARVN) lifted into the fire support base just before inclement weather halted all helicopter operations.

Predictably, enemy-initiated attacks increased during this period of bad weather. On 2 February, FSB Cunningham received approximately 30 to 40 rounds from one or more enemy 122mm field guns located on or near the border. Although one of the 1st Provisional Battery's 155mm howitzers was temporarily disabled by a near hit, and the 3d Provisional Battery's fire direction center was put out of action by a direct hit, the batteries maintained uninterrupted counterbattery fire. The 2d Battalion, 12th Marines sustained

Two Marine UH-1E (Huey) helicopters touch down at the operation's main fire support and logistic base, Cunningham, bringing in additional supplies and personnel in support of the 9th Marines and artillery batteries of the 2d Battalion, 12th Marines.

Department of Defense Photo (USMC) A192655

THE SPRING OFFENSIVE PREEMPTED

Department of Defense Photo (USMC) A192844
Despite rugged terrain and heavy jungle growth, infantrymen of the 2d Battalion, 9th Marines struggle up one of the many ridges in the area of operations.

a total of five killed and an equal number of wounded. Subsequent crater analysis and aerial sightings indicated that the enemy guns were in Laos just beyond the maximum range of the battalion's 155mm howitzers. The Army's 175 guns, located along the coast, proved inaccurate but were used to harass. Therefore the only means of delivering effective counterbattery was by air. If the guns could be visually located, they could be destroyed. However, it soon became apparent that if an aerial observer (AO) remained on station for any length of time, all enemy fire would cease. Therefore, as Barrow later noted, "counterbattery was a simple thing of always having an AO up."[20] The fire support base continued to receive enemy incoming throughout the operation at sporadic but frequent intervals, notably when the observers left the area, even for short periods.

By the 3d, after four days of bad weather, Colonel Barrow had to make a decision. Should present positions be held? Had the regiment overextended itself by placing Company G on Co Ka Leuye? With no relief in sight and helicopter resupply and medical evacuations halted throughout the area, Barrow instructed the 2d and 3d Battalions to pull in their companies and hold them close to areas from which they could be easily supported. The decision proved to be a wise one, since Razor and Cunningham were well-stocked with rations and small arms ammunition. Artillery ammunition, however, was in short supply. The 2d Battalion, 12th Marines had attempted to stock extra shells, but the scarcity of heavy lift helicopters (Marine CH-53s and Army CH-47s), and the weather made it impossible to achieve the initial stockage objectives. Without the reserve, artillery missions had to be reduced. For the first 10 days of February, the battalion fired 6,078 rounds, assisting only engaged units.

Except for Company G, 2d Battalion, all rifle companies assumed a modified defensive position or were quickly moving into one by 4 February: Company L was on Cunningham, while I, K, and M were close by; Company H was on Razor; Company F was on Erskine; and Company E was at LZ Dallas. On the morning of the 5th, Hitzelberger's company began retracing its steps:

> As we came down off of 1175 my point element, which was from the 3d Platoon, observed three NVA off to the right; however, because of the contacts we had the previous day we decided to check out the area a little bit further. So I held the column in place and allowed the point fire team to go out to see if there was any more forces there or take the three NVA if they could. Our point then came under fire.[21]

From what Captain Hitzelberger was able to piece together, the company had been drawn into a classical U- or V-shaped enemy ambush.

The point fire team soon found itself pinned down in the midst of approximately 30 NVA troops scattered in low-lying bunkers and well-camouflaged among rocks and trees. Silhouetted against the sky if it attempted to withdraw, the team waited until the rest of the 3d Platoon was brought up. The 2d Platoon was then moved to the left, and as it started to sweep through the enemy position, came under a hail of automatic weapons and rocket propelled grenade (RPG) fire. With the 2d and 3d Platoons stopped, Hitzelberger decided to commit the 1st by swinging it further to the left and through a small ravine, flanking the enemy. By this maneuver, the 3d Platoon was able to break through and force the NVA to withdraw. The company then pushed through the ambush site to a communications line where it consolidated its position. A cursory check of the immediate area revealed two enemy bodies and several blood trails. Five Marines were killed and 18 wounded. Among those who gave their lives during the battle was fire team leader Lance Corporal Thomas P. Noonan, Jr., of Brooklyn, New York, who was posthumously awarded the Medal of Honor for his daring rescue of a seriously wounded fellow Marine.

With 30 minutes to reorganize for fear of a second attack, there was only time enough to destroy excess equipment and rig stretchers. At 1730, after putting out a strong rear guard and plotting artillery concentrations along the proposed route, the company moved down the ridge. The pace was slow and rest breaks frequent, as half the company was either assisting the walking wounded or carrying stretchers. At 0200 the following morning, Hitzelberger decided to stop and settle in for the night even though the company was split because of a treacherous slope.

Early the next day, the company consolidated and began its trek toward a predetermined rendezvous with a relief platoon from Company E. The terrain, as before, proved to be an obstacle. "At this time the stretcher cases were moving up and down slopes in excess of 70 degrees," reported Captain Hitzelberger, "we had to use six, eight and, at times, ten men to carry a stretcher and it would take us over 30 minutes to move one stretcher case over one bad area."[22] At 1400, the company paused and then began what was to be the most difficult part of its descent. During the next several hours, Marines roped the stretchers and wounded down the face of a rocky cliff without incident. At the bottom the company linked up with the relief platoon which had brought out medical supplies and the first rations the Marines had had in three days. For the next 36 hours, the company wound its way down Hill 1175 toward the river. Once on the Da Krong, Marine aircrews made a heroic effort to extract the most seriously wounded. In dense fog, two medical evacuation helicopters from HMM-161 flew south up the Da Krong, using the river as their guide. Without Huey gunships for cover, and after having been fired on from the high ground during their approach, the two CH-46 helicopters landed, picked up the casualties, and returned to Vandegrift.

On the 8th, Company G returned to LZ Dallas. The ordeal, as Lieutenant Colonel George C. Fox later noted, "was a tremendous performance in leadership and fire discipline . . . . I went out and talked to those

Marine Corps Historical Collection

Capt Daniel A. Hitzelberger, right, and GySgt Charles A. Baker led the Marines of Company G off Co Ka Leuye ridgeline during an extended period of bad weather and heavy fighting when it was impossible to reinforce and resupply the company by helicopter.

young Marines as they came in; every last one of them. They were smiling and laughing. Their clothes were torn, and in some cases completely off of them, but they were ready for a fight."[23]

The two ARVN battalions on FSB Lightning experienced a somewhat similar problem. As the weather closed in on 1 February the battalions' direct support artillery battery and remaining supplies were in the process of being inserted. By the time all helicopter operations halted, only one of the six 105mm howitzers and 400 rounds of ammunition had been delivered. The battalions themselves carried only the basic allowance supplied to each infantryman. With conventional resupply out of the question, it was decided to attempt a helicopter-parachute drop by directing two CH-46s from HMM-161 over the target with the assistance of the Vandegrift air support radar team (ASRT).* Both drops landed within 100 meters of the ARVN position, even though the team's radar equipment was operating beyond its normal range.

From 5 to 8 February, Marine fixed-wing KC-130s made additional ASRT-controlled drops adjacent to Marine positions. Although the "Hercules" could drop greater quantities of supplies, the drops proved to be less accurate, and the percentage of loads recovered fell from 80 to 66. These initial experiences led to a

---

*The ASRT employed a radar-course-directing central computer which consisted of a precision radar and associated computer equipment designed to accurately position aircraft without visual reference to the earth's surface.

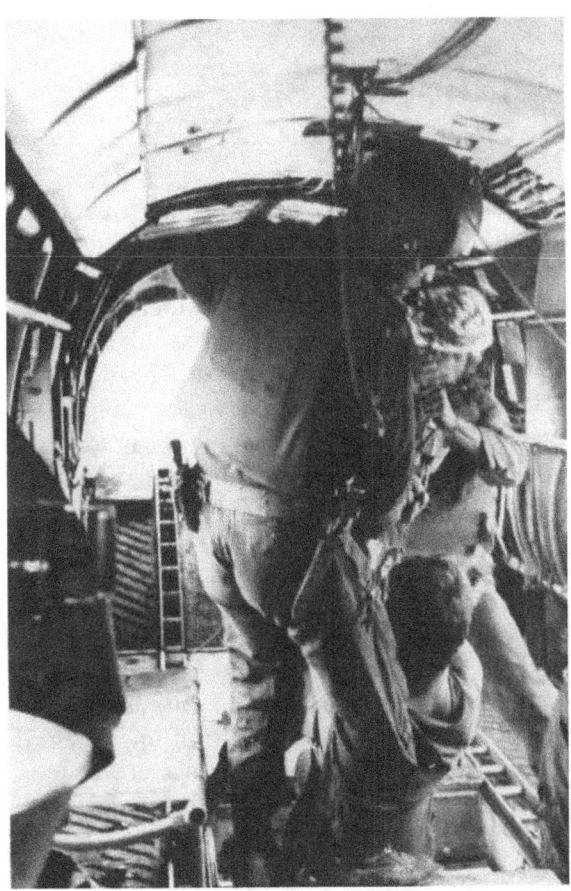

Marine Corps Historical Collection

Using a winch and cable, aircrewmen from Marine Medium Helicopter Squadron 242 hoist a wounded Marine through jungle canopy into a hovering CH-46.

refinement of the Vandegrift facilities and the installation of a second ASRT team at Cunningham on 26 February.[24] Working together, they provided extended radar coverage, increasing the accuracy of subsequent resupply drops and the regiment's counterbattery capability during periods of darkness and inclement weather.

Another innovation that paid high dividends concerned the handling of casualties in the field when poor weather conditions precluded helicopter medical evacuations. In November 1968, the regimental and three battalion surgeons had developed and fabricated a helicopter-transportable aid station, capable of providing maximum lifesaving care as field conditions would allow. One such aid station accompanied the 9th Marines to Cunningham and was placed into full operation soon after the fire support base opened. During the first week of February, when the weather would not permit helicopter evacuation of casualties, the Cunningham station proved invaluable in the number of lives saved.

Nine days of bad weather cost the regiment its momentum. They also permitted the enemy, who by this time had determined the purpose and strength of the Marine attack, to prepare and fortify his defenses. By 10 February, the weather cleared sufficiently for helicopters to move elements of the 1st Battalion from Vandegrift and Shiloh to FSB Erskine, and Battery F from Razor to Erskine. With all battalions in place, the stage was now set for the southward drive across the Da Krong.

CHAPTER 4
The Raid into Laos

Across the Da Krong—The NVA Retaliates—Ambush Along 922—Heavy Fighting Back Into Laos—Persistent Problems—Phased Retraction—Laos: Repercussions

Across the Da Krong

The 3d Battalion, 9th Marines crossed the Song Da Krong early on the morning of 11 February, initiating Phase III of Operation Dewey Canyon. The 1st and 2d Battalions followed the next day. According to the concept of operations, each battalion was given a zone of action approximately five kilometers wide, and an objective about eight kilometers south southwest of the point of departure. To the east, the 3d Battalion was to attack along ridgelines 2,000 meters apart, with one company securing Hill 1228 (Tiger Mountain), and two companies taking Hill 1224 (Tam Boi). The 1st Battalion was to advance over two parallel ridgelines further west, converging on a single objective astride the Laotian border. On the regiment's western flank, the 2d Battalion was to attack through a broad valley with secondary assaults on the ridges to the east. The battalion's final objective also lay on the South Vietnamese-Laotian border.

Tactically, Colonel Barrow divided each battalion: two companies attacking along parallel ridgelines with two companies in trace. The lead company was to attack and if heavily engaged, the company in trace, or its platoons, was to act as the maneuver element, assisting the attacking company and securing a landing zone for resupply and medical evacuation, if necessary. When the situation permitted, the company in trace would assume the lead and the company in the attack would fall back. The scheme of movement, according to Barrow, "was masterfully done." "Battalion commanders went right along with [their troops], no jeeps obviously, or any of that nonsense."[1]

As each battalion moved across Phase Line Red, it made strong contact. Three companies of Lieutenant Colonel George W. Smith's 1st Battalion immediately encountered a sizeable enemy force which had apparently been positioned to mount a ground attack against FSB Erskine. Assisted by well-aimed fire of five artillery batteries, the Marines forced the enemy to withdraw, leaving behind 25 killed in addition to numerous weapons, packs, and explosives. Meanwhile, further east, Company M threw back a mortar-supported ground attack by an estimated NVA platoon, killing 18 while losing two Marines. After fighting a day-long series of minor skirmishes on the 13th, Company C collided with a mortar- and machine gun-reinforced enemy platoon, deployed on a hilltop in a line defense. The ensuing Marine assault forced the enemy from the hill, killing 12 NVA. That night, the Marines employed mortars and artillery to break an enemy effort to retake the hill, claiming an additional 12 NVA during the battle. Company C losses for the day were two killed and 21 wounded.

The opposition the Marines found themselves up against was determined and formidable. Enemy forces, unlike those encountered during Phase II, were well-disciplined and remained in their bunkers or fighting holes until overrun or destroyed. At night they would probe or attack Marine company positions using squads or platoons. Snipers frequently were tied in trees, and would fire at close range or wait until Marines were directly beneath and drop grenades. These suicide techniques seemed to be designed for only one purpose: to prevent or delay the Marines' advance on Route 922, and the important supply area and artillery positions which encircled it.

The enemy's tough resistance achieved little success. Employing a heavy volume of accurate artillery fire and air strikes, the three battalions advanced steadily southward. Attesting to the performance of Marine firepower, two 122mm field guns were destroyed on 15 February—one by air, the other by artillery. Marine scout-sniper teams also contributed to the success of the attack by shooting their NVA counterparts out of trees on several occasions.

Sharp clashes across the entire front marked the action on 16 and 17 February. On the left flank, Company K, 3d Battalion, moving toward an intermediate objective, was attacked from the front and rear by an unknown number of North Vietnamese troops. Using all available supporting arms to silence enemy mortar and rocket propelled grenade fire, the company killed 17 and seized a number of weapons in taking the position, while sustaining few casualties. On the 17th, while advancing along the right flank, Company G, 2d Battalion exchanged small arms and supporting fire with an enemy company in a daylong running

THE RAID INTO LAOS

Riflemen of the 2d Battalion, 9th Marines cross the shallow Song Da Krong below FSB Cunningham, beginning the long-waited-for penetration of enemy Base Area 611.

battle. Thirty-nine NVA lost their lives, while the Marines counted five killed and 12 wounded.

The NVA Retaliates

In observance of *Tet*, the North Vietnamese and Viet Cong unilaterally declared a weeklong truce. The allied countrywide 24-hour truce went into effect at 1800 on 16 February. But as Major Joseph B. Knotts, the regimental operations officer, commented: "out on Dewey Canyon you wouldn't know there was any."[2] At 0345 the following morning, an enemy sapper platoon supported by a reinforced company launched an attack on FSB Cunningham. Dressed in shorts, skullcaps, and weighted down with explosives, the NVA broke through the defensive wire and dashed toward the center of the fire support base, tossing concussion grenades and satchel charges into every open hole. Although initially caught by surprise, the Marines of Company L, securing the fire support base, quickly organized a drive to clear the base in the face of heavy enemy mortar and recoilless rifle fire.

Lieutenant Colonel Scoppa's 2d Battalion, 12th Marines bore the brunt of the attack, suffering major damage within the first minutes; the battalion's fire direction center was put out of action, as was one howitzer. Within 30 minutes, however, the battalion reestablished centralized fire control and batteries continued with their missions. Throughout the night they expended 3,270 rounds on targets of opportunity, suspected assembly areas, and likely escape routes; included among the total were 147 "flechette" and "beehive" rounds of direct fire. In support, the ARVN 105mm battery on FSB Lightning unleashed reinforcing fires totalling 340 rounds.

A sweep of the base and surrounding hillsides at first light revealed 37 NVA bodies, 13 of which were within the perimeter. A number of individual weapons, grenades, and packs were also located, the latter containing quantities of marijuana and other drugs. The use of narcotics, Second Lieutenant Milton J. Teixeira explained, "made them a lot harder to kill. Not one of the gooks we had inside the perimeter had less than three or four holes in him. Usually it took a grenade or something to stop him completely."[3] Four Marines lost their lives and 46 were wounded during the three-hour defense. On the 20th, Companies E, G, and the command group of Lieutenant Colonel James J. McMonagle's 2d Battalion, 3d Marines assumed the mission of providing security for Fire Support Bases Cunningham and Erskine, relieving Companies G and L, which joined their respective battalions in the move southward.[4]

Ambush Along 922

The heaviest fighting of the Da Krong campaign took place from 18 to 22 February, the majority occurring within the sector assigned to Lieutenant Colonel Smith's 1st Battalion. On the morning of the 18th, Company A encountered stiff opposition from an enemy platoon dug into camouflaged, reinforced bunkers on a heavily forested ridgeline, five kilometers southeast of FSB Erskine. Armed with small arms

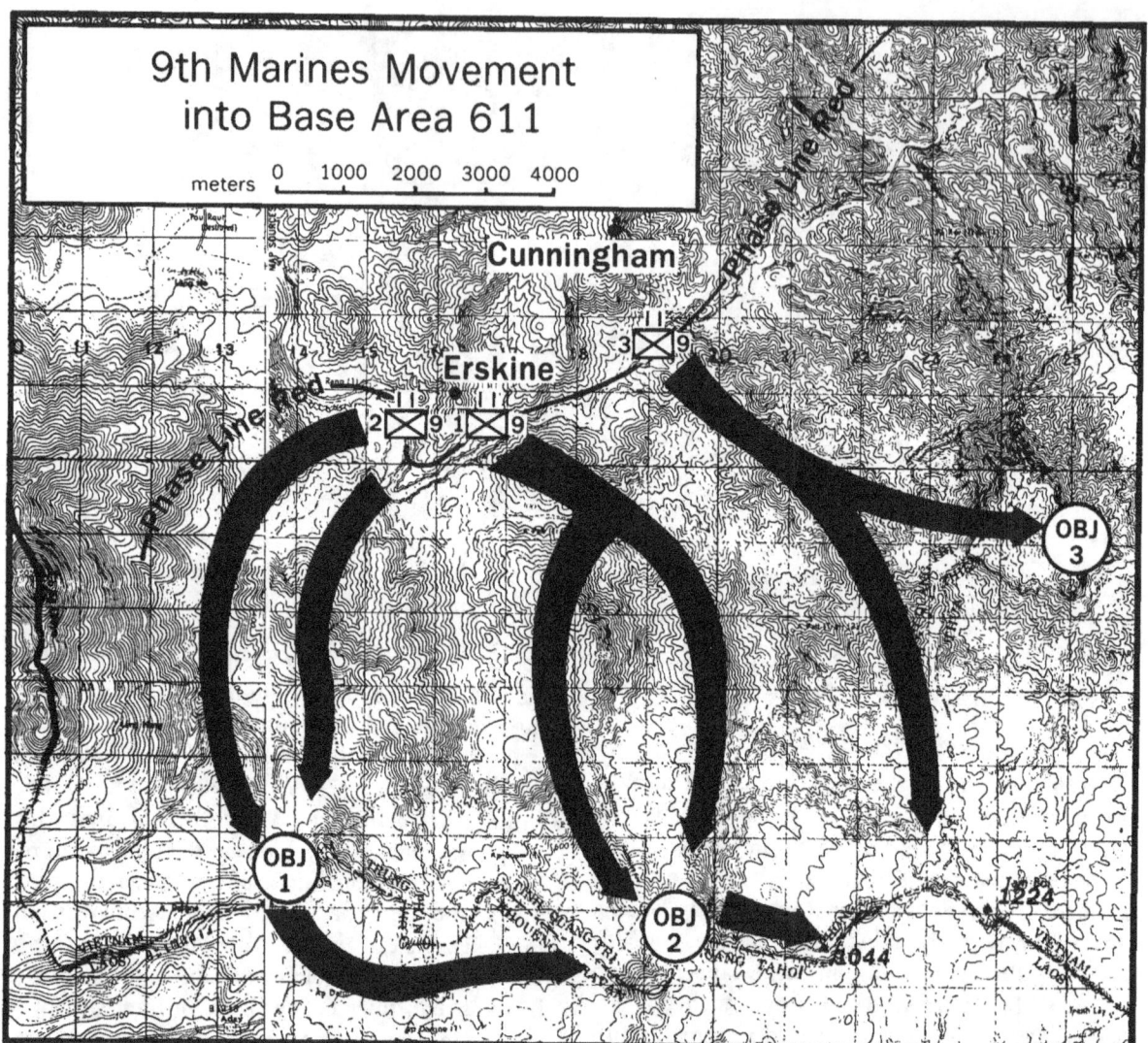

See Reference Map, Sections 16, 17

and automatic weapons, the enemy "appeared to want to hold their position at all cost."[5] Preceded by air and artillery strikes, Company A assaulted and overran the position, counting more than 30 NVA dead. The following morning, Company C moved through Company A's lines and continued the attack against the heavily reinforced hilltop emplacement, killing an equal number of NVA. Friendly casualties resulting from the two actions were one killed and 14 wounded.

Pressing the attack through the bunker complex, Company C again made contact during the late afternoon on the 20th, engaging a large enemy force supported by small arms, grenades, and machine gun fire. Two hours later, the Marine assault, assisted by fixed-wing air strikes with napalm drops within 50 meters of the point element, carried the position, killing 71 NVA. Equipment captured included two Russian-made 122mm field guns, and a five-ton, tracked prime mover.* Employing company rotation tactics, Company A continued the attack through Company C's forward lines and overran yet another enemy emplacement, killing another 17 NVA and seizing a two-and-one-half-ton truck and assorted artillery and antiaircraft ammunition. Marine losses sustained in the two actions were five killed and 28 wounded in Company C, and one killed and two wounded in Company A.

As the attacking forces neared the Laotian border, concern over enemy artillery attacks, protection of the regiment's right flank, and potentially lucrative ene-

---

*The two 122mm artillery pieces, the largest captured during the Vietnam War, subsequently were evacuated. One of the field guns is on display at the Marine Corps Air-Ground Museum, Quantico, Virginia.

my targets generated plans and requests for the tactical deployment of troops across the international boundary. After discussion at division and with XXIV Corps, Major General Davis forwarded a message to MACV requesting that the Special Operations Group (SOG) expand and redirect ground reconnaissance and exploitation operations, codenamed Prairie Fire, being carried out in the Laotian panhandle, toward Base Area 611.[6]* MACV approved and quickly implemented the request.[7] Reacting to the NVA artillery attack of 2 February on FSB Cunningham, Davis had initially requested that the 9th Marines be permitted to enter Laos and destroy the threat: "From the present position of the 9th Marines, a raid by a force of two battalions could be launched quickly and effectively to cut road No. 922 and moving rapidly back to the east, destroy art[iller]y forces and other forces and installations which threaten us."[8]

Davis' request was put aside for a period as current rules of engagement did not permit the introduction of a large combat force into Laos for the purpose of conducting what was in essence a secondary search and destroy operation, and which could possibly be viewed as an expansion of the war. The rules did permit United States and other Free World World Forces to "maneuver, while actually engaged and in contact with enemy forces, into Laos as necessary for the preservation of the force," and employ artillery and air strikes on threatening military targets. The rules in no way prohibited commanders from taking the "necessary counteractions against VC/NVA forces in the exercise of self-defense and to defend their units against armed attacks with all means at their disposal."[9] These exceptions provided the 9th Marines with the justification it needed.

As Barrow's troops moved further south, it became increasingly clear that the enemy was making extensive use of Route 922, either to reinforce or to withdraw his forces. "In either case, interdiction of the road was clearly essential," noted Colonel Barrow. "Efforts by B-52 arc light strikes, fixed-wing attacks, and unobserved artillery had been to no avail; he was continuing to use it. During the day the AOs were reporting fresh vehicle tracks, including tracked vehicle tracks on the road, and as our forces moved fur-

---

*The mission of the Special Operations Group's Prairie Fire program provided for crossborder reconnaissance operations into the panhandle of Laos using combined US/RVN forces to locate, interdict, and destroy enemy personnel and equipment on infiltration routes into South Vietnam.

ther south, we could hear vehicles on the road. This was a pretty unacceptable situation, and it cried out for some sort of action to put a stop to it."[10]

By 20 February, two companies, E and H, of Lieutenant Colonel Fox's 2d Battalion were on the Laotian border. At least two additional companies were expected within the next 24 hours. As Company H sat on the ridgeline overlooking the border and Route 922 beyond, Marines watched as an enemy convoy composed of truck and tracked vehicles moved slowly in a westerly direction along the road. As Captain David F. Winecoff later reported:

> The company, of course, was talking about let's get down on the road and do some ambushing. I don't think they really thought that they were going to let us go over into Laos, . . . I knew if the military had their way we'd be over there in Laos and the company was all up for it . . . . With the Paris Peace Talks going on, I wasn't sure what route was going to be taken.[11]

Winecoff reported the observations and fire missions called, but from "1,700 meters away it is difficult to zero in on movement."[12]

With the information provided by Winecoff's company, and intelligence gathered by SOG teams and 1st Radio Battalion intercepts, indicating that the enemy was evacuating its heavy artillery westward out of the reach of the 9th Marines, Lieutenant General Stilwell revived Davis' initial request. In a message to Lieutenant General Cushman on the 20th, he recommended a limited raid into the heart of enemy Base Area 611 to a maximum depth of five kilometers along a 20-kilometer front. If, however, the proposal was "beyond the realm of political acceptability," he suggested a lesser course of action which would involve the use of a Marine company as an extraction force if SOG reconnaissance teams encountered trouble. According to Stilwell, "this would multiply the number of SOG RT teams which could be deployed simultaneously."[13] Cushman, in a message to General Abrams later the same day, passed on the suggested courses of action and noted that "while recognizing the political implications of Gen Stilwell's proposals, . . . balanced against the military value of this unique opportunity, I fully endorse both."[14] The matter of an incursion into Laos was now left up to Abrams.

Events in the field, however, moved more rapidly. Company H, on the night of the 20th, again observed heavy truck traffic on Route 922. Winecoff reported the observations, and once again the company directed a number of fire missions on the targets, but with unknown results. The following afternoon, Captain Winecoff received a hand-coded message, the result of several days of planning, from Colonel Barrow directing him to set up a company ambush along Route 922 that evening, with specific instructions to be back in South Vietnam no later than 0630 the next morning.[15] "Hotel Company," reported Barrow, "was in the best position; really the only position to do it, and the job fell to them."[16] Winecoff immediately requested a 24-hour postponement because of the limited time available and the condition of his men, most of whom had been on patrol since early morning. Barrow denied his request.

With no time to rehearse and little time to plan, Captain Winecoff decided to use only his 1st and 2d Platoons, as the men of the 3d were exhausted after

The advance of the 1st Battalion, 9th Marines is halted temporarily by a group of North Vietnamese support troops attempting to protect their supplies and road network.

Department of Defense Photo (USMC) A193159

THE RAID INTO LAOS

Marine Corps Historical Collection
One of the 12 captured North Vietnamese Army 122mm field guns. With a range of 14 miles, it was the largest enemy artillery piece captured in Vietnam.

several tiring days of continuous patrol. At 1610, the company command group and the 1st Platoon, reinforced by mortar, forward observer, and machine gun teams, moved out for the 2d Platoon's position at the bottom of the ridge, leaving the 3d as security. Making good time over difficult terrain, they joined the 2d Platoon a little over an hour later, and the 1st passed through the 2d Platoon's position to establish the planned order of march. At 1800, after a meal and a 30-minute forward reconnaissance, the order arrived to execute and Winecoff quickly briefed the company on ambush tactics, signals, and night movement.

Shortly after dark, the company headed toward the road, 900 meters away. Staying off trails and using a creek bed and then a ridge line to minimize noise, the point element reached the small river which paralleled Route 922 at about 2030. Winecoff halted the column and sent his lead platoon commander and the chief scout, an experienced Marine sergeant, forward to find a route across the stream and to select an ambush site. As the company waited, it observed six trucks pass in front of its position; each stopping for a short period to "recon by silence."[17] A tracked vehicle mounting a spotlight also passed. "It was a very exciting moment for Hotel Company because the spotlight was scanning up and down the river and on the bluff, and it was playing over the lead elements of the company, but we were not spotted. Finally it proceeded on down the road."[18]

The two-man reconnaissance team returned around 2215, and after a quick brief, the company moved forward, crossing the river in column formation and then the road. About 35 meters beyond, Winecoff halted the company and set up a hasty linear ambush with the 1st Platoon on the right, and the 2d on the left, and the command group in the center. Within minutes of moving into position, the Marines heard trucks approaching from the west. They passed the word to let the vehicles proceed through the ambush site, as the claymores and flank security were not yet in place. By 0100 in the morning, the ambush was ready.

With the men of Company H about 500 meters inside Laos, Colonel Barrow informed Task Force Hotel of the move, "thinking that even that much of a minor violation might in itself provide a little bit of assurance

Marines move down one of the numerous enemy supply roads which crisscrossed the enemy base area.
Marine Corps Historical Collection

of approval." "There was a little bit of opposition to what we were doing, and much discussion," noted Barrow, "and finally approval came through that, yes, we could do what we were going to do, but the implication clearly was, you had better make it work."[19]

While the 9th Marines' staff obtained approval, Winecoff's men waited. The wait was not long. Less than ten minutes after setting up the ambush, a single NVA appeared, aimlessly walking along the road firing his AK47 assault rifle into the brush. Not wanting to "bag one NVA soldier," Winecoff passed the word to let this "dude" walk through the killing zone. Forty minutes later, flank security detected a single truck approaching. Again not wanting to destroy just one vehicle, Winecoff passed the order to let it through, instructing his forward listening post to visually check its contents. As it turned out, the truck carried a load of lumber.

The next half hour was tense for Winecoff's men; nothing moved, but voices could be heard 800 to 1,000 meters off to the right. "I felt," Captain Winecoff noted, "that sooner or later something was going to be coming along into the killing zone."[20] The company continued to wait. Meanwhile, a radio request came in from the battalion asking for a status report; they were "afraid that we'd blown it," but Winecoff assured them otherwise. At 0230, the lights of eight trucks suddenly appeared off to the east. All positions were alerted. As the trucks moved closer, stopping now and then to "recon by silence," the men of the ambush braced for action.

Three of the vehicles had already entered the killing zone when the entire column stopped. Fearing that the enemy would detect his ambush, Winecoff detonated his claymore. With a loud roar and a boiling cloud of thick, black smoke, the mine disabled the second truck, killing its three passengers. As the smoke cleared, Winecoff could see that the explosion had also set the first truck afire and forced the third off the road. Small arms and automatic weapons fire poured into the vehicles from the flanks; "everybody had been waiting a long time and the excitement was keen."[21] Within seconds the forward observer alerted the artillery and rounds bracketed the company position.

After several minutes of unrestricted fire, Winecoff gave the signal to move forward, making sure everything within the ambush site was destroyed. Once on the other side of the road, the company was given "left face," and "we proceeded in column right back in the same direction we came, crossing the river in the exact area, up the other side, and went about 5 to 600 meters up to a rally point where we . . . hung 'till daylight."[22] Later, the company rejoined the 3d Platoon on the ridgeline where it was resupplied and the men given a rest. In addition to the three trucks destroyed, H Company counted eight NVA dead. Not a single Marine had been killed or wounded by enemy fire.

First reports of the ambush to reach the 3d Marine Division were sketchy and based largely on monitored 9th Marines radio traffic. Colonel Martin J. Sexton, 3d Division Chief of Staff, immediately recommended that only XXIV Corps and III MAF be informed of the incident and that no report would be relayed to MACV until Brigadier General Frank E. Garretson, commanding Task Force Hotel, had prepared a "spot report in compliance with directives pertaining to rules of engagement."[23] On being informed of the ambush, Brigadier General George E. Dooley, III MAF Chief of Staff, was elated: "Hit 'm hard! Good news—who knows where the border is anyway?"[24]

About mid-afternoon on 22 February, a reply to Stilwell's and Cushman's messages of the 20th arrived at III MAF. Responding to their proposals, General Abrams stated emphatically that "all operations in connection with Base Area 611 will be with SOG forces," and that close coordination between Marine units in South Vietnam and SOG teams in Laos was authorized.[25] Although an apparent conflict existed between the action of Company H, 2d Battalion, 9th Marines, and General Abrams' directive, Garretson solved it by making reference to the appropriate rules of engagement permitting a local commander to exercise the right of self-defense in his report.[26] However, larger questions remained. With all three battalions on or just north of the border, and substantial enemy installations and lines of communication directly ahead, what future direction was Operation Dewey Canyon to take? Was the international boundary to remain a permanent barrier to the 9th Marines?

While the ambush itself was dramatic and successful, its real value, according to Colonel Barrow, lay in the leverage it provided to request a continuation of such operations in Laos. "Therefore, the next day I sent a message to higher headquarters stating why we had done what we had done, reiterating the successes achieved, and then my final paragraph made an urgent request for authority to maneuver into Laos as applied from North-South gridline 01 to the North-South [east-west] gridline 02. This generally was about a 2,000 meter extension and included all of Route 922."

Again he stated that his request was based upon the "immediate and constant" enemy threat to his troops and on intelligence which continued to place enemy troops and equipment concentrations in the area. And, noted Barrow, "I put a final comment on my message, which said, quote, 'put another way, my forces should not be here if ground interdiction of Route 922 not authorized.' "[27]

Lieutenant General Stilwell would not give up. Adopting Barrow's recommendations, he requested authority from MACV for "a selected advance south to the east-west 02 gridline—a distance not exceeding two kilometers from the border at any point."[28] Faced with a *fait accompli*, General Abrams finally approved Stilwell's request on 24 February, but placed restrictions on all public discussion of the Laotian incursion, fearing possible adverse effects on international policy.[29] Knowledge of the operation was also to be limited; the American ambassador in Laos, William H. Sullivan, for example, was not informed until the operation was well underway, as was Laotian Prime Minister Souvanna Phouma, who when informed, "expressed understanding of the action and said the essential element was to keep the matter secret," but hoped it would be short.[30]

Heavy Fighting

In the regiment's center, Company A, 1st Battalion, protecting the battalion's left flank, continued to reconnoiter the site of the previous day's contact, and then headed east off the ridge on the morning of 22 February. About 1,000 meters from the battalion command post near Lang Ha on the border, the 1st Platoon encountered an NVA squad in well-positioned bunkers. Under Second Lieutenant George M. Malone, Jr., the platoon quickly overran the position, killing seven while losing one Marine. "At this point," observed First Lieutenant Wesley L. Fox, "it looked like that was all the resistance we had. Everything was quiet, so I radioed up to battalion to send the water details [from Headquarters and Service and C Companies] down to the creek. We were in bad need of water. The helicopters could not get in due to weather, and the battalion was low."[31] A 20-man detail moved down and as they started to fill canteens, they came under enemy 60mm mortar and machine gun fire. Lieutenant Fox immediately ordered the detail back, reoriented his 1st Platoon toward the south, and moved it forward, beginning the last large engagement of Operation Dewey Canyon.

Pushing through triple-canopied jungle, banana

Courtesy of LtCol Wesley L. Fox
1stLt Wesley L. Fox rests at Company A's position overlooking the Ho Chi Minh Trail, a week after the action for which he would be presented the Medal of Honor.

groves, and dense underbrush, Lieutenant Malone's platoon ran up against a reinforced NVA company in a well-prepared, well-camouflaged, and heavily fortified bunker complex. To the rear, on a high ridgeline, the enemy had emplaced RPGs, machine guns, and mortars. Fox moved up the 3d Platoon and placed it on line with the 1st. When the momentum of the assault faltered, the 2d was then committed through the center of the two attacking platoons. Even though casualties mounted, Lieutenant Fox found he could not use air and artillery support as the company was boxed in by a low ceiling, terrain, and vegetation, and so locked in combat that if he withdrew to use artillery, he would run the risk of incurring additional casualties. Momentum nevertheless had to be maintained.

As the three platoons pressed the attack, the company command group took a direct mortar hit, killing or wounding everyone except the executive officer, First Lieutenant Lee R. Herron, who was given command of the 2d Platoon. Lieutenant Fox, despite his wounds, continued to control the advance.* Finally,

---

*First Lieutenant Wesley Lee Fox was awarded the Medal of Honor for his actions during this engagement.

Department of Defense Photo (USMC) A192685

Infantrymen of the 3d Battalion, 9th Marines move up an artillery-scarred slope toward the crest of Tiger Mountain, Hill 1228, one of the regiment's three major objectives.

Company D, which had been ordered to assist, appeared, moving through the banana groves in front of Company A's position. "They had gotten off on the wrong trail and came in behind the enemy position, and then walked into our front." "At this time," noted Lieutenant Fox, "I realized that we had already penetrated the enemy position; we had already pushed through the entire position, and all Delta Company had to do was walk down and help us carry up our wounded."[32] Results included 105 NVA killed and 25 automatic weapons captured; the dead, clad in new uniforms, included several officers, all of whom were highly decorated veterans of other campaigns. Marine casualties were heavy: 11 killed and 72 wounded, 54 of whom required evacuation.

Because of Company A's daylong battle, the 1st Battalion reoriented its direction of search eastward, towards Hills 1044 and 1224 (Tam Boi). During the next four days, it moved along Route 548, just north of the border, encountering small groups of enemy personnel and discovering several minor arms caches. On 27 February, while searching the slopes of Hill 1044, Company D stumbled onto one of the largest enemy weapons and munitions caches of the war. "I was walking along the side of a road," Gunnery Sergeant Russell A. Latona reported, "and there was a bomb crater there and sticking out of the bomb crater I saw the footpod of a mortar bipod." Alerting the company, he ordered several men to start digging. "They dug down about four or five inches and they found boards. They lifted up the boards and they started digging a hole and this is when we found several weapons."[33] A further check of nearby bunkers and bomb craters revealed that the company had moved into the midst of an NVA supply depot, a storehouse which would eventually yield 629 rifles, 108 crew-served weapons (60 machine guns, 14 mortars, 15 recoilless rifles, and 19 antiaircraft guns), and well over 100 tons of munitions. The next two days were spent inventorying and then destroying the cache.

Meanwhile, on the left flank of the regiment's area of operations, although encountering lighter opposition, Lieutenant Colonel Laine's 3d Battalion gained substantial results. Attacking generally down the trace of Route 922 within South Vietnam, elements of the battalion uncovered numerous enemy facilities containing tons of supplies and equipment. On the 18th, Company L located an NVA cemetery containing 185 bodies, most of whom had been buried in June 1968. On the 21st, Company M found a well-camouflaged maintenance installation, complete with six repair pits, a bulldozer, a front-end loader, several disassembled engines, and more than three hundred 50-gallon fuel drums. Pushing southward, the battalion, after securing Hill 1228 (Tiger Mountain), began a detailed search of the Tam Boi mountain complex, discovering on the 23d two spiked 122mm field guns, along with a prime mover and assorted artillery, mortar, and small arms ammunition. Further penetration of the Tam Boi complex revealed a headquarters and administrative facility composed of 11 immense tunnels. Carved into solid rock, these 150- to 250-meter-long, cross-connected tunnels contained extensive repair shops, storage facilities, and a "hospital which they had abandoned very rapidly and left one patient on the operating table to die."[34] All were capable of withstanding direct hits from air and artillery attacks.

With Tiger Mountain secured, Battery E, 2d Battalion, 12th Marines displaced to the top on 28 February, and established FSB Turnage, named after a former 3d Marine Division commander, General Allen H. Turnage. The fire support base, used the year before by the 1st Cavalry Division, was opened primarily to provide balanced artillery support for further operations of the 3d Battalion in the northeast corner of Thua Thien Province.

Back Into Laos

Within hours of General Abrams' approval, Company H, 2d Battalion, 9th Marines was again instructed to move "back down onto the bloomin' Route 922." According to Captain Winecoff, the men's "morale zoomed way down because the company was extremely tired, [and] we were afraid that we were going to have to go off and leave our supplies . . . . This included half a pallet of 60mm mortar ammunition, quite a few C-rations, and of course not the beer; we consumed that."[35] But move out they did.

The plan was for Company H, followed by Companies E and F, to move into Laos, and then drive eastward along Route 922, forcing enemy troops into the waiting sights of the 1st and 3d Battalions. In addition, intelligence indicated that the NVA were desperately trying to evacuate their remaining artillery pieces in the face of the other two battalions' push southward. In essence, the direction of the operation was now toward removing the enemy threat to the regiment's right flank.

Once again on the road, Company H, after a six-hour night march, set up another hasty ambush, and at 1100 on the 24th, engaged six unsuspecting NVA soldiers, killing four. Moving eastward the following day, another 10 were engaged, resulting in eight killed, one 122mm field gun and two 40mm antiaircraft guns captured. Marine losses were two dead and seven wounded. Later the same day, a company patrol was ambushed by an estimated 15 enemy troops in fortified bunkers and fighting holes. Reinforced, the patrol pushed through the enemy position, killing two and capturing a second 122mm gun. Marine casualties were high: three killed and five wounded. Among those who gave their lives was Corporal William D. Morgan, who in a daring dash, directed enemy fire away from two wounded companions, assisting in their rescue. For this action, he was posthumously awarded the Medal of Honor.

Company H and the battalion "jump" or field command group, continued to move eastward, flanked by Companies E and F. "The thought here," noted Colonel Fox, "was to have a force in position to launch a flank attack quickly were we hit from the rear (west) by major enemy units advancing from deeper in Laos."[36] Progress was rapid; too rapid for some: "I felt that if we had been moving slower and had more time to check things out, we probably would have found a heck of a lot more equipment than we did," noted Captain Winecoff.[37] As it was, elements of the 2d Battalion did capture over 20 tons of foodstuffs, and thousands of rounds of ammunition, while killing 48 enemy soldiers.

By 1 March, the three companies were within 1,000 meters of the South Vietnamese border, having covered over 5,000 meters in five days against light enemy resistance. Two days later, they helilifted to Vandegrift Combat Base. The battalion, while in Laos, sustained eight killed and 33 wounded, 24 of whom required evacuation. All dead were officially reported to have been killed "near Quang Tri Province, South Vietnam"; no reference was made to Laos for political reasons.

Persistent Problems

While the 9th Marines enjoyed a number of successes it also experienced two critical and persistent problems during the month-long push southward, resupply of units in the field and casualty replacement. Early in the operation it was found that resupplying rifle companies without halting their forward progress or pinpointing their positions was impossible. To make matters worse, once a company was ready to continue its advance after being resupplied, a squad or platoon often had to remain behind to secure transport nets, water containers, and other items until retrieved. This not only reduced company strength, but unnecessarily exposed the smaller unit to attack. An effort was made to improve this situation through the use of a Helicopter Emergency Lift Pack, designed and fabricated by the 3d Shore Party Battalion. C-rations, ammunition, and other items were placed on wood pallets or bundled in discarded canvas, slung on inexpensive loop-type wire cables, and lifted into the field. Marines were then able to obtain their supplies, dispose of the packaging, and continue the advance with little or no delay.

Initially included among the items of the Emergency Lift Pack were 5-gallon plastic water bottles, which did not supply the need of Marines in the field, and were subject to leakage. Instead of increasing the number of containers, 155mm, 175mm, and 8-inch artillery canisters, each capable of holding approximately 13 gallons of water were substituted, and proved highly successful.[38]

A number of units sustained moderately high casualties, and, as a result, lost some effectiveness in the movement southward. Although anticipated in early planning, the 9th Marines, because of transportation problems, due mostly to weather, was forced to shift personnel already in the field about. Success was achieved, but in most cases units had to operate for several days below the desired strength level before receiving replacements.[39]

Phased Retraction

By the beginning of March, all the battalions of the 9th Marines had obtained their major objectives. Organized enemy resistance had virtually collapsed; most enemy troops not killed or captured had withdrawn westward, deeper into Laotian sanctuaries. There was scattered activity from small groups of enemy throughout the operational area, but it was apparent that no further significant contacts would occur.

The 9th Marines had successfully interdicted Route 922. It had captured or destroyed thousands of tons of enemy food, medical supplies, and ammunition. The equivalent of two medium artillery batteries (twelve 122mm field guns) and one light battery (four 85mm guns) had been seized, along with prime movers and munition carriers. Enemy underground headquarters, storage facilities, hospitals, and troop billeting areas, as well as his fortified positions, had

Marines inspect and inventory a portion of the tons of captured weapons and ammunition in what would be the largest haul of enemy supplies taken during the war.

Department of Defense Photo (USMC) A800583

been overrun and a significant portion of his antiaircraft potential was located and destroyed. In short, by 1 March, with the exception of mopping up, the 9th Marines had accomplished its mission.

The original concept of operations envisioned a leapfrogging retraction from the area of operations, with each element always under a protective artillery fan—the reverse of the technique used to get the regiment into the area of operations. This movement would have required about 10 battery displacements and, since a reasonable level of artillery ammunition had to be maintained during the leapfrog maneuver, it would have entailed approximately 25 heavy lifts per howitzer battery and five heavy lifts for the mortar battery, not including normal resupply lifts. If good weather prevailed, and helicopters were abundant, the leapfrog retraction would be accomplished in seven days.

As the operation drew to a close, however, several factors dictated a reappraisal of the original retraction plan. First, the weather showed no signs of improving. Second, continuation of the operation throughout the retraction phase would require an initial 100 lifts of artillery ammunition to bring stocks up to appropriate levels. That this level of lift support would not be forthcoming was evident from the daily shortfall of normal ammunition resupply during the last week of February and the first few days of March. For example, the 2d Battalion, 12th Marines required 93 lifts on 1 March to sustain normal artillery operations of which it received 35; the battalion required 94 the following day and only two were received. Part of the discrepancy was due to marginal weather; however, a larger part was due to limited helicopter assets. Finally, the 9th Marines was scheduled to relieve the 3d Marines in the Vandegrift-Rockpile-Route 9-Cam Lo area so that the latter could join Operation Maine Crag, which had already begun.

The retraction plan originally had the 2d Battalion scheduled to lift to Vandegrift on 3 March, followed by the 1st Battalion on the 4th. After the 1st Battalion was out, Battery F and the 1st Provisional Battery, which had been covering the 1st Battalion's sector of the area of operations from FSB Erskine, would displace to Vandegrift, and Company G, 2d Battalion, would close Erskine. On 5 March, the 3d Battalion and Battery E would lift to Vandegrift, leaving one company at FSB Turnage as security for the ARVN 105mm battery remaining there. On 6 March, the 2d ARVN Regiment would retract from its area of operations under cover of its battery on Turnage, and FSB Cunningham would be evacuated with all units going to Vandegrift. Finally, on 7 March, the ARVN battery and the one company from the 3d Battalion would be extracted from Turnage under the cover of fixed-wing aircraft, and the retraction of the regiment would be complete.

The first step in the retraction plan—the retrograde of the 2d Battalion—went as scheduled. Everything thereafter changed. The weather turned from marginal to bad. In addition, before clearing the area of operations, III MAF tasked the 9th Marines with linking up with and extracting SOG forces which had been operating in Laos. A third development was the discovery of additional cache sites in the eastern portion of the operational area which had to be searched.

On 8 March, the 1st Battalion, with its huge cache exploited, began to move overland to Tam Boi. In addition, FSB Erskine was evacuated, with Battery F going to Ca Lu and the 1st Provisional Battery going to Vandegrift. Two plans were then developed, designated A and B, for further operations and the extraction of the remaining forces, both of which hinged on whether or not the 1st Battalion linked up with SOG forces by 1300 on 10 March. If it did, Plan B provided for its extraction that day, followed by the displacement of all artillery on FSB Cunningham to Vandegrift before dark. Then on 11 March, Company K, 3d Battalion, would be extracted from Turnage and moved to Vandegrift under cover of fixed-wing aircraft. Plan A provided for the displacement of Mortar Battery to Tam Boi on 10 March to cover the extraction of the 1st Battalion; for the closing of Cunningham by Company K; and, finally, for the employment of Mortar Battery to cover the closing of Turnage. Eventually, the 9th Marines implemented a modified version of Plan A, which essentially followed the same scheme as the original, but which was changed frequently as weather and other factors dictated.

The weather finally broke sufficiently on 15 March to move Mortar Battery to Tam Boi, and to extract all the artillery and most of the 3d Battalion from Fire Support Base Cunningham.* Control centers established helicopter approach and retirement lanes which permitted all batteries to fire a continuous smoke and mortar suppression program until the last gun lifted

---

*During the movement of the 3d Battalion to Cunningham, Company M came under intense automatic weapons fire. During the firefight, Private First Class Alfred M. Wilson was killed protecting a fellow Marine from a grenade. For his heroic action, Private Wilson was posthumously awarded the Medal of Honor.

out. During their displacement, batteries on Cunningham fired over 1,000 rounds, including 547 rounds on active missions and 389 rounds of smoke. A small rear echelon left behind was brought out two days later.

Helicopters lifted the 3d Provisional Battery from Cunningham to Dong Ha. Army CH-47 "Chinooks" carried out the move, the first time that heavy-lift Army CH-54 "Skycranes" had not been used to move the 155mm Marine howitzers. Following the departure of the 3d Provisional Battery, Battery D displaced to Vandegrift, as did the 3d Battalion (-). With all batteries except two out of the area of operations, the 2d Battalion, 12th Marines decentralized tactical control of Battery E on Turnage and Mortar Battery on Tam Boi, and moved to Vandegrift. To provide fire support for the 1st Battalion and Company I, 3d Battalion, Battery E was given the mission of direct support of those units, and tactical fire direction of Mortar Battery; the 1st Battalion FSCC was given responsibility for all fire support coordination within the operational area.

Marginal weather dominated the execution of the withdrawal plan to the finish. Company K and the 2d Battalion, 12th Marines' rear echelon on Cunningham were extracted on the 18th, and the fire support base closed. By this time, the 1st Battalion had joined with SOG forces and was also ready to be extracted, but the weather closed in again, effectively isolating the battalion and exposing it to enemy ground probes and constant mortar fire.

To have followed the planned sequence of events might have required more good weather than it appeared prudent to expect. Therefore, when the weather around Tam Boi broke on the morning of the 18th, Lieutenant Colonel George W. Smith, commanding the 1st Battalion, decided to extract whatever could be lifted out, weather permitting. As a result, Mortar Battery was extracted first, and thus it did not provide covering fires for the evacuation of FSB Turnage as planned. Instead Battery E, in conjunction with fixed-wing and helicopter gunship strikes, covered the withdrawal of the 1st Battalion under heavy enemy mortar and antiaircraft fire, and was in turn covered by fixed-wing. Operation Dewey Canyon terminated at 2000, as the last helicopter touched down at Vandegrift Combat Base.

During Dewey Canyon, supporting arms played a decisive yet somewhat muted role due to weather. Marine fixed-wing aircraft flew a total of 461 close air support missions, expending over 2,000 tons of ordnance. At the same time, Provisional Marine Aircraft Group 39 and Marine Aircraft Group 36 flew nearly 1,200 helicopter sorties, transporting a total of 9,121 troops and 1,533,597 pounds of cargo. On the ground, Lieutenant Colonel Scoppa's artillery fired approximately 134,000 rounds in support of Marine and South Vietnamese infantrymen.

Both sides suffered heavy casualties. The Marines lost 130 killed and 920 wounded, while reporting enemy casualties of 1,617 killed and five captured. Enemy equipment losses were significant: 1,223 individual weapons, 16 artillery pieces, 73 antiaircraft guns, 26 mortars, 104 machine guns, 92 trucks, over 807,000 rounds of ammunition, and more than 220,000 pounds of rice.

The final score, however, reached far beyond mere statistical results. The Marine strike into the Song Da Krong Valley disrupted the organizational apparatus of Base Area 611, effectively blocking the enemy's abil-

Artillerymen of 2d Battalion, 12th Marines load a 4.2-inch mortar round while covering the withdrawal of the remaining elements of the 9th Marines.
Marine Corps Historical Collection

THE RAID INTO LAOS

ity to strike out at civilian and military targets to the east. Attempts to rebuild this base and reorder disrupted supply lines would be long and arduous. In reporting to General Abrams on Dewey Canyon, General Stilwell stated:

> In my possible parochial estimate, this ranks with the most significant undertakings of the Vietnam conflict in the concept and results: striking the enemy unexpectedly in time and place, destroying a NVA base area and LOC center and pre-empting a planned NVA spring offensive somewhere in ICTZ.... The enemy took a calculated risk in massing installations right at the border, misjudging our reach; he lost.... Above all though, a Marine Regiment of extraordinary cohesion, skill in mountain warfare, and plain heart made Dewey Canyon a resounding success. As an independent regimental operation, projected 50KM airline from nearest base and sustained in heavy combat seven weeks, it may be unparalleled. Without question, the 9th Marines' performance represents the very essence of professionals.[40]

Laos: Repercussions

Knowledge of the Laos incursion, ordered kept under wraps by General Abrams, found its way into the press during the first week of March, causing concern in Saigon:

> We have received word from III MAF that a number of correspondents have considerable knowledge of that part of Dewey Canyon that has extended into Laos. Newsmen apparently picked up bits and pieces from troopers while sitting around talking and eating. Media involved are AP, UP, NY Times, Newsweek, AFP, and the New Yorker. We have a rumor that some of the media have photos that they claim were taken in Laos; however, we cannot confirm that any newsman or photographer actually entered Laos in the Dewey Canyon area.[41]

Although the story was out, the official line was to say nothing on the subject, diverting press attention instead to the large amounts of enemy supplies captured.

On 8 March, however, Drummond Ayres, Jr., of the *New York Times* informed MACV that he was filing a story on Marine operations in Laos. Attempts were made to persuade Ayres to ignore the story, but it appeared in the Sunday edition of the *Times* the following day. While noting that Marines had "technically violated Laotian neutrality" guaranteed at Geneva in 1954, and again in 1962, the operations were carried out "to protect the flanks of Marine elements maneuvering nearby along South Vietnam's northwestern border." Concluding, Ayres reported that "Operation Dewey Canyon seems to indicate that allied commanders operating along borders may dip across lines to secure their flanks."[43]

The subject was brought up again during the final news conference of Defense Secretary Melvin R. Laird's fact-finding mission to Vietnam. Asked if American troops had been operating in Laos during the last week, Mr. Laird said:

> I would not confirm that they were there now but I would certainly say that there have been operations in which it has been necessary in order to protect American fighting forces that—that border being a very indefinite border—it may have been transgressed by American forces in carrying out this responsibility.[43]

The Secretary noted that the decision to permit operations inside Laos had been reviewed at the highest level and approved by General Abrams on the basis of the "safety of our men." He further explained that "Marines took up positions in Laos to protect their flank during a sweep of the area near the border."[44]

Secretary Laird's statements acknowledging the American incursion into Laos caused embarrassment in Vientiane. The Laotian Government immediately sought to counter the Secretary's remarks by issuing a communique "clearly designed to confine the controversy to a discussion of a single incident rather than to the general implications for Laotian neutrality." Ambassador William H. Sullivan subsequently apologized to the Laotian Premier for the incident and assured him that the United States would avoid any further extension of hostilities into Laotian territory.[45] The controversy did not end. In 1970 and again in 1973, the Marine incursion into Laos during Operation Dewey Canyon came to the fore, both times in connection with Congressional hearings on Vietnam.[46]

CHAPTER 5
The Quang Tri Border Areas

*No Change in Tactics—The DMZ Front—Brigade Mauls 27th—The 9th Battles the 36th
The Vietnam Salient—Apache Snow—Central DMZ Battles—Eastern Quang Tri and Thua Thien*

No Change in Tactics

Reviewing his tour as Commanding General, 3d Marine Division, shortly before his reassignment, Major General Raymond G. Davis noted, with pride, that the forces under his command were "now in a posture where we totally control Quang Tri Province." "However," he continued, "we cannot lower our guard or decrease our forces one iota so long as the enemy retains his total sanctuary in Laos and in and above the DMZ."[1] On 14 April 1969, General Davis was succeeded by Major General William K. Jones, a hardened veteran of Tarawa, where he earned the Silver Star; of Saipan, where he was awarded the Navy Cross; and of Korea where he commanded the 1st Marines. Unlike Davis, Jones found it unnecessary to reorient the tactical disposition of the division. He completely agreed with General Davis' concept of operations and "simply continued the various actions Davis had initiated."[2]

Neither Davis nor Jones lowered their guard, nor that of the division. Even though the enemy had largely been forced to withdraw to nearby North Vietnam and Laos, General Davis and then General Jones continued to maintain a strong, mobile posture characterized by essentially company-size operations. As General Davis described the tactic:

> A company will be put into an area two or three kilometers on a side, they'll cut an L[anding] Z[one] for resupply and medevac, and they'll work day and night activities until they've thoroughly searched out this area. By thoroughly searching out I mean: on every trail, every hill knob, every draw, every finger—total search-out of the area. Then they'd be lifted to another place.[3]

Relying on this tactic, the division initiated several operations in March throughout the border areas of Quang Tri Province with the aim of preempting enemy efforts to infiltrate major formations and supplies from cross-border sanctuaries or to use northern ICTZ redoubts and lines of communication to stage and move those supplies forward. The March campaign in western and northwestern Quang Tri did not develop heavy contact; rather, the actions were characterized by skirmishes with NVA screening forces and by the seizure of numerous, and often extensive, munitions and supply caches.

The DMZ Front

Combat action along the Demilitarized Zone, from the Laotian border east to coastal Cua Viet, had remained intermittent during January and February. Enemy forces engaged by 3d Marine Division, Army, and ARVN units were, by and large, elements of three independent NVA Regiments, the *27th, 138th,* and *246th,* all tasked with screening the DMZ front. Only occasionally encountered or employed in strength, these units primarily undertook reconnaissance missions, shellings, ambushes, probing and sapper attacks, and assisted in the movement of arms and supplies to local force Viet Cong units and guerrillas. But by the end of February, forward elements of the three regiments had gained key terrain south of the DMZ, especially in northwestern Quang Tri Province, where the *246th NVA Regiment* continued to push slowly southward.

Under the operational control of Task Force Hotel at Vandegrift Combat Base, commanded by Brigadier General Garretson until relieved by Brigadier General Robert B. Carney, Jr. at the end of March, the 4th Marines was given the mission of destroying the *246th* or driving the enemy regiment back into the sanctuary of the Demilitarized Zone. Once the enemy was forced to withdraw, Colonel William F. Goggin's Marines were to secure key terrain features on the DMZ's southern edge, and then move into the southern portion of the zone. The codename assigned to the 4th Marines counterattack was Operation Purple Martin.

The first day of March found the three battalions of Colonel Goggin's regiment patrolling along a broad front, 5,000 to 10,000 meters south of the DMZ. The 3d Battalion, under Lieutenant Colonel William A. Donald, continued to clear the northern portion of the area of operations, north of Fire Support Base Russell; Lieutenant Colonel Joseph E. Hopkins' 2d Battalion conducted search operations north of Fire Support Base Neville; and the 1st Battalion, under

Lieutenant Colonel George T. Sargent, Jr., cleared the northeastern portion of the area of operations, near Elliott Combat Base (Rockpile). First Lieutenant James M. Herron's Company C initiated the first significant engagement with the *246th* as it attempted to reoccupy LZ Mack, north of Elliott, in preparation for the regiment's move deeper into the area.

The action began at 0430 when the company's night defensive position received four rounds of 60mm mortar fire, resulting in three casualties. Shortly after dawn the following morning, Lieutenant Herron's company began its assault. Supported by over 3,000 rounds of artillery fired by batteries of Lieutenant Colonel Eugene D. Foxworth, Jr.'s 3d Battalion, 12th Marines, two platoons first seized a small knoll north of the heavily fortified landing zone and then swept toward the summit. However, when the Marines reached the hilltop, three enemy mortars opened up, forcing the two platoons to withdraw with heavy casualties. During the assault, Company L, 3d Battalion moved up to serve as a reserve force, and overall conduct of the attack placed under the control of Lieutenant Colonel Donald, the 3d Battalion's commanding officer.

Hampered by dense fog and misting rain, and consequently a lack of air support, the two companies consolidated their defensive positions and prepared for a second attack. During the next three days, the enemy subjected Companies C and L to a continuous barrage of 60mm and 82mm mortars, sniper fire, and ground attacks, resulting in more than 15 Marine casualties. Shortly after midafternoon on the 5th, following another extensive artillery preparation, Lieutenant Herron's company again assaulted Mack. Once more two platoons were used, one to secure the small hill north of the landing zone in order to provide covering fire, and the other to move on the summit. The scheme of maneuver proved successful and the assaulting platoon reached the crest of the hill, where squad and fire teams fanned out, methodically clearing one enemy-infested bunker after another.

The enemy's determined defense of Mack characterized the type of engagement experienced by the 4th Marines throughout the area of operations: elements of the *246th* were prepared to fight. Well-equipped and well-supplied, North Vietnamese troops gave up terrain only when physically dislodged.

MajGen William K. Jones, left, assumes command of the 3d Marine Division from MajGen Raymond G. Davis at Dong Ha on 14 April. Jones, like his predecessor, would continue to place major emphasis on blocking enemy infiltration and capturing supplies.

Abel Papers, Marine Corps Historical Center

Department of Defense Photo (USMC) A192537
Infantrymen of the 4th Marines cross a jungle stream just south of the Demilitarized Zone in search of ever-elusive North Vietnamese Army infiltrators.

Sweeping near LZ Catapult on the 9th, Company G, 2d Battalion, engaged yet another large and determined enemy unit in battle. The landing zone, abandoned a year before, was significant as it was located 4,000 meters north of Fire Support Base Neville and dominated the extensive enemy trail network of the upper Cam Lo Valley. With intelligence information which confirmed not only North Vietnamese occupation of the general area, but their intention to hold the landing zone and surrounding terrain, Company G was given the difficult mission of resecuring Catapult.

As Company G, under the command of Captain Joseph M. Dwyer, moved slowly and cautiously from the south along a ridge toward the landing zone, supported exclusively by artillery as air was unavailable due to weather, resistance became increasingly stubborn. Entrenched enemy troops employed snipers, claymore mines, and ambushes to halt or delay the company's progress. On 10 March, Dwyer's Marines broke through the enemy's outer defenses and engaged a number of determined NVA troops in a running firefight which lasted throughout the day.

The next morning, as Dwyer's company continued the assault toward Catapult, the North Vietnamese launched a counterattack. Employing small arms, grenades, and RPG's, the enemy hit Company G on three sides. Fighting at close quarters, at times less than five meters, Dwyer's Marines suffered four killed and 13 wounded, including three killed and four wounded as a result of a 105mm short round. The violent fight, which lasted most of the day, finally broke the enemy's attempt to hold the landing zone. When the company completely secured Catapult on the 14th, Dwyer's Marines discovered 24 enemy bodies, all killed either by artillery or small arms fire.

While Dwyer's Marines were heavily engaged on Catapult, another sharp battle took place 12 kilometers to the east. On 13 March, Lieutenant Colonel Donald's battalion continued its push along the lengthy ridgeline from LZ Mack toward LZ Sierra. Abandoned two months earlier, Sierra was now in NVA hands, and had been used by the enemy as a mortar site in an effort to blunt the Marine assault on LZ Mack, 2,000 meters to the southeast. A dense fog hampered direct air support, forcing the battalion to rely solely on artillery and a small number of radar-controlled bomb drops. The terrain proved rugged. Punctuated by deep draws and steep hills, the ridgeline offered few avenues of approach, and as a result, every meter presented a threat of mines.

Lieutenant Colonel Donald assigned Company M, under the command of First Lieutenant Edwin C. Kelley, Jr., the task of resecuring Sierra, and First Lieutenant John P. Kiley's Company I the taking of a hill north of Sierra, commonly known as Sierra North. Companies K and L would be held in reserve. As Kelley's Marines began their advance, it soon became apparent that the landing zone was defended by a determined NVA platoon, located in well-constructed bunkers, capable of withstanding a direct hit by a 105mm artillery round. Supported by heavy covering fire emanating south of the landing zone, two of Kelley's platoons assaulted from the east through a hail of intense enemy small arms and mortar fire. Once the advance was underway, Kelley's squads and fire teams maneuvered from bunker to bunker, destroying the stubbornly entrenched enemy troops. Company M secured Sierra by late afternoon at a cost of 10 Marines killed and 35 wounded; 23 enemy troops lay dead in the smoldering ruins.

The following morning, Kiley's Marines advanced on Sierra North in a well-executed envelopment from the south. "Two hundred meters from the objective," Lieutenant Kiley recalled, "NVA were spotted on the hill, and there proved to be 11 in number. We were moving in a column; 2d Platoon had the point, followed by the CP group, then 1st Platoon, and then 3d Platoon . . . . I set up the company CP with one platoon as security, moved 2d Platoon up the hill followed by 1st."[4] As Marines of the 2d Platoon emerged from the heavily wooded area surrounding the crest of the hill, they laid down a heavy base of fire in order to permit the 1st Platoon to attack through. The enemy, apparently expecting an attack from the north, as 10-inch claymores were found facing only in that direction, were surprised inside their bunkers.[5]

While Company I was engaged on Sierra North, elements of the *246th* attacked Captain Kelley's company position, initiating the action by downing a CH-46 medical evacuation helicopter with an RPG round. Kelley's Marines beat back the assault, and again, tubes of the 3d Battalion, 12th Marines accounted for all the supporting fires. "After their counterattack failed," reported the battalion executive officer, Major Raymond D. Walters, "what forces they had withdrew and we didn't see any more of them in that area. So it became apparent that we had cleaned them out there and we decided to go on with our primary mission which was to establish our patrol bases in the DMZ . . . . Shortly after we commenced our DMZ patrols, we got an additional mission of constructing landing zones along the DMZ."[6]

On 20 March, the long-anticipated assault on abandoned Fire Support Base Argonne, to secure the regiment's western flank, began. The base, located on Hill 1308, two kilometers east of the border, offered observation into Laos and onto portions of the enemy's infamous Ho Chi Minh Trail. Planned for almost a month, the assault had been postponed due to weather and lack of helicopter support, then heavily committed to the 9th Marines in the Da Krong Valley. By the 19th, the weather cleared and aircraft became available. At 2230, Colonel Goggin decided to conduct the assault the following day.

The proposed scheme of maneuver called for a three company advance, with one company landing on Argonne and two companies moving into the valley to the north. A reconnaissance team would be inserted prior to the assault and would guide the troop-laden helicopters into the landing zone. Goggin gave Lieutenant Colonel Sargent's 1st Battalion the task of securing Argonne, and in anticipation Sargent had moved his companies to FSB Alpine (Lang Hoan Tap), 16 kilometers to the south-southeast. With the Marines of the 1st Battalion came tons of supplies for the support of the Argonne assault and planned operations nearby. The establishment of a mini-logistical supply area on Alpine would prove an asset in the coming days by lessening the distance required for helicopter resupply lifts during periods of poor weather.

At 0930 on the 20th, after an extensive artillery and air preparation, team "Frostburg" from the 3d Reconnaissance Battalion moved toward the upper landing zone on Argonne by air. As the helicopter carrying the team approached the zone, an explosion rocked the area and a volley of small arms fire ripped through the aircraft cockpit, killing the pilot and wounding the copilot. Despite his wounds, the copilot brought the helicopter in and the team jumped out, immediately forming a hasty 360 degree perimeter around the downed aircraft. Within minutes of the crash, the NVA struck. After repelling the enemy's initial charge, the team leader surveyed the situation, and requested an immediate extraction. Following the team's departure, the first transport helicopter attempted to land with Lieutenant Colonel Sargent and elements of Company D on board. The downed UH-1E ("Huey") used by the team prevented the CH-46D transport from entering the upper zone; consequently, Sargent shifted the main assault to the lower zone.

The assault troops of Captain Joe B. Green's Company D received only sporadic sniper fire upon landing in the lower zone, but as the lead elements advanced toward the upper zone, enemy small arms and automatic weapons fire emanating from a mutually supporting bunker system intensified. Like the actions on Mack, Sierra, and Catapult, the Marine thrust on Argonne consisted of destroying the enemy by employing small fire teams methodically to clear each bunker. The company directed a heavy base of small arms fire toward bunker entrances, as one or two Marines crawled to within grenade range, and then assaulted the enemy fortifications. The battle to resecure Argonne continued until dark. Green's company suffered six killed and 11 wounded in the daylong advance, while accounting for 15 NVA dead. Due to the heavy fighting on Argonne, Lieutenant Colonel Sargent cancelled the helilift of the remaining two companies into the valley north of the landing zone.

At 0815 the following morning, an enemy mortar barrage of twelve 82mm rounds fell on the battalion's command post on Argonne, killing Lieutenant Colonel Sargent; Second Lieutenant Carl R. Wilson, Jr., the battalion S-2; two enlisted Marines and wounding 12 others. Later, as a medical evacuation helicopter extracted the casualties of the first attack, 10 more rounds hit the landing zone, resulting in an additional three killed and 11 wounded. The same day, Companies A and C lifted into an area south of the landing zone and began a sweep to the north. But with Argonne under mortar siege, Colonel Goggin modified the mission of the two companies, ordering Company A, under Captain Henry W. "Buzz" Buse III, son of Commanding General, Fleet Marine Force, Pacific, Lieutenant General Henry W. Buse, Jr., to move west, toward the Laotian border, in search of the suspected enemy mortar sites, and Company C to Argonne's relief. On 23 March, while the remainder of the battalion conducted search operations near Argonne in an effort to locate additional enemy harbor and mortar sites, Company B swept six kilometers toward the high ground to the northeast, where it established Fire Support Base Greene, opening the northern portion of the area of operation.

With the regiment firmly established within the area of operations and initial objectives achieved, Lieutenant Colonel Donald's 3d Battalion began reconnaissance operations within the Demilitarized Zone on 25 March. Companies I and K, deployed on hilltops south of the DMZ, overlooking major trail networks, were assigned the task. The size of reconnaissance patrols introduced within the zone were to be limited, according to the rules of engagement, to no more than a reinforced squad. Therefore, a typical 3d Battalion patrol included a squad of 14 Marines reinforced by a forward air controller, forward observer, platoon leader, corpsman, and a machine gun team.[7] Should a patrol become involved in a heavy engagement, a "Sparrow Hawk" reaction force would be deployed to aid in the squad's extraction, and only its extraction.

According to Major Walters, "contact within the DMZ was light. We did find a considerable amount of ammunition, bunkers, complexes, and we blew them as we went. But they weren't there to defend those positions and we never really got into a good fight in the DMZ at all. A couple of times we had to call in a Sparrow [reaction force] and extract the squads, but never did we get into any serious trouble in the DMZ."[8] Lieutenant Colonel Donald's battal-

During a lull in fighting, LCdr Frederick E. Whitaker, chaplain for the 3d Battalion, 4th Marines conducts services for Company M on a ridgeline north of Elliott Combat Base.

Department of Defense Photo (USMC) A192846

Abel Papers, Marine Corps Historical Center

Members of Company D, 1st Battalion, 4th Marines load another 81mm mortar round as the team prepares to fire on an enemy mortar threatening the battalion near Argonne.

ion maintained patrols within the DMZ, as well as in the vicinity of Landing Zones Sierra and Mack, both designed to halt enemy infiltration, until the end of the operation.

Near Argonne, Captain Buse's company continued to sweep northwest toward the high ground, Hill 1154, just east of the Laotian border. After a brief firefight on the 25th, Buse's Marines pushed through a bunker system, suffering only two wounded, but an artillery short round inflicted an additional three killed and 15 wounded. With mortar fire again directed against Argonne, Buse was ordered by Lieutenant Colonel Clair E. Willcox, who had taken command of the 1st Battalion following the death of Lieutenant Colonel Sargent, to take Hill 1154 and silence the enemy tubes. On 28 March, after fighting off an NVA platoon, the Marines of Company A pushed through yet another bunker complex and captured the hill. With Hill 1154 in Marine hands, enemy activity around and harassment of the regiment's western-most fire support base rapidly decreased.

First Battalion Marines continued search operations in the vicinity of Argonne until 3 April when the command group and the remainder of Company B moved by helicopter to Fire Support Base Greene. Company A Marines searched west and then northeast of Argonne, moving to Greene on the 7th. Companies C and D swept north from Argonne, conducting operations along the DMZ northeast of LZ Bell. The two companies maintained search operations in the area for the remainder of Purple Martin. After more than two weeks of fighting around Argonne, Willcox's battalion accomplished its mission; enemy infiltration routes were disrupted, and forces guarding the Ho Chi Minh Trail pushed back into Laos with considerable casualties.

Throughout April and into the first week of May, the number of 4th Marines engagements with screening elements of the *246th NVA Regiment* remained relatively constant. Enemy troops encountered, like the month before, were well-equipped, well-supplied, and prepared to defend key terrain. On 10 April, while searching a section of the upper Song Cam Lo Valley, two kilometers south of the DMZ, Marines of Com-

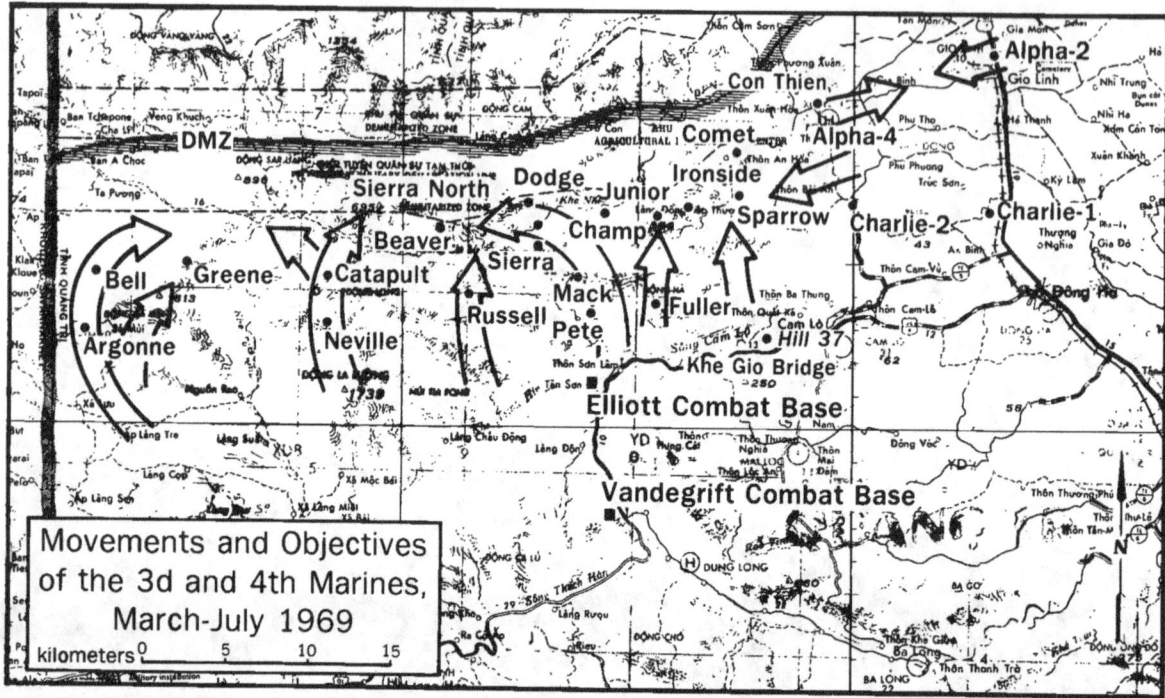

See Reference Map, Sections 1, 2, 3

pany E, 2d Battalion received fire from a well-camouflaged enemy cave complex. Advancing slowly toward the complex, set in towering cliffs bordering the river, Captain Albert H. Hill's company captured two wounded enemy soldiers, one of whom proved to be the commander of the *1st Company, 1st Battalion, 246th Regiment*. Both were extracted immediately and were of considerable intelligence value.

Captain Hill, in order to clear the cave complex, combined both psychological techniques and accepted tactics designed for assaulting a fortified position. A psychological operations team, under the battalion's intelligence officer, was brought in as was a flame section. Using a loudspeaker, the team, in the face of enemy hurled obscenities, endeavored to coax the North Vietnamese troops into surrendering. Three enemy soldiers yielded to the team's entreaties, but the remainder refused, and the company, preceded by flamethrowers, assaulted the complex. After clearing the caves, Hill's Marines began a thorough search of the labyrinth, which yielded a substantial cache of individual weapons and ammunition.

By 25 April, having accomplished their goal of pushing the NVA back into the Demilitarized Zone, Hill's company and the remainder of the 2d Battalion, were ordered south, beyond the range of enemy 82mm mortars emplaced within the DMZ. Colonel Goggin directed the 1st and 3d Battalions to do likewise, but still maintain their reconnaissance efforts within the zone. These positions were being held on 8 May when Operation Purple Martin came to an end.

"Our objectives," noted Major George X. McKenna, the regimental S-3, "were to search and destroy throughout our AO, to push the enemy back, clear him away from our fire support bases, and push him as far north as possible, up to the southern limits of the DMZ. This was accomplished by late April, when all of our units were within 500 meters of the DMZ, strung over 35 to 40,000 meters on an east-west axis."[9] The battle had been hard fought. Before it yielded to the 4th Marines and withdrew into the Demilitarized Zone and westward into Laos, the *246th NVA Regiment* suffered over 347 casualties, three times that of Colonel Goggin's regiment.

Brigade Mauls 27th

With the 4th Marines heavily engaged against the *246th* to the northwest, elements of the 1st Brigade, 5th Infantry Division (Mechanized) began a reconnaissance-in-force operation in the Khe Chua Valley, north of Dong Ha Mountain (FSB Fuller), between Charlie-3 and the Elliott Combat Base. Units of the brigade, up to mid-March, had concentrated on weeding out enemy troops in areas south of Landing Zone Sharon, and along the coastal lowlands from Cua Viet to Wunder Beach. But as elements of the

THE QUANG TRI BORDER AREAS

27th NVA Regiment moved south from the DMZ, west of Cam Lo, with the aim of cutting Route 9, Davis directed units of the brigade to advance westward to counter the enemy threat.

Codenamed Montana Mauler, the counter-infiltration operation called for two tank troops of the 3d Squadron, 5th Armored Cavalry, reinforced with infantry, to enter the Khe Chua Valley and attempt to engage the *27th Regiment*. Once the cavalry troops encountered enemy units, the 1st Battalion, 11th Infantry would be brought in to reinforce.

Troops A and B, 3d Squadron, 5th Armored Cavalry, each with a platoon of infantry from Company D, 1st Battalion, 11th Infantry, swept into the valley from the east on 23 March. The two cavalry troops observed small groups of enemy to the north, and raked them with tank and artillery from fire support bases within range. The troops made few additional sightings as they worked westward along separate axes, finally linking up in mid-valley early in the afternoon.

At 1000 the following morning, lead elements of the cavalry troops encountered an unknown number of NVA soldiers entrenched in bunkers, north of the valley. After an exchange of small arms, automatic weapons, RPG, and tank fire, the brigade units pulled back in order to employ artillery against the enemy force, now estimated to be a battalion in strength. A request was made to Task Force Hotel for reinforcements, which in turn ordered Company I, 3d Battalion, 9th Marines, under Captain Joseph U. Arroyo, immediately airlifted into a makeshift landing zone south of the engaged Army troops. The brigade also alerted two companies of the 1st Battalion, 11th Infantry to prepare for an assault, on order, into an area north of the valley.

The enemy proved surprisingly elusive as Marine and Army units advanced slowly westward along the southern portion of the valley the following day. The two companies of the 1st Battalion, 11th Infantry conducted their planned air assault north of the valley, completing the movement by mid-afternoon. Due to the lack of significant engagements throughout the day, the brigade directed the 1st Battalion, with Arroyo's Marines attached, to sweep northward on the 26th in order to regain contact with the enemy battalion, suspected to have withdrawn further north.

At 0330, 26 March, before the sweep could be initiated, the enemy struck at the night defensive positions of the 1st Battalion, 11th Infantry with small arms, automatic weapons, mortar, and RPG fire, from the north, west, and east, inflicting few casualties. At daybreak, the battalion observed enemy movement to the north. As Army infantry elements probed in that direction, contact was reestablished and air strikes and artillery employed periodically throughout the day on the suspected enemy positions without much success. Experiencing difficulty not only with entrenched enemy troops, but also with the oppressive heat, as temperatures approached 105 degrees, the two companies returned to their positions of the previous night and prepared to resume the attack on the 27th. Meanwhile, Arroyo's Marines advanced northwest without incident, while the two armored cavalry troops searched the area near their previous day's position, finding documents and weapons indicating the presence of the *1st Battalion, 27th NVA Regiment*.

The 1st Battalion, 11th Infantry resumed its northward advance on the 27th, with Company B assigned to secure the high ground on the right flank, supported by Company A. Arroyo's Marines received the task of seizing the high ground on the battalion's left. Shortly after beginning their sweep, Companies A and B fell in with elements of the *27th*, occupying bunkers to the companies' northeast. Air strikes were called, followed by artillery fire on terrain ahead of the line of march. Midday found the two Army infantry companies just short of their objective. Meanwhile, Company C helilifted into blocking positions near Hill 208, the enemy's main position. As Company B moved foward toward the high ground, its objective, the enemy again struck with mortar fire and a ground counter-assault from the north. Again, the Army commander called air strikes and artillery to support the fires of Company B, which repulsed the enemy assault after an hour. Shortly thereafter, Company A too came under attack. And again tactical air struck the disruptive blow. Arroyo's Marines took their objective on the left without incident. The day's heavy fighting accounted for 120 enemy soldiers killed, while friendly losses numbered 13. Company B lost all of its officers except for a forward observer, who took command of the company during the latter stages of the day's fighting.

The three companies of the 1st Battalion, 11th Infantry, supplemented by Company I, 9th Marines, resumed search operations on the 28th, encountering few enemy troops. As added reinforcement, the remaining elements of Company D, 1st Battalion, 11th Infantry helilifted into the area from FSB Sharon. Also during the day, elements of the 3d Squadron, 5th Armored Cavalry moved into the eastern portion of the Khe Chua Valley in support of Company C on the right flank, which occupied Hill 208.

The following day turned out to be one of heavy fighting with considerable losses inflicted on the enemy. While attempting to secure a position in support of the planned helicopter assault by Arroyo's Marines, troops of Company D engaged an NVA force occupying a bunker complex on the right flank. Employing small arms, riot control agents (CS gas), and air strikes, the company accounted for five NVA killed. Moving north along a ridge, west of Company D, Company A also came under heavy attack, estimated at an NVA company. Attacking from the north, the enemy used small arms and RPG fire in an attempt to outflank and isolate the company's northernmost platoon. Expertly directed small arms and helicopter gunship fire, followed by massive air strikes, met the advance. As elements of Company B reinforced Company A, all units then came under mortar attacks from the northwest. In heavy fighting, Army and Marine defenders finally broke the enemy's daylong ground and mortar assault, counting more than 30 NVA dead.

During the next four days, the 1st Battalion, 11th Infantry conducted extensive search and clear operations over the battleground, moving in an east-southeast direction, looking for bypassed enemy positions and personnel. The 1st Battalion, 2d ARVN Regiment, helilifted into the area of operations on the 29th, initially searched along the southern boundary of the DMZ west of Con Thien, and then joined the 11th Infantry in a sweep of the northern half of the battle area. The combined Army, Marine, and ARVN force encountered few enemy troops, and consequently, the operation was terminated on 3 April. Elements of the *27th NVA Regiment* lost close to 300 troops as a result of the short allied strike into the Khe Chua Valley.

With the end of Montana Mauler, Arroyo's Marines returned to the 9th Marines while the 1st Battalion, 11th Infantry split. Company A returned to the coastal lowlands, while Companies B and C, joined by Troop A, 4th Squadron, 12th Cavalry; and Battery B, 1st Battalion, 40th Artillery; formed Task Force 1/11 and moved south. At Ca Lu, east of Vandegrift Combat Base, the task force was joined by Task Force 3/5, composed of Troops A and B, 3d Squadron, 5th Cavalry; elements of Company D, 1st Battalion, 11th Infantry; and Battery B, 5th Battalion, 4th Artillery, in a sweep of the Ba Long Valley. Beginning at the western end of the valley, the two task forces swept eastward along the Song Quang Tri, clearing Route 556, in a five-day

Crouched in elephant grass, a Marine witnesses the results of a close air support mission flown by an F-4 Phantom. From bases at Da Nang and Chu Lai, Marine Phantoms provided air support for allied ground units operating throughout the I Corps Tactical Zone.

Marine Corps Historical Collection

Marine Corps Historical Collection
A veteran of the Combined Action Program, Col Edward F. Danowitz assumed command of the 9th Marines from Col Robert H. Barrow on 9 April 1969.

operation, codenamed Ellis Ravine. The operation terminated on 13 April with disappointing results: one Viet Cong killed and his weapon captured.

The 9th Battles the 36th

The central portion of the Demilitarized Zone remained the main arena in which heavy fighting took place during April, as Marine and ARVN units fought a series of heated engagements with enemy forces concentrated in the region between Con Thien and Mutter's Ridge, 14 kilometers to the southwest. Elements of the *36th NVA Regiment* apparently began infiltrating into the central DMZ region of Quang Tri Province in early April as replacement for the *27th NVA Regiment*, which had sustained severe losses during Operation Montana Mauler. Although provided guides and liaison personnel from the departing *27th*, infiltrating units of the *36th* clearly were unfamiliar with the terrain and the maneuver capabilities and disposition of allied troops in the area, a factor which ultimately was to cost the regiment the equivalent of one battalion.

With the end of Operation Dewey Canyon, Task Force Hotel gave the 9th Marines the mission of securing a number of allied installations within the 3d Division's area of operation, replacing units of the 3d and 4th Marines, heavily engaged in western Quang Tri Province. Although still headquartered at Vandegrift Combat Base, but now under the command of Colonel Edward F. Danowitz, who replaced Colonel Barrow on 9 April, companies of the regiment were scattered from Oceanview on the coast to Fire Support Base Alpine, north of Lang Vei.

The first of a series of separate contacts with the *36th Regiment* took place about seven kilometers northwest of Cam Lo on 9 April, when, at 1030, a 1st Battalion, 9th Marines patrol, moving toward a predetermined helicopter extraction point, encountered an enemy unit estimated at 30 to 40 troops. Engaging the enemy in a day-long running firefight, the patrol killed 19 NVA, before being successfully extracted during the late evening. Two days later, on the 11th, a second patrol from Lieutenant Colonel Thomas J. Culkin's battalion detected 20 enemy soldiers, five kilometers northwest of the 9 April contact.* Artillery fire and fixed-wing air strikes claimed 16 NVA; no Marine casualties resulted from either action.

Minor skirmishes between the 9th Marines and forward elements of the *36th* continued across the central DMZ front until the 21st. At 1440, a reinforced NVA company, armed with automatic weapons, RPGs, satchel charges, and supported by mortars, struck at Company G, 2d Battalion, 9th Marines, under First Lieutenant James M. Horn, eight kilometers northeast of Elliott Combat Base. Horn's company, scattered in three separate, mutually supporting night defensive positions, contained the enemy's initial thrust, then counterattacked behind supporting air and artillery fires, forcing the enemy to flee northward. Results of the night-long battle were 42 NVA killed, 3 taken prisoner, and 27 weapons captured; Company G lost eight killed and 23 wounded.

On 23 April, Captain Donald K. Shockey, Jr.'s Company E, 2d Battalion, 9th Marines encountered an enemy force in the open moving south, midway between Cam Lo and Elliott, three kilometers north of Route 9. Engaging the force with small arms and artillery fire, Shockey's Marines pursued the enemy unit, finally driving it into caves. Launching an assault against the heavily fortified position just before noon, Shockey's company seized the site after two hours of fierce combat, killing 14 NVA troops and capturing an 82mm mortar, while losing eight killed and 17 wound-

---

*Lieutenant Colonel Culkin relieved Lieutenant Colonel George W. Smith as commanding officer of the 1st Battalion, 9th Marines on 31 March.

ed. As the month closed, the 9th Marines began preparing to be relieved by elements of the 3d and 4th Marines.

One day earlier, on the 22d, two battalions of the 2d ARVN Regiment joined the 9th Marines in clearing the front; the 4th Battalion, brought in by Marine helicopters, landed 13 kilometers northwest of Cam Lo and began a sweep to the east, while the 5th Battalion, supported by Marine tanks of Company B, 3d Tank Battalion, attacked from the east. This maneuver, calculated to trap elements of the *36th Regiment* between the two battalions, achieved its first solid contact on the 27th, when an unknown-size enemy force mounted a night attack against the 4th Battalion, deployed on Hill 208, site of heavy action during Operation Montana Mauler. The ARVN battalion held its position, killing 27 enemy troops and capturing 17 weapons.

Five days of heavy combat followed, the brunt of which was borne by the 2d ARVN Regiment. Employing the combined firepower of air, artillery, and tanks of Company B and then Company A, the two Vietnamese battalions pressed the attack, killing nearly 250 enemy troops by 2 May. Action thereafter was limited largely to mopping up isolated pockets of resistance.

While there was evidence of increased North Vietnamese Army presence in crossborder areas of the Demilitarized Zone, and attempts to infiltrate troops into the central region of Quang Tri Province during March and April, the enemy launched no massive effort to contest the region. He instead withdrew his forces into DMZ sanctuaries when pressed by the 4th Marines and the combined efforts of the 2d ARVN Regiment, 9th Marines, and the Army's 1st Brigade, 5th Infantry Division.

The Vietnam Salient

During the 1968 siege of Khe Sanh, the North Vietnamese employed armored elements against the Special Forces camp at Lang Vei, 13 kilometers north of

Col Paul D. Lafond, Commanding Officer, 3d Marines briefs, from left, MajGen Carl A. Youngdale, Deputy Commanding General, III MAF; LtGen Henry W. Buse, Jr., Commanding General, FMFPac; MajGen Raymond G. Davis; and BGen Frank E. Garretson, Commanding General, Task Force Hotel, on search operations in the Vietnam Salient.

Abel Papers, Marine Corps Historical Center

Abel Papers, Marine Corps Historical Center

LtCol James J. McMonagle's 2d Battalion, 3d Marines, in search of North Vietnamese soldiers, patrols an enemy infiltration route littered with vehicle wreckage near Laos.

Route 926, which enters that portion of Quang Tri Province protruding southeast into Laos, commonly termed the "Vietnam Salient." Intelligence gained during early March 1969 from reconnaissance team reports and sensors indicated a sizable increase in truck and tracked vehicle activity in the area, adding credence to the possibility that again enemy support and mechanized units had entered South Vietnam. The enemy's "logistics nose" needed to be blunted once more.

North Vietnamese use of Route 616, an extension of Route 926 from Laos, for the movement and staging of supplies and infiltrating troops, was to be expected. With 9th Marines' Operation Dewey Canyon in Base Area 611 and 101st Airborne Division's Operation Massachusetts Striker in the A Shau Valley clogging the enemy's primary lines of communication to the south, he was obliged to seek an alternate route. Moreover, the area's rugged terrain and position, surrounded on three sides by Laos, offered a major advantage—security.

Terrain within the salient, while providing North Vietnamese Army support and logistical units with a margin of security, posed no major obstacle to Marines. The western area, bordering the Song Xe Pon and Laos, generally consisted of a large 'U' shaped valley, surrounded by high ground with a jungle-covered hill mass at the center. Terrain in the eastern and northern portions of the salient, roughly south of Route 9, consisted of rugged mountains, punctuated by valleys covered with elephant grass and scrub growth. As in Operation Dewey Canyon, Marines would use the now-standard mobile concept of operations; establishing fire support bases on the high ground and then moving out under an artillery umbrella in company search operations.

Elements of the 3d Marine Division had penetrated the salient twice before. In June of 1968, a multi-regiment campaign virtually destroyed two regiments of the *308th NVA Division*. Three months later, a reconnaissance-in-force conducted by the 9th Marines encountered no significant enemy force. Task Force Hotel assigned the mission of confirming the enemy's presence and again clearing the salient to Colonel Paul D. Lafond's 3d Marines, recently returned to Quang Tri Province after participating with units of the 1st Marine Division in Operation Taylor Common, southwest of Da Nang.

The scheme of maneuver for the 3d Marines' thrust into the Vietnam Salient, codenamed Maine Crag, called for the 1st and 2d Battalions to conduct helicopter assaults from FSB Snapper, four kilometers southeast of Lang Vei, to seize and establish fire support bases in the southern portion of the salient, and then fan out in company-size search and clear operations, blocking the western terminus of Route 616 at the Laotian border. Concurrently, a U.S. Army task force, under the operational control of the 3d Marines, would attack westward from the Vandegrift-Ca Lu complex along Route 9 to Lang Vei, thence southward, linking up with the Marines. Subsequently, the 3d Marines in coordination with elements of the 2d ARVN Regiment, would attack eastward along Route 616 in a deliberate search to locate and destroy enemy forces, fortifications, and supply caches. Although as initially planned, the operation was to begin with a two-battalion helicopter advance into the salient, bad weather made it necessary to launch a single battalion by foot from Route 9.[10]

On 10 March, in preparation, Lieutenant Colonel James J. McMonagle's 2d Battalion, 3d Marines helilifted into LZ Hawk, just south of Route 9, and began overland movement to FSB Snapper, seven kilometers to the southwest, by way of the Khe Sanh Plateau. Supported by 155mm howitzers of the 1st Provisional Howitzer Battery on FSB Cates, the battalion reached Snapper after a night's forced march. "It was a moonless night," remembered Lieutenant Colonel McMonagle, "there were quite a bit of streams that we had to cross, a heck of a lot of elephant grass which impeded movement, and the matter of maintaining direction by Foxtrot Company, who had the point on this, was a real task and it was really amazing how they were able to find this place going through elephant grass at that time of the evening, but they did."[11] The following morning, the battalion initiated search operations in the vicinity of the fire support base.

Operation Maine Crag officially began on the 15th, as Battery A, 1st Battalion, 12th Marines lifted into Snapper, and three companies of Lieutenant Colonel McMonagle's battalion pushed overland toward Route 616, reaching FSB Saigon, overlooking the road, the following day. On the 17th, Companies G and H continued southwest to Route 616, leaving Company F as security for Battery C, 1st Battalion, 12th Marines, which had moved from Vandegrift to Saigon.

As elements of McMonagle's battalion probed the salient they encountered few enemy troops; those they did encounter consisted primarily of solitary snipers and ambushers, who quickly disappeared into the heavy jungle growth when engaged by the battalion's point. But on the 18th, these solitary engagements produced tangible results. While in ambush positions along Route 616, Marines of Company G observed two east-bound enemy trucks approach their position. Allowing the first truck, which was empty, to pass, the ambush opened fire on the second, destroying it and its cargo of 122mm rocket and mortar ammunition. The Marines then attacked the security element of the lead truck, which had halted a short distance down the road. The following morning, the enemy sent seven soldiers to check out the ambush site, and Company G ambushed them also.[12]

On the 19th, Colonel Lafond's 3d Marines assumed operational control of Task Force Remagen, under the command of Army Lieutenant Colonel Carmelo P. Milia, which consisted of Company B, 1st Battalion, 61st Mechanized Infantry; Company C, 1st Battalion, 77th Armor; Battery C, 1st Battalion, 40th Artillery (105mm self-propelled); two M42 self-propelled "Dusters" (dual-mounted 40mm cannons) from 1st Battalion, 44th Artillery (AWSP); 4.2mm mortars (self-propelled) from 1st Battalion, 77th Armor; and Army and Marine bulldozers, organized into three teams. The task force, which had advanced along Route 9 from Ca Lu to the Khe Sanh Plateau, was to turn south and establish blocking positions at the western end of Route 616 in the vicinity of the Song Xe Pon and initiate search operations, effectively screening the 3d Marines, operating to the east.

Three companies of Lieutenant Colonel John S. Kyle's 1st Battalion helilifted into FSB Saigon on the 19th, and then moved to the southwest, supported by two Ontos disguised as bulldozers, toward the Laotian border.* Concurrently, Companies G, H, and later E, continued moving eastward along Route 616, searching the draws and ridgelines and encountering a number of squad-size enemy groups in protective bunker complexes. The ensuing firefights were usually of short duration and involved few casualties. On 20 March, however, a water patrol from Company H was ambushed as it approached a stream approximately 1,000 meters north of the road, resulting in three Marines killed and 15 wounded.

Patrolling near the Phou Nhoi Hill mass, the area of the previous day's ambush, First Lieutenant William C. Helton's Company H on the 21st discovered what appeared to be an extensive staging area for approximately 150 enemy troops and a storage site containing rice and other foodstuffs. Between short firefights with security forces, the Marines of Company H eventually found a rice cache totaling over 350

---

*The Ontos was a lightly armored, tracked antitank vehicle armed with six coaxially-mounted 106mm recoilless rifles.

THE QUANG TRI BORDER AREAS

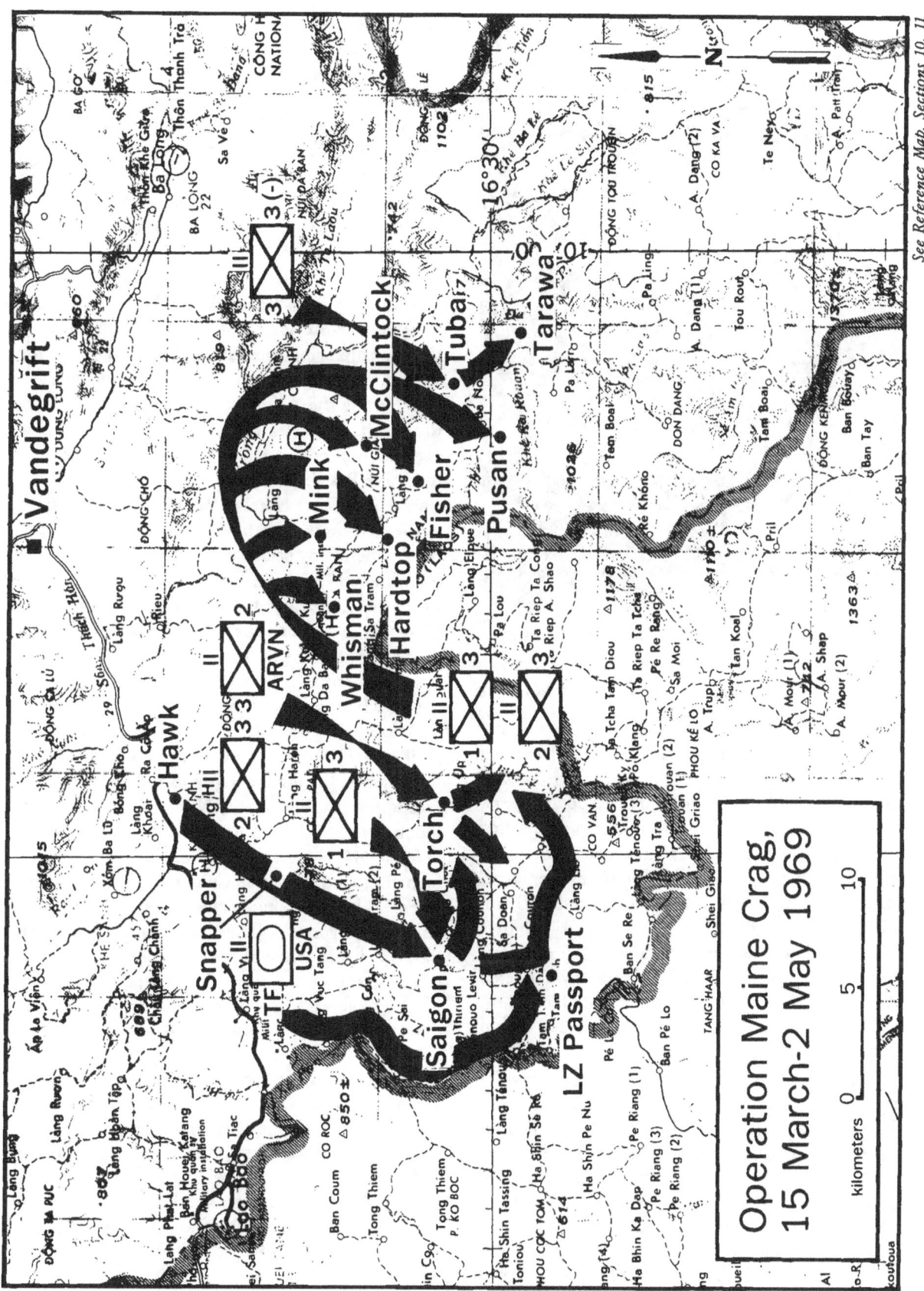

Operation Maine Crag, 15 March–2 May 1969

Abel Papers, Marine Corps Historical Center
A camouflaged Russian truck used by the North Vietnamese to transport supplies from Laotian support bases into South Vietnam that was uncovered by the 3d Marines during operations in the Vietnam Salient.

tons. The significant feature of the rice find was that it was of high quality and contained in bags with Chinese markings—evidence that rice denial operations in the coastal lowlands were having the desired effect on NVA efforts to live off the land. In the same general search area, Lieutenant Helton's Marines found sizeable amounts of small arms, mortar, and RPG ammunition, and 7,000 pounds of salt, loaded in a French truck with Russian tires and American markings. The captured rice was subsequently extracted from the storage site, moved to the coastal lowlands, and distributed to refugees recently resettled within Quang Tri Province.

During the next several days, the three companies of Lieutenant Colonel McMonagle's 2d Battalion continued to search the area bordering the eastern boundary of the salient, finding additional caches of munitions and food while encountering few large groups of enemy troops. "What we had in effect working there," reported Lieutenant Colonel McMonagle, "was Echo Company on the north, . . . Hotel Company on the west, Gulf Company on the south, and the enemy was ricocheting off of these three companies. . . . Those that did manage to get through, and it was very easy for him because the vegetation was thick and there were a number of trails that couldn't be physically covered, the AO [aerial observer] was able to pick them up."[13] After initial enemy attempts to defend the storage sites, the Marines met very little opposition as search operations progressed. Documents and prisoner interrogation confirmed the assumption that the entire area was lightly defended by service units and newly infiltrated troops.

In the first two weeks of April, the NVA launched 14 attacks-by-fire against 3d Marines and ARVN positions, employing mortars, 85mm field guns, and 122mm rockets, all fired from sanctuaries in Laos. However, by this point the principal storage sites in the area had been uncovered, and allied units began sweeping out of the salient. On 6 April, operational control of Task Force Remagen passed from the 3d Marines to Task Force Hotel at Vandegrift Combat Base, as the Army task force moved out of the salient and began operations near the Khe Sanh Plateau. "This force," noted Colonel Lafond, "was a tremendous assist to the 3d Marines and gave us an anti-tank capability that as it turned out wasn't completely necessary in that we received no tank attack from the enemy, but one can never be sure that its very presence didn't deter such an attack."[14] Withdrawal operations continued as the 3d Battalion, 2d ARVN Regiment helilifted to Dong Ha City on the 16th. The ARVN Battalion had made few significant enemy contacts, except for fending off an NVA attack, during its month-long search operation around FSB Torch, north of Route 616. However, "on one occasion which should be highlighted," reported Colonel Lafond, "at a time when 2/3 had temporarily moved outside the artillery fan from Saigon, ARVN artillery from Fire Support Base Torch supported the 2d Battalion, 3d Marines contacts near the rice caches. This support was superb, it was responsive, and it was fast, and it was accurate."[15]

Elements of the 3d Marines, instead of being extracted, moved from the salient in mid-April to an area of the lower Song Da Krong Valley, bordering on Laos. The next two weeks, as companies rotated to Cua Viet for a period of rest and resupply, the regiment swept the area encountering few enemy troops. The last days of April and first two days of May saw the battalions slowly pulled out of the area and helilifted to the central portion of Quang Tri Province, south of the DMZ, where they were positioned for Operation Virginia Ridge.

The seven-week, combined 3d Marines, Army, and ARVN thrust into the Vietnam Salient and lower Da Krong hit the enemy quite literally in the bread basket, where he did not have the wherewithal to resist effectively. In addition to losing over 600 tons of rice, 7,000 pounds each of sugar and salt, and 2,000 pounds each of powdered milk, peanut butter, and miscellaneous canned food, the enemy lost 207 soldiers, over 400 weapons, and 775,000 rounds of assorted ammunition.

Apache Snow

Despite the success of the 9th Marines in Operation Dewey Canyon and the recent accomplishments of the 3d Marines in the Vietnam Salient, reports from Bru tribesmen and North Vietnamese Army defectors (Hoi Chanhs) indicated that several regimental-size enemy units remained located in the northern portion of Base Area 611, south of the salient. It was believed that elements of the *6th* and *9th NVA Infantry Regiments*, the *675th Artillery Regiment*, and various support units, operated within the area. In addition, aerial reconnaissance reports confirmed the belief that Route 922 was under repair, and that the NVA were again moving men and materiel into the northern A Shau Valley and then eastward into Base Area 101, located astride the Quang Tri-Thua Thien provincial boundary.

Under the overall control of Lieutenant General Richard G. Stilwell's XXIV Corps at Phu Bai, elements of the 3d Marine Division and 101st Airborne Division, in coordination with the 1st ARVN Division, were ordered to conduct operations, codenamed Apache Snow, in the northern A Shau and southern Da Krong Valleys, cutting enemy supply and infiltration routes at the Laotian border, and destroying enemy forces, base camps, and supply caches. D-Day was set for 15 May, but subsequently moved forward to the 10th.

XXIV Corps assigned the 1st and 2d Battalions, 9th Marines the task of occupying the southern Da Krong and blocking enemy escape routes into Laos along Route 922. On 3 May, Lieutenant Colonel Thomas J. Culkin's 1st Battalion lifted into FSB McClintock and LZ Tarawa, replacing elements of the 3d Battalion, 3d Marines. From its Tarawa position, the battalion deployed one of its companies, Company D, commanded by Captain Leonard F. Chapman III, son of Marine Commandant Leonard F. Chapman, Jr., overland to reestablish Fire Support Base Razor. "Traveling the tedious and the difficult terrain," reported Colonel Edward F. Danowitz, "Delta Company was

Vietnamese Regional Force soldiers load the tons of rice captured by the 3d Marines in the Vietnam Salient onto trucks for distribution to the refugees of Quang Tri Province. The secured rice was enough to feed more than 5,000 enemy soldiers for one month.

Abel Papers, Marine Corps Historical Center

able to uncover FSB Razor, therefore eliminating the necessity for a heliborne assault, saving the requirement for supporting arms, maintaining the security and secrecy of the operation, and in effect adding to the feasibility of the landing" of the 2d Battalion, 9th Marines, under Lieutenant Colonel George C. Fox, on the 7th.[16] Operation Apache Snow began for the 9th Marines on the 10th, when Culkin's battalion leapfrogged south over Fox's battalion and assaulted into FSB Erskine, overlooking the upper Song Da Krong and Route 922. The lift into Erskine was not without incident, as enemy fire downed a CH-46 transport helicopter, killing seven Marines and wounding five.

During the early stages of the operation, it became apparent that large-size enemy units had yet to reconstitute within the Da Krong Valley following their defeat in Dewey Canyon two months earlier. Culkin's battalion, continuously patrolling in the vicinity of Erskine and Route 922, skirmished with several small NVA units with disappointing results, and towards the end of May swept east, initiating patrol operations near abandoned FSB Lightning. Lieutenant Colonel Fox's 2d Battalion, patrolling from FSB Razor and LZ Dallas, eight kilometers north-northeast of Erskine, encountered numerous small enemy units. On 23 May, for example, a platoon from Company F engaged five NVA, occupying a bunker complex along a stream, five kilometers west-southwest of Razor. As one Marine squad maneuvered against the concealed enemy position, the remainder of the unit massed small arms and automatic weapons fire on the bunkers. The ensuing assault accounted for four enemy killed and one prisoner. The platoon sustained no casualties during the brief encounter.

While the Da Krong remained relatively quiet, the same could not be said for the A Shau where XXIV Corps tasked four battalions of the 101st Airborne Division (Airmobile), in coordination with elements of the 1st ARVN Division, with the destruction of enemy concentrations within the valley. On the morning of 10 May, Army and ARVN battalions helilifted into the valley and began multiple sweeps toward the Laotian border. While patrolling near the border the following day, Company B, 3d Battalion, 187th Infantry encountered an unknown size enemy force, positioned in a well-defended hut and bunker complex at the base of Hill 937 (Dong Ap Bia), three kilometers southwest of A Luoi. Over the next four days, the battalion endeavored to push through the complex toward the summit, supported by heavy volumes of artillery, mortar, gunship, and tactical air fire, without much success. On 15 May, the 1st Battalion, 506th Infantry moved to assist the mired battalion. Both battalions then mounted a counterattack and pursued the enemy up the hill, meeting stubborn resistance as they pushed their way up the jungle-covered slopes. The tempo of the battle increased as the attacking force neared the crest of Hill 937, encountering fresh, well-disciplined NVA forces defending one fortified, mutually supporting bunker complex after another. As a result, elements of the 2d Battalion, 506th Infantry were committed on the 18th, followed by the 2d Battalion, 501st Infantry and 2d Battalion, 3d ARVN Regiment on the 19th.

By the morning of the 20th, with all battalions in position, they joined in the final assault on the contested hill complex. Once taken, the combined Army and ARVN force then pursued the remaining enemy elements southwest down a ridgeline to the Laotian border, less than three kilometers from the crest of the hill.[17] The weeklong battle cost the *9th* and *29th NVA Regiments* more than 500 killed. Testifying to fierce fighting on the hill, later termed "Hamburger Hill" by the remaining infantrymen of the 3d Battalion, 187th Infantry, was the friendly toll—44 soldiers killed and 297 wounded.

Dong Ap Bia secure, the battalions involved reoriented their search operations in an effort to destroy remnants of the two NVA regiments. Although operations throughout the A Shau continued until 7 June, the NVA avoided all but minor engagements.

With Army and ARVN forces heavily engaged in the A Shau, a platoon from Company C, 3d Engineer Battalion completed the first of three cuts of Route 922 in the Da Krong on 25 May. Two were 12 feet wide and 20 feet deep, and the third, 12 feet wide and 10 feet deep. The following day, the platoon caused two 50-meter landslides and blew a 50-meter, enemy hand-constructed revetment. With the interdiction of Route 922 complete, Culkin's battalion lifted out of the area of operations and returned to Vandegrift Combat Base on the 27th, followed by Fox's battalion. "Contact with the enemy during the initial phases of the [three-week] operation," noted Colonel Danowitz, "was light and it continued to be light, mainly against small elements, reconnaissance units or screening force for the major North Vietnamese forces, which according to the progress of the operation, indicated that they had moved into Laos as well as south into the area of the 1st ARVN, but were not to remain to stand and fight against the 9th Marines."[18]

Department of Defense Photo (USMC) A193758

Marine 105mm howitzer crews watch as an Army CH-47 Chinook helicopter hovers after landing ammunition at Fire Support Base Razor. The artillerymen were supporting the joint 101st Airborne-9th Marines attack, code-named Apache Snow, into the A Shau Valley.

The 3d Marine Division's mobile posture, involving the continuous deployment of maneuver battalions in western Quang Tri Province, succeeded in reducing the enemy threat from the west. During June, Colonel Danowitz's 9th Marines continued the effort, participating in Operations Cameron Falls and Utah Mesa. These two concurrent operations were targeted against elements of the *304th NVA Division*, attempting to reestablish a presence south of Route 9.

Evidence from reconnaissance and other intelligence sources suggested that divisional troops had infiltrated into the lower Da Krong Valley, moved east along Route 616, and then north along the river. In addition, the series of rocket attacks on Vandegrift Combat Base in May signaled the start of a period of planned pressure on allied positions by the *57th NVA Regiment, 304th Division*. Task Force Hotel assigned Danowitz's Marines the mission of conducting search and destroy operations in an area bordered on the north by the Song Quang Tri, on the south by the Da Krong, on the east by Fire Support Base Shepherd, and on the west by Fire Support Base Henderson; an area considered critical to the security of not only Vandegrift Combat Base, but of the Ba Long Valley, entryway from the west into the population centers of Quang Tri and Dong Ha.

Operation Cameron Falls, which began on 29 May, shifted the efforts of the 9th Marines from the southern Da Krong to the northern extremities of the mountainous river valley, south of Vandegrift. Movement into the objective area went unopposed as Lieutenant Colonel Fox's 2d Battalion occupied Fire Support Base Whisman and the 3d Battalion, under Lieutenant Colonel Oral R. Swigart, Jr., FSB Shepherd, below FSB Cates, on Route 9. In establishing its position on Whisman, Marines of the 2d Battalion, according to Colonel Danowitz, "rapidly and wisely selected positions for the defense of the fire support base; placing wire, fighting holes, obstacles, and of course, claymores, and tripflares in their protective defense plan. The defensive fire plan was fired and prepared prior to last light." This preparation paid off for at 0215 on the 1st, a small enemy force attempting to probe Whisman hit a listening post, causing the death of two Marines and alerting the fire base. As a result, defenders from Company G ably countered the subsequent heavy attack against the base, killing 19 of the enemy while suffering minor casualties. This attack on Whisman, remarked Colonel Danowitz, "was an unusual aspect of the operation, because never before had the enemy been able to strike within hours of the initial establishment of the fire support base.

But in this case it was attempted and very readily thwarted."[19]

During the attack on Whisman, a prisoner as well as a defector were taken, both of whom acknowledged the existence of a command post of the *57th NVA Regiment* to the southwest of the fire support base. Exploiting this information, Lieutenant Colonel Fox directed Companies F and G toward the area reported to contain the enemy headquarters. But before this could be accomplished, the battalion received fresh intelligence indicating the movement of a large enemy force northeast toward Hill 824 (Dong Cho). Danowitz therefore redirected the attack toward the hill mass, with the two companies of the 2d Battalion moving to the northeast along the Da Krong, and two companies of the 3d Battalion advancing east from Shepherd. "The terrain," reported Lieutenant Colonel Swigart, "was very rough, characterized by triple-canopy rain forest and elephant grass that ran as high as 12 feet . . . . Because of the hot weather, I guess the troops suffered more in the elephant grass than they did in the triple-canopy because down in the 12-foot-high elephant grass, there was no breeze at all, in fact there was the feeling that you couldn't breathe properly."[20]

As elements of the two battalions converged on Hill 824, it became increasingly evident that the enemy was deployed around the hill in strength. Advancing to the northeast on 5 June, Company H encountered a dug-in enemy battalion on the southern banks of the Da Krong. During the initial engagement, which lasted more than 12 hours, 29 enemy troops were killed; subsequent sweeps of the area revealed additional bodies, numerous bunkers, caves, and living quarters, all of which were destroyed. As Marines of Swigart's battalion continued to move toward the hill, they too encountered and engaged sizable enemy forces. "The enemy encountered," noted Lieutenant Colonel Swigart, "were quite effective, they were well-armed, well-supplied, they had on new uniforms, and indications were that they were an enemy force that had been newly introduced into the area of operations."[21]

On 11 June, elements of the 2d Battalion resecured Fire Support Base Henderson in preparation for the positioning of two batteries of the 2d Battalion, 12th Marines. The remainder of Fox's battalion continued search operations along the Da Krong in the southwestern sector of the assigned regimental area, with little success, until the 15th, when the battalion returned to Vandegrift Combat Base.

View of Dong Ap Bia, or Hamburger Hill, after it was secured by elements of the 3d Brigade, 101st Airborne Division, which suffered more than 300 casualties in taking the hill.

Author's Collection

Swigart's Marines continued company sweeps in the Dong Cho Mountain complex until the 18th when ordered to reorient their advance toward the western portion of the area of operations, south of Shepherd, in an effort to exploit a number of reconnaissance sightings. On the 23d, Task Force Hotel shifted operational control of the battalion to Task Force Guadalcanal in anticipation of the battalion's relief of the 1st Battalion, 9th Marines.

Intelligence gained during Operation Cameron Falls, in addition to sensor reports, aerial observation, and reconnaissance patrol reports, indicated that during May and early June, elements of a second regiment of the *304th NVA Division*, the *24th*, and attached support units, had infiltrated south and east, toward the Khe Sanh Plateau. As a result, a joint task force, codenamed Guadalcanal, consisting of the 1st Battalion, 9th Marines and Task Force Mustang from the 1st Brigade, 5th Infantry Division (Mechanized), was established, and in coordination with the 2d and 3d Battalions, 2d ARVN Regiment, directed by Task Force Hotel to drive the NVA out.

The joint Marine, Army, and ARVN effort in the Khe Sanh Plateau, codenamed Utah Mesa, began on 12 June with the helilift of Lieutenant Colonel Culkin's 1st Battalion, 9th Marines into LZ Bison and FSB Cates, and the 3d Battalion, 2d ARVN Regiment into FSB Quantico, northeast of Khe Sanh. Their mission was to conduct offensive sweeps west to Khe Sanh, destroying troops and supplies, securing the division's western flank, and spoiling any enemy attempted buildup which might threaten allied installations and lines of communications. ARVN forces, although considered an integral element, operated in a separate area, generally north of the Marine and Army task force, which gradually advanced to the southwest, along an axis centered on Route 9.

On 13 June, the 2d Battalion, 2d ARVN Regiment, lifted into LZ Cokawa, north of FSB Cates, and began searching to the west. Two days later, Culkin's Company D moved to LZ Horn in order to secure the flanks of Task Force Mustang, which consisted of Companies B and C, 1st Battalion, 61st Mechanized Infantry, and Company B, 1st Battalion, 77th Armor, advancing west along Route 9.

Reacting to the combined thrust, elements of the *24th Regiment* conducted a series of night attacks against allied units, the first taking place on 18th. Between 0335 and 0530, an estimated 100 NVA troops attacked Company B, 61st Infantry's night defensive postion, east of Lang Vei. Using machine gun and RPG fire, the enemy broke through the perimeter and engaged Army troops in heavy close combat. At dawn, the enemy withdrew, leaving 11 bodies inside the defensive wire and 30 outside, in addition to 12 weapons and 100 satchel charges. Company B lost 11 killed and 15 wounded as a result of the attack.

Later that morning, a squad-size reconnaissance patrol from Company C, 9th Marines, while searching an area three kilometers southeast of Khe Sanh, engaged a well-armed, well-entrenched, and well-camouflaged NVA company. The enemy initiated the ambush with a burst of .50 caliber machine gun fire, instantly killing three Marines. The squad returned fire, knocking out the machine gun position, and called for reinforcements. The enemy company then maneuvered to outflank the squad; however, the squad, having linked up with a nearby platoon, struck the enemy's right flank. The remainder of Company C joined the battle and assaulted the enemy position, driving the NVA company southward, into artillery blocking fires.

Continuing the push westward, elements of the task force were again struck on the 20th. Early that morning, the enemy, in three separate ground attacks, hit the combined position of Company B, 61st Infantry and Company D, 9th Marines. With the assistance of helicopter gunship fire, fixed-wing air strikes, and artillery, Army and Marine infantrymen repulsed the assaults, accounting for 27 NVA dead. Two days later, Marines of the 3d Battalion, 9th Marines effected a relief-in-place of Culkin's battalion, which then moved to Vandegrift Combat Base, where it stood down in preparation for redeployment to Okinawa.

Throughout the remainder of the operation, the number of engagements between allied forces and elements of the *24th* remained high, as small enemy units, in an attempt to halt the advance, continued to attack friendly night defensive positions, but without success. On 24 June, two NVA platoons assailed the positions of Company K, 9th Marines, south of Route 9. "On the morning of the 24th at about 0130," reported First Lieutenant Patrick P. Oates, commanding the 1st Platoon, "our ambush, which was out about 75 meters, was hit from three different sides. They were hit mainly by chicoms [grenades] and small arms fire. This alerted the lines, everybody got on stand-to and the ambush started filtering in one by one . . . . Nobody on the sector of the lines where the ambush was, opened-up until after all of the am-

Engineers accompanying the 9th Marines clear a landing zone for resupply and medical evacuation helicopters in heavily wooded terrain south of Vandegrift.

bush was in with the exception of the one Marine who was killed." At about the same time, other sections of the company's position came under fire. "After the last of the ambush came in," continued Lieutenant Oates, "1st Platoon sector started receiving heavy small arms fire, at which time we called in 60mm mortar missions which gave us outstanding support, and knocked out the depth of the attack and broke up the main attack. We had several different occasions where they came very close to the line and then the troops could hear them crawling through the elephant grass on their retreat. This firefight lasted about four and a half hours.... At approximately 7 a.m. we started a sweep of the area and that is when we started coming up with all the bodies and gear. Closest bodies were about 10 to 15 meters from the lines; there we found AKs and Chinese light machine guns."

On the morning of the 26th, Company K moved westward toward a series of knobs where it set-in for the night and where it was again struck. "We had a real fine perimeter that night," reported Lieutenant Oates, "and we were hit . . . by an estimated two companies of NVA. This firefight lasted between two and one half and three hours and we had good support all the way around . . . . On the morning of the 27th, we did find numerous rifles and automatic weapons, and this time two flamethrowers showed up. During both of these fire fights, on the 24th and 26th, the fire discipline that we had was very good."[22] As a result of both actions, the enemy lost 41 killed. In yet another attack, two enemy companies struck at Company I, 9th Marines, on FSB Tenaru, east of Lang Vei, on the 27th, losing another 22 dead. In all attacks, the enemy failed to penetrate beyond the defensive wire.

On 2 July, the 2d Battalion, 9th Marines, under Major Robert L. Modjeski, who had replaced Lieutenant Colonel Fox on the 22d, helilifted 14 kilometers south of Khe Sanh in order to reactivate FSB Spark and conduct sweeps of Route 926 in support of Task Force Guadalcanal. Shortly after reoccupying the base, Modjeski noted, "the NVA immediately began registering 82mm mortars on the position. Towards evening a brisk mortar exchange built up which our artillery also entered into. The battalion sustained about 40 casualties, mostly from mortar shrapnel." The following morning, Modjeski sent his maneuver companies in search of the enemy mortars, which subsequently displaced out of range.[23] With the regiment alerted for redeployment to Okinawa, the 2d and 3d Battalions were pulled out of the Khe Sanh Plateau and returned to Vandegrift Combat Base on the 6th, thus terminating Operation Utah Mesa.

When it appeared that the enemy was seeking to reestablish a strong presence in western Quang Tri Province following the Dewey Canyon defeat, the 3d Marine Division, in conjunction with Army and ARVN forces, fought back. In the four major allied strikes into the area, the North Vietnamese lost over 600 troops and a number of important supply depots. As a result of the continued pressure, the enemy units were again forced to withdraw into their Laotian sanctuaries.

Central DMZ Battles

During May and June, the central and western portions of Quang Tri Province, just south of the Demilitarized Zone and north of Route 9, were again targeted by the 3d Marine Division. The enemy, however, failed to expose his large units, favoring instead sapper and indirect fire attacks against allied installations, while holding his major forces in sanctuaries north of the DMZ.

The *36th NVA Regiment, 308th Division*, which had replaced the *27th* in central Quang Tri following

THE QUANG TRI BORDER AREAS

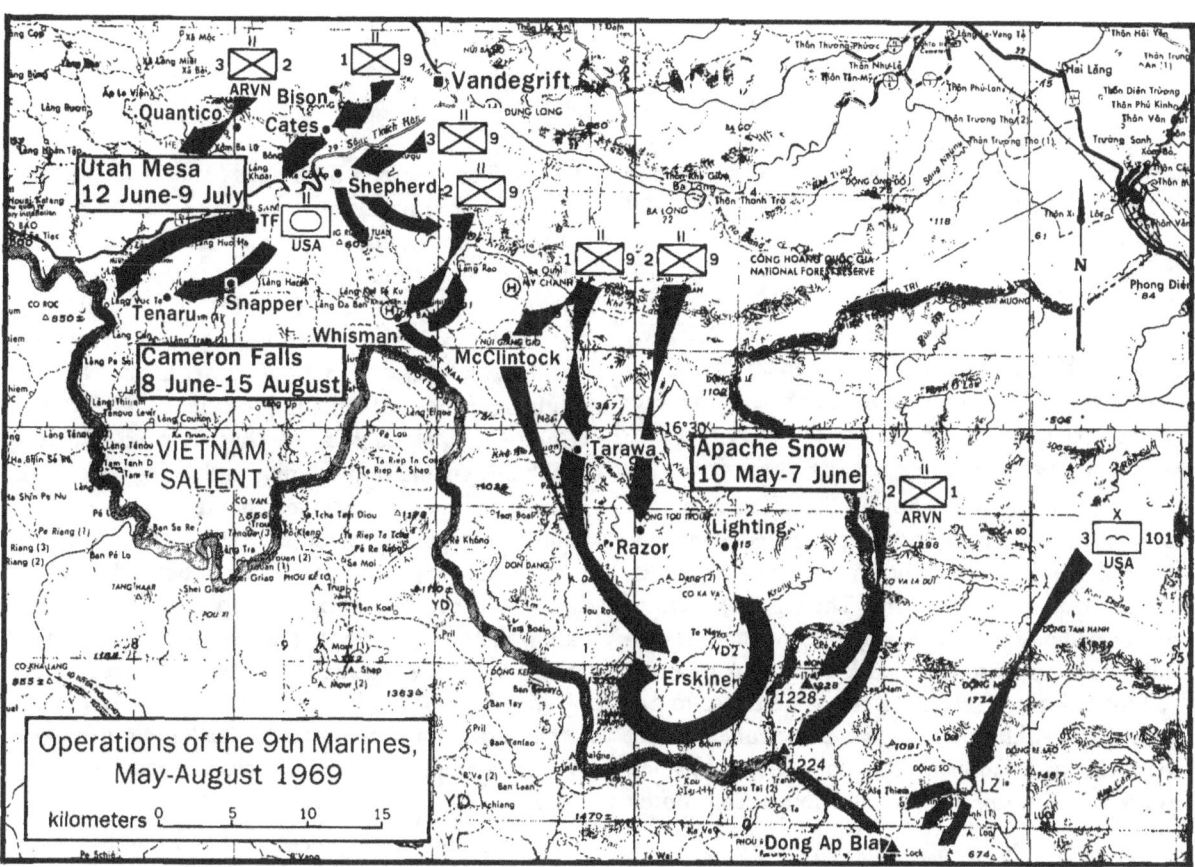

See Reference Map, Sections 10-12, 16, 17

the latter regiment's defeat, was itself driven back into the zone during the successful 9th Marines, ARVN, and 1st Brigade operations in March and April. But by the beginning of May, elements of the *27th* and *36th* again began to filter back into the central portion of the province. Colonel Lafond's 3d Marines, having successfully cleared the Vietnam Salient in Operation Maine Crag, was tasked with destroying the remnants of both regiments, and preventing any enemy attempts at interdicting Route 9 or interfering with the ongoing rice harvest.

On 2 May, Lafond's regiment began Operation Virginia Ridge, as Lieutenant Colonel John S. Kyle's 1st Battalion assaulted into LZ Sparrow, eight kilometers northwest of Cam Lo, immediately engaging small groups of NVA. The 3d Battalion, under Lieutenant Colonel Richard C. Schulze, secured Fire Support Bases Fuller and Pete, northeast of Elliott Combat Base, and began sweeping north toward the DMZ, while the Marines of Lieutenant Colonel McMonagle's 2d Battalion provided security for Con Thien, Charlie-2, Cam Lo Bridge, Cam Lo District Headquarters, Khe Gio Bridge, and Route 9, and furnished contingents for mine sweeps emanating from all fixed installations and roving patrols of the surrounding terrain.[24]

By 6 May, Kyle's battalion had swept west onto Mutter's Ridge, near Landing Zones Ironsides and Junior, three kilometers from Sparrow. Four days later at 0415, Company D, in a night defensive position west of Ironsides, came under attack by an estimated NVA platoon employing RPG, grenades, and small arms fire. After 10 minutes the enemy broke contact and withdrew to the northeast, leaving eight Marines dead and 10 wounded.

Constant patrolling and company sweeps were the rule as Kyle's battalion continued westward and Schulze's 3d battalion move north, engaging small groups of enemy troops. On 16 May, a patrol from Company M, operating north of LZ Champ, received small arms and RPG fire from approximately 10 enemy troops entrenched in bunkers. The platoon-size patrol, using air, artillery, mortars, and CS gas, maneuvered up to and through the bunker complex, killing four and capturing one weapon.

During the remainder of May, the 1st Battalion, now under Lieutenant Colonel David G. Herron, who had replaced Kyle on the 11th, turned and swept east toward LZ Comet and Alpha-4, as did the 3d Battalion. Engagements with infiltrating troops of the *27th* and *36th* remained light except for a number of attacks against Marine positions. Twenty NVA, employing grenades, probed the perimeter of Company C on 20 May without breaching the wire. A search at first light revealed 15 enemy bodies and a number of weapons; Company C lost three killed and eight wounded. Two days later, Company B trapped 30 NVA between the company's night position and a platoon ambush. Using 60mm mortars and small arms fire, the company routed the enemy, killing 19 and capturing two prisoners.

While Herron and Schulze's battalions advanced eastward, just south of the Demilitarized Zone, the division directed both to begin a series of reconnaissance patrols within the zone. These patrols were to collect evidence of enemy troop presence and, if possible, capture prisoners. However, the patrols experienced limited success, as it was necessary to put a company within mortar range of the zone in order to provide patrol support. The supporting companies, as a result, were subjected to numerous enemy mortar attacks, sustaining losses that proved to be unacceptable. The special patrols were thus discontinued and a two- to three-kilometer patrol zone reestablished below the DMZ.

The first of several B-52 raids (Arc Lights) carried out during the operation within the 3d Marines' area of responsibility, just south of the DMZ, occurred on the night of 6-7 June. Based on continuous enemy activity over the previous several weeks, the eastern portion of Mutter's Ridge, Foxtrot Ridge, and Helicopter Valley were struck by six separate Arc Lights. Within an hour of the last bomb drop, Marines of Lieutenant Colonel McMonagle's 2d Battalion conducted heliborne assaults into a number of landing zones near Junior, in an effort to exploit the strikes and conduct bomb damage assessment (BDA). The Marines found few enemy dead, but numerous bunkers destroyed, and the concealing foliage ripped away from several known and suspected enemy redoubts. The destruction was so devastating, that it was suspected many more NVA soldiers lost their lives than were found. After exploiting the area, the 2d Battalion moved south, conducting search and clear operations north of Route 9.

In mid-June, the regiment received a number of intelligence reports from local informants indicating that a large unknown enemy unit was in the process of infiltrating from the DMZ into a portion of Leatherneck Square, southwest of Gio Linh. "It looked to us," reported Captain William J. Quigley, regimental S-2, "like an indication that he was either going to attack C-2, which at that time was in our AO, or he was after C-1 in the ARVN AO. But he was definitely coming down for something. For this operation we selected the 3d Battalion, 3d Marines, and because of being in close proximity to the DMZ as it was where the enemy was building up, we needed to try something unique to see if we could catch the enemy off-balance and not tip our hands."

The battalion loaded on trucks after dark on the 16th and then advanced up Route 1 in column, "brazenly heading right for the DMZ, which had never been done before, and nobody would ever think of doing a thing like this." The bold plan worked; "when the 3d Battalion was moving up Route 1 toward the DMZ, elements of the *27th Regiment* and the *33d Sapper Battalion* were going the other way southward." "Actually," reported Quigley, "what happened was that we passed one another; the 3d Battalion being on the road and them people coming down through the flat-

A CH-46 Sea Knight helicopter lowers a load of supplies at a 3d Marine Division fire base. The supplies, flown out from Force Logistic Support Group Bravo at Dong Ha, included rations, water, and all types of ammunition to sustain not only the artillery battery, but ground forces operating in the surrounding terrain.

Department of Defense Photo (USMC) A193235

lands, heading toward Charlie-1 . . . . The timing was just one of those things, just once in a hundred that you run into, that we hit them on the way down, caught them coming down from the DMZ; he was decimated by artillery fire." "In fact," Quigley continued, "he got hurt so bad that his own sappers from the *33d Sapper Battalion*, when they did reach Charlie-1, they ran into the Charlie-1 minefields. Which of course is a very unusual thing for a sapper to do. The ARVNs on their contact at Charlie-1 hung 56 of the people up in the wire. The 3d Battalion in the meantime sliced in behind them, separating them from the DMZ."[25]

The night sweep by Schulze's Marines from Gio Linh, southwest toward Con Thien proceeded without incident. At 0930 the next morning, Company M engaged an estimated enemy company occupying hedgerows, three kilometers west of the former Marine artillery position. A half hour later, Company L, two kilometers to the south, engaged an unknown-size enemy force in fortified positions on a small hill. Both firefights raged throughout the morning until the enemy broke contact and fled southward, leaving 20 dead.

At midday, Schulze's command group, accompanied by a platoon from Company K and a section of 106mm recoilless rifles, moved westward in trace of the attacking companies. At 1400, while the group established a forward command post, two kilometers east of Company L, an estimated NVA company launched an intense mortar-supported ground attack against the Marines. The command group's security force, employing the recoilless rifles and small arms, repulsed the enemy force, killing 37 and capturing three. During the height of the action, a platoon from Company L, maneuvering from the west to reinforce the command group, engaged an NVA platoon in a bunker complex. Under the cover of air strikes, the platoon assaulted the enemy position, killing eight NVA and seizing 14 weapons.

Throughout the afternoon, aerial observers directed air strikes and artillery fires on the withdrawing enemy force. Fixed-wing strikes accounted for 57 enemy killed, while another 13 were credited to the artillery. Companies F and G, 2d Battalion, the designated division reaction companies, and Companies A and B, 3d Tank Battalion, were committed to the battle late in the afternoon, but the enemy force had fled the area, and significant contact was not reestablished. The action on the 17th resulted in 193 enemy killed, 9 prisoners taken, and 77 weapons seized. Schulze's battalion, although losing 19 killed and 28 wounded, continued

Abel Papers, Marine Corps Historical Center
Carrying an M60, the standard automatic weapon used by American forces, a machine gunner and his assistant from the 1st Battalion, 3d Marines enter a clearing during a patrol south of the Demilitarized Zone.

search operations in the area until the 21st, when it moved to Cua Viet for a period of rehabilitation.

With the enemy limiting his activity during the remainder of Operation Virginia Ridge, which terminated on 16 July, Colonel Wilbur F. Simlik's regiment* continued search operations throughout the area of operations: the 1st Battalion centered on Alpha-4; the 2d Battalion north of Route 9 at FSB Fuller; and the 3d Battalion, after its return from Cua Viet, operating from Cam Lo.

Also operating within close proximity of the Demilitarized Zone, but west of Colonel Simlik's 3d Marines, was the 4th Marines. With the termination of Operation Purple Martin on 7 May, the 4th Marines remained in place, initiating a two-month operation, codenamed Herkimer Mountain. Continually pressured by Colonel Goggin's regiment, the bulk of

---

*Colonel Simlik replaced Colonel Paul D. Lafond as Commanding Officer, 3d Marines on 28 June.

enemy units operating northwest of Elliott Combat Base had been forced to withdraw northward into North Vietnamese havens, leaving behind roving bands of sapper, rocket, and reconnaissance units which attempted to disrupt Marine combat and logistical operations. As in Purple Martin, the regiment's mission remained the same, Major Charles W. Cobb, Jr., S-3 of the 1st Battalion, 4th Marines, noted:

> Our primary mission, of course, was to conduct offensive operations north of, and occupy, Fire Support Bases Neville and Russell. And we had in the back of our minds that the real reason we were out there in this AO was to deny the enemy the use of the avenues of approach from the Laotian border through the west, down around the Lang Ho Valley and the Route that traveled from the northwest to the southeast right through the northern part of our AO and just south of the DMZ, the Cam Lo River Valley. Both of these areas had been used, based on the intelligence information we received, by the enemy over a period of years, and by occupying the areas that we did and by keeping the companies out on the move constantly, . . . I really think we kept them honest and negated their attempts, if there were any, to use these avenues of approach into the 4th Marines AO.[26]

The operation began with the 1st Battalion, 4th Marines relieving the 2d Battalion on LZ Catapult and FSB Neville, which then moved to Cua Viet for a period of rehabilitation. The 3d Battalion, 4th Marines continued to operate from FSB Russell and LZ Sierra, to the northeast, while the 3d Battalion, 9th Marines, awaiting redeployment, manned installations from Vandegrift Combat Base to Hill 950 (FSB Cates), west along Route 9. Participation of the 9th Marines varied during the operation as elements were shifted to other operations throughout the divisional area of operations, and then redeployed.

Enemy activity remained at a low level as 4th and 9th Marines fought sporadic engagements with small groups of NVA. The first significant fight took place at 1610 on 10 May. While moving north from Neville, Company B, 1st Battalion, 4th Marines took small arms fire, wounding five Marines. Pressing the attack, the Marines moved onto the high ground and continued the pursuit until the enemy broke contact. Air strikes and artillery were called, but with unknown results. The following day, a local security patrol from Company K, 3d Battalion, 4th Marines, near LZ Dodge on the DMZ, surprised two well-armed NVA moving toward the company's night defensive position. The enemy soldiers were taken under fire; a sweep the following morning revealed two bodies with TNT strapped to their waists.

Goggin's Marines conducted extensive and continuous patrols throughout the ever-shrinking area of operations during the remainder of May and into June. Engagements with small groups of NVA soldiers were infrequent and of a short duration, as the enemy quickly withdrew when pressed. Noteworthy incidents, however, took place, one of which Major Cobb described:

> A recon insert into the DMZ, which was put in sometime around the 7th or 8th of June, ran into some problems and they had a platoon commander killed and they were surrounded during most of the night. And we received an order from regiment that the "Sparrow Hawk," which is the ready platoon that is maintained at Vandegrift Combat Base under the OP control of the 3d Marine Division and is deployable on short notice to any trouble spots, would be flown up to the LZ located in the vicinity of Bravo Company and join up with them and move into the DMZ and help extract these recon people. While the planning of this was going on, there was another recon team in heavy contact about 4,000 meters from them inside the DMZ. Originally the plan was to take out the recon inserts as they normally do by helicopter, but in the process they had two CH-46s shot down: one of the crews immediately was picked up, the other crew joined one of the recon teams and set in for the night. And it was at that point that the decision was made to not lose anymore helicopters and that we would send B Company up in there, reinforced by the "Sparrow Hawk" platoon and also a reaction force from the 3d Recon Battalion to go up and bring them out of the DMZ. There were many complications in this operation that gave us some trouble. The tremendous heat for one thing down in the valleys and draws without any breeze; the high temperatures; the steep terrain; and the jungle canopy and the growth, the brier and bramble, that resulted in the troops having to cut their way through and it seemed like an endless task to eventually get to these people and then extract them. They had to get resupplied with water and chow and the whole operation took a little better than two days before it was finally over with . . . . The operation went off pretty well without losing any more people.[27]

Month's end found Goggin's Marines fending off no enemy attack other than attacks by fire against the regiment's installations.[28]

Eastern Quang Tri and Thua Thien

While a majority of Marine operations were conducted in central and western Quang Tri Province, responsibility for the coastal lowlands and piedmont was divided between the 2d ARVN Regiment and 1st Brigade, 5th Infantry Division (Mechanized). The ARVN Regiment operated mainly in Leatherneck Square, while the 1st Brigade secured the coast from the DMZ south to the Quang Tri/Thua Thien Provincial boundary. Consisting of the 1st Battalion, 11th Infantry; 1st Battalion, 61st Infantry (Mechanized); 1st

Abel Papers, Marine Corps Historical Center

Two 3d Division Marines escort a captured North Vietnamese Army soldier to the unit's command post where he will be questioned by division intelligence personnel in an effort to obtain information as to his unit's location, strength, morale, and objectives.

Battalion, 77th Armor; and elements of the 4th Battalion, 12th Cavalry; 3d Squadron, 5th Cavalry; 1st Battalion, 40th Artillery; and the Marine 1st Amphibian Tractor Battalion, the brigade operated from Camp Red Devil (Dong Ha Combat Base), LZ Sharon, LZ Nancy, and Wunder Beach. In addition to periodically providing task groups to assist Marines, the brigade conducted a number of independent operations in southwestern Quang Tri Province, while securing major allied coastal installations.

During March and April, elements of the mechanized brigade conducted search and clear operations in Base Area 101, southwest of Quang Tri Combat Base. In May, following Montana Mauler and Ellis Ravine in central Quang Tri, the brigade again moved into Base Area 101, with elements also operating in the coastal lowlands near Landing Zones Nancy and Sharon. The brigade's mission was to prevent enemy forces from entering or leaving populated areas and to deny the enemy rice by destroying his rice-gathering forces. During Operation Massachusetts Bay, which began on 7 May and concluded on 18 June, elements of the brigade saw light contact, consisting of ambushes and probes, and accounted for 61 enemy killed and 50 suspects detained. With the termination of Massachusetts Bay, the brigade began the follow-up operation, Iroquois Grove, in the same area and with an identical mission.

In Thua Thien Province to the south, the 101st Airborne Division prepared to conduct the follow-on division-level operation, Kentucky Jumper, with the termination of Operation Nevada Eagle on 28 February. This operation, begun on 1 March, continued the combined 101st Airborne and 1st ARVN Division effort in support of the Republic's Accelerated Pacification Campaign in the coastal lowlands around Hue, and forays into the mountains of western Thua Thien Province in an attempt to halt infiltration from Laos. Operation Kentucky Jumper (1 March - 14 August) included the following sub-operations: Bristol Boots (25 April - 15 May) directed against elements of the *5th NVA Regiment* in the Ruong Ruong Valley; Massachusetts Striker (1 March - 8 May) in the southern A Shau Valley and northern regions of Quang Nam Province; and Montgomery Rendezvous (7 June - 14 August), directed against Viet Cong forces operating in Phu Loc and Hien Doc Districts, south of Hue.

Also during this period, the 3d Brigade, 101st Airborne Division participated in the XXIV Corps operation, Apache Snow (10 May - 7 June), in the northern A Shau Valley. In addition, the 1st Brigade joined the Americal Division in southern I Corps, assisting the division for three months in Operation Lamar Plain.

Throughout the first six months of 1969, Marine, Army, and ARVN troops continued the relentless and successful pursuit and destruction of enemy forces in northern I Corps. From the Da Krong Valley and Vietnam Salient in the west to Leatherneck Square in the east, and along the Demilitarized Zone within Quang Tri Province, troops of the 3d, 4th, and 9th Marines aggressively and repeatedly forced the enemy to withdraw into cross-border sanctuaries, thereby spoiling any attempt at a military victory in far northern I Corps.

PART II
SOUTHERN I CORPS BATTLEGROUND

CHAPTER 6
Destruction of Base Area 112

Defense of Da Nang — Attack into 112 — "A Little Urban Renewal" — Americal's TAOI

Defense of Da Nang

The surge in enemy ground combat activity witnessed during the last months of 1968 in the provinces of Quang Nam, Quang Tin, and Quang Ngai, which composed southern I Corps Tactical Zone, moderated somewhat as 1969 began. The eastern portion of Quang Nam Province, however, again produced the highest level of enemy action as NVA and VC forces subordinate to the *4th Front Headquarters* pursued a limited tactical course of ground, rocket, and mortar attacks against friendly installations, in preparation, many allied intelligence analysts thought, for a major thrust against Da Nang. In addition, the enemy persisted in attempts to control the civilian population and major rice-producing areas of the province by resorting to terrorism, intimidation, kidnappings, and the assassination of local government officials. Operating within the boundaries of Quang Nam, and subject to the *4th Front*, was the *2d NVA Division* and its subordinate regiments: the *1st Viet Cong*; *21st NVA*; *31st Independent*; *36th NVA*; *38th NVA*; *141st NVA* ; *68B NVA Artillery (Rocket)*; and the *368B NVA Artillery (Rocket)*. All were thought to be located in the mountains either southwest of Da Nang, or those astride the provincial border with Quang Tin.

In the southern two provinces of I Corps, Quang Tin and Quang Ngai, regiments controlled by *Headquarters Military Region 5* and the *3d NVA Division* — the *2d Viet Cong*, *3d NVA*, *22d NVA*, *31st NVA*, and the *401st VC (Sapper)* — continued to confine their activities primarily to scattered attacks by fire, interdiction of friendly lines of communication, and the harassment of villages, hamlets, and refugee camps surrounding the cities of Tam Ky and Quang Ngai.

Facing the estimated 37,300 enemy troops in the three provinces at the beginning of 1969, were two major United States combat units: the Army's 23d Infantry (Americal) Division under the command of Major General Charles M. Gettys, and Major General Ormond R. Simpson's 1st Marine Division.

A Texan by birth, Major General Simpson entered the Marine Corps in 1936 and served in the Pacific during World War II. When the Government of

Department of Defense Photo (USMC) A372782
MajGen Ormond R. Simpson, as Commanding General, 1st Marine Division, coordinated the activities of four Marine regiments in the defense of Da Nang.

Thailand requested American troops during the Laotian Crisis in 1962, CinCPac ordered then-Brigadier General Simpson to Southeast Asia as Commanding General, 3d Marine Expeditionary Brigade, as well as Naval Component Commander, Joint Task Force 116. Following a tour as Commanding General, Marine Corps Recruit Depot, Parris Island, he assumed command of the 1st Marine Division from Major General Carl A. Youngdale on 20 December 1968.

Under Simpson, the division performed a variety of missions. The division's general task, like that of all other United States combat units, was to locate and destroy enemy forces, installations, and LOCs [lines of communication] within its assigned area of responsibility, in coordination with South Vietnamese and other allied forces. Its primary mission was the defense of Da Nang and the more than one million South Vietnamese living within the city or nearby. As General Simpson later commented: "The 1st Marine Division was, far beyond all else, tied to the defense of the Da Nang Vital Area. This was exactly as it should have been. Da Nang was clearly a textbook example of a 'Vital Area.' Here were military headquarters, political headquarters and officials, a great seaport, a splendid airfield, a vast array of logistical support apparatus including supplies of every variety, equipment, medical establishments, to say nothing of nearly one million Vietnamese. U.S. Forces could not have operated in ICTZ without Da Nang." Therefore, the division's infantry units and supporting arms were to be "disposed to provide maximum security for the Da Nang vital area, installations and LOCs of greatest political, economic and military importance."[1]

Among the secondary tasks assigned the division were to provide security for the continuing engineer effort to improve National Route 1 and logistics craft operating in inland waterways, and to assist Vietnamese forces in the pacification effort. In addition, it was to carry on surveillance, reconnaissance within its tactical area of responsibility (TAOR), and "such other places as assigned."* Elements of the division were also required to furnish support for combined action platoons, Civilian Irregular Defense Group camps, and government district headquarters. Finally, the division was to provide one reinforced battalion for deployment anywhere in South Vietnam on 12-hour notice, and two additional battalions within 24 hours.[2]

Stretching from above the strategic Hai Van Pass in the north to the rugged Que Son Mountains in the south, the division's TAOR encompassed approximately 1,100 square miles and included most of Quang Nam and small portions of Thua Thien and Quang Tin Provinces. From the flat sand beaches along the South China Sea and the wide bay of Da Nang, the terrain rose westward into the jungle-covered mountains of the Annamite Chain and opened out to the south and southwest into the flat, treeline-broken, rice-paddy country of the An Hoa-Song Thu Bon basins, and Go Noi Island. It was heavily populated terrain which offered the enemy numerous places of defense and concealment, and the Marines a difficult chore of routing them out.

The type of warfare carried on in southern I Corps Tactical Zone was in marked contrast to that fought in northern I Corps, where, as Colonel Robert H. Barrow later noted, "anything that moved you could shoot at because he was the enemy; you did not have to separate the armed threat from the civilian population." Barrow came to appreciate "the most difficult; the most arduous; dirty; psychologically bad situation that confronted those who fought the kind of war that was necessary to fight down in the Da Nang" area. "Those Marines who went out day after day conducting, . . . combat patrols, almost knowing that somewhere on their route of movement, they were going to have some sort of surprise visited on them, either an ambush or explosive device . . . . I think that is the worst kind of warfare, not being able to see the enemy. You can't shoot back at him. You are kind of helpless. It is easy to become fatalistic, as indeed a lot of our young men did."[3]

Centered on Da Nang, the division deployed its four infantry regiments, the 1st, 5th, 7th, and elements of the 26th Marines, in a series of radiating belts. To the north, Colonel Clyde W. Hunter's 26th Marines secured portions of the Hai Van Pass and sections of Route 1. Colonel Herbert L. Beckington's 7th Marines patrolled the scrub-covered piedmont and mountainous jungle that rose to the west. To the southwest, the 5th Marines, under the command of Colonel James B. Ord, Jr., scouted the An Hoa and Song Thu Bon basins. Included within the regiment's area of responsibility was the infamous Arizona Territory, that rice paddy-dotted, enemy-infested region set between the Song Thu Bon and Song Vu Gia. South of Da Nang and north of the area assigned the Korean Marines was Colonel Robert G. Lauffer's 1st Marines, whose area of operations included Dodge City, Go Noi Island, and portions of the coastal lowlands. A reinforced artillery regiment, the 11th Marines, provided fire support for the four infantry regiments, while the 1st Reconnaissance Battalion and 1st Tank Battalion supplemented and reinforced their efforts, as did contingents of engineer, transport, and service troops.

Like all allied forces, the 1st Marine Division coor-

---

*TAOR, as defined at this time, was "the area assigned to the 1st Marine Division in which the responsibility and authority for the development and maintenance of installations, control of movement, and the control of tactical operations involving troops under division control is vested in the Commanding General, 1st Marine Division. All fire and maneuver conducted within the TAOR, or the effect of which impinge upon the TAOR, must be coordinated with the Commanding General, 1st Marine Division." TAOR differed from an area of operations (AO), which was "an area where forces conduct operations during specific periods of time," and which could be an area within or outside of an existing TAOR. (Anx C, 1stMarDiv OpO 301-YR, dtd 6Feb69, in 1stMarDiv ComdC, Feb69).

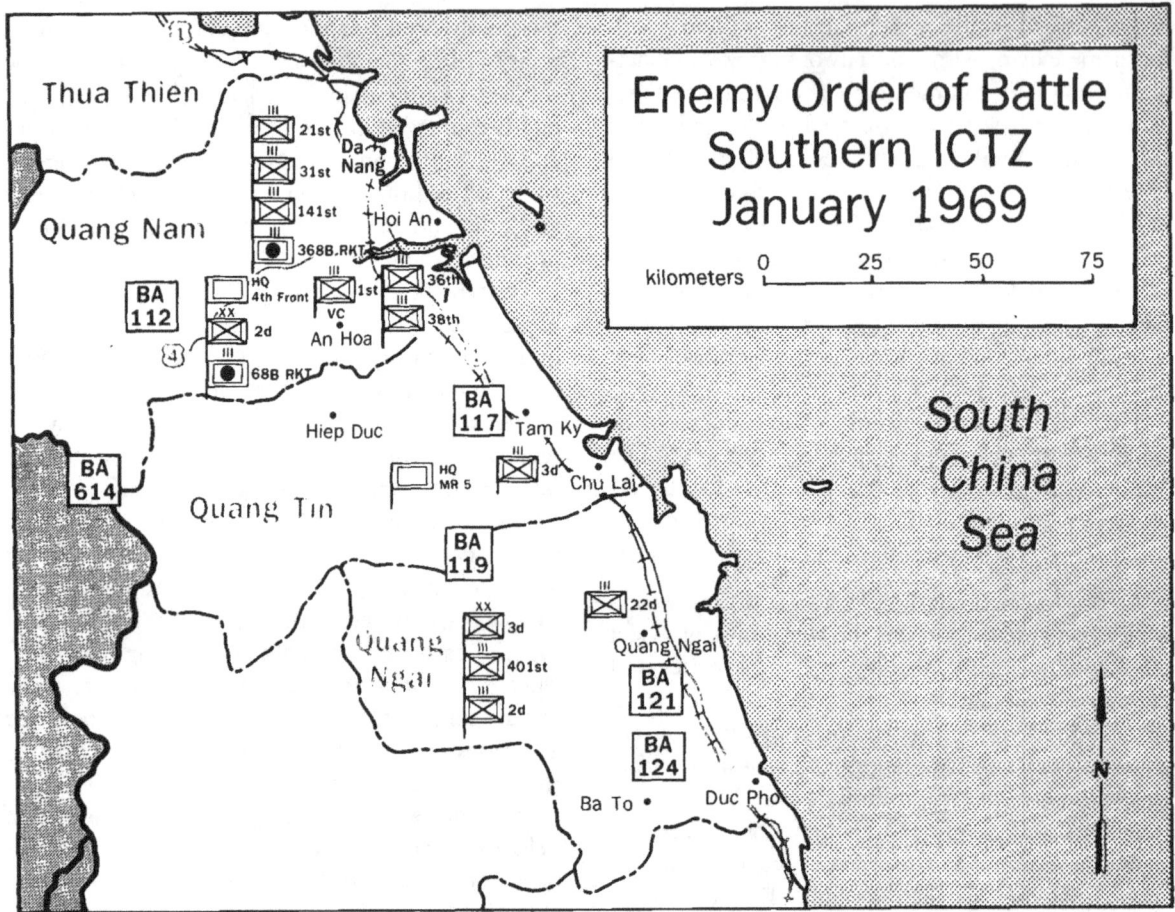

See Reference Map, Sections 18-36

dinated its efforts with South Vietnamese and Korean Marine forces within Quang Nam Province. The four battalions of the Republic of Korea's 2d Marine Brigade, based at Hoi An, about 27 kilometers southeast of Da Nang, defended a small TAOR stretching from the South China Sea inland to the foothills of the Que Son Mountains. South Vietnamese forces within the province were considerable. Regular ARVN forces consisted of the four-battalion 51st Regiment; the 1st Ranger Group of three battalions; and supporting armor, artillery, and service troops. Civilian Irregular Defense Groups based at Thuong Duc and at Nong Son, deep in the mountains, interdicted important enemy infiltration routes. Protecting the populated areas were Regional Force companies, Popular Force platoons, and a large contingent of the National Police Field Force.

Despite four years of bitter warfare in Quang Nam as the new year began, Marines, together with South Vietnamese and Korean units, faced an estimated force of 24 enemy infantry and support battalions. Although massing from time to time, the enemy generally adhered to a defensive pattern established during late summer 1968, a posture of consistent refusal to engage friendly forces in a large-scale confrontation. Clearly the enemy was attempting to reconstitute and conserve his troops by holding his formations to relatively secure areas. But the enemy was to be afforded no respite, as 1st Division Marines carried the war into the areas the Viet Cong and North Vietnamese considered safe from attack.

Attack into 112

Numbered among the goals assigned III MAF by both CinCPac and MACV in 1968, was the neutralization of eight enemy base areas within ICTZ. Although not sharply defined, these eight geographic regions were known to harbor training and logistical support facilities of enemy regular and guerrilla forces. Since these areas often covered hundreds of square kilometers of mountainous hinterland and piedmont, and were criss-crossed by thousands of hidden paths, roads, and waterways, absolute neutralization was impractical, if not impossible. It was the destruction and dislocation of the enemy's logistical facilities within

An infantryman of the 1st Battalion, 7th Marines examines several captured 140mm enemy rockets, positioned on earthen firing ramps and ready for launch against Da Nang.

these areas, and the eventual degradation of his combat capabilities, to which CinCPac referred when defining "neutralization" as a condition when the areas were "no longer able to be used for their intended purpose."[4]

During 1968, III MAF conducted 21 operations in the eight enemy base areas. As a result of these operations, two base areas were "neutralized": Base Area 100 in Quang Tin Province; and Base Area 116 in Quang Nam. However, one new base area was established. Designated Base Area 112, it was located in the mountainous region of Quang Nam Province southwest of An Hoa, directly threatening the heavily populated coastal region between Da Nang and Tam Ky.

Neutralization of Base Areas 100 and 116 in mid-1968 had forced the enemy to shift his training and logistical support facilities eastward into the mountains between the Song Thu Bon and Song Cai, and beyond. Early intelligence provided by the U.S. Army Special Forces "Delta Force" confirmed the relocation.*

---

*Under the Military Assistance Command and the Special Forces, Project Delta was given a long-range reconnaissance and intelligence-gathering mission. Organized into a reconnaissance element and a reaction force, at full strength Project Delta would comprise about 600 men, both U.S. and South Vietnamese. The typical reconnaissance element consisted of eight road patrol teams, and 16 six-man reconnaissance teams.

On 25 October 1968, a number of Delta Force reconnaissance and road teams entered the area in order to determine the identity and location of enemy units. The Army intelligence collection effort, codenamed Operation Warbonnet, continued until 14 November when it was terminated prematurely and the Delta Force teams diverted to other areas within South Vietnam. Defectors and prisoners rounded up by Marines during Operation Meade River in November provided additional intelligence regarding unit identification.

Taken together, reconnaissance and prisoner interrogation reports provided a somewhat accurate list of enemy units and probable locations within Base Area 112. Among the units identified were the two main command elements which controlled NVA and VC activities within Quang Nam, Quang Tin, and Quang Ngai Provinces: *Front 4 Headquarters* and *Headquarters Military Region 5*. Attached and directly subordinate to the two headquarters elements, and also located within the base area were the *21st Regiment, 2d NVA Division, 220th Transport Regiment, Q81st (Deux Xuan)* and *Q83d (Dai Loc) Local Force Battalions*, and *2d Battalion, 141st NVA Regiment*. Reinforcing the estimated 3,500 enemy troops were another 6,000 located just outside the base area in the Que Son Mountains and on Go Noi Island to the east.

Situation appraisals based on the intelligence reports, indicated that the enemy units within Base Area 112 would not defend in strength, but would withdraw their headquarters, supplies, and personnel to the west and southwest, while attempting to delay friendly forces. In addition, the III MAF appraisals expected the enemy to continue to harass allied lines of communication, make maximum use of surprise firing devices, and mount attacks by fire against allied installations, specifically An Hoa Combat Base.[5]

Desirous of eliminating the threat to Da Nang, MACV suggested that an operation be conducted against the enemy base area as a follow-up to the highly successful operation, Meade River.[6] Preliminary discussions and planning began in late November, as Brigadier General Ross T. Dwyer, Jr., Assistant Division Commander, 1st Marine Division, noted:

> There were some planning sessions between respective 1st Division staff and III MAF staff, and then we had some of our own discussions in the 1st Division. It was our view that this was something that a regiment could handle itself. The action officer level of III MAF indicated we'd have to have a task force go out there . . . . We didn't think it was really warranted . . . from what they were describing to us. We argued that a reinforced regiment, beefed up out of the existing command structure that was at An Hoa at the time—then the 5th Marines—could do the job. But subsequently, it was determined, and I think at the III MAF level, that one, the task force would be formed and would conduct the operation, and that additional forces would be made available to perform the mission.[7]

III MAF passed word to the 1st Division on 1 December to form the required task force organization. "We started from absolute zero," General Dwyer remembered:

> Since no task force staff and its equipment was in existence, the rapid organization of a task force headquarters was an immediate requirement. Under Major General [Carl A.] Youngdale's guidance (he was then CG, 1st Mar Div), I selected Colonel Bob Nichols, then an assistant G-3, as my Chief of Staff. He supervised and directed the formation of the task force headquarters from officers serving in the various division staff sections, from Headquarters Battalion and from the Communications Company. It was purposely designed as a small headquarters because we felt we could satellite on existing facilities at An Hoa. We had our initial meeting of the hastily assembled staff and commenced planning for the operation and for briefing General Abrams. Time was of the essence since the deadlines were short.[8]

On 4 December, the 1st Marine Division activated the temporary command, codenamed Task Force Yankee, designating General Dwyer, a World War II and Korean War veteran and former commanding officer of the 1st Marines, as its commander.* Later the same day, task force staff section heads briefed General Creighton Abrams on details of the operation at III MAF Headquarters. With no comment or question during the entire briefing, General Abrams at the conclusion turned to General Dwyer and said, "It sounds fine. Go!"[9]

Assigned to the task force were three battalions of Colonel James B. Ord's 5th Marines—Lieutenant Colonel Richard F. Daley's 1st Battalion, Lieutenant Colonel James W. Stemple's 2d Battalion, and Lieutenant Colonel Harry E. Atkinson's 3d Battalion—as were Battalion Landing Team 2/7 under Lieutenant Colonel Neil A. Nelson, and elements of the 1st Force Reconnaissance Company. A small field artillery group was formed from elements of Force Artillery, the 11th, and later the 12th Marines, consisting initially of one 8-inch, two 155mm, four 105mm, and two howtar batteries.** Operating in coordination with Task Force Yankee would be the 1st ARVN Ranger Group, consisting of the 21st, 37th, and the 39th Ranger Battalions, and one brigade of the Americal Division.

The plan for the upcoming operation, codenamed Taylor Common, hammered out two days before the formal activation of Task Force Yankee, called for units of the task force to conduct a three-phase operation to destroy enemy forces, caches, and installations in Base Area 112 and adjacent areas, and to prepare a series of fire support bases extending along likely avenues of approach to the base area from the Laotian border. During phase one, task force units were to conduct search and clear operations from Liberty Bridge to An Hoa in coordination with the 1st ARVN Ranger Group's Operation Le Loi in the An Hoa-Arizona area, in order to destroy elements of the *2d NVA Division*. A series of fire support bases would then be prepared along the approaches to 112. Penetration of the enemy base area by four Marine battalions and the establishment of bases required to support the extensive search and destroy operations would be carried out in phase two. During the final phase, task force units were to conduct reconnaissance and surveillance operations

---

*At this time there were two assistant division commanders of the 1st Marine Division. General Dwyer was stationed with the division, while Brigadier General Carl W. Hoffman was assigned to III MAF as Assistant Chief of Staff for Operations.

**The howtar resulted from the blending of two existing weapons: the tube of a 4.2-inch mortar mounted on the carriage of a 75mm pack howitzer. The result was a helicopter-transportable, high-trajectory weapon. With the increased evolution toward heavy-lift helicopters and more mobile artillery, the howtar was deleted from the Marine Corps' artillery inventory.

Department of Defense Photo (USMC) A371820

Aerial photograph looks east down the runway at An Hoa Combat Base, the 1st Division's western-most logistical facility and home of Task Force Yankee, commanded by BGen Ross T. Dwyer, Jr., and the 5th Marines, under the command of Col James B. Ord, Jr.

deep into the mountains west of the Song Cai, develop fire support bases to sustain forces completing the neutralization of 112, and interdict the avenues of approach from the Laotian border. Vital to all phases of the operation would be the maintenance of a continuous reconnaissance screen to the north, south, and west of the maneuvering battalions as they progressed westward into the enemy base area.

The weather was a major consideration in the planning as the monsoon season was in full swing. Since Marines would be operating in rugged terrain far from their bases and thus dependent on helicopters, there was thought of waiting for better flying weather. As General Dwyer noted, "we couldn't have picked a worse time weatherwise for helicopter operations in Base Area 112; we were going to be weather sensitive." But, he continued, "we were at the stage where we were told to run an operation, and the climatic conditions were such they said go ahead and run it."[10]

With the activation of Task Force Yankee on 4 December, Nelson's Marines, four companies and the command group were released from Operation Meade River, and reembarked on board the *Tripoli* (LPH 10), where all personal gear and organizational equipment was packed for debarkation. The following day, as operational control of the landing team passed to the 1st Marine Division and then to the 5th Marines, Companies E, F, G, H, and the command group moved by helicopter to An Hoa Combat Base. Simultaneously, the team's rear echelon moved ashore to Camp Love, the 7th Engineer Battalion's command post at Da Nang, where the battalion's administrative and logistical facilities were to be established.

Operation Taylor Common began two days later, on the morning of the 7th, with a heliborne assault by Lieutenant Colonel Nelson's Marines into the southwestern corner of the Arizona Territory, three kilometers west of the Song Thu Bon, opposite An Hoa.* The first wave of Marines from Company H experienced no contact as they landed at LZ Champagne, and were followed immediately by the remaining companies and the command group. In trace, the four companies moved northeast across swollen streams, rice paddies, and through dense treelines, conducting search and clear operations throughout the widely scattered Phu Loi village complex. The 1st ARVN Ranger

---

*"Arizona Territory," or simply Arizona, was the name given to the rice paddy regions of Dai Loc and Duc Duc Districts lying between the Song Vu Gia and Song Thu Bon. Origin of the term is unknown.

Group assaulted into the northeast corner of the same area on the 10th, and began search and clear operations to the southwest, eventually passing through blocking positions established by Nelson's Marines, who then swept southeastward across the Song Thu Bon to My Son, and then to An Hoa. Meanwhile, elements of Colonel Ord's 5th Marines, following their return from Meade River, conducted a thorough search of their northern area of operations, from Liberty Bridge to An Hoa.

These three operations, in conjunction with the 196th Infantry Brigade's search of the Que Son Mountains to the south, completed the initial phase by sweeping major enemy units from areas adjacent to An Hoa, Liberty Bridge, and Liberty Road, the main supply route between the two. But the operations were not without cost. Although engagements with enemy units were light and scattered during the first four days, surprise firing devices or boobytraps, usually consisting of M26 grenades rigged as antipersonnel mines, wounded eight. Friendly fire killed five and wounded an equal number of Marines. Both of these problems were to plague task force Marines throughout the operation, especially those working in the lowlands.

While search and clear operations were in progress around An Hoa, task force Marines made preparations for the move into Base Area 112. On 9 December, with no additional combat resources available from the 1st Marine Division, Task Force Yankee assumed operational control of the 1st and 3d Battalions, 3d Marines, under Colonel Michael M. Spark, from the 3d Marine Division: the 1st would join Operation Taylor Common on the 13th, and the 3d the following day. According to General Davis, the two battalions were provided to assist the 1st Marine Division in its "first 'high mobility' operation out into the hills."[11]

Also in preparation for the assault, Task Force Yankee established a main logistical area with 10-day supply levels of rations and ammunition at An Hoa, in addition to a forward direct air support center (DASC). Located near the artillery fire support coordination center (FSCC), in order to pool "Save-a-Plane" information for the protection of aircraft, the DASC would not only control Marine fixed-wing and helicopter support, but also Air Force transport aircraft provided by the 15th Aerial Port Squadron, fireship (AC-47) or "Spooky," and AC-119 or "Shadow" assistance furnished by the 14th Special Operations Wing, and special mission aircraft for heavy ordnance drops by the Seventh Air Force within the area of operation. During this period of preparation, the first four fire support base sites were selected and bombarded by B-52, fixed-wing, and concentrated artillery fire with the heaviest barrages directed against the sites designated Lance and Pike. But due to the distance (eight kilometers) between Lance, the main artillery support site, and An Hoa, a temporary mobile fire support base, close to Lance and oriented southward, was opened. Its mission was to provide complementary fire support to the Nong Song Civilian Irregular Defense Group and two Mobile Strike Force companies operating along the Song Thu Bon and southern Taylor Common boundary. Battery K, 4th Battalion, 13th Marines, a self-propelled 155mm Howitzer (M109) bat-

A tank of the 1st Tank Battalion conducts a sweep of Liberty Road, the main thoroughfare between Da Nang and An Hoa, in preparation for the build-up at the combat base.
Marine Corps Historical Collection

Marine Corps Historical Collection
Photograph provides an overhead view of An Hoa logistics operations center and the passenger and cargo pad beyond. The center coordinated the helicopter movement of personnel and supplies in support of combat operations in Base Area 112 and the Arizona.

tery, supported by Company L, 5th Marines, moved overland on the 10th to establish Fire Base Marne on the eastern shore of the Song Thu Bon, five kilometers from Lance.[12]

Phase two of Operation Taylor Common began on 11 December with an assault against Hill 575, the site selected for Lance. The location had been visually reconnoitered prior to preparatory fires by Zone Interpretation, Planning, Preparation, and Overfly (ZIPPO) and Fire Base Interpretation, Reconnaissance, Planning, Preparation and Overfly (FIRPPO) Teams to determine its suitability as a landing zone and subsequent development as a fire support base.* Although the preparatory fires cleared a large proportion of the vegetation from the landing zone, a few large tree trunks remained, necessitating the use of rappel techniques to land engineers and a small security force, who cleared an area large enough to accommodate a helicopter. Within two hours, division engineers created an adequate zone and the main assault element

---
*ZIPPO and FIRPPO Teams, composed of air, artillery, engineer, and infantry representatives, determined the selection and suitability of a fire support base, and the subsequent placement of guns, command bunkers, and storage areas.

of Lieutenant Colonel Atkinson's 3d Battalion, 5th Marines landed and established perimeter security for the engineers, who then began construction of artillery positions, ammunition and command bunkers, and further enlarged the base.

Once the security force was in position and the supporting artillery batteries in place, rifle companies of Atkinson's battalion radiated from Lance, initiating deliberate search and clear operations. The established patrol pattern resembled a clover leaf, expanding as Marines secured areas near the fire support base. This pattern of operation characterized the establishment of the next three support bases: Pike (Hill 214), opened by the 2d Battalion, 5th Marines on 13 December; Spear (Hill 558), occupied by the 1st Battalion, 3d Marines on the 15th; and Mace (Hill 375), taken by the 3d Battalion, 3d Marines on the 19th. In constructing Spear and Mace, Spark's Marines encountered problems. The initial clearing fires were insufficient and had to be augmented by 10,000-pound demolition bombs (MK121), known as "Combat Traps," dropped by Air Force C-130 aircraft manned by personnel of the 434th Air Division from Tan Son Nhut Airbase, near Saigon. Although partially successful on

Spear, the explosive force of the bombs was not strong enough to completely clear the required area on the extremely narrow ridgelines selected for Spear and Mace. Standard 500- and 1,000-pound bombs, rockets, and napalm then were used to clear away the multilayered, 70- to 80-foot canopy, and thick secondary growth which generally covered the terrain in Base Area 112.[13]

With the establishment of four Marine battalions, under the operational control of the 3d Marines, in the eastern zone of Base Area 112, search and destroy operations against an area of reported enemy activity and concentrated installations began. During the next two weeks, Marines, in their search, found and destroyed several enemy base camps, fighting positions, hospitals, and an enemy prison camp: all of which had been vacated before the Marines arrived. Engagements were few as the enemy withdrew westward, leaving only a handful of troops to slow the advance. For many Marines, this was their first experience operating in mountainous terrain, as Lance Corporal Rick L. Wackle related:

> This was completely new for me because I had never operated up in the canopied areas. It was a whole new type of warfare up there. The density of the woods, vines, jungle; it's really thick and it's nagging and tiresome to work in, and everything is against you up there . . . . Being it was so thick up there, it was very easy to walk past a ville; the foliage and coverage was unbelievable; you couldn't detect anything from what was right or wrong.[14]

In conjunction with the search and destroy mission, Task Force Yankee mounted ground operations against Hills 1050 and 551, subsequently designated Dagger and Cutlass. Lieutenant Colonel Richard C. Schulze's 3d Battalion, 3d Marines secured the former and assisted in the establishment of a communications retransmission site. Lieutenant Colonel Richard B. Twohey's 1st Battalion, 3d Marines took the latter and began to exploit a major trail network identified near Mace. The battalions of the ARVN Ranger Group, meanwhile, continued search and clear operations in the Arizona area, relieving Lieutenant Colonel Nelson's battalion landing team, which assaulted into the northwestern portion of Go Noi Island on 17 December. Sweeping south, the battalion displaced to An Hoa Combat Base two days later, having met only light resistance. On the 23d, the 21st and 39th Ranger Battalions, operating in the piedmont west of Phu Loi, encountered and then fought an estimated NVA battalion, killing 158 and capturing 18 individual and 10 crew-served weapons.

Abel Papers, Marine Corps Historical Center
Fire Support Base Lance was the first of many infantry and artillery positions constructed in support of Task Force Yankee operations in the enemy base area.

Near Taylor Common's southern boundary, the two Special Forces Mobile Strike companies and the Nong Song Irregular Company continued reconnaissance operations along the upper Song Thu Bon. Although these forces were relatively small, they did provide timely intelligence and proved to be an impediment to the flow of enemy supplies and troops that previously had used the area as a route into the Que Son Mountains and the flatlands beyond. Further south, the 196th Infantry Brigade continued to maintain blocking positions, as well as search operations in the Que Sons in order to prevent an enemy escape.

With the new year, Taylor Common moved into the third and final phase of operations. Combat action centered on two regions, the An Hoa basin, the scene of constant enemy activity throughout most of 1968, and Base Area 112, the high ground lying to the west and southwest.

On 1 January, the 3d Battalion, 5th Marines lifted into Combat Operations Base (COB) Javelin, signaling the initiation of operations in the western zone of Base Area 112; more specifically, the penetration of the large basin between the Ong Thu slope and the Nui Gaing-Yang Brai ridgelines near the Song Cai.* Following the establishment of Javelin, the bombardment of Hill 508, future site of FSB Maxwell, began. Although

---

*A combat operations base was similar in character to a fire support base, but did not include artillery.

more than 177 tons of high explosives were used to clear a landing zone, the number of exposed tree trunks and the continued enemy small arms fire, prevented Marines from being inserted by air. As a result, Lieutenant Colonel Twohey's 1st Battalion, 3d Marines landed on nearby Hill 728 and attacked toward Hill 508 over Hill 401, finally securing the objective on the 15th. With the six 105mm howitzers of Battery C, 12th Marines in position on Maxwell, Spark's Marines were ready to pursue enemy forces westward, searching and clearing the remainder of 112.

Executing heliborne assaults from fire support and combat bases into selected landing zones, the infantry battalions fanned out in local search operations, upon the successful completion of which they moved still deeper into the base area: the 3d Battalion, 3d Marines conducting clearing operations south and west of Cutlass through COB Dart to COB Battle-Ax and FSB Bolo; the 3d Battalion, 5th Marines, under Lieutenant Colonel Atkinson, continuing operations through COB Broadsword toward FSB Tomahawk; and Lieutenant Colonel Twohey's 1st Battalion conducting search operations with companies advancing on parallel axis north and west of Maxwell, and then developing COB Scimitar on Mai Guy ridgeline overlooking the confluence of the Song Cai and Song Boung. By 5 February, units of Task Force Yankee were operating along the entire length of the Song Cai within Base Area 112, while 1st Force Reconnaissance Company teams penetrated deep into the western approaches.

The four Marine battalions, radiating from the widely dispersed combat and fire support bases, developed numerous contacts with evading enemy units no larger than platoons, resulting in an undramatic, but steady, attrition of enemy troops. Beyond the generally light ground combat, they uncovered abundant evidence confirming substantial enemy strength within the base area. Patrolling units continued to locate many base camps, supply stores, weapons, and ammunition caches. On 5 January, for example, Company E, 5th Marines unearthed an arms cache containing 166 rifles and three crew-served weapons, 11 kilometers west of An Hoa near FSB Pike. A logistics complex discovered by Companies C and D, 1st Battalion, 3d Marines, 10 kilometers southwest of Thuong

A Marine patrol pauses in the dense jungle undergrowth. Fighting not only the terrain but also excessive heat and humidity, Marines found the search of Base Area 112 exhausting.

Marine Corps Historical Collection

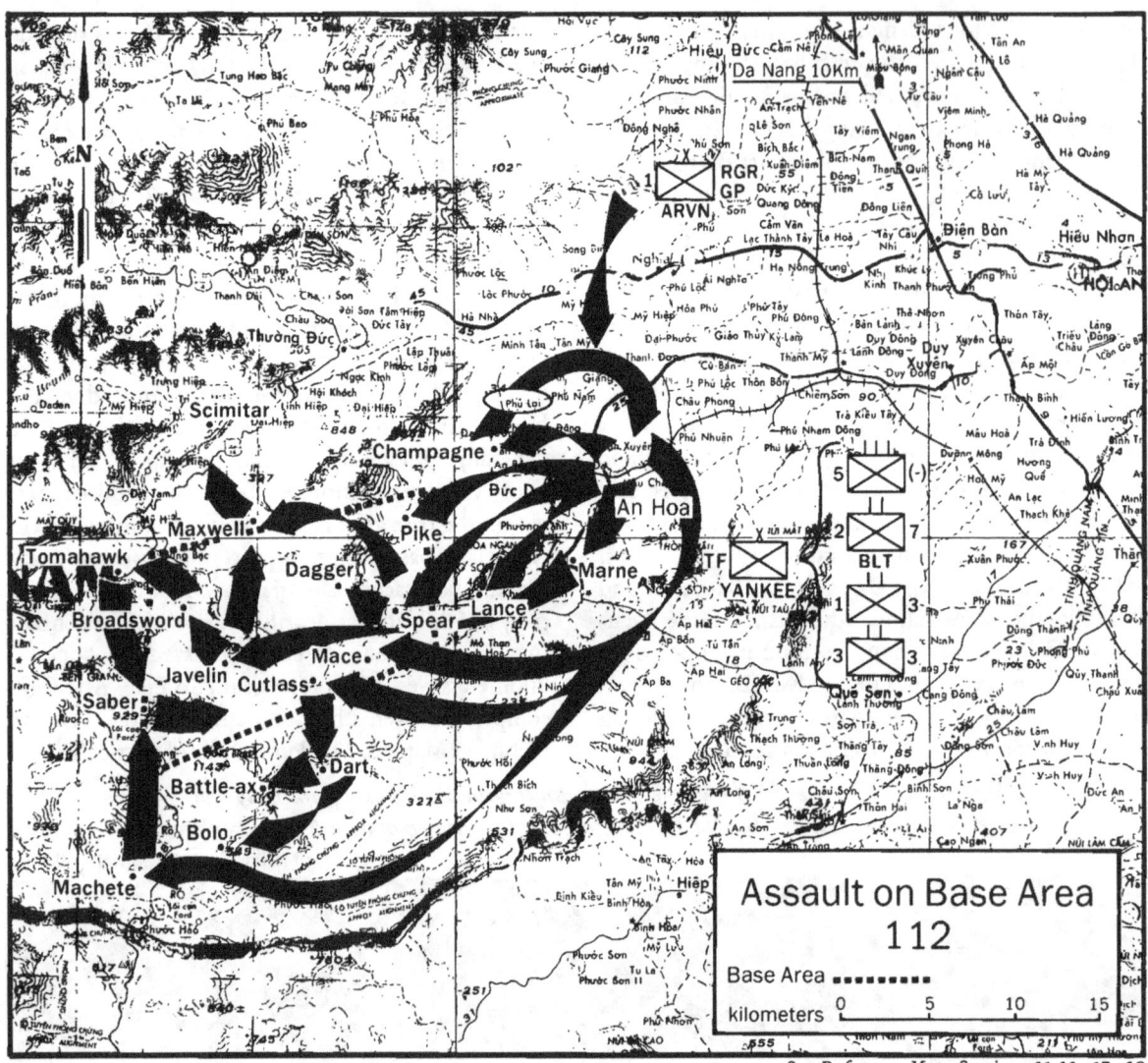

See Reference Map, Sections 31-33, 37, 38

Duc on the 22d, yielded twenty-two 122mm rockets, a thousand 82mm mortar rounds, 501 RPG rounds, 25 rifles, 17 cases of small arms ammunition, nearly 12 tons of rice, and a pen containing 65 live pigs.

It was during this period that the 3d Marines suffered a profound loss. While on visual reconnaissance south of FSB Maxwell on the 15th, an Army UH-1H helicopter received automatic weapons fire causing it to crash and burn. On board were Colonel Michael M. Spark; the regimental sergeant major, Ted E. McClintock; the commanding officer of the 1st Battalion, 12th Marines, Lieutenant Colonel Ermil L. Whisman; and Colonel Spark's radio operator, Lance Corporal Fredrick D. Kansik. All, including the helicopter's Army crew, were killed. Colonel Paul D. Lafond assumed command of the 3d Marines, while Lieutenant Colonel Roddey B. Moss took over the 1st Battalion, 12th Marines.

Detailed search operations within Base Area 112 continued throughout the remaining days of January and into February. On the 6th, Task Force Yankee initiated operations west of the Song Cai as the 2d Battalion, 5th Marines, following a short rest at An Hoa, assaulted Hill 435, later named Machete, and began searching north-northwest along the river toward Fire Support Base Saber.

In the An Hoa basin, the new year was marked by occasional skirmishes with small enemy units moving between An Hoa and Go Noi Island, 10 kilometers to the northeast. Assigned to secure the area was Lieutenant Colonel Richard F. Daley's 1st Battalion, 5th Marines. Combat patrols were the order of the day, as described by First Lieutenant Ronald E. Pruiett:

> The normal way we operate is to go out and set up a company PPB [platoon patrol base] and operate out of that, sending out platoons and squad-size patrols. The normal

patrol covers an area anywhere from 500 meters to a click and a half [1,500 meters], depending on terrain and type of contact which we expect to make.... Normally the only contact we do make is a small unit also. Normally we run into groups of maybe three, four, or five. The way contact is normally initiated, they, in most instances, initiate the contact by firing a few sniper rounds at us and then we will go ahead to commence to maneuver. Again, they are very slippery, and by the time we maneuver into the area which they are at or where we think they are at, they have already made their bird [escape].[15]

The most intense action to occur took place during the night of 29 January in the far western sector of Go Noi Island. At 2200, a squad ambush of Company C, 1st Battalion, 7th Marines, not a participant in Operation Taylor Common, observed approximately 300 enemy troops cross to the southern bank of the Song Ky Lam, six kilometers west of Dien Ban. The enemy unit, apparently forced south by 7th Marines Operation Linn River and ARVN Operation Hung Quang 1-03, was taken under artillery fire, while the company launched an attack to block the enemy's advance. Engaging the Marines with automatic weapons and RPG fire, the enemy attempted to escape westward, but was intercepted by Company D, 5th Marines, moving from the southwest through head-high elephant grass. Fierce firefights continued throughout the night, with Marines employing 155mm artillery fire and air strikes in support of the attack. By dawn,

LtCol Richard B. Twohey, center, Commanding Officer, 1st Battalion, 3d Marines, and LtCol Ermil L. Whisman, right, Commanding Officer, 1st Battalion, 12th Marines, brief Task Force Yankee commander BGen Ross T. Dwyer on operations of the battalions.

Abel Papers, Marine Corps Historical Center

the enemy had broken into small groups and scattered. A search of the battle area turned up 72 NVA dead, while numerous drag marks and blood trails punctuated the dense growth of elephant grass. Friendly casualties resulting from the night's action were seven wounded.

On 7 February, operational control of Battalion Landing Team 2/26, under Lieutenant Colonel William F. Sparks, was shifted from the 7th to the 5th Marines and the BLT joined Operation Taylor Common. Continuing the cordon and search of Go Noi Island begun early during Operation Linn River, the team's Marines encountered sniper fire and a large number of boobytraps as they moved across their assigned area, destroying tunnel systems, bunkers, and other enemy-prepared fighting positions. Completing its short sojourn ashore, the battalion landing team returned to the amphibious assault ship, *Okinawa* (LPH 3), where after a vigorous training period, it was placed in reserve for the expected *Tet* Offensive.

During this same period, BLT 2/26 was joined in Operation Taylor Common by her sister landing team. On 10 February, by way of a vertical envelopment, codenamed Defiant Measure, Lieutenant Colonel J. W. P. Robertson's BLT 3/26 deployed to the Arizona, relieving the 1st ARVN Ranger Group. Due to the size of the team's area of operation (100 square kilometers), Robertson assigned each company a separate area in which to conduct search and destroy missions. Constant sniping at the moving companies, with five or six NVA tracking each company, characterized action during the first two weeks. Any halt in movement would result in sporadic sniper and incoming M79 grenade fire. Near the end of February, Company L made heavy contact killing 75 enemy soldiers and destroying two .50-caliber antiaircraft positions. Over the next several days, Robertson's Marines found approximately 20 rockets, mortars, and recoilless rifles in positions from which they could be fired, line-of-sight, at An Hoa Combat Base. With the close of the operation, BLT 3/26 remained in the Arizona, concentrating on the southern portion of its assigned area while being subjected to continuous daylight sniper and night mortar, RPG, and suicide-squad attacks.

By mid-February, Task Force Yankee essentially had neutralized Base Area 112 and established fire support and combat operations bases on the western approaches from the Laotian border. Upon order of the 1st Marine Division, General Dwyer, who was replaced on the 14th by Brigadier General Samuel Jaskilka, reduced the scale of operations by ordering the withdrawal to An Hoa of all forces in 112 with the exception of two companies (L and M) of the 3d Battalion, 5th Marines, each with one battery of direct support artillery, located on Fire Support Bases Tomahawk and Maxwell. Due to increased enemy activity in the DMZ, the 3d Marines command group and its 3d Battalion withdrew from Base Area 112 to An Hoa Combat Base on 16 February, and redeployed immediately to Dong Ha. The 1st Battalion, 3d Marines displaced to Hill 55 the following day, and subsequently airlifted to Dong Ha after participating in a short operation in the 5th Marines' northern area of operations.

On 21 February, following three days of rehabilitation and refurbishment at An Hoa, Lieutenant Colonel Stemple's 2d Battalion, 5th Marines moved by truck to the Phu Loc (6) Refugee Hamlet, northeast of the combat base on the Song Thu Bon. There, in coordination with the 1st ARVN Ranger and local Regional Force Groups, the battalion initiated blocking operations in conjunction with the ARVN attempt to again find, fix, and destroy enemy forces, fortifications, and installations on far western Go Noi Island.

Abel Papers, Marine Corps Historical Center
Two Marines enter a bamboo hut in one of the several enemy base camps and storage sites discovered during the thorough search of Base Area 112.

On one of many patrols carried out in the Arizona, Marines of Company D, 1st Battalion, 5th Marines search an abandoned hut for hidden enemy troops and supplies.
Marine Corps Historical Collection

Marines of Company D, 1st Battalion, 5th Marines rush a fellow Marine, wounded by a boobytrapped grenade, to a waiting helicopter for evacuation to a nearby medical facility.

Limited land-clearing operations, using high explosives, medium dozers, and Rome plows, were to be conducted after the sweep of the island, but a predawn enemy attack carried out against An Hoa Combat Base during the *Tet* holidays forced their cancellation.*

Shortly after midnight on the 23d, the northeast corner of the combat base, near the ammunition storage area, was hit with enemy 82mm mortar fire. Under cover of the mortar and small arms fire, enemy troops cut and entered the base's defensive wire, and from that position, using bamboo poles, were able to lob satchel charges into one of the ammunition dumps, causing a fire which ignited the remainder. Small arms and mortar fire broke the probe, and the enemy fled to the northeast, continually engaged by "Spooky" and artillery fire. But the enemy force had done its job. In addition to the extensive loss of ammunition, base personnel sustained numerous casualties from the night-long series of explosions which rocked the ammunition dumps. As a direct result of the enemy attack on An Hoa, and minor probes at Liberty Bridge and on other allied installations within the Da Nang Vital Area, Colonel Ord ordered Stemple's battalion to Liberty Bridge, where the battalion assumed a local security mission.

As the number of enemy-initiated ground and indirect fire attacks around An Hoa rose, so did the number experienced by the units which remained in Base Area 112. Almost nightly, Companies L and M, operating near Fire Support Bases Tomahawk and Maxwell, reported enemy ground and mortar attacks against their defensive positions. The companies requested reinforcements and General Jaskilka ordered the remainder of Atkinson's battalion redeployed to the base area in late February. But with the attacks against An Hoa and other allied units operating nearby on the increase, Jaskilka again ordered the the 3d Battalion to withdraw in early March.

Planned as a one-day operation, the withdrawal of Lieutenant Colonel Atkinson's battalion became a three-day battle of disengagement. On 3 March, Com-

---

*Of the various types of land-clearing equipment tested in Vietnam, the standard military D7E tractor, equipped with a heavy-duty protective cab and a special tree-cutting blade manufactured by the Rome Company of Rome, Georgia, proved to be the most versatile and effective. The tractor took its name from the imposing blade attached to the front, which sheared off most vegetation six inches above the ground.

pany M, while on a sweep near Maxwell, received small arms and automatic weapons fire from an estimated entrenched enemy platoon. Three Marines were killed in the attack, two of whose bodies could not be recovered due to heavy enemy fire. Forced to maintain its position, the company requested additional air and artillery support. The following day, the Marines made another attempt to retrieve the bodies, but they were successful in recovering only one. On the 5th a third attempt was made to recover the remaining Marine body, but as the company attacked the enemy position, two more Marines were killed and their bodies left on the battlefield.

Meanwhile, operations to close Tomahawk and Maxwell began. As originally conceived, helicopters were to extract the infantry companies and two artillery batteries simultaneously from both fire bases, but low clouds and sporadic enemy mortar fire around Maxwell forced the airborne helicopter controller to concentrate all lifts on Tomahawk instead. Four 105mm and two 155mm howitzers of the 11th Marines, along with one infantry company, airlifted to An Hoa; Company L remained to provide security for a downed CH-53 helicopter. The following day, Company L lifted to An Hoa and Tomahawk closed.

On 6 March, the Marines of Company M made one last attempt to recover the bodies of their comrades. In their final drive, enemy fire proved to be too intense to warrant the risk of losing additional men, and the company withdrew. A force reconnaissance team subsequently recovered the bodies of the fallen Marines without loss.[16] Carrying their wounded, the Marines of Company M advanced through the dense jungle foliage toward Maxwell, encountering sporadic enemy resistance along the way. In one instance the company's point element was taken under fire by an enemy squad, resulting in the wounding of one Marine, who required immediate evacuation. While the company maintained its position, a medical evacuation helicopter extracted the wounded Marine by hoist. Poor visibility, additional enemy contact, rugged terrain, and the slow movement due to the wounded resulted in Company M arriving at Maxwell after dark, too late to be lifted to An Hoa along with the artillery. The following day, the last of Atkinson's tired Marines lifted out through sporadic small arms fire, and the fire support base was closed. With the later extraction of all reconnaissance teams operating within the base area, Operation Taylor Common came to an end on 8 March.

Results of the three-month-long operation were impressive: the destruction of enemy manpower in excess of a regiment; the capture of 206 tons of rice, 430,000 rounds of ammunition, and 1,100 weapons; and the neutralization of Base Area 112. But as General Dwyer was later to observe:

> We knew when we went in—and we pushed these fire bases all the way out as far as they'd go, almost to the border—we knew we couldn't stay. And we had pretty much cleaned out the area . . . . But when you have to pull out, they just filtered back in—that was, of course, the nature of the war.[17]

Marine casualties were 183 killed and 1,487 wounded; boobytraps killed 27 and wounded 386 Marines, while 26 Marines were killed and 103 wounded by friendly fire. The ARVN Ranger Group suffered 100 killed and 378 wounded, most occurring during operations in the Arizona and on Go Noi Island.

Despite poor flying weather and rough terrain, Marine airpower played a major role in the neutralization of Base Area 112, and the repeated security sweeps of the lowlands. The F-4 Phantom, A-4 Skyhawk, and A-6A Intruder pilots of Major General Charles J. Quilter's 1st Marine Aircraft Wing flew numerous tactical support missions in marginal weather. During the operation the Da Nang and Chu Lai-based fixed-wing aircraft flew 3,702 sorties, striking targets with 7,042 tons of bombs, killing 155 enemy troops, and destroying 624 installations.

Marine helicopters made an equally important contribution to the operation. The 10 helicopter squadrons of Colonel Warren L. MacQuarrie's Marine Aircraft Group 16 at Marble Mountain, and Colonel Bruce J. Matheson's Phu Bai-based MAG-36, flew 32,619 sorties, carried 61,995 troops, and transported 10,489 tons of supplies. Besides providing battlefield mobility to the infantry and close air support when fixed-wing aircraft were unable to attack targets due to poor visibility, the pilots of these squadrons accomplished medical evacuation, reconnaissance, resupply, and other operational and administrative missions. Army CH-54 "Crane," CH-47 "Chinook," and UH-1E "Huey" helicopters, "loaned" to the Marines by the Americal Division supplied additional support. Air support for Taylor Common was not without problems. While fixed-wing support was well-coordinated and "very timely," helicopter support oftentimes was not. Like Colonel Barrow during Operation Dewey Canyon, General Dwyer was critical: "The helicopter support I would have to judge overall mixed in performance. It ranged from outstanding, courageous, superb helicopter work, to the other end of the spectrum where it did not arrive on time, left before it should have, [or] went to wrong zones.

"It got to a point," he continued, "that we started recording the times that they were supposed to be on hand, the times they actually arrived, by type of aircraft, so that we kept a plotted curve on them—their performance." A frustrating problem for General Dwyer and his ground commanders were lunch breaks. "It was remarkable," he commented, "when they finally did arrive, they would disappear around noontime—at lunchtime—for a variety of reasons. It was a startling coincidence of bad radios that had to be fixed at lunchtime."[18] A number of Marine pilots, both fixed-wing and helicopter, took exception to the remarks of General Dwyer. Among them was Colonel Edwin H. Finlayson, who served as the 1st Wing's operations officer at the time. "The fact of this matter is," he explained, "the helicopters as a physical characteristic ran short of fuel after about four hours' operation and had to return to Marble Mountain for fuel since the First Division at the time had not provided for any at their forward bases as the Third Division had. BGen [Henry W.] Hise [Assistant Wing Commander] investigated this complaint and arranged to move refueling facilities into more forward locations for subsequent operations which greatly reduced the problem."[19] Despite the problems and resultant criticism, Marine aviation, specifically helicopter support, significantly influenced the results on the battlefield.

"A Little Urban Renewal"

"At first light, I told my [lead] platoon to move in there and do that village a job; and take a little bit of Tecumseh Sherman into Chau Son (1)." After all the civilians, mostly women and children, were rounded up, put on amtracs, and sent to the processing center adjacent to Hill 55 before resettlement, the Marines of Company D, 1st Battalion, 7th Marines moved swiftly through Chau Son (1) destroying bunkers, fighting holes, and tunnels, and burning huts found to contain fighting gear. The actions of Company D at Chau Son (1) characterized the conduct of the other companies involved in the short cordon and search operation, codenamed Linn River.[20]

While battalions of the 3d and 5th Marines searched the lowlands near An Hoa and Base Area 112, the 1st Marine Division gave elements of Colonel Herbert L. Beckington's 7th Marines the task of cordoning and searching an approximately 10-kilometer-square area south of Hill 55, between Route 4 and the Song Thu

Elements of Company D, 1st Battalion, 3d Marines inventory a portion of the tons of enemy food, supplies, and ammunition captured during Operation Taylor Common.

Department of Defense Photo (USMC) A800567

Bon, in support of the Accelerated Pacification Campaign. This task was in addition to the regiment's normal missions of patrolling the Da Nang rocket belt, with emphasis on the Song Vu Gia infiltration corridor, and bridge and installation security. Except for scattered treelines and a few small hamlets, fallow rice paddies dotted the area. Long considered a haven for local guerrilla forces, the area had witnessed several allied operations: Linn River would be no different.

At midday on 27 January, the 1st Battalion, 7th Marines departed Hill 65 and moved east on Route 4, accompanied by half a dozen amphibious assault vehicles. Once in the objective area, Lieutenant Colonel William F. Bethel's battalion would be joined by the 2d Battalion, 26th Marines, under Lieutenant Colonel William F. Sparks, which was to assault two separate landing zones the following day, link up with the 1st Battalion, and establish the initial cordon. Although eight Sea Knight (CH-46D) helicopters from HMM-165 did arrive on schedule, their air filters swiftly clogged with sand, and the lift portion of the operation had to be postponed. Meanwhile, Bethel's battalion arrived in the objective area, and not wishing to disclose the target and mission, moved further east and established a temporary blocking position.

The feint to the east "might have fooled some of the gooks," noted the acting commanding officer of Company B, Second Lieutenant Wyman E. Shuler III, "but it sure didn't fool all of them," as the assault elements of Lieutenant Colonel Sparks' battalion discovered the following morning. The first wave landed at LZ Owl without problem; the second, however, received heavy small arms fire as it attempted to land at LZ Hawk. Four of the six helicopters in the flight sustained heavy damage and were forced to return to Hill 55, halting the heliborne assault for three hours while Marines awaited replacement aircraft. By late afternoon on 29th, with the lifts completed, all units moved into position, establishing the initial cordon.[21]

Supported by three 105mm artillery batteries, 5-inch guns of the heavy cruiser *Newport News* (CA 148), and two platoons of tanks from the 5th Tank Battalion, the 7th and 26th Marines successively cordoned and then searched the objective area. Engagements during the remainder of the 12-day operation were light, consisting of Marines intercepting enemy troops attempting to flee the cordon. These small groups of enemy troops were sighted and then engaged by air and artillery; however, the majority of casualties resulted from mortar and sniper fire. Although 53 enemy troops were killed, the destruction of for-

Marine Corps Historical Collection
As elements of the 7th Marines look on, a South Vietnamese Air Force "Skyraider" drops its ordnance on an enemy position during Operation Linn River.

tifications and tunnel complexes carried out by the two battalions and accompanying engineer detachments overshadowed the loss of enemy personnel.

While multi-battalion operations such as Linn River and Taylor Common gathered a majority of the laurels, small-unit, counter-guerrilla operations were consistent in achieving success. When not participating in major operations far afield, elements of Beckington's 7th and Colonel Clyde W. Hunter's 26th Marines joined Colonel Robert G. Lauffer's 1st Marines in saturating the coastal lowlands and piedmont, north, west, and south of Da Nang with day and night patrols, ambushes, and company-size operations, denying the enemy the freedom of action necessary for tactical successes within the Da Nang Vital Area.*

As the new year began, elements of the three regiments launched an around-the-clock assortment of 10,600 patrols and ambushes, in coordination with 78 company-size cordon operations, during the month

---
*The 26th Marines, task-organized as a regimental landing team, was under operational and administrative control of the 9th Marine Amphibious Brigade. The regiment's in-country composition at the beginning of the year included a command group and the 1st Battalion. The remaining two battalions formed the infantry element of the Seventh Fleet's Special Landing Force.

against suspected enemy harbor sites and areas of intense combat and logistical support traffic with meager results. But the relative calm observed in January, to a degree reminiscent of the period preceding the wave of offensive thrusts of *Tet* 1968, gave way the following month to the first significant rise in enemy activity since August 1968. Attempting to counter the expanding South Vietnamese influence and to provide stronger political leverage, the Quang Nam enemy leadership again struggled to stage its combat strength in the populated piedmont and lowlands preceding the *Tet* holidays, but were once more trapped in the maze of 1st Marine Division patrols and ambushes.

Acting on locally obtained intelligence, a patrol from Company D, 1st Battalion, 26th Marines, on 7 February, found an enemy base camp containing equipment and messing and billeting facilities near the Nam O Bridge on the Song Cu De, 13 kilometers northwest of Da Nang. Reporting the find, the patrol departed, leaving the site untouched. Shortly after dark, the full company returned and set up a series of ambushes in order to catch any enemy troops using the facility. Twenty soldiers attempting to move into the base camp activated the first trap shortly before midnight. By 0200 the following morning, Company D had surprised two additional NVA units. Of a total of 45 enemy observed and engaged, the company killed 18 and captured two prisoners.

Enemy attempts to move rockets within range of Da Nang during early February, also fell victim to the numerous Marine patrols and ambushes. On the 8th, Company L, 3d Battalion, 7th Marines found seven complete 122mm rockets concealed along the banks of the Song Yen, 14 kilometers southwest of the city. On the same day, and two kilometers west, another 3d Battalion patrol discovered thirteen 140mm rockets, temporarily stored in a waterhole. And shortly before midnight on the 18th, a Company F, 2d Battalion, 1st Marines ambush, directing artillery on suspected enemy movement, five kilometers south of Marble Mountain, reported 21 secondary explosions, presumably enemy rockets being destroyed.

By mid-February, encounters with larger enemy units around the periphery of the Da Nang Vital Area rose. Company D, 1st Battalion, 7th Marines, while patrolling 22 kilometers south-southwest of the city, located an NVA platoon occupying a bunker system. Under cover of artillery, the company assaulted the position, forcing the enemy to withdraw, leaving 16 dead. A squad was left in the area, and at dusk it ambushed another enemy platoon attempting to reoccupy the bunker complex, killing 14 more. Earlier in the day, four kilometers to the east, the 2d Battalion, 51st ARVN Regiment engaged an estimated enemy battalion moving north from Go Noi Island. Pinned against the Song Suoi Co Ca, the enemy lost 49 killed.

Despite the lack of strength necessary for a full-scale offensive, enemy units within range of Da Nang committed themselves to action on the morning of the 23d, the first day of *Tet*. Rocket and mortar teams were the first to strike. Attacks against the Da Nang Vital Area began with a 25-round, 122mm rocket mission directed at the Deep Water Pier and continued with sporadic attacks throughout the vital area until dawn. Principal allied losses included the destruction of an ARVN ammunition dump near III MAF Headquarters and a 450,000-gallon fuel tank near the airbase. One A-6A fixed-wing aircraft and six helicopters sustained light damage during the attacks.

In addition to a rocket and mortar attack on Logistic Support Unit-1 supply areas at An Hoa, which des-

Col Robert G. Lauffer, Commanding Officer, 1st Marines, maps out the movement of patrols south of Da Nang with his operations officer, Maj James K. Reilly.
Marine Corps Historical Collection

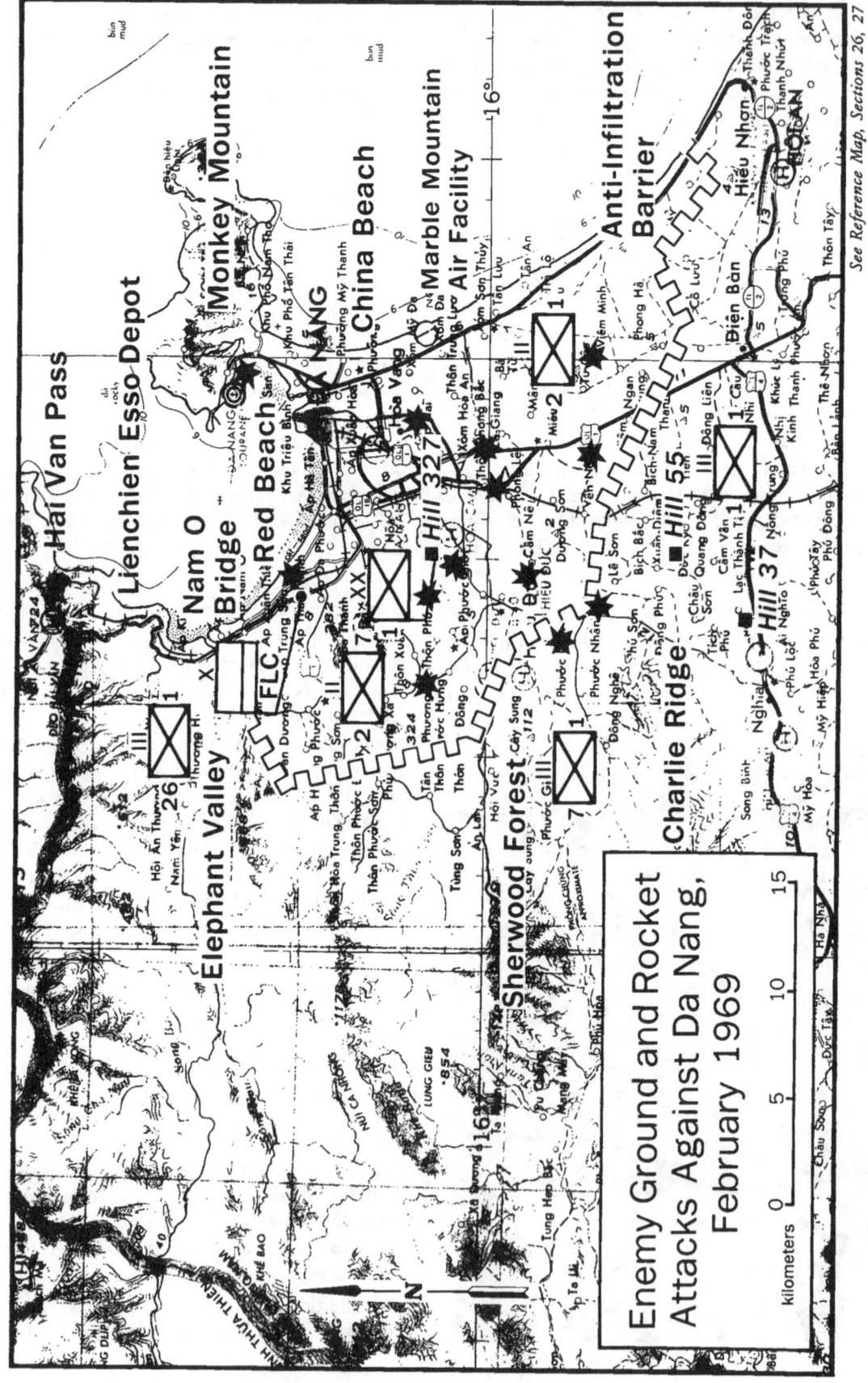

Enemy Ground and Rocket Attacks Against Da Nang, February 1969

troyed 15,000 rounds of artillery ammunition and 40,000 gallons of aviation fuel, enemy units also targeted the Chu Lai complex. The largest rocket mission of the day—fifty 122mm rockets—targeted the Da Nang Force Logistic Command and Naval Support Activity installations. Over half the rounds, however, fell into the ocean with the remaining inflicting limited damage on the LST ramp and one empty fuel tank.

As rocket and mortar teams attacked allied command and logistic facilities within the vital area, enemy sapper units attempted to disrupt major infantry command installations, while still other units moved to cut the principal approaches to the city. Like previous attempts against Da Nang, the effort was detected and repulsed, forcing the enemy to withdraw again to avoid total destruction.

Ground action south of Da Nang began shortly after midnight on the 23d, when Company K, 3d Battalion, 1st Marines and Company D, 1st Military Police Battalion detected enemy troops approaching the two Song Cau Do bridges. Attacking the yet-unassembled enemy units, the two companies killed 47 Viet Cong and captured 11, halting any enemy attempt at closing the two critical highway approaches. A short time later, an estimated 70 Viet Cong attacked the command post of the 2d Battalion, 1st Marines, six kilometers south of Marble Mountain. Repelled and forced to withdraw, the enemy left 17 dead and 4 wounded in the hands of the 1st Marines.

Shortly after dawn on the 23d, a Viet Cong unit was detected in a factory complex near the Hoa Vang District Headquarters, site of the heavy fighting during the abortive attempt to take Da Nang in August 1968. Marine units from the airbase forced the enemy into an isolated, bamboo-encircled cemetery after killing six and capturing two others. In a two-hour firefight the following day, the 21st ARVN Ranger Battalion assaulted the enemy force, then in the process of withdrawing southward, killing another 57.

After less than 12 hours of fighting, enemy units sent north to attack Da Nang were in retreat. Their efforts to escape unscathed were shattered by elements of the 1st Marines and 1st Battalion, 51st ARVN Regiment, who found them 11 kilometers south of Da Nang and struck hard. Maintaining almost constant contact for three days, the ARVN and Marine troops killed 139 and captured 38 weapons.

West of Da Nang, Lieutenant Colonel Francis X. Quinn's 3d Battalion, 7th Marines intercepted and then blunted a major three-pronged thrust into the vital area by elements of the *141st NVA Regiment*. The central and southern thrusts aimed at seizing the village of Tuy Loan and destroying nearby Cobb Bridge in order to prevent allied reinforcements from moving north along Highway 540. The northern thrust attempted to secure a route through Dai La Pass and then into the 1st Marine Division Command Post on Hill 327. Shortly after midnight on the 23d, a squad ambush from Captain Paul K. Van Riper's Company M trapped an enemy force moving east of Hill 10, killing 10 and capturing numerous weapons. Several hours later, another of Van Riper's patrols spotted 40 NVA troops in the same area and engaged them with artillery. A company search at first light the following morning revealed that the patrol had ambushed an enemy mortar company. In addition to securing two complete 82mm mortars, the enemy company's first sergeant was captured. He later indicated that a major NVA offensive was underway.

During the morning of the 23d, as elements of the *141st* continued to advance, Colonel Quinn first committed Van Riper's company and then the remainder of the battalion. The constant pressure applied by Quinn's Marines, which at times approached hand-to-hand encounters, forced the enemy to separate in small groups which, by the end of the day, congregated in three pockets along the Song Tuy Loan. The pocket east of Hill 41 was eliminated on the morning of the 24th by Captain Fred T. Fagan, Jr.'s Company K, whose Marines captured the acting regimental commander during the engagement.* Van Riper's Marines, in close fighting, reduced the second pocket centered around the village of Tuy Loan the same day. The third pocket, nestled between the An Tan ridgeline and Song Tuy Loan, proved to be more difficult. Under Captain James K. Hall, Marines of Company L, supported by artillery and air strikes, assaulted the position several times but were unable to dislodge the enemy from the thick stands of bamboo and dense growth of elephant grass that covered the area. Suffering numerous casualties, included among them Captain Hall, the company was forced to withdraw and regroup.[22]

At first light on the 26th, Company M and the two effective platoons of Company L prepared to move for-

---

*Under interrogation, the captured regimental commander provided information which eventually led to the destruction of his own regiment, and to that of the *31st* during Operation Oklahoma Hills. (LtCol Merrill L. Bartlett, Comments on draft ms, 1Sep86 [Vietnam 69 Comment File, MCHC, Washington, D.C.]).

Marine Corps Historical Collection

Sgt Howard J. Johnson, a member of Detachment A, Marine Air Support Squadron 3, displays a North Vietnamese Army flag captured during one of the several enemy attacks on Da Nang-area Marine and other allied positions, which began on 23 February.

ward against the enemy position. Following air strikes, which consisted of 500-pound retarded bombs ("Snake Eyes"), napalm, and artillery fire, the assault began under a blanket of riot control agent (CS gas). In a series of coordinated squad assaults, Van Riper's Marines carried a portion of the objective before stalling in the face of stiffening enemy resistance at nightfall. The following morning, again under cover of CS gas, Company M renewed the attack. Moving rapidly, Van Riper's lead platoon reached the Song Tuy Loan, cutting the objective in two while the trace platoons turned east and west, clearing the remainder of the area and hunting down surviving enemy troops. "The commanding officer was a prisoner and nearly 200 of his men were dead," noted Captain Van Riper, "remnants of the unit struggled desperately to break contact and move to the relative safety of the mountains . . . . With the collapse of resistance at An Tan Ridge, the *141st NVA Regiment* ceased to exist as an effective fighting force."[23]

Two other predawn *Tet* attacks centered on major allied command complexes west of Da Nang. On the northern slope of Hill 327, security elements for Headquarters, 26th Marines and 1st Marine Division repulsed a nocturnal assault by satchel charge-equipped NVA sappers. A similar attack targeted the 2d Battalion, 7th Marines compound to the northwest. Although the sappers breached the defensive wire, 2d Battalion Marines drove the attackers back. At least 75 enemy troops were killed or captured in the two futile attempts. Reflecting the intensity of the rocket- and mortar-supported suicide raids, Marine defenders lost 18 killed and 80 wounded.

Although Marine patrols and ambushes continued to engage remnants of the enemy force through March, the attacks on the Da Nang Vital Area during *Tet*, in essence, were met and broken on 23 February. Stranded in the Da Nang-Hoi An-Dai Loc triangle, the enemy hid, hoping to escape area saturation by Marine small units and increased employment of the deadly scout/sniper teams.* Despite the enemy's reluctance to engage 1st Division Marines, nearly 500 NVA and VC were taken out of action—a clear gauge of the continued effectiveness of the 1st Marine Division's small-unit campaign in Quang Nam Province.

Americal's TAOI

Headquartered at Chu Lai, about 45 kilometers south of Da Nang, was Major General Charles M. Gettys' Americal Division. The division's Tactical Area of Operational Interest (TAOI), one of the largest in Vietnam, encompassed all of Quang Tin and Quang Ngai Provinces and the Que Son District of Quang Nam Province. Spanning the relatively flat coastal lowlands and mountainous central highlands, the division's area contained approximately 1.2 million South Vietnamese centered around Tam Ky and Quang Ngai cities. Sharing the TAOI was the 2d ARVN Division headquartered at Quang Ngai and numerous provincial forces.

Tactically, the three infantry brigades of the division were deployed throughout the TAOI in separate areas of operation. To the north was the Oregon area of operation; in the center, the Chu Lai; and, to the south was the Duc Pho area of operation. In addition, there were a number of areas created for specific combat operations.

Operations within the Chu Lai TAOI, as the year began, centered on small unit patrols, ambushes along infiltration routes, and security operations along major lines of communications, designed to locate and eliminate enemy forces, enhance security of friendly installations, and ensure the safety of the local population. Employment of patrols in the Chu Lai rocket belt and detailed searches of Ky Hoa Island successfully prevented attacks by fire against the airbase and the city of An Tan. In addition, a series of preemptive operations was conducted in late January and early February north of the Song Tra Khuc to deny the enemy use of the area as a base from which to launch attacks against Quang Ngai City. Encounters remained light during the first two months of the year and in early March the Chu Lai area of operation was incorporated into that of Operation Geneva Park.

Americal Division forces conducted combat operations within the Duc Pho area of operation during the first two months of the year with emphasis on securing the heavily populated coastal plains, using saturation patrols and preemptive assaults in suspected enemy staging areas. Like those within the Chu Lai area, engagements remained light until late February when a series of joint Army-ARVN operations were launched along the coastline east of Mo Duc and into the foothills of the Nui Tam Cap Mountains, all aimed at preventing enemy troops from approaching the city of Quang Ngai. As with the other areas, in early March military actions within the Duc Pho area of operation were terminated and its area incorporated into the Iron Mountain Operational Zone.

Created in early November 1968, the Oregon area encompassed the northern portion of the Americal Division TAOI—Quang Tin Province and Que Son District of Quang Nam. Engagements were few as elements of two infantry brigades and one cavalry squadron conducted saturation patrols, reconnaissance-in-force, and rice-denial operations to locate and destroy enemy troop and supply concentrations. On 23 February, elements of the *2d NVA Division* launched simultaneous attacks on Tam Ky and against the Civilian Irregular Defense Group camp at Tien Phuoc. Americal Division forces were committed to these two areas and engaged the attacking enemy forces, turning them back before they could achieve any success. On 18 March, as part of the realignment of forces within the Americal Division TAOI, the Oregon area of operation was incorporated into the operational zone of Frederick Hill.

In addition to operations conducted within the Oregon, Chu Lai, and Duc Pho areas, four separate operations were carried out. As a complement to Operation Taylor Common conducted by Task Force Yankee against Base Area 112, elements of the 196th Infantry Brigade initiated Operation Fayette Canyon on 15 December against the *1st Viet Cong Regiment* in Antenna Valley and the Nui Mat Rang Mountains to the southeast. Operation Russell Beach was carried out on the Batangan Peninsula, in conjunction with Special Landing Force Operation Bold Mariner, to rid the area of enemy troops and to reintroduce South Vietnamese control. In support of the Accelerated Pacification Campaign, Operation Hardin Falls was initiated in the Thang Binh District of Quang Tin Province in De-

---

*Marine two-man scout/sniper teams, observer and rifleman, were deployed along heavily traveled enemy infiltration routes. Using the standard sniper weapon, a Model 700 Remington rifle with a variable-power telescopic sight, the teams were often credited with first-round kills at distances exceeding 1,000 meters.

cember and was aimed at destroying local Viet Cong forces, rebuilding war-ravaged hamlets and villages, and reestablishing South Vietnamese control of the area. Further south, in Quang Ngai Province, Operation Vernon Lake II continued in the Song Re Valley against elements of the *3d NVA Division*, preventing the enemy force from launching offensive operations against Quang Ngai City and the populated coastal lowlands. Due to aggressive Americal operations during the first two months of 1969, the enemy was unable to achieve a single military or political objective within the division's TAOI.

CHAPTER 7

The Battle for Quang Nam Continues

*Rockets Equal Operations—5th Marines and the Arizona—Securing the Southern and Northern Approaches
Americal Battleground—Operation Oklahoma Hills*

Rockets Equal Operations

As it was standing operating procedure (SOP), both of FMFPac and III MAF, that there be a five-day overlap of commanding generals, Generals Youngdale and Simpson did a lot of talking before the formal change of command. Rather prophetically, General Youngdale told his replacement as Commanding General, 1st Marine Division, that the biggest concern he would have to face when rockets fell on the Da Nang Vital Area, was answering the inevitable question posed by III MAF: "What the hell are you doing about it?" "Well," as General Simpson later recounted, "of course they knew what we were doing about it because we had an SOP which they clearly understood, and we always mounted an operation."[1]

The 122mm rocket was an excellent weapon. Using the designated mount and sight from a surveyed position, it was the equivalent of light to medium tube artillery. By 1969, noted General Simpson, "the NVA were firing the 122mm from crossed bamboo sticks. This was adequate for them since the density of the Da Nang complex was such that, for any rocket that got over the surrounding hill mass, a complete 'miss' was next to impossible."[2]

The psychological damage, and to a minor extent, the physical damage, that rockets could inflict on Da Nang was of major concern. Defense of the Republic's second-largest city and surrounding allied military installations from attack, either by rocket artillery or infantry, was the division's main task. The immediate, and most obvious, response to a rocket attack was counterbattery fire, tapping any number of the division's 178 artillery tubes. But, to prevent the rockets from being launched, daily patrols, numbering 500 or more, were sent out to search the "rocket belt": the great arc, anchored at Hai Van Pass in the north and Marble Mountain in the south with Da Nang at its center, whose maximum and minimum limits corresponded to the maximum and minimum range of an enemy 122mm rocket. In addition, Americal Division LOH observation helicopters swept the area twice daily in search of possible launching sites. A third response was to prevent the rockets and their crews reaching sites from which an attack could be launched: to move out into the hinterlands and not only server the enemy's infiltration routes and supply lines, but also destroy his materiel caches and base camps. So mount operations Simpson did.[3]

Operation Oklahoma Hills

The large mountainous region west of Da Nang, encompassing such well-known areas as Charlie Ridge and Happy Valley, had long been suspected as a region that not only harbored enemy troops, but major base camps and infiltration routes, all of which posed a direct and ever-present threat to the Da Nang Vital Area. Considerable information on those routes had accumulated since October 1968, when the last major Marine operations in the area, Mameluke Thrust and Maui Peak, ended. Defectors and prisoners of war captured during Operation Taylor Common and subsequent operations around Da Nang and throughout the An Hoi basin during *Tet* provided additional information. One such prisoner, the senior captain and temporary commander of the *141st Regiment*, captured by Lieutenant Colonel Quinn's 3d Battalion, 7th Marines during the heavy fighting around Hill 41 on 23 February, furnished intelligence on the major base camps and infiltration routes leading toward Da Nang and An Hoa. During his extensive interrogation, he related that the major supply routes for the *141st NVA Regiment*, and in all probability the *31st Infantry* and *368B Artillery Regiments*, originated far to the west in the Ai Yen area, 20 kilometers east of the Laotian border, and could be traced east along Route 614. At the point where the road divided west of the Song Con, one supply route continued east along 614 into Happy Valley, while the other route began at the meeting of the Song Con and Route 614 and followed the river south to its intersection with the Song Yang at An Dien, eight kilometers northeast of Thuong Duc, and then east to the Song Vu Gia. From there supplies and men were either diverted to Base Area 112 and then into the northern Arizona or north onto Charlie Ridge and into Happy Valley. From the terminus of Route 614 in Happy Valley, the enemy shifted supplies and men to units operating near the Song

Department of Defense Photo (USMC) A371933
A 2d Battalion, 7th Marines patrol on Charlie Ridge carefully maneuvers through triple-canopied jungle, typical of the terrain found throughout the area of operations.

Tuy Loan, or to other units located in the northeast Charlie Ridge-Sherwood Forest-Worth Ridge area, overlooking Da Nang.[4]

Enemy infiltration and supply routes described by other prisoners of war and ralliers were of a general nature, but two common areas continued to emerge — Charlie Ridge and Happy Valley. Both regions contained not only major enemy supply routes, but also suspected base camps and storage facilities at the terminus of those routes. Both were to become prime targets for the Marines of the 1st Division. As Colonel Robert L. Nichols, who replaced Colonel Beckington as Commanding Officer of the 7th Marines on 7 February noted: "This terrain mass has provided a haven for the enemy in which he could assemble his forces and then institute his infiltration tactic into the Da Nang Vital Area. Of particular concern in recent months has been his tactic of using this infiltration approach to launch rockets into the Da Nang Vital Area."[5] Once Task Force Yankee had neutralized Base Area 112 and secured the southern flank of the Thuong Duc corridor as a result of Operation Taylor Common, clearing the hills west of Da Nang and securing both the western approaches to the vital area and northern flank of the Thuong Duc corridor was the next logical step.[6]

First Division Marines would find it difficult operating within the region. Both Charlie Ridge and Worth Ridge were high, narrow ranges, cut by numerous steep-sided valleys, ravines, and gorges, and covered by multi-canopied jungle, and dense undergrowth. Movement throughout Happy Valley, blanketed by dense underbush and elephant grass seven to ten feet high, likewise would be arduous. The irregular terrain and density of vegetation would thus make foot movement a necessity, but yet impede it. Supporting arms would have to be used sparingly because of the dense overhead cover, and helicopter operations, especially medical evacuations, would have to be restricted due to the lack of suitable landing zones. Although terrain often favored the enemy, in this case, both Marine and NVA soldier would be on equal footing, as Colonel James B. Ord, Jr., noted:

> The enemy always has the advantage, as I see it, of operating in the jungle, in the canopy. You only get a point to point contact. You cannot maneuver on a broad front, so you are on a parity with him as far as the infantry is concerned. Since your observation is limited and your fields of fire are limited, it is difficult to make use of supporting arms in which we have a distinct advantage. And the enemy can always break contact and he can always evade. And so this being the case, we are just about equal; we have no advantage.[7]

The initial concept of operations, as outlined by General Simpson, called for two battalions of Nichols' 7th Marines to be helilifted into the southwestern and northwestern portions of the area of operations, one battalion to attack northwest from Hill 52 along Route

4, and the other to attack south from R.C. Ba Na, Hill 467, overlooking Happy Valley. A third battalion was to attack west along the axis of Worth Ridge and Charlie Ridge, placing pressure on the enemy from all directions. As the 7th Marines began planning for the operation, a number of potential problems arose. A landing on R.C. Ba Na, followed by a sweep south from the ridge onto Charlie Ridge would be hazardous and time-consuming due to the rough terrain. In addition, the third battalion would find it difficult to conduct effective search and destroy operations over the broad expanse of terrain formed by Charlie and Worth Ridges. In light of these two problems, Colonel Nichols and his staff presented a revised concept of operations to General Simpson on 27 March, calling for two battalions to attack west along the axis of Worth and Charlie Ridges instead of landing a battalion on R.C. Ba Na. Nichols predicated the revised concept on the assumptions that R.C. Ba Na would act as an effective barrier to north-south movement of enemy troops and that at least two battalions would be necessary to ensure adequate coverage of the two main ridgelines. General Simpson approved the modification to the initial concept, and Nichols proceeded to develop the detailed scheme of maneuver and fire support plan to sustain it.

The final plan of attack into Happy Valley and the surrounding terrain, codenamed Oklahoma Hills, called for the 7th Marines, reinforced, in coordination with the 51st ARVN Regiment, to conduct the phased movement of three battalions into the area of operations, establishing fire support bases and landing zones, and conducting reconnaissance-in-force operations, destroying all enemy forces, caches, and installations. Simultaneously, reconnaissance elements were to conduct screening operations to the north and west, as well as within the area of operations. A fourth Marine battalion would conduct screening operations south of Charlie Ridge, astride Route 4 and the Song Vu Gia, to prevent enemy troops from crossing into the Arizona area and vice versa, while a fifth Marine battalion would be available on two hours' notice as a reaction and exploitation force if needed.

Preparatory operations directly in support of Oklahoma Hills began on 21 March with the advance of Lieutenant Colonel John A. Dowd's 1st Battalion, 7th Marines west from Fire Support Base Rawhide (Hill 65) along Route 4. Assigned the mission of securing the route between Hill 65 and Hill 52, a distance of 10 kilometers, Dowd's Marines also were to establish a major fire support base, later named Mustang, at the latter site. Early on the morning of the 24th, Company C seized the hill and began local security patrols. The following day, a platoon from Company B and a platoon of engineers from Company C, 1st Engineer Battalion, began sweeping Route 4 of mines and upgrading the roadbed. By noon on the 26th, Hill 52 was secure and the 10-kilometer stretch of Route 4 between Hills 65 and 52 was clear and ready to support the heavy logistical traffic necessary to sustain Mustang. Engineer work on gun positions began on 28 March and by the 30th, Mustang was ready to receive Battery K, 4th Battalion, 11th Marines, and a platoon of 8-inch howitzers.

It also would be necessary to relieve the 2d and 3d Battalions, 7th Marines of their normal responsibility of patrolling the rocket belt west of Da Nang. On the 29th, the 26th Marines assumed responsibility for the area controlled by the two battalions, as Colonel Nichols ordered a number of final preparations for the operation. Among them was the establishment of an automatic retransmission site on R.C. Ba Na to provide adequate communications throughout the area of operations. The 2d Battalion, 7th Marines initially provided a security element for the relay station, but as the operation progressed, and various battalions phased out, the 3d Battalion, 26th Marines followed by the 3d Battalion, 7th Marines provided this support.

Shortly after sunset on 30 March, Lieutenant Colonel Neil A. Nelson's 2d Battalion, 7th Marines departed Hill 10 (FSB Stallion), and began moving on foot into the area of operations. Concurrently, the 3d Battalion under Lieutenant Colonel James O. Allison, who had relieved Lieutenant Colonel Quinn on the 23d, initiated a similar advance to the west from Hill 41. "This was a very unique move," recalled Captain Paul K. Van Riper, Company M's commanding officer, "in that we took the whole company well up into the jungled mountains during the nighttime. We moved out at 2000 and by early the next morning we were up under the canopy and the NVA forces in the area had no idea that we had moved this far and of our present location." As both battalions pushed westward, "searching out base areas, looking for caches, fortifications, any enemy that we could locate and destroying all of the same," Operation Oklahoma Hills began.[8]

Events moved smoothly on the morning of the operation's first day, with all landing zone preparations, delivered by tubes of the 11th Marines, the *Mullinnix* (DD 994), and later *Newport News* (CA 148), com-

MajGen Ormond R. Simpson, center left, discusses movement by foot into the area of operations by 2d Battalion, 7th Marines with its commanding officer, LtCol Neil A. Nelson.

pleted on schedule. The lift by HMM-165 helicopters of the 2d Battalion, 51st ARVN Regiment into LZ Hawk (three kilometers northeast of the Thuong Duc CIDG Camp), and the 3d Battalion, 51st ARVN Regiment into LZ Eagle (three kilometers northwest of Thuong Duc), began at 1100 and was accomplished without incident within an hour. The following morning, Lieutenant Colonel Edward W. Snelling's 3d Battalion, 26th Marines (BLT 3/26) assaulted, along with a 4.2-inch mortar battery from 1st Battalion, 13th Marines, into LZ Robin, overlooking Happy Valley. These landings, coupled with the overland movement of the 2d and 3d Battalions, 7th Marines on the night of the 30th, completed the introduction of all major allied units into the area of operations.

Confronted with the ever-present problem of helicopter availability, Colonel Nichols deliberately decided to establish fire support bases initially around the periphery, instead of throughout the objective area. Additional bases would be established as the maneuver battalions moved beyond the range of their artillery support, and on prominent terrain features in anticipation of future operations in the area.[9]

Once established, Nelson and Allison's battalions attacked to the west along Worth and Charlie Ridges, while the 3d Battalion, 26th Marines and the two 51st ARVN Battalions attacked to the southeast and northeast into the high ground. Movement was slow, and as Colonel Nichols related, "very tiring on the troops; the progress was so slow that it became very apparent that there was not a real benefit to be obtained in attempting to maneuver in any basic skirmish-attack formations through the thick jungle canopy. Accordingly, it became the standard practice to restrict movement to the trail networks." Once on the trails, it also became apparent that not more than a platoon could maneuver with any degree of efficiency. Thus, noted Colonel Nichols, "it became the general practice to . . . establish a temporary company base camp and then maneuver with platoons from that company base camp, largely restricting the maneuver to trail networks." Only when searching a specific target area did Marines move "cross-compartment, through the virgin jungle."[10]

The capture on 1 April of an enemy soldier and the rallying of another was to have an immediate effect upon the five maneuver battalions. In widely separated engagements, a reconnaissance insert detained a master sergeant from the *8th Company, 2d Battalion, 141st NVA Regiment*, and Company K, 3d Battalion, 7th Marines captured a warrant officer from the *18th Company* of the *31st NVA Regiment*. Both enemy soldiers identified specific sites within the area of operations where their regimental base camps were located; the master sergeant being most definite in locating his base camp during a helicopter reconnaissance flight. This firm and timely information posed two alternative courses of action: the attacking units could continue their present movement toward the central high ground, conducting a thorough search of draws and ravines within their areas of responsibility; or the maneuvering battalions could advance rapidly toward the base camps, bypassing other suspected camps and caches, in order to quickly exploit the specific intelligence, trapping enemy troops in the camps or, at least, preventing them from evacuating materiel. Colonel Nichols decided to pursue the latter course and directed Lieutenant Colonel Allison and Snelling's battalions to close as rapidly as possible on the area believed to contain the base camp of the *141st Regiment*. Concurrently, he initiated planning for a second phase of the operation in order that all units might reverse their direction of advance, and conduct detailed searches of the areas bypassed.

After completing FSB Rattlesnake (Hill 749), two kilometers southwest of Robin, Snelling's 3d Battalion, 26th Marines moved as quickly as terrain and vegetation would permit up the long ridgeline towards Hill 1166 and the base camp of the *141st*. As Company I, with L in trace, swept up the ridge using the enemy's trail network, small groups of NVA soldiers repeatedly attempted to slow the Marines' advance without success.

To the northeast, Allison's battalion accelerated its movement to the west along Charlie Ridge in an effort to reach the enemy base camp while it was still occupied. At the same time, Nelson's 2d Battalion, 7th Marines reached the western extreme of its 105mm howitzer coverage from FSB Stallion, and was forced to halt and begin construction of FSB Buckskin (Hill 502) to support its move further west.

By late afternoon on 7 April, Company K, 3d Battalion, 7th Marines reached its intermediate objective, Hill 1062, with Company L a kilometer behind. Simultaneously, Company I, 3d Battalion, 26th Marines reached its objective, Hill 1166, with Company L not far to the rear. The forward elements of both battalions continued to close on the deep ravine below both objectives, believed to contain the base camp of the *141st*. At first light on the 8th, it appeared that

LtCol Edward W. Snelling's 3d Battalion, 26th Marines boards a Marine CH-46 helicopter, as elements of the Special Landing Force were called upon to support operations ashore.

Department of Defense Photo (USMC) A374209

Courtesy of Col Fred T. Fagan, Jr.
A Kit Carson Scout pauses at the entrance to a tunnel within the base camp of the 141st *NVA Regiment, that led to an extensive underground medical facility.*

Snelling's Marines were in the best position to close rapidly on the main objective. Consequently, Lieutenant Colonel Snelling assumed operational control of Company K, 3d Battalion, 7th Marines, and led the battalion on a coordinated attack on the enemy base area.

As Company L moved down the ravine, its lead element uncovered the first of what were to be many enemy base camps. Advancing into the camp area, subsequently identified as the *Q-79 Dispensary*, they observed and engaged approximately 20 North Vietnamese soldiers attempting to flee to the southwest. The camp, like those later discovered, was "cleverly put together," Colonel Nichols noted:

> It was not uncommon to go into a bunker which was reinforced with logs, eight to 15 inches of earth, another layer of logs, well-covered, . . . and find in turn a trap door and a subterranean space below that, dug into the earth, providing additional individual protection. These generally would accommodate anywhere from four to ten enemy soldiers, and in some instances tunnel complexes connecting these, running very extensively throughout the camp. Very careful preparations were made to ensure that cook houses were well-camouflaged and that smoke conduits to abort any evidence of smoke from coming up through the jungle had been laid throughout."[11]

The following day, Companies I and L, on line with squads in column, swept deeper into the complex from the north and west, while Company K, 3d Battalion, 7th Marines remained above, on Hill 943, prepared to block any enemy escape to the south. Movement during the next several days was exceedingly slow due to numerous skirmishes with small bands of enemy soldiers, the oppressive heat, rugged terrain, and the number of separate camps to be searched.

While Lieutenant Colonels Allison and Snelling's battalions combed the base camp of the *141st*, Lieutenant Colonel Nelson's 2d Battalion, 7th Marines continued to search the valley floor north of Worth Ridge. Once completed, Nelson's Marines then moved up the ridge toward Hill 745, into an area suspected to harbor the base camp of the *31st Regiment*, as revealed in the interrogation of the warrant officer captured on 1 April. On the 11th, Company E discovered the base camp, approximately four kilometers southwest of FSB Buckskin. As the lead platoon entered, it received a burst of machine gun fire as the residents departed. Initial reports indicated the camp to be the largest yet discovered, containing well in excess of 200 structures.

The next several days represented a period of relative stability in the movement of all major units, each having essentially reached its final objective. The 2d Battalion, 7th Marines continued its search of the *31st NVA* base camp, engaging small pockets of tenacious defenders. Lieutenant Colonel Allison's battalion occupied Hills 1235 and 1062 and conducted local patrols which produced no significant results, and Snelling's Marines continued to sweep through the base camp of the *141st Regiment*, discovering a massive network of interconnected enemy facilities. By 15 April, engagements with enemy forces remaining within the areas assigned to the 3d Battalion, 7th Marines and 3d Battalion, 26th Marines had evaporated, while the 2d Battalion, 7th Marines encountered a number of small groups of enemy contesting its advance.

Materially supporting the operation throughout this period, as Marines worked deep under the canopy, proved to be a challenge. Tiny holes were cut in the jungle into which skillful Marine helicopter pilots lowered supplies and extracted those in need of medical attention. On at least one occasion, the pilots brought a surprise—ice cream and beer packed in large styrofoam containers, previously used to ship aviation ordnance. "You can imagine," Colonel Nichols report-

THE BATTLE FOR QUANG NAM CONTINUES

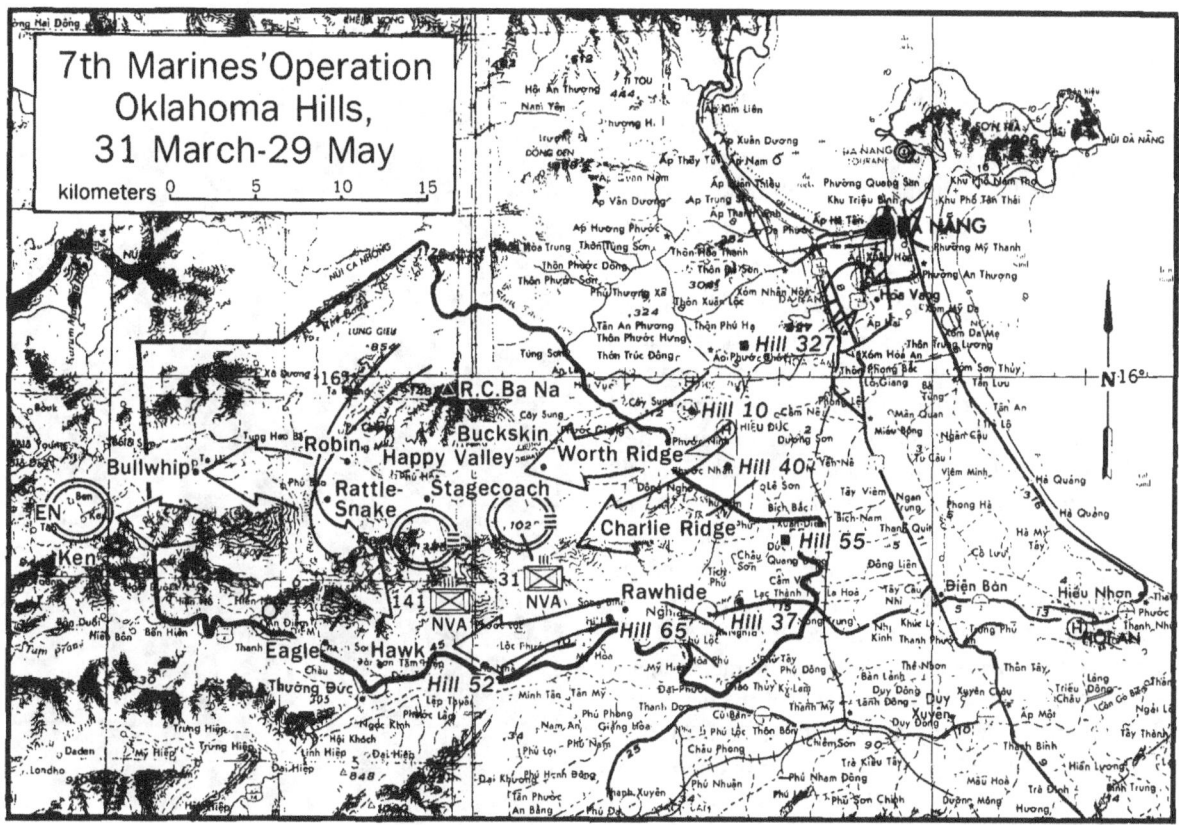

See Reference Map, Sections 25-27

ed, "the shouts of joy from some weary Marines who received this surprise."[12]

On 19 April, Nichols directed Nelson's Marines to withdraw to Hills 785 and 502 (FSB Buckskin) in preparation for a helilift out of the area of operations, since the 1st Battalion, 26th Marines was to rejoin the Special Landing Force, and a battalion would be needed to cover that portion of the vacated Da Nang TAOR. With the 2d Battalion, 7th Marines' withdrawal, coordination was made with the 51st ARVN Regiment in order that a relief in place might be conducted between Nelson's battalion and a battalion of that regiment. Two days later, in a combined effort involving Marine and Vietnamese helicopters, Nelson's Marines and Battery H, 3d Battalion, 11th Marines withdrew and were replaced by the 1st Battalion, 51st ARVN Regiment and a supporting 105mm howitzer battery. The ARVN battalion assumed a mission similar to that of 2d Battalion, 7th Marines; one company protecting the battery on Buckskin, while the remainder of the battalion patrolled the surrounding terrain.

On the southern edge of the area of operations, Dowd's 1st Battalion, 7th Marines maintained patrols along the Song Vu Gia, and provided security for the fire support bases on Hills 52 and 65, while securing Route 4, ensuring its viability as a main supply route. Major emphasis continued to be placed on interdicting enemy movement between Charlie Ridge and the northern Arizona area. Among the assigned tasks was the setting of daily ambushes at known river crossings. This tactic produced results on the night of 13 April when a platoon from Company B, set in along the northern bank of the river, observed 30 NVA soldiers entering the water from the opposite bank. The platoon withheld its fire until the enemy had almost crossed before releasing a heavy volume of small arms and machine gun fire, catching 14 NVA soldiers in the water.

With the relief of the 2d Battalion, 7th Marines by 1st Battalion, 51st ARVN Regiment, Operation Oklahoma Hills shifted into a second phase. Instead of the specific objectives which charaterized phase one, battalions were now given general zones and ordered to conduct coordinated and systematic searches to destroy enemy forces, uncover caches and installations, and at the same time construct helicopter landing zones and a series of mutually supporting fire bases.

In anticipation of phase two, Colonel Nichols directed Company L, 3d Battalion, 7th Marines to move the four kilometers eastward from Hill 1062 to Hill 866 on foot, and there construct FSB Longhorn. Arriving at midday on 20 April, the company began local search operations in the nearby draws and ravines while providing security and assistance for the engineers constructing the base. On the 25th, with Longhorn completed but unoccupied, Company L rejoined the battalion in a general sweep to the east.

Lieutenant Colonel Allison's Marines, during the second phase of Operation Oklahoma Hills, conducted a detailed and methodical search of their assigned zone from west to east, retracing their original move along Charlie Ridge. While Company L searched areas near FSB Longhorn, Companies I and M moved from Hill 1235, three kilometers to the southeast, searching ravines as they progressed on foot. On 24 April, Company I helilifted four kilometers further to the northeast, to Hill 722, and Company M and the battalion command group moved by helicopter an equal distance, but further north. Spaced two kilometers apart, both units began a thorough search of the new areas. The following day, the 3d Battalion, 26th Marines released Company K which rejoined its battalion. Engagements with enemy forces within the zone assigned to Allison's battalion were almost nonexistent during the second phase of the operation.

The 3d Battalion, 26th Marines continued search operations within its primary objective area assigned during the first phase of Operation Oklahoma Hills; it being necessary for the battalion to ensure that all base camps in the vicinity of the *141st* were discovered and destroyed. With the release of Company K, 3d Battalion, 7th Marines, Company M, 3d Battalion, 26th Marines concentrated on conducting combat patrols in the draws and ravines near FSB Rattlesnake, while Company K conducted extensive patrol and search operations from Hill 1066. Contact with small groups of enemy troops remained sporadic, consisting of harassing sniper and mortar fire within the North Vietnamese camp complex. Toward the end of April, the battalion made preparation to withdraw, and on 2 May Companies K and L, with their supporting artillery, Battery C, 1st Battalion, 13th Marines, lifted out of the area of operations. The following day, a platoon from Company K, 3d Battalion, 7th Marines moved into Rattlesnake and then pushed southwest toward Hill 1166 to secure a landing zone for the remainder of the company. Four tubes from Battery G, 3d Battalion, 11th Marines lifted from Mustang to Rattlesnake to provide 3d Battalion, 7th Marines with

Marine Corps Historical Collection

Infantrymen of the 2d Battalion, 7th Marines move cautiously across a small enemy bridge through an area containing the base camp of the 31st NVA Regiment.

direct artillery support, and by nightfall, as the remaining company of Lieutenant Colonel Snelling's command withdrew, the area was turned over to Allison's Marines.

The area assigned to Lieutenant Colonel Dowd's battalion witnessed considerable troop realignment and enemy activity during the second phase of Oklahoma Hills. In standby reserve since the operation began, Lieutenant Colonel Thomas E. Bulger's 3d Battalion, 1st Marines was called upon to conduct a search and clear operation south of Camp Muir (Hill 55), an area void of friendly forces since the end of March. The operation, which began on 26 April, was the first step for the battalion in assuming responsibility for the eastern portion of 1st Battalion, 7th Marines' area, enabling Dowd's Marines to move west and begin further work on Route 4. In addition, the 4th Battalion, 51st ARVN Regiment, operating above Thuong Duc in an area northwest of Dowd's battalion, withdrew on 1 May, leaving a void on the western flank.

In coordination with the 3d Battalion, 1st Marines,

or alone, Lieutenant Colonel Dowd's men conducted numerous ambushes in the low ground at the base of Charlie Ridge and along the Song Vu Gia in the continuing effort to prevent the north-south movement of enemy forces. Early on the afternoon of 21 April, intelligence sources reported the movement of enemy troops south of the Song Vu Gia, in the Arizona. The mission of the concentrated enemy force was unknown, but suspected to be an attack on friendly forces and outposts north of the river, or to sever Route 4 between Mustang and Hill 65.

After assembling and assessing the intelligence reports, First Lieutenant William L. Culp, the battalion S-2, alerted the patrols and ambushes established by Companies B, C, and D of possible enemy movement south of the river. Shortly after dark on the 21st, patrols from Captain Joseph M. A. Romero's Company C reported sighting a number of North Vietnamese troops on the southern bank of the river, who appeared to be moving from west to east. Company B, under Captain James W. Huffman, Jr., and elements of Company D, led by Captain Brian J. Fagan, located in heavy hedgerows skirting the water's edge, were alerted, but instructed not to fire due to the lack of information concerning the location of the enemy's main forces. At 1945, the 2d Squad, 2d Platoon, Company B observed seven NVA soldiers on a sandbar directly opposite its ambush site, located near Ban Tan (1). Approximately 1,000 meters in length and 200 meters in width, the sandbar was 3,000 meters east of the earlier sighting by Romero's company. Based on the information provided by Company C, Huffman instructed his Marines to withhold their fire, even if the small group should attempt to cross the river, while preparing to interdict the sandbar with organic and supporting arms. A second squad, located in the same area, moved to reinforce the already positioned ambush, and Huffman's 3d platoon, located 600 meters to the west, was ordered to set up a 106mm recoilless rifle and a .30-caliber machine gun so as to direct enfilade fire along the sandbar in front of the two squads. Direct and general support artillery batteries plotted fires to the south and southwest on other possible crossing sites, and along avenues of approach and es-

Despite an oftentimes abundance of rations, Marines frequently foraged off the land, as in this case where a group of Marines prepare to roast and eat several snakes.

Marine Corps Historical Collection

Department of Defense Photo (USMC) A371941
A 1st Battalion, 7th Marines machine gunner and his assistant, in the continuing effort to secure Route 4 to Thuong Duc, assault a hut from which they had received enemy fire.

cape. In addition, the companies alerted a reconnaissance team located south of the river to the situation and instructed it to keep the area under observation.

At 2025, Huffman's ambush lost sight of the original seven, but continued to wait. About 30 minutes later, a large enemy force, divided into several groups of 40 or more, suddenly emerged from the underbrush along the southern bank of the river and took up positions on the sandbar previously occupied by the seven. Carrying small boats, the NVA force moved to the water's edge and began crossing. Using starlight scopes, Huffman's Marines watched as the NVA placed 17 boats into the water; each contained three to five troops guided by two or three wading soldiers. An additional group of 25 brought up the rear.

As the craft approached the center of the river, Huffman called for illumination and as they passed mid-stream, Company B opened up with all the organic and supporting arms at its command. During the ensuing ambush, elements of Companies C and D moved to the flanks and rear of Huffman's company in order to assist if necessary.

Caught completely by surprise, the enemy scattered. The 25 composing the rear guard continued to cross, while others broke and ran for cover, dragging the dead and wounded. Huffman's Marines caught the troops in the river with small arms and 81mm mortar fire, while the preplanned artillery barrage cut down those running south. At the height of the ambush, Company B reported 150 to 200 troops attempting to cross, and of that number, 57 were later found floating in the water or scattered along the opposite shore. Unfortunately, illumination was not continuous throughout the night, and the enemy was successful in removing a majority of the dead and wounded.

In order to exploit the ambush and ensure the integrity of Route 4, Huffman requested tanks and LVTs. During the remaining hours of darkness, Romero and Fagan's companies advanced to relieve Huffman's Marines, who began preparation for a river crossing at first light the following morning. Artillery fire continued throughout the night, while the tanks, when they arrived, were placed along the northern shore, their tubes directed at the opposite bank.

Shortly after dawn, Marine fixed-wing aircraft struck the treeline south of the sandbar, and at 0930 Company B boarded the LVTs and, under cover of supporting arms, crossed the river and began a sweep of the southern shore. Once on the opposite shore, Huffman's men found 14 more bodies, clad in new uniforms and equipment. Although Marines of Company B counted less than 100 bodies, they estimated that the actual number of enemy killed was much higher. Two Marines received minor wounds during the successful blocking ambush on the Song Vu Gia.

The large enemy crossing of the Vu Gia on the night of the 21st confirmed numerous intelligence reports received during April, indicating a strong enemy presence south of the river, in the northern Arizona area. During this period, reconnaissance teams and 1st Battalion patrols made 14 separate sightings. Reacting to the threat against Mustang, Hill 65, and Route 4, the battalion planned a quick thrust south of the river into the Arizona to find and destroy the enemy forces. On the 29th, the 5th Marines granted the 7th Marines a seven-kilometer-wide by two-kilometer-deep area of operations extension into the northern Arizona, south of the Song Vu Gia.

That night, Huffman and Fagan's companies and the battalion command group crossed the river opposite the village of My Hoa and, at first light, began to attack east-southeast when Company B, on the right flank, became heavily engaged. The remaining attack force immediately swung to the northwest toward the river, assaulting into an estimated two NVA companies. Fighting was fierce as the enemy directed heavy small arms and mortar fire at Dowd's advancing Marines. After again reaching the river, the two companies turned left and continued the attack to the southwest along the shore. Company A, deployed along the northern bank of the Song Vu Gia as a reserve force, maintained its assigned blocking positions. Both Companies B and D continued their attack throughout the day and into the next, fighting through a series of hedgerows and treelines, supported by artillery, air, and CS gas.

On the morning of 1 May, heavy enemy small arms and automatic weapons fire drove off helicopters attempting to resupply the two companies, forcing Company A to resupply the companies by LVT. The resupply complete, the 3d Battalion, 1st Marines, then operating to the northeast of Liberty Bridge, moved overland by truck and amphibious vehicles, made a river crossing, and established blocking positions to the west of Dowd's Marines, near the village of Minh Tan.

While Bulger's Marines moved toward the Song Vu Gia, elements of the 1st Battalion, 7th Marines resumed the attack to the west, meeting heavy resistance from each enemy-infested treeline, and succeeded in covering only 200 meters. By late afternoon, the 3d Battalion had crossed the river and turned east, attacking toward Lieutenant Colonel Dowd's battalion.

Capt James W. Huffman, Jr., takes time to enjoy a bath. The "tub" was one of several boats captured by his Marines, who caught close to 200 enemy troops crossing the Song Vu Gia.

Marine Corps Historical Collection

Darkness found the two battalions one kilometer apart.

During the night, the two battalions made preparations for the next day's attack. The mutually agreed upon plan called for Dowd's Marines to hold their position, while Bulger's Marines drove to the east. Once the 3d Battalion closed with the 1st, Dowd's battalion was to turn about and both battalions were to attack to the east-northeast, destroying enemy forces suspected to be east of Dowd's position.

At 0600 on 2 May, the 3d Battalion, 1st Marines began its drive to the east toward the 1st Battalion. The attack proceeded as planned without contact, and Bulger's Marines closed with Dowd's about midday. Both battalions then began a methodical drive to the east-northeast, prepping each successive treeline with artillery as they moved. Both battalions reached the southern bank of the Song Vu Gia by late afternoon, and by dark had crossed the river without incident. The four-day, two-battalion incursion into the northern Arizona cost the North Vietnamese at least 60 killed, and the Marines nine dead and 60 wounded.

On 3 May, the 1st Battalion, 7th Marines began operations along Route 4 to the west of Hill 52. To facilitate the move, the 3d Battalion, 1st Marines assumed responsibility for the eastern portion of the 1st Battalion's TAOR, enabling Dowd's battalion to shift its attention west toward Thuong Duc. Concurrently, the 1st Engineer Battalion began the long-awaited improvement of Route 4 from Hill 52 to Thuong Duc, while elements of the 7th Engineer Battalion began reconstruction of the bridge at the CIDG Camp. Lieutenant Colonel Dowd's battalion assumed responsibility for the security of both engineer efforts; Company C was to occupy the high ground north of Route 4 and Thuong Duc, while Company A deployed along Route 4 to provide close security. The remainder of the battalion continued to provide security for FSB Mustang and Route 4 east to Hill 65. Dowd's Marines maintained these general deployments until 9 May, by which time both Route 4 and Thuong Duc Bridge had been upgraded and were in use by the local Vietnamese. On 9th, the 1st Battalion shifted companies to the east, relieving the 3d Battalion, 1st Marines, which returned to the operational control of the 1st Marines the following day. With the departure of Bulger's Marines, Dowd's battalion reassumed its originally assigned mission of providing blocking forces along the Song Vu Gia and security for FSB Mustang and Route 4.

Phase three of Oklahoma Hills found one ARVN battalion, 1st Battalion, 51st ARVN Regiment, and one Marine battalion, 3d Battalion, 7th Marines, the only units remaining within the area encompassing Charlie and Worth Ridges. While the South Vietnamese conducted operations in the northeastern portion of the area of operations, around Hills 785 and 502 (FSB Buckskin), the 3d Battalion, 7th Marines continued searching the remainder of the high ground. The concept of maneuver during the third phase was for Lieutenant Colonel Allison's battalion to conduct widespread operations throughout the area in order to establish contact with the enemy, believed to have reentered. Consequently, when Company K returned after a period of rehabilitation on 3 May, it lifted onto Hill 1166, within striking distance of the *141st Regiment's* base camp. The following day, Company L joined K around Hill 1166 and began patrolling the high ground to the east, while Company K advanced southeast into the enemy complex. The remainder of the battalion provided security for the direct support artillery battery at Rattlesnake.

Reconnaissance teams operating along the western and northwestern periphery of the area of operations reported not only an increase in the number of enemy sighted, but also an increase in the number of small engagements. This rise in enemy activity during early May provided the catalyst for inserting Company I along the Song Tan Khong, west of Happy Valley on the 6th. Lieutenant Colonel Allison directed the company to land at LZ Dry Gulch, conduct a reconnaissance-in-force, and then advance south to the high ground, providing security for the construction of FSB Bullwhip, designed to project a 7th Marines presence further west. In a similar move three days later, Company L helilifted from Hill 1166 to Rattlesnake, relieving Company M, which assaulted into the northern portion of the area of operations, eight kilometers north of Rattlesnake, and began to search north of Happy Valley. This move, like that of Company I, was in direct response to the recent reconnaissance reports indicating an enemy presence in the area.

Events in the Da Nang TAOR again dictated the loss of another unit from the operation due to the need for increased security in the area then patrolled by the 26th Marines. On the morning of 12 May, Company I pulled out of Bullwhip, where it had operated for six days, and returned to Hill 10, ten kilometers southeast of Da Nang. To replace Company I, Allison shifted a platoon from Company L to the western fire support base from Rattlesnake.

A Marine with the 1st Battalion, 7th Marines, grenade launcher in hand, pauses for a rest outside a partially destroyed temple in the village of Ban Tan (1), south of Route 4.

The period between 12 and 20 May was one of relative stability as Company M continued to conduct reconnaissance-in-force operations north of Happy Valley, while Companies K and L searched the base camp of the *141st* and surrounding hills. At the same time, the 7th Marines began preparations for yet another shift westward, specifically, an assault into the Ken Valley. The valley, southwest of Bullwhip, had long been mentioned in prisoner interrogations as a main arms and ammunition storage facility. Prisoners reported making trips to the area to pick up 140mm and 122mm rockets, which would eventually be launched at Da Nang. With the establishment of a widespread system of fire support bases during Oklahoma Hills, an assault into the Ken Valley was now possible.

Between 18 and 20 May planning proceeded for the operation; coordination was carried out with the 51st ARVN Regiment and arrangements made for the use of the regiment's reconnaissance company. Attached to the company would be a Vietnamese-speaking Marine officer, an artillery forward observer team, and a helicopter support team from the 3d Battalion. Companies L and M plus the battalion command group were to make the assault. On 20 May, Company K assumed responsibility for securing both Rattlesnake and Bullwhip, and a provisional battery of four 105mm howitzers helilifted into the westernmost fire support base.

At 0930 on the 21st, Company L boarded CH-53s at Rattlesnake, and then assaulted into the valley. Following the company into the objective area were the 51st ARVN Reconnaissance Company and Company M. From the several landing zones, Company L began reconnaissance-in-force operations to the northeast, while the ARVN reconnaissance company advanced to the southeast and Company M conducted search operations to the southwest. Over the next five days, the three companies conducted a thorough search of the valley with little contact. Evidence of enemy presence in the area proved scarce, and the companies engaged NVA troops only on two occasions with minor results; they discovered no supply facilities or caches. As a result, on 25 May, all units withdrew by helicopter.

With the completion of operations in the Ken Valley, Lieutenant Colonel Allison's battalion command group and Companies K and L lifted to Hill 785 to assist the 2d Battalion, 51st ARVN Regiment in the final destruction of the *31st NVA Regiment* base camp. The effort continued until the withdrawal of the ARVN battalion on the 26th, and that of the two Marine companies on the 28th. Company M, following operations in the Ken, returned to Rattlesnake and began the destruction of the fire support base. Battery G, 3d Battalion, 11th Marines withdrew from Rattlesnake on the 28th, followed by Company M the next day. With the evacuation of all units, Operation Oklahoma Hills came to an end.

Although the enemy had avoided major confrontation, Marines of the 7th and 26th Regiments, in coordination with troops of the 51st ARVN Regiment, drove him from his base camps, destroying the sanctity of Charlie Ridge and inflicting a total of 596 casualties. "Had he chosen to fight," noted Colonel Nichols, "hold his position and defend, . . . he could have done so and levied a very severe price on us in our efforts to take it."[13] "The relatively low level of enemy initiated attacks from the southwest against the Da Nang Vital Area" since the end of May, continued Colonel Nichols, "must in part be attributed to the disruptive effect of Operation Oklahoma Hills." As the city and its military installations would continue to be of prime importance, he suggested that "similar operations be conducted into this area periodically in the future."[14]

Operations in the rough terrain and heavy vegetation took its toll on the Marines. Forty-four lost their lives and another 439 received wounds requiring medical evacuation. The number of nonbattle casualties reported, a figure usually forgotten, was high during Operation Oklahoma Hills, exceeding the number of those wounded in action. A total of 456 nonbattle injuries occurred, most, if not all, attributable to the rugged, often slippery terrain and thick jungle vegetation. These injuries consisted of broken bones, sprains, and lacerations, of which a majority were sustained during the first two weeks of the operation as units maneuvered into the area and began construction of the needed fire support bases; 93 percent of the casualties returned to duty within six weeks.

5th Marines and the Arizona

With the termination of Operation Taylor Common and the passing of direct control of Task Force Yankee, under Brigadier General Samuel Jaskilka, to the 1st Marine Division on 8 March, Colonel Ord's 5th Marines returned to the Arizona and An Hoa basin and normal operations designed to provide security for allied military installations and the South Vietnamese industrial complex, the pacification effort, and the approaching rice harvest. In the eastern portion of Duc Duc and western section of Duy Xuyen Districts, Lieutenant Colonel Richard F. Daley's 1st Battalion continued operations begun during Taylor Common, concentrating its efforts on protecting Liberty Bridge and the nearby Seabee battalion compound, and securing Liberty Road between the bridge and An Hoa Combat Base. Daley's Marines, in seemingly endless patrols, ambushes, and sweeps along the road and near the bridge, endeavored to blunt the enemy's attempts at counteracting the growing allied presence in the area. In mid-March it was learned that the primary target of the enemy effort would be Liberty Bridge, at that time well on its way toward completion. At approximately 0245, under cover of mortar and rocket fire, an estimated battalion of NVA launched a coordinated attack against the bridge and then against 1st Battalion, 5th Marines and Battery D, 2d Battalion, 11th Marines positions at Phu Lac (6), south of the bridge.

Using flamethrowers, satchel charges, bangalore torpedoes, and AK47 fire, the enemy penetrated both the infantry and battery positions, methodically destroying most above-ground structures and inflicting a number of casualties.[15] A reaction force, hastily organized, halted further enemy penetration and prevented a link-up of the attacking forces within the perimeter. Confused and disorganized, the enemy then attempted to withdraw and were destroyed, as Captain Wayne A. Babb, commanding officer of Battery D, later noted:

> The reaction group, growing in strength and without the previous uncertainty and confusion caused by the violent enemy assault, was everywhere, emphasizing the destruction of enemy in ammunition bunkers. The battalion command post to the east had effectively contained the enemy forces located there and had further canalized them into the mess hall complex. Here, the remaining enemy within the battalion command were destroyed.[16]

Lieutenant Colonel Daley's Marines killed over 75 of the enemy attackers, while sustaining 16 casualties.[17]

As with Liberty Bridge, the enemy maintained constant pressure against An Hoa Combat Base, defended by elements of Lieutenant Colonel Harry E. Atkinson's 3d Battalion, primarily employing attacks by fire rather than attempting an all-out infantry attack. During the month, the base received some 430 rounds of mixed rocket, mortar, and recoilless rifle fire, far more than reported during any month since III MAF established the position in April 1966. The enemy effort achieved little effect other than harassment,

Aerial view of strategic Liberty Bridge under reconstruction by Seabees of the 3d Naval Construction Brigade shows, in the center, the temporary vehicle ferry, and to the left, guarding the bridge's southern approach, the 5th Marines' compound at Phu Lac (6).

as his gunnery was not distinguished by a marked degree of accuracy.

Throughout the remainder of the 5th Marines area of operations, east of An Hoa in the Phu Nhuans, the 2d Battalion, commanded by Lieutenant Colonel James W. Stemple until 14 March when relieved by Lieutenant Colonel James H. Higgins, continued land-clearing operations. Employing T18 bulldozers and an Eimco tractor with an attached Rome plow, engineers with the battalion concentrated on clearing treelines, trenches, bunkers, and fortifications, in an effort to reduce the number of enemy harboring sites. Although engagements with enemy units were few, Higgins' Marines discovered and disarmed numerous surprise firing devices before they could do their damage. Later in the month, the battalion crossed the Song Thu Bon into the Arizona and began search and clear operations to the west.

In response to intelligence information garnered from captured documents exhorting enemy units to step up the campaign to replenish diminished rice stocks, the 5th Marines initiated Operation Muskogee Meadow on 7 April, a combined search and clear and rice-denial operation in the fertile An Hoa basin. Expanding upon techniques developed during the Golden Fleece operations of 1966, the Marines coordinated their search and clear efforts with the rice harvest, cooperating closely with district officials involved, in this instance with those of Duc Duc and Duy Xuyen.

While division reconnaissance teams maintained a screen along the southern and western approaches into the area, Colonel William J. Zaro's three battalions ranged across the basin's lowlands.* The Marines of Lieutenant Colonel Daley's battalion were given the task of providing security for the Vietnamese rice harvesters of Duy Xuyen District, and transporting the rice, once harvested. The 2d Battalion performed a similar task within the Arizona, while the 3d Battalion secured the rice harvest of Phu Nhuan and Thu Don Districts, south of the Song Thu Bon. Generally, both NVA and VC forces avoided Zaro's Marines; however, during a sweep of the Arizona, three of Lieutenant Colonel Higgins' companies engaged a large enemy force on the 13th, five kilometers north of An Hoa.

Company E, advancing toward blocking positions established by Companies G and H, flushed an estimated company of NVA out of hiding sites on the morning of the 13th and pushed it toward Company H. Company B, 1st Battalion, 7th Marines, then engaged in Operation Oklahoma Hills, supported the

---

*A Texan by birth and former Chief of Staff, Task Force Yankee, Colonel William J. Zaro replaced Colonel Ord as Commanding Officer, 5th Marines on 23 March 1969.

action from positions across the Song Vu Gia to the north, as did elements of the 3d Battalion, 1st Marines. All three of Higgins' companies remained engaged until darkness, when units of the 1st Battalion, 7th Marines and 3d Battalion, 1st Marines ambushed the enemy company attempting to cross the river, killing 14 troops. At daybreak on the 14th, Company E closed the trap, encountering only sporadic resistance. Results of the combined 1st, 5th, and 7th Marines engagement were over 100 NVA killed and a considerable number of weapons captured, including seven individual rifles, a 12.7mm antiaircraft machine gun, and a short-range rocket launcher.[18]

Operation Muskogee Meadow ended on the 20th with the successful conclusion of the rice harvest, which added in excess of 171 tons to South Vietnamese storage bins. In comparing the two district harvests, security operations were more successful in Duy Xuyen than in Duc Duc. Under the watchful eyes of Zaro's Marines, Vietnamese farmers harvested 271,150 pounds in Duy Xuyen District against only 67,600 pounds in Duc Duc; unharvested rice was napalmed to prevent it falling into enemy hands.[19] The reason for the wide variance in harvested rice between the two districts, was due, as Colonel Zaro noted, to Duc Duc District officials, whose "planning began late, and the Duc Duc plans were neither well-thought-out nor well-executed," nor were they coordinated with 5th Marine units.[20] Despite the shortfall, both allied and South Vietnamese officials considered the harvest operations highly successful.

Combat action by Marines of Colonel Zaro's regiment in the An Hoa basin during May centered on the increased use of small unit patrols and ambushes along that well-used and preferred approach to Da Nang. With the end of Operation Muskogee Meadow, the regiment retained responsibility for a majority of the basin, including the Arizona, west and north of An Hoa Combat Base, across the Song Thu Bon. Deploying companies independently, Zaro saturated the area with platoon- and squad-size patrols and cordons. In one such cordon on 2 May, Company B, 1st Battalion and Company M, 3d Battalion joined in a well-concealed and skillfully executed night movement on the La Thap village complex, south of Liberty Bridge. Approaching the village from all directions, the company caught the La Trap Village guerrilla force, killing 36 of the enemy and capturing 14 prisoners and 18 weapons.

A sharp rise in the tempo of enemy activity in the Arizona during the first week of May, coupled with information gleaned from various intelligence sources suggested that one NVA battalion and elements of an undetermined number of other enemy units were using the northeastern portion of the area as a staging point for attacks on Marine installations both north and east of the Song Vu Gia. This intelligence information was to force an immediate shift from independent small unit operations to a regimentally controlled, five-company operation.

Following a careful review of the intelligence estimates, Colonel Zaro directed that a plan of attack into the northern Arizona be formulated. Drafted by Lieutenant Colonel Higgins, the scheme to destroy enemy troops in the area called for three of his companies to sweep from southwest Arizona into blocking positions established by two companies of 1st Battalion in the northeast Arizona. The sweeping companies would then turn north and attack toward the Song Vu Gia where elements of the 1st Battalion, 7th Marines and 3d Battalion, 1st Marines, in blocking positions on the north bank of the river, would cut off the enemy's escape.

All units involved in the operation moved to their attack positions prior to first light on 9 May. Designated to attack east and then north, Companies E, F, and H, accompanied by the battalion command group and a heavy section of tanks took up positions just north of the Song Thu Bon, following a deceptive move to the east as if to vacate the central and western portions of the Arizona. Also on the night of 8 May, Companies A and D began their night advance from the battalion command post at Liberty Bridge to prearranged blocking positions. By 0200 on the morning of the 9th, Company D had established a three-platoon block on Football Island, with Company A to the north, forming a two-company block in eastern Arizona.

At 0645, a tower lookout at Liberty Bridge spotted approximately 200 enemy troops moving to the north, apparently flushed out by the maneuvering companies. Within an hour, the enemy force had grown in size and split into two groups of about 200 each, one moving to the northeast and the other to the northwest. Subsequently, both groups broke into smaller units which were joined by additional enemy forces.

Preceded by alternating artillery fires and napalm drops by F-4 Phantoms, Companies E, F, and H began their attack shortly after dawn. As each company took a series of objectives, supporting arms fire was shifted from one to another with the intention of softening the new objective and inflicting heavy casualties on the retreating enemy troops. As the intensity of the operation increased, Colonel Zaro, with a hastily assembled command group, moved to a vantage point near Liberty Bridge in order to better control the commitment of other units of the regiment.[21] During the day's battle, the carefully coordinated Marine ground assault and air attack not only surprised the enemy, but also sent him reeling into the guns of one Marine unit after another, as First Lieutenant Victor V. Ashford reported:

> As the friendly elements began their push, the cowpokes [air controllers] virtually took over completely all coordination of supporting arms. They called in continuous artillery barrages in front of the friendly elements while they were on the move, and at the same time the cowpokes were running continuous air strikes to the north, pushing the enemy into a disorganized retreat toward our ground units. Information from POWs indicated that the enemy communications structure broke down quickly under the hundreds of tons of ordnance dropped on them and this apparently resulted in a chaotic and a completely disorganized enemy withdrawal in all directions.... As the enemy broke down into groups of five to twenty, the cowpokes kept all friendly elements advised of their movements, resulting in what must be called a "turkey shoot" as the day wore on.[22]

By 1800, Companies E, F, and H, with the assistance of Companies G and K, brought in during the day by amphibian vehicles and helicopters from Liberty Bridge, had established a cordon anchored on the southern bank of the Song Vu Gia, encompassing the My Hoa village complex.

On the morning of the 10th, following an evening during which the enemy probed but did not penetrate the positions of all four companies on the cordon, the companies renewed the assault by sweeping through the cordon and destroying or capturing the remaining enemy troops. Again, air observers played a key role as forward air controller Ashford noted:

> Throughout the day on numerous occasions, the cowpokes became airborne platoon commanders as small units assaulted enemy-held treelines and heavily dug-in machine gun bunkers. They were passing on tactically sound information concerning the positioning and type of fire maneuver best to be employed against a variety of enemy objectives, based on their excellent observation capabilities. This undoubtedly lessened the number of friendly casualties and increased the number of enemy killed.[23]

The area was again saturated with small unit patrols on the 11th, as elements of both battalions searched out the remaining pockets of enemy resistance and directed supporting arms fire toward their destruction. The heaviest fighting of the day occurred when Com-

Infantrymen of the 1st Battalion, 5th Marines guard local rice-gatherers in the continuing effort aimed at preventing the twice-yearly harvest from falling into enemy hands.
Department of Defense Photo (USMC) A374230

Department of Defense Photo (USMC) A374224
Preceded by tanks, riflemen of Company H, 2d Battalion, 5th Marines push toward an enemy-infested treeline during the battalion's sweep and block of southwestern Arizona.

pany H sent a platoon-size patrol to the southeast in order to link up with a platoon from Company D, which had secured a disabled tank. At 0930, the patrol made contact with an enemy force located in mutually supporting bunkers encompassed within a treeline. Artillery and mortars were called for as the platoon closed on the enemy position. The ensuing firefight, which lasted throughout the day, was fought at close range as Marines, sometimes fighting hand-to-hand, moved from bunker to bunker until the position was neutralized and enemy fire finally silenced.

By the 12th, enemy resistance had diminished sufficiently for the 5th Marines to return the assembled units to their parent organizations, where they again took part in independent small unit operations. Later intelligence indicated that a planned enemy attack on Marine positions at Hill 65 was aborted because of the heavy losses the enemy suffered in northeastern Arizona. Lieutenant Colonel Higgins' 2d Battalion, 5th Marines was awarded a Meritorious Unit Citation for its outstanding performance in the action, which resulted in over 230 enemy casualties.

The first half of May saw allied installations within the 5th Marines area of operation again come under enemy indirect fire attacks. While An Hoa Combat Base experienced a number of rocket and mortar attacks, resulting in only minor damage and light casualties, on the night of 11-12 May, enemy sappers attacked the eastern portion of the base's defense perimeter. Fourteen enemy troops penetrated the outer wire, but were killed before moving further. Marine snipers equipped with night observation devices or starlight scopes had been moved into the area soon after the sappers were discovered cutting their way through the wire. According to Colonel Zaro, "they were 'dead ducks' when they reached the final strands, having been under observation the entire time. Much was learned about their wire penetration techniques and the value of the starlight scope was enhanced." Night observation was improved to such an extent that during a subsequent use, Colonel Zaro noted, "a number of Marines were observed enjoying the coolness of the water in the base's water supply tower. They were much surprised that they were detected on such a dark night and subsequently apprehended."[24]

During the same night, sappers using small arms, automatic weapons, grenades, rockets, and flamethrowers also attacked Liberty Bridge. Marines met the attack with a strong counterattack, resulting in 12 enemy killed and numerous weapons captured.

With 5th Marines successes in the Arizona, and at An Hoa and Liberty Bridge, the enemy shifted tactics, concentrating his effort instead on an intensified mine and boobytrap campaign throughout the area of operations, particularly in western Go Noi and Phu Nhuan along Liberty Road. Despite the effort, all 5th Marines units continued their aggressive search and destroy operations within the basin.

Securing the Southern and Northern Approaches

As Operation Taylor Common ended, units involved resumed their conventional posture; each regiment returning to its regimental area, and each battalion to its distinct battalion area. "We had, in the Division," reported General Simpson, "what I called a 'blue line' syndrome and — blue meaning our own boundaries — every battalion had an area and every battalion was committed." As a result, there was no division, nor regimental reserve upon which to draw. Boundaries had become so fixed, that, as Simpson observed, "a battalion would begin to think that their piece of ground was the whole war as far as they were concerned. If the enemy was in that area, they were engaged, but if he was in somebody else's area, that wasn't any of their business." This situation had to be corrected, and, due to the urging of its commanding officer, the 1st Marines would be the "guinea pigs."[25]

Under Colonel Charles S. Robertson, a troop commander during World War II and Korea, who had replaced Colonel Lauffer on 24 February, the mission of the 1st Marines had changed little since the beginning of the year. Emphasis continued to be placed on company- and platoon-size combat patrols and ambushes, security of allied lines of communications, and small search and destroy operations, all aimed at the destruction of enemy forces and the support of the pacification and hamlet upgrading programs so as to secure the sourthern approaches into the Da Nang Vital Area. During February, the regiment conducted nine cordon, block, and search operations, four of which were joint 1st Marine and ARVN ventures conducted on the Man Quan Peninsula, near the villages of An Tu (1), An Tra (1), Bich Nam (2), Giang Dong, and Tanh Hanh, south of Da Nang. In addition, Lieutenant Colonel Harold G. Glasgow's 2d Battalion initiated a land-clearing operation within its area of

Employing a variety of supporting arms, including 106mm recoilless rifles, here directed by SgtMaj Clifford M. Burks, the 5th Marines crushed the enemy's attempt at Hill 65.

Marine Corps Historical Collection

operation. With the cooperation of the Hoa Nam District Headquarters, Glasgow's Marines assisted the civilian population of Tra Khe and Tra Lo in their move to the new resettlement village of Xuan Tre, and then began, and successfully completed, a clearing operation of the vacated area with the intent of turning the previously contested village complex into a "free fire zone," denying the enemy yet another primary infiltration route.

With little enemy activity in the 1st Marines area of operations, Colonel Robertson put the experimental realignment of forces into effect in early March. On the 12th, Lieutenant Colonel Alphonse A. Laporte, Jr.'s 1st Battalion assumed responsibility of the 3d Battalion's TAOR, relieving the 3d to become a reserve force, thus providing increased flexibility within the entire regimental area of operation. The realignment resulted from a number of factors, as Robertson noted:

> Lieutenant Colonel Hal Glasgow had initiated a platoon reinforced training program in 2/1; I had observed serious deficiencies in the performance of small units, reflecting training requirements; and, Colonel Adolph G. Schwenk, Div G-3, had informed me that the 1st Marines would be required to furnish one battalion for Oklahoma Hills. Further conferences with Colonel Schwenk also revealed that the 27th Marines, while occupying present 1st Marines TAOR had utilized only two battalions and retained a reserve. All of these facts, and the results achieved by Lieutenant Colonel Glasgow's modest training program, led to the presentation and General Simpson's approval of the plan for a mobile battalion in the 1st Marines.[26]

The designation of the 3d, under Lieutenant Colonel Thomas E. Bulger, as the mobile battalion, now made it unnecessary to shift units from one command to another, forming a composite fighting unit when special operations were to be conducted. It also provided a reserve battalion which could swiftly respond to regimental orders. Additionally, the mobile battalion was to carry out a concentrated two-month training program, rotating all rifle companies through a series of courses with appropriate support weapons attached. Ideally, at the end of eight weeks, the mobile battalion would have not only conducted several effective operations, but also would have accomplished progressive unit training in subjects vital to its assigned mission. Assignment as the mobile battalion would alternate among the three battalions of the regiment every eighth week.

Strings were attached. The mobile battalion could not be committed without General Simpson's knowledge, and he would also be free to move it from one regimental area to another. Eventually, Simpson expanded the realignment to include all regiments within the division, and as he noted, "we became considerably more fluid and the [regimental and battalion] boundaries didn't make that much difference."[27]

On 3 April, Lieutenant Colonel Bulger's 3d Battalion was put to the test, when Colonel Robertson ordered the battalion to conduct a detailed search of northern Dodge City, centering on Phong Nhat, an area within the Korean Marine TAOR. After Company D, 1st Battalion, 1st Marines, established blocking positions on the northern bank of the Song La Tho, Company K moved by foot and established another block along the north-south railroad berm, south of the river. Companies I and L, with the battalion command group, assaulted by CH-46s east of the berm and began searching south to north, then east to west, finally reassembling with Company K near the railroad berm.

To this point, the enemy proved elusive, and Bulger decided to resweep the area. Utilizing maximum deception, Company K swept west and then north out of Dodge City, while Companies I and L counterswept to the east. This maneuver caught the enemy force, later identified as comprising elements of the *Q-82d Local Force Battalion* and *36th NVA Regiment*, unawares. Company L engaged the combined VC and NVA force, not expecting another search, as Company I and the battalion command group maneuvered north across the Song La Tho, flanking and then destroying over 70 troops. As Robertson later noted, intelligence largely obtained from a captured NVA captain "revealed that 3/1 had chanced upon a conference of VC local force commanders and had succeeded in destroying the local VC leadership. The captured NVA captain had been sent to Quang Nam to reorganize and reestablish the VC Infrastructure."[28]

On the 9th, while the remainder of Bulger's battalion returned to its normal area of operations, Company K remained behind in an area just to the east of Dodge City. As Company K secured its positions by sending out numerous small patrols, remnants of the shattered enemy force responded with ever-increasing amounts of RPG and sniper fire. Preceded by air and artillery bombardments, the full company swept back into Dodge City, through a region peppered with hedgerows and treelines. Sweeping and then countersweeping, the company counted over 30 dead, most of whom had been killed by air or artillery. On the 12th, Company L relieved Company K for the mop-up. During the nine-day sojourn in Dodge City, the battalion accounted for 119 enemy killed and the

Marine Corps Historical Collection

LCpl Robert Redd, a fire-team leader with 3d Platoon, Company L, 3d Battalion, 1st Marines, temporarily occupies an enemy spider hole while on one of the numerous daily patrols launched south of Da Nang.

capture of numerous weapons, foodstuffs, and miscellaneous documents, including a sketch plan of attack on the command post of the 3d Battalion, 51st ARVN Regiment and enemy codes. The local ARVN commander, noted Lieutenant Colonel Bulger, "was so enthused over the results of this battle that he awarded 30 Vietnamese medals to members of 3/1."[29]

During the remainder of the month, while regimental combat patrols and ambushes from company- and platoon-size bases continued to be emphasized, a number of hamlet cordon and searches were carried out in coordination with South Vietnamese units in order to capture or destroy enemy infrastructure members. On 22 April, Company H, 2d Battalion, 1st Marines, in conjunction with the Provincial Reconnaissance Unit from Hoi An, cordoned the village of Viem Tay (1), capturing 12 suspects, seven of whom were later confirmed as infrastructure members. Again on the 28th, Company H and elements of the newly formed 34th Regional Force Battalion and a platoon of National Police Field Forces converged on Ngan Cau (2), discovering over 4,000 pounds of rice and detaining 17 suspects, most of whom were identified as members of the village enemy infrastructure.

In addition to patrols, ambushes, cordons, and searches, land-clearing efforts continued throughout the regimental area of responsibility in an effort to remove enemy harbor sites and neutralize concentrations of surprise firing devices. Focusing on "No Name Island," which had been used as a staging area for sapper attacks on allied positions, Lieutenant Colonel Glasgow's 2d Battalion, 1st Marines expended several hundred bangalore torpedoes in clearing treelines beneath which the battalion found spider and individual fighting holes. Likewise, battalion Marines cleared the vacated areas once known as Cam Le (1) and Cam Le (2) of numerous surprise firing devices. Once reclaimed, the area was to be made available for refugee resettlement.

While the regiment's mission remained unchanged in May, the enemy organized a major effort against 1st Marines installations. In the early morning hours of 12 May, an estimated enemy company, supported by 82mm mortars, B40 rockets, and automatic weapons, attacked the 2d Battalion command post at Cau Ha, five kilometers east of Highway 1. The battalion rallied to a quick defense, returning fire with organic weapons, mortars, direct artillery fire, and gunships. At dawn, 19 NVA soldiers lay dead around the perimeter, in addition to an assortment of individual weapons, equipment, and ordnance.

On the same night, only 10 minutes after the 2d Battalion came under attack, the command post of Lieutenant Colonel Wendell P. Morgenthaler, Jr.'s 1st Battalion (also the regimental command post), astride the railroad between the Son Yen and Song Bau Xau, came under a mortar and RPG-supported ground attack directed at the positions of Battery D, 11th Marines. Bolstered by direct support artillery, combined with that of OV-10s, Huey gunships, and "Spooky" airships, Morgenthaler's Marines repelled the enemy assault with minor casualties.[30] In addition to leaving over 30 dead and three wounded, the enemy abandoned a large number of individual weapons, B40 rocket launchers, ordnance, miscellaneous equipment, and documents.

As a result of the early morning attacks, and also information indicating that an enemy force of two companies had moved into Quang Chau, northeast of the regimental command post, three companies of Bulger's 3d Battalion, moving under cover of darkness, launched an attack at first light. Crossing the "Anderson Trail," Bulger's Marines searched from south to north, as far as Quang Chau, when Company I met resistance from an unknown size enemy force entrenched in a treeline bordering the village. Companies K and L moved to the west side of the village, while two companies of the 59th Regional Force Battalion closed the cordon to the north and east. Tanks and amtracs provided additional support throughout

Elements of the 3d Battalion, 1st Marines, supported by a tank from Company C, 1st Tank Battalion, take up positions in preparation for the assault on an enemy-held treeline.

the day and into the evening, pounding the cornered enemy force and finally forcing it to withdraw from the area, leaving over 150 dead.

Operations, carried out with and in coordination with ARVN forces, also continued in efforts to pacify hamlets and destroy the Viet Cong Infrastructure. On 8 May, Company F, 2d Battalion, 1st Marines, with two companies of the 4th Battalion, 51st ARVN Regiment, established a cordon of Viem Dong hamlet, resulting in the detention of seven suspects. On the 23d, Company G, 2d Battalion, with a platoon of National Police Field Forces, conducted a cordon and detailed search of Viem Tay (1), between Highway 1 and the Song Vinh Dien, detaining six Viet Cong suspects. Land-clearing operations likewise were carried out, particularly in the Cam Ne area, resulting in the destruction of enemy bunkers, fighting holes, trenches, and tunnels, and the clearing of 967,000 square meters.

The 1st Marines successfully carried out all operations within its TAOR despite the ever-present threat of mines and boobytraps. "In fact," Colonel Robertson noted, "the bulk of casualties resulted from the abundance of surprise firing devices," instead of engagements with enemy forces. As a result of a seminar conducted by General Simpson on the subject, a directive dealing with the threat was developed and implemented by all 1st Marines patrols. Scouts would henceforth be provided sticks or metal rods with which to probe suspected areas. Upon detonation of a surprise firing device the patrol would freeze in place so as not to detonate additional devices. Marines not wounded, after posting security, would then probe the area of the explosion in search of other boobytraps, provide emergency treatment and evacuation of the wounded, and then proceed with their mission.[31]

While Colonel Robertson's 1st Marines covered the south and southeastern approaches into the Da Nang Vital Area, to the northwest of Da Nang, the 1st Battalion of Colonel Ray N. Joens' 26th Marines, continued small unit patrols and ambushes aimed at preventing enemy rice gathering operations and infiltration into the villages of Kim Lien and Quan Nam. Along Highway 1, and throughout the Hai Van Pass, the extensive patrolling of Company B prevented NVA units from delaying or halting allied convoys on the main north-south line of communication.*

On 1 April, Lieutenant Colonel George C. Kliefoth's battalion was reinforced to become BLT 1/26, but remained in its defensive positions along the

---

*Throughout most of March, BLT 2/26 was controlled by the 5th Marines, participating in Operation Taylor Common, Eager Pursuit I, and Eager Pursuit II, and search and clear operations on Go Noi Island. On 29 March, the battalion landing team assumed responsibility for the 2d and 3d Battalions, 7th Marines area of responsibility, relieving the two battalions for Operation Oklahoma Hills. On the 31st, BLT 3/26, following Bold Mariner and Defiant Measure, joined Oklahoma Hills.

northwestern portion of the Da Nang perimeter until 25 April when it loaded on board ships of the fleet's amphibious ready group. During the month, the 1st Battalion assisted in the rice harvest, and cordon operations in the Nam O village area. Also on the 1st, Battalion Landing Team 2/26 lost its attachments and became 2d Battalion, 26th Marines, but continued to occupy former 7th Marines areas of responsibility west of Da Nang. On 25 April, Lieutenant Colonel George M. Edmondson, Jr.'s battalion moved into the area formerly occupied by the 1st Battalion.

The 1st of May found the 26th Marines with operational control of the 2d Battalion and the 2d Battalion, 7th Marines, reinforced by Company M, 3d Battalion, 1st Marines. Occupying a TAOR formerly assigned to three infantry battalions, the regiment continued to conduct extensive patrols and night ambushes in an attempt to halt enemy infiltration. The regiment remained in this posture until the 29th, when Operation Oklahoma Hills was terminated, resulting in the return of the 2d Battalion, 7th Marines to its parent regiment, and the realignment of the regimental areas of operation.

Americal Battleground

With the end of Operations Fayette Canyon, Hardin Falls, and Vernon Lake II on 28 February, the Americal Division moved into a short period of force and boundary realignment throughout southern Quang Nam, Quang Tin, and Quang Ngai Provinces.* Previously, the Americal and 2d ARVN Divisions had operated in separate areas in which they had unilateral responsibility. After 18 March, as a result of the realignment, "combined planning, combined operations, and combined responsibility" was, as Major General Charles M. Gettys noted, "the rule throughout the TAOI. It is expected that this concept will give ARVN greater responsibility . . . and will upgrade the operational capability of the 2d ARVN Division through constant operation with U.S. units and more ready access to Americal combat support and combat service support assets."[32]

Tactically organized, the Division's Tactical Area of Operational Interest (TAOI) was divided into combined operational zones. Within the northern sector, the 196th Infantry Brigade shared an operational zone with the 5th ARVN Regiment. In the center sector, the 198th Infantry Brigade operated with the 6th ARVN Regiment, while south of Quang Ngai City, the 11th Infantry Brigade cooperated with the 4th ARVN Regiment in its operational zone. The division cavalry squadron, 1st Squadron, 1st Cavalry, occupied a large zone in the northern sector along the coastal plain. With the creation of the four operational zones, the Oregon, Duc Pho, and Chu Lai areas of operation were discontinued.

During the 12-day realignment period, the only major division operation to continue was Russell Beach. Initiated in January in an effort to cleanse the Batangan Peninsula, the combined Army, Marine, and ARVN force maintained a constant series of search and security operations. With the building of new roads and hamlets, and following a careful screening to eliminate elements of the local infrastructure, the population was moved back onto the peninsula in April along with South Vietnamese governmental authority. Allied security operations were maintained throughout the remainder of April and into May to protect the newly established village and hamlets and prevent the reintroduction of Viet Cong units into the area.

Following the realignment, three new operations were initiated simultaneously within the combined Americal and 2d ARVN Division area of interest on 18 March. Within the northern sector, the 196th Infantry Brigade, 5th ARVN Regiment, and elements of the 1st Cavalry began Operation Frederick Hill designed to secure population centers in the coastal plain and to destroy enemy troop concentrations, base camps, and infiltration routes in the adjacent mountains. Engagements were few as Cavalry and ARVN troops began operations against enemy staging areas, notably Pineapple Forest and Barrier Island, in the coastal lowlands and would remain so. In the mountains to the west, the 196th Brigade and elements of the 5th ARVN Regiment launched two successive preemptive strikes. The first against Antenna Valley and the surrounding mountain ranges was designed to neutralize the *1st Viet Cong Regiment*, and the second, launched on 25 April, was against elements of the 2d NVA Division believed to be harbored within Base Area 117 in the Ba Su Mountains. Fighting was light throughout both areas searched.

---

*In February, the division was reorganized under the infantry division MTOE to standardize it along the same lines as the 1st, 4th, and 25th Infantry Divisions. The division had evolved from Task Force Oregon which was composed of the 11th, 196th, and 198th Infantry Brigades, deployed to Vietnam as separate units. They were organized into the 23d Infantry (Americal) Division on 25 September 1967. The reorganization under standard MTOE reduced the combat service elements of the division, which were redistributed to other units within USARV.

In the center sector, the 198th Infantry Brigade and 6th ARVN Regiment launched operation Geneva Park in order to secure major lines of communication and to locate and destroy enemy forces attempting to attack Quang Ngai and Chu Lai. In addition to small unit patrols, ambushes, and roving sweep teams, a number of preemptive strikes were launched against suspected enemy concentrations in the Nui Ne Mountains, along the Song Tra Khuc, and on all approaches to the Batangan Peninsula. As in the northern sector, skirmishes were few as enemy forces avoided engagement with Americal and ARVN troops.

Operation Iron Mountain, conducted by the 11th Infantry Brigade and 4th ARVN Regiment, was initiated in the southern sector, and was designed to protect coastal population centers and to destroy enemy units operating in the western mountains before attacks against population centers could be launched. To accomplish this mission, three large-scale preemptive operations were carried out against Base Area 121, mountainous areas northeast of Duc Pho, the Song Ve Valley, and bordering Nui Hoat Mountains. All three operations accomplished their mission, and prevented the enemy from massing in order to attack major coastal population centers during the spring.

Despite the enemy's continued capability to surface for harassing attacks within southern I Corps Tactical Zone, troops of the 1st Marine and Americal Divisions, and their ARVN counterparts, continued to operate along enemy lines of communication and within his staging and assembly areas, scoring substantial gains against Viet Cong and North Vietnamese efforts to attack major population centers. Small unit counter-guerrilla actions, focusing on approaches to the coastal lowlands, denied the enemy access to rice and other supplies, sorely needed by forces occupying the sparsely populated hinterlands. Within southern I Corps, the enemy's capacity to initiate large-scale offensive operations during the spring deteriorated substantially.

PART III
THE THIRD'S FINAL MONTHS

CHAPTER 8
Redeployment: The First Phase

Keystone Eagle—"A Turning Point"

Keystone Eagle

Post-hostilities planning by MACV began shortly after the seven-nation Manila Summit Conference of October 1966. The communique released at the close of the conference contained the conditions under which it was envisaged that Free World forces could be withdrawn from South Vietnam: "allied forces . . . shall be withdrawn, after close consultation, as the other side withdraws its force to the north, ceases infiltration, and the level of violence thus subsides, those forces will be withdrawn as soon as possible and not later than six months after the above conditions have been fulfilled."[1] Although the communique stipulated that the withdrawal of forces would take place not later than six months after the necessary conditions had been met, it did not specify a length of time during which the conditions would be assessed and numerous preparatory actions accompanying a major withdrawal of U.S. forces would be accomplished; nor did it address the question of a residual U.S. presence.

With the announcement of a number of bombing halts and the initiation of discussions with the North Vietnamese in Paris in May 1968, the development of detailed plans for the withdrawal of U.S. and allied forces was given increased emphasis. In addition to general planning based on the Manila Communique, a number of plans, identified as T-Day, were developed to support specific withdrawal alternatives. Once the essential conditions for a cessation of hostilities had been met, either as a result of formal agreements at the Paris negotiations, informal mutual understandings, or the enemy's unilateral withdrawal from South Vietnam, Laos, and Cambodia, U.S. and allied forces would be phased down and then withdrawn over a six- or twelve-month period, depending upon the progressive expansion and modernization of the South Vietnamese Armed Forces. Two major considerations would determine the sequence of redeployment: those units slated to reconstitute the Pacific Theater's reserve would be withdrawn first; and, the phasing out of the remaining units would be governed by the objective of maintaining a balanced force posture. In addition, the alternative plans specified that the withdrawals could be suspended at any stage should the situation change, and that the residual force would vary from a military advisory assistance group to a group with a combat force of two divisions.

While both MACV and I Corps Combined Campaign Plans for 1969 assumed that there would be no major increase in United States force strengths in Vietnam "beyond those provided in existing programs," neither addressed the question of troop withdrawals during the year.[2] However, the changing political environment would point up the possibility that selected U.S. forces might be withdrawn from South Vietnam prior to the cessation of hostilities and not under the terms of the Manila Communique.

In January 1969, a new administration took office committed to finding a solution to the nagging question of Vietnam. In order to maintain public support, as well as carry on the war in the face of imminent Congressional cuts in defense appropriations, the administration had to reduce substantially or end American involvement in Vietnam. Ideally, President Richard M. Nixon hoped to achieve a negotiated settlement and the mutual and simultaneous withdrawal of all outside forces from South Vietnam. Failing this, the option remained for the orderly, progressive withdrawal of American forces and their replacement by South Vietnamese troops. Proceeding with ongoing efforts toward a negotiated mutual withdrawal, the administration also began consideration of unilateral United States force reductions should the negotiations fail.

The idea of withdrawing American combat forces and replacing them with South Vietnamese troops was not new. The intent of the RVNAF improvement and modernization program, launched by President Lyndon B. Johnson in mid-1968, was that the South Vietnamese would eventually relieve U.S. and allied forces of the combat role. In his New Year's address, President Thieu also raised the prospect.[3] In Washington, the possible replacement of American troops by South Vietnamese was seriously considered at a meeting of the National Security Council (NSC) in late January. Again taken up at a February meeting of the NSC, it was proposed that Vietnamese forces replace U.S. troops as soon as possible, but faced with the possibility of yet another enemy offensive similar to the one launched during *Tet* 1968, the administration chose

Department of Defense Photo (USA) SC649484

President Richard M. Nixon, accompanied by Melvin R. Laird, center, Secretary of Defense, and Gen Earle G. Wheeler, USA, right, Chairman, Joint Chiefs of Staff, visits the Department of Defense for an orientation briefing shortly after taking office in January 1969.

to postpone action until after Secretary of Defense Melvin Laird's visit to Vietnam in March.

Among the purposes of the Secretary's visit was not only to observe the situation, but to inform both U.S. military commanders and South Vietnamese officials of the new administration's desire that a greater share of the fighting be assumed by the RVNAF. Assured by both General Abrams and President Thieu that the Republic's armed forces were improving, Laird returned to Washington convinced that the United States could prepare to replace American combat troops with Vietnamese. Accordingly, he recommended that plans be drawn up for the redeployment of not only 50,000 to 70,000 troops from South Vietnam in 1969, but of additional forces the following year. As the Secretary's plane took off on the return flight to Washington, General Abrams ruefully remarked that he "certainly had not come to Saigon to help us win the war."[4] Based on the Secretary's recommendation, MACV began planning for a tentative force reduction of 50,000, or two divisions, during the latter half of 1969.

In March meetings of the National Security Council, the question of Vietnam again arose. With regard to the withdrawal of U.S. forces, it was the consensus of those involved that the combat effectiveness of the RVNAF had been improved to such a degree as to justify the initiation of redeployment planning; the actual decision would be delayed until mid-year. At the direction of the President, the Secretary of Defense was given the responsibility for overall planning which was to cover all aspects of United States involvement and would be grounded on the following assumptions: a starting date of 1 July 1969; continuation of current NVA and VC force levels; use of current projections of South Vietnamese force levels; maintenance of the current level of allied military operations, except for drops resulting from the phased withdrawal of American and other allied forces not fully compensated for by the South Vietnamese; and, the equipping and training of South Vietnamese forces which would be assigned the highest national priority. Based on these assumptions, timetables were drawn up for the transfer of the United States combat role and the restriction of the American effort to combat support and advisory missions, with alternative completion dates of 31 December 1970, 30 June 1971, 31 December 1971, and 31 December 1972. As was done with all force-level planning, input was sought from MACV, CinCPac, and other concerned agencies within the Federal Government.

Although there was neither official announcement nor comment that a troop reduction was under consideration, public speculation had become so prevalent by mid-March, that the President was forced to dampen it. On the 14th, he publicly stated that there was "no prospect for a reduction of American forces in the foreseeable future," listing three factors upon which any decision to reduce the American troop commitment would have to be based: the ability of the South Vietnamese to defend themselves; the level of hostilities imposed by the enemy; and, the progress of the Paris talks. A month later, Mr. Nixon said he saw "good prospects that American forces can be reduced," but noted that "we have no plans to reduce our forces until there is more progress on one or all of the three fronts that I have mentioned."[5]

Speaking to the nation on 14 May, the President gave his assessment of the Vietnam situation. While reiterating his call for a phased mutual withdrawal based upon a negotiated settlement, he did indicate that a unilateral reduction of American forces might be possible. He noted that General Abrams had informed him of the excellent progress made in training South Vietnamese forces, and that, "apart from any developments that may occur in the negotiations in Paris, the time is approaching when South Vietnamese forces will be able to take over some of the fighting fronts now being manned by Americans."[6]

In late May, an initial plan for the phased withdrawal of American forces from Vietnam was submitted by the Joint Chiefs of Staff to the Secretary of Defense. Calling for the transfer of the U.S. combat and support roles to the South Vietnamese to the maximum extent possible, the plan provided timetables for a total reduction of 244,000 personnel from the current authorization of 549,000, leaving approximately 306,000 in South Vietnam. For reductions to be carried out during the latter half of 1969, the plan provided four alternatives: 50,000 (two divisions, one Marine, one Army, plus limited support); 50,000 (one Marine division plus support); 100,000 (three divisions, one Marine, two Army, plus limited support); and, 100,000 (two divisions, one Marine, one Army, plus support). In order to avoid the redeployment of a major combat unit from I Corps, where the enemy threat was still considered greatest, a fifth alternative involving a countrywide cut of 50,000 was suggested.

Should any forces be withdrawn during 1969, the Joint Chiefs of Staff recommended that the first alternative be adopted. In addition they urged that any reduction be in two increments, with a pause between to assess the results. The Joint Chiefs also favored the reconstitution of the Pacific reserve, in favor of the redeployment of combat forces to the United States and their subsequent demobilization, and opposed any reduction in 1969 of out-of-country forces supporting the war.

The Secretary of Defense forwarded the JCS proposals to the President in early June, recommending an initial withdrawal of 20,000 to 25,000 troops beginning in July with the total reduction for the year limited to 50,000. Composition of the initial redeployment was to be determined by the Joint Chiefs of Staff in coordination with CinCPac, MACV, and the South Vietnamese. The President made no immediate decision, but took the plans to Midway where he was scheduled to meet with President Thieu on the 8th to assess the progress of the war.

Troop reduction planning by MACV was carried out concurrently with that of the Joint Chiefs of Staff. A number of conditions, suggested by planners in Saigon, would bear directly on the feasibility of any reductions: pacification to continue to make definable progress; improvement in the performance of the South Vietnamese Armed Forces to continue to achieve programmed goals; enemy troop strength in or near South Vietnam not to exceed present levels; no new weapon systems to be introduced into South Vietnam or be capable of reaching the Republic; infiltration rates from North Vietnam to remain constant, as was enemy logistical support; and, current levels of B-52 sorties, tactical air, helicopter, and nondivisional artillery support were to be maintained. By mid-April, MACV planners produced a tentative plan, with the concurrence of III MAF, specifically suggesting the redeployment of the 9th U.S. Infantry and 3d Marine Divisions. The divisions were selected because they were both considered "first-rate" combat units and as such would make the reduction credible to both the enemy and

U.S. and South Vietnamese publics. The 3d, according to General Abrams, was selected "because it could go to Okinawa; because it would be leaving the area to the 1st ARVN Division, recognized by all as the strongest and best ARVN division; and finally, because northern I Corps has one of the best security environments in the country for the people." As for the 9th Infantry Division, it was picked because "the war there [in the Delta] has been largely fought by the Vietnamese and has been going well for several months."[7]

Although MACV planners suggested alternatives, in every case the first unit deployed out-of-country would be the 3d Marine Division, reinforced, combat-loaded on board amphibious shipping destined for Okinawa, where it would constitute the most readily available strategic reserve.[8] The plan provided for the redeployment of the division in the following phases:

Phase	Unit	Date of Deployment	Strength
1	RLT	1 July 1969	7,132
2	RLT	1 August 1969	6,803
3	RLT	1 September 1969	6,823
4	SvcBn (-)	15 September 1969	916
5	MarDiv(-)	30 September 1969	574
		Total Strength	22,248

The MACV proposal, however, did not reflect the desire of Lieutenant General Herman Nickerson, Jr., Commanding General, III MAF, nor that of Lieutenant General Henry W. Buse, Jr., Commanding General, FMFPac, that it embody the relocation of a typical Marine air-ground team. As General Buse later noted:

> The initial troop lists on all this super-duper planning for withdrawal, didn't have any Marine air in it. The initial guidelines were that no air would come out-of-country and no heavy artillery. We took up the cudgel, and first of all we had to have helicopters go out; they were not even in it at all. Secondly, in order to reconstitute the Strategic Reserve we wanted air with our package that came out. So we had it actually put in there, and we didn't get too much opposition.[9]

In addition to air, Nickerson and Buse suggested other modifications. In order to support the division, once on Okinawa, a full-strength service battalion would have to be created from the 9th Provisional Service Battalion, with the augmentation of approximately 150 men from Force Logistic Command at Da Nang. Also, as the mount-out blocks of supplies carried by each regimental landing team were low or nonexistent, both Nickerson and Buse recommended that current operating stocks be used to replenish the 30-day blocks. General Abrams approved both suggested

Department of Defense Photo (USMC) A419099
As a member of the Joint Chiefs of Staff, Gen Leonard F. Chapman, Jr., Commandant of the Marine Corps, lobbied for the maintenance of the Marine air-ground team during initial planning for redeployment.

modifications.[10] The question as to whether Marine air would accompany the 3d Division remained unresolved for the moment.

The MACV proposal gained quick approval from Admiral John S. McCain, Jr., following which both CincPac and MACV representatives journeyed to Washington where they presented it to the Secretary of Defense and Joint Chiefs of Staff. During the briefing of the Joint Chiefs, the Commandant of the Marine Corps, General Leonard F. Chapman, Jr., again pointed out the fact that although Marine helicopters and fixed-wing aircraft were not organic to the 3d Division, as in the Army, they were essential if the division was to be used in reconstituting the Pacific reserve. In addition, Marine air would be necessary from a training standpoint. The MACV plan was given tentative approval by the Joint Chiefs; however, it was suggested that one helicopter group and two jet fighter squadrons, together with supporting detachments, be included in the final troop list, in case the division was to be deployed elsewhere within the Pacific Command.[11]

With debate raging in Congress over troop withdrawals, Secretary of Defense Melvin Laird expressed concern that "political realities may force a decision on troop withdrawals sooner than anticipated."[12] By 5 June, after extensive discussion of a number of additional alternatives, and incorporating Army Chief of Staff General William Westmoreland's suggestion that the complete removal of the 3d Division was dangerous, in that an attack by the NVA would escalate the war, and recommendation that the division be withdrawn in increments, a plan for the two-phased pull-out of the division was approved. Phase one was to include one 3d Marine Division regimental landing team with air and support units, and two brigades of the 9th Infantry Division, while phase two would encompass the remaining two landing teams and their support units, both air and logistics.[13]

On 8 June, President Nixon and South Vietnamese President Thieu met on Midway Island. Thieu, initially opposed to any proposed plans for a large American withdrawal from Vietnam in 1969, as it would signal the beginning of an irreversible policy, was persuaded to accept the immediate redeployment of approximately 25,000 men. In a brief statement following the meeting, both Nixon and Thieu noted that further troop withdrawals in the months ahead would be based on the three previously stated variables, periodically assessed: the level of North Vietnamese infiltration and enemy battlefield activity; the ability of South Vietnam to carry the burden of fighting its own war; and, progress at the Paris peace negotiations.[14] With the decision to begin unilateral redeployment, a number of conferences were held at CinCPac Headquarters in order to plan the actual movement of men and materiel.

The initial redeployment, codenamed Keystone Ea-

President Richard M. Nixon welcomes South Vietnamese President Nguyen Van Thieu to Midway Island in the Pacific where they discussed and decided upon the withdrawal of 25,000 American combat forces and their replacement by South Vietnamese units.

Department of Defense Photo (USN) K74369

gle, would involve the incremental deployment of a 3d Marine Division regimental landing team: one-third to be pulled out on 15 July and the remaining two-thirds by 31 August. A problem soon developed. The number of men in the RLT, its direct support elements, and the two air squadrons, did not meet the 8,388 spaces finally allotted by MACV. As a result, III MAF was forced to "add-on" another 1,294 men from a wide variety of engineer, headquarters, and logistical support units to meet the MACV allocation. By mid-June all was ready.[15]

"A Turning Point"

III MAF selected Colonel Edward F. Danowitz's 9th Marines as the first regimental landing team to redeploy. "We drew out the 9th Marines," recalled Major General William K. Jones, "because they were the Swing/Ready regiment; the regiment that was sort of a Division reserve, or not occupying a fire support base. The 4th and the 3d Regiments were occupying [positions] so we drew back the 9th Marines and they started the process, a battalion at a time."[16] The regiment's supporting artillery, the 2d Battalion, 12th Marines, would accompany it, as would small engineer, motor transport, reconnaissance, shore party, headquarters, medical, and logistical detachments. III MAF also designated the 3d Anti-Tank Battalion; the 1st Amphibian Tractor Battalion; Company C, 3d Tank Battalion; and the 1st Searchlight Battery for withdrawal.

The 1st Marine Aircraft Wing would relinquish one jet and one helicopter squadron, in addition to the 1st Light Antiaircraft Missile Battalion and Marine Air Traffic Control Unit 68 (MATCU-68). Lieutenant Colonel Edwin C. Paige, Jr.'s Marine Fighter Attack Squadron 115 (VMFA-115), with its 15 F4Bs ("Phantoms"), would be deployed to the Marine Corps Air Station, Iwakuni, Japan, while Lieutenant Colonel Thomas E. Raines' Marine Medium Helicopter Squadron 165 (HMM-165), with its 14 CH-46s, would accompany the 9th Marines to Okinawa.

"On the 14th of June," noted Colonel Danowitz, "I was apprised about 1000 by General Jones that it would be the regiment that would be moved out. I knew that someone was going out of the division, but certainly not the regiment until that time."[17] The following day, III MAF Operational Plan 182-69 was issued which prescribed procedures for the withdrawal of units during continuing hostilities. Under the plan, each redeploying unit would cease combat operations, move to a designated base camp well before the actual date of departure, and prepare men and equipment for sea and air transportation out of country. Although its mission and area of operations would be assumed by other organizations according to prearranged plans, each redeploying unit was to "retain sufficient combat ability for security and self-defense."[18]

While Marine units were to leave Vietnam as "balanced combat units," fully organized and equipped, they would rarely leave with the same men who had served with them in combat. Instead, with each redeployment, a system of personnel transfers, nicknamed "Mixmaster," was put into effect. In this process, the departing unit would be manned with Marines from all III MAF units who had completed more than one tour in Vietnam and were nearing the end of their current one-year tour, or were nearing the completion of their first tour. Those Marines with the most months left in-country would be transferred to units not designated to redeploy. Those units whose final destination was the United States were to undergo "Mixmastering" to a greater extent than the 9th Marines, which experienced little shift in personnel. "We endeavored," as General Buse later stated, "to avoid any mixmaster approach in this move; that is, any extensive intra-III MAF personnel shuffles. There will be some exceptions, but in the main, all units and detachments are redeploying with their on board personnel in order to minimize confusion and to retain unit integrity for contingency readiness."[19]

The troop and equipment movements of Keystone Eagle began on 15 June when the *Iredell County* (LST 839) departed Vietnam for Okinawa with the first increment of the 1st Amphibian Tractor Battalion's equipment, accompanied by a nucleus of maintenance and headquarters personnel. The shipment, which General Buse characterized as "jumping the gun," included 14 LVTP-5s and three forklifts.[20] On the 23d, the 1st Battalion, 9th Marines, following its participation in Operation Utah Mesa, stood down at Vandegrift Combat Base. On 12 July, Lieutenant Colonel Thomas J. Culkin's battalion moved by truck to Quang Tri and then by C-130s to Da Nang.

At Da Nang's Deep Water Pier, two days later, with the *Paul Revere* (LPA 248) standing by, Lieutenant General Nickerson thanked the officers and men of the 1st Battalion for their performance and dedication. "But," as General Nickerson noted, "this day goes beyond honoring the officers and men of the 9th Marines. It represents a turning point . . . when victories on the battlefield and progress in the pacification struggle now permit the GVN/ARVN to say to their

Department of Defense Photo (USMC) A800469

The 1st Battalion, 9th Marines waits to board the amphibious transport Paul Revere *at Da Nang, initiating the first phase of the withdrawal of American forces from Vietnam.*

LtGen Herman Nickerson, Jr., left, and LtGen Hoang Xuan Lam, right, talk with 1stSgt James L. Langford of the 2d Battalion, 9th Marines prior to the battalion's departure.

Abel Papers, Marine Corps Historical Center

The MACV List: Composition of Keystone Eagle

Unit	Strength	Departure Date	Destination
1st Bn, 9th Mar	1,166	14 Jul	Okinawa
Co B (Rein), 3d Med Bn	42	15 Jul	Okinawa
Co A-C (Rein), 3d Motor Trans Bn	167	13 Jul	Okinawa
Co D (Rein), 11th Engr Bn	175	15 Jul	Okinawa
3d Anti-Tank Bn (C)	19	29 Jun	Okinawa
Co C (C) (Rein), 3d Tank Bn	74	13 Jul	Okinawa
Co C (Rein), 3d Shore Party Bn	144	15 Jul	Okinawa
Det, 3d Dental Co	1	13 Jul	Okinawa
1st AmTrac Bn	135	13 Jul	Okinawa
1st Armed Amphib Co	42	15 Jul	Okinawa
Hq Btry, Fld Arty Gp	24	15 Jul	Okinawa
Btry D, 2d Bn, 12th Mar	139	13 Jul	Okinawa
107 Btry, 2d Bn, 12th Mar	84	19 Jul	Okinawa
Co C, 11th Engr Bn	180	13 Jul	Okinawa
1st Search Light Btry	116	14 Jul	Okinawa
Det, Mar Air Traffic Control Unit	23	15 Jul	Okinawa
2d Bn, 9th Mar	1,166	1 Aug	Okinawa
Hq Co (-), 9th Mar	234	1 Aug	Okinawa
Co C (Rein), 3d Engr Bn	257	30 Jul	Okinawa
Det, Hq Btry, 12th Mar	21	31 Jul	Okinawa
Btry E, 2d Bn, 12th Mar	139	31 Jul	Okinawa
Hq Btry, 2d Bn, 12th Mar	161	31 Jul	Okinawa
3d Bn, 9th Mar	1,166	13 Aug	Okinawa
Btry F, 2d Bn, 12th Mar	139	13 Aug	Okinawa
Btry L, 4th Bn, 12th Mar	112	13 Aug	Okinawa
Det, Hq Bn, 3d Mar Div	354	5 Aug	Okinawa
Co C (Rein), 3d Recon Bn	120	13 Aug	Okinawa
Det, Force Log Comd	150	12 Aug	Okinawa
Det, Hq Co, 9th Mar	20	13 Aug	Okinawa
Co A (Rein), 9th Motor Trans Bn	130	14 Aug	Okinawa
1st Light AA Missile Bn	661	16 Aug	Okinawa
Mar Atk Sqdn 334	388	30 Aug	Japan
Med Helo Sqdn 165	279	14 Aug	Okinawa

American friends, 'We can do more. We ask you to do less.' " With the conclusion of General Nickerson's remarks, the battalion, by company, boarded the *Paul Revere*, and then sailed for Okinawa.[21]

On 6 July, Lieutenant Colonel Robert L. Modjeski's 2d Battalion concluded its participation in Operation Utah Mesa, and moved by air to Vandegrift, where it stood down in preparation for redeployment. The battalion then moved to Quang Tri Combat Base, where on 25 July, tribute was again paid to the men of the 9th Marines. Following remarks by General Jones, the honored guests, General Creighton Abrams, Lieutenant General Nickerson, Lieutenant General Melvin Zais, and Lieutenant General Hoang Xuan Lam, watched as representative Marine, Army, Navy, and ARVN forces massed colors as they passed in review. Colonel Danowitz, the regiment's commanding officer, invited Colonel Robert H. Barrow, who had commanded the regiment during Operation Dewey Canyon, to join him in this final honor.[22]

During the last two days of July, the battalion moved to Da Nang, and on the first day of August, accompanied by the regimental headquarters and colors of the 9th Marines, departed Vietnam. Lieutenant Colonel Donald E. Wood's 3d Battalion followed on the 13th. With the standdown and departure of the

Marine Corps Historical Collection

Personnel of Marine Fighter Attack Squadron 334 board C-130 transport aircraft at Chu Lai, destined for Iwakuni, Japan, where they would join Marine Aircraft Group 15.

9th Marines, Task Force Hotel was disbanded and the area of operations formerly occupied by the regiment, as well as its missions, divided between the 3d and 4th Marines which were placed under the direct operational control of the division.

The loss of one-third of the division's combat power resulted not only in a tactical realignment of forces, but in a series of administrative moves designed to consolidate the remaining units and to provide for greater efficiency and control. The 3d Marines extended its area of operations westward to include Elliott Combat Base. The area assigned the 4th Marines now included Fire Support Bases Russell and Cates, Hill 950, Vandegrift Combat Base, and the Ba Long Valley. The 1st Brigade, 5th Infantry Division (Mechanized) continued to maintain control of the coastal lowlands, while the 101st Airborne Division (Airmobile) extended its boundary northward into Quang Tri Province to include all of enemy Base Area 101. The division designated the extreme western portion of its area of operations a reconnaissance zone, and in early August, Detachment B-52 (Project Delta) began surveillance operations in the area. In order to increase unit integrity and control, the rear echelons of the 3d and 4th Marines and various combat support and service support units, which had long been maintained at Quang Tri Combat Base, moved to Dong Ha and Vandegrift Combat Bases.

The jet aviation redeployment of Keystone Eagle posed a problem. Lieutenant Colonel Paige's VMFA-115, with its F4Bs, was originally selected for withdrawal, but subsequently replaced by Lieutenant Colonel John R. Braddon's VMFA-334, with its 13 F4Js. The problem revolved around the use of the two aircraft. Both Headquarters Marine Corps and the Navy were concerned about the high usage, attrition, and cost of the F4J, equipped with the Westinghouse AWG-10 pulse Doppler radar (data link) fire control weapons system. Both recommended the maximum utilization of the F4J in an air-to-air role in Japan, instead of air-to-ground, more suited to the F4B and combat in Vietnam. In addition, as the F4J required special support equipment, readily available in Japan, it was suggested that instead of splitting resources between Vietnam and Iwakuni, the F4J be based at a single site, Japan, thus enhancing Marine Aircraft Group 15's air-to-air commitment with the improved weapons system.[23]

On 13 August, VMFA-334's equipment left Chu Lai by sea, followed by its personnel and avionics van on the 30th by air. On 24 August, Lieutenant Colonel Braddon led the command echelon of 13 F4Js from Vietnam to Naha, Okinawa, with a refueling stop at Naval Air Station, Cubi Point, Philippines. All 13 Phantoms arrived at Iwakuni, Japan, on the 27th. In a move unrelated to redeployment, but bearing upon the Marine Corps and Navy's desire to replace all F4Js in Vietnam, Lieutenant Colonel Ralph J. Sorensen's VMFA-232 (F4J) turned over its slot in MAG-13 at Chu Lai to Lieutenant Colonel John K. Cochran's VMFA-122 (F4B) in early September.

Meanwhile, in mid-August, Lieutenant Colonel Raines' HMM-165 embarked its 14 CH-46 "Sea Knight" helicopters on board the former carrier, now amphibious assault ship, *Valley Forge* (LPH 8), for shipment to Okinawa. During the same period, the 1st Light Antiaircraft Missile Battalion, under Major Edward L. House, Jr., boarded the *Belle Grove* (LSD 2), *Tortuga* (LSD 26), and *Tulare* (LKA 112) at Da Nang, ultimately destined for Twentynine Palms, California.

By the end of August, all units of III MAF scheduled for Keystone Eagle had left Vietnam. The 3d Marine Division now consisted of the 3d and 4th Marines with the 1st Brigade, 5th Infantry Division (Mechanized) under its operational control. The strength of III MAF was reduced by 8,388 to 72,355. With the addition of 14,000 Army troops from the 1st and 2d Brigades, 9th Infantry Division, and 2,000 reservists and Navy personnel, the goal of 25,000 out-of-country by 31 August was met.

CHAPTER 9
'A Strange War Indeed'

Company Patrol Operations — Idaho Canyon — "A Significant Step" — Specter of Anarchy

Company Patrol Operations

With the standdown and redeployment of the 9th Marines Regimental Landing Team, Major General William K. Jones' 3d Marine Division, composed of Colonel Wilbur F. Simlik's 3d Marines and the 4th Marines under Colonel William F. Goggin, embarked upon the final four months of combat operations in Quang Tri Province. Despite the loss of one regiment and the resultant shrinkage of the division's tactical area of responsibility, its mission changed little. As stated in a revised letter of instruction, issued in July, the 3d Marine Division, in cooperation and coordination with the 1st and 2d Regiments, 1st ARVN Division, was to:

> Conduct offensive operations to destroy NVA/VC main forces, VCLF [Viet Cong Local Forces], and VCI [Viet Cong Infrastructure] within AO, and to interdict enemy LOCs [Lines of Communications] and neutralize enemy base areas within AO; conducts surveillance and interdiction of DMZ and Laotian border; assists GVN forces in the defense of Dong Ha and Quang Tri cities; provides support for the Pacification Development Plan, other civil activities, and the GVN resources control and denial program within the AO; be prepared to provide forces in support of CIDG and resettlement areas within the AO; be prepared to assume 101st Airborne Division (AM) task as Corps Reserve on order.[1]

Tactically, the division moved away from the large multi-battalion search and destroy operations in the Khe Sanh Plateau, Song Da Krong Valley, and other areas of far-western Quang Tri Province, characteristic of its operations during the first six months of 1969. In attempting to maintain its mobile posture, the division began to concentrate instead on company search, patrol, and ambush operations that would still provide protection for all lines of communication within the area of operations and for virtually 100 percent of the population without tying down an excessive number of companies from any one unit to fixed positions. With fewer troops to practice "much economy of force" throughout the province, noted Colonel Robert H. Barrow, former commanding officer of the 9th Marines, and III MAF Deputy G-3, "Charlie is going to be able to stick his logistics nose in country with less chance we will find it."[2] And that he did.

As a result of the numerous beatings inflicted on the NVA during the first six months, enemy activity of battalion-size or larger throughout the province decreased markedly in mid-summer, and company-size ground and indirect fire attacks became more common. Of approximately 30 battalions available, only elements of the *9th*, *24th*, *27th*, and *31st Infantry*, and the *84th Artillery (Rocket) Regiments* remained consistently active. These units, in conjunction with minor elements of the *7th Front*, not only continued selective attacks by fire over a wide front in eastern and central Quang Tri, favoring such targets as Vandegrift Combat Base, Elliott Combat Base, Route 9 strongpoints, and the Alpha and Charlie outposts south of the DMZ, but also increased infiltration of men and supplies with the aim of interdicting Route 9. In an effort to halt these attempts, the 3d Marines continued Operation Virginia Ridge and launched Operation Idaho Canyon.

Idaho Canyon

The first day of July found Colonel Simlik's 3d Marines engaged in Operation Virginia Ridge. Enemy activity within the area of operations, south of the DMZ, was relatively light, consisting of sporadic rocket attacks against Marine installations at Alpha-4 and Charlie-2, north of Cam Lo, point and sniper contacts, and attempts at interdicting Routes 9 and 561 with mines and other surprise firing devices. Countering the enemy, Lieutenant Colonel David G. Herron's 1st Battalion continued search and destroy operations in the vicinity of Mutter's Ridge and Helicopter Valley, north of Fire Support Base Fuller, while the 2d Battalion, under Lieutenant Colonel James J. McMonagle, generally deployed to the southwest, provided security for Khe Gio Bridge, Route 9, and conducted extensive search and destroy operations within the northern portion of the Mai Loc TAOR to the south. Lieutenant Colonel Richard C. Schulze's 3d Battalion occupied and provided security for fixed positions along Route 561, from Alpha-4 to the Cam Lo District Headquarters on Route 9, conducted search and destroy operations west of 561, and deployed Company L for one week along Song Rao Vinh, south of Route 9.

Although Simlik's Marines caught an ever-increasing number of enemy troops, small groups of

Infantrymen of Company B, 1st Battalion, 3d Marines patrol the hills surrounding Khe Gia Bridge and Route 9, the vital road linking Dong Ha with Vandegrift Combat Base.

NVA continued to infiltrate the DMZ and move south. Aggressive 1st Battalion patrols north of Fuller, in the Mutter's Ridge-Helicopter Valley area, however, discouraged any attempt to bring in larger units. When engagements did take place, hit-and-run and attacks by fire remained the enemy's main tactic. In order to limit this small but steady stream of infiltrators, the 3d Marines adopted a new technique, the Denial Stingray Concept.

Under the concept, the regiment established a denial zone centered on Mutter's Ridge, three kilometers south of the DMZ. Seismic intrusion devices then were implanted along known infiltration routes, and beginning on 7 July, CS gas crystals dropped along streams, in valleys, and on any possible redoubt area within the zone: an average of three gas drops were made per day. The enemy, upon encountering the gas, would, it was thought, be forced to use well-known infiltration trails, along which the sensor devices were planted. As the seismic instruments were activated, massive air and artillery fires would be brought to bear. To detect infiltration through or around the denial zone, squad-size "hunter-killer" or Stingray patrols, possessing the capability of operating in the field for four days without resupply and of directing air and artillery, would be deployed, one per 1,000-meter square, south of the zone.

Simlik's Marines employed the denial technique for approximately two weeks, beginning 9 July. Although there were no sensor activations indicating enemy attempts at infiltration within the zone, Lieutenant Colonel Herron kept Captain James M. McAdams' Company A and Captain Gary E. Carlson's Company C continually engaged in checking the zone for any signs of enemy activity, and in measuring the persistency of the gas. With the discovery, on 22 July, that the air-delivered gas was lightly persistent CS1 instead of the requested, more persistent CS2 crystals, it became imperative that the denial zone and the area north, between it and the DMZ, be physically searched by Marines on foot to determine if an enemy build-up had taken place. Consequently, the following day, Colonel Simlik ordered the two companies to move north, through the zone, toward the DMZ. This shift resulted in a number of significant engagements, during which the companies killed a total of 43 NVA troops.

Moving west toward Mutter's Ridge at dusk on the 26th, McAdams' 2d Platoon observed five enemy soldiers approaching its position through the thick stands of elephant grass which covered the region. The pla-

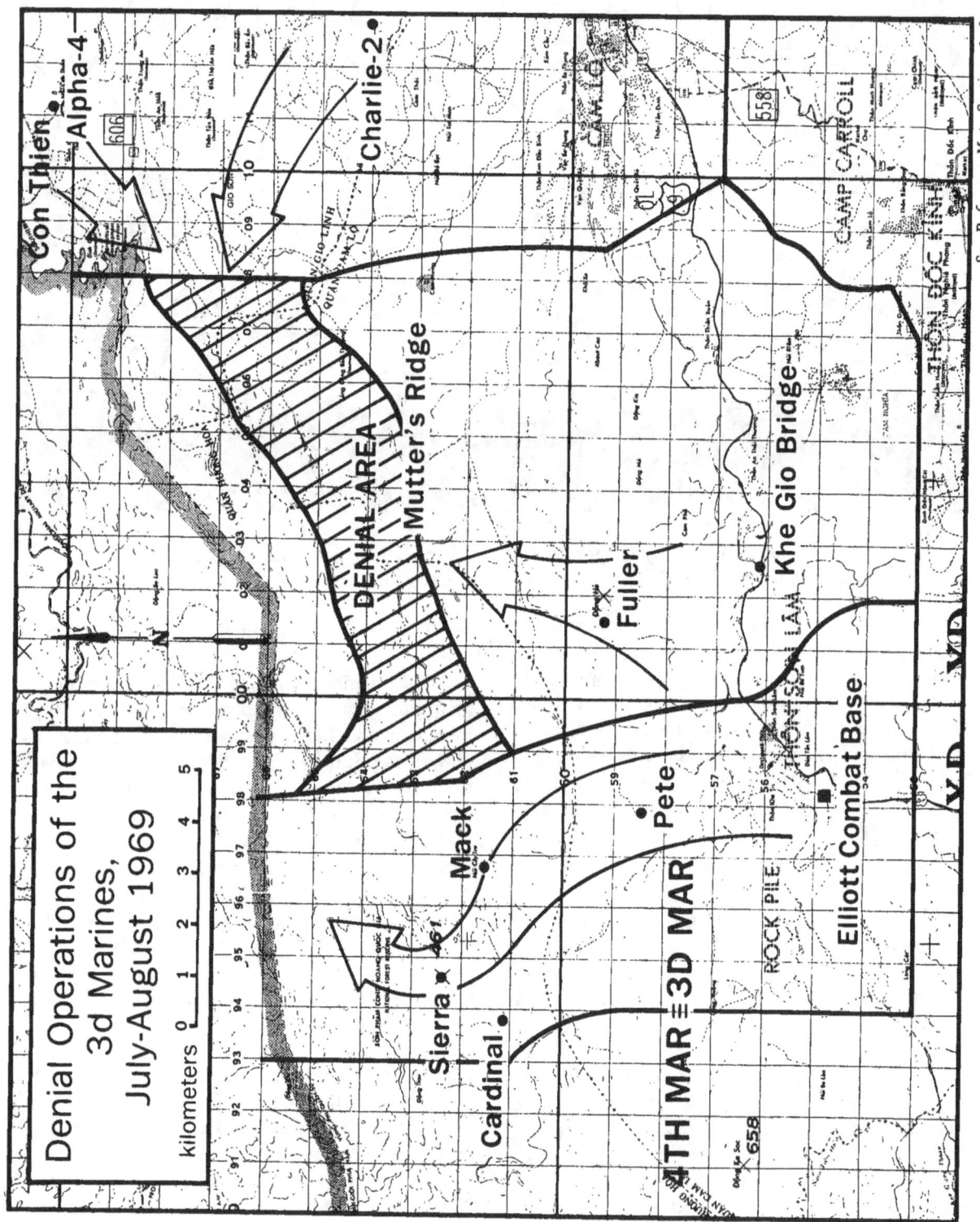

toon halted its advance, and took the five under fire with small arms and grenades, driving them into a ravine approximately 100 meters southwest of its position. Moving in squad blocking forces, the platoon commander then directed 60mm mortar fire on the enemy position. The platoon maintained its positions throughout the night in an effort to halt any enemy attempt at escape.

The following morning, as the 2d Platoon resumed its southwestward advance toward the 1st Platoon, it engaged an enemy force of undetermined strength. Batteries of Lieutenant Colonel Morgan W. West's 1st Battalion, 12th Marines fired missions to the north, blocking possible escape routes, while fixed-wing aircraft strafed the enemy position, "blowing bodies apart."[3] By noon, the 1st Platoon had killed five and the 2d three; the dead were clean shaven, with close haircuts, and dressed in fresh green uniforms, indicting recent infiltration from the North. Preceded by two additional flights of fixed-wing, both platoons then pushed north in pursuit. During the next two days, McAdams' company searched a six kilometer-square area bordering the DMZ, counting 40 NVA killed—17 by small arms, 10 by air, and 13 by artillery.

Having successfully searched the denial zone and the area lying between it and the DMZ, the two companies then reoriented their advance toward the southeast in order to serve as a mobile blocking force for a combined search and destroy operation through the Cam Hung Valley. At month's end, Lieutenant Colonel Herron's 1st Battalion remained split; two companies saturated the northern portion of the area of operations with patrols and ambushes, while two companies provided security for FSB Fuller, Khe Gio Bridge, Route 9, and Seabee road construction crews.

With the end of Operation Virginia Ridge on 16 July, Simlik's 3d Marines moved immediately into Operation Idaho Canyon. Although the concept remained essentially the same as that of Virginia Ridge, a number of changes were made within the area of operations. Due to the redeployment of the 9th Marines and the assumption of its area of operations by the 4th Marines, an extension of the regiment's western boundary took place. The expanded area of operations resulted in the minor realignment of the regiment's three battalions: while the 1st Battalion continued its role in the Denial Stingray Concept, the 2d Battalion began search and destroy operations north of Elliott Combat Base, and Lieutenant Colonel Schulze's 3d

Marine Corps Historical Collection
The point man with a rifle squad from the 1st Battalion, 3d Marines carefully moves through the jungle while on patrol south of the Demilitarized Zone.

Battalion continued operations west of Charlie-2 along Route 561.

Enemy activity within the eastern third of the area of operations at the beginning of Operation Idaho Canyon was generally small in scale and brief in duration, consisting of encounters with NVA reconnaissance teams of two to three men. In the latter part of July, NVA soldiers became more daring, launching strong attacks against elements of Lieutenant Colonel Schulze's 3d Battalion, operating in the Cam Hung. On 25 July, while searching four kilometers west of Charlie-2 for a reported large enemy force, First Lieutenant Terry L. Engle's Company I received fifteen 60mm mortar rounds, RPG, and small arms fire from a treeline north of its position. Engle's Marines countered with small arms while batteries of the 12th Marines shelled and then three fixed-wing flights raked the area with napalm, 750-pound, and Snakeye bombs. Coordinating with Company C, 1st Battalion to the west and Company K, supported by Company A, 3d Tank Battalion, to the north, Engle moved his platoons out in a systematic search of the area following the brief but fierce exchange. "The whole area," reported Lieutenant Engle, "reeked of burning flesh and the stink of dead. We could find only small bits of flesh and guts laying in all the trees," grim testimony to the ferocity of the air attack. As the company moved through the area, hindered somewhat by "still burning timber and napalm," the Marines counted 20 NVA dead, possibly more, killed by air; large amounts of mortar ammunition; and two complete 60mm mortars.[4]

The following morning, as Company I swept west and then east toward Charlie-2, Captain Paul B. Goodwin's Company K, supported by tanks, moved south, encountering heavy 82mm mortar fire on the 27th, and strong enemy resistance the following night. Shortly after midnight, while occupying sites south of the destroyed village of Gio Son, a platoon from Goodwin's company ambushed a small group of NVA moving down a trail, killing six and capturing two AK47 assault rifles. Two hours later, in presumed retaliation for the beating two days before by Engle's company, 35 to 40 NVA attacked the night defensive position of Goodwin's company. Concentrating their heaviest fire on the tanks, the attackers hit three, killing an equal number of Marines while wounding six. Goodwin's Marines repulsed the attack with strong machine gun and small arms fire, suffering few additional casualties. A search of the perimeter the following morning revealed numerous blood trails and drag marks, but only two enemy dead.

On 28 July, the 3d Marines assumed operational control of the 1st Brigade's 1st Battalion, 11th Infantry, supported by Company C, 1st Battalion, 77th Armor. In addition to providing security for Con Thien and Route 561, elements of the two Army battalions moved west, conducting search and destroy operations in the northern reaches of the Cam Hung Valley. As the infantry progressed, searching within one to two kilometers of the DMZ, the number of engagements with increasingly larger groups of NVA infiltrators rose. On 7 August, while Company D, 1st Battalion, 11th Infantry searched through an extensive bunker complex, 1,000 meters south of the zone's southern boundary, an estimated two enemy companies attacked. Although the intensity of combat varied throughout the day, a number of sharp exchanges of small arms and automatic weapons fire did take place, resulting in a total of 56 NVA killed and 26 weapons captured. Three Army infantrymen lost their lives and 13 received wounds in the daylong engagement.

With the beginning of a new month, the enemy shifted his effort away from the eastern portion of the Idaho Canyon area of operations to the western third. While enemy rockets and mortars intermittently pounded Con Thien and Charlie-2, and as elements of Lieutenant Colonels Herron's and Schulze's battalions continued their aggressive patrols, Marines of Lieutenant Colonel William S. Daniels' 2d Battalion engaged an ever-increasing number of fresh, energetic NVA troops.*

Operating northwest of Elliott Combat Base, Daniels' battalion centered its attention on Mutter's Ridge: Company H operated south of the ridge; Company E moved to the northwest; Company F searched to the northeast; while Company G provided security for Elliott. Each company in the field established a primary patrol base and then sent out squad-size patrols, ensuring maximum coverage of the area to be searched. Enemy activity during July had been extremely light as the NVA avoided contact and appeared to be skirting the battalion's area of operation; all was to change in August.

On the 7th, Captain Shawn W. Leach's Company F, while moving onto high ground two kilometers east of LZ Mack, atop Nui Oay Tre, encountered an estimated two companies of NVA in fortified positions. Aided by fixed-wing and artillery, Captain Leach ordered his 1st and 2d Platoons to seize the terrain. But with each heavily fought Marine gain, the enemy counterattacked with at least a reinforced platoon, forcing both Marine platoons to again withdraw. Although additional artillery and air strikes softened the enemy position, Leach's Marines could not make headway due to shortages of ammunition, high casualties, and a napalm-ignited brush fire which eventually drove the 2d Platoon into a heavily wooded area devoid of landing zones for the evacuation of wounded and resupply. Prior to dusk, a platoon from Company A, 1st Battalion helilifted into a landing zone several kilometers to the rear of Company F to reinforce the company's advance the following morning.

Company F resumed the attack on 8 August, meeting unexpectedly light resistance. By dusk, Leach's Marines seized the high ground, counting 46 NVA dead

---

*Lieutenant Colonel William S. Daniels replaced Lieutenant Colonel James J. McMonagle as Commanding Officer, 2d Battalion, 3d Marines on 2 August.

Meanwhile, less than 1,000 meters to the southwest, other elements of the *9th* hit Sinnott's 1st Platoon with a heavy ground and mortar attack from the west. The platoon returned fire, held its position with the assistance of accurate artillery and air strikes, and, accounted for 19 NVA dead. During the firefight, the platoon reported observing women removing enemy wounded from the battlefield. The 1st Platoon suffered six killed and 17 wounded in the predawn attack.

Soon after sunrise on the 10th, Lieutenant Colonel Daniels ordered Company A, 1st Battalion to link up with the three beleaguered platoons. But a number of problems were to delay the consolidation. Medical evacuation helicopters, given priority over those to be used in the troop lift, suffered a number of mechanical difficulties forcing them to return to Vandegrift. At the same time, accompanying Huey gunships repeatedly ran out of fuel and left station prior to the arrival of backup medical evacuation helicopters, again prolonging the evacuation of casualties. The shifting of landing zones due to incoming mortar rounds and the aircrafts' need to refuel delayed the lifts another six hours. It was not until late afternoon that Company A arrived in the objective area. During the interval, Sinnott consolidated his 1st and 2d Platoons, and with the arrival of Company A, the company, with the remnants of the 3d and Mortar Platoons, established a night defensive position in preparation for a coordinated attack the following morning.

Before an assault could be launched, the division ordered the battalion to withdraw. Under cover of darkness, the battalion moved south, leaving Company A to ensure the evacuation of the dead. The following morning, helicopters extracted Sinnott's company, lifting it to Cua Viet for a period of rest, reorganization, and subsequent security duty under the operational control of the 1st Brigade, 5th Infantry Division (Mechanized). The remainder of Daniels' battalion continued moving south on foot. Several days later, it shifted its operations to the eastern portion of the Idaho Canyon area, west of Cam Lo.

As a result of the attacks on Companies E and F and the increased enemy activity in the western sector of Idaho Canyon, Colonel Simlik issued an order which prevented any but platoon-size day patrols within the area three kilometers south of the DMZ, and also ordered that within five kilometers of the zone, company night defensive positions would be established after dark with all platoons physically consolidated. There were no size requirements placed on

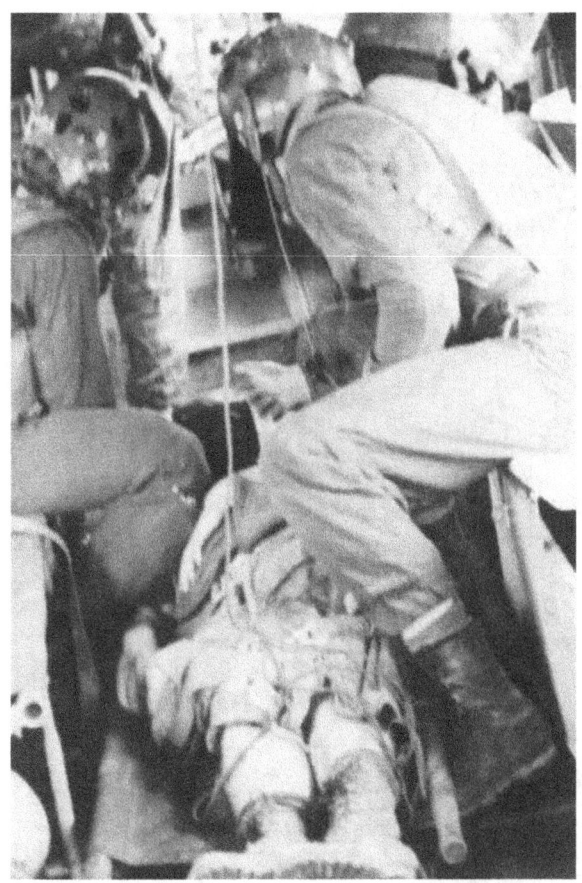

Marine Corps Historical Collection
A Marine Medium Helicopter Squadron 262 crew chief and Navy corpsman aid a wounded rifleman, who within minutes would be flown to a division medical facility or Navy hospital ship offshore.

and capturing 10 weapons. Documents found on the battlefield indicated that the NVA were members of the *1st* and *3d Battalions, 9th NVA Regiment, 304th NVA Division*, units new to the area of operations.

Two days later, while in night defensive positions northwest of LZ Sierra, a second reinforced company of the *9th Regiment* attacked the battalion's 81mm Mortar Platoon and 3d Platoon of Captain Paul J. Sinnott's Company E with grenades, satchel charges, and small arms fire. All communication with the platoons was lost for approximately an hour, forcing Batteries A and B, 1st Battalion, 12th Marines at Elliott to cease fire. Although the enemy company penetrated that portion of the perimeter manned by the mortar platoon, Sinnott's Marines staged a vicious fight, finally reestablishing their lines at sunrise. Within the perimeter lay 13 Marine dead and 58 wounded along with 17 NVA bodies.

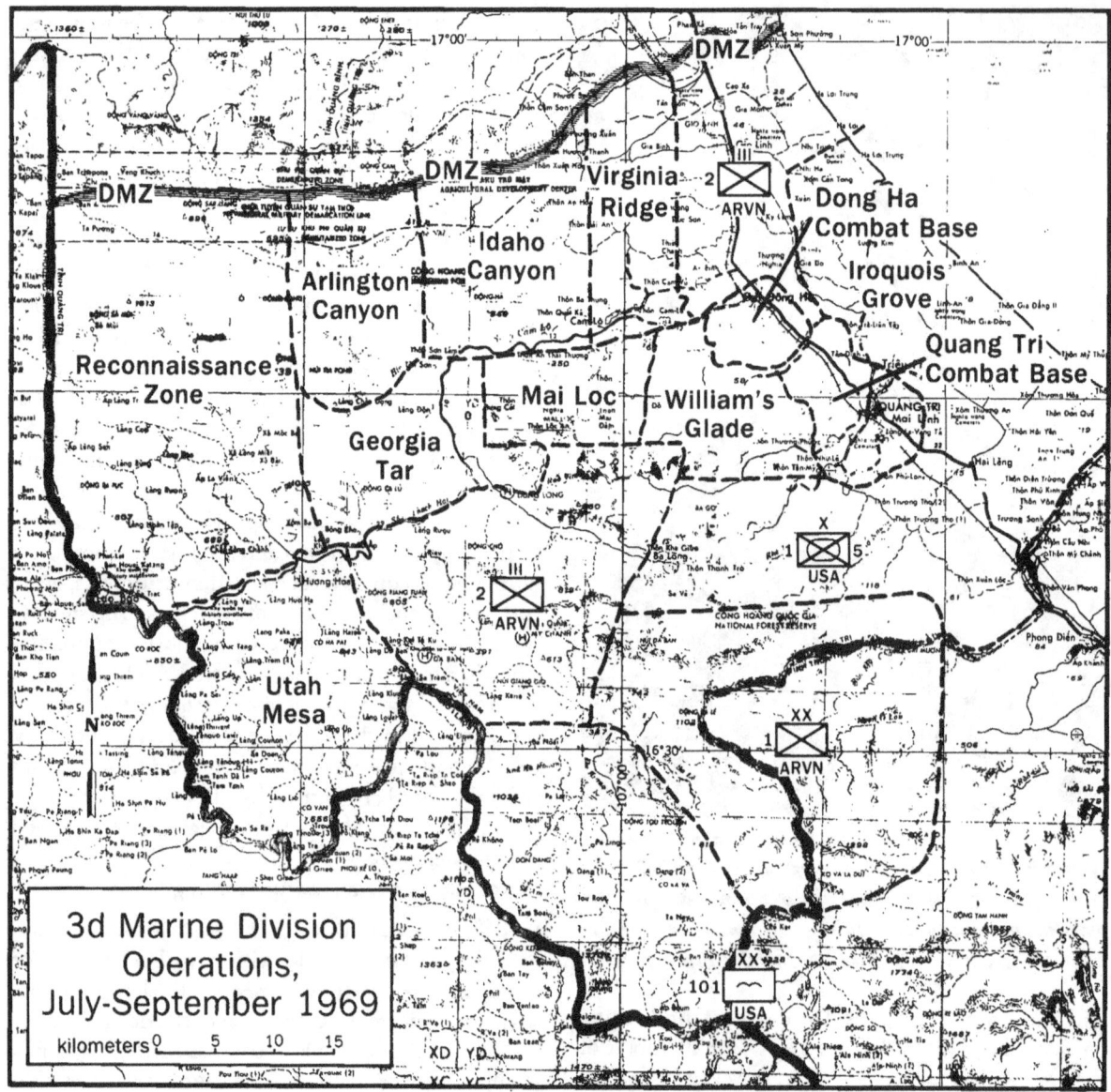

See Reference Map, Sections 1-8, 10-13, 16-18

movement south of the five-kilometer line. Simlik's orders later were incorporated into a division regulation which also directed all companies to move at least 1,000 meters per day and prohibited independent platoon operations. The forced movement of 1,000 meters was not well received by Marines in the field, as First Lieutenant Engle noted: "this got to be quite tiring. I believed it helped a few times, but many times it put my company in jeopardy, because I was starting to form a routine . . . . I felt it was stupid tactics, but this came all the way from the top."[5]

In mid-August, Lieutenant Colonel Schulze's battalion moved north and west of Charlie-2, its security mission at the outpost having been assumed by elements of the 1st Brigade, 5th Infantry Division (Mechanized). On the 11th, prior to the move, while sweeping west of the base, Company K engaged a small group of NVA. The enemy immediately broke contact. Continuing its sweep, the company, a short time later, surprised two NVA sapper platoons in the process of constructing bunkers. While artillery, gunships, and fixed-wing aircraft strafed the area, Captain Paul B. Goodwin's Marines fought the enemy sappers with mortar and small arms. A reaction force, consisting of one platoon from Company I with tanks, moved out from Charlie-2 and linked up with Goodwin's Marines, as elements of Company M secured blocking positions. The combined force assaulted and then searched the enemy redoubt, the battle raging throughout most of the day. Goodwin's Marines eventually found 19 enemy dead and large stocks of enemy equipment, while suffering 23 wounded in the engagement.

Following the brief but heavy fighting west of Charlie-2, Schulze's battalion shifted its operations into the western portion of the Idaho Canyon area on the 13th, replacing Lieutenant Colonel Daniels' battalion. The 3d Battalion, in addition to be being ordered to conduct search and destroy operations in the area of Mutter's Ridge, assumed responsibility for securing Elliott Combat Base and Route 9. Daniels' battalion, once again consolidated, moved into the southeastern portion of the area of operations and provided security for the Cam Lo District Headquarters, Charlie-3 Bridge, engineer construction crews on Route 558 south of Cam Lo, and portions of Route 9. The 1st Battalion, under Lieutenant Colonel Herron, remained in the center third of the area of operations conducting search and destroy operations east of Mutter's Ridge and Helicopter Valley, while providing security for Khe Gio Bridge, Fire Support Base Fuller, and its portion of Route 9. The 1st Battalion, 11th Infantry, along with the northeastern portion of the area of operations centered on Con Thien, was returned to the Army's 1st Brigade.

Few engagements took place throughout the area of operations following the mid-August shift in battalions. Although Herron's Marines sighted large groups of enemy infiltrators west of Dong Ha Mountain (Fire Support Base Fuller), and artillery and fixed-wing strikes were called, subsequent searches revealed comparatively few bodies in view of the numbers reported. As a result, Colonel Simlik increased the number of patrols and ambushes north of Fuller in order to lessen the possibility of enemy troops filtering down to interdict Route 9.

While Daniels' Marines engaged few enemy troops once they left Mutter's Ridge and moved east, 3d Battalion Marines under Lieutenant Colonel Ernest E. Evans, Jr., who had replaced Schulze on the 20th, were not as lucky. On the 22d, Company L, operating near LZ Sierra, 1,200 meters west of the 2d Battalion's encounter earlier in the month, came upon two reinforced NVA platoons occupying well-constructed, camouflaged bunkers situated in extremely steep, heavily vegetated terrain. Although one platoon of First Lieutenant James A. Burns' company was pinned down for a short time by two enemy .30-caliber machine guns, AK47s, and grenades, aggressive attacks by the remainder of the company, aided by air and artillery, enabled the platoon to withdraw with few casualties. The next day, following air and artillery fires, the company swept through the extensive complex, destroying the enemy redoubt along with 10 troops and an equal number of weapons.

Toward the end of the month the level of enemy activity again rose in the western two-thirds of the area of operations. On the 28th, Captain Gerald H. Sampson's Company B, 1st Battalion began a five-day-long series of engagements, resulting in 13 enemy killed. The first occurred approximately two kilometers north of Fuller when a reinforced NVA sapper platoon probed the company's night position. A vicious grenade, RPG, and small arms battle then ensued, during which the Marines of Company B repulsed the attack at a cost of three casualties—among them Captain Sampson. Three days later and 700 meters further north, Marines manning the perimeter observed seven to 10 NVA moving toward the company's night position, preparing again to attack. The Marines took the enemy under small arms fire, killing three and capturing their weapons. As the company swept north near the crest of Mutter's Ridge on the 1st of September, four more enemy troops were caught by Marine sharpshooters.

As Company B and the remainder of the regiment settled into night defensive positions on 2 September, Typhoon Diane swept ashore with 50-knot winds, wreaking havoc throughout the province. Despite little warning, the companies weathered the two-day storm. As First Lieutenant Terry Engle, Commanding Officer, Company I, 3d Battalion, later reported: "Somebody had failed to inform us that a typhoon was on the way.... Being ill prepared and not having any time to set up good hootches or dig real good holes, I suffered some casualties, mainly eight cases of trenchfoot, and felt I was going to suffer a lot more because of the cold, the rain, and the people standing in the water all night long.... The weather also hurt the NVA quite a bit, so I didn't worry about being attacked, at least during the typhoon."[6]

Installations, however, suffered most; roofs were blown off buildings, tents leveled, and there was extensive water damage to supplies and equipment. Fortunately, casualties were few throughout the regimental area: one Marine was seriously injured in a bunker collapse, and one killed when a watchtower at Cua Viet in which he was standing toppled to the ground.

After the short hiatus caused by Diane, enemy activity around LZ Sierra and LZ Mack in the western

Marine Corps Historical Collection

Despite rough terrain and suffocating temperatures, men of Company H, 2d Battalion, 3d Marines were required by division order to cover 1,000 meters per day while on patrol.

third of the Idaho Canyon area of operations again increased, although incidents were generally small in scale and brief. On the morning of 5 September, as First Lieutenant Engle's Company I occupied a night position near LZ Mack, company Marines detected movement beyond the perimeter. One NVA, thought to be point for a larger unit, was taken under fire. The call then went out, "we have movement on the lines," and Engle's Marines immediately went to 100 percent alert, donning their flak jackets, helmets, and manning the perimeter. Engle then called artillery, 61mm mortar, and three flights of fixed-wing within 400 meters of the company's position. The 3d Platoon then swept the area, finding three wounded enemy soldiers, two of whom were evacuated. During later interrogation of one of the prisoners, it was learned that he was part of four 10-man teams from the *1st Company, 1st Battlion, 9th NVA Regiment* who were under orders to attack and overrun Company I. The prisoners, whose ages ranged from 14 to 16, had spent one month training in Quang Binh Province, North Vietnam, and one month in combat below the DMZ. He also stated that morale in his unit was low due to the lack of food and supplies, destroyed by American air strikes, and that few of his comrades were willing to fight because they had received no mail from home in months. As later events would show, the prisoner spoke only for himself.

Another pause occurred between 8 and 11 September due to a ceasefire agreement, in observance of Ho Chi Minh's death on 3 September. A division order directed companies in the field to continue to move at least 1,000 meters per day, maintain a "defensive attitude," and not to call for artillery or air unless engaged. With his company on Mutter's Ridge, First Lieutenant Engle felt the order unjustified due to the "dangerous" location. His fears for the safety of his men proved accurate for on the 10th, as Company I swept through a site below LZ Sierra where several enemy troops had been observed, his 1st Platoon unknowingly walked into a typical "U"-shaped ambush, initiated by command detonated mines, small arms, and automatic weapons fire. Returning fire, Engle's Marines withdrew and called for artillery, but due to the truce, they were informed they would be limited to two rounds per gun, after three adjustments to register on target. Huey gunships, although under similar truce restraints, pounded the area with rockets, killing six NVA. Sweeping the ambush site, Engle's troops found an extensive complex of fighting holes and one additional NVA, all of which they destroyed. Company I then moved east, "that continual click, . . . to get out of the area," off Mutter's Ridge and south to Elliott Combat Base, where the Marines received beer, got haircuts and shaves, and relieved Company L on the base perimeter.[7]

Three days later, as Company L moved towards Mutter's Ridge to replace Company I, a scout dog alerted to enemy troops ahead, and First Lieutenant James A. Burns ordered a machine gun brought to the front. An unknown size NVA force then opened fire with small arms, RPGs, and grenades. The point platoon immediately withdrew after taking a number of casualties, including the company's commanding officer, Lieutenant Burns, and artillery, 81mm mortars, and a fixed-wing C-47 "Spooky" gunship was called on the enemy position. A sweep the following morning revealed eight enemy killed and numerous weapons scattered about the ambush site. Later the same day, Company L, now under Captain William D. Wester, moved south to LZ Bird where it joined Company M, and picked up a section of 81mm mortars for whom the company was to provide security.[8]

Meanwhile, a reinforced NVA platoon waylaid First Lieutenant Richmond D. O'Neill's Company K, while it moved toward LZ Sierra from Mack on the 15th, with claymore mines hung in trees, .30-caliber machine guns, grenade, RPG, and small arms fire. Initial casualties among O'Neill's Marines were two killed and 11 wounded. Forty-five minutes after the first firefight, the company began receiving 60mm enemy mortar fire which lasted approximately four hours, adding two more killed and 25 wounded. Lieutenant O'Neill then pulled his Marines back and allowed artillery, mortars, gunships, and fixed-wing to pound the ambush site and suspected enemy mortar positions. The Marines of Company K, in a sweep of the area, found eight NVA bodies, most killed by air.[9]

Shortly after midnight two days later, on Hill 154, adjacent to LZ Bird, a reinforced NVA company firing RPGs, small arms, and throwing grenades struck at Company L, now under the command of First Lieutenant Richard C. Hoffman. After two hours of vicious fighting, the enemy penetrated the 2d Platoon's lines, but soon were pushed back. Although Hoffman's Marines reestablished the perimeter, they continued to receive a heavy volume of RPG and machine gun fire from the northeast, despite the accurate support of five batteries of the 12th Marines, two "Spookys," and three flights of gunships. The assault and subsequent attack by fire lasted until first light when Hoffman sent out patrols to clear the field. As

Department of Defense Photo (USMC) A800600

Swollen by heavy monsoon rains, one of the many streams in the zone near Mutter's Ridge is forded by the men of 3d Battalion, 3d Marines during Operation Idaho Canyon.

the company's executive officer, First Lieutenant James P. Rigoulot, reported:

> The whole area was littered with chicoms [grenades], pieces of flesh, skin; we found a leg down the trail. There were quite a few of them out there. One machine gun hole had 13 gooks stacked up in front of it; the nearest one was about ten feet away. That one machine gun probably saved us from being overrun; they were right on us. The area was literally infested with them all over the place. We had numerous sightings from our position on the high ground; we could see them crossing rivers and milling around the area below.[10]

Hoffman's men killed a total of 41, while suffering 13 dead and 23 wounded.

At 0805 the following morning, a "Bald Eagle" reaction force, Captain David M. Jordan's Company I, 3d Battalion, 4th Marines, helilifted from Vandegrift Combat Base into LZ Cardinal, southwest of Sierra. Moving out of the landing zone and then along a ridgeline to the southeast toward the beleaguered company near LZ Bird, Jordan's point element spotted and then took two enemy troops under fire. Once engaged, the NVA blew a claymore mine, forcing the rest of the company to withdraw a short distance, set up a 360-degree perimeter defense, and lay down a heavy base of fire in support of the marooned point. Gaining immediate fire superiority, Jordan ordered a squad to bring the 11-man point element, nine of whom were casualties, back into the company position. Gunships and artillery strafed and bombarded the suspected enemy position and a helicopter arrived to evacuate the dead and wounded.

The exchange continued throughout the day as Jordan's Marines countered the hail of enemy grenades, heavy automatic weapons, and accurate sniper fire. Late in the afternoon, before the company could again move, enemy mortar rounds began impacting on the company's position, killing four more Marines. At dusk, another medical evacuation helicopter removed the second group of casualties, after which the company settled in for the night without the requested ammunition resupply, denied by the 3d Battalion, 3d Marines. With a "Spooky" gunship on station and artillery on call, Jordan's Marines spent an "extremely quiet" night; not a shot was fired. It was so quiet that Jordan figured the 3d Marines "wrote us off the books; they thought they had lost another Marine company up there" on Mutter's Ridge.[11]

The following morning, the company swept unopposed through the evacuated enemy position, finding nine bodies, numerous arms, and a large quantity of equipment. As Captain Jordan later reported, "the enemy had a tremendous amount of Marine 782 gear [packs, cartridge belts], or at least U.S. issue-type, whether it came from Marine units is unknown. But they had so many Marine-type haversacks that they were using them for sandbags. They would fill the haversacks with dirt and were using these for sandbags around their positions." Not wanting to retrace its previous route of advance, Company I moved southeast along the ridgeline and then onto Hill 154, from where it lifted to Vandegrift. During their two-day sojourn with the 3d Marines, Jordan's Marines suffered nine killed and 38 wounded.[12]

After the heavy ground attack on the 17th, First Lieutenant Hoffman's company and a 63-man reaction platoon from Company H, 2d Battalion, moved off Hill 154 and onto a small hill, 300 meters southeast of LZ Bird, overlooking the Song Cam Lo. Early on the morning of the 19th, Hoffman's Marines awoke to the sound of explosions, signaling yet another attack. Shortly after 0400, an estimated NVA platoon hit the company with a heavy volume of grenades and RPG rounds; the enemy employed no small arms. Although Hoffman requested artillery, there was no illumination to adjust the rounds; "they hit all over the place." The company, even though heavily engaged for more than an hour, took no casualties in the attack. However, later that morning, after observing and then killing three NVA crossing the river below, the company took two RPG rounds, one of which detonated a friendly mortar round, killing one Marine and wounding eight. These nine proved to be the last casualties the company took. That night the company moved to LZ Pete, linked up with Company M, and the next morning, lifted out of the area of operations. "When we left LZ Pete," the executive officer reported, "we lifted out with a fighting strength, counting attachments, of 92 people, and we walked in [on 13 August] with 156."[13]

Although a majority of the activity within the area of operations centered around Landing Zones Sierra and Mack during the last weeks of Idaho Canyon, the 1st and 2d Battalions persisted in their pursuit of the NVA. Working north of Fire Support Base Fuller, Lieutenant Colonel Herron's 1st Battalion continued to conduct aggressive search and destroy operations east of Mutter's Ridge and Helicopter Valley, meeting light enemy resistance. Lieutenant Colonel Daniels' 2d Battalion, occupying the easternmost portion of the area of operations, saturated the Cam Lo District with patrols and ambushes, and like the 1st Battalion, it too had little contact. Both battalions continued their efforts until mid-September when the regiment alerted Daniels' battalion and then directed it to relieve the 3d Battalion at Elliott Combat Base and on Mutter's Ridge on the 19th. But before the shift could take place, the division ordered the 3d Marines to cease all offensive operations and to stand down in preparation for redeployment from Vietnam.

During the 68-day operation, a marked change occurred in the character and tactics of the enemy. At the outset, the NVA operated in small units, concentrating on ambushes, stand-off attacks by fire, and minelaying along roads, all under the cover of darkness. By the 23d day, 7 August, Colonel Simlik's Marines faced well-equipped, well-trained enemy units of battalion size, later determined to be the three battalions of the *9th NVA Regiment*. Surprise, use of heavy firepower, and a violent determination to maintain contact now characterized enemy initiated attacks. Engagements, previously terminated at sunrise, continued into daylight, where the enemy would be most vulnerable to Marine supporting arms. To counter the effects of these tactical changes, the 3d Marines employed deliberate, careful, and methodical search and destroy techniques, coupled with the intelligent use of artillery and air power, which left the NVA only three options: move to a new position, thereby exposing troops; remain in position and fight; or attack. And as the final totals, 563 enemy killed and 201 weapons captured, indicated, the 3d Marines proved ready and eager to meet the NVA in whichever course of action the enemy chose.

"A Significant Step"

The standdown of the 3d Marines signaled the beginning of the second phase of redeployment. In the midst of the first United States troop withdrawal from South Vietnam, consideration was given to further troop reductions. At Midway in early June, President Nixon had suggested that a decision on future withdrawals would be made in August or shortly thereafter. Others recommended an accelerated withdrawal. Writing in the summer issue of *Foreign Affairs*, former Secretary of Defense Clark Clifford proposed the withdrawal of 100,000 troops by the end of the year and all ground combat troops by the end of December 1970.[14] On 19 June, in commenting on Clifford's proposal, President Nixon stated: "We have started to withdraw forces. We will withdraw more. Another decision will be made in August." Refusing to indicate a specific number, the President did note that "as far as how many will be withdrawn by the end of the year, or the end of next year, I would hope that we could beat Mr. Clifford's timetable."[15]

As a result of the President's comments at the June news conference, planning for additional troop reductions began at all levels. MACV was to assess progress and submit a proposal on further reductions together with a detailed troop list by 10 August in preparation for a presidential announcement on the subject around the 15th, and withdrawal in September. Both MACV and the Joint Chiefs of Staff assumed that the second withdrawal would be 25,000, although the President and Secretary of Defense Laird had expressed a desire that the total reduction for the year was to exceed the Clifford figure of 100,000.

On 30 July, President Nixon paid an unscheduled visit to South Vietnam during the course of a trip to the Pacific and then to Europe. There he talked with both President Thieu and General Abrams not only about the current situation, but also about further United States troop reductions.[16] In Abrams' conversations with Nixon, the general noted that while a second withdrawal of 25,000 was feasible, considering the improvements made by the RVNAF, he was opposed to a larger figure. Nevertheless, the President returned to Washington convinced that the next reduction could be more than 25,000 combat troops, with headquarters and support forces making up the difference.

Early in August, MACV and CinCPac submitted their assessments of the initial troop withdrawal and their views on future reductions. Both recommended a maximum reduction of 25,000. The Joint Chiefs of Staff, likewise, recommended a withdrawal of 25,000 which could begin in late September and be completed by the end of November, barring a significant change in the enemy situation. They could not recommend a higher figure due to current enemy disposition throughout South Vietnam and status of the RVNAF, still overly dependent on extensive American support.

Unwilling to limit the reduction to 25,000, both the President and Secretary Laird asked the Joint Chiefs to reconsider their recommendations and to propose an alternative that would reduce the troop ceiling well below that of 499,500 proposed by MACV. What emerged at the end of August was a revised Phase II package that reduced the Vietnam authorization to 484,000 by 15 December. Of the 40,500 spaces included, 9,500 would not be filled, meaning an actual reduction of 31,000. In submitting the revised package to the Secretary of Defense, the Joint Chiefs of Staff warned that such a reduction without substantial decline in the enemy threat placed not only the remaining troops, but the Government of South Vietnam at serious risk and was without justification on military grounds.

Planning for redeployment went hand-in-hand with that of Vietnamization. On 25 August, the Joint Chiefs submitted the final Vietnamization, or T-Day plan to the Secretary of Defense, completing the exercise begun with the preparation of the initial plan in May. In addition to the objectives set forth in the initial plan, the final plan included a number of military guidelines: emphasis was to be placed on combined military operations, protection of populated areas, pacification, and improvement of the RVNAF in accordance with the "one war" concept; combined United States-South Vietnamese operations would

Two riflemen of Company M, 3d Battalion, 3d Marines pause for a rest and cigarette during a heavy thunderstorm while on patrol just below Mutter's Ridge.
Department of Defense Photo (USMC) A800598

continue out of necessity and in order to improve the effectiveness of the RVNAF; as feasible, as United States units and then South Vietnamese were withdrawn from selected areas, Regional and Popular Forces and then internal security forces were to assume responsibility; American residual forces were not only to furnish the South Vietnamese with combat and service support, but to relieve South Vietnamese forces of responsibility for pacification and be prepared for emergency reinforcement; as combat responsibility progressively was transferred to the RVNAF, U.S. forces would be redeployed; and current programs whose goal was to expand South Vietnamese forces would be continued. Incorporating the timetables included in the initial plan, the Joint Chiefs proposed a reduction of 264,000 in 18 months and 282,000 in 42 months. As in the initial plan, they concluded that Vietnamization should proceed on a "cut-and-try" basis, with periodic assessments of the situation determining the pace.

By early September, President Nixon had reviewed both the final plan for Vietnamization and Phase II redeployment recommendations. On the 12th, he met with his political and military advisers and informed them that he had accepted the Joint Chiefs of Staff revised redeployment package and that he would announce it formally on the 16th. As to the final plan for Vietnamizing the war, the President made no decision, but he did specify that any further troops withdrawals would be based on full consideration of the three previously set-forth criteria. By postponing a decision, the President in effect adopted the Joint Chiefs' "cut-and-try" approach to redeployment.[17]

In a televised statement on the night of the 16th, the President announced that "after careful consideration with my senior civilian and military advisers and in full consultation with the Government of Vietnam, I have decided to reduce the authorized troop ceiling in Vietnam to 484,000 by December 15." Under the newly authorized ceiling, he noted, a minimum of 60,000 troops would be withdrawn by mid-December. It was, he concluded, "a significant step" in which "both sides turned their faces toward peace rather than toward conflict and war."[18] With the President's announcement, movement planning within the Pacific Command got underway.

Planning by FMFPac and III MAF for Phase II, codenamed Keystone Cardinal, of the division's redeployment had been carried out simultaneously with the deployment of the 9th Marines and was completed with the departure of the last elements of the regimental landing team. The timing and composition of the Marine contingent of the 31,000-man reduction, however, remained unresolved until the President's announcement, despite the fact that only two choices existed: Colonel Simlik's 3d Marines or Colonel Goggin's 4th Marines. Once FMFPac and III MAF had made the decision, it remained closely held, as Colonel Simlik later remembered:

> We were in the ridiculous situation of the Division commander being forbidden to tell the Regimental commander that his regiment would be deployed out of Vietnam. But there were rumors, and I let the Division staff know that I knew that my regiment would be moving. There were some comic-opera exchanges. I guess the administration, Washington that is, was afraid the press would break the news before the event took place. But the press was not fooled. I recall reporters coming to my CP and saying, "Well, what is your reaction about the withdrawal?" And I had not been informed, officially, and I had to play it awfully dumb. And of course rumors got down to the troops, and this had an impact upon the fighting morale of the troops because nobody, of course, wanted to be the last man killed. And I'm convinced the enemy had some wind of it, too, because during that time they staged a couple of vicious local attacks against our patrols.[19]

With the president's announcement on the 16th, III MAF ordered the 3d Marines and its direct support elements (1st Battalion, 12th Marines; Company B, 3d Engineer Battalion; Company B, 11th Engineer Battalion; Company C, 3d Medical Battalion; Company B, 3d Motor Transport Battalion; Company B, 9th Motor Transport Battalion; Company A, 3d Reconnaissance Battalion; Company A, 3d Shore Party Battalion; and the 3d Bridge Company), making up the regimental landing team, to stand down in preparation for redeployment on 1 October to the United States.

On 20 September, elements of the 3d Battalion, 3d Marines lifted out of the field to Vandegrift Combat Base, and then moved by truck to Quang Tri Combat Base. "It was not an ordinary withdrawal from lines," noted Colonel Simlik, "no unit came on-line to relieve us. Other on-line units extended their lines in order to fill the large gap when we pulled out. And it was a large gap."[20] During the next two days, the remaining elements of the regiment and its support units withdrew from combat and moved to either Dong Ha or Quang Tri Combat Bases, where, because of the weather, they found themselves "hip high in mud."[21]

As elements of the 3d Marines withdrew, the 4th Marines shifted east, occupying Elliott Combat Base and Fire Support Base Fuller, and the 1st Brigade, 5th Infantry Division (Mechanized) moved west, closing the gap. A large portion of the 4th Marines area of operations was then redesignated a reconnaissance zone, and Fire Support Bases Russell, Cates, Shepherd, and Hill 950 leveled. After a short period, Vandegrift Combat Base, too, would be closed, as both the 1st ARVN Division and the 101st Airborne Division, which was to assume the mission of screening the western portion of Quang Tri Province, rejected the offer of occupying the vacated Marine bases, wishing instead to build new ones, as Major General William K. Jones later recalled:

> We started closing back on Vandegrift. That meant closing down fire support bases, and it became obvious that the last one we wanted to close was Fuller because that was defending Vandegrift from the north there, of course, and Cates which was a brand new one that we'd built that overlooked Khe Sanh that was controlling Route 9 coming from west to east. At that stage of the game, the 101st Airborne was directed to take over. They were to have a screening mission in front of the 1st ARVN Division which was to take over the 3d Division headquarters at Dong Ha and the whole area that we were vacating in Quang Tri. So, the 101st took a look and they decided they didn't want to keep any of our fire support bases. I don't understand why because they opened up some new ones and they weren't as good. It didn't make sense, but it was just one of those things. So we had to close down these bases.[22]

Although preparations for the regimental landing team's redeployment went well, despite the limited time available, a number of problems arose. During the few days at Quang Tri and Dong Ha before either being flown to Da Nang for departure or transferred to another Marine unit under the "Mixmaster" program, 3d Marines tempers flared. "Marines who had fought a common enemy just a few days earlier, now fought each other." "I'm convinced," Colonel Simlik later recounted, "that part of the problem was caused by a group of journalists who came up while we were on-line and asked to interview troops . . . . I later learned that they asked a number of racially inflammatory questions. They segregated some black Marines,

President Nixon and South Vietnamese President Thieu, accompanied by, from left, Special Advisor Henry Kissinger, Vice President Nguyen Cao Ky, and American Ambassador Ellsworth Bunker, descend the steps of Independence Palace during the American president's unannounced visit to Saigon in July, when troop withdrawals were again discussed.

Department of Defense Photo (USA) SC651157

Department of Defense Photo (USA) C55922

Discussing the planned withdrawals, Gen Earle G. Wheeler, left, Chairman of the Joint Chiefs of Staff; Gen Creighton W. Abrams, center; and Adm John S. McCain, Commander in Chief, Pacific, meet at MACV Headquarters in Long Binh, outside of Saigon.

for instance, and asked, 'Isn't it true that you've done more than your share?' and this sort of thing. This eventually planted seeds of discontent which erupted in violence in the rear areas," resulting in the murder of one Marine.[23]

With Simlik's ability to control the regiment "lessening rapidly in the fast moving events," the division requested that the troops be moved "out of the explosive environment as quickly as possible." Although FMFPac complied with the requested change in movement schedules, many continued to question the underlying reason. In answer, Colonel Raymond C. Damm, chief of the division's Redeployment Planning Group said that he "thought the Marine Corps could ill afford a racially inspired riot in the middle of a redeployment that the world was watching." With that response, all questioning ceased.[24]

One of the most aggravating problems proved to be passing Department of Agriculture inspection. All gear, all equipment, and all vehicles being returned to the United States had to be spotless, so as to prevent the introduction of any foreign insect or plant disease. But with "the mud of Vietnam, with vehicles that had been in combat only a few days before, this was a very difficult task to accomplish." As a result, Marine engineers quickly set up hosing-down facilities at the Cua Viet embarkation point where all equipment was scrubbed before being loaded on board ship. It "was one of those little things which you don't ordinarily think of that gave us headaches," noted Colonel Simlik, "but it created all sorts of scheduling problems and initially slowed down our operations quite a bit."[25]

Five days prior to the embarkation of the equipment and troops, III MAF informed the regiment that President Nixon was interested in journeying to the Marine Corps Air Station at El Toro to welcome the 3d Marines. As Colonel Simlik later recounted:

> We wiped the mud from our boots, and took 150 Marines eligible for rotation to the States down to the airbase at Da Nang. The word was that when we disembarked from the airplane at El Toro we were to be in starched utilities, bright new helmet covers, and spit-shined boots. FLC [Force Logistic Command] somehow rounded up the gear for us, and for three days we practiced getting on and off a 707 airplane so we would look sharp for the President.... We brought 150 from Dong Ha to Da Nang, and pared this down to 135, a 707 load.... When we landed at Okinawa, the first stop on the way back, we confounded the air controllers by staging a dress rehearsal. And so we flew back to the States, changing into new uniforms 15 minutes from El Toro. Of course, the President was not there; [Under] Secretary [of the Navy] John Warner was.... It was a strange war indeed.[26]

Colonel Simlik, having not completed his tour, flew back to the 3d Marine Division and the mud of Dong Ha.

On 1 October, the rest of the 3d Marines departed Dong Ha for Da Nang where, on the 5th, they boarded the *Washburn* (LKA 108), *Iwo Jima* (LPH 2), and the *Bexar* (LPA 237). The majority of the regimental landing team's support elements remained behind, being scheduled to depart from Cua Viet. The following day, as the amphibious ships departed Da Nang Harbor, III MAF passed command of the 3d Marines to the 5th Marine Amphibious Brigade, Camp Pendleton, California. Of the 3d Marine Division's infantry regiments in Quang Tri Province, only the 4th Marines remained.

Specter of Anarchy

The incident of violence which erupted among the Marines of Colonel Simlik's regiment was symptomatic of the gradual deterioration of discipline and unrest affecting all the Armed Services. By late 1969, riots and acts of sabotage had occurred at a number of military bases and on board ship; officers and enlisted men alike had refused assignment to Vietnam; small groups of troops had refused to fight; drug abuse and minor defiance of regulations had become commonplace; and officers and noncommissioned officers had faced the threat of assassination ("fragging") by their own men. In addition, an ever-increasing number of servicemen had joined radical groups whose aims included ending the war and revolutionizing the Services, and militant blacks had set themselves apart by the use of "Black Power" symbols, and had actively challenged authority citing alleged discrimination as the basis of their discontent.

These problems facing the military resulted not only from the carrying over of the divisions and tensions then existing within American society, but from the nature of the Vietnam War itself. Unlike other conflicts, active combat in Vietnam was not continuous, resulting, as the war progressed, in increasing periods of boredom and restlessness. This boredom and restlessness oftentimes manifested itself in excessive drinking, drug abuse, and violence, especially among those troops occupying secure rear areas. Length of assignment, frequent personnel turnover, and inadequate training also had an affect, as did the prospect of redeployment. Men found it increasingly difficult to maintain a sense of purpose in a war that was unsupported at home and coming to an end without decisive results.

For III MAF Marines in 1969, the most disruptive and difficult to understand problem was that of violence among their ranks, violence toward officers and NCOs and violence among white and black Marines. "This war has produced one form of felony that no other war has ever had; more despicable and inexplicable thing [than] in any wars that I have ever seen," noted Colonel Robert H. Barrow. "And that is the felonious attack of one Marine against another, very often with a hand grenade." During World War II and Korea, he recalled, "you always heard these stories about somebody allegedly said that if so-and-so didn't do such-and-such in the next battle, he would get it in the back. I don't think this ever happened. I don't think anyone ever recalls some officer or some NCO being killed in combat by his own troops intentionally. In Vietnam, yes. We had several of these."[27]

The number of "fraggings," the attempted murder of an officer or NCO by an enlisted man, often by means of an M26 fragmentation grenade, increased dramatically in 1969. During the first five months of the year, the 3d Marine Division reported 15 such incidents.[28] Similar incidents also occurred in the 1st Division, 1st Aircraft Wing, and Force Logistic Command.* Of the 15 fraggings which took place in the 3d Marine Division, most occurred in secure rear areas such as Vandegrift and Quang Tri Combat Bases, and were committed by enlisted men against NCOs and junior officers. Motives varied from drug disputes and racial hatred to the desire to rid the unit of a particularly aggressive commander.

Of the 3d Marine Division incidents, the most indicative was that of the murder of First Lieutenant Robert Timothy Rohweller, Commanding Officer, Company K, 3d Battalion, 9th Marines on 21 April. As Lieutenant Colonel Elliott R. Laine, Jr., commanding the battalion, recalled:

> [Lieutenant Rohweller] was a mustang and, as a matter of fact, had a previous tour in Vietnam as a sergeant in Recon. He was a hardcharger and widely recognized as a superior leader . . . . As it happened, there were six Marines in the rear who didn't care to go forward and the 1stSgt was apparently unable to force them to do so. This continued for several days until Lt Rohweller left FSB Vandegrift for the company rear. Upon confronting the recalcitrant six, . . . the six conspired to kill the Lt by fragging him. Apparently aware that the confrontation was not finally resolved, Lt Rohweller was wary enough that he went to chow that evening with his .45 stuck in the waistband of his cammies, under his shirt, and later to the club, similarly armed. A frag grenade was acquired and two of the six . . . went to the hut where the Lt was sleeping . . . . The fragging itself involved one of the six [who] . . . rolled the grenade into the hootch . . . . Though he was quickly evacuated by jeep, [Lieutenant Rohweller] died within an hour or so.[29]

The company executive officer immediately held a formation and the accused were apprehended. Of the six Marines involved, four were charged with the murder and of the four, one was granted immunity in exchange for his testimony against the others. The re-

---

*Records are nonexistent or incomplete as to the number of fraggings which took place in 1969 among the Marine units of III Marine Amphibious Force.

maining three were tried by courts-martial and two convicted and one found not guilty.

Procedures to deal with the apprehension and conviction of the perpetrators varied. Whether out of fear or friendship, Marines hesitated to turn in their peers, despite appeals which pointed out that it was "against their family upbringing, against their religion, against their concept of America and fair play, and of the Marine tradition." Initially, each individual commander had his own "pet idea" of what should be done, ranging from an immediate response to any intimidation, no matter how minor, to looking the other way. But by mid-1969, Major General William K. Jones, Commanding General, 3d Marine Division, felt that the problem had grown to such an extent that a formal response was necessary, even demanded. "Basically," he recalled "it was that you just don't put up with this stuff and you go after these guys and you don't allow them to utilize the technique of intimidation to hide behind and to terrorize their fellow Marines."[30]

In July, Jones issued a set of procedures to deal with the apprehension of individuals involved in acts of violence against Marines of the command. Under the procedures, any fragging or other act of violence would be met with a swift, massive reaction which was to be thorough, serious, and determined in detecting and apprehending violators. Military police or an infantry reaction force immediately would isolate the area of the incident. Commanders would assemble their men and conduct a roll call, so as to determine who was missing and who was in that area that should not be. All sergeants and below would then be ordered to their living quarters and directed to stay there until called for, while teams led by an officer searched the incident site and each tent or hut. Meanwhile, an interrogation area would be set up where Criminal Investigation Division personnel, assisted by the unit legal officer, would question each Marine about the incident privately, assuring him of the commanding general's promise to protect those who would identify the guilty and testify. This process would continue until

Marines of Headquarters and Service Company and Maintenance Company, Logistic Support Group Bravo meet in an intramural football game at Dong Ha. An active intramural sports program was one of many means used to defuse rising tensions in rear areas.

Abel Papers, Marine Corps Historical Center

all suspects had been identified and arrested. All leave and personnel rotations were to be postponed until the process was complete.[31] In addition to the SOP, Jones also ordered all division clubs closed by 2130 and imposed a 2200 curfew; the Military Police Company to be carried overstrength; the creation of an intramural athletic program; and institution of regularly-held commander's conferences on the subject.[32]

These changes had an effect, as did the redeployment of the division to Okinawa, later in the year. Jones' SOP would be used as a basis for developing Operation Freeze, instituted by III MAF the following year. The operation and its associated measures produced not only a decline in the number of fraggings, but a rise in the number of cases solved.

Equally troubling to Marine commanders was the problem of racial tension. Since the integration of the Services in the late 1940s and early 1950s, all military specialties were open to Marines of all races; formal discrimination in promotions and assignments was forbidden; and the command structure, on-base housing, and recreational facilities were completely desegregated. While white and black Marines lived and worked together in integrated units, *de facto* segregation remained. On and off duty, Marines resegregated themselves. In dining facilities, recreational areas, and clubs, Marines tended to break up into small groups along racial lines. In spite of the formal abolition of discrimination in duty assignments, black Marines tended not to be assigned to the more highly technical military specialties because of educational and social disadvantages, and possibly prejudice. In liberty areas near Marine bases, there were facilities which catered exclusively to one race or the other, as did a majority of off-base private rental housing.

By the late 1960s, after years of civil rights agitation and progress, a large proportion of blacks entering the Marine Corps were unwilling to accept these remaining vestiges of real or perceived discrimination and prejudice. Imbued with a feeling of racial pride, they requested "soul" food in the messhalls and "soul" music in the clubs, wore "Afro" haircuts, and used "Black Power" salutes. A small minority, however, aggressively challenged the chain of command by attempting to form an alternative power structure and actively created or intensified racial grievances. These groups of militants also singled out whites and nonconforming blacks for retribution. Typically, quarrels broke out in enlisted men's clubs and culminated in groups of blacks roaming the base attacking white Marines. In retaliation, whites assaulted blacks.

Such outbreaks of racial violence by late 1968 were common to most major Marine bases throughout the world. In October, III MAF experienced a series of incidents with racial overtones, varying in degree of violence from large-scale riots to individual fights, muggings, and robberies. In response to the serious situation, General Cushman established a system of committees to monitor and recommend appropriate action on racial tensions, the rising number of incidents, and to serve as focal points for problems in race relations. The I Corps Tactical Zone Watch Committee, composed of representatives of each major subordinate and component command, was to meet to discuss incidents and the proposed responses. Subordinate command committees were to receive, discuss, and take action on reports received from "Action Committees," composed of junior officers and NCOs of varying ranks and races. The local action committees were to advise the command on race relations, serve as a focal point for the collection of information bearing on racial activities, and act as a sounding board for possible injustice and prejudice.[33]

The III MAF committee structure remained in effect throughout 1969. Although meeting regularly, the local action committees soon seemed to degenerate into debating platforms for militants or into general "gripe" sessions on nonracial issues. As a result, the local committee system was revamped in 1970 to deal almost exclusively with race relations and not with "gripes," which could better be handled through the normal chain of command.

In an effort to deal with the problem Corps-wide, General Chapman, on 2 September, issued ALMAR 65, a directive to all Marines on "Race Relations and Instances of Racial Violence within the Marine Corps." Prefacing his remarks with the admonition that acts of violence between Marines "cannot be tolerated, and must stop," the Commandant declared:

> It is now and has long been our policy in the Marine Corps that discrimination in any form is not tolerated. It has similarly been our policy that a fighting organization such as ours must have a solid foundation of firm, impartial discipline. It is in the context of these two basic policies that we must take measures to dispel the racial problems that currently exist.

Chapman instructed all Marine commanders to make "positive and overt efforts to eradicate every trace of discrimination, whether intentional or not." He directed them to identify the "causes of friction, rather than the symptoms," to discuss them frankly and openly, and to eliminate them wherever possible. Chapman urged all officers and NCOs, in their roles as leaders and instructors, to combat racial strife and ensure that every Marine understands that the Marine Corps "guarantees equal rights, equal opportunity, and equal protection, without regard to race, and will continue to do so." In what was to become the most controversial portion of the directive, the Commandant instructed commanders to permit the wearing of the "Afro/Natural haircut provided it conforms with current Marine Corps regulations." In addition, he forbade any "actions, signs, symbols, gestures, and words which are contrary to tradition" to be used during formations or in rendering military courtesies to the flag, the national anthem, or individuals. However, he declared that "individual signs between groups or individuals will be accepted for what they are—gestures of recognition and unity; in this connection, it is the Marine Corps policy that, while such actions are to be discouraged, they are nevertheless expressions of individual belief and are not, in themselves, prohibited."[34] Chapman's sanctioning of "Afro" haircuts and "Black Power" salutes was to draw immediate criticism from many Marines who viewed the approval as divisive and constituted the granting of special privileges to a minority.[35]

In addition to ALMAR 65, Headquarters Marine Corps established the Equal Opportunities Branch to deal with minority group problems affecting the entire Corps and began a concerted drive to recruit more black officers.[36] Although progress in resolving racial conflicts was slow in 1969, III MAF's committee system and ALMAR 65 established the basic framework upon which the Corps could build in the area of race relations into the 1970s.

Next to fraggings and racial tension, the rapidly increasing use of drugs troubled Marine commanders. In 1967, MACV identified 1,713 military personnel who possessed or used illegal drugs out of a total troop strength of 468,000. The problem at that time was considered minor; "there is no epidemic of marijuana use," reported III MAF.[37] By 1969, the opposite was true; drug abuse among American troops had reached crisis proportions. As Colonel Peter J. Mulroney, Commanding Officer, 12th Marines, told a group of his peers at FMFPac Headquarters in July 1969, the use of drugs, especially marijuana, "is more widespread than anyone would care to admit. Every one of my battalions has investigations going on all the time. It is almost impossible to keep somebody that wants to get marijuana from getting it. [It is] sold at every roadside ville and peddled by all the civilians."[38] Unit commanders conservatively estimated that half their men were involved with drugs.

Among III MAF Marines, marijuana was the most prevalent narcotic, followed by illegally obtained stimulants and barbiturates. Heroin use remained rare. Marines from all racial, social, economic, and education levels used drugs in about equal proportions. Troops in the field commonly avoided drugs, while among those in rear areas and support units drug use at times raged out of control. "To keep it out of the boonies is easy enough," noted Colonel Barrow, "I don't know who the hell is going to bring it to them unless the helicopter drivers get into the business of pushing. But in the rear is the real problem. It is kind of very easy to come by. The rear produces a certain amount of boredom; it's a way of looking for excitement, or they think so."[39]

In an effort to deal with the problem, III MAF, like other Vietnam commands, relied heavily on troop education. Commanders were to impress upon the individual Marine the moral evils, legal consequences, and physical hazards of drug use. When education failed, as it often did, III MAF resorted to the strict enforcement of Naval Regulations and the Uniform Code of Military Justice which prohibited the possession and use of narcotics. "There is no need to talk about if it is a drug, habit forming, or injurious to the health," noted Colonel Mulroney, "these are medical considerations that most people, and I am one of them, are not qualified to talk about . . . . The way it has to be attacked, I feel, is that there is a military regulation that prohibits the possession and use; . . . that has to be enforced."[40]

Commanders and noncommissioned officers routinely searched vehicles as well as troop living quarters and work areas. Strict controls were placed on the movement of personnel in rear areas and increased emphasis was placed on troop supervision; "you have to have the officers, staff NCOs, and the sergeants constantly checking, knowing what their men are doing, and supervising them, so that there is a constant fear that somebody is looking over your shoulder when you go to pull out that marijuana cigarette."[41] Whenever possible, pushers and users were arrested and prosecuted. Finding the offenders, however, proved difficult. Peer pressure, threats, and "misplaced loyalty" hampered the collection of evidence and successful prosecution. Some young officers and staff NCOs excused drug use during off-duty hours by Marines needed in the unit. Those caught received courts-martial or were recommended for an administrative discharge. The administrative discharge would come into ever-increasing use during the early 1970s, not only to rid the Service of drug users, but those that did not meet the Marine Corps' performance and disciplinary standards.

In spite of drug use, racial tension and violence, and occasional fraggings, III MAF and its subordinate commands remained unaffected in the accomplishment of its varied combat missions during 1969. Nevertheless, these problems did draw the command attention necessary to deal effectively with a number of social and personnel issues that previously had been ignored.

CHAPTER 10
'A Difficult Phase'

Maintaining a Protective Barrier—"You Shouldered Us"—The Brigade Takes Over

---

Maintaining a Protective Barrier

The last regiment to be redeployed as part of the incremental withdrawal of the 3d Marine Division was the 4th Marines. Its final months of combat before standing down, like those of the 3d, were characterized by the launching of numerous company sweeps and patrols aimed at blunting the introduction of enemy personnel and equipment.

The first day of July found Colonel William F. Goggin's regiment engaged in the last phases of Operation Herkimer Mountain in an area of operations generally extending from the Demilitarized Zone south to Route 9, and from Vandegrift Combat Base west to the Khe Sanh Plateau. Lieutenant Colonel Clair E. Willcox's 1st Battalion, with three companies of the 3d Battalion under its operational control, had responsibility for securing Vandegrift and patrolling the rocket belt to the west. Assigned the mission of securing Fire Support Base Russell and the surrounding terrain, a 60-square-kilometer area northwest of Elliott Combat Base, was the 2d Battalion, under Lieutenant Colonel William C. Britt. Lieutenant Colonel James W. Wood's 3d Battalion, with the 2d Battalion, 9th Marines attached for a short period, secured a portion of Vandegrift, Elliott Combat Base, Fire Support Base Cates, and a number of other Marine outposts stretching west along Route 9.

On the 3d, Wood's battalion, less the 2d Battalion, 9th Marines, which began the process of standing down for redeployment, ended its participation in Herkimer Mountain and simultaneously began Operation Arlington Canyon. Its new area of operations centered on Nui Tia Pong and the contiguous valleys, nine kilometers northwest of Vandegrift. With a dual mission of locating and destroying enemy caches and rocket sites in the area, Company I conducted a heliborne assault into LZ Uranus on the 3d; followed by the battalion command group on the 7th; Company M's assault into LZ Cougar, six kilometers to the northwest, on the 8th; and the helilift of Company K into LZ Scotch on the 10th. Company L and Company D, 1st Battalion, walked into the area of operations from Vandegrift.

Enemy activity in the area proved to be "disappointingly slow"; sightings and any resultant engagements were light, being limited to small NVA patrols and reconnaissance teams of two to four soldiers. During extensive search operations centered on Uranus, Wood's five companies did discover a multitude of enemy bunker complexes and small ammunition caches, all of which indicated a lack of recent enemy activity.

With the area around Nui Tia Pong well-patrolled, Colonel Goggin ordered the 2d Battalion to replace the 3d, which he then directed to move south. Wood's command group had already displaced to Fire Support Base Cates, and Company D, 1st Battalion to Cua Viet, when the remaining four companies moved out of the Arlington Canyon area of operations and into that of Georgia Tar on the 23d. Previously occupied by the soon-to-be-redeployed 3d Battalion, 9th Marines, the new area of operations included Fire Support Base Cates, Hill 950, and a majority of Rocket Valley, east of Vandegrift. Once the battalion joined the new operation, Company K was assigned to the defense and improvement of Cates and Hill 950, while Companies I, L, and M moved north into the rocket belt and began an extensive sweep to the south.

Meanwhile, Colonel Goggin alerted Lieutenant Colonel Willcox's 1st Battalion on the 8th to be prepared to move to the Cua Viet In-Country R&R Center the following day. The move of Company D from the Arlington Canyon area of operation and the remainder of the battalion from Vandegrift to Cua Viet went without incident. There the battalion enjoyed two days of rest and rehabilitation before joining elements of the 1st Brigade, 5th Infantry Brigade in Operation William's Glade. The joint Army and Marine operation, designed to "sweep the backyard," was to take place in an area generally south of Dong Ha, west of Quang Tri, and east of Mai Loc.

On 12 July, Willcox's battalion began a sweep south from Dong Ha Combat Base, while elements of Task Force 1-61 (1st Battalion, 61st Infantry) established blocking positions east of Fire Support Base Angel and conducted reconnaissance-in-force operations to the west of the fire base. At the same time, Task Force 1-11 (1st Battalion, 11th Infantry) set up a second blocking position southwest of Dong Ha Combat Base, while

Troop A, 4th Squadron, 12th Cavalry completed the circle by establishing positions near LZ Pedro, west of Quang Tri.[1] Four days later, Willcox's battalion swept through the lines of Task Force 1-61, swinging southwest, searching the high ground between the Song Thach Han and Route 557. The terrain, consisting of small rolling hills and valleys, bisected by dry streambeds and covered with six-foot-high savannah grass proved to be no obstacle, but the hot and humid weather did, resulting in a large number of heat casualties. Although a couple of NVA were sighted and one caught in a daylight ambush, enemy activity was all but nonexistent.

Once Willcox's Marines completed their southward sweep, company-size patrols were organized for operations in the hills, north of the Ba Long Valley and south of FSB Angel. The battalion patrolled the area, with no sightings or contact, until the 22d when it returned to Vandegrift and joined Operation Georgia Tar. Elements of Task Force 1-61 continued William's Glade until the 26th, when the operation was merged with that of the brigade's primary operation, Iroquois Grove.

Upon the termination of Operation Herkimer Mountain on 16 July, Colonel Goggin's 4th Marines began Operation Georgia Tar within the same area of operations, excluding the northern portion reserved for Arlington Canyon. The operation was prompted by numerous rocket attacks against both Vandegrift and Elliott Combat Bases; Vandegrift alone had received over sixty 107mm mortar and 122mm rocket rounds during the month of June. Elements of the regiment were to locate and destroy the suspected rocket launch sites, and then thoroughly search the remaining areas of the rocket belt, west of the two combat bases.

Initially assigned to the operation was the 3d Battalion, 9th Marines, then under the operational control of the 4th Marines. The battalion secured Vandegrift and Ca Lu, while also searching north of Cates and Hill 950, east of Khe Sanh. But on 22 July, with the standdown of the 3d Battalion, 9th Marines, Willcox's 1st Battalion helilifted to Vandegrift, upon leaving William's Glade, and assumed security of the position, while initiating continuous sweeps of Route 9 and maintaining one company as the regimental

Men of Company D, 1st Battalion, 4th Marines prepare to fire an 81mm mortar in support of company-sized patrols operating in the vicinity of Vandegrift Combat Base.

Department of Defense Photo (USMC) A800622

reaction force. The following day, Lieutenant Colonel Wood's 3d Battalion, 4th Marines joined the operation, securing Cates and Hill 950 with one company, sending two companies on patrol into the rocket belt, and one across Route 9, to the south.

Although both battalions made use of extensive patrol operations, ambushes, and hunter-killer teams, Colonel Goggin instituted a number of precautions in response to the violent enemy attacks experienced by elements of Colonel Simlik's 3d Marines. These precautions required that all companies move at least 1,000 meters a day; that all move into night defensive positions under the cover of darkness; that all platoons be located at the company patrol base during hours of darkness; and, that there be no independent platoon operations.

Enemy activity throughout the large area of operations, however, proved to be very light during the remainder of July and into August, as reported by the battalion's operations officer, Captain Henry W. Buse III:

> The enemy employed small groups of recon-type forces to simply harass us in our movement. We found out that whenever we left, pulled a company out of the rocket belt, which lay west of VCB [Vandegrift Combat Base], the enemy would rocket VCB, so consequently we tried to keep a rifle company maneuvering in that area at all times. The majority of contacts that we made, the sightings that were made, were made by reconnaissance units rather than by the infantry companies working on the ground.[2]

This lack of significant enemy activity and the dramatic decrease in the number of rocket attacks and mining incidents suggested to Captain Buse and others that the enemy was avoiding the area by moving south along the Khe Sanh Valley and then east through the lower Da Krong.

On 26 August, the two battalions switched primary missions and area of operations. During the day, Lieutenant Colonel Joseph A. MacInnis' 1st Battalion command group moved from Vandegrift to Cates.* The following morning, three companies of the battalion conducted a vertical assault onto the high ground, three kilometers north of Hill 950 and began a sweep of the rocket belt. Meanwhile, Lieutenant Colonel Wood's 3d Battalion assumed control of Vandegrift, Ca Lu, and that portion of the Georgia Tar area of operations contiguous to the installations. In addition to the defense and improvement of the two facilities, the battalion was to provide security for road sweeps and Seabee road repair crews, while maintaining one rifle company as a reaction force and another as a reserve for the operations of "Project Delta" being conducted within the division's reconnaissance zone to the west.**

Enemy activity throughout the Georgia Tar area of operations continued at the same low level into the month of September. Although there were signs of heavy trail use and a number of bunker sites discovered indicating recent occupation, the NVA limited themselves to small-unit patrols, instead of massing for a direct confrontation with sweep elements of MacInnis' or Wood's battalions.

Towards the middle of the month, another major shift in regimental units took place. On the 11th, Lieutenant Colonel Wood's battalion, minus one rifle company, returned to the Arlington Canyon area of operations, west of the Rockpile and south of the DMZ. At the same time, the 2d Battalion, 4th Marines, under Lieutenant Colonel Donald J. Garrett, who had replaced Lieutenant Colonel Britt on the 5th, helilifted out of Arlington Canyon and was given the responsibility of securing Vandegrift and Ca Lu, and of providing rifle companies for the regimental reaction and reserve forces, in addition to the search and destroy operations conducted around both installations. To accomplish these varied missions, rifle companies of both the 1st and 3d Battalions were assigned for varying lengths of time to the battalion.

With the standdown of the 3d Battalion, 3d Marines on the 21st, Colonel Goggin ordered Garrett's Marines pulled out of Georgia Tar after only 10 days, and directed them to secure Elliott Combat Base, Khe Ghia Bridge, Fire Support Base Fuller, and conduct sweeps of a truncated area of operations, north of Elliott. As Garrett's battalion moved east, the 1st Battalion assumed control of the entire Georgia Tar area of operations, and with it the varying security missions.

As the division prepared for Phase II redeployment in late September, continued occupation of the

---

*On 5 August, Lieutenant Colonel Joseph A. MacInnis relieved Lieutenant Colonel Willcox as Commanding Officer, 1st Battalion, 4th Marines.

**"Project Delta," composed of Detachment B-52, 5th Special Forces Group (Airborne), 81st Airborne Ranger Battalion (-), two platoons, 281st Army Helicopter Company, and attached Air Force liaison and Army air relay personnel, was under the operational control of the 3d Marine Division from 4 August to 1 October. Assigned to the division's reconnaissance zone during this period, the 19 reconnaissance and 17 road runner teams, 6 Ranger companies, and 4 bomb damage assessment platoons were directed to locate and destroy enemy forces, caches, infiltration routes, and lines of communication in western Quang Tri Province. (Det B-52, 5th SpForGp, 1stSpFor AAR 3-69 [Operation Trojan Horse], n.d., in 3dMarDiv ComdC, Aug69)

Department of Defense Photo (USMC) 192539
With full packs, infantrymen of Company B, 1st Battalion, 4th Marines cross a stream while on search operations in the mountainous jungles west of Elliott Combat Base.

western fire support bases appeared infeasible, and Goggin directed MacInnis' Marines to destroy and then close Cates, Shepherd, and the observation post atop Hill 950. In addition, they were to prepare for the future evacuation of Vandegrift and Ca Lu.

The slow and deliberate shift east of the 4th Marines brought with it the termination of Operation Georgia Tar on the 25th. During two months of sweeping the rocket belt and securing major western outposts, the regiment only accounted for 40 enemy dead and 15 weapons captured, while losing one killed and 23 wounded. "Overall," as Captain Buse later summarized, "Georgia Tar was relatively successful, in that it was designed to keep the enemy away from VCB, and to keep him, of course, out of that area of operations. And, he did stay away, for the most part, from the Cates area, and he very rarely bothered VCB."[3] With the close of Georgia Tar, the 4th Marines continued Operation Idaho Canyon and Arlington Canyon.

While participants and reports alike characterized enemy activity within the Georgia Tar area of operations as insignificant, the same term could not be applied to the actions of NVA troops operating within the area of Arlington Canyon, to the north. Captured documents, agent reports, and strategically placed sensor strings indicated that elements of four enemy battalions, the *3d Battalion, 246th Independent Regiment*; *3d Battalion, 9th NVA Regiment*; *1st Battalion, 84th Artillery (Rocket) Regiment*; and an unnumbered battalion of the *24th Independent Regiment*, were using the area's extensive trail network to move men and supplies further south in order to support a buildup in the central portion of the province. While avoiding a massive, direct attack, screening and reconnaissance elements of these four battalions did not hesitate to protect their parent units, installations, or infiltration routes by employing indirect fire attacks and small unit probes against advancing 4th Marines patrols.[4]

The original task assigned Marines involved in Arlington Canyon was to halt the enemy's numerous rocket attacks against fire support bases and other major allied installations throughout the central and western portions of the division's area of responsibility. But, as the operation progressed, this mission was expanded by the need to locate and destroy enemy units known to be operating in, or moving through, the area to the southeast. To accomplish these two missions, Lieutenant Colonel Britt's 2d Battalion, 4th Marines, which had replaced Lieutenant Colonel Wood's 3d Battalion in the area on 24 July, employed extensive patrols and ambushes. With one company assigned to secure and improve the defensive works of Fire Support Base Russell, Britt's remaining three companies moved out into the surrounding, heavily-jungled, mountainous terrain. Division orders, however, prohibited offensive patrols within three kilometers of the DMZ, thus limiting operations of the three companies to the upper Cam Lo River Valley, immediately north of Russell. A second limitation imposed by division was that each rifle company move its command post and all platoons the standard one kilometer per day. This forced movement in mountainous terrain not only taxed the companies, reported the battalion's operation officer, Major James J. O'Meara, but "in order to make that click [1,000 meters] they would not effectively search any area. It became sort of a road race; you must make your click."[5]

Despite these limitations, the overburdened companies established a total of 360 ambushes and ran 270 patrols during the month of August. Contact was made on 12 different occasions, most of which resulted from sighting small groups of four to six NVA soldiers. Two, involving larger units, were significant. The first took place as Captain Harry C. Baxter, Jr.'s Company E secured its night defensive position atop Hill 715, five kilometers west of Russell, on 12 August. Shortly after midnight, two NVA sapper squads attacked that portion of the perimeter manned by Baxter's 3d Platoon. Firing AK47s and throwing satchel charges, the sappers killed two and wounded five Marines before withdrawing. Later, as a CH-46 helicopter attempted to land and evacuate the casualties, it came under heavy small arms fire, and the sappers again attempted to penetrate the perimeter. Baxter called for mortar fire and adjusted it on the enemy's position, forcing the sappers to withdraw a second time. After the completion of a second medical evacuation, "Spooky" gunships circled the perimeter, pounding the remnants of the enemy sapper squads. Baxter's Marines made a complete search of the area at first light, finding three NVA bodies and a large cache of hand grenades and satchel charges.

A week later, as Captain Francis Zavacki's Company H advanced from Dong Tiou, four kilometers northeast of Russell, towards LZ Sierra, his 1st Platoon walked into an "L"-shaped enemy ambush, initiated by claymores, grenades, and followed with small arms fire. The enemy killed three Marines outright and seriously wounded eight more. The platoon returned fire with small arms and called upon artillery and 81mm mortars for additional support. Zavacki's 3d Platoon then maneuvered toward the 1st to render assistance and evacuate the casualties to a nearby landing zone, secured by the 2d Platoon. Under pressure, the NVA withdrew and began a mortar attack which artillery fire and fixed-wing strikes quickly surppressed. In a subsequent search of the area, the Marines found three enemy bodies.

Lieutenant Colonel Britt's, later Lieutenant Colonel Garrett's, Marines continued search and destroy operations in the 60-square-kilometer Arlington Canyon area, conducting numerous day and night squad- and platoon-size patrols and ambushes, with mixed results until 12 September, when replaced by Lieutenant Colonel Wood's 3d Battalion. On that date, Wood's command group and one rifle company displaced to Russell as two companies helilifted into the surrounding terrain: Company M into the northwest quadrant and Company K into the southern half, west of Elliott. During the next 10 days, the rifle companies, operating from patrol bases, showed little result. Offensive operations in the Arlington Canyon area of operations ceased on the 20th, when Wood directed the command group and Companies K and M to return to Vandegrift. The company on Russell remained one more day in order to begin the destruction of the fire support base, but an accidental fire, which later spread to exposed artillery ordnance, forced the premature evacuation of the hill before the mission could be completed.

The battalion command group, following its move to Vandegrift, immediately lifted to Cam Lo village, where it established a command post at the district headquarters. Companies I and K then trucked into a new, unnamed area of operations astride Route 9, which stretched from the Vinh Dai Rock Crusher to the Khe Gio Bridge, where Company K was to provide security for the command group, Cam Lo District Headquarters, and the tactically important Charlie-3 Bridge at Cam Lo; Company I was to conduct search and destroy operations north of Route 9 and west of the village. On the 22d, however, Lieutenant Colonel Wood ordered Company I temporarily into the Arlington Canyon area of operations in order to examine the damage to Russell, recover missing equipment, and complete the destruction of the fire support base, a mission which the company accomplished the following day by the blowing of all remaining structures and much of the excess ammunition. With the leveling of Fire Support Base Russell, Operation Arlington Canyon came to an end. During nearly three months of searching the rough mountainous terrain northwest of Elliott, the 2d and 3d Battalions, 4th Marines gained meager results, accounting for only 23 enemy killed and eight weapons captured, while sustaining 10 killed and 28 wounded. The operation, according to Major James J. O'Meara, was a success, "in that the area we were assigned, . . . was thoroughly covered by 2/4, even though the rifle companies had to make that magic click a day."[6]

During the last week of September, the 4th Marines assumed control of the 3d Marines' tactical area of responsibility (Idaho Canyon), as the last elements of Colonel Simlik's regiment moved to Dong Ha in preparation for redeployment to the United States. In doing so, the 4th Marines took the responsibility of securing major installations while closing others. It was, as Colonel Gilbert R. Hershey, who had replaced Colonel Goggin on 10 August, later remembered, "one of the most difficult phases that a regiment can go through . . . picking up the brass and policing everything else that people had left for five years while you were trying to maintain a tactical posture."[7]

Tactically, Colonel Hershey positioned his three battalions strategically throughout the now diminished regimental area of operations. Lieutenant Colonel MacInnis' 1st Battalion, earlier responsible for an area of operations west of Vandegrift, on 20 September, was directed to defend the combat base and dismantle Cates, Shepherd, and the outpost atop Hill 950. The 3d Battalion, under Lieutenant Colonel James W. Wood, after closing Operation Arlington Canyon, relieved the 2d Battalion, 3d Marines of its responsibilities at Cam Lo, and was also given the task of leveling Fire Support Base Russell. On the 28th, the battalion again transferred its command post and two rifle companies, this time from Cam Lo to Dong Ha. Company M provided security for a portion of the combat base's perimeter, while Company I secured the northern bank of the Cua Viet River. The battalion's vacated area near Cam Lo later passed to the 1st Brigade, 5th Infantry Division. Lieutenant Colonel Garrett's 2d Battalion moved, following the announced plan for the withdrawal of the 3d Marines from Vietnam, to Elliott Combat Base, where it assumed responsibility for 3d Battalion, 3d Marines area and a portion of the 1st Battalion's, including Fire Support Base Fuller and Khe Gio Bridge.

At the close of the month, enemy activity throughout the regiment's new area of operations again centered on Landing Zones Sierra and Mack, near Mutter's Ridge. There were indications that the *9th NVA Regiment*, which had engaged the 3d Marines over the past several months, was continuing to infiltrate personnel and equipment along the Song Cam Lo in an effort to cut Route 9. Elements of Lieutenant Colonel Garrett's battalion sighted units of the elusive enemy regiment on nine different occasions, but made contact only once.

On 20 September, First Lieutenant William H. Stubblefield's Company G and a sister company helilifted into an area just north of the Song Cam Lo, near LZ Pete, in order to secure the northern approaches to Elliott Combat Base and at the same time bar enemy infiltrators from moving toward the southeast. Six days later, while the companies occupied a night defensive position on LZ Dixie Pete, 1,000 meters north of Pete, four sensor devices registered movement outside the companies' perimeter. An ambush, not far away, then reported sighting three figures moving across their front and tossed several hand grenades in the direction of the movement, which soon ceased. "I figured," noted Lieutenant Stubblefield, "OK, it stopped; whatever was causing it was gone or maybe the [sensor] batteries wore out or something. I wasn't sure how these things operated or if they were reliable at all. At that time, I said, OK, if anything desperate happens, wake me up."[8]

Two hours later, Stubblefield awoke to the crackle of enemy small arms and automatic weapons fire, followed by a heavy 60mm and 82mm mortar barrage. He called for artillery on a series of preplanned targets, but batteries delayed firing for over an hour due to the loss of original grid coordinates. Meanwhile, Stubblefield's Marines countered with heavy fire of their own, finally halting the attack and forcing the enemy sappers to withdraw. Shortly after sunrise, fixed-wing aircraft came on station and pummelled the enemy's escape routes, subsequently spotting over 11 bodies beyond the wire. A later ground search of the surrounding area revealed numerous grenades, spent shell casings, and fresh blood trails, but no bodies.[9]

The attack on Company G, in which two Marines lost their lives and 59 received wounds, proved to be one of the last enemy-initiated assaults on elements of the 3d Marine Division prior to the implementation of the final phase of Keystone Cardinal. Division intelligence analysts suspected that the enemy intended to pull his major forces back into North Vietnam in order to exploit and then fill the vacuum which he thought might occur with the division's departure and its replacement by the 1st Brigade, 5th Infantry Division (Mechanized) and elements of the 1st ARVN Division. Statistics kept of enemy activity during October and November would partially support this assumption, for enemy attacks of all kinds carried out within the division's area of operations during the redeployment of the 4th Marines fell by more than 50 percent in comparison to previous months. The enemy had indeed withdrawn, but whether he was preparing for a future offensive or allowing the last elements of the 3d Marine Division to withdraw undisturbed, was not then known.

"You Shouldered Us"

The beginning of its final month in Vietnam found Colonel Hershey's 4th Marines fully operational with three battalions positioned in the north central portion, south of the Demilitarized Zone, of Quang Tri Province. But as the month progressed, each battalion would be withdrawn from combat, moved to Quang Tri Combat Base where each was to assemble with the remaining support elements of the battalion landing team, and then embark on board amphibious shipping for Okinawa. Lieutenant Colonel MacInnis' 1st Battalion, which had been assigned the task of defending Vandegrift and Ca Lu, and securing Route 9 from the combat base north 3,000 meters to the boundary between the 1st and 2d Battalions, was the first to stand down.

On 5 October, MacInnis' battalion disengaged from combat, stood down from its tactical commitments, and displaced to Quang Tri Combat Base in order to prepare for redeployment to Okinawa. Company D, however, remained behind. Assigned to the operational control of the 2d Battalion, the company was to provide security for the 2d Battalion, 2d ARVN Regiment so that the ARVN battalion could devote all of its time to the dismantling and salvaging of material from Vandegrift to be used in the construction of a new combat base at Camp Carroll. The company secured Vandegrift until relieved by a platoon from Company G on the 10th, and then it rejoined the battalion at Quang Tri. On 22 October, MacInnis' battalion boarded the *Dubuque* (LPD 8) and *Vancouver* (LPD 2) at Cua Viet, while the remainder of the battalion landing team, made up of elements of the 3d Engineer Battalion; 3d Tank Battalion; 3d Battalion, 12th Marines; 3d Bridge Company; 3d Motor Transport Battalion; and detachments of Headquarters Battalion, 3d Marine Division, and Headquarters Battery, 12th Marines, embarked on board six landing ships. By the end of the month, the landing team had arrived in Okinawa and settled into garrison duty.

The 2d Battalion, 4th Marines, commanded by Lieutenant Colonel Donald J. Garrett, continued its primary missions of defending Elliott Combat Base, Fire Support Base Fuller, Khe Gio Bridge on Route 9, and conducting offensive operations north to the

A CH-46 helicopter inserts the men of Company G, 2d Battalion, 4th Marines at Pete in preparation for a two-company search and block of the ridges north of the landing zone.

Department of Defense Photo (USMC) A193489

DMZ. In order to assist Garrett's battalion in accomplishing these missions, Colonel Hershey assigned Companies L and K, 3d Battalion, and Company D, 1st Battalion to the battalion for short periods of time. With these three additional companies, the 2d Battalion continued to conduct aggressive operations to within 1,000 meters of the Demilitarized Zone's southern boundary, uncovering numerous North Vietnamese graves and a large number of small weapons and ammunition caches. It was during this period that the regiment experienced its last engagement.

On the night of 9 October, Second Lieutenant Danny G. Dennison's 3d Platoon, Company L, stationed atop a hill three kilometers northeast of Elliott overlooking the Song Cam Lo, received a heavy barrage of 82mm mortars followed by a surprise ground attack by two reinforced platoons of NVA infantry and sappers. As Lieutenant Dennison later recalled:

> The enemy at first seemed to have moved up with two two-man [teams] using AKs, to set up more or less a security force. Three men moved up to the main part of the wire throwing Chicoms and satchel charges, and then to the left of the CP [command post], a 10-man engineer team moved up also employing satchel charges and Chicoms. By watching the way the enemy was moving it seemed apparent that they had been more or less spotting our position for a week or so because they hit every key position we had.[10]

Soon after the first bursts of enemy grenades and satchel charges, a number of Dennison's machine gun and "blooper" (M79 grenade launcher) positions were put out of action, the wire penetrated, and the platoon's ammunition dump destroyed. With the help of a reaction force from Khe Gio Bridge, two kilometers away, "the men began moving up to set up a defensive perimeter, and grenades were used to force the enemy from the defensive wire, back out into the bush where we could get small arms fire on them." The enemy broke contact at sunrise after taking an hour of heavy artillery, mortar, and "Spooky" gunship fire on their position. A head count revealed that Dennison lost eight men killed and 17 wounded, and a search of the battlefield disclosed 10 enemy bodies.[11]

On 22 October, Garrett's battalion disengaged from combat and displaced to Quang Tri Combat Base to prepare for embarkation to Okinawa. Company G, reinforced with a platoon from Company H, remained at Elliott Combat Base under the operational control of the 3d Marine Division in order to police and then destroy the base's fortifications, a task completed on the 25th. Company G then moved to Quang Tri, rejoined the battalion, and prepared for embarkation.

Company K, under the operational control of the 2d Battalion, returned to its parent unit, but Company L remained on Fire Support Base Fuller, under 3d Marine Division's control, until relieved by elements of the 1st Brigade, 5th Infantry Division on 5 November. Garrett's battalion, following two weeks of training, inspections, and cleaning equipment, joined the remainder of the battalion landing team and sailed for Okinawa on 6 November.

The first days of October found Lieutenant Colonel Wood's 3d Battalion, the last slated to leave, conducting offensive operations out of Dong Ha Combat Base. Company I occupied and defended a sector of the base's perimeter, while Company M operated in a separate area north of the Song Cua Viet. Company M's area of operations, established by the division, and its aggressive small-unit patrol activities and company-size search and destroy operations proved vital in keeping the river free from enemy activity. The Cua Viet was of primary interest to the regiment and division for two reasons: first, the river was the main supply route for all logistical materiel supporting the division, and second, it provided an avenue of departure for half the Marines redeploying to Okinawa. The remainder of the battalion, Companies K and L, were under the operational control of the 2d Battalion as the month began.

On 5 October, the battalion assumed complete responsibility for the defense of Dong Ha Combat Base, while at the same time continuing its security mission along the north bank of the Cua Viet. The battalion maintained this tactical posture through 22 October when Company K rejoined the battalion, and its operational control transferred from the 4th Marines to the 3d Marine Division. A month later, Wood's Marines disengaged from combat operations and began preparations for redeployment. At the same time, Company L, which had secured Fuller, under the operational control of the division since 22 October, rejoined the battalion.

Two days after terminating combat operations, Lieutenant Colonel Wood and his command group flew to Da Nang in order to participate in departure ceremonies for the division. Gathering before the Da Nang City Hall on the banks of the Song Han, a large number of dignitaries spoke of the 3d Marine Division's contributions to the war effort and the people of I Corps, principal among them Lieutenant General Hoang Xuan Lam, Commanding General, I Corps Tactical Zone. During his speech, General Lam recalled:

I still remember that memorable date of the 8th March 1965, at which I had the honor to welcome the forward elements of the 3d Marine Division landing on the beaches of Da Nang and marking the arrival of the first large scale ground combat units of U.S. Armed Forces to South Vietnam. Today, five years and more than 120 operations later, the 3d Marine Division is completing its process of redeployment, and in a few moments its last elements will embark for a journey back to the U.S., leaving behind in the memory of the South Vietnamese people the resounding echoes of a splendid combat record, with glorious names of successful operations such as Starlite, Khe Sanh, Golden Fleece, Scotland, Lancaster, Napoleon Saline, Dewey Canyon and countless others.

Concluding his remarks, General Lam noted that while gallant Marines had fallen, they had not died in vain:

You have shouldered us at the critical moment we needed you most, and now we are entirely capable of assuming the burden of this war and nothing can deter us from achieving all our cherished goals; that of defeating the Communists and bringing peace to South Vietnam. You will depart from South Vietnam, but you will leave behind a strong and prosperous nation.[12]

Among the other speakers were Lieutenant General Herman Nickerson, Jr., Commanding General, III Marine Amphibious Force; Major General William K. Jones, Commanding General, 3d Marine Division, who delivered his remarks in Vietnamese; General William B. Rosson, Deputy Commander, U.S. Military Assistance Command, Vietnam; and Mr. Nguyen Xuan, Chairman of the Citizens Council of Da Nang. Following the presentation of traditional Vietnamese leis, made of yellow and red cloth, the ceremony concluded, and Major General Jones and his principal staff officers left. At Da Nang Airfield, Jones and his staff boarded awaiting aircraft; the last to board was Division Sergeant Major Clyde M. Long, carrying the division colors. The 3d Division was on its way to Okinawa and new headquarters at Camp Courtney.[13]

On 20 November, the final division battalion landing team, the 3d Battalion, 4th Marines, along with the remaining elements of the 3d Reconnaissance Battalion; 3d Medical Battalion; 11th Engineer Battalion; 3d Dental Company; 4th Battalion, 12th Marines; Company C, 9th Motor Transport Battalion; and Headquarters Battalion, 3d Marine Division; moved by truck to Quang Tri Combat Base from where they flew to Da Nang and then embarked on board the *Tripoli* (LPH 10). Four days later, the battalion landing team arrived on Okinawa, after more than four years of combat service in South Vietnam.

The MACV List: Composition of Keystone Cardinal

Unit	Strength	Departure Date	Destination	Unit	Strength	Departure Date	Destination
1st Bn, 3d Mar	1,166	6 Oct	CONUS	Det, 7 Comm Bn	193	6 Oct	CONUS
Co B, 3d Engr Bn	159	2 Oct	CONUS	Co B, 9th MT Bn	91	2 Oct	CONUS
Co C, 3d Med Bn	24	2 Oct	CONUS				
1st Bn, 12th Mar	662	2 Oct	CONUS	Det 1st Bn, 4th Mar	118	7 Oct	CONUS
3d Bridge Co (-)	102	4 Oct	CONUS	Det 2d Bn, 4th Mar	118	6 Oct	CONUS
				Det 3d Bn, 4th Mar	118	6 Oct	CONUS
2d Bn, 3d Mar	1,166	6 Oct	CONUS	Det Hq Co, 4th Mar	100	6 Oct	CONUS
Hq Co (-), 3d Mar	230	7 Oct	CONUS	Det, 1st SSCT	4	6 Oct	CONUS
Det 3d Bn, 12th Mar	91	6 Oct	CONUS				
Det Hq Btry, 12th Mar	61	6 Oct	CONUS	Det, Hq III MAF	70	30 Sep	CONUS
Det Hq Bn, 3d Mar Div	436	6 Oct	CONUS	OOCNE	724	30 Sep	CONUS
Det, 11th Engr Bn	622	4 Oct	CONUS	OOCNE	14	6 Oct	CONUS
3d Bn, 3d Mar	1,166	7 Oct	CONUS	1st Bn, 4th Mar	1,048	22 Oct	Okinawa
Det 4th Bn, 12th Mar	150	6 Oct	CONUS	Det Hq Bn, 3d Mar Div	200	22 Oct	Okinawa
Det Hq Co, 3d Mar	24	6 Oct	CONUS				
Co B, 3d MT Bn	68	4 Oct	CONUS	7th Comm Bn (-)	190	20 Oct	Okinawa
				Btry G, 3d Bn, 12th Mar	133	23 Oct	Okinawa
Co B, 3d SP Bn	84	2 Oct	CONUS	3d Engr Bn (-)	341	23 Oct	Okinawa
Det, FLC	400	6 Oct	CONUS	3d MT Bn (-)	41	20 Oct	Okinawa
Co A, 3d Recon Bn	143	4 Oct	CONUS	3d Tk Bn (-)	345	23 Oct	Okinawa

Unit	Strength	Departure Date	Destination	Unit	Strength	Departure Date	Destination
Plt, 3d Bridge Co	21	20 Oct	Okinawa	H Btry, 3d Bn, 12th Mar	110	27 Nov	Okinawa
Hq Btry (-), 12th Mar	100	20 Oct	Okinawa	7th ITT	11	24 Nov	Okinawa
2d Bn, 4th Mar (-)	1,048	9 Nov	Okinawa	HMM-265	249	7 Oct	CONUS
Hq Bn (-), 3d Mar Div	308	9 Nov	Okinawa	OOCNE	123	6 Oct	CONUS
Hq Co (-), 4th Mar	130	6 Nov	Okinawa	Det, VMO-6	8	6 Oct	CONUS
3d Bn, 12th Mar (-)	328	5 Nov	Okinawa	Det, HMM-164	8	6 Oct	CONUS
K Btry, 4th Bn, 12 Mar	100	10 Nov	Okinawa	Det, MABS-36	89	6 Oct	CONUS
17th ITT	11	5 Nov	Okinawa	Det, H&MS-36	164	6 Oct	CONUS
11th IT	6	5 Nov	Okinawa	Det, MABS-11	20	6 Oct	CONUS
9th IT	6	5 Nov	Okinawa	Det, MABS-12	20	6 Oct	CONUS
Det Hq Btry, 12th Mar	83	9 Nov	Okinawa	Det, MABS-13	20	6 Oct	CONUS
9th MT Bn	88	4 Nov	Okinawa	Det, MABS-16	22	6 Oct	CONUS
Co B, 3d Tk Bn	140	6 Nov	Okinawa	VMA-533	304	7 Oct	CONUS
3d SP Bn (-)	228	10 Nov	Okinawa	Det, H&MS-12	69	7 Oct	Japan
1st SSCT (-)	6	8 Nov	Okinawa	HMM-164	258	20 Oct	Okinawa
15th CIT	16	3 Nov	Okinawa	VMO-6 (-)	234	22 Oct	Okinawa
3d Bn, 4th Mar	1,048	20 Nov	Okinawa	Det, VMO-6	32	22 Oct	Okinawa
Det Hq Bn, 3d Mar Div	200	24 Nov	Okinawa	HMH-462	233	20 Oct	Okinawa
Det Hq Co, 4th Mar	24	20 Nov	Okinawa	1st MAW Hq (Rear)	353	3 Nov	Japan
3d Recon Bn	309	24 Nov	Okinawa	H&MS-36 (-)	324	7 Nov	Okinawa
3d Med Bn (-)	86	24 Nov	Okinawa	MABS-36 (-)	318	23 Nov	Okinawa
11th Engr Bn (-)	103	21 Nov	Okinawa	MASS-2 (-)	123	23 Nov	Japan
3d Dental Co	3	24 Nov	Okinawa	Det, H&HS-18	18	3 Nov	Japan
4th Bn, 12th Mar (-)	152	19 Nov	Okinawa	Det, MASS-2	39	8 Nov	Okinawa
Co C, 9th MT Bn	83	22 Nov	Okinawa	Det, MABS-36	87	23 Nov	Japan

Note: All CONUS destinations refer to Camp Pendleton, California.

The departure of the 3d Marine Division brought with it a shift in Marine air assets committed to Quang Tri Province. As the division's area of operations shrank and the 3d and 4th Marines pulled back and then stood down, Colonel Owen V. Gallentine's Provisional Marine Aircraft Group 39 did the same. On 23 September, the wing directed the air group to shift its units from Quang Tri Combat Base to Phu Bai. Four days later, Major Richard W. Carr's Marine Medium Helicopter Squadron 161 began its move, followed on the 30th by Marine Medium Helicopter Squadron 262, commanded by Major Donald J. Meskan. Both helicopter squadrons continued to support 3d Marine Division units through 15 October, when operational control of both passed to Marine Aircraft Group 36 at Phu Bai.

Marine Observation Squadron 6, under Lieutenant Colonel Albert K. Charlton, stood down on 2 October in preparation for redeployment to Okinawa. On the 8th, the squadron's 18 OV-10A aircraft left Quang Tri on a four-leg trip to Marine Corps Air Facility, Futema, while the squadron's remaining aircraft, 11 UH-1E helicopters, and pilots moved to Phu Bai to await amphibious shipping and at the same time assist HML-367. Twelve days later, the squadron loaded its personnel and helicopters on board the *Cleveland* (LPD 7), and departed for Okinawa the following day. Of the remaining two air group units, Headquarters and Maintenance Squadron 39, commanded by Major Joseph F. Golden, was reduced to cadre strength and moved to Phu Bai, and Marine Air Traffic Control Unit 62 transferred to Marine Aircraft Group 13 at Chu Lai.*

Phase II withdrawal of U.S. forces from South Vietnam proceeded without interruption. Joining the

---

*For redeployment of other 1st Marine Aircraft Wing units during Phase II of Keystone Cardinal, see Chapter 13.

Department of Defense Photo (USMC) A1933636

Marine engineers using heavy bulldozers level and then bury accumulated debris at Vandegrift Combat Base during the standdown and withdrawal of the 4th Marines.

18,500 Marines of the 3d Division and 1st Marine Aircraft Wing were 14,000 Army personnel, including the 3d Brigade, 82d Airborne Division, and 2,600 members of the Air Force and 5,400 Navy personnel. By mid-December, American strength in Vietnam stood at 472,442—well below the goal of 484,000.

On the evening of 3 November, President Nixon reported to the American people on his administration's efforts to end the Vietnam war. Recapitulating the unsuccessful American peace initiatives and noting that 60,000 troops would be withdrawn by mid-December, the President turned to future U.S. action:

> We have adopted a plan which we have worked out in cooperation with the South Vietnamese for the complete withdrawal of all U.S. combat ground forces on an orderly scheduled timetable. This withdrawal will be made from strength and not from weakness. As South Vietnamese forces become stronger, the rate of American withdrawal can become greater.

A specific timetable was not mentioned, as it would remove any incentive for the enemy to negotiate: "They would simply wait until our forces had withdrawn and then move in." The timing, he said, was flexible and would depend on the three factors previously mentioned—progress at the Paris talks, the level of enemy activity, and the improvement of the RVNAF.

He warned the North Vietnamese not to misinterpret American intentions:

> Hanoi could make no greater mistake than to assume that an increase in violence will be to its advantage. If I conclude that increased enemy action jeopardizes our remaining forces in Vietnam, I shall not hesitate to take strong and effective measures to deal with the situation.

Concluding his remarks, the President said the United States had two choices in ending the war: "an immediate, precipitate withdrawal of all Americans from Vietnam without regard to the effects of that action"; or, persistence in the search for "a just peace through a negotiated settlement if possible," and continued implementation of the Vietnamization plan. Because of his belief that an immediate withdrawal would widen the war, he stated that he would proceed on the path of negotiation and orderly withdrawal.[14]

During November the President's chief military advisers undertook a review of the military situation in Vietnam and consideration of a number of redeployment plans in preparation for the presidential decision on further troop reductions expected to come in mid-December. At the end of the month, they submitted their conclusions to the Secretary of Defense. Recognizing that the enemy retained the capability of launching a significant, yet unsustainable, offensive, especially against III Corps and northern I Corps, they noted that continued progress was being made in pacification and Vietnamization, albeit at varying rates. Informing the Secretary that they had considered two alternatives—a 50,000 reduction by mid-March or April 1970, or a reduction of 100,000 by mid-July— they counseled against any decision at that time, based on military grounds. They believed that a troop reduction during the first months of 1970 would burden allied capabilities in meeting the enemy threat, especially during the *Tet* holiday period. Nevertheless, they recognized that "other considerations" might necessitate a withdrawal, and therefore recommended a reduction of 35,000. However, should the enemy escalate military operations, they strongly suggested that any announced troop withdrawal be cancelled or, if necessary, reversed, and that a prompt air and naval campaign against North Vietnam be launched.

With other than military considerations apparently influencing his decision, President Nixon, on 15 December, announced that 50,000 more troops would be withdrawn by 15 April 1970. Although acknowledging that enemy infiltration had increased substantially, he noted that it had not reached a point where "our military leaders believe the enemy has developed the capability to mount a major offensive." There would be risks, but they would be risks taken in search of peace. The President again cautioned Hanoi against misinterpreting U.S. actions by repeating his November warning that he would not hesitate to take strong and effective measures against any increased enemy activity that threatened the remaining American forces in Vietnam.[15] With the President's announced withdrawal of an additional 50,000 troops, planning began as to the composition of the force to be withdrawn.*

The Brigade Takes Over

At 1500 on 22 October, operational control of the 1st Brigade, 5th Infantry Division (Mechanized) passed from the 3d Marine Division to XXIV Corps at Phu Bai. With the departure of the division, the brigade became the senior allied combat unit in the northernmost region of I Corps Tactical Zone. In assuming this role, the brigade took on the responsibilities of defending Quang Tri Combat Base, and in conjunction with elements of the 1st ARVN Division, Dong Ha Combat Base, and of securing a limited tactical area composed of the eastern and central portions of Quang Tri Province. Should the brigade prove incapable of accomplishing its assigned mission in the face of a major enemy offensive, it, like the division before it, could call upon an infantry regiment of the 1st Marine Division, a two-battalion brigade of the Americal Division, an infantry or airborne brigade of the Army's I Field Force, or elements of the special landing force for reinforcement, depending on the severity of the situation.[16]

The 1st Brigade, since the end of June, had concentrated a majority of its efforts in the eastern portion of the province, an area extending east from Dong Ha and Quang Tri to the Gulf of Tonkin, and south from the 2d ARVN Regiment's area of operations on the DMZ to the provincial boundary. Organized into three task forces, Task Force 1/11 Infantry, Task Force 1/61 Infantry (Mechanized), and Task Force 1/77 Armor, the brigade began Operation Iroquois Grove on 19 June. Conducted within the brigade's normal area of operations, Iroquois Grove was designed to protect the civilian population and the rice crop, and also to assist the South Vietnamese in their Accelerated Pacification Program. While a majority of the brigade conducted search and clear operations, saturation ambushes, and patrols in conjunction and coordination with provincial and district forces, individual task forces were spun-off to assist or work with Marine units in two separate operations, Utah Mesa and William's Glade. Iroquois Grove ended on 25 September with enemy losses put at 134 killed, while the brigade lost 13 dead and 130 wounded.

During the month between the end of Iroquois Grove and the beginning of Fulton Square on 22 October, the 1st Brigade conducted a series of search and clear, reconnaissance-in-force, pacification, and rice denial operations in the eastern portion of the province. In addition, it conducted defensive operations to cover the withdrawal of the 3d Marine Division and progressively absorbed portions of the vacated Marine areas of operations.

On the 22d, the brigade launched its first combat operation under the control of XXIV Corps into an area composed of Trieu Phong, Hai Lang, Gio Linh, Cam Lo, and Mai Linh Districts in the lowlands. Operation Fulton Square was highlighted by heavy contact with elements of the *27th NVA Regiment* in the vicinity of LZ Sparrow during November, and as a result, the 101st Airborne Division and ARVN deployed units

---

*For a detailed discussion of the 15 April 1970 reduction see Graham A. Cosmas and LtCol Terrence P. Murray, USMC, *U.S. Marines in Vietnam: Vietnamization and Redeployment, 1970-1971*, (Washington: History and Museums Division, Headquarters, USMC, 1986).

'A DIFFICULT PHASE'

to assist. Enemy activity soon subsided, changing from frequent mortar and heavy ground attacks to sporadic engagements, and the operation terminated on 18 January 1970 with 384 enemy killed.

To the south, in Thua Thien Province, the 101st Airborne Division, which was also to take over a portion of the vacated 3d Marine Division area of operations, continued combined actions with the 1st ARVN Division to defeat NVA and VC main forces and infrastructure, interdict the A Shau Valley, and assist Vietnamese forces in assuming greater responsibility for combat and pacification operations within the province. On 17 August, the division launched the umbrella operation, Richland Square, a continuation of Kentucky Jumper with the 3d Brigade conducting reconnaissance-in-force in the A Shau Valley (Operation Louisiana Lee). The division's 2d Brigade continued local patrol and security missions along Route 1 (Operation Clairborne Chute), and on 18 August, the 1st Brigade began Operation Cumberland Thunder in conjunction with the 3d Regiment, 1st ARVN Division, to locate and destroy elements of the *5th NVA Regiment*, known to be operating in the southern portion of the Province.

During the last week of September, XXIV Corps issued plans for the repositioning of forces due to the deployment of the 3d Marine Division. By the 21st, 101st Airborne Division Operation Plan 10-69 (Republic Square) was approved, calling for the withdrawal of all forces from the A Shau Valley; the positioning of a control headquarters and two maneuver battalions to screen the final move of the Marine division; and the concentration of division forces in the coastal and piedmont areas of the province. In order to implement Republic Square, Operations Richland Square, Cumberland Thunder, Clairborne Chute, and Louisiana Lee were brought to an end and work began of the back-hauling of personnel, supplies, and

Greeting MajGen William K. Jones, right, shortly after the division's arrival on Okinawa were, from left, BGen Robert H. Barrow, Commanding General, MCB, Camp Butler; MajGen Robert B. Smith, Deputy Commanding General, U.S. Army, Ryukyu Islands; and BGen Robert B. Carney, Jr., Commanding General, 9th Marine Amphibious Brigade.

Marine Corps Historical Collection

equipment from the westernmost portion of the division area of operations. In addition, a number of boundary modifications among the 1st Brigade, 5th Infantry Division; 1st ARVN Division; and 101st Airborne Division were made. These changes included larger areas of responsibility for the 2d ARVN Regiment and reconnaissance elements of the 101st Airborne Division in Quang Tri Province.

Operation Republic Square, begun on 29 September, was characterized by extensive airmobile, reconnaissance-in-force, and search and ambush operations to destroy enemy forces within the division's area of operations; interdiction of enemy infiltration routes and base camps; the capture or elimination of the local Viet Cong Infrastructure; disruption of enemy supply routes from the rice producing lowlands to mountain base camps; and support for the Accelerated Pacification Program within the province. During the operation, which ended on 6 December, the 1st and 2d Brigades concentrated on the coastal and piedmont areas near Hue, while the 3d Brigade deployed to Quang Tri Province, northwest of the now closed Vandegrift Combat Base, initiating operations (Norton Falls) to screen the withdrawal of the 4th Marines.

As the year drew to a close in northern I Corps Tactical Zone, the enemy generally avoided major contact with allied forces, concentrating his efforts instead on rice collection and undermining government pacification efforts in the heavily populated lowlands near the old imperial city of Hue. In the western portions of both Thua Thien and Quang Tri Provinces, now devoid of all but reconnaissance forces, he slowly began to rebuild the large base areas along the Vietnamese-Laotian border, destroyed earlier in the year. The year, however, had witnessed the defeat of NVA and VC forces at every turn, frustrating their attempts to terrorize and victimize the inhabitants of the two provinces, and denying the rice, supplies, and personnel so vital to their survival. The redeployment of the 3d Marine Division was testimony not only to this defeat, but to the great strides made in the pacification and Vietnamization of northern I Corps.

PART IV
QUANG NAM: THE YEAR'S FINAL BATTLES

CHAPTER 11
Go Noi and the Arizona

Vital Area Security—Pipestone Canyon: The Destruction of Go Noi Island
1st Marines: Protecting the Southern Flank—The Arizona

Vital Area Security

In conformity with III MAF's corps-wide strategy for 1969, the 1st Marine Division, during the last six months of the year, continued to concentrate its efforts on keeping the enemy away from the city of Da Nang and its heavily populated environs. Its infantry units and supporting arms were disposed to provide maximum security for the Da Nang Vital Area and other important political and economic sites, military installations, and lines of communication. Simultaneously, the division directed its offensive operations against enemy forces and base areas which posed the most immediate threat to these centers or to allied military installations.

At midyear, Major General Ormond R. Simpson continued the general scheme, adopted earlier, for deploying his four infantry regiments. Supported and reinforced by artillery batteries of the 11th Marines, the 1st Reconnaissance Battalion, 1st Tank Battalion, and strong contingents of engineers, transportation, and service troops, the 1st, 5th, 7th, and 26th Marines were positioned in a series of concentric circles centered on Da Nang. Although not directly involved in the defense of the city itself, the division's responsibility began just outside the Da Nang Vital Area and radiated in all directions. To the north and northwest the 26th Marines patrolled the rocket belt, and spread out to the west and southwest was the 7th Marines. Elements of the 1st Marines were deployed to the southwest, south, and southeast of the city, while further to the southwest, the 5th Marines operated in a TAOR encompassing An Hoa Combat Base and major enemy infiltration routes along the Song Thu Bon and Song Vu Gia, and throughout the region between the two rivers, the Arizona.

From the outskirts of Da Nang to the remote mountain valleys, small detachments of North Vietnamese and Viet Cong regulars and guerrillas continued to move throughout the division's TAOR, despite the series of successful major allied operations and constant counterguerrilla patrols conducted during the first half of the year. Likewise, enemy rocket, mortar, and ground assault teams persisted in attacks against allied installations and population centers, while planting mines and boobytraps, gathering food and tribute, and maintaining an unrelenting campaign of terrorism against the civilian population. Division military operations, from the squad ambush and platoon patrol to multi-battalion sweeps, during the latter half of 1969, aimed at the complete destruction of this endless cycle of harassment by elements of 21 enemy infantry and support battalions known to infest Quang Nam Province.

Pipestone Canyon: The Destruction of Go Noi Island

For a number of years, the Viet Cong and North Vietnamese Army had used the Dodge City and Go Noi Island areas, south of Da Nang, as haven sites and staging areas for attacks into the coastal lowlands between Hoi An and Vietnam's second largest city. In response, the allies conducted a series of operations to rid both areas of enemy troops; the last two were Operation Allen Brook in May and Operation Meade River in December 1968. A classic example of a deliberately executed cordon and search, the 1st Marines' Meade River and its ARVN counterpart, accounted for over 1,200 enemy killed or captured, 72 of whom were identified as members of the local Viet Cong Infrastructure.

Although previous operations in the area produced significant results, the enemy stuck to the accepted technique of withdrawing his forces when pressed and then reintroducing them into their original operating areas once friendly forces shifted to a new zone of action. During the first five months of 1969, the 1st Marines saturated the fringes of the region with company-size and small-unit patrols with notable success, but these maneuvers, while effective in curtailing the enemy's free passage northward, lacked the scope necessary to produce a lasting effect on enemy forces using the area. Ridding the area of enemy troops was to become the major task of the 1st Marines during the final six months of 1969.

The contiguous areas of Dodge City and Go Noi Island, located approximately 10 to 20 kilometers south of Da Nang and 6 to 20 kilometers west of Hoi

An, constituted the western portion of Dien Ban and the eastern half of Dai Loc Districts, and included 19 villages or portions thereof. The combined area was bordered on the west by the south fork of the Song Vu Gia; on the north by the Song Ai Nghia, Song Lo Tho, and Song Thanh Quit; on the east by Route 1; and on the south by the Song Thu Bon, Song Ba Ren, and Song Chiem Son. Although bisected by the one- to two-meter-high, north-south railroad berm, the area consisted of semi-open, flat terrain, covered by numerous rice fields and grave mounds bounded by hedgerows, brush, and expanses of elephant grass.

Intelligence agencies estimated that Dodge City and Go Noi Island harbored seven to nine enemy battalions with a maximum strength of 2,500 troops, in addition to 200 to 500 local force Viet Cong and hamlet guerrillas. The enemy's main battle units were tentatively identified as the *36th NVA Regiment*, consisting of three battalions, and *District II Da Nang* forces made up of the *T-89th Sapper, D-3 Sapper, T-3 Sapper*, and *R-20th Battalions*, and elements of the disbanded *38th NVA Regiment*. Although battered, these enemy units still were considered capable of sniping, harassing, and attacking in mass, and then retreating to well-constructed camouflaged defensive positions in Dodge City, Go Noi Island, and the Que Son Mountains beyond. The time had come to rid, once and for all, Dodge City and Go Noi Island of enemy forces.

In mid-May, General Simpson called Colonel Charles S. Robertson, Commanding Officer, 1st Marines, and his operations officer, Major James K. Reilly, to Headquarters, 1st Marine Division for a briefing on the concept, mission, and forces of a planned operation in Dodge City and Go Noi Island. The operation, codenamed Pipestone Canyon, explained Colonel James B. Ord, Jr., Division Assistant Chief of Staff, G-3, was designed primarily to deny the North Vietnamese and main force Viet Cong safe haven in the two areas and to open Route 4 from Dai Loc to Dien Ban, closed to civilian and military traffic for several years. It was, he noted, the "natural sequel" to Operations Taylor Common and Oklahoma Hills. To accomplish the mission would require a sizeable amount of infantry, heavily reinforced with artillery, naval gunfire, and air. It would also require a land-clearing effort, which "we had never really been able to do." Specifically, as Colonel Ord pointed out, a combined Marine, Korean, and ARVN force amounting to 10 infantry battalions supported by a large artillery, naval gunfire, and armor force and including a Provisional Land-Clearing Company, composed of personnel and equipment from the 7th and 9th Marine Engineer Battalions and the Army's 687th Land-Clearing Company, would be task organized and placed under the control of the 1st Marines. This would ensure enough troop density and supporting arms, he noted, "to really clear it out."[1]

On the 16th, General Simpson and his staff presented the concept of operations to Lieutenant General Herman Nickerson, Commanding General, III MAF, who approved the mission and forces, authorized direct liaison with Korean and ARVN units involved, and ordered execution on or about 27 May. Following approval, detailed and coordinate planning began.[2]

During the month, 1st Marine staff planning progressed in secret. As the operation was to be multiphased, only those with a need to know were informed, and then only concerning the phase in which they would participate. When it came time to inform the Korean forces, Colonel Robertson and his staff visited the 2d Brigade, Republic of Korea Marine Corps Headquarters at Hoi An and briefed Brigadier General Dong Ho Lee, initiating a period of coordinated planning between the two Marine staffs. The ARVN forces, to be led by Colonel Thien, commanding officer of the Quang Da Special Zone (QDSZ), a loosely formed, division-level organization tasked to defend Da Nang, were not to be brought into the planning until 48 hours prior to their participation so as to forestall disclosure.

On 24 May, Colonel Robertson approved and directed publication of 1st Marines Operation Order 001-69 (Pipestone Canyon), selecting the 26th as D-Day. Beginning at 0600, two battalions would attack eastward: Special Landing Force Alpha (1st Battalion, 26th Marines) from Hill 37 toward Dodge City, and, 3d Battalion, 5th Marines from Liberty Bridge toward western Go Noi Island. The attack, aimed at forcing the enemy into both areas and at the same time deceiving him as to allied intentions, would conclude with the establishment of blocking positions on the western edge of the area of operations. During the second phase, scheduled to begin five days later, five battalions (1st and 2d Battalions, 1st Marines; 37th ARVN Ranger Battalion; and the 1st and 4th Battalions, 51st ARVN Regiment) were to attack southward through Dodge City, coordinating with the 1st and 2d Battalions, 2d Korean Marine Corps Brigade, occupying positions on the area of operation's eastern flank. When

Marine Corps Historical Collection
Company B, 1st Battalion, 1st Marines, supported by tanks, sweeps and countersweeps scrub-covered Dodge City in preparation for the attack on Go Noi Island to the south.

the battalions reached the Song Ky Lam, engineering work would begin on upgrading and then eventually opening Route 4 from the railroad berm east to Route 1. At the same time, the Provisional Land-Clearing Company would be formed and staged at Liberty Bridge and one battalion would be lifted from the area of operation to provide security for the attack east across the island. In phase III, while blocks were maintained along the north bank of the Song Ky Lam, the railroad berm on Go Noi, and engineering efforts continued on Route 4, three battalions were to attack across the eastern portion of the island, followed by land-clearing operations, denying the enemy access and use of the area for staging and infiltration. Should circumstances warrant, Colonel Robertson retained the option of ordering additional phases.[3]

On Monday the 26th, Lieutenant Colonel George C. Kliefoth's 1st Battalion, 26th Marines, under the operational control of the 7th Marines, and Lieutenant Colonel Harry E. Atkinson's 3d Battalion, 5th Marines launched eastward, moving over ground pummeled by artillery fires of the 1st Battalion, 11th Marines and 8-inch guns of the *Newport News* (CA 148). Except for surprise firing devices, the Marines discovering fewer than were tripped, the two battalions generally met very light resistance during the advance. But as they drew closer to Dodge City and Go Noi Island, enemy activity picked up, the companies reporting an ever-increasing number of engagements, enemy killed, and weapons and equipment discovered or captured. By 30 May, both battalions had reached their blocking positions just west of the railroad berm and begun to dig-in in preparation for phase II. To this point, Kliefoth's and Atkinson's Marines had killed a total of 16 enemy troops, but the price was high: 10 dead and more than 100 wounded, all as a result of mines and boobytraps.

Following a 24-hour ceasefire in honor of Buddha's birthday, control of Operation Pipestone Canyon was passed to the 1st Marines and the five attacking battalions began to move toward the line of departure, the Song La Tho, on the morning of the 31st. South of the river, artillery and naval gunfire, designed to detonate expected heavy concentrations of surprise firing devices as well as prevent enemy interference with the attack, began. With the forward shift of the 1st Marines' command post to Phong Luc (3), and the exchange of liaison personnel among U.S., ARVN, and Korean units, all five battalions crossed the Song La Tho in rapid succession. Sandwiched between the

ARVN Ranger battalion in the west and two battalions of the 51st ARVN Regiment in the east, Lieutenant Colonel Wendell P. Morgenthaler's 1st Battalion, 1st Marines and Lieutenant Colonel Harold G. Glasgow's 2d Battalion moved cautiously into Dodge City. Soon after crossing the river, both battalions reported locating numerous recently occupied, well-constructed bunker and tunnel complexes, and areas peppered with mines and boobytraps; devices which would become all too familiar as the Marines moved further south. Activity, however, was light, as enemy troops fled south and west into the sights of the blocking forces. Meanwhile, the 1st and 4th Battalions, 51st Regiment, on the eastern flank in companion Operation Vu Ninh 05, busied themselves screening civilians with the help of teams composed of Quang Nam Provincial Reconnaissance Units (PRU), National Police Field Forces, and counterintelligence personnel assigned to the 1st Marines. The Korean Marine battalions, south of Go Noi, experienced no initial enemy activity.

Sweeping south toward the island, the battalions generally moved out in the early morning, taking advantage of the coolest part of the day. As Lieutenant Colonel Morgenthaler explained: "at times it would reach temperatures of approximately 115 degrees and with the gear we were carrying, we figured that by moving out early in the morning, we would negate any heat casualties, and at that time the troops would be extremely fresh and more observant."[4] The pace was slow as every bunker and tunnel complex was searched, and every hedgerow, paddy dike, grave mound, and riverbank probed for surprise firing devices and caches. As each battalion closed on the first of several successive phase lines, a small force would be positioned along the line while the remainder began a detailed and deliberate countersearch of the area just covered and naval gunfire pounded deeper targets. In addition to the forward attack and countersweep tactics, a large number of independent patrols and ambushes were deployed every evening.

Movement became more difficult as the advancing battalions neared the second phase line. Not only did both ARVN and Marines encounter a large band of mines set across their paths, but enemy activity picked up. On 2 June, as Company G moved south in mid-morning, it received a number of 60mm mortar rounds followed by bursts of AK47 fire from a group of enemy troops occupying a small bunker complex. Supported by a section of tanks, elements of the com-

Three artillerymen of the 11th Marines provide 105mm howitzer support for the joint Marine, ARVN, and Korean search of enemy-infested Dodge City and Go Noi Island.

Marine Corps Historical Collection

pany maneuvered forward, pounding the enemy position. Sweeping through the complex, the Marines discovered seven killed and one wounded, in addition to a number of weapons and propaganda leaflets. Later that same day, both the ARVN Ranger battalion and western blocking forces reported increasing activity in their zones of action as enemy troops tried to escape west, but were forced instead to move south across the Song Ky Lam onto Go Noi.

Two days later, after an early morning artillery preparation by the tubes of 1st Battalion, 11th Marines, Morgenthaler's and Glasgow's battalions again moved south. Meanwhile, the two battalions of the 51st ARVN Regiment remained in their initial positions and continued civic action and screening operations in order to identify members of the local Viet Cong Infrastructure. The Korean Marines, having yet to engage any enemy troops, initiated several local company-size search and block operations south of Go Noi. By 5 June, elements of the 1st Marines reached the Song Ky Lam, separating Dodge City and the island. During the next three days, the remaining attack forces closed on the river and then counterswept, while observing wing aircraft dropped 1,000- and 2,000-pound bombs on eastern Go Noi Island. Before the air bombardment ceased, nearly 750,000 pounds of ordnance had been dropped.

With the sweep through Dodge City complete, Company A, 1st Engineer Battalion, with security provided by the 39th ARVN Ranger Battalion, began upgrading Route 4. Simultaneously, the advancing forces began repositioning themselves for the third phase. The 1st Battalion, 26th Marines, which had occupied blocking positions west of Dodge City, withdrew from the operation and helilifted to its amphibious shipping in the South China Sea. In addition, Morgenthaler's battalion, less Company D, moved by air to Liberty Bridge where it took command of tanks and tracked vehicles and began an advance overland toward Go Noi Island.

On 10 June, the third phase of Operation Pipestone Canyon began. General Simpson, Colonel Charles E. Walker, interim commander of the 1st Marines in the absence of Colonel Robertson, who was on emergency leave, and their tactical command group staffs were atop Hill 119, just south of Go Noi. Observation was excellent. Morgenthaler's battalion could be seen advancing from Liberty Bridge. Colonel Atkinson's 3d Battalion, 5th Marines could be seen occupying blocking positions along the railroad berm, and the positions of the Korean Marines, south of eastern Go Noi, were also in view. Although they were dug in and could not be observed from 119, the ARVN forces were in position north of the island. As the command groups watched, wing attack and fighter aircraft strafed selected landing zones and surrounding areas. Finally, the fighter aircraft moved out and the attack aircraft, flying 200 feet above ground, laid down a thick stream of smoke, dividing the island. As scheduled, 22 troop-loaded CH-46s appeared and headed for two landing zones on the southern banks of eastern Go Noi. Minutes later, the combined force of Glasgow's men and Korean Marines alighted from the helicopters, formed up, and began a sweep to the north. That afternoon, Morgenthaler's armored column passed through Atkinson's lines on the railroad berm, picked up Company D, and joined in the coordinated attack.

Again advancing by numbered phase lines, the three battalions reached phase line II on 11 June. At this line, the 1st Korean Marine Battalion encountered several bunker complexes and a large number of rice and equipment caches. The brigade's liaison officer informed Colonel Walker that the battalion wished to search the area, and it was agreed that Morgenthaler's and Glasgow's battalions would continue north while the Koreans carried out the search. The decision proved to be correct, for in each of the numerous tunnels and bunkers searched, the Koreans discovered enemy troops or substantial caches of rice, weapons, and equipment. The 1st and 2d Battalions, 1st Marines also added to these totals, uncovering many discarded weapons, large rice caches, and an increasing number of dead enemy troops, killed by the heavy air and artillery bombardment.

Squeezed between the blocking forces and the advancing Marines, the enemy scattered, breaking into smaller and smaller groups, hoping to be bypassed and thus able to make their escape south into the Que Son Mountains. Some did escape, but many were found and either captured or destroyed, if they resisted. Those captured were troops unable to move—the wounded and the starving. Ironically, a number of these undernourished North Vietnamese soldiers were discovered within a short distance of substantial caches; all were unaware of the existence of the concealed food.

On 13 June, the Provisional Land-Clearing Company assembled at Liberty Bridge. An armored column was dispatched with a platoon from Company M, 3d Battalion, 5th Marines to provide security for the 10 Marine Eimco (M64) tractors and nine Army D7E

Col Charles E. Walker, acting Commanding Officer, 1st Marines, discusses tactics with his battalion commanders in preparation for crossing one of the many phase lines that marked the advance southward.

Caterpillars. At midday, as the column moved out across country toward Go Noi Island, one of the tanks hit a mine, resulting in the wounding of two Marines and causing a temporary halt in the column's pace. After resuming the advance, a second mine disabled yet another tank and the column halted. Additional security was requested and the combined infantry, tank, and tractor column dug in for the night to make repairs. The following morning, the land-clearing unit resumed its eastward march.[5]

On Go Noi Island, the two battalions of the 1st Marines reached the Song Ky Lam and turned, beginning countersweep operations. At the same time, the Korean Marine battalion established company-size areas and began a series of detailed searches. Colonel Walker notified Lieutenant Colonel Atkinson that his battalion, then in blocking positions along the railroad berm, would no longer be needed and that the participation of the 3d Battalion, 5th Marines would terminate on 15 June, as land-clearing operations would soon get underway. Just north of the island, the 1st and 4th ARVN battalions moved from their blocking positions along the Song Ky Lam and initiated countersearch operations in Dodge City and areas west of Route 1.

Twenty days into the operation, Atkinson's battalion ceased its participation in Pipestone Canyon; Morgenthaler's battalion, in turn, assumed responsibility for the railroad berm and an area 500 meters west, while at the same time continuing to provide security for the land-clearing company, which was beginning the complete destruction of all vegetation and the filling and leveling of all enemy installations on eastern Go Noi. Clearing 250 acres at a time to a depth of six inches, the blades of the combined company eventually would leave behind over 8,000 dirt-brown and flat acres. The enemy, as a result, lost a long-used, major elephant grass- and bamboo-covered, bunker-saturated haven and staging area.[6]

With the clearing effort well underway, the countersweep of eastern Go Noi and adjacent islands nearly complete, and enemy activity decreasing by the day, Colonel Robertson, having reassumed command on the 14th, decided to begin company-size search and clear operations in the western portion of the island. At first light on the 19th, Morgenthaler's Company C, later joined by Company B, moved out from the railroad berm, searching in a westerly direction toward Bao An Dong. A homemade mine was tripped, then another, and another; western Go Noi was saturated with surprise firing devices. Evidence of this was borne out over the next several days as Morgethaler's Marines continued the search from Bao An Tay to An Quyen, in the northwest corner, taking additional casualties. Solutions to the recurring problem of mines and boobytraps consisted of bombarding the areas with artillery fire, peppering with bombs and napalm, conducting all movement mounted on tanks or tracked vehicles, and continually stressing the threat, ensuring that the troops maintained maximum dispersion while moving. These solutions, however, did not eliminate the threat and casualties continued to mount. The only way to avoid the surprise firing devices, Colonel Morgenthaler later noted, was to "avoid the area which meant avoiding the mission . . . . We did *not* stay inside our compounds like the Korean Marines in order to avoid casualties."[7]

The 1st Battalion, 1st Marines' sweep of western Go Noi continued until the 21st, when the battalion returned to its base at Dong Son (2). With the departure of Morgenthaler's Marines, the 2d Battalion, 1st Marines assumed security for the land-clearing company and responsibility for most of the island, except for the area assigned the Korean Marines. Now it was Glasgow's battalion's turn to work western Go Noi.

Operating with three companies, Lieutenant Colonel Glasgow was determined to find and destroy the remaining enemy hiding on Go Noi. Conducting search and clear operations day after day, Marines of

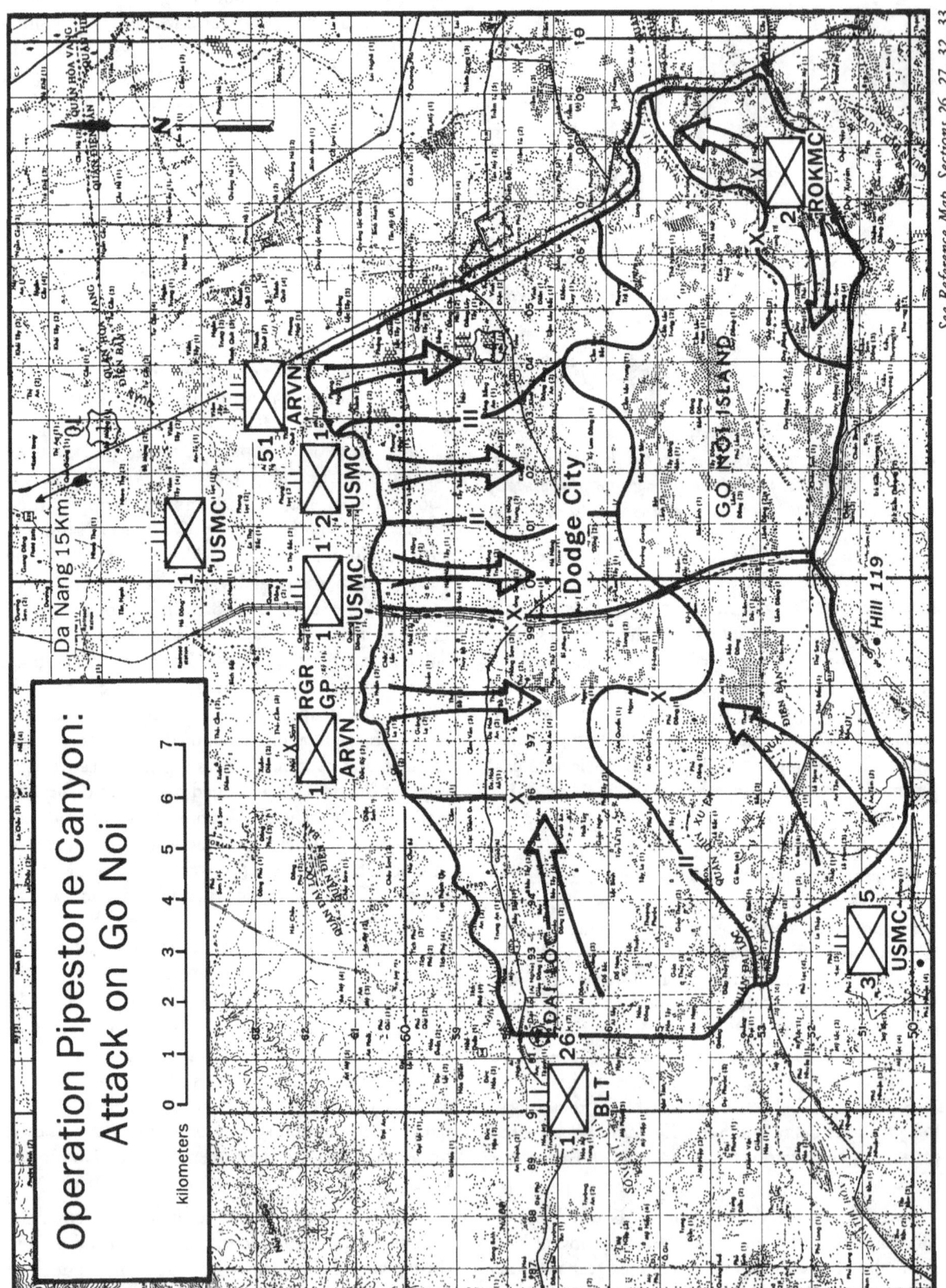

the 2d Battalion, 1st Marines encountered numerous surprise firing devices, but flushed out few troops. The continuing problem of boobytraps and mines not only took its toll in casualties, but also on the morale of those left behind. Company G's Commanding Officer, Captain Frank H. Adams, observed the effects. Losing 59 men killed and wounded to boobytraps out of a casualty total of 70, his company neared the breaking point during its sweep of western Go Noi, as he later recounted:

> When you do encounter boobytraps and you continue to trip them, it gets to the point where each individual within that unit—regardless of the leadership that you have—it gets to the point where the troops say: "They put them out there, we have got to sweep it, ultimately I'm going to hit that son-of-a-bitch that they put out there. I don't know who is going to hit it tomorrow, but one of these days I'm going to hit one myself." When you get to that point as a troop leader, as a squad leader, as a platoon leader, as a platoon sergeant, and a company commander . . . you're lost . . . . When a trooper feels he is going to get it, you have had the weenie.
>
> So we went back in [after taking several boobytrap casualties], . . . sat down, got the company together, put the security out, and we got together for about a 15-minute talk. That is what I had planned, but I kind of choked up on them, so I only made it three and a half to four minutes. After talking to them, explaining to them, that these are the things of war that we have to encounter—that we will encounter—the things we have to take—you don't enjoy it, you don't like it, but these are the things you do encounter. Then we said the Lord's Prayer, prayed for those that we had lost, and passed the word . . . that all of us are going back, . . . that we have the same sweeps tomorrow that we had today, and we are going to find every boobytrap out there without tripping it. Troop morale raised, . . . we jumped off into the operation the next day and continued to march, and continued to sweep.[8]

While Glasgow's Marines swept western Go Noi, elements of the 1st Battalion, 1st Marines were reintroduced into the Pipestone Canyon area of operations on the 27th. Conducting a short search and clear operation in northern Dodge City, they turned up additional enemy equipment and dead, killed by air and artillery, but encountered only those few enemy troops who had remained behind. The ARVN forces, adjacent to Morgenthaler's Marines, made no contact and continued the process of screening the civilian population in search of infrastructure members as they moved south.

By the end of June, the entire tempo of the operation slowed. Few enemy troops were found, and those who were were either the wounded or those missed in the initial sweeps. As the land-clearing effort on eastern Go Noi neared completion, security for the unit passed from Glasgow's battalion to the Korean

Several Marines help a wounded comrade to a waiting medical evacuation helicopter. Surprise firing devices accounted for a number of casualties during Operation Pipestone.

Marine Corps Historical Collection

Marines for a short period. In addition, elements of the 1st Engineer Battalion officially opened Route 4 from the railroad berm to Dien Ban, meeting a major goal of the province's yearly pacification plan and of the operation. During the month-long effort, the engineers had not only constructed a road capable of accommodating two-way traffic, but a series of large culverts also, and cleared an average of 500 meters on either side of the thoroughfare, totaling more than 6,000,000 square meters.

As a result of a number of coordinating meetings held earlier in the month, General Simpson determined that eastern Go Noi would be permanently occupied. With the help of the land-clearing company, work began on two combat bases—the first to be occupied by the 3d Battalion, 51st ARVN Regiment, and the second by the Korean Brigade's 1st Battalion. He also decided that once the bases' initial defenses were completed, western Go Noi would be cleared and at least one U.S. Marine company would be tasked to patrol the area. He hoped, as a consequence, that the island would never again be returned to enemy hands, unless the North Vietnamese and Viet Cong were willing to commit the major forces required and accept the heavy casualties that would result from such an attempt.

The opening days of July saw the operation enter its second month with the third phase still in progress. In the Dodge City area, elements of the 51st ARVN Regiment continued to patrol and screen. Morgenthaler's Marines, having completed their search and clear operation, returned to the regiment's western area where they secured the Cau Do and Ha Dong railroad bridges. On Go Noi, Glasgow's battalion pursued search operations in the western portion of the island, while again providing security for the land-clearing effort. Across the railroad berm, the 3d Battalion, 51st ARVN Regiment and the Korean Marines continued building their combat bases and conducting company-size clearing operations.

On the 6th, Colonel Robertson decided to reduce the effort on western Go Noi to a rifle company, which was to provide security for the Provisional Land-Clearing Company, and, as a consequence, the 2d Battalion, 1st Marines, less one company, withdrew and returned to its permanent base at Phong Luc (2) for rehabilitation. Company E, which had spent several days at "Stack Arms," the division's in-country rest and recreation center south of Da Nang, returned to Go Noi, and resumed patrol and ambush activities. Two days later, another realignment took place; the 4th Battalion replaced the 1st Battalion, 51st ARVN Regiment in southwestern Dodge City, and the 37th Rangers withdrew. With a reduction in size of the operation, Colonel Robertson decided to close his forward headquarters and return the command group to Duong Son (2).

Weather reports received on the 8th indicated that Typhoon Tess would come ashore near Da Nang on the 10th. Go Noi Island, especially the western portion, had been inundated during a similar storm in October 1968, and it was decided to withdraw the land-clearing company and its security force from the island until the typhoon passed. The move took place the following day. Just prior to reaching the high ground along Route 1, where the forces would wait out the storm, the rear of the column came under heavy small arms fire. Two Marine engineers were killed and an equal number wounded before the fighting ended.

Activity throughout the Pipestone Canyon area of operation ground to a halt as Typhoon Tess brought heavy rains to Quang Nam Province for the next two days. By the 12th, the weather cleared and Company E, with tracked vehicles and tanks attached, moved from Route 1 back across Go Noi to await the bulldozers. During the move, one of the tanks accompanying Company E detonated a land mine which resulted in a ruptured gas tank and the severe burning of 12 Marines. The 7th Engineers, instead of following, decided it would place the tractors on low-bed trucks and drive them around to Liberty Bridge to conserve the dozers' engines and tracks. That afternoon, the forces to continue the land-clearing were back on western Go Noi and operations began the following morning.

Meanwhile, an increasing number of intelligence reports concerning enemy presence in eastern Dodge City, east of the Song Suoi Co Ca, convinced Colonel Robertson that the area required additional attention. Arrangements were made on 14 July for a battalion-size heliborne assault into four landing zones surrounding the former village of Tay Bang An, the area suspected of harboring a company-size sapper unit. In preparation for the assault, assisted later by armor, Colonel Glasgow requested that Company H relieve Company E as security for the land-clearing operation, and that Company D, 1st Battalion, 1st Marines join

A Marine engineer levels enemy fortifications on Go Noi Island in preparation for the reintroduction of a stable population and the return of the land to rice production.

his battalion in order to provide a four-rifle-company operation.

Early on the morning of the 15th, the lift went off as planned, but as troop-laden CH-46s approached the four landing zones, all began receiving enemy small arms fire. Seven of the helicopters were hit and one eventually forced to land near a Korean Marine compound on Route 1. Although all zones were hot, two insertions were carried out as planned, but two others were shifted to alternate sites, forcing an hour's delay in closing the cordon around the abandoned village. Once on the ground, aerial observers circling above reported sighting 30 to 50 enemy troops inside the area to which Glasgow's Marines were moving from all directions. By 0830, Company D had captured one Viet Cong and was engaging a small pocket of enemy troops in its sector; Company G had detained a male who later was classified as a Viet Cong; and Company E had detonated a boobytrap, causing several casualties, and reported taking several bursts of small arms fire from its front. Company F met the heaviest resistance. As it closed on its cordon positions, the company received a large volume of automatic weapons and RPG fire from enemy-occupied bunkers on the west side of the Suoi Co Ca, killing two Marines and wounding seven. Eventually pushing through the complex, the assaulting platoons captured one NVA, counted four enemy bodies, and spotted seven more soldiers withdraw across the river. Meanwhile, a platoon of tanks and tracked vehicles made its way down Route 1, then turned west onto the recently upgraded Route 4, and joined Glasgow's Marines in the cordoned area.

Throughout the 16th, as the Marines tightened the cordon and established defensive positions, the entrapped enemy sappers conducted several probes in a vain attempt to discover a vulnerable area in the battalion's lines. Following these initial attempts, the enemy initiated a breakthrough which Company G successfully repelled. Late in the day, it was decided to slightly shift the cordon, under cover of darkness, to the north along the Song Tam Giap into an area where Company D had captured several enemy troops the day before. After tightening the cordon and conducting a number of searches on the morning of the 17th, the area proved to be devoid of enemy troops and Colonel Glasgow reported the search complete, the battalion having killed 20 and captured 14. Later in the day, the battalion helilifted out of the area and returned to its base at Phong Luc.[9]

With the level of operations slowing on Go Noi Island as the enemy avoided contact, but again picking up in Dodge City, Colonel Robertson initiated planning for an additional phase. Robertson met with Colonel Thuc, Commanding Officer, 51st ARVN Regiment, and together they agreed to conduct a search of Dodge City south of Route 4, where it was suspected the enemy was hiding. Following approval by General Simpson, Colonel Robertson ordered the operation scheduled for 21 July and assigned the 1st Battalion, 1st Marines and 4th Battalion, 51st ARVN

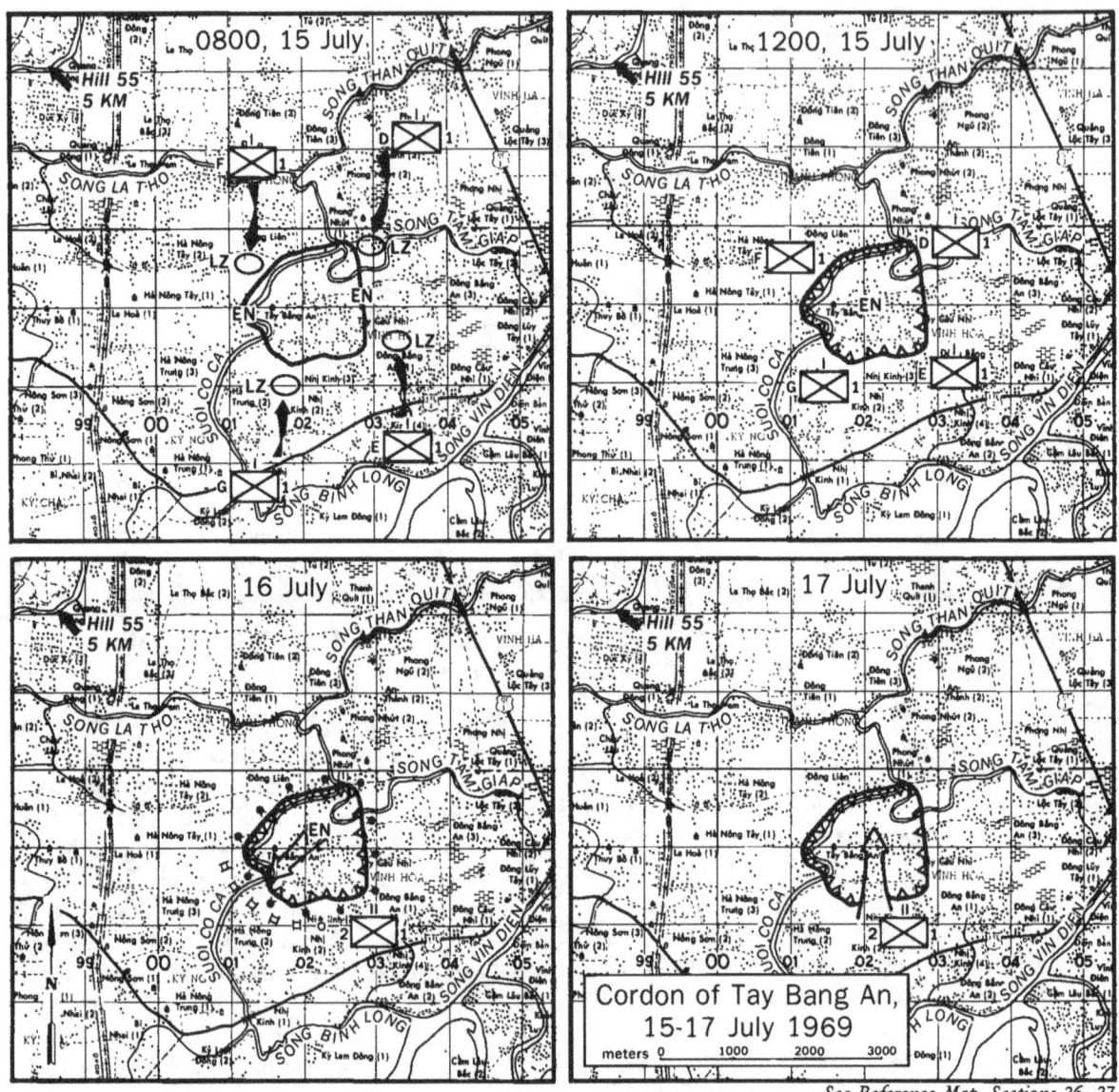

At 0800 on 15 July, four companies of the 2d Battalion, 1st Marines establish landing zones near Tay Bang An, five kilometers southeast of Hill 55. By noon, the cordon of the village is complete, trapping a company-size enemy sapper unit. On the 16th, the enemy unit attempts to break through the battalion's lines, fortified with mines, tanks, and mortars. The battalion completes the search of the area on the 17th, having found no survivors.

Regiment the task. A realignment of forces within the 1st Marines' normal area of responsibility, however, was necessary before Morgenthaler's Marines could be released for the operation. The 1st Marines, as a result, assumed control of 1st Battalion, 26th Marines and assigned it control of the regiment's western area of operations. Lieutenant Colonel Thomas P. Ganey's 3d Battalion, 1st Marines extended its lines to cover the remainder of the area of responsibility as Lieutenant Colonel Glasgow's battalion prepared to join Operation Durham Peak.

At midnight on 20 July, following the completion of land-clearing operations on western Go Noi, the third phase of Pipestone Canyon came to a close. In nearly three months, the combined force logged 734 enemy killed, 382 weapons captured, and 55 prisoners taken. Marine casualties were 57 killed and 394 seriously wounded.

Pipestone Canyon's fourth phase began with the move of Morgenthaler's Marines into an area of southern Dodge City, south of Route 4 and west of the railroad berm on the 21st. While two companies occupied blocking positions along the southern bank of the Song Ky Lam, the remainder of the battalion began search and destroy operations in the assigned area. Although no engagements with enemy forces took place during the three-day operation, the Marines continually encountered mines and boobytraps. In one mine incident, occurring on the 23d, a Marine from Company C detonated a "daisy chain," composed of three dud artillery rounds set as antipersonnel mines, resulting in the severe wounding of six men. At midday on the 24th, the 1st Battalion, 1st Marines closed the short search of southern Dodge City, and again returned to its base at Phong Luc.

As July ended, Company L began moving patrol forces onto western Go Noi in relief of Company I, which returned to Ha Dong Bridge, northwest of Hill 55. Like Marines of the 1st Battalion operating in southern Dodge City several days before, Company L encountered a high number of surprise firing devices. On the 25th, an LVT carrying a squad from the company onto the island detonated a small antipersonnel mine, damaging the vehicle. After temporary repairs were made, the LVT moved out again, striking yet another mine, thought to be a 250-pound bomb, which killed three and severely wounded seven other squad members. Most, if not all, of the surprise firing devices encountered on western Go Noi were fabricated from discarded or dud American ordnance, such as grenades, mortar and artillery rounds, bombs, or cans filled with the explosive C-4. On the average, 60 percent of all devices were defused and 40 percent detonated; that 40 percent continued to inflict a majority of all Marine casualties.

Company M, under Captain Donald J. Robinson II, relieved Company L on western Go Noi at the beginning of August, continuing the cycle of patrol and short cordon and search operations. Throughout the rest of the island, the 3d Battalion, 51st ARVN Regiment conducted similar operations in the central third, while elements of the 2d Republic of Korean Marine Corps Brigade operated in the eastern third. To the north, other Korean Marines drove through eastern Dodge City, while the 4th Battalion, 51st ARVN Regiment searched the central portion. On 6 August, Lieutenant Colonel Ganey's 3d Battalion, 1st Marines began a search and clear operation in Dodge City. After some difficulty, caused by an LVT throwing a track, the battalion initiated an attack with Company L on the left flank, Company I on the right, the battalion command group in the center, and Company K pro-

Department of Defense Photo (USMC) A374597
A radioman with the 1st Marines takes a break while on one of the numerous patrols that swept and then reswept both Dodge City and Go Noi Island.

viding rear security. Few engagements occurred as Ganey's Marines swept north from Route 4, between the railroad berm and the Suoi Co Ca and, as a result, the battalion returned to Duong Son (2) on the 9th.

During the remainder of the month, Robinson's Marines continued sweep operations in western Go Noi, as other elements of the regiment periodically returned to Dodge City to conduct short search operations in conjunction with their Korean and ARVN counterparts. Again, no significant engagements took place. This respite allowed companies opportunity to train in all elements of offensive and defensive combat and use all available supporting arms in the process.[10] In addition, efforts were made to keep Route 4 open to traffic despite repeated enemy attempts to mine the road and destroy major culverts. Also during August, the Provisional Land-Clearing Company, after a period of maintenance, returned to southwestern Dodge City. Plowing a total of 2,594,000 square meters in one week, the company leveled a suspected enemy staging area bounded on the north by

Route 4, on the west by the Phong Thu hamlet complex, on the south by the Song Ky Lam, and on the east by the north-south railroad berm, before returning to the 7th Engineer Battalion's permanent base.

Major enemy activity throughout the Pipestone area of operations had all but ceased by the beginning of September. Although Viet Cong and North Vietnamese troops avoided encounters with friendly forces, they did continue to concentrate their limited available resources on harassing allied units by continuing to lay surprise firing devices. But as the month passed, aerial sightings of small groups of enemy soldiers north of Route 4 increased, signaling the presence of an unknown size force in that area of Dodge City. These sightings prompted the commitment of three of Morgenthaler's four companies to the area in late September. At 1120 on the 25th, Companies C and D helilifted into two separate landing zones, approximately 1,000 meters south of the Song La Tho. Simultaneously, Company A and the battalion command group, reinforced by a section each of tanks and amphibian tractors, crossed Route 4 and advanced north, blocking enemy attempts to escape southward. Morgenthaler's Marines encountered few enemy troops during the operation, although numerous bunkers, small caches, and extensive mine fields were discovered and destroyed as the battalion's effort shifted east. On the 29th, after only four days in the area, the companies withdrew and returned to Phong Luc.

Heavy rains fell as the month of October began, turning the area into a quagmire. By the 5th, the rising flood waters of the Song Ky Lam inundated western Go Noi forcing Company L, which had replaced Company M, to withdraw by air and return to Hill 37. The rains also forced the withdrawal of the 2d Battalion, 51st ARVN Regiment from Dodge City. Five days later, as flood waters subsided and the units returned to the field, the fourth phase of Pipestone Canyon came to an end and the final phase began.

Pipestone Canyon's fifth phase, like the fourth, was characterized by a number of separate search and clear operations. On the 11th, the 1st Battalion, 1st Marines again returned to Dodge City, initiating operations in the La Tho Bac, Dong Tien, and Duc Ky hamlet complex, north of the Song La Tho. Although Morgenthaler's battalion detained a number of Vietnamese as suspected members of the local Viet Cong Infrastructure, no combat engagements took place and the operation terminated two days later.

By far the most significant of the series of searches conducted by the 1st Marines within the Pipestone Canyon area during the latter stages of the operation was the multi-battalion cordon and search of the La Huan and Giang La hamlet complex, located in northwestern Dodge City. Based on intelligence reports which indicated that elements of the *Q-82d Battalion* and a large number of infrastructure members had moved into the area, planning for the cordon began. Shortly after sunrise on the 18th, Morgenthaler's battalion, composed of Companies A, B, and C, in addition to two platoons from Company G, assaulted two landing zones, just south of the Song La Tho, following an artillery and air bombardment of the zones and nearby railroad berm. Simultaneously, elements of the 3d Battalion, 51st ARVN Regiment moved into blocking positions along the northern bank of the river, between the berm and the Song Ai Nghia. To the southeast, elements of the ARVN regiment's 2d Battalion took up positions extending from the hamlet of La Moa (1) south to Route 4. To the west, three of Ganey's four companies, plus Company H, 2d Battalion, 5th Marines, moved into positions stretching along Route 4, then north along Route 1-D to the Song Ai Nghia, south of Hill 55. Once all were in place, Morgenthaler's Marines, supplemented by 50 men of the National Police Field Force from Dien Ban District, attacked westward. By late afternoon, the cordon was set and civilians began their exodus of the area, filing across "Golden Gate Bridge" on the Song Ai Nghia toward the collection point at the base of Hill 55. By noon the following day, district Phoenix and intelligence personnel had processed 813 civilians, of which 19 were identified as Viet Cong and 50 classified as Infrastructure members.* Meanwhile, Morgenthaler's battalion conducted a thorough search of the hamlet complex, destroying every bunker and other enemy installations, while police field forces burned every house on order of the province chief. Battalion Marines completed the search on the 21st. The residents of the La Huan and Giang La complex eventually were resettled in the village of Bich Bac, two kilometers northeast of Hill 55.

A day before the completion of the La Huan-Giang La search, the 1st Marines conducted yet another company-size reconnaissance-in-force on western Go Noi Island. At 0630 on 20 October, control of Com-

---

*The secret Phoenix, or Phung Hoang, program was carried out by Vietnamese police and intelligence agencies under the advice and supervision of the U.S. Central Intelligence Agency. Its objective was the "neutralization" of the Viet Cong Infrastructure, Communist clandestine government, and political movement members by death or capture.

pany C passed from the 1st Battalion to the 3d Battalion, 1st Marines, and the company helilifted to the island, where it patrolled for the next week. Although the Marines encountered and sighted a number of small groups of enemy troops, most were observed south of Go Noi, outside the area of operations, and thus could not be engaged. On the 27th, Company C ended its search of the western portion of the island and returned to control of the 1st Battalion. Eleven days later, Operation Pipestone Canyon was brought to a close.

During the 164-day operation, each of the interrelated objectives was met. All major Viet Cong and North Vietnamese units were driven out of Dodge City and Go Noi Island. Route 4 was not only upgraded, but opened to traffic from Dien Ban west to the railroad berm, permitting access to western Quang Nam Province. Land-clearing operations had transformed Go Noi Island from a heavily vegetated tract to a barren waste, free of treelines and other cover long used by the enemy to conceal his movement across the island. And, through a series of combined cordon and search operations, the ranks of the local Viet Cong Infrastructure were depleted, especially in Dodge City. In the accomplishment of these goals, 852 enemy soldiers were killed, 58 taken prisoner, and 410 weapons, along with large quantities of equipment, ordnance, and foodstuffs, captured. The successes achieved during the operation were not, however, attained without friendly losses. A total of 71 troops, Marines and Navy Corpsmen, died, while 498 others were wounded, most by surprise firing devices, and evacuated, and 108 received minor wounds.

1st Marines: Protecting the Southern Flank

Although heavily committed to Operation Pipestone Canyon throughout the latter half of the year, the 1st Marines retained responsibility for the regimental TAOR. As the 1st and 2d Battalions moved into Dodge City at the end of May, Lieutenant Colonel Thomas E. Bulger's 3d Battalion, reinforced by Company A, 1st Battalion, 7th Marines, took the burden of patrolling the remainder of the regiment's assigned area.

Throughout the fertile-rice-paddy- and sand-dune-dotted region, roughly stretching from the Song Yen to the South China Sea, south of Da Nang, Bulger's Marines fanned out in company- and platoon-size combat patrols, hoping to engage elements of the *R-20th* and *Q-82d Local Force Battalions*, known to be operating in the area. The enemy, however, proved to be illusive as they attempted to avoid Bulger's ever-present maze of small-unit, counterguerrilla operations.

Although enemy activity throughout Quang Nam Province remained relatively high during the month of June, the majority of action within the 1st Marines' TAOR consisted of attacks directed against 3d Battalion patrols, command posts, and bridge security elements. The largest of these occurred shortly after midnight on the 7th, when approximately 70 North Vietnamese troops moved against a platoon of Company K, positioned near No Name Island within the Tre Khe hamlet complex, six kilometers east of Route 1. Under heavy enemy 60mm mortar, CS-gas, RPG, grenade, and small arms fire, the platoon held its position and returned fire, while calling in artillery missions and directing "Spooky" gunship support. As a result of the attack, the enemy lost over half his force.

Towards the end of the month, as emphasis shifted from the multi-battalion search to the land-clearing effort in the Pipestone Canyon area of operations, the 1st Battalion returned to the regimental area and assumed responsibility for the western sector, including security for the Cau Do and Ha Dong Bridges. Bulger's Marines, as a consequence, were given the eastern sector and security of the Tu Cau Bridge. This arrangement continued until 20 July, when 1st Battalion, 26th Marines replaced Bulger's Marines, who then shifted operations to the regiment's western zone. The following day, as the 5th Marines assumed control of the 2d Battalion in preparation for an assault into the Que Son Mountains, Morgenthaler's battalion was assigned the mission of regimental or mobile reserve and returned to Pipestone Canyon. Little changed during this period with respect to enemy tactics as both Viet Cong and North Vietnamese troops, heavily battered on Go Noi Island and in Dodge City, avoided other regimental cordon and search operations, patrols, and ambushes.

During the month of August, the 1st Marines, when not engaged in Pipestone Canyon, continued aggressive patrol and ambush operations, placing heavy emphasis on clearing the Song Yen within the rocket belt and assisting the 5th Marines in Operation Durham Peak. In addition, the regiment carried out cordon and search operations in the hamlets of An Thanh (1), Viem Tay (1), An Tra (1), Bo Mung (2), Tan Luu, and La Huan (2), all designated for upgrading under the Accelerated Pacification Campaign. At mid-month, a major shift in forces involved in the counterguerrilla campaign near Da Nang and the surrounding

Infantrymen of the 2d Battalion, 1st Marines, responsible for the security of Tu Cau Bridge, south of Da Nang, conduct a daily patrol through one of the surrounding villages.

coastal lowlands occurred. Following successful operations against enemy forces in the Arizona Area, the 7th Marines redeployed to a new area of operations, encompassing the Que Song District of Quang Tin Province. This redeployment, along with the concurrent repositioning of the 5th Marines, 26th Marines, and Vietnamese forces, who assumed a larger role in the pacification and counterguerrilla effort closer to Da Nang, resulted in the expansion of the 1st Marines' area of responsibility.

While retaining control of the eastern, that area generally east of Route 1 between Marble Mountain and Hoi An, and southern (Dodge City and Go Noi Island) sectors, a portion of the regiment's northern zone was transferred to the 26th Marines and its western boundary expanded into an area previously occupied by the 1st and 3d Battalions, 7th Marines. The regimental command post, as a result, shifted southwestward from Dong Son (2) to Camp Muir (Hill 55), and at the same time Colonel Herbert L. Wilkerson assumed command of the regiment, replacing Colonel Robertson, who was promoted to brigadier general and given the position of assistant division commander.

Within the expanded area of responsibility, the 1st Marines was committed to a wide range of interrelated activities, including Operation Pipestone Canyon, during September and October. Despite monsoon rains during the first two weeks of October, the regiment launched vigorous patrol, ambush, and cordon and search operations, with increased emphasis placed on combined operations with elements of the 51st ARVN Regiment and local Regional Force units in support of the pacification effort, defense of the Da Nang Vital Area, and security of the rocket belt. In addition, the 1st Marines concentrated its rice denial efforts during the beginning of harvest season in the heavily cultivated area flanking the Song Cau Bien, south of Nui Kim Son, and the rich rice-producing regions flanking the Song Yen, north of Hill 55. The regiment directed a special effort to denying the enemy rice grown east of Hill 22 in the Bo Ben and Duyen Son areas, where the rice fields were declared as belonging to the Viet Cong by the Hieu Duc District Chief.

As elections generally coincided with the rice harvest, Wilkerson tasked his Marines with assisting provincial forces in providing polling place security for the provincial elections on 28 September and hamlet elections a month later. Extensive patrols and ambushes were run near polling sites the day before each election. On election day, Marine security operations shifted at least 500 meters from the sites, while Regional and Popular Forces provided close-in protection. In addition, a platoon with two CH-46 and two AH-1G helicopters stood by to provide immediate reaction to any terrorist incident which might threaten the security of elections within the 1st Marines' TAOR.

During the final two months of the year, the 1st Marines, in addition to its normal responsibilities of defending the Da Nang Vital Area, securing the rocket belt, protecting allied installations and lines of communication, and participating in the rice denial effort, focused much of its attention on the support of the Accelerated Pacification Program through the Infantry Company Intensive Pacification Program (ICIPP), later renamed the Combined Unit Pacification Program (CUPP). Loosely based on the Combined Action Program (CAP), the ICIPP, or CUPP concept called for an entire Marine rifle company to merge with Regional and Popular Force platoons into a combined Marine-Vietnamese pacification effort. One Marine rifle squad and one Vietnamese platoon would work together to pacify one specific area, with their combined efforts augmented by provincial forces, including Census Grievance Teams, National Police Field Forces, Provincial Reconnaissance Units, and Revolutionary Development Cadre Teams, when available. When the area was considered pacified, and when a sufficient number of People's Self-Defense Forces had been trained and armed, the Marines would be withdrawn and sent to other targeted areas.

On 7 November, the regiment assumed direct operational control of Captain Donald J. Robinson's Company M and assigned it to the Combined Unit Pacification Program. As early as the 3d, selected officers and NCOs began an intensive two-week training course conducted by the 2d Combined Action Group at Da Nang in order to prepare themselves for duty with Regional and Popular Forces. Training completed, the first unit, composed of one platoon from Company M and one platoon from the 759th Regional Force Company, along with a Revolutionary Development Team, moved into Chau Son Hamlet, two kilometers southwest of Hill 55 on the 9th. The following day, the regiment dispatched a second unit to Binh

A Marine from Company M, 3d Battalion, 1st Marines stands watch with two members of the local Popular Forces. The joint Marine-Popular Force unit was tasked with providing security for the village of Binh Boc as part of the Combined Unit Pacification Program.

Marine Corps Historical Collection

Bac Hamlet, a kilometer northeast of the regiment's command post, and on the 30th, a third moved into Le Son (1) Hamlet, five kilometers to the northeast. During December, the 1st Marines installed five additional combined platoons in hamlets designated by the South Vietnamese Government for pacification status upgrading, as the program continued to show promise.

In late December, to supplement the usual ground patrols and ambushes, the 1st Marines instituted a new system of helicopter-borne combat patrols, codenamed Kingfisher. These patrols, the latest variant in a long series of quick-reaction infantry-helicopter combinations, were intended to seek out the enemy and initiate contact rather than exploit engagements or assist ground units already under fire. As Colonel Wilkerson noted, they were "an offensive weapon that goes out and hunt[s] them . . . . They actually invite trouble."[11]

The initial Kingfisher patrol was to consist of one rifle platoon loaded on board three Boeing CH-46D Sea Knight helicopters which would then fly over the regimental TAOR accompanied by two Bell AH-1G Cobra gunships and a North American OV-10A Bronco carrying an aerial observer. In the air at first light, the patrol was to search the terrain for targets of opportunity, attacking enemy formations, destroying enemy installations, and detaining persons acting in such a manner as to warrant suspicion. If the Marines found enemy troops, the Cobras would provide close support and the aerial observer would call for fixed-wing air strikes and artillery if necessary. Kingfisher operations required careful coordination once in the air. Each patrol included a UH-1E Huey command helicopter. This aircraft carried the company commander, a regimental staff officer, both in radio contact with the 1st Marines' command post, and the air commander. These officers mutually would decide when and where to land the troops. Each time a Kingfisher patrol went out, the battalions would be informed as to which areas within their TAORs were likely targets to be investigated, so that the battalion's own patrols could avoid them. This same information was to be supplied the artillery, which then would suspend all fire in those areas unless called upon to support the patrol.

The regiment's first patrol, composed of a platoon from Captain Jimmie L. Adkins' Company H, lifted off at 0645 on 26 December with 10 targets of primary interest throughout the TAOR. The patrol landed on a target in the Ngan Cau area, three kilometers east of Route 1, to establish a block for the rest of the company. As no engagement ensued, Kingfisher I spent but 35 minutes on the ground. The patrol later assaulted a target in the area of Dong Lien, between the Song La Tho and Suoi Co Ca, following an air bombardment by Cobra gunships. Although the patrol initially encountered small arms fire, there was no ground action and the patrol took off 55 minutes later—this being the first time a platoon-size unit entered Dodge City alone. After the Dong Lien landing, the patrol then secured, returned to base, and key personnel assembled at the regimental command post for a debrief and critique of the initial operation. Although Kingfisher I engaged no enemy troops, 1st Marines and Marine Aircraft Group 16 participants expressed enthusiasm about the concept, suggesting that additional trials be conducted in order to refine a number of command and control techniques. Kingfisher patrols would, during 1970, become a valued tactic for the regiment and division, especially against small enemy units operating in the rocket belt. In augmenting the regiment's tactical arsenal, the patrols would aid the 1st Marines in successfully inflicting significant losses and reducing the enemy's freedom of movement within its assigned area of responsibility.

Despite the institution of several tactical innovations during the year, the frustrating war south of Da Nang had changed little over the years, as the 1st Battalion's commanding officer, Lieutenant Colonel Godfrey S. Delcuze, noted:

> The war had moved on except for sporadic, murderous local force mining. Brave men died "pacifying" old men, women, and children who refused to be pacified. Too heavy infantry armed, equipped, and supplied to engage [Viet Cong] main force units, slogged through paddies and scrub brush past farm folk who mined trails from time to time. They—the peasants—wreaked their havoc from time to time with M16 bounding mines from fields U.S. forces had laid. Our only identifiable "military" service was a two-day lay out ambush. The ambush netted one enemy "soldier." He came walking down a trail with an M16 bounding mine in each hand. We shot him in the gut. He was a 12-year old boy.[12]

The Arizona

Southwest and west of the 1st Marines' TAOR, the 5th Marines continued to defend the large broad plain dominated by the confluence of two major rivers, the Song Vu Gia and Song Thu Bon. Commanded by Colonel William J. Zaro, the regiment began the latter half of the year with Lieutenant Colonel William E. Riley, Jr.'s 1st Battalion operating in the Arizona area; Lieutenant Colonel James H. Higgins' 2d Battalion, deployed from the Arizona action, protecting Liberty Bridge and Road and conducting patrols in the surrounding terrain; and Lieutenant Colonel Harry E. Atkinson's 3d Battalion participating in Operation Pipestone Canyon under the operational control of the 1st Marines.

The pattern of battalion activities varied according to region. In the Arizona, between the Song Vu Gia and Song Thu Bon, the 1st Battalion defended no fixed positions, but continually moved in company-size formations from place to place, patrolling, setting up night ambushes, searching for food and supply caches, and frequently conducting multi-company sweeps with ARVN forces in this long-time enemy stronghold. Companies of Higgins' 2d Battalion not only manned the strategic outpost of Liberty Bridge and other strongpoints, and cooperated with Vietnamese forces to secure Routes 540 (Liberty Road) and 537, but also launched company-size sweeps of the surrounding terrain. Although temporarily assigned to the 1st Marines, the 3d Battalion normally operated in the regiment's eastern area, centered on the Phu Loc Valley and northern tier of the Que Son Mountains, where it saturated the countryside with patrols, ambushes, and occasional multi-company sweeps.

Enemy activity throughout the 5th Marines' area of responsibility, although light during the last week of May and the first days of June, increased sharply both in frequency and intensity as the month progressed with coordinated attacks by fire against An Hoa Combat Base and units in the field. In the early morning hours of 7 June, the enemy subjected An Hoa to a company-size sapper attack, supported by small arms fire, grenades, RPGs, B40 rockets, and approximately 10 rounds from 82mm mortars. Concentrating the attack in two sectors, the enemy broke through the defensive wire, but were driven back and forced to retreat under heavy volumes of Marine small arms, automatic weapons, 81mm mortar, and artillery fire. The action cost elements of the *3d NVA Sapper Battalion* 19 dead and two captured. The captured sappers, according to Colonel Zaro, grateful for their treatment, demonstrated and revealed many of their infiltration techniques.[13]

At approximately the same time, but six kilometers to the west, near the heavily fortified hamlet of An Bang (2) in the Arizona, an unknown-size enemy unit, subsequently identified as an element of the *90th NVA Regiment*, attacked the night defensive position of Lieutenant Colonel Riley's 1st Battalion command

Marine Corps Historical Collection
Marines of Company B, 1st Battalion, 5th Marines cross a rice paddy dike while on patrol in the Arizona in search of remnants of the 90th NVA Regiment.

group and Company A. Over the next 10 days, in a series of battles reminiscent of those fought by the 7th Marines along the Song Vu Gia a month before, Riley's Marines would batter the enemy regiment, finally forcing it to withdraw to the Ong Thu Slope in Base Area 112 to recover.

The attack began shortly after midnight, as the grenade-throwing enemy force, supported by mortars and heavy automatic and small arms fire, came at Riley's Marines from three directions. Employing organic weapons, artillery, and "Spooky" gunship support, the Marines broke the enemy ground attack. A search of the battlefield at first light revealed 11 enemy bodies and three wounded soldiers, who had taken refuge along a rice paddy dike. Throughout most of the next day, the enemy harassed the command group and Company A with mortar and recoilless rifle fire, which Riley's Marines were unable to silence. Late in the afternoon, further east, Company B executed a hasty ambush of 25 NVA troops, resulting in 19 enemy, but no friendly, casualties.

On the morning of the 8th, elements of the *90th Regiment* again attempted to drive Riley's battalion out of the Arizona. Shortly before sunrise, the enemy

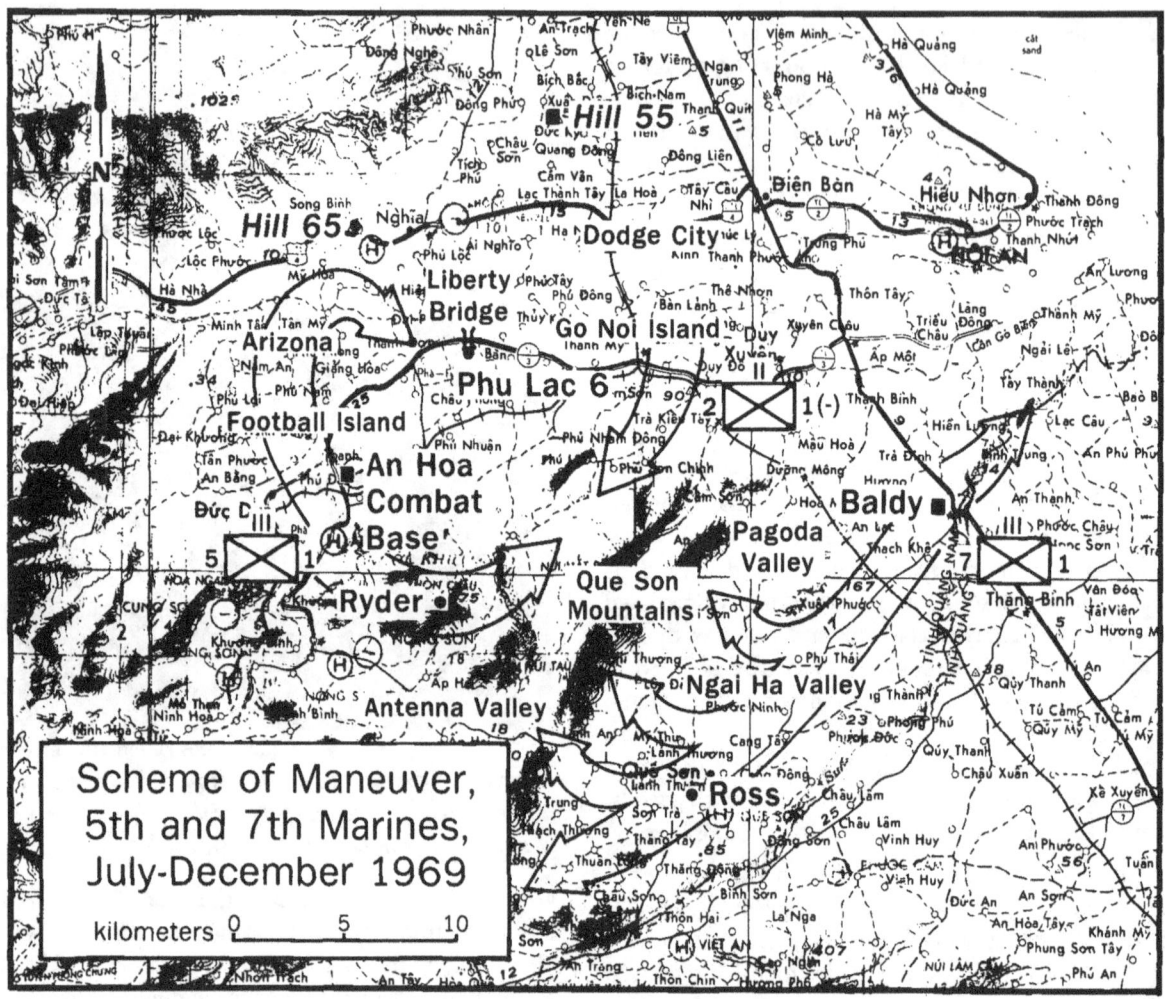

See Reference Map, Sections 31-33, 37-39

struck at the command group and Company A, and again the aggressive attack was broken with the assistance of accurate artillery and air support. Later in the day, as the battalion command post attempted to relocate, lead elements of Captain Philip H. Torrey's Company A, acting as security for the move, came under very heavy .30- and .50-caliber machine gun fire. A hasty perimeter was set up while fixed-wing aircraft and artillery peppered the suspected enemy weapons site. With the lifting of supporting arms fire, Company A moved out in the attack, but again came under heavy automatic weapons fire, this time supported by 60mm mortars. In spite of the fire, a platoon of the company was able to establish a toehold on the southern flank of the enemy's perimeter, and batter his positions with machine gun, small arms, and handheld rocket fire for 90 minutes before being ordered to withdraw because of continued resistance and impending darkness. Once contact was broken, air and artillery moved in and pounded the enemy position throughout the night.

Following a heavy air, artillery, and mortar bombardment the next morning, the attack resumed. Reinforced by a platoon from Company C, Company A seized and secured the enemy position despite continued resistance. A detailed search of the complex, believed to be the site of the NVA battalion's command post defended by two well-entrenched infantry companies supported by at least one heavy weapons company, revealed 80 enemy bodies.

While Company A continued searching the enemy position, Company B, under Captain Gene E. Castagnetti, moving to assist, came under intensive fire. Sizing up the situation, Castagnetti ordered two of his platoons into the assault, with the remainder of the company providing cover fire for the advance. Expertly maneuvering across 300 meters of fire-swept rice paddies, the two platoons stormed the enemy position, killing another 75 NVA troops, including the battalion commander, and capturing over 50 small arms weapons and one 12.7mm antiaircraft gun.[14] During the next four days, the battalion command group and Company C again came under a series of large-scale enemy attacks. Although supported by a seemingly endless supply of ordnance, in the form of B40 rockets, RPGs, 82mm and 60mm mortars, recoilless rifles, and heavy machine guns, Riley's Marines forced the North Vietnamese to sacrifice heavily. As a result of these engagements, the enemy lost another 71 troops, among them a company commander, and numerous individual and crew-served weapons.

After the beating on 12 June, enemy activity subsided throughout the Arizona for the next several days as elements of the *90th Regiment* consciously avoided encounters with Riley's patrols. Shortly after midnight on the 17th, they again struck in force. Supported by mortars, B40 rockets, and RPGs, two companies assaulted the battalion's night defensive position from the north and west. Relying on heavy concentrations of artillery, 81mm mortar, and "Spooky" gunship fire, which at times fell within yards of the perimeter, 1st Battalion Marines again beat back the attack in bitter fighting, which lasted over five hours. At midmorning, a sweep of the battlefield found 32 enemy dead, two wounded, and a large quantity of weapons and miscellaneous equipment. Losing over 300 troops in 10 days, major elements of the *90th NVA Regiment* withdrew into Base Area 112, and activity throughout the southern Arizona subsided.

While Lieutenant Colonel Riley's battalion fought the *90th Regiment* in the Arizona and Lieutenant Colonel Higgins' 2d Battalion secured Liberty Bridge and Road (North), Lieutenant Colonel Atkinson's 3d Battalion ended its participation in Operation Pipestone Canyon and began an unnamed, 13-day, search and clear operation in the Phu Loc Valley, aimed at catching enemy troops driven south by the 1st Marines. On 15 June, two companies of Atkinson's Marines crossed the Song Chiem Son from Go Noi and moved up the valley on foot. There they were joined the following day by the command group and the rest of the battalion, which air assaulted into the area. The battalion then searched the rugged, mountainous terrain, south of Alligator Lake, until the 28th, finding only empty base camps, caves, fighting positions, and encountering few enemy troops. On the 28th, Atkinson's Marines withdrew from the valley and flew to An Hoa where they assumed security duty for the base and Liberty Road (South).

During the first week of July, the 5th Marines initiated a cordon and search operation, Forsyth Grove, with the 1st and 2d Battalions, 5th Marines and 1st Battalion, 7th Marines. Conducted in a two-kilometer-square area of the northern Arizona, the objective was successfully cordoned on the south when Riley's Marines moved under cover of darkness into their assigned blocking positions from the southern Arizona. Similarly, the 2d Battalion covertly completed a crossing of the Song Thu Bon and occupied blocking positions to the east. Before sunrise on the 1st, the 1st Battalion, 7th Marines forded the Song Vu Gia and closed the trap. Although the combined Marine force encountered token resistance during the search, the 5th Marines reported that the local Viet Cong again were "denied the use and exploitation of a natural sanctuary."[14]

Following the close of the three-day operation in the northern Arizona, the 1st Battalion, 5th Marines remained in the area and continued offensive patrol operations while Lieutenant Colonel Higgins' Marines returned to Phu Lac (6) and reassumed security for Liberty Bridge and Road (North), and the 1st Battalion, 7th Marines recrossed the Song Vu Gia. The 3d Battalion, 5th Marines now under the command of Lieutenant Colonel John M. Terry, Jr., continued its assigned tasks of defending An Hoa Combat Base, securing the southern portion of Liberty Road, and conducting patrols within the regiment's southern area of operations, southeast of the combat base.

On 18 July, a shift among the regiment's three battalions occurred in preparation for the 5th Marines' last multi-battalion operation of the year on the southern fringe of its area of operations. In order to free the 2d Battalion, two of Lieutenant Colonel Riley's companies moved from the Arizona to Phu Lac (6). At the same time, the remainder of the 1st Battalion airlifted to An Hoa Combat Base, there relieving Lieutenant Colonel Terry's 3d Battalion. Joining the two battalions would be Lieutenant Colonel Glasgow's 2d Battalion, 1st Marines. Site of the 5th Marines-controlled operation was to be a 20-kilometer-square area encompassing Antenna Valley, Phu Loc Valley, and the Que Son Mountains, location of the enemy's old Base Area 116, approximately 10 kilometers southeast of An Hoa Combat Base.

Protruding like spikes into the Quang Nam lowlands, the Que Son Mountains range in height to over 900 meters. Covered with single-canopy jungle and thick underbrush, the chain is punctuated by narrow ridges which drop off into deep ravines. Along the chain's entire base runs a natural corridor from Antenna Valley in the southwest to Phu Loc Valley in the northeast; the corridor then opens onto Go Noi Island and the Dodge City area, the broad plain south of Da Nang. Scattered along the ridges and in the ravines of the chain were suspected enemy base camps, hospitals, fighting positions, storage areas, and an extensive trail network. Although no enemy force was known to have actually occupied the area since the departure of the *1st VC Regiment* in March, intelligence sources suspected that the elusive headquarters and service elements of *Front 4* and the *36th NVA Regiment* had moved into the region, having been driven out of Dodge City and off Go Noi Island by the 1st Marines during the first month of Operation Pipestone Canyon.

In preparation for the attack and search of the Que Son Mountains, codenamed Durham Peak, two 105mm howitzer batteries of the 11th Marines moved from An Hoa Combat Base on the 19th and established a temporary fire support base on the southern edge of Go Noi Island. As a deceptive measure, they trained their guns northward. Offshore stood the *Boston* (CAG 1), her six 8-inch 55s at the ready. The following morning, Batteries B and F shifted their tubes 180 degrees, and with the guns of the *Boston*, unleashed a barrage against preselected targets throughout the operational area. Simultaneously, the 37th Battalion, 1st ARVN Ranger Group assaulted into a previously prepared fire support base and several landing zones in the upper reaches of Antenna Valley, establishing positions aimed at blocking enemy escape routes out of the valley. Later in the day, Lieutenant Colonel Terry's 3d Battalion joined the ARVN Rangers in the area of operations and set up blocking positions to the west and southwest. Both assaults went unopposed, the day being marred only by the crash of a MAG-16 CH-46 helicopter in which several Rangers were killed. The following day, Lieutenant Colonel Glasgow's 2d Battalion helilifted into three landing zones in the Phu Loc Valley and established positions astride known enemy escape routes from the Que Son Mountains to the north and northeast. Elements of the Americal Division's 196th Brigade set up blocking positions to the east and southeast, in the Que Son Valley, completing the circle. Lieutenant Colonel Higgins' 2d Battalion, 5th Marines, designated regimental reserve, remained at Phu Lac (6).

As company patrols moved out from their initial landing zones, they discovered extensive bunker com-

Elements of the 2d Battalion, 5th Marines find the terrain difficult during search operations for the elusive headquarters of Front 4 *thought to be in the Que Son Mountains.*

Department of Defense Photo (USMC) A372128

plexes, caves, hootches, supply caches, and numerous NVA graves. Most bunkers and hootches, however, showed damage as a result of B-52 bombing raids (Arc Lights), carried out in the Que Son Mountains prior to the operation. Enemy resistance was light, stemming primarily from small groups attempting to evade ARVN and Marine forces. But as the Marines moved to higher ground, specifically toward Nui Mat Rang and Nui Da Beo, activity intensified as enemy troops employed an ever-increasing number of sniper teams and ambushes.

On 25 July, as Marines of Company H, 2d Battalion, 1st Marines moved up a narrow, well-used trail toward the top of Nui Mat Rang (Hill 845), they came under heavy sniper fire from a rock ledge, 100 meters above. Responding with small arms, and rocket and machine gun fire from an orbiting Rockwell OV-10A (Bronco), the company forced the snipers to withdraw. The following morning, the company's 3d platoon moved back to the area of the previous day's encounter, and was ambushed by an estimated company of NVA soldiers. As Second Lieutenant Robert A. Lavery, of the 1st Platoon, later reported:

> They had set up foxholes and positions off to one side of the trail . . . . As the point man came up they shot him. They couldn't see much of the killing zone because of the heavy vegetation, but the field of fire was cleared so low that they originally shot everybody in the legs that came into it. As people would come into it to assist a wounded person, . . . they would get shot in the legs. Then once they were down, they had one sniper that would either shoot them in the head or the back.[16]

As a result of the tactic, NVA sharpshooters killed six and wounded 16 without, it was thought, losing a man.

Efforts to extract the embattled platoon proved difficult as communications had broken down, causing confusion as to the platoon's exact location. Air and artillery were called in on what was thought to be the enemy's position, but, as it was later determined, the air strikes and artillery rounds impacted more than 1,000 meters to the southwest. In addition, a medical evacuation helicopter, endeavoring to bring out the dead and wounded, was shot down, compelling reinforcements which otherwise would have been sent to assist the 3d Platoon, to be diverted away in order to establish security for the downed CH-46. Despite these unfortunate events, reinforcements eventually reached the embattled unit and the platoon, with its casualties, returned to the company's position near the summit of Hill 845, where a jungle penetrator extracted the wounded.

As the month drew to a close, both Terry's and Glasgow's Marines continued to push deeper into the mountains, following the extensive enemy trail network instead of moving cross-country through the thick jungle terrain. "The NVA travel the trails," noted Lieutenant Lavery, and "everything they have is along the trails. If we are going to find them or any of their gear, it is going to be along the trails, not on cross-country sweeps."[17] Lavery's observation proved correct: discoveries of bunkers, caves, and hidden encampments along the trails increased with elevation, as did the number of brief firefights with small groups of enemy troops, employing a wide range of delaying tactics. Simultaneously, enemy sightings by elements of the Americal's 196th Light Infantry Brigade and 5th ARVN Regiment, providing flank security in the Que Son lowlands, increased as a result of the Marines' push to the southeast. It was Colonel Zaro's belief that the blocks by these units were ineffective and permitted groups of enemy to escape to the south and east.[18]

Operating along the ridgelines and among the draws of the Que Son's created a number of problems for the two Marine battalions, chief among them, resupply. The rugged terrain, high winds, and small landing zones atop mountain peaks forced many Marine helicopter pilots to cancel direct landings and concentrate instead on resupply drops, which they often lost, forcing both Terry's and Glasgow's Marines to exist for extended periods on Long Range rations and to obtain water from local streams. The lack of purified water and adequate supplies of malaria pills produced an abnormally high incidence of the disease and related fevers in the Marines participating in the operation.[19]

On 31 July, Colonel Zaro committed Lieutenant Colonel James H. Higgins' 2d Battalion, 5th Marines to Durham Peak, which immediately established blocking positions near Hill 848 in the center of the area of operations. Three days later, the 1st Battalion, 1st Marines relieved its sister battalion in place, continuing patrols in the Que Son highlands in search of enemy units and base camps.

By the end of the first week of August, the ground had been covered and encounters had dwindled to a few short, sporadic, but fierce, hit-and-run attacks. Based on all available intelligence, the enemy remaining in the area consisted largely of the sick and wounded—the able-bodied having fragmented into

Marine Corps Historical Collection

Members of the 106mm Recoilless Rifle Platoon, Headquarters and Service Company, 2d Battalion, 5th Marines fire at an enemy target from a position on Hill 848.

small groups and fled into the lowlands. On the 7th, the withdrawal began with the return of the 1st Battalion, 1st Marines and a battery of the 11th Marines to their bases in the Quang Nam lowlands. The next day, the 1st ARVN Ranger Group began its withdrawal to An Hoa Combat Base, followed by the 2d Battalion, 5th Marines and elements of the 3d Battalion, 5th Marines on the 12th. The final phase of the measured withdrawal took place on the 13th, when the remaining batteries of 2d Battalion, 11th Marines and companies of 3d Battalion, 5th Marines helilifted from the Que Son Mountains to the regimental combat base at An Hoa.

With the termination of Durham Peak, the 5th Marines returned to a changed area of operation brought about by the southward shift of the 7th Marines. Of particular significance was the assumption of responsibility for the Thuong Duc Valley, north of the Song Vu Gia, including the outpost at Hill 65 and the southern slope of Charlie Ridge. On 14 August, elements of the 2d Battalion, 5th Marines relieved the 3d Battalion, 7th Marines on Hill 65, while the 3d Battalion, 5th Marines moved into the southern Arizona two days later.

Under the leadership of the new regimental commander, Colonel Noble L. Beck, who relieved Colonel Zaro on the 16th, the three battalions of the 5th Marines concentrated on a variety of missions within their respective areas of operation. At Liberty Bridge, Lieutenant Colonel Riley's 1st Battalion continued defensive operations in areas adjacent to the vital river crossing, while providing security patrols for truck convoys along Liberty Road, north of An Hoa Combat Base. To the northwest, the 2d Battalion, under the command of Lieutenant Colonel Higgins, relieved on the 24th by Lieutenant Colonel James T. Bowen, confined its operations to company-size patrols and participation in the district pacification program, north of the Song Vu Gia, within the villages surrounding Hill 65. Lieutenant Colonel Terry's 3d Battalion, operating within the Arizona, initially concentrated its efforts on destroying NVA and guerrilla havens and on interdicting enemy movement throughout the Phu Loi and Nam An village complexes, south of the Song Vu Gia and east of the Finger Lakes, and then in areas of central and southern Arizona.

Contact within the regimental area was unusually light during the remainder of August, but with the new month, enemy activity intensified, most notably within the boundaries of the Arizona. Operating in terrain characterized by low hills, numerous tree lines, and rice paddies, Lieutenant Colonel Terry's Marines, first independently and then in conjunction with elements of the 1st ARVN Ranger Group, experienced a number of sharp, violent clashes with units of the reintroduced *90th NVA Regiment*, while continually being subjected to a large volume of harassing small arms, mortar, and rocket fire. On 11 September, while Company I moved across an open rice paddy toward a tree line between the villages of Ham Tay (1) and Ben Dau (3), near the Song Thu Bon, approximately 30 enemy troops took the company under heavy automatic weapons, rocket grenade, and mortar fire. Almost simultaneously, the battalion's S-3, Major Martin J. Dahlquist, stepped on a well-concealed enemy mine, that shattered his leg and slightly wounded two other Marines. Although periodic sniper fire hampered helicopter operations, the medical evacuation was accomplished without damage to aircraft or loss of additional personnel.[20]

The Marines of Company I quickly returned fire, and called for air strikes, interspersed with artillery. Following a shift of artillery fire onto likely escape routes, Captain William M. Kay ordered a frontal assault and simultaneous flank envelopment. Kay's Marines moved rapidly through the enemy position, searching tree lines, bunkers, and spider holes, finding 12 NVA bodies and 16 weapons, including a Soviet carriage-mounted, heavy machine gun. Later in the day and early the next morning, Captain Kay's company again came under intense mortar and small arms fire, resulting in an additional 18 casualties. Two days later, the company, in addition to the rest of the battalion, withdrew from the Arizona and moved by air to Phu Lac (6), where it assumed responsibility for the security of Liberty Bridge and Liberty Road. The 1st Battalion, 5th Marines, in turn, helilifted into the Arizona.

Towards the end of September, all three battalions began rice denial and destruction operations within their respective areas of responsibility. Working in conjunction with ARVN and district forces, designated 5th Marine units were to protect Vietnamese farmers during the fall rice harvest, assist in the removal of the crop to secure storage areas, and aid in the destruction of enemy-controlled fields identified by district officials. In addition, on 27-28 September, 5th Marine units provided security for elections to the Quang Nam Lower House of Representatives through screening operations, extensive patrols, and ambushes, while regional, provincial, and National Police forces provided close-in security. During the two days of election security operations, there was no attempt by the enemy to disrupt the voting within the 5th Marines area of operations.

Conditions during the month of October within the

Navy Corpsman Anthony Fodale checks the pulse of one of four wounded North Vietnamese Army soldiers found in an abandoned hospital complex by elements of the 3d Battalion, 5th Marines while on a patrol 11 kilometers east of An Hoa Combat Base.

Department of Defense Photo (USMC) A372184

regiment's area of responsibility could only be characterized by one word—wet. The northeast monsoon dumped a total of 40 inches of rain, raising river and stream levels as much as eight feet above normal. Flood conditions made movement in the lowlands difficult if not impossible. As a result, the 1st Battalion, now under the command of Lieutenant Colonel Joseph K. Griffis, Jr., pulled out of the Arizona and moved to An Hoa where it conducted defensive patrol operations in and around the combat base, cordon and search operations with Combined Action Company 29 and Duc Duc District forces near the villages of Mau Chanh (2) and Thu Bon (5), and company patrols near Tick Lake, southeast of An Hoa. On the 18th, Griffis' Marines returned to the rain-soaked Arizona and resumed search and rice denial operations begun the previous month.

To the north in the high ground, the 2d Battalion, 5th Marines continued, despite the monsoon, search and destroy operations in the Thuong Duc Valley and security patrols along Route 4. The scene was different at Liberty Bridge. The Song Thu Bon quickly rose to 17 feet above normal, covering the bridge with six feet of water and forcing Lieutenant Colonel Terry's battalion to higher ground. Flood waters rose so rapidly on the night of 5 October that a security platoon and a four-man watchtower guard were cut off and had to be rescued by lifeline and helicopter. As a result of flood conditions and subsequent bridge and road damage, truck convoys were halted and resupply of An Hoa Combat Base carried out by Marine helicopters and Air Force C-130 transports. The river subsided enough for Terry's battalion to return to normal security positions, and for elements of the 7th Engineer Battalion to begin repair of the bridge's southern approach on the 13th. By 21 October, with temporary repairs completed, "Rough Rider" truck convoys again moved down Liberty Road toward An Hoa Combat Base. The regiment reported no injuries as a result of bunker, fighting position, and other field emplacement cave-ins.[21]

Following the two weeks of heavy monsoon rains, enemy activity within the regimental area of operations progressively increased, notably within northern Arizona. Situated north of An Hoa, west of Dai Loc, and south of Hill 65, between the Song Vu Gia and Song Thu Bon, this small triangular area had long been a region of intense enemy activity as it sat astride major east-west infiltration routes. In addition, intelligence sources reported that local guerrillas of the

Q83d Battalion, recently resupplied with ammunition from Base Area 112, were about to attack across the Song Vu Gia into heavily populated Dai Loc District. Consequently, plans for a multi-battalion search and clear operation were drawn up, to be put into effect at the end of the month.

Early on the morning of the 30th, Lieutenant Colonel Griffis' Companies A and D moved out of the southern Arizona and established two blocking positions paralleling a stream which ran from My Hoa (3) to Phu Long (1) in northern Arizona. Simultaneously, Company I, 3d Battalion, 5th Marines crossed the Song Thu Bon by LVTs near "Football Island," secured a landing zone for elements of 2d Battalion, 5th Marines, and then moved into blocking positions near the eastern tip of the Arizona. With the insertion of Lieutenant Colonel Bowen's command group, Companies G and H, and the establishment of an additional block by Regional Force Company 369 along the Song Thu Bon, aggressive search operations began in the loosely cordoned area.[22]

Concentrating on squad-size patrols, the combined force searched the paddy-dotted area, discovering numerous bunkers, food caches, dud rounds, and boobytraps. With the exception of two clashes with 10 to

Members of the 2d Platoon, Company C, 1st Battalion, 5th Marines ford a monsoon-swollen stream while searching the Arizona during operations in November.
Marine Corps Historical Collection

15 enemy troops, engagements consisted of numerous encounters with small units of three to four rice-gatherers. After 10 days of successful small-unit engagements, during which the combined force accounted for more than 100 enemy troops killed, elements of Lieutenant Colonel Bowen's battalion withdrew to the Thuong Duc Valley, and Lieutenant Colonel Terry's Marines moved out of their blocking position, back across the Song Thu Bon and resumed operations near Liberty Bridge; Lieutenant Colonel Griffis' Marines returned to their normal area of responsibility in southern Arizona.

Late on 17 November, operations within northern Arizona began anew with the reinsertion of two companies of the 2d Battalion in the guise of resupplying the 1st Battalion. Under cover of darkness, Lieutenant Colonel Bowen's Marines then moved into the attack, while both Griffis' and Terry's Marines entered the area and reoccupied their original blocking positions. Three days of maneuvering followed during which the three battalions pushed a large number of enemy troops onto Football Island in the Song Thu Bon. An intensive search of the island followed on the heels of massed, pre-planned, time-on-target artilleryfire by the 11th Marines.* Forced into an ever smaller area, approximately 40 enemy troops attempted to escape the island on the night of 20 November, but were ambushed by Griffis' blocking forces, who killed 18 and captured a large quantity of arms and foodstuffs. With the ambush of the remnants of the *Q83 Battalion*, operations in northern Arizona ceased and all regimental units, with the exception of the 1st and 3d Battalions which exchanged areas of responsibility, returned to their normal operational areas.

Throughout the final month of the year, the 5th Marines continued aggressive search operations throughout the An Hoa basin aimed at blocking enemy infiltration and destroying his sources of food. North of the Song Vu Gia, 1st Battalion Marines, in conjunction with Regional Force Company 193, concentrated on small-unit patrols in the Thuong Duc Valley and company-size operations in the thick canopy and steep hills of Charlie Ridge, while supplementing An Hoa base defenses. The 2d Battalion carried out similar operations in the Arizona. Until relieved on 23 December by the 3d Battalion, Lieutenant Colonel Bowen's Marines, in close coordination with elements of the 51st ARVN Regiment, employed company- and platoon-size patrols and night ambushes in an effort to counter small groups of enemy moving through the region on food-gathering missions. The combined effort, which would last into the new year, achieved limited gains due to the highly successful operation carried out in November.

During the first two weeks of December, 3d Battalion Marines under Lieutenant Colonel Johan S. Gestson, who relieved Lieutenant Colonel Terry on the 9th, continued to provide security for Liberty Bridge and Liberty Road, while conducting patrols and ambushes throughout the expanse of the regiment's eastern area of operations. On the 16th, the battalion displaced to An Hoa in preparation for the transfer of its area of responsibility to the 2d Battalion. While at the combat base, the regiment received intelligence reports indicating that enemy forces in the Que Son Mountains were preparing to attack the base. As a result, Colonel Beck ordered a preemptive strike, directing Lieutenant Colonel Gestson to split his force into two provisional battalions: Command Group Alpha, consisting of Companies I, K, and M; and Command Group Bravo, composed of Companies L, E, 2d Battalion, 5th Marines, and C, 1st Battalion, 5th Marines. Group Alpha, commanded by Gestson, jumped off on 17 December for a five-day search and clear operation in the northern Que Sons, while Group Bravo, commanded by the battalion's executive officer, Major Denver T. Dale III, assumed complete responsibility for the security of Liberty Bridge, Liberty Road, and the regiment's eastern area of operations.

On 23 December, following several days of very little activity in the Que Sons, Command Group Alpha helilifted into the Arizona, relieving the 2d Battalion, 5th Marines of responsibility for the area. The next day, Colonel Beck deactivated both command groups and ordered Lieutenant Colonel Bowen's Marines to assume control of the eastern area of operations. Throughout the remainder of the month, Gestson's Marines conducted extensive patrols and rice denial operations within the Arizona, employing a denial technique, codenamed "Operation Butterfly," pioneered earlier.** Split into 10-man teams and equipped with detonation cord, elements of the battalion helilifted into areas containing enemy controlled

---

*Time-on-target denotes the method of firing on a target in which various artillery units so time their fire as to assure all projectiles reach the target simultaneously.

**For a detailed discussion of Operation Butterfly, see Colonel Noble L. Beck, "Rice Krispies Nipped in the Bud," *Marine Corps Gazette*, May70, p. 50.

seedling beds. With the "det" cord and gasoline, Gestson's battalion destroyed the seedlings before they could be transplanted into paddies—maximizing destruction in a minimum amount of time. Utilizing this technique, the battalion and the regiment destroyed 760 rice seedlings beds, averaging 400 meters square: potentially enough rice to supply a company-size unit for months. This rice denial technique, combined with extensive patrols and night ambushes and the rotation of battalions into the Arizona at approximately one-month intervals, would continue to aid the 5th Marines in inflicting significant losses and reducing the enemy's freedom of movement throughout the An Hoa basin during the coming year.

CHAPTER 12

Da Nang and the Que Son Valley

The 7th Marines—26th Marines: Protecting the Northern Flank
Quang Tin and Quang Ngai Battleground—Results

The 7th Marines

North of the 5th Marines' TAOR and west of that of the 1st Marines, the 7th Marines defended a large area of responsibility stretching from Elephant Valley in the northwest to the Thuong Duc Valley in the southwest, west of Da Nang. Although dominated by Charlie Ridge, a hill mass that projected from the Annamite Mountains and constituted a much-used enemy base area, the regimental area included a variety of terrain. To the north, the rolling, brush-covered foothills, interspersed with few hamlets and patches of woods, predominated, while to the south were the steep-sided, jungle-covered walls of Thuong Duc Valley and the broad, rice-paddied flood plain of the Song Vu Gia and Song Yen. Besides Routes 4 and 540, few roads crisscrossed the TAOR. The same could not be said for enemy infiltration routes. The regiment's area of operations, elongated as it was, sat astride all known routes from the western mountains into the Da Nang Vital Area.

With the end of operations in the mountains to the west, Colonel Robert L. Nichols' 1st and 3d Battalions returned to the regiment's TAOR at the beginning of June, where they rejoined the 2d Battalion, which had maintained a screen in the piedmont throughout Operation Oklahoma Hills. Based at Dai La Pass, Lieutenant Colonel Marvin H. Lugger's 2d Battalion, reinforced from time to time by two additional companies of the regiment, continued its mission of providing security for the Da Nang Vital Area by aggressively patrolling and ambushing throughout its TAOR, while strengthening and improving the Da Nang Barrier.

III MAF envisioned the barrier, or as it was later known, the Da Nang Anti-infiltration System (DAIS), as the first line of defense for the city, its vital military installations, and surrounding populated areas. In June 1968, the 1st Marine Division, at the direction of III MAF, began construction of a physical barrier along the outer edges of the rocket belt, a 12,000-meter semicircle centered on the Da Nang airfield whose radius was the maximum range of the enemy's 122mm and 140mm rockets. The project, as initially conceived, was to consist of a 500-meter-wide cleared belt of land containing two parallel barbed wire fences, concertina wire entanglements, 23 observation towers, and minefields which would halt or at least delay enemy infiltrators. Although work continued throughout the remainder of 1968, by the beginning of 1969, the barrier remained uncompleted.

Under a revised plan prepared by General Simpson in March 1969, the final sections would be completed, and five Marine rifle companies and a supporting artillery group of two 105mm howitzer batteries, the entire force under the direct operational control of the 1st Division, would be assigned to guard the barrier. According to General Simpson's proposal, the system, when completed, would require no more than 1,800 Marines to keep the enemy out of the rocket belt, freeing nearly 5,000 Marines for offensive operations elsewhere.

By the beginning of June, Marine, ARVN, and Korean engineers had cleared the land, and had finished laying barbed wire, minefields, and over 100 line sensors, but little else. Divided responsibility, poor site planning, and the lack of manpower, materiel, and a well-coordinated fire support plan continued to prevent completion of the system. The installation of the elaborate array of sensors and indirect observation devices had not been accomplished, nor had the forces to monitor them or guard the barrier been assembled. Older portions of the barrier now were deteriorating. Brush, in places 18 feet high, covered portions of the cleared strip, and numerous cuts had been made by farmers bound for their rice fields through the unguarded wire. "Unless radical improvements are made," General Simpson stressed, "the Da Nang Barrier will prove to be ineffectual in countering enemy infiltration into the Da Nang Vital Area."[1] It was this concern which prompted the assignment of elements of Lieutenant Colonel Lugger's battalion to the barrier. Likewise, Lieutenant Colonel James O. Allison's 3d Battalion, designated the regiment's mobile strike battalion, initially was assigned to the barrier following Operation Oklahoma Hills, and tasked with repairing the wire and installing a string of sensors from the Song Tuy Loan to the Song Yen, before moving on to a number of short, swift strikes into Dodge City, Bo Ban-Duong Lam villages, and Sherwood Forest-An Tan Ridge areas later in the month.

While work on the barrier consumed a portion of the efforts of the 2d and 3d Battalions, Lieutenant Colonel John A. Dowd's 1st Battalion, following its return to the lowlands, concentrated on operations along Route 4 and the Song Vu Gia from Hill 37 near Dai Loc, west to Thuong Duc, in order to reestablish a presence along the road and to block major river fords. These efforts bore fruit on the night of the 19th, when a Company D platoon ambush spotted an equal number of Viet Cong crossing the Song Vu Gia, 10 kilometers west-northwest of Liberty Bridge. The ambush, waiting until the enemy reached midstream, employed organic weapons and artillery fire, killing 20 of the infiltrators. Three nights later, three kilometers downstream, another ambush was sprung, catching eight more Viet Cong and capturing over 1,000 pounds of tea. On 30 June, Allison's 3d Battalion relieved Dowd's Marines in place, as the 1st Battalion, reinforced by one company of the 3d, joined elements of the 5th Marines in the northern Arizona for Operation Forsyth Grove.

Following the three-day Arizona operation, Lieutenant Colonel Dowd's Marines moved back across the Song Vu Gia, relieved the 3d Battalion, and immediately began extensive patrols along the western sections of Route 4. By the end of the first week of July, the 1st Marines, working to the east, completed upgrading the route from Hoi An to the railroad berm, and Dowd's battalion had secured the road and its bridges from Dai Loc to Thuong Duc. On the 10th, the Marines officially opened Route 4 and the first civilian convoy in four years made its way across Dodge City to Dai Loc and then up the Thuong Duc Valley, accomplishing a major goal of the 1st Division's Operation Pipestone Canyon.

Dowd's Marines continued to maintain security for Route 4 until 17 July, when the battalion, relieved by Allison's Marines, again crossed the Song Vu Gia into the Arizona, this time freeing 5th Marines units for operations in the Que Son Mountains. "We landed across the Vu Gia River," reported First Lieutenant Raymond A. Hord, Commanding Officer, Company C, and then "deployed four companies abreast of one another and had a coordinated sweep to the south; two companies through the My Binh region, about 4,000 meters to the east."² Once established on the high ground, 3,000 meters into the Arizona, each company sent out squad-size patrols and night ambushes which encountered numerous enemy reconnaissance and small foraging and ammunition-carrying parties. On occasion the companies combined for sweeps and cordons of specific areas. In one instance, while Companies B and D provided deep security, Company C advanced into the Nam An (5) village complex to conduct a cordon and achieved unexpected results. Lieutenant Hord noted:

Marine Corps Historical Collection

Col Gildo S. Codispoti, right, assumes the helm of the 7th Marines from Col Robert L. Nichols at change of command ceremonies held at Hill 55 on 9 July.

> We moved very late at night, had a good night move during which the forward elements of my company moved very quietly, and we had a good sound plan in setting up on the objective once we got to it. The second platoon, commanded by Second Lieutenant [Anthony H.] Yusi, moved into the right side of the objective, tied in at 12 o'clock, using north as our direction of advance, set his people down very quietly and waited for the first platoon to move in with him. The first platoon, led by [Second] Lieutenant [Ronald W.] Costello, effected the move nicely, did tie in at 12 o'clock and this led for the CP group, led by myself, and the battalion CP group with [Lieutenant] Colonel Dowd and his staff to move right in behind us. We moved into the center of the village that was encompassed by the two platoons to our north and the third platoon tied in to our rear, so we had a very sound cordon in a matter of minutes. And much to the surprise of five NVA ammo humpers sleeping, we woke them up while they were in their bunker and in a matter of about 15 minutes had five POWs.³

This constant, although low-keyed, patrol and sweep activity continued throughout the remainder of July and into the first 10 days of August.

Beginning late on the 11th, conditions worsened. That evening, every major unit throughout the 1st Marine Division area of operations was hit by either mortar or rocket fire, accompanied in most instances by a predawn enemy sapper attack. The heaviest fighting occurred in the Arizona, where Lieutenant Colonel Dowd's battalion initiated a three-day battle, reminiscent of the 1st Battalion, 5th Marines encounter in June with a large enemy force, later identified as composed of the *8th* and *9th Battalions, 90th NVA Regiment* and *1st Battalion, 368B Artillery (Rocket) Regiment*, which again was attempting to move through the area under cover of the intense series of indirect fire attacks.

At 0415 on the 12th, a Company D listening post and a Company B squad ambush engaged two enemy soldiers sighted midway between their positions, whereupon 15 to 20 enemy directed small arms fire against the two Marine security elements, who then withdrew once reinforced. As the security elements returned to their positions, each of Dowd's companies simultaneously came under heavy, but sporadic, enemy fire, which continued throughout the night. Activation of preplanned artillery concentrations about the friendly positions staved off a major enemy attempt to mass against a single company target. At first light, with air strikes and artillery fire placed on suspected routes of escape, Dowd's Marines swept the site of the predawn firefights. In the vicinity of the initial action, sweeping units found 58 NVA killed, 2 wounded, who were taken prisoner, and 16 AK47 rifles, 3 light machine guns, 3 grenade launchers, and a large assortment of ordnance.

In an effort to relocate the enemy force, Lieutenant Hord's company began sweeping to the northeast shortly after sunrise. At 0830, Hord's Marines regained contact. The enemy was by then deployed in bunkers within a tree line near the villages of Phu An (1) and (2), some six kilometers northwest of An Hoa Combat Base. Consolidating his position for a subsequent assault, Lieutenant Hord directed a coordinated air and artillery attack against the enemy's fortified positions. By 1330, Lieutenant Colonel Dowd committed Company D to cover Hord's right flank, and both companies then prepared to assault. Despite the results of the heavy air and artillery concentration, which made movement through the thick tree line difficult, the enemy mustered enough strength to oppose the Marine assault. Lieutenant Hord observed:

> In essence we had four platoons on line with awesome firepower going into this objective. We got the people up and we moved forward and got inside the tree lines, through the first initial trench networks. In the first trench line we found several NVA bodies, well-equipped NVA, quite young, well-equipped with web gear, grenades, AK47s, helmets, and B40 rocket launchers. In one bunker complex, as we moved through there, we had to assault one with two machine guns which had excellent grazing fire over our positions, and it is very hard to describe the efforts and the courage that each individual Marine displayed in the company as we moved forward assaulting these positions: throwing grenades, shooting LAWs, trying to envelop, getting pinned-down, getting up and moving again. This was just head-on-type stuff, grenade throwing, and almost hand-to-hand combat. On each occasion, as soon as we would secure 10 meters of ground we would come under attack again from the next network of trenches. The NVA were very well dug in and they were waiting for us.[4]

At 1430, Company A, maneuvering toward the battle area, caught a portion of the enemy force, either attempting to outflank the two Marine companies or to flee. By late afternoon, the main assault had broken through the tree line and routed the defenders. Air and artillery peppered the remnants as they fled to the north and northwest. All fighting ceased shortly before sunset, and the 1st Battalion established night defensive positions. Enemy losses for the daylong battle were 145 killed and 50 individual and automatic weapons captured.

Ordered to reinforce Dowd's Marines, Company L, 3d Battalion, 7th Marines moved by helicopter, and Company I, 3d Battalion, 5th Marines advanced overland by foot on the afternoon of the 12th. Neither was committed immediately, but instead held in blocking positions as a reserve. Beginning at dawn on the 13th, and preceded by an air and artillery preparation, Company I joined 1st Battalion Marines in a four-company-front, northeasterly attack through the Finger Lake region of the Arizona. At midday, the attacking force engaged an estimated 100-man NVA unit in a skirmish which lasted some seven hours. Like the previous days' battles, the fighting was again at close quarters, with Marines inflicting 73 casualties, while sustaining 5 killed and 33 wounded. Included among the dead was Lieutenant Colonel Dowd, subsequently awarded the Navy Cross, who was felled by a burst of enemy automatic weapons fire as he and a portion of his command group endeavored to maneuver toward the site of the day's heaviest fighting. Thirty-nine-year-old Lieutenant Colonel Frank A. Clark assumed command of the battalion the following day.

On the 14th, the enemy again attacked. Just after midnight, a remnant of the scattered NVA force attempted to breach the battalion command group's night defensive position, overlooking the Song Vu Gia, near the village of My Hoa (3). Employing the full spectrum of organic and supporting arms, Clark's Marines beat back the attempt, breaking what was to be the enemy's final and somewhat feeble bid to gain a victory at any cost in the Arizona during August. A sweep of the perimeter at dawn revealed 13 bodies and 10 weapons. In three days, the reinforced 1st Battalion had inflicted over 220 casualties, severely disabling the *90th NVA Regiment* and forcing it again to withdraw in order to regroup.

Within hours of the last engagement in the Arizona, the 7th Marines, under World War II and Korean combat veteran, Colonel Gildo S. Codispoti, who had

A Marine shoulders an M79 grenade launcher and fires into a treeline suspected of harboring several Viet Cong guerrillas during the heavy Arizona fighting.
Department of Defense Photo (USMC) A371757

taken over the regiment in July, received final orders from III MAF and the division to stand down in preparation for a move south into the Que Son Valley, also known as the Nui Loc Son basin. Recent Marine multi-battalion and special landing force operations had denied the enemy use of his traditional infiltration routes through the An Hoa basin, as well as access to Dodge City and Go Noi Island, forcing him to shift a larger portion of his operations into the Que Son Mountains and Valley, where elements of the Army's Americal Division likewise had disrupted his movement. This southward expansion of the 1st Marine Division area of responsibility was the next step in the continuing battle to deny the enemy access to the populated and rice-rich coastal lowlands of Quang Nam and Quang Tin Provinces. In addition to allowing Vietnamese regular and territorial forces a greater role in the defense of the Da Nang Vital Area, this shift not only brought the whole of Quang Nam Province, but also key terrain features, previously divided between the two divisions, under control of the 1st Marine Division.

The move of the 7th Marines 54 kilometers to the southeast was fraught with problems from the beginning. This was not to be a short tactical move, but a permanent one. In addition to men and equipment based at the regiment's seven cantonments scattered throughout the soon-to-be-vacated area of operations, all property assigned to the regiment would also be moved, necessitating use of the division's entire rolling stock. First to go would be the 2d Battalion. By the morning of the 15th, Lieutenant Colonel Lugger's Marines and their equipment were loaded on board 120 trucks at Dai La Pass and ready to head down Highway 1. "This was," according to Major Peter S. Beck, regimental S-4, "the greatest single mistake we could have made, since it became readily apparent that it was absolutely impossible to control 120 vehicles in one convoy on a narrow dirt road, many sections of which were only passable one way at a time."[5]

What occurred later in the day on the 15th could only be termed a fiasco. As Lugger's Marines moved south, without the aid of control vehicles or military police stationed at obvious choke points, unbeknownst, a 35-truck, 9th Engineer convoy, loaded with wide-angle-bladed Eimco tractors, was moving north from Chu Lai. They met at the one place on Route 1 that could have precipitated the worst bottleneck possible: a one-way, one-vehicle-at-a-time, pontoon bridge. Riding in front of the 120-truck convoy was Major Beck, and as he later reported:

Infantrymen of the 1st Battalion, 7th Marines patrol a Vietnamese village near Landing Zone Baldy, while the rest of the regiment pushes westward into the Que Son Valley.

Needless to say, the tractor-trailers going north completely blocked the road so that the southbound convoy could not cross and could not pass if they could cross. And the northbound convoy, which was the tractor-trailers with the bulldozers, completely blocked their portion of the road. Consequently, we had a four-and-one-half-hour bottleneck at this bridge, which ate up most of the day, and additionally, at one point in the road, concentrated in excess of 150 pieces of large rolling stock plus all the equipment that they were carrying and troops . . . . We finally managed to unsnarl the bottleneck, by allowing the northbound convoy, with the wide-load angle blades, to pass first because there was no way possible for the southbound convoy to pass. In doing this we had to back up the 120 trucks off the right shoulder of the road, so that the truck convoy going north could pass. This was an unbelievable task, since Marines who can't move in either direction become very frustrated and all of a sudden we had 1,000 traffic control personnel; everybody thinking they knew exactly what they were doing.[8]

The Marines finally resolved the problem and the convoy continued; however, it was so late in the day when it arrived at LZ Baldy that it could not proceed to its final destination, LZ Ross, 16 kilometers inland.

Again, this presented an unacceptable tactical situation: 120 trucks and a large proportion of Lugger's Marines sitting on Baldy's landing strip—a lucrative mortar target. The battalion convoy was in fact mortared on the night of the 15th, but fortunately only one Marine was wounded. The following morning, the convoy traveled the 16 kilometers along Route 535 to LZ Ross without incident.

With one battalion's move completed, the movement procedures and schedule of the remaining two had to be revised due to the problems encountered on the 15th. In discussions which followed the move, division and regimental planners decided that instead of trucks, CH-53 helicopters would be used to move troops, while equipment would be carried by 30-truck convoys spaced over a period of days, instead of a single, 120-truck convoy. In addition, military police would be assigned to each bridge, choke point, and curve, and "roadmaster" jeeps would patrol Highway 1, regulating the flow of traffic. Beginning on the 17th, men and equipment of the 3d, and then the 1st Battalion, moved without incident to LZ Baldy, and by 23 August, the regiment had settled into its new area of operations, which encompassed a large portion of the Que Son Valley.[7]

Lying south of the rugged, jungle-covered Que Son Mountains, the fertile Que Son Valley spread northeastward from its head at Hiep Duc into the coastal plain between Hoi An and Tam Ky. Running through its center, in an easterly and then northeasterly direction, was the Song Ly Ly which marked the boundary between Quang Nam and Quang Tin Provinces, and also the new areas of responsibility of the 1st Marine and Americal Divisions.

As a major enemy thoroughfare, the region had experienced much warfare. In the Que Son Mountains, ridgelines, ravines, and caves hid enemy base camps and harboring sites, all within easy striking distance of the populated coast. The valley, with its many Viet Cong-controlled hamlets, was a major source of food and manpower. From the war's earliest stages, Communist main force elements roamed the area, and as a result, it was the site of one of the Marines' first large-scale operations in 1965. The Marines returned in 1966 and again in 1967, but as North Vietnamese pressure along the DMZ pulled the Marines northward, the Army took over responsibility. On 20 August 1969, the Army officially handed back the defense of the northern portion of the Nui Loc Son Basin, as the 7th Marines moved into the Que Son Valley.

From the Army, the 7th Marines inherited two combat bases, both located on Route 535, a narrow dirt road which ran westward from Route 1 to the district headquarters at Que Son. There the road divided, with Route 535 continuing southward into the Americal TAOR, while the northern fork, Route 536, climbed over the Que Son Mountains, through Antenna Valley, and then into the An Hoa basin. LZ Baldy, formerly the command post of the Army's 196th Infantry Brigade and now site of the 7th Marines' Headquarters, was the easternmost of the two bases, located at the intersection of Route 535 and Route 1, about 30 kilometers south of Da Nang. Sixteen kilometers west, near Que Son District Headquarters, was Fire Support Base Ross, which commanded the Que Son Valley.

Within days of the arrival of the 7th Marines, heavy fighting erupted in the rolling foothills around Hiep Duc, some 32 kilometers west of Tam Ky, at the head of the Que Son Valley. Triggered by elements of the 196th Infantry Brigade endeavoring to reach a downed helicopter, the Army's 4th Battalion, 31st Infantry locked horns with elements of the *1st VC Regiment* and *3d Regiment, 2d NVA Division*, both of which were attempting to destroy the government's model pacification effort at Hiep Duc. By 20 August, the 31st Infantry had killed over 300 enemy troops, and was still heavily engaged. The following day, the Army battalion requested the 7th Marines provide "any size unit" to relieve the pressure by sweeping a finger of the Que Son Mountains to the east of their position. At 1400, in over-100-degree heat, two of Lieutenant Colonel Lugger's companies, F and G, in addition to the battalion's Alpha command group, left FSB Ross and advanced down Route 535 towards the hill mass, thought to contain an NVA battalion and regimental command post.[8]

Early on the morning of the 22d, Company F moved up Hill 441, north of the village of Phu Binh (3), and then back down where it joined Company G in a sweep of the hill's southern slope. As the companies moved westward, the only difficulty encountered was the heat, which caused numerous nonbattle casualties, requiring several emergency evacuations. Later in the day, again at the request of the 31st Infantry, Lugger's two companies moved off the slopes of Hill 441, and by the morning of the 23d, had set up a 1,500-meter blocking position, stretching across the valley floor. The following day, Companies F and G were to begin moving slowly forward in an effort to relieve enemy pressure on the Army battalion, pushing eastward from Hiep Duc. In the interim, forward and flank patrols were sent out. On the left, Company F made no contact as it reconnoitered the area to the front of its position, but on the opposite flank, as Lieutenant Colonel Lugger reported, Company G encountered stiff resistance:

> The hill mass located to my immediate right front was a very heavily covered small hill . . . . I ordered Golf Company to send a reconnaissance force forward to determine what was on that hill, and they sent a reinforced squad. The squad moved up the slope, and was about one-third of the way up when it came under intensive sniper fire. The enemy, firing from very well-concealed and very heavy sniper positions, inflicted wounds on two men and then, with his normal tactics, he covered the bodies with fire so that anyone who attempted to go forward to assist or to aid or to retrieve the bodies would himself come under very intensive fire. Before the day was out, we had about three bodies that we could not retrieve.[9]

At 1700, Company H moved by air to reinforce Company G and the two units attempted to recover the dead Marines, but failed. On the 24th, after air and artillery had stripped away the heavy foliage and destroyed the enemy's positions, the two companies made another attempt during which they retrieved the three bodies.

All three companies of Lugger's battalion moved out on the morning of the 25th, but ran headlong into elements of the two enemy regiments. On the right, Companies G and H encountered the same heavy resistance they had on the 23d, and spent most of the day attempting to both move forward and recover their casualties. On the left, elements of Company F came under intensive mortar, RPG, and automatic weapons fire, as did Lugger's command group in the center. With the enemy less than 50 meters away, noted Lieutenant Colonel Lugger, "every man in the CP had to fire his weapon in order to protect himself." Lugger requested air strikes—napalm within 50 meters, 250-pound bombs within 200 meters, and 500-pound bombs "as close as we dare get them"—breaking the attack on the battalion command post. By late afternoon, with Companies G and H still heavily engaged on the right, and the forward elements of Company F unable to move on the left, Lugger requested reinforcements. At dusk, Company E helilifted into the area, and in what was a daring rescue, Huey gunships, supported by AH-1G Cobras, extracted the battered remnants of Company F, returning them to the command post while evacuating the casualties.[10]

That night, as the Marines of Companies E and F huddled around the battalion command post, the enemy attacked with a heavy mortar barrage which killed four and wounded 26. It appeared that all efforts to spread the Marines out and dig them in was to no avail, and as Colonel Lugger remarked:

> It was a very grim lesson that was learned. Unit leaders at every level must pay more attention; especially after an intensive fight there is a tendency for people to let down because they feel they have given their all. This is not the time to let down. You must even intensify your efforts in order to spread people out and dig people in, especially when the enemy seems to have had some advantage over you. These enemy forces will press the advantage.[11]

Later that evening, the battalion received another mission. Once all casualties were retrieved and evacuated, Lugger's Marines were to push forward 2,000 meters, link up with the 4th Battalion, 31st Infantry, and act as rallying point for its scattered companies.

At first light on the morning of the 26th, as Companies G and H secured the high ground on the right, Companies E and F moved forward and immediately came under heavy small arms and mortar fire. By afternoon, both companies had advanced only 600 meters, and once again had come under heavy enemy fire. Digging in, the companies requested air and artillery support, but it had little effect. Under constant orders to push forward, no matter the cost,

A machine gun crew from Company G, 2d Battalion, 7th Marines opens up on a fleeing enemy force during several days of fierce fighting east of Hiep Duc at the end of August.

Marine Corps Historical Collection

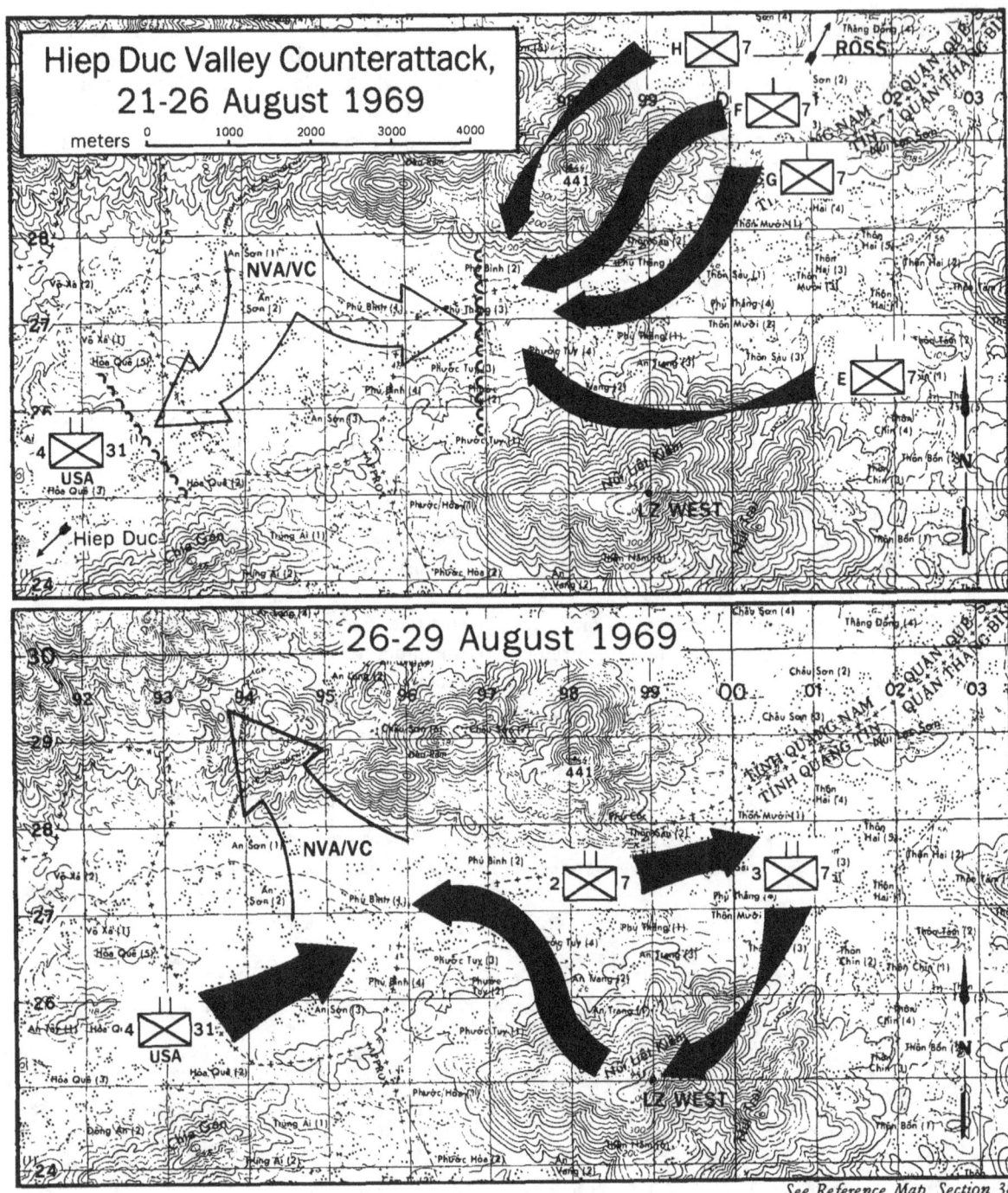

Company G was brought down to reinforce the beleaguered companies, but it too took intense mortar fire, suffering numerous casualties. With all forward movement blocked, Colonel Codispoti ordered Lugger's battalion to hold its positions, retrieve all casualties, and assist the 3d Battalion, which would be moved up in relief. In the interim, Lieutenant Colonel Joseph E. Hopkins, transferred from the 3d Marine Division to the 1st Marine Division, had assumed command of 2d Battalion, 7th Marines. Hopkins, with Colonel Codispoti's approval, issued revised orders for the battalion to "move forward to certain selected objectives . . . and recover all casualties lying in front of their positions." Second Battalion Marines accomplished the mission as ordered, noted Hopkins, "albeit reluctantly in at least two instances."[12]

Following its arrival in the Que Son Valley on the 17th, the 3d Battalion, 7th Marines, under Lieutenant

Colonel Ray G. Kummerow, who had relieved Lieutenant Colonel Allison on the 16th, was assigned by Colonel Codispoti the tasks of securing LZ Baldy and the 9th Engineer rock crusher to the west, and patrolling Barrier Island to the east. On the 26th, following several days of sweeping the island and encountering nothing but enemy snipers, Kummerow's Marines helilifted to LZ West, atop Nui Liet Kiem, overlooking the upper Que Son Valley, and ordered to relieve the 2d Battalion, heavily engaged below. After coordinating with Lieutenant Colonel Lugger by radio on the relief, the battalion moved off the hill, guided by an Army reconnaissance unit. Lieutenant Colonel Kummerow described the relief:

> The going was very slow, with numerous halts and very little progress. It turned out that the Army had never been off the hill on foot before, and had become helplessly lost. I instructed my point of the mile-long battalion column to use a compass heading to the rendezvous point. Approaching dusk, we finally emerged on the stream bed where I expected to pick up 2/7 guides and found to my surprise 2/7 on the march, heading back to FSB Ross. I deployed the point company to establish security for a bivouac area just short of the 2/7 furthest point of advance and closed in the battalion as darkness fell.

The next morning, following a passage through the 2d Battalion's lines, Kummerow's Marines headed west toward a planned linkup with the 4th Battalion, 31st Infantry.[13]

Straddling a small stream with two rifle companies abreast followed by the remaining two in trace, the 3d Battalion began sweeping the valley floor. Almost immediately, Company L, on the right flank, became engaged and eventually unable to maneuver, all the while suffering heavy casualties from an entrenched enemy automatic weapons position. Kummerow ordered Company K to pass through Company L's lines and continue the attack. Surmounting a series of rice paddy dikes, the Marines of Company K, in a number of violent assaults, overran the NVA platoon, killing 13 and capturing two 12.7mm heavy and one 7.62mm light machine guns.

There were numerous displays of personal valor as Company K furiously pushed against the base of the Que Son Mountains into which the NVA had withdrawn. Among them was that of Lance Corporal Jose Francisco Jimenez, who, while shouting encouragement to his fellow Marines, plunged forward, attacking a group of enemy troops and silencing one heavy machine gun. Moving forward toward yet another position, he became the object of concentrated enemy fire and was mortally wounded. Second Lieutenant Richard L. Jaehne, meanwhile, ordered his platoon to attack. When one of his squads was halted by heavy fire, the young Marine officer inched his way through a rice paddy toward the enemy position. After lobbing hand grenades, Jaehne ran forward firing his .45-caliber pistol, killing those of the enemy who had survived the grenade explosions. Although subsequently wounded, the lieutenant continued to lead his men during the engagement.

In another action, Private First Class Dennis D. Davis raced across 10 meters of open ground, leaped atop an enclosed, fortified bunker, and tossed a grenade into a rear aperture. Although seriously wounded by an enemy grenade which landed nearby as he released his own, Davis crawled to the front of the bunker and pushed another grenade through a firing port. He entered following the explosion and seized an enemy machine gun which he then used to fire on another nearby position. Seeing a fallen Marine about 20 meters away, Davis dashed from the bunker and dragged the man to a covered position only to discover that he was dead. Picking up the Marine's rifle he charged another fortification, but was cut down by enemy fire before he could reach it. For their heroic actions, Lance Corporal Jimenez received a posthumous Medal of Honor, while Private First Class Davis and Second Lieutenant Jaehne were awarded Navy Crosses, the former posthumously.[15]

By nightfall on the 27th, Kummerow's Marines had linked up with elements of the 4th Battalion, 31st Infantry in preparation for the push into the Que Son Mountains. Before moving out the following morning, the Marines, in a customary search of areas adjacent to their night defensive positions, came upon a grisly scene. Apparently during their hasty retreat the night before, the NVA had executed a number of civilian prisoners—two males, one female, three young children, and a baby. All were lying side by side, shot once in the head. Continuing the search, 3d Battalion Marines moved into the high ground later in the day and discovered numerous large bunkers with connecting tunnels, all capable of holding in excess of 10 enemy troops. Most were protected by rock outcroppings or nestled among huge boulders, making them impervious to artillery and air strikes.

On the 29th, Colonel Codispoti ordered Companies K, L, and M, together with the 2d Battalion, 7th Marines into blocking positions in preparation for a multi-battalion assault to trap the two fleeing NVA regi-

Nestled among the boulders which dotted the Que Son Mountains, the 7th Marines discover an enemy hide-out. These temporary way stations could accommodate one or more North Vietnamese Army or Viet Cong troops, who would then move into the valley below.

ments. As 3d Battalion Marines moved deeper into the mountains and Marines of the 2d Battalion deployed west from FSB Ross, Lieutenant Colonel Clark's 1st Battalion, in conjunction with the 1st Battalion, 51st ARVN Regiment, assaulted landing zones along the mountains' main ridgeline. During the next three days, the four battalions searched the ridgelines and ravines leading into the valley, finding caves, bunkers, and tunnels, but few enemy troops. The remnants of the two NVA regiments, it was later surmised, had scattered to the west, instead of northward, after being beaten near Hiep Duc.

September found the 1st and 3d Battalions, 7th Marines still in pursuit of the two enemy regiments, and the 2d Battalion patrolling the regiment's western TAOR, centered on the district headquarters at Que Son. In the mountains to the northwest of FSB Ross, ARVN troops and Marines of the 1st Battalion continued search operations begun the previous month, but encountered few enemy troops. To the northeast of the western fire support base, Kummerow's Marines, following their withdrawal from Hiep Duc, conducted sweep operations up the Nghi Ha Valley, and like the 1st Battalion, participated in no significant engagements. As the month progressed, the regiment gradually shifted its operations to the northeast as Clark's Marines, still in pursuit, established blocking positions along the draws leading into Phu Loc Valley on the northern slope of the Que Sons, and 3d Battalion Marines conducted reconnaissance-in-force operations through the mountains toward the blocks.

On 16 September, Clark's Marines withdrew from the Que Son Mountains and reassumed responsibility for the regiment's eastern TAOR, centered on LZ Baldy, where they concentrated on rice denial operations and security assistance in support of Vietnamese elections held in the 28th. Behind, remained Marines of the 3d Battalion, who, as Lieutenant Colonel Kummerow was later to recount, found fighting the environment more difficult than fighting the enemy:

[It] was a "billy goat" type scramble from peak to peak, trying to maintain communications and cover of supporting arms.... We failed to find the main force and facilities of the [NVA] Regiment, however, which was hunkered in along the base of the mountains in caves and tunnels protected by rock outcroppings and huge boulders against which our artillery and air strikes were harmless.... We were surprised at the casualties sustained from malaria and other diseases after a month of continuous fighting in that environment. The battalion dwindled to half field strength. India Company lost all its officers save the company commander, ... who requested relief because of fatigue.[16]

At the end of the month, Kummerow's Marines pulled out of the mountains and moved back to FSB Ross, under the command of Major Samuel J. Marfia, who temporarily replaced the wounded Kummerow. At Ross, the battalion began the task of refurbishing the fire support base's defenses and patrolling the approaches to the town of Que Son.[17] As an added security mission, companies periodically rotated to FSB Ryder, atop Hill 579, from which Battery H, 3d Battalion, 11th Marines conducted "pinpoint accurate fire missions, ... shooting at anything that moved in the valley below."[18]

While Kummerow's Marines maintained watch over the regiment's western TAOR for the next month, 1st and 2d Battalion Marines took on the tasks of ferreting out the enemy and his supplies, first in Antenna Valley, between An Hoa and Hiep Duc, and then in Pagoda Valley, northeast of LZ Baldy. During the month, the regiment employed over 2,000 patrols, ambushes, and company sweeps which not only blocked enemy lines of communications and destroyed base areas, but significantly disrupted the enemy's rice-gathering activities. In the Pagoda Valley alone, Clark's Marines, reinforced by elements of the 1st ARVN Armored Brigade, captured over 17 tons of rice, 75 percent of the regiment's monthly total, which they subsequently distributed among the local civilian population. During November, as the regiment employed more than 2,400 patrols, ambushes, and company sweeps, encounters increased. Lieutenant Colonel Clark's 1st Battalion experienced the sharpest fighting in the mountains overlooking Antenna Valley, a rugged, heavily vegetated area which severely limited both visibility and maneuver. Assisting Clark's Marines in locating enemy troops and their main lines of communications was the Integrated Observation Device (IOD), introduced throughout the division in late October. Sited at FSB Ryder, this highly sophisticated, line-of-sight device used a laser range-finder in conjunction with high-powered binoculars and a night observation device to locate and pinpoint enemy movement during both daylight and darkness at ranges up to 30,000 meters. The primary asset of the IOD was its range and azimuth accuracy, which, when coupled with the Field Artillery Digital Automatic Computer (an aid for solving firing problems), produced a 70 percent probability of first-round-on-target hits by supporting artillery. The device at FSB Ryder accounted for at least 83 NVA killed during an eight-day trial period, primarily along trail networks in the Antenna Valley.*

Scouring the mountains until relieved by the 3d Battalion in mid-December, Clark's Marines pursued elements of an NVA regiment, subsequently identified as the *36th*, discovering several significant ordnance and logistical complexes. While the *36th NVA Regiment* was not encountered in strength, Marines of the 1st Battalion did chance upon several large groups of the regiment's troops. On 12 November, as Company D moved toward the summit of Hill 953, northeast of Ryder, it encountered about 40 entrenched enemy troops, supported by automatic weapons. In an action that was to gain him the Medal of Honor, Private First Class Ralph E. Dias, on his own initiative, assaulted one of the machine gun emplacements. Although severely wounded by heavy enemy fire, he continued to crawl for 15 meters toward a large boulder from which he threw grenades at the enemy gun position. Unsuccessful in destroying the gun, Private Dias left his cover, moved into the open to hurl more grenades, and was shot once again—this time fatally. His last grenade, however, destroyed the machine gun position and its crew.[19]

The nearly two-month-long sojourn in the Que Son Mountains proved to be extremely lucrative for Clark's Marines. In searching almost every cave and ravine, they captured over 200 individual weapons, as well as 40,000 rounds of small arms ammunition, 3,000 grenades, twelve 122mm rockets, and huge stockpiles of food, field equipment, and assorted ammunition. On 9 December, 1st Battalion Marines withdrew from the Que Sons, moved to FSB Ross, and assumed control of the regiment's western area of operations from the 3d Battalion, under Lieutenant Colonel Kummerow, following his return to command. The 3d Battalion then returned to the Que Sons.

By year's end, the 7th Marines had tramped over virtually every square meter of ground from Barrier Island on the coast to Antenna Valley, near the western

---

*For additional detail on the use of the IOD, see Chapter 14.

edge of the Nui Loc Son Basin. In four months of hard fighting, the regiment, as Lieutenant Colonel Kummerow was later to report, had turned the area around militarily:

> Up to the time the 7th Marines had moved into [lower] Quang Nam Province in August 1969, there had been little, if any, patrolling done by the Army (US and ARVN) outside of the Fire Support Bases and cantonments. The enemy had used the terrain from the Barrier Island to Elephant Valley [sic], lowlands and mountains, without interference .... [But] we had succeeded in stabilizing the region militarily. Elections went off without a hitch in the province and attacks against heavily populated An Hoa failed to materialize.[20]

Although badly beaten and forced to suffer severe losses in both men and materiel, the Viet Cong and North Vietnamese were not defeated, as the 7th Marines would discover in 1970.

26th Marines: Protecting the Northern Flank

Protection of Da Nang's northern flank required the constant efforts of Marine infantrymen, and in June 1969, the 26th Marines continued to shoulder the task. Under the command of Colonel Ray N. Joens, who was relieved on the 14th by Colonel Ralph A. Heywood, the regiment held the vital northern half of the rocket belt, through which Route 1, South Vietnam's only north-south highway, and the railroad parallelling it, passed. Composed of only a headquarters unit and the 2d Battalion with its direct support elements, the two other battalions having been assigned to Special Landing Forces Alpha and Bravo, Joens' 26th Marines was thinly scattered from Camp Perdue in the south to Hai Van Pass in the north. Between the two, the regiment maintained platoon- and company-size positions at the Lien Chieu Esso Depot, Lang Co Bridge, Nam O Bridge, and Hill 190, overlooking the Song Cu De flood plain.

During the first two weeks of June, Lieutenant Colonel George M. Edmondson, Jr.'s 2d Battalion maintained a constant round of day and night ambushes, concentrating on the area east of Hill 190, north of the Song Cu De. Marines of the battalion also cooperated with Regional Force troops in providing security for hamlet and village elections, while

Among the weapons captured by the 7th Marines in the Que Son Mountains was a 12.7mm antiaircraft gun, here being presented by MajGen Ormond R. Simpson, left, and Col Gildo S. Codispoti to MajGen William G. Thrash, right, Commanding General, 1st Marine Aircraft Wing, and BGen Ralph H. Spanjer, Assistant Wing Commander, center right, in appreciation of the timely and accurate air support provided the regiment.

Marine Corps Historical Collection

In addition to weapons, food, and ammunition captured in the Que Sons, a cache of bicycles, here displayed by members of the 1st Battalion, 7th Marines, was uncovered.

launching occasional company-size reconnaissance-in-force operations along known infiltration routes in Elephant Valley. On the 12th, the 3d Battalion, which had come ashore the day before, relieved Edmondson's Marines of the responsibility for the regimental TAOR. The 2d Battalion was then redesignated Battalion Landing Team 2/26 and assigned to Special Landing Force Bravo.

Throughout the remainder of June and into July, Lieutenant Colonel Edward W. Snelling's 3d Battalion, reinforced for a period by one medium tank platoon, one amphibian tractor (Ontos) platoon, and attached engineer, truck, reconnaissance, and artillery units, continued to provide security through patrols and ambushes for the area's vital installations. In addition, the battalion conducted cordon and search operations with local Popular Forces and actions designed to deny the enemy use of Elephant Valley as an avenue of approach into the Da Nang area. Although enemy activity, characterized by sniper and harassing fire, remained fairly constant, there were a number of sharp exchanges. In June, for example, Company M caught and severely mauled a group of 50 enemy troops crossing the Song Cu De with automatic weapons fire, supplemented by artillery and Air Force C-47 "Spooky" missions. Again in July, Company M patrols and ambushes in the Elephant Valley, west of Route 1, snared another 25 enemy rice carriers, and captured large quantities of field equipment and food. The 3d Battalion's aggressive cordon and searches, patrols, and ambushes were so successful that by August, enemy infiltrators and rice gatherers made obvious attempts to avoid encountering Snelling's Marines.

In August, with the southward expansion of the 1st Marine Division's TAOR and the 7th Marines' move into the Que Son Valley, the 26th Marines assumed a portion of the latter regiment's area of operations. On the 10th, after periods of training on Okinawa and in the Philippines, and participation in Landing Force Operation Brave Armada in Quang Ngai Province, near Chu Lai, Lieutenant Colonel Edmondson's Battalion Landing Team 2/26 again moved ashore and into positions vacated by the 2d Battalion, 7th Marines, west of Da Nang. By 15 August, the BLT completed the relief and split its rifle companies into heavy platoons and squads, sent out on day patrols and night ambushes in an area of operations stretching from Hill 41 in the south to Hill 22 in the northwest. In addition to defending static positions and blocking avenues of approach into the Da Nang Vital Area, Colonel Heywood tasked Edmondson's Marines with maintaining and responding to intrusions along the regiment's portion of the Da Nang Barrier. Armed with readouts from the balanced pressure system sensors, night observation devices, and large spotlights, 2d Battalion Marines and their supporting artillery responded with both direct and indirect fire to any break in the barrier.

Throughout the remainder of August and most of September, encounters with enemy forces in the expanded 26th Marines TAOR was light and sporadic, with the exception of an attack by 15 sappers on the command post of Company F at Hill 10. The continued employment of a Marine rifle company and a Regional Force platoon from 1/25 Regional Force Company in the high ground west of Hai Van Pass, kept enemy fire in the area at a minimum. To the south, the 2d Battalion, in addition to monitoring and assisting in the continued construction of the barrier, participated with ARVN forces in securing the Hoa Vang and Hieu Duc Districts' rice harvest, not only denying the enemy a source of food, but blocking infiltration routes into the two districts.

In mid-September, another battalion "flip-flop" took place. On the 20th, Lieutenant Colonel James C. Goodin's Battalion Landing Team 1/26 disembarked by helicopter and landing craft from the *Iwo Jima* (LPH 2) and began the relief of the 2d Battalion, which in turn embarked on board the *New Orleans* (LPH 11). Ten days later, Battalion Landing Team 2/26 made a practice amphibious landing within the regiment's TAOR. On the morning of the 30th, one reinforced rifle company landed by LVTs over Nam O Beach, while three reinforced rifle platoons helilifted into a landing zone near the rock crusher at Dai La Pass, and three waves of combat support elements made turnaway landings in assault craft. The exercise terminated at midday and all elements returned to Amphibious Ready Group Bravo's shipping.

During the first two weeks of October, despite swollen streams and flooded lowlands due to the monsoon rains, the 1st and 3d Battalions continued patrol and ambush operations throughout the regiment's TAOR. On the 19th, the 26th Marines reassumed command of BLT 2/26, now under Lieutenant Colonel William C. Drumright, who relieved Lieutenant Colonel Edmondson on 9 September. The 2d Battalion relieved elements of the 3d Battalion and 101st Airborne Division (Airmobile) in the subsequent northward expansion of the regiment's area of operations. The following day, the 3d Battalion passed responsibility for securing Route 1 in the Hai Van Pass and the Lieu Chieu Esso Depot to the 2d Battalion. At the same time, the 9th Marine Amphibious Brigade transferred administrative control of the 26th Marines to the 1st Marine Division. The division redesignated and deactivated the regimental and battalion landing teams, except for planning purposes. With the assumption of responsibility for Observation Post Reno, in the foothills west of Da Nang, Observation Post Eagle Eye, overlooking the Song Cu De, and security for the Da Nang Barrier construction effort by the 3d Battalion on the 23d, the division completed the internal realignment of forces and boundaries. At the conclusion of the realignment, the new area of operations of the 26th Marines encompassed some 711 square miles.[21]

As was the case with the preceding five months, enemy activity during the final two months of the year continued to be light and sporadic throughout the 26th Marines' TAOR. The enemy continued to devote the bulk of his efforts toward gathering food and supplies, but the regiment's aggressive patrol and ambush operations again severely restricted these endeavors. In an effort to locate, interdict, and destroy enemy lines of communication and base camps, Heywood's Marines carried out several company-size search and clear operations in the western and southern portions of the regiment's area of operations. Landing by helicopter, elements of the 1st Battalion began a three week operation in Happy Valley and Sherwood Forest areas on 3 December. Marines of Lieutenant Colonel Goodin's battalion found several tunnels and bunkers, but enemy activity, on the whole, was nonexistent. The regiment carried out similar operations in Rumor Valley, south of Dai La Pass; Leech Valley, along the Song Lo Dong; and in the foothills below Dong Den, all with the same disappointing results.

December, while not a lucrative month in terms of enemy troops destroyed or supplies captured, did witness the introduction of a number of innovations. Under the leadership of Colonel James E. Harrell, who relieved Colonel Heywood on the 12th, elements of the regiment began planning for participation in the division's Infantry Company Intensified Pacification Program and Kingfisher patrol operations, slated to

On a mountaintop northwest of Da Nang, Col James E. Harrell, center, Commanding Officer of the 26th Marines, discusses the movement of Company L with its Commanding Officer, 1stLt John K. Robb, right, and LtCol William A. Simpson, Commanding Officer of the 3d Battalion, who had replaced LtCol Edward W. Snelling in September.

begin in Janaury 1970.* In addition, the 11th Marines installed an Integrated Observation Device on Hill 270, enabling the regiment to have a continuous observed fire capability within Happy Valley, Worth Ridge, and Charlie Ridge—all areas crisscrossed by well-known enemy infiltration routes. By integrating the new equipment with changes in tactics, the 26th Marines found itself better equipped to carry out the mission of defending Da Nang's northern flank in the coming year.

Quang Tin and Quang Ngai Battleground

On 1 June, command of the Americal Division passed from Major General Charles M. Gettys to Major General Lloyd B. Ramsey. In reviewing the accomplishments of the division during his tenure and its future prospects, General Gettys noted:

> Although the enemy continues to present a significant threat in this area, because of aggressive Americal operations he has been unable to achieve a single military or political objective. His future looks no brighter. As GVN forces continue to grow stronger and to dominate the coastal plain, Americal will turn its attention further to the west, targetted against his staging areas and command and control installations, the objective of completing his destruction in the southern I Corps Tactical Zone.[22]

During the previous five months, emphasis was placed on maintaining a flexible offensive posture poised to counter enemy threats anywhere within the division's TAOI. The principal enemy targets, however, continued to be the heavily populated provincial capitals of Quang Ngai and Tam Ky. As a result, a majority of the significant battles fought were in response to the enemy threats against these two cities and were preemptive in nature, engaging the enemy well west of the cities, leaving him to resort only to stand-off attacks by fire. In addition to these preemptive coastal operations, the division also placed emphasis on operations into the mountainous hinterland of southern I Corps to locate and destroy previously immune enemy

---
*For a detailed discussion, see Chapter 11.

units and base camps. These operations, during the latter half of 1969, would be intensified in order to provide a screen behind which South Vietnamese forces could consolidate and expand their control of the strategically important populated coastal lowlands.[23]

As General Ramsey took command, Americal Division forces were engaged in five major operations throughout the two provinces of southern I Corps. To the north, Operation Frederick Hill continued as elements of the 196th Infantry Brigade and 5th ARVN Regiment conducted combat operations designed to secure population centers along the coastal plain and to destroy enemy concentrations, base camps, and infiltration routes in the Que Son Mountains to the west. Within the center sector of the combined Americal-2d ARVN Division area of operations, elements of the 198th Infantry Brigade and 6th ARVN Regiment continued to protect major allied lines of communication and to locate and destroy enemy forces attempting to attack the city of Quang Ngai and the Chu Lai Base complex in Operation Geneva Park. In the mountains west of Tam Ky, the 1st Brigade, 101st Airborne Division, under the operational control of the Americal Division since 16 May, continued Lamar Plain, designed to destroy elements of the *2nd NVA Division* in Base Area 117. To the south, the 11th Infantry Brigade and 4th ARVN Regiment, in Operation Iron Mountain, secured population centers south of Quang Ngai City and continued to destroy other elements of the *2d NVA Division* operating in the mountains to the west. And, on the Batangan Peninsula, Marine Combined Action teams in conjunction with elements of the 6th ARVN Regiment and U.S. 46th Infantry

Feeling that the Marines under his command had accomplished much in providing a secure environment for the inhabitants of Quang Nam Province, MajGen Simpson, right, relinquished command of the division to MajGen Edwin B. Wheeler on 15 December.

Department of Defense Photo (USMC) A372305

continued population security, guerrilla interdiction, and nation-building efforts in this long-time enemy stronghold in Operation Russell Beach.

Enemy activity during June and July was light and sporadic throughout Quang Tin and Quang Ngai Provinces, consisting of sapper and indirect attacks by fire against Americal Division installations. Within the Frederick Hill operational zone, the division continued to place emphasis on preemptive operations designed to deny enemy forces the use of base areas, infiltration routes, and supply caches. Barrier Island was the scene of four such major preemptive operations in an effort to neutralize the area thereby increasing security for South Vietnamese pacification programs. South, within the Iron Mountain operation zone, the division conducted a series of combat sweeps and reconnaissance-in-force operations in the Song Tra Cau Valley and surrounding mountains in order to blunt a possible enemy attack upon Duc Pho. On 20 July, the Americal initiated Operation Nantucket Beach in an area north of the Batangan Peninsula in conjunction with Marine Special Landing Force operation Brave Armada to increase population security in the area, northeast of Quang Ngai City. The following day, Operation Russell Beach came to an end.

With the termination of Operation Lamar Plain in mid-August, enemy activity throughout the division's operational area rose dramatically. During 18-29 August, elements of the 196th Infantry Brigade, 5th ARVN Regiment, and 7th Marines engaged elements of two NVA regiments near LZ West, southeast of Hiep Duc. In fierce fighting the combined allied force drove the enemy from the area, inflicting over 540 casualties. Two weeks later, elements of the battered enemy force returned and attempted to launch an attack on Hiep Duc, but were again driven back by the 2d Battalion, 5th ARVN Regiment.

As the monsoon season began during the latter half of September, both allied and enemy activity declined. Continuous heavy rains during the remaining three months of the year limited combat operations in the Frederick Hill, Geneva Park, Iron Mountain, and Nantucket Beach operational zones by curtailing the effectiveness of visual reconnaissance causing delay or cancellation of close air support missions and limiting both air and ground mobility. Nevertheless, Americal forces continued to concentrate on combat operations, however limited, to increase the level of security for pacification efforts near the major population centers of southern I Corps Tactical Zone.

Results

Measuring the results of six months of large- and small-unit action within the 1st Marine Division's area of responsibility was not an easy task. By the end of 1969, the division could point to many indications that it was inflicting more casualties on the enemy than it was taking. Casualty figures for the six-month period shed some light: 5,503 Viet Cong and North Vietnamese killed against 419 Marines killed, and 4,623 wounded. To these figures one would have to add those of the ARVN and Korean forces. The Marines could also point to the large quantity of weapons, the tons of rice and other foodstuffs, and countless rounds of assorted ammunition captured. And they could add the number of base camps, installations, and enemy fighting positions destroyed.[24]

Statistics tell only half the story. The other half is

PFC David A. Wosmek drops a round into a mortar tube held by LCpl Jose L. Rodriguez during an attack in progress by Company I, 3d Battalion, 26th Marines upon an enemy base camp north of Da Nang.

Marine Corps Historical Collection

told by how well allied forces did in restoring South Vietnam to an era of peace in which the people were allowed to resume their normal pursuits. Using this measure, Major General Ormond R. Simpson thought his 1st Marine Division had done well indeed:

> We achieved limited success by that measure in the Da Nang defensive area . . . the percentage of people that were voting in elections and the very high percentage of children that were in school. I counted that as a successful type of thing. At one time I had available the hectares or the acreage, as we used to have to do it, because that was the only thing we knew, or square kilometers of ground that was made safe enough for people to return to farming and to fishing and that sort of thing. It would be a rough guess, but I would suppose that area that I was responsible for during the year I was in Vietnam, the 1st Marine Division Reinforced must have doubled the area. Now, that doesn't mean anything . . . but it was a significant amount of acreage in which people were able to return and start in a very rudimentary fashion to rebuild their villages, to go ahead with rice farming, and the other kind of crops that they did . . . . Those are the kind of things that you measure success in.[25]

PART V
SUPPORTING THE TROOPS

CHAPTER 13
Marine Air Operations

*1st MAW Organization and Deployment — Single Management: Relations with the Seventh Air Force
Upgrading of Aviation Assets — I Corps Fixed-Wing Support — The Interdiction Campaign — Air Control
Helicopter Operations — Improving Helicopter Support — Air Defense — Accomplishments and Costs*

1st MAW Organization and Deployment

In January 1969, MACV had at its disposal approximately 2,000 United States fixed-wing aircraft and 3,700 helicopters, in addition to the support of Strategic Air Command B-52 bombers scattered from Guam to Thailand and naval aircraft on carriers stationed in the South China Sea. Of these aircraft, 258 fixed-wing and 270 helicopters were under the control of the 1st Marine Aircraft Wing (MAW).[1]

The fixed-wing aircraft of the 1st MAW were concentrated at two bases in I Corps Tactical Zone. At Da Nang, where the wing headquarters, support, and air control groups were located, Colonel Robert D. Slay's Marine Aircraft Group (MAG) 11 included four jet squadrons: Marine All Weather Attack Squadron (VMA[AW]) 242; Marine Fighter Attack Squadrons (VMFAs) 334 and 542; and Marine Composite Reconnaissance Squadron (VMCJ) 1. Two other fixed-wing aircraft groups operated from Chu Lai. Under Colonel Rex A. Deasy, MAG-12 consisted of Marine Attack Squadrons (VMAs) 221, 223, and 311, and VMA(AW)-533. MAG-13, commanded by Colonel Norman W. Gourley, included VMFAs -115, -314, and -323. Three of the four attack squadrons were equipped with McDonnell-Douglas A-4E Skyhawk bombers and the fourth with the older A-4C Skyhawks; the all-weather attack squadrons used Grumman A-6A Intruders. Three fighter attack squadrons flew the McDonnell Douglas F-4B Phantom II, while a fourth was equipped with the improved F-4J Phantom. The primary task of the attack and fighter squadrons was to provide close air support for ground combat units; a secondary mission was interdiction. The reconnaissance squadron flew a mixed complement of RF-4Bs, Phantom IIs modified for aerial reconnaissance and photography; EA-6A Prowlers carrying electronic warfare devices; and the electronic versions of the McDonnell-Douglas F-3D Skyknight, known as EF-10s.

Three aircraft groups controlled the wing's helicopters, divided among three airfields at the beginning of 1969. Based at Marble Mountain Air Facility was Colonel Warren L. MacQuarrie's MAG-16 with six squadrons: one light helicopter squadron, HML-167, with Bell UH-1Es; three medium squadrons, HMMs-164, -165, and -364, the first two equipped with Boeing CH-46A Sea Knights, and HMM-364 with Boeing's improved Sea Knight, the CH-46D; and one heavy squadron, HMH-463, with Sikorsky CH-53A Sea Stallions. Marine Observation Squadron (VMO) 2, in addition to Bell UH-1Es, was equipped with fixed-wing North American OV-10A Broncos. MAG-36, commanded by Colonel Bruce J. Matheson, was at Phu Bai Airfield with four helicopter squadrons: the heavy squadron, HMH-452, with CH-53As; the light, HML-367, flying UH-1Es; and two medium squadrons, HMM-265 equipped with CH-46Ds, and HMM-363, using Sikorsky UH-34D Seahorses. Flying in support of the 3d Marine Division was Colonel Walter Sienko's Provisional Marine Aircraft Group (ProvMAG) 39, created and based at Quang Tri in April 1968. Colonel Sienko's command included two medium helicopter squadrons, HMM-262, equipped with CH-46As, and HMM-161 using CH-46Ds, and VMO-6, which flew UH-1E helicopters, OV-10As, and Cessna O-1 and O-1G observation aircraft.

Not assigned to the operating squadrons, but attached to the 1st MAW, were a number of other aircraft. Headquarters and maintenance squadrons (H&MSs) employed seven aging Douglas C-117Ds on a variety of transport missions. Three of the headquarters and maintenance squadrons also operated 11 TA-4Fs, two-seat trainer versions of the A-4 Skyhawk, and three Grumman TF-9J Cougars, for reconnaissance and forward air control missions. H&MS-17 used four Grumman US-2Bs for aerial monitoring of sensors, and employed two Grumman C-1A Traders in reconnaissance flights. A detachment of Lockheed KC-130F Hercules refueler-transports from Marine Aerial Refueler/Transport Squadron (VMGR) 152, based on Okinawa, flew refueling, transport, and illumination missions from Da Nang Airbase.

Department of Defense Photo (USMC) A422115
As Commanding General, 1st Marine Aircraft Wing during the first half of the year, MajGen Charles J. Quilter devoted much effort to facilitating the wing's adjustment to single management and the support of two Marine divisions, and at times two Army divisions.

In addition to Marine aviation units, aircraft of the U.S. Air Force's 366th Tactical Fighter Wing and the 41st Wing, 1st Vietnamese Air Force Air Division also were based in I Corps, as was the organic helicopter support for the 101st Airborne and Americal Divisions.[2] These units were not under Marine control.

Three groups supported the personnel and aircraft attached to the wing. Headquartered at Da Nang was Colonel Thomas H. Nichols, Jr.'s Marine Wing Headquarters Group (MWHG) 1 which provided administrative and logistical support. Furnishing maintenance were the squadrons of Colonel Richard S. Rash's Marine Wing Support Group (MWSG) 12, also located at Da Nang. Marine Wing Control Group (MWCG) 18, under the command of Colonel Edward S. Fris, provided air control and antiaircraft support.

Major General Charles J. Quilter commanded the 1st MAW at the beginning of 1969. Quilter, a highly decorated veteran of World War II and Korea, took over the wing soon after MACV's imposition of single management of fixed-wing aircraft and the movement of large contingents of Army forces into I Corps. During his tenure as wing commander and III MAF deputy commander for air, Quilter devoted much of his time to facilitating the wing's adjustment to single management and to the increased demands for air support by the two United States Marine and two Army divisions, South Vietnamese units, and the Korean Marine Brigade.

Among the highlights of Quilter's tenure was the activation of an auxiliary wing headquarters in northern I Corps in an effort to improve coordination and response. Headed by Assistant Wing Commander Brigadier General Ralph H. "Smoke" Spanjer, who possessed delegated command authority over all wing aviation and base resources north of Hue, the new headquarters, which replaced the less formal liaison staff headed by Assistant Wing Commander Brigadier General Homer S. Hill, was collocated with Headquarters, 3d Marine Division at Dong Ha Combat Base. The new organization, in addition to ensuring ground commanders more responsive air support and permitting more effective use of air assets, particularly helicopters, reduced the span of control necessary to command the air units and airfields responsive to wing headquarters.

In July 1969, Major General William G. "Gay" Thrash relieved General Quilter in command of the 1st MAW. A native Georgian, Thrash served with distinction during World War II and Korea where, while serving with MAG-12, he received the Silver Star for gallantry in action before being shot down, captured, and held prisoner for two years. General Thrash, during the remaining months of 1969, labored to improve the working relationship between the wing and the two Marine divisions, which gradually had deteriorated during the first year of single management.[3] By late December, his efforts appeared to be succeeding, as Marine Major General George S. Bowman, Jr., Deputy Commanding General, III MAF, informed Major General Keith B. McCutcheon, the Deputy Chief of Staff for Air at Headquarters Marine Corps:

> Here in III MAF we have a very fine relationship between our Ground and Air . . . . Gay spends a great deal of time to make it so. He is bending every effort to use more of the Air capability in support of the Ground effort. And I mean this from a planning point of view, and not just having it available should someone call up. Every adverse comment is thoroughly examined, and in almost every case, there wasn't a problem when all the details were exposed. We still have a ways to go.[4]

In addition to strengthening the air-ground relationship, General Thrash also supervised the initial

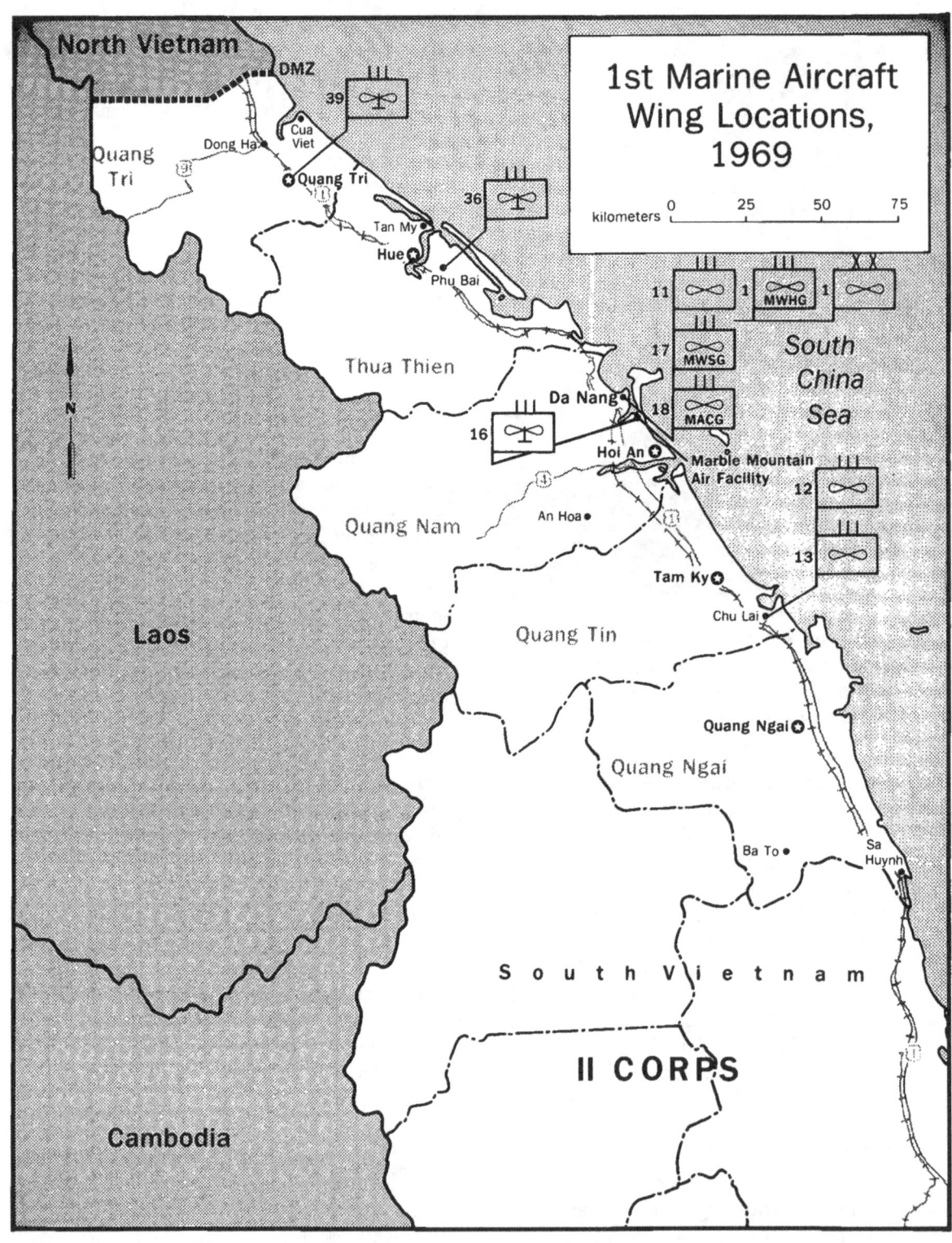

redeployment of 1st MAW air and support units. As a portion of the 25,000-man United States force reduction announced by President Nixon in June 1969, the four 1st MAW units selected for departure represented a cross section of Marine aviation in I Corps. Marine Air Traffic Control Unit 66 left Vietnam for Okinawa on 14 July, followed in August by Marine Fighter Attack Squadron 334, which moved to Iwakuni, Japan; Marine Medium Helicopter Squadron 165, which deployed to Futema, Okinawa; and the 1st Light Antiaircraft Missile (LAAM) Battalion, which joined its sister battalion, the 2d, at Twentynine Palms, California. Both the traffic control unit and two aircraft squadrons joined MAG-15, the air component of the 9th Marine Amphibious Brigade. As a result of the Keystone Eagle redeployment, the wing lost approximately 1,300 personnel and 29 aircraft.

The movement of Marine air units designated as part of the second troop withdrawal, Keystone Cardinal, took place in early October. Marine All Weather Attack Squadron 533 departed Chu Lai on the 5th, enroute to Marine Corps Air Station, Iwakuni, Japan for assignment to MAG-15. Later in the month, Marine Observation Squadron 6 and Marine Heavy Helicopter Squadron 462 left Vietnam for Okinawa. The transfer of wing units imposed by Keystone Eagle and Keystone Cardinal culminated during November in the creation of a wing headquarters (rear) in Japan. With the establishment of the I Marine Expeditionary Force (I MEF), for command and control of Marine combat units in the Western Pacific not committed to Vietnam, FMFPac activated the 1st Marine Aircraft Wing (Rear) on 7 November as the senior I MEF aviation component. Under 1st MAW (Rear), which was not associated in any way organizationally with the 1st MAW, Vietnam, were MAG-15, which retained operational control of fixed-wing units; MAG-36, which assumed control of all helicopter, OV-10A, and KC-130 aircraft; and selected headquarters, maintenance, and air control elements.[5]

A second consequence of the late 1969 troop redeployment was the consolidation of remaining 1st MAW aviation resources in I Corps. With the departure of the 3d Marine Division, helicopter needs north of Hai Van Pass were reduced significantly. Beginning in October, those helicopter squadrons not involved in the withdrawal began moving to Marble Mountain Air Facility in order to adequately support the 1st Division. By early December, all but three squadrons, HMM-161, HMM-262, and HML-367, which were to remain at Phu Bai, had moved south. The Army then assumed operational responsibility for the Quang Tri, Dong Ha, and Hue-Phu Bai airfields although certain wing equipment remained at Quang Tri and Marine helicopter squadrons continued to operate from the Phu Bai airfield until the end of the year.

Single Management: Relations with the Seventh Air Force

Since March 1968, in their capacity as Deputy Commander USMACV for Air Operations, the Commanding Generals, Seventh Air Force, General William W. Momyer, and his successor, General George S. Brown, exercised "fragging and operational direction" of all 1st MAW fixed-wing strike and reconnaissance aircraft.* Prior to that time, the 1st MAW assigned its own aircraft to particular missions and then reported to the Seventh Air Force the number of available fixed-wing sorties not needed to support Marine operations. The Seventh Air Force could then use the extra sorties for its own purposes. Under the new arrangement, the wing reported all preplanned, fixed-wing sorties for Air Force approval and assignment.[6] This new system, outlined in a letter from General William C. Westmoreland to the Commanding General, III MAF, on 7 March 1968, was termed "single management," and justified on the basis of providing adequate air support for the Army divisions reinforcing the Marines in I Corps during the siege of Khe Sanh and *Tet* Offensive, in addition to improving the efficiency of United States tactical airpower as a whole.

The decision to place Marine aircraft under Air Force control required a fundamental change in the Marine Corps' basic principles of combat organization. III MAF was designed and equipped as a combat entity, in conformity with the Marine air-ground principle of exploiting, under a single tactical command, the capabilities of infantry maneuver, helicopter mobility, and the immediate control and coordination of organic attack aircraft and artillery. By means of an uncomplicated and responsive system of air and ground control, the Marine infantry commander was able to weave artillery and air support quickly and effectively into his pattern of ground maneuver, in addition to coordinating naval gun fire support and the movement of supporting helicopters and reconnaissance aircraft within the battle zone.

---

*The daily orders assigning an aircraft to a particular mission are known as fragmentary orders, hence the slang verb "frag" as applied to air operations.

Sheltered within a steel-reinforced concrete revetment, a versatile McDonnell Douglas F-4B Phantom II awaits assignment to a close air support or interdiction mission.

Most Marine commanders believed that while both systems employed similar organizational terminology, there existed a fundamental difference between the two. The single management system was primarily a producer effort, while the one it supplanted was oriented toward the consumer. This consumer orientation was essential to the Marine Corps system and underlaid the complete responsiveness of Marine air to the desires of the supported ground commander.

Preplanned requests for air support under the Marine system involved only three processing steps and 18 hours from the submission of the initial request to receipt of air support. In contrast, the single management system imposed intervening layers of processing between I Corps units and the Seventh Air Force Tactical Air Control Center (TACC) in Saigon. Six steps were now required to process requests from the 1st Marine Division and seven for the 3d Marine Division. Under the Air Force system, request times varied from a minimum of 36 hours advanced notice for radar-controlled aircraft to over 50 hours for preplanned visually controlled aircraft attacks.

Requests for immediate air support under the Marine system likewise involved three processing steps: the originating battalion or regiment; the direct air support center (DASC), collocated with the division; and III MAF Tactical Air Control Center. The TACC then scrambled waiting aircraft. The single management system relied upon diverting aircraft already assigned to other missions. This often resulted not only in the requestor being deprived of support, but the questionable ability of the diverted aircraft to perform the mission properly. Where the Marine system focused on the division, the single management system focused on the corps.

Despite Westmoreland's assurances that Marine aircraft would support Marine ground units, "consistent with the tactical situation," Marines viewed single management as yet another bid by the Air Force for operational control of Marine fixed-wing aircraft, and an expanded role in the tactical support of Marine ground forces.[7] The issue resurrected bitter memories of what the Marine Corps considered inadequate and inefficient air support of Marine ground forces during the Korean War, under the single management system directed by the Fifth Air Force.

The III MAF commander, Lieutenant General Robert E. Cushman, Jr., with the full support of the Commandant, waged a relentless campaign during the remainder of 1968 to overturn Westmoreland's directive. For his part, the Commandant, General Leonard F. Chapman, Jr., took the issue to the Joint Chiefs of Staff, declaring, as he later stated, that it was unnecessary for two reasons:

> The Marine Corps did not battle roles and missions, did not use roles and missions as an argument in battling sin-

gle management, but battled it rather on two other issues. First, that it was unnecessary. There was already a good system in effect that supported Marines and supported the Army . . . . And secondly, that it destroyed the immediate responsiveness of Marine close air support to the Marine infantry and that's a fact. Under the Marine techniques, the Marine infantry commander can state at night what he wants for tomorrow morning and get it in the way of close air support. Under single management, he had to state 72 hours ahead of time what he wanted, see, 72 hours hence. Well, at that point he didn't know. Well, of course that's the Army-Air Force system you know, the air is programed three or four days in advance in their system. They don't have any concept of immediately responsive exigency-type air support for the infantry, and it was on those two grounds that the Marine Corps battled single management.[8]

The controversy resulted in a split among the Joint Chiefs; the Army and Navy Service Chiefs supported the Marine position, while the Air Force and Chairman supported single management. The issue went to the Secretary of Defense, who turned it over to Deputy Secretary Paul Nitze for resolution. A compromise, according to General Chapman, who took the question to the President, eventually was reached:

[General Earle] Wheeler [Chairman of the Joint Chiefs of Staff] made a special trip to Vietnam to talk it out with MACV with the end result that single management was rearranged in a fashion that permitted the Marines to get their immediately responsive close air support as they needed it, and the surplus to go to the Army—just the way it had been before, but with a different name.[9]

Although grudgingly accepting single management, Marine Corps leaders continued to insist that the system destroyed the concept of the Marine air-ground team and at the same time violated existing inter-Service agreements on the conduct of joint operations. Emotions ran high on both sides.[10] Both General Quilter and his successor, General Thrash, however, by working informally with the Seventh Air Force, attempted to modify the system and recover as much control of Marine fixed-wing aircraft as was possible. This pragmatic approach eventually succeeded and by the end of 1969, the 1st MAW had regained much of the ability to assign its strike and reconnaissance aircraft to missions in support of Marine ground operations, and exercise a degree of supervision over the sorties surrendered to the Air Force. The wing, however, was stymied in its efforts to compel the Air Force into supporting the two Army divisions in I Corps to a greater extent than it had in the past.[11]

"On a strictly working day-to-day basis," General Quilter noted, "we hardly . . . knew of single management, because we got everything we wanted. We could negotiate, and the stuff we proposed was invariably bought."[12] Others, however, continued to view the system as a failure despite the increasing amount of flexibility gained by Marine Corps prodding. Among them was Brigadier General Homer S. Hill, Assistant Wing Commander, who stated:

There is some indication that there is beginning to be a degree of respectability and acceptability for single management. And I want to go on record right now as saying, that if this is true, it is a sad, sad day for the Marine Corps, because single management is no better than it was the first day it was implemented. It is no damn good for the Marine Corps, and for Marine aviation. And if we are getting lulled into a sense of false security, it is about time we wake up. And there is some indication from people we have talked to that say, well hell that is not bad, it is working isn't it? Well sure it is working. It is working because the Marine Corps had provoked so many changes to the original single management concept that it pretty well parallels the old Marine Corps system. We have managed to prod some flexibility out of this thing, but the disease is still there. It has got to be cured.

It is not working all right. If you are following the close air support statistics every morning, . . . you will see what the hell is happening. You talk to the 3d Marine Division and you will find it is not all right, because they are nowhere near getting the amount of close air support that they requested every day, and they are not getting what they used to get. And every morning on the board you will see 50, 60, 70 Marine close air support sorties going to the Americal, or you will see 40 or 50 close air support sorties going to the 101st. So there are some people that are smelling like a rose in this business, because these Army units not only have their organic ARAs [Aerial Rocket Artillery], gunships, as well as their Huey gunships, but now they are getting the world's finest close air support, in considerable proportions. So, we don't like this thing from two standpoints. One, is that we don't have control of our organic air, and it is affecting the support to our Marine divisions, and likewise their capability to fight this war. And secondly, the Army never had it so good.[13]

Although opinions on single management still varied widely, Marines had, by the end of 1969, come to terms with the system and had modified it enough in practice to keep the air-ground team substantially intact. These arrangements, growing in part out of the tactical situation and from the conciliatory attitude of both Marine and Air Force commanders on the scene, especially that of Air Force General George S. Brown, had yet to be formalized in a MACV directive or an Inter-Service agreement for joint operations. The only official description of the system remained General Westmoreland's letter of March 1968 to General

Cushman, although MACV attempted to incorporate the basic principles of single management into a December 1968 revision of Directive 95-4, which prescribed the rules of air operations throughout Southeast Asia. MACV abandoned the attempt after III MAF, in a sharply worded response, refused to concur in the draft. Throughout 1969, Marines remained steadfast in their opposition to any attempt to formalize single management. This stance would change in 1970, as Marines, in order to protect their position in Vietnam and in future joint operations, would finally agree to the revision of MACV Directive 95-4, incorporating a description of the system as it actually existed, not as it was originally proposed.[14]

Upgrading of Aviation Assets

"Aviation is a dynamic profession," explained General McCutcheon. "The rate of obsolescence of equipment is high and new aircraft have to be placed in the inventory periodically in order to stay abreast of the requirement of modern war."[15] New aircraft had been introduced periodically into the 1st MAW's inventory since the unit arrived, and 1969 was to be no exception.

The Marines' fifth year in Vietnam witnessed the steady upgrading of the wing's aviation inventory, both fixed-wing and helicopter. In January, eight additional light attack and forward air control OV-10A Broncos, designed to replace the Cessna O-1, were ferried to Da Nang, where they were divided between Marine Observation Squadrons 2 and 6. The detachment brought the total number of OV-10As assigned to the wing to 24. The month also saw the trans-Pacific deployment to Vietnam of Marine All-Weather Attack Squadron 225, with its Grumman A-6A Intruders, a low-level, long-range attack aircraft capable of penetrating enemy radar defenses and hitting small targets in any weather. VMA(AW)-225 was assigned to MAG-11 at Da Nang, where it replaced Marine Attack Squadron 121, and its older light, single-engined, McDonnell Douglas A-4C Skyhawks, scheduled to be reassigned to the 2d MAW at Cherry Point, North Carolina. In a similar trans-Pacific deployment in February, Marine Fighter Attack Squadron 232, with 15 improved F-4J Phantom IIs, relieved VMFA-323, equipped with older

Gathered to discuss aviation requirements for the 3d Marine Division are, from left, BGen Frank E. Garretson, Commanding General, Task Force Hotel; MajGen Raymond G. Davis; and BGen Homer S. Hill, Deputy Commanding General, 1st Marine Aircraft Wing.

Courtesy of BGen Frank E. Garretson (Ret.)

model F-4Bs, bringing the number of 1st MAW F-4J aircraft to 32.*

April witnessed the continued improvement in the wing's helicopter gunship and lift capabilities. Equipped with new engines producing greater shaft-horsepower, additional Boeing CH-46Ds arrived to replace original CH-46A models, scheduled to be modified during the year. The benefits of the larger engine could be seen when payload weights were compared under combat conditions—operating at sea level, in 95 degree weather, the CH-46D was able to lift 2,720 pounds, while the older model was limited to 1,710 pounds. On 10 April, the first increment of a total inventory of 24 Bell AH-1G Cobra gunships arrived at Da Nang. The four Cobras, assigned to VMO-2 (Marble Mountain Air Facility, Da Nang), began medical evacuation and reconnaissance escort, and strike and fire suppression missions, within six days of their acceptance by the squadron.

The tandem-seat Cobra supplied to the 1st MAW in order to meet the continued need for helicopter gunships, provided several advantages over the support available from the armed UH-1E, the aircraft it was to replace.** A 45 percent faster cruise speed allowed the AH-1G to maintain pace with the CH-46 troop carriers and lead them into combat landing zones. In addition, the Cobra, possessing a 3.4-hour endurance compared to slightly less than two for the UH-1E, could remain on station longer, providing required fire suppression. An augmentation system incorporated into the aircraft's gunsights, gave the Cobra added stability as a weapons platform. The resultant increase in accuracy permitted steeper attack angles, while reducing the aircraft's exposure to ground fire at low altitudes. Armed with a 7.62mm mini-gun, a chin turret-mounted 40mm grenade launcher, four externally mounted 2.75-inch rocket pods, and able to carry 2,000 pounds of ordnance, the Cobra provided the wing with a significant increase in firepower. Monthly accessions by December equipped VMO-2 with 21 aircraft.***

In May, the wing's lift and troop transport capability again was increased with the arrival of the first CH-53D Sea Stallions, one of the largest helicopters produced by Sikorsky. Designed to augment the CH-53A, the newer model, like the CH-46D, was equipped with a more powerful shaft-turbine engine, increasing by 4,000 pounds the payload capacity of the "A" model. In addition, internal rearrangement made it possible for the CH-53D to accommodate up to 55 troops, compared with 38 in the CH-53A. Despite a number of transfers and combat losses, the wing by the end of year possessed a total of 79 CH-53D aircraft.

June witnessed the first of 10 trans-Pacific deployments, codenamed Key Quoit, by which new-production Grumman A-6A Intruders were delivered to the 1st MAW, replacing older models scheduled for progressive aircraft rework in the United States.**** The newer models, like the old, provided exceptional bomb-carrying capacity and a significant measure of versatility to the wing's in-country attack effort. The all-weather capability of the Intruder—supplied by automated navigational and attack problem-solving systems—complemented the varied radar modes for acquiring hostile targets. Using the aircraft's moving target indicator, the two-man crew could direct strikes against moving vehicles, while the aircraft's search radar could locate significant structures. In addition, the development and use of the radar beacon system allowed the Intruder to provide all-weather coverage against targets—whether radar significant or not—while under control of a ground observer.

Included in the Key Quoit deployments were a number of new-production EA-6A Prowlers, the electronic warfare version of the Intruder. Assigned to Marine Composite Reconnaissance Squadron (VMCJ) 1, the newer EA-6As were to replace older models scheduled for rework and subsequent transfer to the 2d MAW, and the McDonnell Douglas EF-10. Utilized to

---

*The McDonnell Douglas F-4J Phantom II, like its predecessor the F-4B, was a twin-seat, supersonic, all-weather fighter aircraft, designed primarily for interception and air superiority, but used as a close support aircraft in Vietnam. The improved F-4J, in addition to possessing more powerful engines and larger wheels, which permitted heavier ordnance loads, carried sophisticated bombing and radar fire-control systems, enabling it to strike targets with improved accuracy.

**Assignment of the AH-1G aircraft to Vietnam was an attrition replacement and not a force level increase. The introduction coincided with anticipated losses and the exhaustion of the UH-1E. Total authorized operating UH-1 and AH-1 aircraft remained at 72 for the 1st MAW.

***Initially, the 1st MAW assigned the AH-1Gs to VMO-2, but in December the wing activated HML-367, an all-Cobra squadron, in order to assure better maintenance and efficient use of the aircraft.

****The Key Quoit deployments involved the flight-ferrying of two to five aircraft at a time from Naval Air Station (NAS), Whidbey Island, Washington, to Da Nang, with intermediate stops at NAS, Barber's Point, Hawaii; Johnston Island; Wake Island; NAS, Agana, Guam; and NAS, Cubi Point, Philippines. The total ferrying effort involved 24 Intruders and 12 Prowlers.

Marine Corps Historical Collection

The first of more than 20 tandem-seat AH-1G "Cobra" gunships, scheduled to replace the slower UH-1E "Huey" gunships through attrition, is off-loaded from a C-130 transport at Da Nang in early April for assignment to Marine Observation Squadron 2.

counter hostile antiaircraft, missile control, and surveillance radar, the EF-10 had, since its arrival in 1965, served as the wing's only electronic warfare aircraft until the introduction of the Prowler. After more than 9,000 sorties, the aircraft was to be reassigned to the 3d MAW, El Toro, California.

Early in August, the last 1st Wing Sikorsky UH-34D Seahorse squadron, Marine Medium Helicopter Squadron 363, terminated combat operations in preparation for redeployment to the United States, completing the phased withdrawal of the aircraft. Initially used to put the vertical envelopment concept, perfected by Marine air and ground units during the 1950s and early 1960s, into practice, the UH-34 eventually became the workhorse of the Marine helicopter effort in I Corps until increasing numbers of CH-46 and CH-53 aircraft assumed the lead role in troop and cargo lifts. The Seahorse, however, compiled an impressive record. From its arrival with HMM-162 and -163 in March 1965 until its August standdown, the UH-34s assigned to the 1st Wing and Special Landing Forces of the Seventh Fleet flew over 917,000 sorties in support of I Corps combat operations, proving to be the most dependable aircraft in the wing's helicopter inventory. Designated to replace the outgoing Seahorses were 18 new CH-53D aircraft of Marine Heavy Helicopter Squadron (HMH) 361. Unloaded from the *New Orleans* (LPH 11) at Da Nang on 27 August, the Sea Stallion squadron joined MAG-36 at Phu Bai in support of the Army and remaining Marine forces in northern I Corps.

Despite the redeployment of helicopter and fixed-wing squadrons during the latter half of the year, the 1st Wing, by December, had completed the replacement of a majority of the aircraft it had arrived with four years before. The all-weather A-6A Intruder had replaced a substantial portion of the A-4 Skyhawks, and a majority of the F-4B Phantoms had given way to more capable F-4Js. Likewise, the EA-6A electronic warfare Prowler had replaced the Korean War vintage EF-10, and the OV-10A Bronco had superceded the Cessna O-1. In addition, the UH-34 transport helicopter was replaced by the CH-46, whose lift capability was further enhanced by the CH-53, and the AH-1G Cobra was introduced to provide a true attack helicopter capability, permitting the UH-1E to return to its mission of observation. Of the wing's aircraft, only the KC-130 refueler-transports remained unaffected.

I Corps Fixed-Wing Support

American fixed-wing air operations in Southeast Asia, following the bombing halt, changed dramatically. No longer concerned with the struggle for air superiority and the defense of strike formations over North Vietnam, the role of airpower in interdiction and ground combat support in Laos and South Vietnam intensified.

Within the confines of I Corps Tactical Zone, the 1st MAW's fixed-wing aircraft, aided by United States Air Force, Navy, and small contingents of the Australian Air Force, performed a variety of missions in support of III MAF ground operations. While in-country interdiction of enemy troops and supplies was a continuous task, as were reconnaissance, airborne forward air control, and landing zone preparation, the wing's most significant function was that of providing close air support. Assisting troops on the ground, according to wing bombardier, First Lieutenant Earl C. Smith, was Marine aviation's basic mission: a task which he and other aircrew members found to be "the most gratifying mission" flown in Southeast Asia.[16]

Throughout the first eight months of 1969, Marine aircraft flew about 80 percent of the daily tactical air strikes and combat support missions in I Corps, assisting six divisions and two brigades. During this period, wing A-4Es, A-6As, and F-4Bs completed a monthly average of 6,480 attack and combat support sorties; the latter category included interdiction, reconnaissance, artillery and air strike control, the bulk of which fell to the wing's OV-10As. By the end of September, with the reduction of aerial support requirements created by the redeployment of the 9th Marines from northern I Corps and the resultant lower level of combat activity, the number of monthly attack and combat support missions plummeted to 4,017. Over the next three months, as the remainder of the 3d Marine Division and three fixed-wing squadrons redeployed, the monthly in-country sortie total dropped further to a December figure of 3,084—less than 41 percent of the January to August average.

While the decline of sortie requests was common to all forces throughout I Corps, there was a marked change in the distribution. Having received an average of 2,890 sorties during the first eight months of 1969, Marine units in October accumulated but 862, a majority of these going to the 1st Division. Conversely, as the 101st Airborne Division expanded its responsibility from Thua Thien Province into Quang Tri, and the Americal Division continued operations in the southern two provinces of the corps tactical zone, the two Army units accounted for 60 percent of the wing's sorties during the last four months of the year. Air support rendered Korean and South Vietnamese units followed a similar pattern to that of the Marines, dropping from 282 sorties in January to 97 in December.*

With alterations in both the intensity and distribution of the wing's attack effort, as the level of combat diminished, a change came in mission assignment. As a result of the action generated during the numerous large unit operations of early 1969, close air support missions between January and August averaged 4,630, accounting for 90 percent of the 1st MAW fixed-wing operations. The remaining months of the year witnessed an inverse commitment. As combat activity decreased and troop density thinned, the requirement for air-delivered munitions in support of ground elements dropped significantly. Although redeployment affected the wing's capabilities, sufficient fixed-wing assets remained to shift greater emphasis to deep air support. By year end, the 1st Wing directed nearly 1,200 sorties a month (48 percent of the fixed-wing effort) on enemy base areas and lines of communications throughout the I Corps hinterland.

An example of the versatility of fixed-wing aircraft in support of and coordination with ground action can be seen in the assistance given a 1st Marine Division reconnaissance team, conducting operations in the Que Son Mountains south of Da Nang in late August. Capitalizing on persistent enemy movement through the Phu Loc Valley toward Go Noi Island, the patrol organized an air-supported ambush. Selecting a site centered on a portion of the well-traveled trail flanked by a lake and opposing steep terrain, the tactics envisioned initial detection by seismic intrusion devices, followed by surprise air strikes.

Shortly after sunset on the 28th, the team, situated on Hill 425 overlooking the valley from the southeast, began monitoring the seismic recorders, while the patrol's forward air controller initiated radio contact with all aircraft involved: a flight of three A-6As orbiting well to the north, and an OV-10A, carrying an airborne controller, on station to the east. Standing

---

*Reported air support sorties furnished South Vietnamese units during the year were somewhat deceiving, as the units increased participation in combined operations with U.S. Forces, to whom the sorties were primarily allocated.

by to provide radar-controlled bombing guidance was an air support radar team (ASRT) at An Hoa Combat Base. Additional aircraft, on alert status, waited at the Da Nang Airbase.

Within a short time, the sensors indicated movement within the target area, whereupon the team using night observation devices confirmed over 60 enemy troops moving east, directly into the killing zone. Selecting an initial impact point ahead of the enemy column, the team's ground controller immediately relayed the target information to the An Hoa ASRT. As the enemy moved forward, the radar team, using the TPQ-10 all-weather radar, vectored the first A-6A on target. Observing the initial string of twenty-eight 500-pound bombs strike the end of the enemy column, the ground controller made adjustment, bringing the next two strikes directly on the dispersing troops.

As the A-6s departed the target area, the Bronco moved in to illuminate the zone, and then called in a flight of three F-4 Phantoms, which had launched from Da Nang when the ambush was triggered. Circling the ambush site, the airborne controller gave each of the incoming F-4s a target until all enemy movement within the valley ceased. With the departure of the Phantoms, An Hoa-based artillery took over, responding to sensor activations as the enemy attempted to retrieve the bodies of their fallen comrades. In the morning, the reconnaissance team counted 48 enemy soldiers killed.

During 1969, 1st MAW attack aircraft operated under no formal sortie limit, and "continually overflew the program," noted Brigadier General Homer S. Hill, Assistant Wing Commander. Under single management, daily attack sorties were subject to Seventh Air Force assignment, which "fragged" 1st MAW fixed-wing aircraft at a utilization rate of 100 percent (one operational flight by one aircraft per day). Combat support, emergency requests from troops in contact, and other wing-generated missions were not included. As a result, the wing's average daily utilization rate hovered around 150 percent, much to the distress of CinCPac air planners who were finding it increasingly difficult to finance excess flight hours and aircraft repairs and replacement during a period of growing economic constraints. Throughout the year efforts were made to cut the number of Air Force fragged sorties by 25 to 30 percent in order to provide a cushion for the wide variety of wing missions, but without success. The tactical situation, however, provided some relief.[17]

Results of the wing's in-country support of ground maneuver units can be viewed in a number of ways. In terms of statistics, wing aircraft accounted for 1,614 enemy troops killed and over 20,400 bunkers and enemy structures razed. Less tangible were results accruing from strike missions which enabled ground units to reduce enemy strongpoints and to secure operational objectives rapidly and effectively with minimal friendly losses. Whether trapping the enemy in fortifications or driving him into the open, air strikes softened his resistance to allied ground attacks considerably. In addition, the psychological value of air support was evident as friendly morale rose and enemy morale plunged, resulting in increased enemy defections

Originally conceived of as an observation aircraft, the OV-10A "Bronco" gradually assumed a close air support mission, at times replacing both the F-4B Phantom and A-6A Intruder.

Department of Defense Photo (USMC) A373942

directly attributable to the fear of air strikes throughout I Corps.

The Interdiction Campaign

With the termination of the United States bombing campaign in North Vietnam in November 1968, the American air interdiction effort in Southeast Asia shifted to the southern panhandle of Laos, which was divided into two strike areas, Commando Hunt and Steel Tiger. Here the system of supply roads, known as the Ho Chi Minh Trail, crossed the western border of North Vietnam through three major passes—Nape, Mu Gia, and Ban Karai—in the Annamite Mountains, and then turned south, branching off into the Communist base areas of South Vietnam and southeastern Laos. Over this road network, North Vietnamese troops, supplies, and munitions moved by foot, bicycle, pack animal, and by truck through a region of Laos rich in hidden natural limestone caves and dense jungle. Traveling mostly by night, the convoys vanished into the numerous well-camouflaged camps and storage depots protected by antiaircraft weapons at daybreak or at the first sign of danger, making interdiction difficult.

The flow of enemy troops and supplies along the road network, and the American effort to restrict it, was tied to the annual monsoon seasons. Between October and February, the northeast monsoon brought dry, clear weather west of the Annamite Mountains, while cool, foggy, rainy weather settled in along coastal North Vietnam and northern South Vietnam. The North Vietnamese customarily increased their activity in Laos by moving large amounts of supplies through the passes and down the road network during this period, requiring a corresponding increase in the American interdiction effort. With the beginning of the southwest monsoon in May, moisture-laden air from the southwest backed up against the mountains, resulting in frequent heavy rains in southern Laos. The poor weather not only posed obstacles to enemy truck traffic, turning the cratered and unimproved trails and roads that comprised the infiltration system into quagmires, but to American air operations as well.

Adapting interdiction efforts to the cyclical weather changes, MACV and the Seventh Air Force in November 1968 launched a series of air campaigns known as Commando Hunt, designed to disrupt the enemy supply lines in Laos, substantially increasing the time required to transport materiel and troops into South Vietnam. United States Air Force, Navy, and Marine tactical aircraft and Air Force B-52s struck at exposed vehicles, storage areas, and truck parks with blast and delay fuzed munitions, while seeding passes and river fords with MK36 air-delivered mines. By January 1969, the Seventh Air Force allotted 40 percent of all preplanned tactical air sorties and 60 percent of all B-52 bombing missions to the Commando Hunt campaign.

In addition to strikes into southern Laos, American aircraft flew other missions further north and, to a lesser extent, in North Vietnam. Over northern Laos, Air Force, Navy, and Marine aircraft flew armed reconnaissance missions and participated in Operation Barrel Roll, providing tactical air support to friendly Laotian forces. Over North Vietnam, American aircraft continued reconnaissance flights following the bombing halt, confirming a gradual buildup in the number of enemy fighter aircraft, surface-to-air missile (SAM) sites, airfields, and antiaircraft artillery positions.

The 1st Marine Aircraft Wing, at the beginning of 1969, provided an average of 35 sorties out of a total of 198 per day in support of the Commando Hunt area raids in Laos, and other air operations outside South Vietnam; an average that was maintained throughout the northeast monsoon season. During the southwest monsoon, beginning in late May, the daily sortie rate fell below 25, but rose again in November with the advent of the dry season. While F-4B Phantoms and A-4E Skyhawks carried the major burden of conducting daylight conventional bombing and strafing attacks at the beginning of the year, increasing reliance was placed on the night missions of the A-6A Intruder as the year progressed.

Described as "the finest all-weather bombing aircraft in the world," the Intruder, with its elaborate target acquisition radar and computer-controlled navigation and bomb-aiming systems, proved to be ideal for night and poor-weather bombing along the Ho Chi Minh Trail.[18] Carrying as many as twenty-eight 500-pound bombs, Rockeye II cluster, or delayed-fuzed MK36 mines, the wing's A-6As were guided to selected targets by Air Force forward air controllers or the sensor readout station at Nakhon Phanom, Thailand, which monitored strings of seismic and acoustic sensors airdropped along the main branches of the trail network. An A-6A assigned to the Commando Bolt, Commando Hunt, or Steel Tiger areas of Laos, would take off from Da Nang and fly to a prearranged point where it would orbit, awaiting target assignment. As trucks, known to pilots and bombardiers as "movers," activated sensors, the Nakhon Phanom station would notify the Intruder of the target location. The aircrew

Department of Defense Photo (USMC) A422876

Described as the finest all-weather bomber, a Grumman A-6A Intruder heads for targets along the Ho Chi Minh Trail, the North Vietnamese Army's main supply route.

would then feed the relayed data into the craft's computer system and head for the truck convoy or storage site, destroying it by using offset bombing techniques or the aircraft's ability to pick up a moving target. In the course of the Commando Hunt series of air operations, Intruders destroyed or damaged an average of 300 moving or stationary targets per month.[19]

Marine Intruders flying missions along the Ho Chi Minh Trail encountered a number of persistent problems, among them the Air Force's failure to understand and appreciate the capabilities of the aircraft itself. As First Lieutenant Earl C. Smith pointed out in describing an average mission over Laos:

> We went over and we had to orbit 25 minutes, waiting to get on the route. They would not allow us on the route. We had the capability . . . to pick up moving targets. An Air Force FAC [forward air controller] was trying to work a couple of [Air Force] F-4s visually at night to pick up three trucks. We waited for 25 minutes; they were unable to find their trucks; they were dropping flares. Periodically through this 25 minutes we called and asked to go on the route to see if we could pick them up. We were rejected. Finally they had to hit the tanker and we were allowed on the route. We were on the route approximately five minutes, picked up the three movers, and wiped all three of them out. And it was confirmed by their F-4s as they were pulling off target.[20]

Air Force controllers, despite their preference for visually controlled aircraft such as the Phantom and Skyhawk, grew to appreciate the capacity of the A-6 to loiter for longer periods without refueling and its capabilities during periods of darkness and poor weather.

Another major problem was heavy antiaircraft fire controlled by North Vietnamese gunners who aimed and fired either at the sound of an aircraft or the general area above a target.[21] While inaccurate, the flak was potentially dangerous and the 1st MAW, in early December, began assigning F-4B Phantoms of VMFA-542, codenamed Commando Bolt Assassins, as escorts for the patrolling A-6s. The Phantom crews received the same briefing as the crews of the A-6As with which they were paired, but flew independently to the assigned orbiting point. When the Intruders were given a target and began the bombing run, the F-4Bs followed, watching for enemy antiaircraft gun flashes. If the A-6s were fired upon, the Phantoms attacked the Communist gun position with Zuni rockets or cluster bombs, and if not, the ordnance was expended on the Intruders' target.[22] Accompanying an Intruder on a night bombing mission on the Ban Karai Pass or any one of the surrounding roads was no easy task, as Captain Laurence G. Karch pointed out:

> Our escort mission over there is the most difficult of all. The A-6 has terrain-following radar and has all the goodies to do all-weather, night interdiction missions. Well, we don't. We have got an air-to-air radar which we can do air-to-air and all-weather work, but following this dude around right on the ground and then going in for a visual attack on a gun at night . . . it's really quite challenging . . . . If you don't have radar you're really in a bind because he turns his lights out when he starts going into the pass. The only way you have of keeping up with him is have your navigational computer work and hope you can dead-reckon yourself to the target.[23]

The use of the F-4 in flak suppression proved successful as both A-6A and F-4 pilots reported a dramatic decrease in antiaircraft fire directed at the Intruders.

Acquiring targets for, and at times controlling, Marine attack aircraft in Laos were the McDonnell-Douglas TA-4Fs of Headquarters and Maintenance Squadron (H&MS) 11. The aircraft's high speed and maneuverability made this small, two-seat plane ideal for conducting low-level reconnaissance, first over North Vietnam and then of the Ho Chi Minh Trail following the bombing halt. Flying between 2,500 and 5,000 feet, altitudes well below those later permitted the slower Cessna O-1, O-2, and North American OV-10A, and at speeds over 400 knots, the TA-4F could remain on station for about 40 minutes before refueling. By constantly maneuvering up and down and from side to side, and shifting from one section of the route to another, the aircraft avoided most hostile antiaircraft fire. Even with these tactics, two aircraft from H&MS-11 were shot down in more than 1,700 sorties conducted over Laos in 1969, and a number received extensive damage to their wing fuel tanks.[24]

While Air Force OV-10As, F-4s, and F-100s monitored the overall trail network from altitudes above 7,500 feet, the TA-4F concentrated on small portions of the enemy supply system by making repeated passes. Using binoculars and hand-held cameras loaded with high resolution or infrared film, the pilot and his accompanying observer searched for individual trucks, truck parks, supply depots, rest areas, and troop concentrations. During Operation Dewey Canyon, for example, TA-4F aircrews located a number of the enemy's 122mm field guns and trucks, which were subsequently destroyed by Marine attack aircraft. Despite a number of successes, thick jungle canopy and enemy camouflage techniques continued to prevent the location and destruction of a majority of lucrative targets in the area.[25]

While interdiction of enemy lines of communications and supply was severely limited above the DMZ following the bombing halt, Marine pilots of Marine Composite Reconnaissance Squadron (VMCJ) 1 continued to conduct both intelligence gathering and electronic countermeasure (ECM) flights. The primary mission of VMCJ-1 aircrews during the year was the maintenance of an electronic screen above the DMZ to protect III MAF air operations in northern Quang Tri Province and reconnaissance sorties along Route 1 in North Vietnam from the enemy surface-to-air missile and radar-directed antiaircraft threats. Flying orbits parallel to the DMZ and southern coast of North Vietnam, squadron aircrews piloting the EA-6A (and the EF-10 before its phaseout in early October) provided continuous electronic support.

Further north, over the Gulf of Tonkin, VMCJ-1 aircraft, especially the versatile EA-6A Prowler, supported

Col Norman W. Gourley, Commanding Officer, Marine Aircraft Group 13, flying an F-4B Phantom, and Col Rex A. Deasy, Commanding Officer, Marine Aircraft Group 12, in the smaller A-4 "Skyhawk," team-up on a mission to destroy enemy supply positions.

Marine Corps Historical Collection

Navy and Air Force reconnaissance programs centering on Vinh and the Hanoi-Haiphong complex. Protection for both manned missions near Vinh and unmanned (drone) operations in northern North Vietnam was possible since the Prowler, configured with jamming devices, electronically targeted radar-controlled antiaircraft, missile, and enemy fighter threats.

Although the allies possessed total command of the air, both over North and South Vietnam during 1969, North Vietnamese MIG fighter aircraft posed a continuing threat to friendly planes operating over Laos, North Vietnam, and to the Navy's Attack Carrier Striking Force (Task Force 77) in the Gulf of Tonkin. While maintaining a continuous airborne alert over Laos (MIGCAP), an average of 110 wing sorties a month were devoted to the Seventh Fleet's barrier combat air patrol (BARCAP) operations. Forming a screen across the primary North Vietnamese air threat axis, extending southeast from Hanoi and Haiphong, the barrier patrol provided 24-hour protection for American naval shipping and aircraft in and above the Gulf of Tonkin. In addition, rotational support of the barrier afforded wing F-4 aircrews the necessary experience in order to maintain proficiency in intercept techniques. Supporting the fighters deployed over the gulf and elsewhere were Marine KC-130 refueler/transports orbiting nearby, providing a day and night refueling capability.

While these two missions placed a strain on the wing's fighter-bomber and financial resources, Major General Quilter and his deputy, Brigadier General Hill, considered them essential. Speaking of the wing's air-to-air capability, General Quilter noted:

> There was nothing like putting a hot shot NFO [naval flight officer] and a good pilot alongside Haiphong, looking into that beautiful scope and seeing MIGs flying out there.... It's meaningful that if we are going to ever tangle with them in an air-to-air way, and we may well, nobody knows, but you had better keep your hand and your foot in the door on this kind of capability, because things could deteriorate very rapidly.[26]

Of the same mind, General Hill declared that participation in the barrier patrol maintained not only pilot proficiency, but the wing's close relationship with the fleet, a relationship that would continue with the end of the Vietnam conflict:

> If you go so long in the air-ground role with these birds and with these crewmen that we have got here, we lose a hell of a lot of our capability, particularly true as far as the radar is concerned and the aircraft is concerned.... If you don't exercise these things, and you don't keep your crew members exercised you lose the capability. If the Vietnam War was over tomorrow and we had to sail off to Timbuktu or Zamboanga, we would need this air-to-air capability, and as a matter of fact, it is part of our mission.[27]

Despite the drain on resources, the 1st MAW actively maintained an around-the-clock participation in the allied interdiction, reconnaissance, and air defense campaign. American intelligence officers estimated that the wing's effort, while small, along with that of the Air Force and Navy, produced an overall reduction of approximately 30 percent, when compared to 1968, in the amount of materiel reaching enemy troops in South Vietnam during 1969.

Air Control

Requesting and controlling fixed-wing air support throughout I Corps Tactical Zone, although complex, was an ever-increasingly-efficient process. All missions, except those specifically generated by the 1st MAW for specific purposes, were controlled by the direct air support control center (DASC) at Camp Horn, Da Nang. The senior tactical air control agency for I Corps, this combined U.S. Air Force, Marine, and Vietnamese Air Force control center could divert any preplanned fixed-wing mission assigned to the tactical zone, launch aircraft held on alert, or request additional Air Force or Navy aircraft for tactical emergencies. Working in close cooperation with the Horn DASC was the 1st MAW air control system, consisting of a tactical air direction center (TADC) at the Da Nang Airbase, responsible for command and control of all wing aircraft; a tactical air operations center (TAOC) on Monkey Mountain, tasked with conducting air surveillance and antiair warfare operations; and direct air support control centers (DASC) at both 1st and 3d Marine Division Headquarters, a wing agency controlling all aircraft assigned in support of the two divisions.* Victor DASC at Phu Bai, subordinate to the Horn DASC, controlled air support assigned to XXIV Corps units, although it was often bypassed by the 3d Marine Division.[28]

Marine or Army ground units needing preplanned air support submitted requests at least 24 hours in advance to the division air officer, who ranked the requests. The consolidated division requests would then be sent to the wing where they were combined with other corps unit requests and transmitted to the MACV Tactical Air Support Element (TASE) and Seventh Air Force Tactical Air Operation Center (TAOC) in Saigon. Seventh Air Force, with MACV su-

---

*Both the Americal and 101st Airborne had control centers similar to the Marine DASC, as did the Air Force.

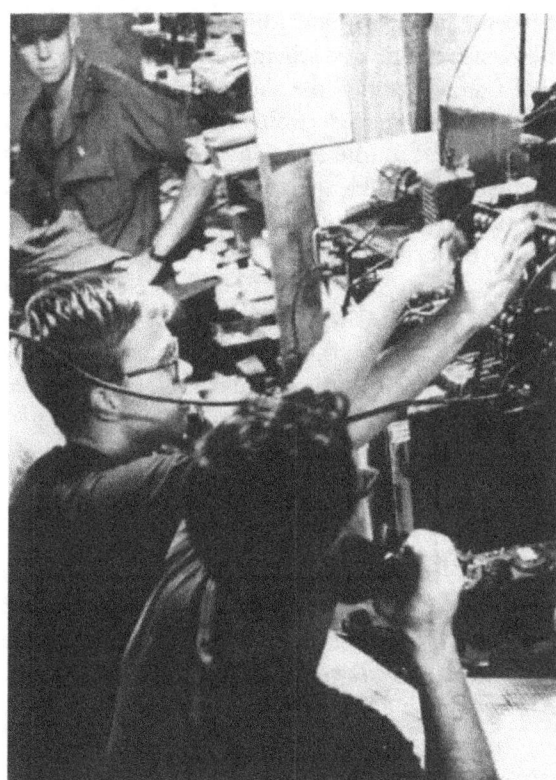

Marine Corps Historical Collection

Collocated with the headquarters element of each division was a direct air support control center where wing radio operators coordinated flights of both jet and helicopter aircraft with the needs of ground troops.

pervision, apportioned available sorties among the corps areas, almost always assigning 1st MAW aircraft to missions in I Corps. These mission assignments were transmitted to the wing in the form of daily or weekly "frag" orders on the basis of one mission per aircraft per day. To these allotted Seventh Air Force missions, the wing added special missions such as the BARCAP and landing zone preparations, which it directly controlled. The wing TADC would then inform the division DASC originally requesting the mission of the number, type, ordnance load, radio call signs, and time-on-station of the aircraft assigned. Once in division airspace, the division DASC took responsibility for establishing initial contact with the aircraft and turning it over to the forward air controller, either on the ground or airborne, who would direct the requested air strikes.

In cases of tactical emergency, the DASC, on its own authority, could divert preplanned flights already assigned to the division. If none were available, the division DASC would request the wing's TADC for additional strikes. The TADC then would scramble any available Marine aircraft or pass the request on to the Horn DASC which would scramble Air Force aircraft based at Da Nang. If additional assistance was needed, the DASC could go to Saigon. Such was the case during Operation Purple Martin in fierce fighting around Fire Support Base Argonne. Air strikes over and above those already allocated were needed to blunt a number of heavy enemy attacks and the requests made their way to Saigon which scrambled both Thailand-based Air Force and Navy carrier-based fighters in the South China Sea.[29] As the tempo of ground action slackened during the year, commanders placed increased reliance on preplanned missions and less on emergency sorties, but as Brigadier General Hill continually stressed: "when our Marines get in trouble during the day and they need more air, of course we start scrambling, . . . You have no alternative. We are not going to let our own Marine units go short of support, if we have got the capability to do it."[30]

All fixed-wing and helicopter fire support furnished Marine ground units was controlled by a ground or airborne forward air controller (FAC), or an air support radar team. Each Marine battalion had a tactical air control party which transmitted air support requests and controlled strikes; however, ground FACs were of limited value due to the mobile nature of combat operations resulting in a heavy dependence upon airborne FACs, flying OV-10As or Cessna O-1s. When not conducting visual and photographic reconnaissance, or directing artillery, these airborne controllers established contact with the ground unit, determined the type and amount of air support required, and then directed the assigned aircraft, passing on changes or additional targeting information received from the supported ground unit.

While ground and airborne air controllers were often limited by darkness or poor weather, AN/TPQ-10 radar course directing centrals, operated by the air support radar teams (ASRTs) of Marine Air Support Squadron (MASS) 3, were not. These combined radar and computer devices, located strategically throughout I Corps, could track an aircraft at distances up to 50 miles and direct it to the desired target in any weather condition. The air support radar teams normally received target assignments from the division DASC and when an aircraft was within range, the ASRT took control of the attack mission, determining the aircraft's relative position to both the target and TPQ-10, and then plotted a course to the objective, as well as bomb release time over the target.

At the beginning of 1969, MASS-3 maintained six

ASRTs deployed at Vandegrift; Quang Tri; Fire Support Base Birmingham, west of Phu Bai; Da Nang; An Hoa; and Chu Lai. Although routinely used for fixed-wing, low-visibility ordnance delivery missions, the teams also positioned helicopters for medical evacuations, reconnaissance runs, and supply drops. In February, when northeast monsoon conditions threatened the lift and logistical support of the 9th Marines during Operation Dewey Canyon, air support radar teams provided assistance. During a typical mission from Quang Tri or Dong Ha into the Da Krong Valley, the helicopter pilot, after an instrument-assisted departure and climb to a position above the cloud cover, would request flight clearance and ASRT assignment from the Vandegrift DASC. The assigned ASRT then tracked the helicopter with TPQ-10 radar, providing the pilot enroute navigational guidance. Arriving over the destination, the pilot, taking advantage of an opening in the clouds, would then proceed to the landing zone or to the release point for parachute supply drops. During the operation, team-controlled helicopters conducted 1,552 evacuation, command and control, and support missions, delivering 2,113 tons of supplies.

A less reliable, but more sophisticated all-weather electronic air strike control system was the radar beacon forward air control (RABFAC), known simply as the "Beacon," used in conjunction with the A-6A Intruder. The core of the system, introduced in 1968, was a six-pound, battery-powered transponder, carried by the ground forward air control team. Emitting a distinctive signal which was picked up by the Intruder's radar, the beacon provided the pilot with the approximate location of friendly troops. By radio, the ground FAC then provided target bearings and bombing direction in relation to the beacon's position. With this information, the Intruder's on-board attack-navigation computer system guided the aircraft to the objective where the aircrew employed off-set bombing techniques to destroy the target.

While A-6A Intruders flew numerous beacon sorties per day for both Marine and Army units, use of the system during 1969 was limited. Ground controllers, especially those unfamiliar with the aircraft, had difficulty in accurately determining target bearings, not only forcing the strikes to be adjusted like artillery fire, also but causing a number of accidents. As a result, distance restrictions eventually were placed on the use of the system when supporting troops in close combat.[31] Equipment failure proved to be the most annoying problem. Poor radio performance, attributed to battery wear or discharge, prevented the ground unit from contacting the supporting aircraft, or the Intruder's elaborate electronic systems oftentimes fell victim to the Southeast Asian environment. "When it worked," noted Lieutenant Colonel George C. Fox, commanding officer of the 2d Battalion, 9th Marines, the RABFAC "was beautiful. We used it inside 300 meters, contrary to division SOP, to repel the attack on Fire Support Base Whisman on 29 May during Operation Cameron Falls. It and 'firecracker' artillery ammunition were instrumental that night."[32] Despite the problems, the A-6A accounted for nearly 20 percent of the wing's in-country attack sorties and over 45 percent of the high-explosive ordnance expended.

Helicopter Operations

Despite the steady decline in combat operations over the year, there was little reduction in the demands placed on MAG-36, ProvMAG-39, and following the first redeployment, on MAG-16 for helicopter support. As Deputy Wing Commander, General Hill observed:

> Viewing the nature of this war, the terrain, and the enemy, ... we never have enough helicopters to satisfy the needs and requirements of the two divisions, and they are honest requirements. And so we have been attempting to do the best we can and satisfy as many of these needs as we can, and we have been doing it by overflying the program. This can only do one or two things; it can get you in trouble real fast, or sooner or later, it can drive you off the deep end. As [Major] General [Paul J.] Fontana said when he was out there, "you are eating your young."[33]

The year began with the wing's fleet of helicopters flying 47,346 sorties a month, carrying 83,630 troops and passengers, and lifting 11,550 tons of cargo. Monthly sortie rates soared to over 52,000 in April, May, and June due to the heavy commitment of ground troops to enemy base areas in both Quang Tri and Quang Nam Provinces, but fell back to 46,303 in July. Over 90 percent of these sorties were consistently flown in support of Marine units, with the remainder divided among the Korean Marines, ARVN, and United States Army Special Forces.

Although each of the wing's helicopter pilots and aircraft types operated under maximum number of monthly flight hours prescribed by the Navy Department, the 1st MAW constantly overflew both. The standards, ranging from 31.5 hours for the CH-53 to 66.6 for the UH-1E, and 80 to 100 hours for pilots, were used by the Navy as a basis for the purchase of fuel, spare parts, and the training and allocation of pilots. By mid-1969, wing helicopters routinely were flying at a rate of 150 percent of their authorized utilization, and during periods of heavy commitment, approached 200 percent. While these high usage rates created a shortage of spare parts, maintenance problems, and an excessive incidence of pilot fatigue, they were considered necessary. Speaking of the heavy use of the CH-53, General Hill remarked:

> [Ground units] have been encouraged, and rightly so, to move into these inland base areas that have become sanctuaries over in the mountainous areas. As they do this, as we build these fire bases, and move over in there, it becomes necessary, of course, to support them with heavy artillery, ammunition; and you can't do this very well with a [CH]-46, you need a heavy lift helicopter. So we have ourselves on the horns of a dilemma here now. We are attempting to root the enemy out of these base areas next to the border of Laos and we need the heavy lift helicopters to support it, and at the same time, we are going to have to reduce flying time of these 53s.[34]

The vexatious cycle of high usage rates and resultant supply and repair problems continued throughout the remainder of the year despite attempts at flight hour reduction.

As a consequence of Keystone Eagle redeployments and the coming of the monsoon season, the monthly sortie rate began a steady and continuous decline in July. From a summer high of 46,303, the number of monthly helicopter sorties fell to 30,957 in October, and to 28,292 by December. During this same period flight hours were cut by over 40 percent, from 13,289 in July to 8,965 by the end of the year.

The mission and tactics of the wing's helicopter fleet changed little. After four years of constant combat, missions and tactics had been refined and by the beginning of 1969 were set. The "workhorse" of the fleet was the CH-46 Sea Knight, which had gradually

Providing the bulk of troop lifts, medical evacuations, and routine supply missions, the CH-46 "Sea Knight" was the workhorse of the 1st Marine Aircraft Wing's helicopter fleet.

Department of Defense Photo (USMC) A372127

replaced the UH-34. Flying over 60 percent of the wing's monthly helicopter sorties, the medium transport performed the bulk of both assault and routine trooplifts, resupply missions, medical evacuations, search and rescue, and the insertion and extraction of reconnaissance teams. Support by this versatile, tandem-rotor aircraft increased during the year as "D" model aircraft replaced the original CH-46A versions, which by June were assigned primarily to special landing force squadrons.

Like the CH-46, older model CH-53A heavy-lift helicopters were augmented and replaced during 1969 by the more powerful CH-53D. The first of these new model helicopters arrived in May, and by December, 20 were assigned to HMH-361, joining an equal number of "A" model aircraft in HMH-463.* The Sikorsky Sea Stallions, to the frustration of the aircrews, were restricted to nonassault trooplifts and supply missions, and to the recovery of downed aircraft. Because it was an expensive and difficult-to-maintain aircraft, Marine commanders hesitated to expose the CH-53 to hostile fire. The aircraft, however, provided the wing with much needed lift capability, as it endeavored to support Marine ground units operating far from their established bases.

The UH-1E, or as it was more commonly termed, "Huey," was an aircraft in continual demand. Assigned initially to four squadrons, VMO-3 (redesignated HML-367), HML-167, and VMO-2 and -6, the unarmed Huey's (known as "slicks") performed a variety of tasks. Slicks allotted to III MAF Headquarters, the 1st MAW, the 1st and 3d Marine Divisions, Force Logistics Command, and the Korean Marine Brigade, not only carried out administrative and command and control missions, but transported an endless stream of visitors, from allied service commanders, to U.S. Congressmen and government officials, to traveling performers. These "VIP" missions were a continual drain on the helicopters' availability, consuming as much as 25 percent of the aircrafts' flight hours.

Hueys also flew reconnaissance missions. While 1st MAW fixed-wing aircraft could provide ground commanders with detailed surface intelligence, such as terrain conditions and camouflaged enemy areas, they often lacked the capability to detect the presence of enemy formations concealed by heavy jungle canopy. To provide such intelligence, a number of wing UH-1E helicopters were equipped with the XM-3 "People

---

*HMH-361 joined MAG-16 in August, eventually replacing HMH-462, which departed Vietnam in November with MAG-36.

Sniffer" Airborne Personnel Detector (APD). As the pilot flew at tree top level, the 65-pound device monitored the air rising from beneath the jungle canopy, detecting human ammonia effluence, or the combustion products associated with human activity, such as fires and vehicle exhaust. Normally employed along trail networks, ridgelines, and stream beds, the APD was able to scan 100 square kilometers an hour, picking up evidence of enemy troop concentrations, as it did preceding Operation Dewey Canyon around an area which would later be developed into Fire Support Base Cunningham.

Although the primary mission of the Huey was observation, an armed version of the aircraft was used most often as an escort. Until the introduction of the AH-1G Cobra, Huey gunships carried the burden of escorting transport and resupply helicopters into hostile areas, and of supporting troops in contact. But the Huey's role as a gunship was considered a limiting factor in overall helicopter operations, as General Hill observed:

> As the war seems to go on, we get more and more dependent on gunships, Huey gunships. The Marine Corps' position has come about 180 degrees since 1964, when we had no gunships and we subscribed to the theory . . . that we could escort all of our helicopters with the U-4 [UH-34A] or the fixed-wing aircraft. The greatest limiting factor in helicopter operations, right now—and this is substantiated by both division commanders—the greatest limiting factor is the availability of gunships. Their tempo of operations . . . to a large degree is based upon the availability of helicopters, and the operational helicopters are largely based upon the availability of gunships.[35]

The AH-1G Cobra gunship, like its predecessor, played an ever-increasing role in Marine helicopter operations following its introduction in April 1969. Initially assigned to VMO-2 and -6, but later placed in HML-367 due to replacements and to ensure better maintenance support, the Cobra's primary task, like the Huey, was to escort transport, medical evacuation, and resupply helicopters. On flights into hostile landing zones, the lead gunship located and scouted the zones, and directed the transport helicopters into the LZs. If opposition was encountered, Cobras, circling above, immediately attacked enemy positions with minigun, grenade, and rocket fire. The AH-1G also was used to break up enemy attacks on Marine positions, firing within 15 to 30 yards of friendly forces. From their arrival, wing Cobras maintained a grueling flight schedule, compiling 21,310 sorties during six months of air combat operations.

During 1969, Marine helicopters flew a total of

MARINE AIR OPERATIONS

Marine Corps Historical Collection

Marine Medium Helicopter Squadron 362 crewmen salute after folding the blades of a UH-34D, retiring the aircraft after seven years of service in Vietnam. With the arrival of CH-53 Sea Stallions, HMM-362 was recommissioned as a heavy helicopter squadron.

547,965 sorties, raising the total support provided forces in I Corps since March 1965 to over 2,300,000. The wing's transport effort accounted for the movement of 895,000 passengers and 115,000 tons of cargo by December. These lift totals represented a substantial improvement, as the average payload per cargo flight exceeded 2,200 pounds, a 23 percent increase over the 1968 figure. This increase benefited both ground and helicopter units, allowing ground elements, now unencumbered by numerous resupply requests, greater mobility, and permitting helicopter squadrons more economical use of time and aircraft by cutting the number of sorties and reducing exposure time to enemy fire.

Improving Helicopter Support

As Marine ground forces moved into enemy base areas with greater frequency following the 1968 *Tet* Offensive and thus became more and more dependent upon the helicopter for support, incidents of mutual recrimination between aviation and ground Marines arose during this period of maximum effort and high stress.[36] The frustration reached a climax early in 1969, when the wing, operating with an inadequate number of helicopters, endeavored to support not only two reinforced and widely scattered Marine divisions, but Korean and South Vietnamese units as well. As Major General Carl A. Youngdale, III MAF Deputy Commanding General, observed:

You would be surprised at the frustrations that exist today in the Marine Corps in our air-ground team. Let me give you some examples of what we got. Here are air quotes: emergency Medevacs: "we get up, we get out, we finally get down, all of a sudden the patient comes running from the bush and jumps in the airplane"; "we get word we got a clear zone, we come in and get our tail shot off"; "we have a patient to move, we try two or three times to get in, but they won't move him 50 yards in order to get a clear zone to move him out on"; "they are using us to haul water right up to their front line units." Dirty fire bases: one pilot was telling about coming into a fire base and all of a sudden this poncho sails up in the air just even with his rotor heads and came moving right over into his head. Said he just closed his eyes and figured he had it. Fortunately a down draft caught it and pushed it on down and didn't wrap in his rotor heads and he didn't crash. "Nobody is in charge at the fire base; some PFC is telling me how to bring this million dollar airplane in"; "troops are not ready when they say they have to go at a certain time." Now here are some ground quotes: "planes don't arrive on time or in the numbers they say they are going to send"; "they quit in the middle of the day and don't come back"; "they are too cautious in bad weather"; "pilots differ in the load they will carry"; "Army will fly when Marines won't"; "no control over what they will or will not do."[37]

These notions eventually moved from Vietnam throughout the Marine Corps, raising doubts about the Marine system of helicopter command and control, and at times threatening the cohesion of the air-ground team as a whole.

In April, Lieutenant General Nickerson convened

a board of six officers headed by Major General Youngdale, and directed it to "examine the utilization, command and control of Marine Corps helicopter assets in III MAF."* During several weeks of inquiry, the board interviewed 64 witnesses, headed by the commanding generals, 1st Marine Division, 3d Marine Division, and 1st Marine Aircraft Wing. Each III MAF unit provided a cross-section of experienced officers from the regimental and group commander down to the company commander and individual pilot. In addition to officers, the board heard from a number of enlisted personnel, one of whom was a reconnaissance patrol leader with a record of 54 patrols.[38]

After careful consideration, the board reaffirmed the basic Marine Corps concepts of the air-ground organization and helicopter command and control, declaring that most of the air-ground difficulties in Vietnam stemmed from the shortage of aircraft and from the fact that one wing was doing the work normally given to two. The board nevertheless found a number of deficiencies. Primary among them was a lack of understanding on the part of both air and ground commanders of the capabilities and limitations of the other, a deficiency which the board noted could be remedied by improved training at all levels, and by again requiring the assignment of naval aviators to the Amphibious Warfare School at Marine Corps Base, Quantico. While rejecting the Army's system of permanently attaching helicopters to ground units, the board recommended strengthening the wing's DASC at each division, in order to facilitate the rapid exchange of flight information between the division and the wing, and to permit the more timely response of helicopters to tactical emergencies. To improve support of the 3d Marine Division specifically, the board recommended the establishment of a 1st MAW auxiliary headquarters to be located with the division at Dong Ha.[39]

Among the first recommendations implemented by Lieutenant General Nickerson was the creation of the wing auxiliary headquarters and the assignment of Brigadier General Ralph H. Spanjer as its commanding officer. Both produced immediate and beneficial results.[40] Among the other recommendations instituted were two exchange programs. The first was an exchange of staff officers. "We started sending," noted General Youngdale, "infantry company commanders to aviation units and we started sending [aviation] captains to ground units, not as air liaison officers, but simply as extra staff officers in the staff itself, battalion, or regiment or whatever it might be."[41]

Although the rapport between aviator and infantryman was slow to be reestablished, the program did go a long way in increasing the understanding of the other's tasks and problems. To further enhance understanding, the wing and divisions began short orientation visits. Lieutenants from the division periodically spent a single or several days with the CH-46 squadrons of ProvMAG-39 or MAG-16, participating with pilots and aircrew in the daily routine of mission briefings and lift or supply sorties. Aviators, both fixed-wing and helicopter, in turn visited infantry regiments and battalions, touring positions, attending operational briefings, and viewing weapons demonstrations.

Other recommendations, while approved, took more time to implement. In the interval, the withdrawal of the 3d Marine Division during the second half of 1969 resulted in the pairing of a single division with the wing, and a more favorable ratio of air support to ground troops. Taking full advantage of this new sufficiency of helicopters, Major General Thrash began experimenting with the delegation of the task of assigning helicopter missions by increasing the authority of the wing DASC, and making increased use of helicopter "packages." While not new, helicopter packages were now placed under the direct operational control of infantry regiments. Among the first of these quick-reaction packages was that established by the 1st Marines, codenamed "Kingfisher."** With the success of these patrols, additional innovative helicopter packages were created in 1970.

With the initial steps taken in 1969 to correct a number of deficiencies in helicopter support, the 1st Wing moved to provide greater flexibility and innovative assistance to ground operations. In this process, both ground and air commanders grew to understand and appreciate the capabilities and limitations of the other within the war zone. Changes also occurred outside of Vietnam, among them the greater integration of aviation and ground members within Headquarters Marine Corps and Fleet Marine Force staffs. In addition, the military education of Marine Corps aviators, especially of junior officers, was given greater emphasis as was cross training and duty assignment,

---

*In addition to Major General Youngdale, the board included Brigadier General Frank E. Garretson, Brigadier General Homer S. Hill, Brigadier General Samuel Jaskilka, Lieutenant Colonel William D. Bassett, Jr., and Lieutenant Colonel Albert N. Allen, recorder.

**For a detailed description of "Kingfisher" patrols see Chapter 11.

all of which aimed at promoting understanding among the members of the air-ground team.[42]

Air Defense

Although Marine, Air Force, and Navy aircraft possessed total command of the air in Southeast Asia during 1969, the American command still found it necessary to maintain defensive arrangements in the event of North Vietnamese air strikes on vulnerable allied targets. In I Corps, while fighter aircraft and antiaircraft weapons could be alerted, major responsibility for ground antiair defense centered on the 1st Marine Light Antiaircraft Missile (LAAM) Battalion, armed with Hawk ground-to-air missiles.

Deployed to Vietnam in February 1965, followed by its sister 2d Battalion, which was withdrawn in October 1968, the 1st LAAM Battalion established its base of operations at Da Nang. Composed of three firing batteries and a fire assault unit, possessing 118 missiles, although authorized 252, the battalion came under administrative control of Marine Air Control Group 18, while operational control was vested in the Air Force's control and reporting center (CRC), codenamed "Panama," located east of Da Nang on Monkey Mountain.

Commanded at the beginning of 1969 by Lieutenant Colonel John W. Drury, relieved in July by Major Edward L. House, Jr., the battalion's batteries were strategically positioned around Da Nang. Located within the Da Nang Airbase itself was Headquarters Battery, while Battery A was atop the Hai Van Pass, Battery B at Monkey Mountain, and Battery C on Hill 327, west of the airfield. The battalion's fire assault unit "E" was deployed on Hill 55, south of Da Nang. Throughout the first six months of 1969, until withdrawn in mid-July, the battalion conducted numerous antiair exercises and practice raids using available Marine fixed-wing aircraft as targets to test the proficiency of the battalion's control and communications system. In January, the battalion engaged 1,375 targets during 75 exercises with a successful engagement rate of 99.8 percent. During the remaining months of its stay in Vietnam, as the number of exercises fell, so did the battalion's success rate. On 19 July, the battalion ceased operations and began preparation for redeployment to Marine Corps Base, Twentynine Palms, California, where in September the battalion was reduced to cadre strength and its firing batteries deactivated.

Accomplishments and Costs

Despite the initial phase of unit redeployments, the 1st Marine Aircraft Wing continued to provide a vari-

Two Marines of the 1st Light Anti-Aircraft Missile (LAAM) Battalion check out the battery of Hawk ground-to-air missiles located on Monkey Mountain, east of Da Nang Airbase.
Department of Defense Photo (USMC) A422857

ety of air support, responding fully to the diverse combat conditions experienced in I Corps Tactical Zone. Marine fixed-wing aircraft furnished attack and reconnaissance assistance, contributing to the continued success of Marine and other United States, South Vietnamese, and Korean ground forces. Likewise, wing helicopters provided the necessary ingredient, and at times the sole means, for the increase in tactical mobility. The wing's versatility was also reflected in the successful out-of-country interdiction campaign, and the electronic warfare, reconnaissance, and air defense assistance furnished Navy and Air Force operations.

While 1969 witnessed the continued modernization and increased flexibility of the 1st Wing's aviation assets, the year also saw the first sustained drop in aircraft losses. As the tempo of ground and air combat operations decreased so did the number of aircraft lost to hostile fire. By year's end, the 1st Wing had lost a total of 44 helicopters and 34 fixed-wing aircraft. In human terms, 92 wing officers and crew members had been killed, 514 wounded, and 20 were listed as missing in action.

CHAPTER 14
Artillery and Surveillance

Artillery Operations—Surveillance and Reconnaissance Activities

Artillery Operations

As 1969 began, all Marine artillery units within I Corps Tactical Zone were either under the control of the 11th Marines, the artillery regiment of the 1st Marine Division, or the 12th Marines, the artillery regiment of the 3d Marine Division.

The 11th Marines, commanded by Colonel Harry E. Dickinson consisted of four organic battalions and the attached 1st Field Artillery Group (1st 155mm Gun Battery, Self-Propelled [SP], later redesignated 1st 175mm Gun Battery); 1st Battalion, 13th Marines; Battery K, 4th Battalion, 13th Marines; 3d 8-inch Howitzer Battery (SP); Battery G, 29th Artillery (USA); Battery B, 8th Battalion, 4th Artillery (USA); and the 1st Armored Amphibian Company. Attached specifically for Operation Taylor Common, which was to conclude on 17 February, were elements of the 1st Battalion, 12th Marines in direct support of the 3d Marines.

Colonel Peter J. Mulroney's 12th Marines was composed of its three organic battalions and the attached 1st 8-inch Howitzer Battery (SP), under the operational control of XXIV Corps and assigned to the Army's 108th Field Artillery Group; 1st Searchlight Battery; 5th Battalion, 4th Artillery (USA); and the 3d Provisional 155mm Howitzer Battery.* Also operating within Quang Tri Province, but not under the direct control of the 12th Marines, was the 5th 155mm Gun Battery (SP).** Headquartered at Dong Ha Combat Base, with its 155mm guns at Vandegrift and a reinforcing platoon of 8-inch self-propelled howitzers at Elliott Combat Base, the battery operated under the control of the 108th Field Artillery Group.

The two artillery regiments' 105mm howitzer batteries were deployed offensively in direct support of Marine infantry units. The 1st Battalion, 11th Marines, with its command post on Hill 55 and batteries at fire support bases scattered about the flatlands south of Da Nang, supported the 1st Marines. From positions at An Hoa Combat Base, Liberty Bridge, and mountainous fire bases to the west, the 2d Battalion, 11th Marines and three batteries of the 1st Battalion, 12th Marines supported the 5th and 3d Marines, while the 3d Battalion, deployed at bases centered on Dai Loc and Da Nang, fired missions for the 7th Marines. The 4th Battalion, 11th Marines, headquartered on Hill 34 and batteries at the Northern Artillery Cantonment, west of Red Beach, Hill 55, and Hill 65, fired in general support of the 1st Marine Division. The 1st Battalion, 13th Marines, which administratively controlled Battery K, 4th Battalion, 13th Marines, fired missions from the Northern Cantonment and the Hai Van Pass in support of the 26th Marines.*** Of the general support artillery units, most were temporarily under the control of the 1st Field Artillery Group at An Hoa Combat Base in support of forces engaged in Operation Taylor Common.****

To the north, Colonel Mulroney's 12th Marines supported infantry units of the 3d Marine Division; 1st Brigade, 5th Infantry Division (Mechanized), and to a lesser extent the 101st Airborne Division (Airmobile); the Navy's Task Force Clearwater; and elements of the 1st ARVN Division. The 2d Battalion, 12th Marines, headquartered at Vandegrift, fired missions for the 9th Marines, while the 3d Battalion, with batteries at Fire Support Bases Neville, Russell, Fuller, and Elliott, supported the 4th Marines. The 4th Battalion, with its command post at Dong Ha and batteries stretching in an arc from Cua Viet west to Elliott Combat Base, fired in general support of the division, as did units of the

---

*In general support, the 108th Field Artillery Group included the 8th Battalion, 4th Artillery (SP); 1st Battalion, 40th Artillery (SP); Battery C, 6th Battalion, 33d Artillery; 2d Battalion, 94th Artillery (SP); and, Marine 1st 8-inch Howitzer and 5th 155mm Gun Batteries.

**With the arrival of 175mm guns in March and April, the battery was redesignated the 5th 175mm Gun Battery (SP). The 1st 155mm Gun Battery likewise was redesignated following the retubing of its guns during the same period.

***Throughout most of the year, two batteries of the 1st Battalion, 13th Marines were in direct support of Special Landing Forces Alpha and Bravo.

****Following Operation Taylor Common, units attached to the 1st Field Artillery Group were released and the group reduced to cadre strength. On 14 July, administrative control of the group was passed from 11th Marines to Regimental Landing Team 9 and the unit departed Vietnam for Okinawa and eventual transfer to Twentynine Palms, California.

108th Field Artillery Group. Although under the control of the 12th Marines, the Army's 5th Battalion, 4th Artillery directly supported the 1st Brigade, 5th Infantry Division from positions at Fire Support Bases Sharon, Hai Lang, and Nancy. Attached to each of the direct support battalions of the regiment was a provisional, four-howitzer, 155mm battery, which Colonel Mulroney noted, "we could not get along without."[1]

Combined, the 11th and 12th Marines possessed a total of 242 howitzers, guns, and mortars at the beginning of the year. Three firing batteries in each direct support battalion were armed with the M101 A1 105mm towed howitzer, which had a maximum range of 11,000 meters and could be transported by CH-46 helicopters to distant fire support bases throughout the corps tactical zone; the fourth firing battery had six 107mm (commonly termed 4.2-inch) mortars with a range of 5,600 meters. The 4th battalion of each artillery regiment was equipped with M109A self-propelled 155mm howitzers, capable of striking targets at ranges up to 14,600 meters. Twenty-four helicopter-transportable, towed 155mm howitzers remained in both regiments' inventories in order to reinforce fires of the smaller caliber howitzers. Allocated among the direct support battalions, these heavy weapons normally were attached to either the 105mm or mortar batteries. The 155mm gun batteries initially were equipped with the M53 self-propelled 155mm gun, maximum range of 14,600 meters, but later replaced by the M107 175mm self-propelled gun, with a maximum range of 32,700 meters. Using the same tracked, motorized carriage as the 175mm gun, the fourteen M110 8-inch howitzers attached to the Force Artillery batteries were capable of hitting targets at a range of 16,800 meters.*[2]

Beginning in midyear, Keystone Eagle and then Keystone Cardinal spawned the redeployment of the 12th Marines and relocation of a number of artillery units. The 2d Battalion, 12th Marines left Vietnam with the 9th Marines, the infantry regiment it supported, in August, followed in October and November by the 1st, 3d, and 4th Battalions, which accompanied the remaining elements of the 3d Marine Division. With the departure of the 12th Marines, control of the 1st 8-inch Howitzer Battery passed to the 11th Marines, and the battery relocated to Quang Nam Province and its gun platoons to An Hoa Combat Base, Landing Zone Baldy, and Landing Zone Ross. Of Marine artillery units in Quang Tri Province, only the 5th 175mm Gun Battery and the 1st Platoon, 5th 8-inch Howitzer Battery remained. Under the operational control of the 108th Artillery Group and the administrative control of the 11th Marines, the batteries continued to fire long-range missions in support of elements of the 101st Airborne Division, 1st Brigade, 5th Infantry Division (Mechanized), and the 1st ARVN Division.

Within the expanded area of operations controlled by the 1st Marine Division, the 3d Battalion, 11th Marines moved to Landing Zone Baldy and then westward to fire support bases dotting the Que Son Mountains and Valley, as the 7th Marines assumed responsibility for that portion of southern Quang Nam Province vacated by the Americal Division in August. On the northern extreme of the division's area of operations, two batteries of the 1st Battalion, 13th Marines, which had supported the 1st and 2d Battalions, 26th Marines serving with the Seventh Fleet's Special Landing Force, moved ashore in October.** Initially located at the division's Northern Artillery Cantonment, northwest of Da Nang, the batteries later moved to Fire Support Base Los Banos, a former Army fire base overlooking the Hai Van Pass, as the division assumed control of the area from the 101st Airborne Division. By December, the 11th Marines and attached general support batteries controlled 152 artillery pieces.

The basic mission assigned to both the 11th Marines and 12th Marines was to "provide fires in support of offensive operations within and beyond the TAOR's, AO, and RZ [Reconnaissance Zone]" for Marine, other American, South Vietnamese, and South Korean forces. In support of the mission, the artillery's primary task was to respond to calls for fire from engaged units, and to prepare landing zones and fire support bases for occupation, which often consumed a minimum of 1,000 rounds of artillery, in addition to air delivered ordnance. Among the collateral functions were base

---

*In addition to the standard artillery weapons, the two regiments possessed a number of "howtars," a weapon which combined the tube of a 4.2-inch mortar and the carriage of the 75mm pack howitzer. Although a high trajectory, helicopter-transportable weapon which could "deliver a round with more punch than a 105mm howitzer," the howtar was phased out during 1969 due to its inflexibility. See "Howtar is Phased Out," *Marine Corps Gazette*, vol. 53 (Oct69), p. 1.

**Although the 11th Marines had had operational control of 1st Battalion, 13th Marines and Battery K, 4th Battalion, 13th Marines since November 1968, administrative control of the units was passed from the 9th Marine Amphibious Brigade to the regiment on 20 October with the redesignation of Regimental Landing Team 26.

ARTILLERY AND SURVEILLANCE

Artillerymen of 3d Battalion, 11th Marines on Hill 63 prepare to fire a 105mm howitzer, the most common piece of artillery used in Vietnam, in support of the 7th Marines.

defense and countermortar, rocket, and artillery missions. As part of this function, the 11th Marines controlled the Northern Sector Defense Command (NSDC), which consisted of various headquarters and support units, artillery and infantry, organized as an outer defensive shield for the Da Nang Vital Area.

In accomplishing the defensive mission, both regiments expended large amounts of ammunition on actual or suspected enemy rocket, artillery, and mortar sites, suspected Communist base camps, infiltration routes, assembly areas, sensor activations, and in efforts to neutralize concentrations of surprise firing devices.[3] These essentially unobserved fires, or harassing and interdiction fires as they were commonly termed, were carried out in response to either specific intelligence from informants, radar, strings of antiinfiltration devices, radio intercepts, or according to specific fire plans to thwart periodic enemy concentrations, and accounted for approximately 85 percent of the total amount of artillery rounds fired by both regiments at the beginning of the year.* As the tempo of ground combat operations slowly declined, the proportion of artillery fire devoted to unobserved missions increased, and by December these fires consumed over 95 percent of artillery ammunition fired by the 11th Marines.

Much of the unobserved fire was planned with information from the 1st and 3d Marine Divisions' Fire Support Information Systems (FSIS). Inaugurated in 1968, the system was located within the target information section of each division's fire support coordination center. Gathering input on enemy troop sightings, movement, cache sites, and rocket launching positions from a wide variety of sources, the section coded

---

*To prevent enemy infiltration of the Demilitarized Zone, the 12th Marines and the Army's 108th Artillery Group maintained a number of ground and counterbattery radar sites south of the zone at Alpha-4, Charlie-2, and Gio Linh.

and stored the information on computer tape, and on request provided artillery commanders with reports, plotting recurrent patterns of enemy movement in a given area. Using these reports, the artillery regiments placed unobserved fire on the most heavily traveled enemy infiltration routes and concentrations of cache sites in order to block movement and preempt an enemy attack.

Sensor activations also provided a number of lucrative targets. The 3d Marine Division, for example, monitored approximately 125 seismic and accoustical sensor strings, emplaced by reconnaissance teams and helicopters throughout the division's area of responsibility. Strings were assigned to certain batteries and upon activation the battery would fire a concentration a short distance from the end of the string. Excellent results were achieved, according to Colonel Wallace W. Crompton, who relieved Colonel Mulroney as commanding officer of the 12th Marines: "I recall the OIC [Officer in Charge] of the sensor unit telling me that one string which had been very active suddenly ceased. A team went out to see what had happened to the devices. They were surprised to see a sign on the trail warning not to use that trail as it 'led to death.' A new trail by-passed it, so the team moved the devices to that trail."[4] The 1st Division used anti-infiltration devices more for gathering intelligence, than for delivering an immediate, preemptive response.

Despite the steady rise in unobserved fires, both regiments continued to conduct a large volume of direct support and observed fire support missions. As Marine infantry units found themselves operating in mountainous, jungle terrain, far from established cantonments and lines of communications, in areas accessible only by helicopter, a method of direct fire support was needed. Developed during late 1968 from Army techniques by the 3d Marine Division under Major General Raymond G. Davis, the mobile fire support base concept envisioned the rapid construction of temporary artillery positions in remote areas, defended by a minimum of infantry. Under a series of protective, overlapping artillery fans, infantry units could then rapidly search the designated terrain, always being assured of immediate artillery support.[5]

By 1969, this technique for landing reconnaissance and security elements, engineers, construction equipment, guns, crews, ammunition, and infantry on a remote peak in the midst of an enemy base area was perfected and used to such an extent that existent or abandoned fire support bases dotted the high ground

Department of Defense Photo (USMC) A371877
With each round weighing close to 150 pounds, loading a 175mm gun required two Marines. The gun was the largest weapon in the Marine artillery arsenal.

throughout the corps tactical zone and batteries could be emplaced and firing within hours of the initial insertion. This welding of artillery and infantry into teams allowed for much more flexibility on the battlefield, as General Davis was later to observe:

> It was soon discovered that the NVA could not cope with this kind of highly mobile warfare when artillery batteries were positioned on razorbacks and high pinnacles throughout an area, eight kilometers apart so as to provide mutually supporting fire plus 3,000 meter overshoot to hit mortars beyond the base, with infantry battalions operating under the artillery fan. In brief, an infantry battalion with its direct support artillery battery formed a team . . . . In addition, the companies themselves operate independently as far as mutual support is concerned. As long as they're within the 8,000 meter fan of the artillery, there is no requirement for the rifle companies to operate together; they can be several kilometers apart.[6]

The normal application of this flexible team approach was to assign each infantry company a two to three kilometer-square area within which an artillery fire support base would be established, where helicopters could resupply and lift out casualties, and from which patrols could thoroughly search the area. Once

ARTILLERY AND SURVEILLANCE

cleared, the company would then be lifted by helicopter to another area within the artillery fan. Using this method, detailed searches were made, revealing, as General Davis noted, "major trail networks and cache areas that the NVA had been using for the better part of ten years," and accounting for the success of such operations as Dewey Canyon in Quang Tri, and Taylor Common and Oklahoma Hills in Quang Nam Province.[7]

During Operation Taylor Common, conducted by Task Force Yankee from 7 December 1968 to 8 March 1969, for example, artillery batteries of the 11th and 12th Marines occupied 13 fire support bases in enemy Base Area 112, Go Noi Island, and the Arizona. Several batteries occupied as many as four different temporary bases during the course of the operation when almost all artillery displacement and resupply were accomplished by helicopter. Throughout the remainder of the year, the 11th Marines fired from an additional 52 positions, and by year's end artillery units of the regiment occupied 17 bases stretching from Alpha-2 near the DMZ, to FSB Ryder in the Que Son Mountains.[8]

In addition to direct support and combat missions, observed artillery fire was used to supplement, and to a limited extent, replace the search and blocking activities of infantry patrols. All of these observed fires were directed to a degree by the traditional eyes of the artillery, the forward observer teams assigned to each infantry company. Often blinded by double and triple canopied jungle, elephant grass, mountainous terrain, climatic conditions, and distance between units, the artillery was forced to use additional means to supplement the eyes of the forward observers. Among these was the establishment of permanent observation posts in towers and on commanding terrain.

Although observation posts had been in use by the 11th and 12th Marines for some time, it was Colonel Don D. Ezell who, shortly after taking command of the 11th Marines in September 1969, instituted greater reliance on the technique, as he stated:

Typical of the numerous 11th Marines' mountaintop artillery positions was Fire Support Base Cutlass, constructed to support the 3d Marines' search of enemy Base Area 112.

Marine Corps Historical Collection

It appeared to me that when we first went in, the [Viet Cong] infrastructure and the organized units were lying together in the coastal plains, and that the Marines, through offensive operations, had disengaged the organized units from the infrastructure, knocking them back into the west and to the hills where they formed base camps. Now the infrastructure had to remain . . . to control the population. But they also had a great deal of dealings with the organized units in their mission; they reconned for them, they stored caches for them, they got food and medicine . . . . And it would appear if there was a disengagement that there must be . . . a lot of travel back and forth across the battlefield by both the infrastructure and the organized units to perform their missions. My artillery was not in position to control this. My F[orward] O[bservers] were with the rifle companies, and they were certainly forward, but they weren't observers in six feet of elephant grass.[9]

Taking "100 people out of my hide," as Colonel Ezell noted, he initiated a regimental observation post system in an effort "to destroy the enemy as far away as

In addition to forward observers with each infantry company and electronic sensors, Marine artillery battalions relied on observation towers such as this one at Landing Zone Ross to provide accurate fire.

Marine Corps Historical Collection

possible, to diminish his capabilities across the battlefield to perform his mission."[10]

These observation posts, each manned by a team of artillerymen and protected by infantry or reconnaissance elements, commanded the main infiltration routes into the populated lowlands surrounding Da Nang. The post atop Hill 190 covered Elephant Valley, north of Da Nang, while Hill 270, to the west, commanded routes leading from Happy Valley, Mortar Valley, Sherwood Forest, and Charlie Ridge. Covering the Thuong Duc corridor and the northwestern portion of the Arizona Territory were Hills 250 and 65. Farther south, Hill 425 in the Que Son Mountains watched Phu Loc Valley and the An Hoa basin, while artillerymen atop Hill 119 observed Go Noi Island and Dodge City. A post on FSB Ryder covered Antenna Valley and the northern section of the Que Son Valley to the south. Artillery observers at each of these positions searched the countryside for enemy movement and called fire missions on promising targets.[11]

In mid-October, the regiment's ability to control the battlefield with observation and fire was further enhanced by the introduction of the Integrated Observation Device (IOD).* This 400-pound instrument, valued at $225,000, consisted of a high-powered Kollmorgan ships' binoculars, combined with an infrared night observation device and a laser range finder. Using the IOD, a trained observer could locate targets up to a maximum range of 30 kilometers in daylight and, employing the infrared observation device, 4,000 meters at night. Once the observer identified a target and determined its distance and direction from the observation post, firing batteries could fire for effect without the usual preliminary adjustment rounds and achieve accuracy of five meters in range and one mil in azimuth.[12] The IOD, with its ability to achieve first round hits, was, as Colonel Ezell observed, "just what we needed." "We were losing targets because during the adjustment phase while we were trying to bracket them they were jumping in

---

*The Integrated Observation Device was a product of the Marine Corps' Special Procedures for Expediting Equipment Development (SPEED) program, administered by HQMC and coordinated by the Marine Corps Development and Educational Command (MCDEC). Initiated in late 1968, the program was designed to identify the operational hardware requirements of Marine forces in Vietnam, followed by quick procurement and delivery to the field. Production and delivery of the IOD, a combination of three existing devices, spanned approximately six months. Of the initial 10 devices constructed, four went to the Army and six to the 11th Marines. For details of other items developed and procured under the SPEED program see FMFPac, MarOpsV, Jan-Feb71, pp. 37-39.

holes." It proved to be the "missing ingredient as far as good fire support was concerned."[13]

Initially two teams, consisting of an officer and five enlisted men, were selected from the 11th Marines' pool of forward observers, trained in the use and maintenance of the device by intelligence personnel of the division, and then assigned to observation posts commanding the Arizona and Que Son Mountains. Eventually expanded to six by December, the IOD-equipped teams were positioned at observation posts on Hills 270, 250, 65, 119, 425, and FSB Ryder. Scanning the same countryside constantly, the trained observers in the course of time became so proficient in anticipating enemy evasive action that they could call in artillery fire so as to "lead" a moving enemy formation.

With the initial deployment of two teams in late October, IOD-equipped observation posts reported achieving considerable success. During the first 10 days of operation, the teams were credited with 72 kills, amounting to 28 percent of the total number of NVA and VC casualties reported by the 1st Marine Division for the same period. With the placement of four additional devices in November, enemy casualties mounted. On 10 November, the IOD team on Ryder observed nine enemy troops carrying packs and rifles in the Que Son Valley; Battery H, 3d Battalion, 11th Marines responded and killed all nine. Four days later, Battery E, 2d Battalion claimed 11 enemy killed of 16 sighted by the IOD team on Hill 65. In November, sightings by the six teams resulted in the deaths of 463 troops, 72 percent of the enemy casualties credited to the artillery and 42 percent of all enemy casualties reported by the division. December results were equally impressive, but as Colonel Ezell was later to report, confirmed enemy casualties probably did not accurately reflect the actual number of enemy killed:

> Colonel [Gildo S.] Codispoti, who had the 7th Marines, had a valley called Antenna Valley which he used to keep one entire infantry battalion operating in. We were able to release that battalion for other operations . . . with one FO team with an IOD [on FSB Ryder]. In the first month they were there they had 300 confirmed kills. The infantry went back . . . and found hundreds of skulls, bones and they told us the place was stinking down there. It was interesting to find out that we were probably killing more than we thought.[14]

Another vital link in the control and surveillance of the battlefield was the artillery aerial observer. Supported by Marine and Army light observation helicopters (LOH-6A), UH-1E gunships, Cessna O1-G "Bird Dog" and OV-10A aircraft, aerial observers attached to the 11th and 12th Marines flew numerous low-level

Department of Defense Photo (USMC) A372433
The Integrated Observation System was one of many new devices created during the war that enhanced Marine artillery's ability to control the battlefield.

reconnaissance and artillery registration missions in support of ground operations throughout the year. During Operation Dewey Canyon, for example, it was an airborne artillery observer attached to the 12th Marines who spotted the enemy's long-range 122mm field guns and directed their destruction. Similarly, aerial observers of the 11th Marines, supported by light observation helicopters from the Americal Division's Company A, 123d Aviation Battalion and gunships from the 282d Aviation Battalion, made three daily flights over the Da Nang rocket belt, searching for potential launch sites. On numerous occasions sites were located and destroyed before rockets could be launched at Da Nang or surrounding military installations. "The deterrent effect of aerial observers," noted Colonel Mulroney, "has been apparent in all types of counterfire. The enemy does not fire when a AO is in the vicinity. Enemy artillery, rocket, and mortar attacks have all been obviously timed during gaps in AO coverage. Continued thorough coverage by aerial observers is an important part of the defensive program against enemy fire of all types."[15]

No less important was illumination provided Marines of the 1st Division by Battery G, 29th Artillery and to the 3d Marine Division by the 1st Searchlight Battery. Often transported to the remotest fire support bases, battery searchlights were used to illuminate suspected enemy infiltration routes and rocket sites, as well as camp and fire support base perimeters and bridges, to place small arms and artillery fire on enemy positions.[16]

For each of the varied tasks assigned Marine artillerymen, target clearance, both air and ground, continued to be a complicated and often frustrating process. Except for specified or "free" fire zones, where artillery and other supporting arms could be used without restriction, a call for artillery fire had to be cleared at the province and district levels and through the division, regiment, and appropriate South Korean commands before the mission could be executed. Using well-established procedures, division fire support coordination centers (FSCCs) synchronized all artillery, air, and naval gunfire support within the division TAOR, as did each regiment and infantry battalion. The regiments and battalions were primarily responsible for maintaining contact with allied military and civil headquarters within their respective areas of operation and for obtaining the proper fire clearances from each. The division fire support coordination centers, in close coordination with the 1st Wing DASC, operated the Sav-a-plane system to prevent aircraft from flying into the artillery's line of fire. The safety system, however, became a point of contention between air and artillery as the commanding officer of the 12th Marines, Colonel Peter J. Mulroney, pointed out:

> There is too much of a tendency to go to automatic check firing. The decision for check firing must be made by the regimental commander concerned, it can't be made by an AO, . . . it can't be made by the DASC, it can't be made by some pilot. We can have artillery and air at the same time . . . . The pilot must have, which they don't have now, faith in the artillery. The principle that XXIV Corps works on is that with troops in contact and taking casualties, artillery fire should not be held up while they take more casualties on the slim chance that an aircraft will be hit. None were hit in the 13 months that I served in the 3d Marine Division.[17]

A number of changes instituted during 1969 further simplified the clearance procedures and reduced delays in initiating fire missions. Among them were preclearing of areas void of allied patrol activities, instituting a permanent restrictive fire plan during daylight hours, codenamed "California," across division TAORs while still permitting fire support to be employed, and demanding careful fire planning and preclearance of likely target areas for planned reconnaissance team operations. These changes reduced clearance delays to a minimum, while maintaining appropriate safety requirements.

Throughout most of 1969, the volume of Marine artillery rose steadily. In January, the 11th and 12th Marines fired 329,500 rounds during 35,916 missions. By June, the amount of fire had risen to 358,816 rounds for 34,860 missions. The volume of fire remained about that level throughout August, but fell precipitously in September with the redeployment of the 12th Marines. By December, the 11th Marines, in an expanded TAOR, fired 163,574 rounds during 14,421 missions.

Augmenting the fires of the artillery regiments were tanks of the 1st and 3d Tank Battalions, and the long-range guns of ships of the Seventh Fleet. The primary mission of the Marine tank battalion was combat support during amphibious assault and subsequent operations ashore. In Vietnam, Marine tanks were employed in direct support of the infantry. The usual assignment was one tank company per regiment, with further assignment of tank platoons to battalions as required. The Marine command, however, often assigned tank companies to the direct or general support of separate task forces.

The M48A3 tanks of the 1st Battalion, under Lieutenant Colonel Maurice C. Ashley, Jr., and 3d Battalion, commanded by Lieutenant Colonel Joseph Sleger, Jr., attached to the 1st and 3d Division respectively, performed a variety of missions, the most important being direct support of infantry in the assault, perimeter defense, road, bridge, and strongpoint security, and convoy escort. They also supplemented artillery fires, providing unobserved missions when needed. In addition, when in support of infantry operations, they undertook the destruction of enemy fortifications by direct fire. As an added task, the 1st Tank Battalion coordinated and controlled all activities within the Southern Sector Defense Command, aimed at delaying or denying enemy penetration of the Da Nang Vital Area.

As elsewhere in Vietnam, the greatest concern of Marine tankers were mines or RPG ambushes. In addition to box mines, which were difficult to detect and thus detonated by the vehicle, the enemy employed command-detonated artillery rounds and aircraft ordnance. All were successful according to Lieutenant Colonel Sleger, who reported that between January and May 1969, the "3d Tank Battalion incurred a total of 38 mining incidents to organic tracked vehicles. Of the 50 M48A3 tanks on hand, 30 had been mined one time, 9 had been mined twice, and one had been mined three times."[18]

Reinforcing the two tank battalions were elements of the deactivated 1st and 3d Anti-Tank Battalions. Equipped with the Ontos, a lightly armored tracked vehicle mounting six 106mm recoilless rifles, four .50-caliber and one .30-caliber machine guns, the primary mission of the battalions was the destruction of enemy armor. But in Vietnam, as a result of the

Marine ground commanders, in addition to artillery and air support, relied on naval gunfire provided by ships of the Seventh Fleet, such as the battleship New Jersey (BB 62).

lack of such a threat, the vehicle initially was employed in support of infantry operations and convoy escort, and then only in perimeter defense due to the vehicles' vulnerability to mines.

Led by the battleship *New Jersey* (BB 62), until recalled in March, and then individual cruisers and destroyers, ships of the Seventh Fleet continued to provide accurate and timely fires in support of ground operations. Whether firing in support of engaged units, softening targets for advancing infantry, suppressing active enemy firing positions, or interdicting enemy lines of communication, the combat record of the ships was impressive. Hundreds of enemy fortifications, storage facilities, and firing batteries were destroyed, roads cut, and numerous previously occupied positions seized without opposition and friendly casualties. In addition, the availability of naval gunfire support allowed III MAF on several occasions to redistribute artillery assets in order to support mobile operations in the western reaches of the I Corps Tactical Zone.

The *New Jersey*'s contribution was noteworthy. Firing in support of III MAF Marines, her battery of nine 16-inch guns enabled her to attack targets at a range of 24 miles with a shell weighing 2,750 pounds. The weight of metal, range, and penetration of the 16-inch round far exceeded that of the heaviest Marine artillery weapon—the 175mm gun. In addition, the battleship's secondary battery of 20 5-inch guns provided a fire support capability roughly equal to that of four destroyers. During her six month tour in Vietnam, the *New Jersey* fired over 3,000 16-inch rounds and nearly 11,000 5-inch rounds, the bulk in support of the 3d Marine Division.

Surveillance and Reconnaissance Activities

The key to all successful military operations lay in timely, accurate information about the enemy. In Vietnam, the guerrilla nature of the struggle made timely intelligence even more essential, and at the same time more difficult to collect and evaluate. By 1969, the Marines' intelligence effort had evolved from an initial reliance on conventional techniques into a multifaceted, highly sophisticated intelligence gathering system that combined traditional air and ground reconnaissance methods with a number of new technological advances.

The majority of intelligence obtained by III MAF and its subordinate units was derived from air and ground reconnaissance. Marine Observation Squadrons 2 and 6 served as the airborne eyes of the 1st and 3d Marine Divisions. Each month the squadrons' UH-1E helicopters, OV-10As, and Cessna O-1 and O-1G light aircraft flew hundreds of observation missions. In addition, wing helicopters provided a platform for the Airborne Personnel Detector, Detector Concealed Personnel, and the Side Looking Airborne Radar. The mixed complement of RF-4Bs, Phantom IIs, EA-6A Prowlers, and F-3D Skyknights attached to Marine Composite Reconnaissance Squadron 1 also flew numerous conventional and infrared photographic survey missions. When the 1st MAW was unable to fulfill requests for photographic missions, the Seventh Air Force and Army aviation companies provided support. Rapid, expert interpretation and dissemination of aerial photographs was accomplished by III MAF's G-2 Photo Imagery Interpretation Center (PIIC), which included an automatic data processing system and a direct teletype link between III MAF and XXIV Corps. In addition, photo interpretation teams were assigned to tactical units to assist in the planning and execution of combat operations.[19]

Although small-unit infantry patrols continually provided information, the division's organic reconnaissance battalions generated the bulk of ground intelligence. III MAF reconnaissance forces consisted of two reconnaissance battalions and two force reconnaissance companies in January 1969. The 1st Reconnaissance Battalion supported 1st Marine Division operations, while the 3d Reconnaisance Battalion supported the 3d Marine Division. Attached to each battalion was a force reconnaissance company. The original doctrinal purpose of force reconnaissance companies was to operate in an amphibious operation under the landing force commander (III MAF), providing preassault reconnaissance and long-range reconnaissance after landing. In Vietnam, the force reconnaissance companies were originally used for deep reconnaissance under III MAF control. But by 1969, the 3d Force Reconnaissance Company had become totally absorbed by the 3d Reconnaissance Battalion during its support of operations undertaken by Task Force Hotel. Although attached to the 1st Reconnaissance Battalion, the 1st Force Reconnaissance Company remained a separate entity.

Realizing the need for reconnaissance information beyond that provided division commanders by their respective reconnaissance battalions, Lieutenant General Herman Nickerson, Jr., shortly after assuming command of III MAF in March, directed that the force reconnaissance companies be returned to the control of III MAF. 1st Force Reconnaissance Company became the first, beginning deep patrol operations for the MAF in June, followed by the reconstituted 3d Force Reconnaissance Company in October.

Although deep reconnaissance missions were conducted by units of the Army's Special Operations Group within I Corps, the information provided did not meet the specific tactical needs of III MAF. As a result of III MAF's desire for more coordination as well as coverage of areas not targeted by other operations, III MAF reassumed control of the 1st and 3d Force Reconnaissance Companies, which then were placed under the direction of the newly created Surveillance and Reconnaissance Center (SRC), established in October. Under the SRC, the following missions were assigned to the force reconnaissance companies: perform deep reconnaissance to determine location and current usage of enemy base camps, storage sites, and lines of communication; fix and identify enemy units tentatively located by sensor devices and agent reports; provide specific targeting and bomb damage assessment for B-52 Arc Light strikes; execute POW recovery missions and wiretap operations; and emplace sensors across enemy trails and in other critical areas.[20]

Based at An Hoa Combat Base initially and then at Da Nang, Major Roger E. Simmons' 1st Force Reconnaissance Company concentrated its efforts during the first half of the year in support of Task Force Yankee and 1st Marine Division operations. Conducting missions in areas surrounding Charlie Ridge and enemy Base Area 112 to the west, patrols, usually inserted and extracted by helicopter, attempted to locate enemy troops, base camps, and storage areas. In addition they spotted targets for artillery fire, assessed bomb damage, and occasionally engaged enemy forces. During January, for example, the company ran 116 patrols, sighting 1,339 enemy troops and killing 88, while sustaining 7 killed and 37 wounded. The company also directed 88 artillery fire missions and 25 air strikes. Following its transfer to III MAF, the company shifted operations to the far reaches of Quang Nam and Quang Tin Provinces, and as a result the number of patrols gradually declined, totaling only five during December.

The 3d Force Reconnaissance Company, based with and essentially absorbed by the 3d Reconnaissance Battalion at Quang Tri, supported 3d Marine Division operations, conducting 20 patrols and observing or engaging 62 enemy troops while suffering one Marine wounded during January. With the redeployment of the battalion and the division in October, the company was brought up to authorized strength, control passed to III MAF, and the company relocated to Phu Bai Combat Base. During the remaining two months of the year, 3d Force Reconnaissance Marines concentrated on patrolling the Demilitarized Zone and the newly created western reconnaissance zones of Quang Tri and Thua Thien Provinces, focusing on the A Shau Valley and surrounding terrain.

At the beginning of 1969, Lieutenant Colonel Larry P. Charon's 1st Reconnaissance Battalion was overstrength, possessing five lettered companies, and the 1st Force Reconnaissance Company, instead of the normal four.* In support of Task Force Yankee and the 1st Marine Division, the battalion performed a variety of missions: furnishing teams to support regimental search operations; securing fire support bases and artillery observation posts; and training scuba divers to check bridges within the division TAOR for demolitions and searching waterways for obstructions and weapons caches. However, the principal function of the reconnaissance battalion was to patrol the western fringes of the TAOR. Operating in six-man teams, each composed of an officer or NCO patrol leader, a radioman, three riflemen, and a Navy corpsman, battalion Marines normally spent half their time in the field and the remainder preparing for the next operation or participating in refresher training.

Reconnaissance patrolling, by 1969, had become somewhat standardized. Each team member packed food, water, ammunition, and equipment to sustain him for up to six days in the field. The radioman carried the AN/PRC-25 and extra batteries, while the corpsman took charge of the medical supplies. After several hours of rehearsals and briefings, helicopters lifted the team to its assigned operating area. Upon insertion, a radio check was made with the aircraft, radio relay, and company command post, and then the team departed the landing zone, following a prearranged route. Carefully noting and then reporting details of terrain and enemy activity, or calling in artillery and air strikes, the patrol attempted in most cases to avoid contact. At the end of its assigned mission, or when discovered or attacked, helicopters extracted the team. On return, each member of the team was debriefed and all reports of the patrol were reviewed and then distributed to the appropriate regiment or battalion.

Patrolling during the year by 1st Reconnaissance Battalion Marines resulted in a steady stream of sightings and engagements. During April, for example, the battalion conducted 177 patrols, sighting 2,746 enemy troops, and directing 88 artillery fire missions and 31 air strikes. During the month, battalion Marines killed 177 at a cost of 7 dead and 39 wounded.

Like the 1st Reconnaissance Battalion, the 3d Reconnaissance Battalion, under the command of Lieutenant Colonel Aydlette H. Perry, Jr., was also overstrength as 1969 began.** Instead of the usual four lettered

---
*Lieutenant Colonel Charon was succeeded in February by Lieutenant Colonel Richard D. Mickelson, who was in turn replaced in October by Lieutenant Colonel John J. Grace.

**Lieutenant Colonel Perry was replaced in May by Lieutenant Colonel Richard R. Burritt.

companies, five were present plus the attached 3d Force Reconnaissance Company under Major Robert W. Holm. Supporting Task Force Hotel and the 3d Marine Division, battalion Marines performed the same missions as those assigned to the 1st Battalion. Concentrating their efforts in the DMZ, in western Quang Tri, and in the piedmont west of Quang Tri City and Dong Ha, meant that "every indication of enemy activity," General Davis recalled, was "explored by the insertion of reconnaissance teams."[21]

Generally, two types of patrol missions were conducted by reconnaissance Marines within the 3d Marine Division TAOR. As General Davis explained:

> Under the artillery fan as established at the time, we would use Sting Ray techniques with 8 to 10 men in a team, seeking the enemy, seeking opportunities to deliver fire upon

A patrol from Company B, 3d Reconnaissance Battalion moves along a trail south of the Demilitarized Zone in the continuing search for evidence of North Vietnamese infiltration into Quang Tri Province.
Department of Defense Photo (USMC) A192449

Although the primary purpose of reconnaissance patrols was to gather information, direct artillery and air strikes, and not to fight, teams often found themselves involved in intense combat. Firefights erupted from ambushes, chance meetings with small enemy units, or from efforts to take prisoners. One such encounter took place in March in the southwestern corner of Quang Nam Province.

On the 23d, a team from 1st Force Reconnaissance Company, identified by its radio call sign "Report Card," consisting of two officers, seven enlisted Marines, and a corpsman, was inserted by helicopter, shortly after noon, near the Song Thu Bon, southwest of Antenna Valley. The following morning, the team moved up to a trail where they were to set an ambush in an effort to snatch a prisoner. Once in position it became apparent that the trail was one of the enemy's main routes for moving supplies from western base camps, through Antenna Valley, into the An Hoa basin. During the first half hour in position, a group of approximately 32 enemy troops passed two to three meters in front of the team's ambush. Waiting for an enemy officer or NCO, the team let most pass. The last, dressed in full utilities, a pith helmet, boots, and "strutting along holding his rifle at port arms," appeared to be a good target and was ambushed. As the Marines dragged the enemy soldier into their ambush, they heard movement down the trail, both north and south of their position. Pulling back five meters into deep elephant grass, the team engaged two enemy soldiers, killing both. Then six more appeared to the front. While taking these under fire, and endeavoring to move down to a streambed, the patrol was hit from all sides by approximately 80 to 100 troops.

For 30 minutes, the team fended off probes by the large enemy force until two Huey gunships arrived; the only time the Marines used small arms was when an enemy soldier was actually sighted, otherwise they employed their grenades and the M79 launcher. The fighting continued for another two-and-one-half hours while the gunships were on station and then suddenly stopped. Searching the area around their position before being extracted, the patrol counted 10 enemy killed by Huey machine gun fire. "I learned," the team leader, First Lieutenant Wayne E. Rollings, later reported, "that with a small unit, if you keep good security, 360, that you can hold off a very large force that outnumbers you considerably, and suffer very few casualties. We had no casualties."[23] Although the patrol did not get its prisoner, who had been killed

Department of Defense Photo (USMC) A192444
Concealing himself in a grove of bamboo, a reconnaissance Marine surveys the terrain and then directs artillery and air strikes on enemy troops and base camps.

them. Well-out, smaller teams—four or five men—going on the basis of secrecy: only to observe, stay out of sight. If the enemy is encountered, they attempt to escape. These are not normally reinforced unless we are able to insert artillery at the time. Under the artillery fan, normally they would be reinforced if the enemy presented an adequate target. On contact the team hangs in and fights it out or if it's a small contact and they start to take casualties, we might extract them. However, if it's a large contact and under the artillery fan and the opportunity presents itself, they are reinforced in order to attempt to destroy the enemy force in its entirety.[22]

Using Stingray and deep reconnaissance techniques, 3d Reconnaissance Battalion in May, for example, conducted 194 patrols during which 68 contacts with enemy troops were made, resulting in 80 enemy killed and the loss of 4 Marines killed and 31 wounded.* During this same period, battalion Marines directed 60 artillery missions, 35 air strikes, and conducted 14 scuba missions.

---

*For details of the Stingray concept of operations, see MajGen Raymond G. Davis and 1stLt J. L. Jones, Jr., "Employing the Recon Patrol," *Marine Corps Gazette*, May69, pp. 41-45.

by an enemy grenade during the fight, they did leave behind 22 NVA dead.

Two-and-one-half weeks later, Lieutenant Rollings and seven men were again on patrol. "The name of our reconnaissance patrol was 'Lunchmeat,' and with 150 North Vietnamese soldiers surrounding us, that's just how I felt, like a piece of lunchmeat in a sandwich." The mission assigned Rollings' patrol was to reconnoiter a trail and ridgeline, four kilometers southwest of An Hoa.

Near noon on 10 April, Rollings and his team were inserted into the area and began checking the ridgelines for enemy activity. Shortly after dusk the following day, they spotted 35 to 40 lights moving in a northeasterly direction, approximately 800 meters from their position. Before the team could move, they heard movement to their front and rear. "We hurriedly set up a defensive perimeter in some dense undergrowth on the side of the trail," noted Rollings, "and called in Spooky [Air Force C-47 aircraft equipped with mini-guns]."

With the enemy moving ever closer, Rollings called an artillery mission on a base camp spotted earlier in the day with the hope of forcing the NVA to call off the search and then radioed for Spooky to make a pass. As Lieutenant Rollings continued:

> His first burst landed about 400 yards from us and I began to direct him in. He warned me to tell him when he was hitting within 50 to 75 yards of our position and that he would then start working out toward the enemy from there. But the enemy would still be between us and his fire so I waited until the outer fringe of his fire, which had a 25 yard radius, was within five yards and then told him to start working away from us. I didn't tell him how close his fire was to us, because I knew he wouldn't have gotten that close if he couldn't mark our position.[24]

Patrol members counted more than 30 instances where they heard screams and groans as artillery and mini-guns scored hits. In one instance, related Rollings, "we saw 10 NVA get within 40 yards of our position before 'arty' caught them with a barrage that finished them all off."

At first light the patrol got word to move out, but within 100 meters of its position, it encountered 20 NVA troops. Spooky again called for, the Air Force's C-47 began working in from the rear while the team hit the enemy from the front. "We had them sandwiched between us, but after about a half-hour, the NVA . . . took off." The patrol continued to search the area, but without success, and was extracted on the 13th with one minor casualty.[25]

Other teams were not so lucky. On 4 June, a patrol from Company D, 3d Reconnaissance Battalion, fought the battalion's most severe action of the year and lost. The team, identified as "Flight Time," consisted of six Marines. Helicopters inserted the patrol, which carried two strobe lights for illumination, at 0930 on the 2d near Hill 471, overlooking Khe Sanh and Lang Vei, in western Quang Tri Province. The team's arrival went unopposed and the Marines moved northward from the landing zone toward the high ground, finding evidence of recent enemy occupation in the area. The following day, after setting up its harbor site for the evening, the team observed five enemy troops in brown utilities and helmets, but did not take the troops under fire.

At 0250 the next morning, the team began receiving small arms fire and grenades from an unknown size enemy force. Reporting one killed and five wounded, the team leader requested an emergency extraction and all available "on call" air. When the aerial observer arrived on station 10 minutes later, he saw that the enemy was within 10 meters of, and surrounding, the team's position. He immediately requested that a reaction force be inserted to assist the team. At 0315, the observer expended his ordnance, heard a secondary explosion, and then lost all communications with the team.

The 12-man reaction force arrived in the area at 0620 and reported sighting three, and possibly five, members of the team in terrain which looked as though it had been "hit by a flame thrower." On the ground, the force found the bodies of five members of the team in an enemy trench and the sixth approximately 10 meters down the hill. An on-sight investigation indicated that the enemy had come up the northeast side of the hill, firing grenades, small arms, and throwing satchel charges and bangalore torpedoes. The reaction force leader surmised that the burn marks on the ground and bodies, and the way in which the equipment was scattered, indicated that the team must have been involved in hand-to-hand fighting before being overrun.[26]

Enemy troops were not the only hazard faced by reconnaissance Marines when patrolling deep in mountainous terrain. In May, a seven-man team, again from the 3d Reconnaissance Battalion, codenamed "Centipede," while patrolling the steep, triple-canopied hills surrounding the Ba Long Valley, observed numerous tiger tracks. On two occasions during the four-day patrol, a tiger came within 10 meters of

Marine Corps Historical Collection
Cpl Sandy R. Reid of the 3d Reconnaissance Battalion applies additional camouflage paint to his face and neck in order to blend in with the jungle and thereby avoid detection.

the team's position and had to be driven off with CS grenades.[27] Among other nonhostile hazards were lightning, friendly fire, the rugged terrain itself, and equipment failure. Although reconnaissance Marines did suffer a number of noncombat casualties, losses in most cases were a direct result of clashes with enemy troops.

With four years of experience behind them, reconnaissance Marines had, by 1969, developed tested techniques and equipment in order to supply the division they supported with accurate and timely intelligence. To assure prompt artillery support when needed and at the same time prevent accidental shelling, special reconnaissance zones were established for each deployed team in which only the patrol could call fire missions. The 11th and 12th Marines designated a battery or platoon of howitzers to support each team and assigned a liaison officer at the reconnaissance battalion's command post to assist in fire planning and coordination. To ensure the rapid extraction of a team under fire or in a tenuous situation, the 1st Marine Aircraft Wing designated helicopters as part of a quick-reaction package, that at times included division infantry forces to assist.

When not on patrol, reconnaissance Marines continually trained for their exacting task. In addition to the initial indoctrination program for newly arrived personnel, which included instruction in the use of the AN/PRC-25 radio, map reading, first aid, rappelling from helicopters, observer procedures, and intelligence reporting techniques, the battalions conducted periodic refresher courses with special emphasis on weapons training, scuba diving, physical conditioning, and the use of new equipment such as extraction ladders. Selected personnel also were sent to the Army's Recondo School at Nha Trang for more specialized training.

With the redeployment of the 3d Marine Division, Marine reconnaissance strength was halved. What had been the reconnaissance zone of the 3d Battalion was passed to reconnaissance elements of the 101st Airborne and 1st ARVN Divisions. The 3d Force Reconnaissance Company, now a separate entity under III MAF, moved to Phu Bai and was given the task of patrolling the A Shau Valley. The 1st Force Reconnaissance Company and 1st Reconnaissance Battalion continued to concentrate on Quang Nam Province, although by December, fewer patrols were assigned to deep missions in the western reaches of the province.

While direct air observation and ground reconnaissance provided the bulk of intelligence, the artillery's system of observation and target acquisition also produced information. Scattered throughout the divisions' areas of responsibility were numerous observation towers which not only directed artillery fire, but permitted general surveillance of enemy movement. Supplementing the artillery's intelligence gathering capability were Integrated Observation Devices and the computerized Fire Support Information System.*

Captured enemy documents and prisoners yielded additional information. To extract the intelligence, the divisions relied heavily upon specially trained Marines attached to interrogation-translation teams, interpreter teams, and counterintelligence teams. Working within the division G-2 sections, the interrogation and interpreter teams, as their names implied, interviewed NVA and VC prisoners and suspected civilian detainees, and reviewed all captured documents for information on enemy unit strength; designations; attack and withdrawal routes; staging, rally, and base areas; mines and surprise firing devices locations; and enemy combat effectivenss and morale. In September 1969, a typical month, teams attached to the 1st Marine Division interrogated 1,397 detainees, 18 of whom were classified prisoners of war, 45 as civilian defendants, 13 as returnees, and 1,321 as innocent civilians. During the same month, the teams screened 3,107 documents for translation.[28]

Counterintelligence teams, in addition to performing normal security and counter-espionage tasks at every Marine cantonment where South Vietnamese civilians were employed, accompanied Marine units to the field in search of their primary target, the Viet Cong Infrastructure. Working closely with ARVN intelligence agencies, National Police, National Police Field Forces, Provisional Reconnaissance Units, and Revolutionary Development Cadre in numerous cordon operations, they checked the identities of civilian detainees against lists of known infrastructure members and carried out immediate exploitative operations.[29]

The Marines also employed numerous South Vietnamese interpreters and informants, tasked with ferreting out the local infrastructure. Many in the intelligence community, however, thought Marines should not be involved in such activity because, as the 1st Division's G-2, Colonel Anthony J. Skotnicki, pointed out, "we didn't have the skill or language ability," and that others among the near dozen agencies involved in such activity were better qualified.[30]

Marines in the field also relied heavily on Kit Carson Scouts, due to their proven loyalty and knowledge of the people and terrain. In addition, some Marine units, especially those operating in the heavily populated lowlands, worked closely with South Vietnamese Armed Propaganda Teams. Although primarily involved in psychological warfare, the teams, through informal contacts with villagers, did collect information concerning local guerrilla and infrastructure activity, which was passed on to the appropriate Marine unit.

Under the Voluntary Informant Program (VIP), Marines enlisted the assistance of South Vietnamese civilians in the intelligence gathering effort. Administered by the division's G-2 staff, battalions were provided funds with which information could be purchased. A majority of the funds, however, went to rewarding Vietnamese who brought in or pointed out munitions, such as grenades, dud artillery rounds, and aircraft ordnance, which could be used by the enemy

---

*For additional detail on artillery targeting and operations, see pp. 245-249.

Marine Corps Historical Collection

Under the Voluntary Informant Program, South Vietnamese civilians turned in dud ammunition, mortar rounds in this instance, that might otherwise be used to make boobytraps.

in constructing surprise firing devices. During May 1969, for example, 1st Marine Division units spent a total of 1,502,454 piasters (approximately 1,200 dollars) in 764 separate payments for the return of ordnance, while making two payments for "casual information."[31]

As an adjunct to the VIP program, the 3d Marine Division Psychological Operations Office established its own program, dubbed "Circuit Rider." Composed of a psyops officer and an explosive ordnance disposal team, Circuit Rider traveled Route 1 weekly purchasing ordnance local children had found. The program, continually advertised by audio-visual trucks, leaflet drops, and aerial broadcasts, was considered highly successful. The area of greatest activity during the year, proved to be along Route 1, between Dong Ha and Gio Linh, where it was thought children had found and ransacked a number of enemy caches.

Marines also relied on information generated by signal intercepts. During the year, Lieutenant Colonel Patrick J. Fennell, Jr.'s 1st Radio Battalion provided III MAF with this capability. Headquartered at Camp Horn, with its Headquarters and Service Company at nearby Camp Hoa Long and Operations Company at Dong Ha, the battalion's six task-organized platoons, deployed at fire support bases and observation posts throughout Quang Tri and Quang Nam Provinces, provided immediate tactical support for both regimental and division operations. Using both ground installations and airborne platforms supplied by the Army and Air Force, Marine radiomen listened to enemy verbal and message communications in an effort to determine the location of transmitter sites. As a result of these efforts, the battalion passed on an average of 4,000 fixes each month to tactical commanders who in turn used artillery, air, or ground operations to destroy them. In addition to monitoring enemy communications, the battalion also monitored friendly transmissions to ensure against security violations or compromises. During March, for example, the battalion reported 194 violations in 118,920 messages monitored.[32]

Electronic sensors provided yet another source of intelligence information. Products of the aborted Demilitarized Zone barrier project initiated by Secretary of Defense Robert S. McNamara and abandoned in October 1968, sensors, by 1969, were being employed tactically throughout South Vietnam under a new program, Duffle Bag.* These "24-hour silent sentinels" not only contributed to economies in force, but provided early warning of attacks on base camps and cities, and contributed to the reduction of rocket attacks. "It appears," noted a MACV message, "that . . . sensor technology may be one of the more important developments to come out of the Vietnam war. At the present time, the only limitations on successful sensor-supported operations are the availability of sensors, and the degree of imagination, initiative, ingenuity, and resourcefulness of tactical commanders."[33]

The Marines first used sensors during the siege of Khe Sanh in early 1968. At that time, Air Force Igloo White aircraft—dedicated EC-121s in orbit over Laos—provided readouts from out-of-country sensors. The sensor information was relayed to Nakhon Phanom where it was assessed and targets passed to Khe Sanh and Dong Ha. Towards the end of the siege, some local readout and assessment capability was given the Khe Sanh Marines. As a result of the experience at Khe Sanh, coupled with the onset of the rainy season in the Laotian Panhandle, sensors became available for limited test and evaluation in support of ground combat operations. Upon completion of the evaluations, codenamed Duck Blind, in August 1968, it became apparent that sensors, originally designed to impede or substantially reduce infiltration from North to South Vietnam, could make significant contributions in surveillance and target acquisition operations in South Vietnam.

A majority of the sensors employed by III MAF were of the radio-type, which transmitted information electronically directly to monitoring stations. These small, camouflaged, battery-powered devices could be dropped from aircraft or implanted by hand. Once in position, the sensors reacted to minute physical changes in the surrounding environment. Seismic sensors, known as Seismic Intrusion Devices (SIDs), responded to ground vibrations, such as human footsteps. Magnetic sensors, or Magnetic Intrusion Devices (MAGIDs), detected moving metallic objects, and infrared sensors (PIRIDs) reacted to heat emanating from bodies, vehicle engines, and campfires. Accoustic sensors picked up audible sounds. Once activated, the sensors sent a signal to a receiver from which the operator could determine the location and probable nature of the object. Accoustic sensors transmitted the sounds they detected directly to the monitoring stations.

Sensors were generally planted in groups, or "strings" as they were more commonly termed, along enemy infiltration routes from the mountains into the lowlands. A typical string, designed to detect movement, consisted of several seismic and a few magnetic and accoustical sensors. Once activated, the monitoring station operator could request an artillery fire mission, alert a nearby ground unit, or simply record the time and direction of movement for later analysis. Seismic, magnetic, and infrared line sensors also were employed around fixed installations such as fire support or combat bases. The Da Nang Barrier contained 106 such sensors and plans called for the future implantation of an additional 775. By mid-1969, each division had over 100 sensors, maintained and monitored by the divisions' G-2 staffs.

Whether obtained by sensors, air and ground reconnaissance, or from a paid agent, intelligence information had to be quickly evaluated, correlated, and transmitted to units in the field to be of any value. In order to facilitate this process, III MAF established the Surveillance and Reconnaissance Center at Da Nang in late 1969, under Assistant Chief of Staff, G-2, Colonel John S. Canton. The center, according to Colonel Canton, was to "physically and functionally integrate and coordinate all intelligence collection means in ICTZ, thus reducing the time lapse between the initial collection of intelligence information and the dissemination of processed intelligence to tactical commanders." In addition to directing deep surveillance missions of the force reconnaissance companies, the SRC "monitored all intelligence collection in ICTZ. This ensured round-the-clock, timely and reliable communication of perishable intelligence data to using units, thus producing a quantum increase in the immediate utilization of intelligence assets."[34]

"In this war, like no other war in the past generation" noted Colonel Anthony J. Skotnicki, "we never worked under a lack of information. We actually acquired so much intelligence information we couldn't handle it." Despite advances in processing and organization, there remained "a considerable amount of difficulty in manually recording it and manually extracting it in order to put it together into useful intelligence."[35]

---

*The use of sensors within South Vietnam, nicknamed Duffle Bag, was one of four continuing sensor programs carried out by MACV in Southeast Asia. The remaining three were: Igloo White, which involved the out-of-country use of sensors; Duel Blade II, the sensor supported anti-infiltration system in and along the DMZ; and, Tight Jaw, the combined US/GVN border surveillance operation.

CHAPTER 15

Supplying III MAF

*Force Logistic Command—Naval Support Activity, Da Nang—Engineer Support
Motor Transport—Medical Support—Communications—Logistics of Keystone Eagle and Keystone Cardinal*

Force Logistic Command

For supply, maintenance, and service support, III MAF relied on Force Logistic Command (FLC). At the beginning of 1969, Brigadier General James A. Feeley, Jr. commanded the logistical arm supporting Marine operations in Vietnam. A Massachusetts native, combat veteran of World War II and Korea, and trained as an aviator, General Feeley assumed command of the FLC in October 1968.*

Composed of 430 Marine and 22 Navy officers and 9,164 Marine and 150 Navy enlisted men, Force Logistic Command was headquartered at Camp Jay A. Books, part of the expansive Red Beach support complex, northwest of Da Nang. Under the operational control of III MAF and command and administrative control of FMFPac, FLC was organized around the Headquarters and Service, Supply, and Maintenance Battalions of the 1st Force Service Regiment and included 1st Service Battalion/Force Logistic Support Group Bravo (FLSG-Bravo), 3d Service Battalion/Force Logistic Support Group Alpha (FLSG-Alpha), 1st and 3d Military Police Battalions, 5th Communication Battalion, and 7th Motor Transport Battalion.

The three battalions of the Force Service Regiment performed a majority of the logistical functions of Force Logistic Command. Headquarters and Service Battalion provided administrative, communication, and motor transport assistance for elements of the FLC and units of III MAF. In addition to operating graves registration and maintaining internal and perimeter security for Camp Books, it also managed the III MAF Transient Facility, through which passed all incoming and outgoing personnel, and the R&R Processing Center. The Supply Battalion received, stored, distributed, and accounted for all supplies, while operating ammunition supply points (ASPs), baking most of III MAF's breadstuffs, and providing personnel for the logistical support subunit at Chu Lai. Maintenance Battalion repaired all types of Marine ordnance and equipment, with the exception of aviation items or equipment requiring extensive overhaul. The battalion transferred these items either to 3d Force Service Regiment facilities on Okinawa or Japan, or to maintenance depots in the United States.

Force Logistic Support Group Alpha, initially headquartered at Phu Bai but moved to Camp Books on 5 January, directly supported the 1st Marine Division. Composed of the Headquarters and Service, Maintenance, Supply, and Truck Companies of the 3d Service Battalion, the FSLG maintained logistic support units (LSUs) at Hill 55, An Hoa, and Phu Bai, which served the 1st, 5th, and 7th Marines. Each LSU drew rations, fuel, and ammunition from the FLC for issue to its supported regiment, repaired equipment and ordnance, and operated a laundry. On 15 July, FLSG-Alpha assumed control over the logistic support subunit at Chu Lai, which provided rations, ammunition, and maintenance support for Marine Aircraft Groups 12 and 13, 9th Engineer Battalion, and the 1st Combined Action Group.

During November 1969, Force Logistic Support Group Bravo, which in like manner had supported the 3d Marine Division, assumed the support of the 1st Marine Division and portions of the 1st Marine Aircraft Wing. On the 7th, FLSG-Bravo adopted FLSG-Alpha's mission and initiated standdown procedures at Quang Tri, Vandegrift, and Dong Ha Combat Bases prior to moving to Camp Books. At the same time, FLSG-Alpha's organizational colors moved to Okinawa with the remaining elements of the 3d Marine Division. FLSG-Bravo continued to provide support for the 1st Marine Division through the operation of three logistic support units located at Hill 55, An Hoa Combat Base, and LZ Baldy (established in August), and the subunit at Chu Lai (FLSG-Bravo Sub-Unit 1).[1]

Under the amphibious concept, each division and the wing possessed its own logistical support capability. But as the war intensified, the accretion of troops and equipment necessitated a change. A viable, semipermanent logistic support organization, Force Logistic

---

*Brigadier General Mauro J. Padalino replaced General Feeley in November 1969. As a colonel in 1965, he headed FLC's predecessor, the Force Logistic Support Group.

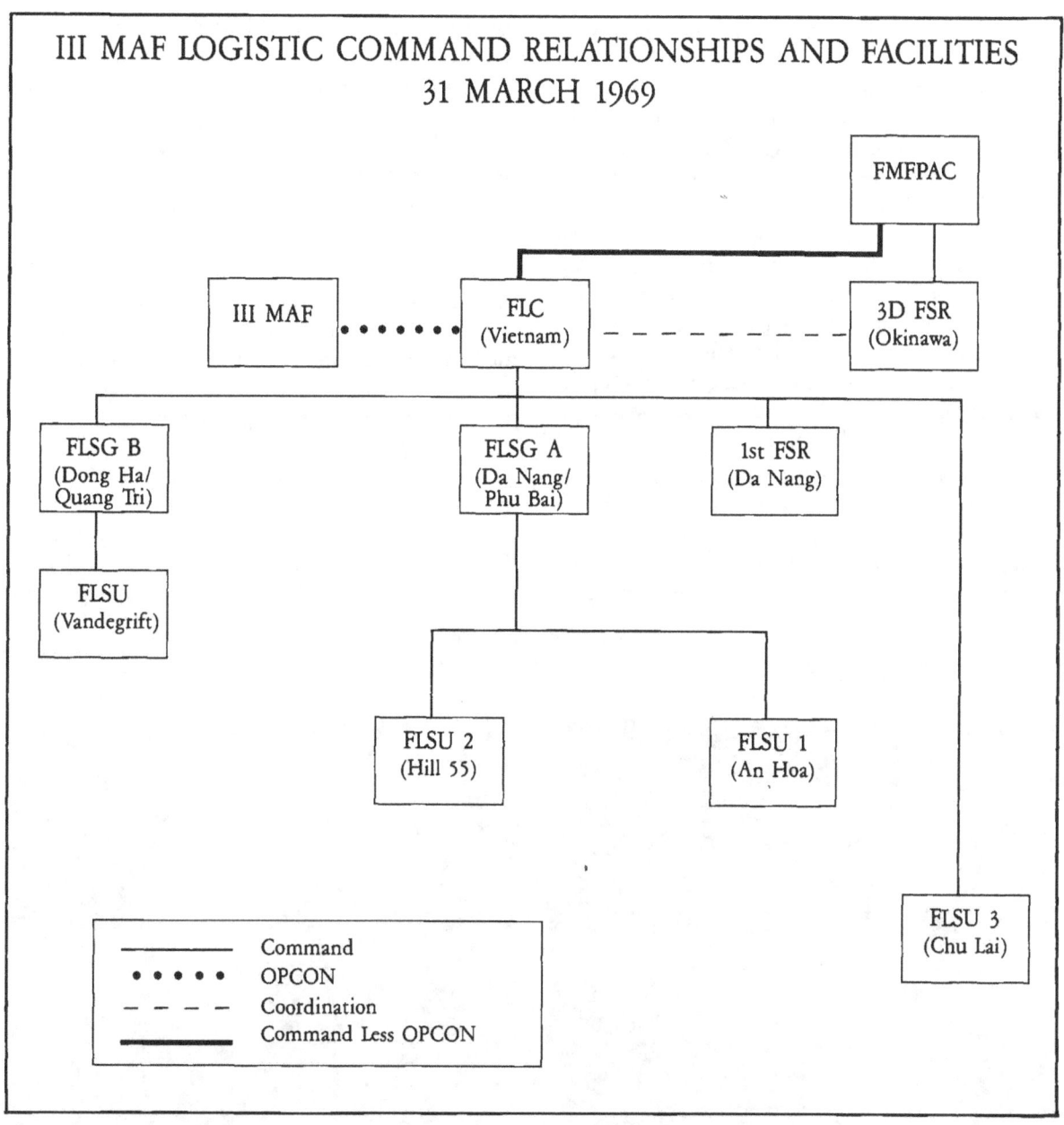

Command, was thus created from the previously fragmented logistic command and control structures. As a result, the divisions gave up their organic service battalions and thus maintained no separate supply or accounting facilities. Many Marines continued to view this loss as detrimental to the divisions' capabilities to perform their missions. Among them was Colonel Frank R. DeNormandie, G-4, 3d Marine Division, who noted that with the creation of FLC and subordinate groups, division control over logistical support moved from direct management to one of cooperation and coordination. "As a result, supply support rapidly changed from unit distribution to supply point distribution. In addition, changes in priority for either unit supply or equipment repair had to be effected at the highest level." The division commander now not only had no readily available source of supply, but no established third echelon maintenance and supply or materiel storage capability. "We make a division that is supposed to be self-sufficient," noted Colonel DeNormandie, "that is capable of taking care of itself, that is capable of supporting itself far removed from any other headquarters and yet we take away from that division commander the thing that makes him tick, and the thing that makes any military organization really tick and really able to fight is its logistics support capability."[2]

Despite the lack of direct division control and the imposition of additional management levels, the logistics of support, on the whole, remained rather simple. Individual battalions of the 1st Marines, for example, radioed their supply requests to their representatives on Hill 55 each day prior to 1500. Battalion support personnel then drew supplies from FLC, either directly or through a logistic support unit and staged the loads for next-day delivery. Trucks or helicopters then transported passengers and supplies to the battalion and on the return trip, removed retrograde equipment and troops.[3]

As helicopter resupply became more prominent, each division became more dependent upon the activities of its shore party battalions. Originally established to facilitate the movement of men and equipment across the beach, the battalions expanded their mission to include support of heliborne assaults. Organic to each division, these battalions deployed a company with each infantry regiment. Shore party support teams located with each LSU assembled and prepared supplies for helicopter pickup, while control teams with the rifle companies marked the landing zones, briefed the incoming helicopter crews, and supervised unloading.

Supply and maintenance support for the 1st Marine Aircraft Wing was more complex since the wing drew upon both Navy and Marine sources. Force Logistic Command provided non-aviation supplies and ammunition, while a variety of Navy agencies supplied replacement aircraft, spare parts, vehicles, and maintenance support. Commander, Naval Air Force, Pacific Fleet, a subordinate of CinCPacFlt, was responsible for aviation logistic support of the wing. As a result, the wing requisitioned its Navy material from the Naval Supply Depot at Yokosuka, Japan, which also contracted for and oversaw major repair and

BGen James A. Feeley, Jr., right, Commanding General, Force Logistic Command, guides LtGen Herman Nickerson through the command's data processing center at Camp Books.

Department of Defense Photo (USMC) A193236

rebuilding of Marine aircraft. Within the wing, each aircraft group stored and issued supplies and performed routine maintenance and limited repair of aircraft. Augmenting the groups' organic battle damage repair capabilities were civilian teams from naval aircraft repair facilities. Marine Wing Support Group 17 provided Marine Corps supply, postal, post exchange, and disbursing services for all wing elements, while maintaining group equipment, aircraft launch, and recovery systems, and overseeing the shipment of aircraft into and out of Vietnam.

The logistic supply and repair system supporting Marine units within I Corps ran smoothly during 1969. It responded quickly and effectively to III MAF's highly mobile, wide-ranging offensive maneuvers with the establishment of expedient positions in rugged, mountainous terrain in order to sustain extended combat operations. Temporary shortages of ordnance, spare parts, radio batteries, wet weather gear, and malaria and salt tablets did occur, but these shortages were quickly remedied by borrowing from the Army or by emergency shipments from Marine supply facilities on Okinawa or in the United States. Despite these occasional shortages, Marine units experienced few supply system problems. As Major General Wilbur F. Simlik, former commanding officer of the 3d Marines and later III MAF G-4, noted: "never have troops been supported in such abundance as in the Vietnamese war. The chow, the ammunition, the supplies, the transportation, were there when we needed it, in abundance; as a matter of fact, probably too much."[4]

As a direct result of abundance of support, the problem of supply discipline arose. It varied from the solitary Marine who abandoned his gas mask along a trail because it was too bulky or heavy to carry and was issued a replacement in preparation for an inspection, to the battalion commander who requested a dozen sets of utilities be issued per man when only three were authorized. "As a practical matter," noted 1st Marine Division Supply Officer and later division Assistant Chief of Staff, G-4, Colonel John L. Schwartz, supply discipline "is non-existent. It does not make any difference whether it is ammunition, fuel, chow, or what it is. There is gross extravagance . . . . There seems to be in the minds of many many commanders three questions: How much stuff have I got? How soon can I use it? and Where can I get some more?"[5] Although numerous attempts were made, the problem continued to defy solution.

On 27 April 1969, the III MAF logistic support system was tested severely when a grass fire brought about the destruction of Ammunition Supply Point (ASP)-1, three kilometers southwest of the Da Nang Airbase. The fire first ignited unserviceable ammunition slated for disposal, and the resultant explosions spread in chain reaction to the two main ground and air ammunition storage areas and a nearby fuel storage area. Colonel William D. Bassett, Jr., FLSG-Alpha's commanding officer, described the effects:

> On that Sunday afternoon, the Helicopter Utilization Review Board was in session at III MAF Headquarters. The smoke and fire could be seen across Da Nang at a distance that I would guess to be 10 to 12 kilometers. There were two significant explosions which were far greater than the rest. Both produced fire balls similar to small nuclear explosions, complete with shock waves which could be seen moving out in a circular pattern through the smoke and haze. The first of these two exceptional blasts hit III MAF Headquarters at approximately 1430. The meeting was in a converted single story warehouse with a solid wall toward ASP-1. The seaward side of the building had two large warehouse-type doors which closed together and had steel drop-bar closures into the concrete floor. The reverse, counter pressure actually pushed the doors in, breaking the concrete around the holes that the bars were in . . . . The second similar blast took place around 2200 and was not as strong as the first, but the shock wave did hit III MAF Headquarters.[6]

Major destruction occurred in the ammunition supply point, the fuel storage area, and a nearby Air Force bomb dump, while extensive damage caused by the blast and flying debris was done to FLC facilities between the ASP and the airfield. Continuous secondary explosions forced the temporary closing of the Da Nang Airbase to all but emergency traffic; normal airfield operations were resumed within 18 hours. Casualties were limited to one American and one Vietnamese killed and 65 wounded, while 1,500 Vietnamese were left homeless when the nearby village of Hoa Phat was destroyed by the fire and explosions.

Approximately 38,000 short tons of ground and air munitions, valued in excess of 75 million dollars, were destroyed; an amount equal to 40 percent of the total Marine munitions on hand at FLC facilities throughout I Corps.[7] Nevertheless, the destruction of the supply point caused no interruption in ordnance support for continuing combat operations. As the commanding officer of the 11th Marines, Colonel Samuel A. Hannah, noted:

> When the ammo dump started going, we put a little restriction on our shooting to slow it down a little bit and keep it down because we weren't sure exactly the extent of it. But within a day or so, this cleared up and we got a general feeling about what the ammo supply was and we were able to go

Department of Defense Photo (USMC) A422546

The large mushroom cloud produced by exploding ordnance stored at Force Logistic Command Ammunition Supply Point 1 was visible for several miles. While close to half of III MAF's ammunition was destroyed, Marines experienced no interruption in support.

back to what might be called a normal rate of fire . . . . From a shooting standpoint, no great problems with it. There may have been one or two cases where we ran a little short of a certain type of fuze, but it was of no great consequence to the actual support.[8]

Immediate action was taken on the 28th when FLC shifted munitions storage operations to nearby ASP-2 and ordered replenishment stocks from storage areas in the Western Pacific and the United States. Although ground stocks for four months remained below the 45-day level authorized, and the ASP was idle for six while repairs were made, there was no degradation in ordnance support for continuing III MAF operations.[9]

Naval Support Activity, Da Nang

The United States military logistic system in I Corps was composed of three elements, of which Force Logistic Command was one component. For most standard supply items and for a wide variety of support services, III MAF depended upon Naval Support Activity (NSA), Da Nang, headquartered at the "White Elephant" within the city until 15 August, and then at the China Beach Public Works Compound ("Wooden Elephant") in East Da Nang.

Commanded by Rear Admiral Emmett P. Bonner, who was replaced in December by Rear Admiral Robert E. Adamson, Jr., Naval Support Activity, Da Nang consisted of close to 11,000 United States Navy officers and enlisted men and a civilian work force of over 6,700 South Vietnamese. An equal number of Americans, Vietnamese, and other Asians worked for the activity's private contractors. Established in late July 1965 to support the initial elements of III MAF, NSA Da Nang was under the immediate operational control of Commander, United States Naval Forces, Vietnam, while overall command was exercised by Commander in Chief, Pacific Fleet through Commander, Service Force, Pacific Fleet.[10]

The Naval Support Activity operated the port of Da Nang as well as transshipment points at Cua Viet/Dong Ha and Hue/Tan My in northern I Corps and Sa Huynh and Chu Lai in the southern provinces. With a fleet of over 350 ships and other small craft, vast warehouses, storage lots, and tank farms, NSA handled, stored, and issued all incoming and outgoing military cargo. NSA's public works department provided electricity, water, and ice to American cantonments, while its civilian contractors maintained over 700 miles of roads and the attending construction equipment. In addition, the activity managed Navy and Marine real estate holdings and operated the 720-bed naval hospital at Da Nang.[11]

Army units operating within I Corps Tactical Zone received logistical support from the U.S. Army Support Command, Da Nang, an organization which performed functions similar to those of Force Logistic Command. Under the operational control of the Commander, 1st Logistical Command, the Da Nang Support Command, by 1969, had grown to a strength of about 7,500 supply and transportation troops. The command included a field depot at Da Nang and two general support groups, the 26th, located at Phu Bai, and the 80th at Da Nang, which supported Army units in northern and southern I Corps.[12]

At its peak in 1969, the Navy by way of the Naval Support Activity, Da Nang, provided 98 percent of the commonly used supplies, construction materials, and service support for the 190,000 troops in I Corps. Marines and Army troops, through the Force Logistic Command and U.S. Army Support Command, distributed supplies drawn from the NSA to their own units, and procured, stored, and issued their own ammunition and those other supplies unique to the particular service. In addition to supporting the 1st and 3d Marine Divisions and 1st Marine Aircraft Wing, FLC supported the 2d ROKMC Brigade, while Army Support Command maintained petroleum pipelines used by all Services, as well as providing mortuary assistance and property disposal. With the redeployment of the 3d Marine Division and the relocation of FLSG-Bravo to Da Nang in November, the Army Support Command assumed the function of furnishing supplies and services for the remaining Marine elements in northern I Corps.[13]

With the implementation of plans for the withdrawal of Marine units from I Corps, the Army would assume a greater role in supporting the remaining forces. As redeployment planning began, Vice Admiral Elmo R. Zumwalt, Commander of U.S. Naval Forces, Vietnam, proposed that the Army, which already furnished support for all United States forces outside of I Corps, assume the missions of Naval Support Activity, Da Nang. With a proviso that the Navy would end its support only in conjunction with the redeploy-

Marine Corps Historical Collection
A Force Logistic Command forklift unloads artillery ammunition from a Navy LST. The Naval Support Activity, Da Nang, provided Marines most standard supply items and a wide variety of support services.

ment of Marine units, Zumwalt secured approval for his proposal from the Chief of Naval Operations and the Commander in Chief, Pacific Fleet. Also endorsing his plan, General Abrams, in late May 1969, ordered U.S. Army, Republic of Vietnam to make a study of the cost and manpower requirements of an Army logistics takeover in I Corps.[14]

When informed of these preliminary steps in early June, Lieutenant General Nickerson, III MAF commander, protested the move. Expressing complete satisfaction with Navy support, he urged that the present logistical structure in I Corps not be dismantled at a time when major redeployments and realignment of allied forces were to take place and the threat of enemy action remained high.[15] General Marine reaction to the possible loss of Navy support was one of apprehension. As Major General Simlik later recalled:

"We had great misgivings of losing Navy support. Naval Support Activity, Da Nang (NSA) had done such a marvelous job for a number of years and had given us such magnificent support. All of a sudden with NSA leaving we had a sinking feeling—almost one of despair."[16]

The Navy-Marine Corps team had worked well and few were willing to see the formal and informal relationship dissolved. According to General Simlik:

> It wasn't as simple as writing a contract for janitorial services.... NSA had been supporting the Marines in Vietnam for 5 years or so. Both NSA and the Marines knew the major areas of support. But there were so many areas that were covered by the Marine gunnery sergeant-Navy chief routine. For example,... a gunnery sergeant may have gotten a chief to take care of certain functions—to render certain support, small that it may be—by seeing that he got a couple bottles of booze or a case of beer at the right time. It was an informal, unwritten agreement of course, passed on from gunnery sergeant to gunnery sergeant, and chief to chief. Undoubtedly, there were a number of such agreements—difficult to discover, impossible to reduce to written form for a formal contract. And we were apprehensive, a psychotic apprehensiveness, that the Army would not respond if the written contract didn't include it.[17]

The greatest area of concern was the possible loss of the naval hospital. As Lieutenant General Leo J. Dulacki, then a brigadier general and III MAF G-3, later commented:

> When the redeployment plans were first drawn up, it was envisioned that substantial Marine forces would be redeployed out of country in the very first phases. Consistent with those plans, the Navy developed a plan for the early redeployment of the Naval Support Activity (Da Nang) concurrent with the redeployment of the Marines. However, the original plan was modified, as a result of which, the Marines forces would be redeployed on a slower and more extended time schedule. Nevertheless, the Navy determined that it would continue with its original plans regardless of any changes in the timing of the Marine redeployment. Suddenly we were faced with the prospect of some 40,000 Marines continuing operations in ICTZ but without naval support which had been such an integral part of the overall campaign in ICTZ. Of particular concern was the closure of the Naval Hospital (Da Nang) since it was prudent to assume that the enemy might attempt to exploit reduction of forces in ICTZ by launching increased offensive operations; if the latter eventually occurred, the availability of the hospital was essential. Formal representations were made to Admiral Zumwalt, Commander of Naval Forces, Vietnam, and Admiral Adamson, the Commander Naval Support Activity (Da Nang) to no avail; the Navy intended to proceed with its original redeployment plans. The situation was also discussed with General Abrams, COMUSMACV; General Abrams, as he stated, "preferred not to get involved in a 'Navy-Marine Corps controversy' "; he then gave his personal assurances that, if the enemy embarked on large-scale offensive operations, at the outset, a hospital ship would be made available off the coast of ICTZ, and if necessary, a MASH would be moved into ICTZ to render medical support to the Marines.

"It was my understanding," General Dulacki continued, "that CG, FMFPac made a similar representation to CINCPacFlt in Hawaii for the continuation of hospital support in Da Nang, but also to no avail."[18]

Despite Marine protests, planning for the Army takeover of the activity's support functions continued. In September 1969, MACV established a joint Army-Navy planning group, at Admiral Zumwalt's suggestion, to work out the practical details of the gradual transfer to the Army as the Marines pulled out. The group, chaired by the Army and located at Da Nang, included representatives of MACV, USARV, NavForV, III MAF, 1st Logistical Command, NSA Da Nang, Army Support Command Da Nang, and Force Logistic Command. Divided into fuctional subcommittees, MACV tasked the group with determining requirements for personnel and equipment, costs, and defining problems and proposing solutions.

With Marine redeployments and joint studies underway, General Abrams, in mid-November, instructed the Army and Navy to develop a support turnover schedule for formal presentation to MACV by 1 January 1970. Noting that particular functions not directly required for the support of III MAF could be transferred earlier, Abrams directed that the final assumption of common support by the Army would follow the complete removal of Marine combat units.

Discussions dragged on past the 1 January MACV deadline with Zumwalt pressing for early Army takeover of ports and activities not needed by Marines in northern I Corps, and indicating that once the Army assumed the common support mission, NSA Da Nang would be replaced by a smaller naval support facility, whose primary concern would be small-craft maintenance and assisting the South Vietnamese Navy. At the same time, III MAF stressed the need for the slow and deliberate transfer of functions to the Army, while reemphasizing that Navy support continue until all Marine combat forces were withdrawn from Vietnam. USARV sought the loan or outright transfer of Navy facilities and equipment to supplement Army logistical resources in I Corps, while all the Service components sought to minimize the cost of supporting the remaining forces.

On 21 January, General Abrams set 1 July 1970 as the date for final turnover of common service support to the Army. The changeover would take place even if Marine combat units remained. Preliminary turnovers of equipment and minor facilities in northern I Corps began in November 1969, following the redeployment of the 3d Marine Division, but not until February 1970 did the first of a series of major transfers occur. On the 15th, Naval Support Activity, Da Nang disbanded its detachments at Sa Huynh and Cua Viet and transferred the port facilities to the U.S. Army Support Command. Additional transfers were made during March, April, and May, and on 30 June 1970 NSA Da Nang was disestablished. The following day U.S. Naval Support Facility, Da Nang came into being.[19]

Engineer Support

At the beginning of 1969, five Marine combat engineer battalions were deployed in I Corps. The 1st Engineer Battalion, organic engineer element of the 1st Marine Division, reinforced by a platoon of Company A, 3d Engineer Battalion, and a platoon of Company A, 5th Engineer Battalion, performed light construction throughout the division's area of responsibility, maintained water points, swept roads of mines, and conducted the division's Demolitions, Land Mine Warfare, and Viet Cong Boobytrap School. The 3d Engineer Battalion, organic to the 3d Marine Division, performed similar functions in Quang Tri Province. Assisting the 3d Engineer Battalion was the 11th Engineer Battalion, reinforced by the 3d Bridge Company. Of III MAF's two force engineer battalions, the 7th, with attached 1st Bridge Company, worked almost exclusively for the 1st Marine Division, performing heavy construction in the Da Nang area, maintaining and improving roads, and conducting sweeps in search of enemy mines. The 9th Engineer Battalion, with its command post and three companies at Chu Lai and part of the fourth at Tam Ky, concentrated its main effort on maintaining and upgrading Route 1 between Chu Lai and the Song Cau Lau. The battalion also provided secondary road maintenance and other tactical support to the Americal Division. The battalions, in addition to normal combat tasks, carried out an extensive civic action program, that included repair of local school and government buildings, irrigation canals, and plowing acres of rice paddies.

In addition to the five Marine engineer units, naval construction forces (Seabees) of the 3d Naval Construction Brigade and the four-battalion U.S. Army 45th Engineer Group operated in I Corps at the beginning of 1969.[20] The Seabees rotated battalions in and out of I Corps throughout the year and had 10 battalions at the beginning of 1969, 12 at midyear, and 5 at the end of the year. Like the 1st and 3d Marine Divisions, the Americal and 101st Airborne Divisions, and the 1st Brigade, 5th Infantry Division, had organic engineers. The Air Force relied on a heavy repair squadron, located at the Da Nang Airbase.[21]

With Marine, Army, Navy, and the public works division of NSA Da Nang involved in large and varied construction projects, the lines of responsibility among the engineer elements, specifically between Marine direct and general support battalions and the Seabees, became "blurred," noted Colonel Nicholas A. Canzona, G-4 of the 1st Marine Division. "I never saw so many engineers in all my life working in a given area," Canzona continued, "and I must admit that I don't think I've ever seen so much attendant confusion as to who is supposed to do what and why and who is in charge of this and that. And this can get somewhat exasperating at times."[22]

Redeployments during the last months of 1969 reduced the III MAF engineer force by two Marine battalions: the 3d Marine Division's 3d Engineer Battalion and the 11th Engineer Battalion, a force unit. Among the principal contributions of the battalions in northern I Corps was development and perfection of the fire support base concept. With the increased dependence on mobile operations to exert maximum pressure on enemy formations, there occurred a requirement to provide close artillery support for combat units deployed beyond the range of guns at existing support bases. The solution was to establish small fortified positions on defensible terrain, large enough to accommodate the required artillery and service units supporting the maneuver elements. The construction of these sites proved to be a major engineering task, requiring first a detailed reconnaissance and then the formation of a task-organized engineer unit. Engineer equipment and troop requirements varied according to the nature of the terrain and the amount of clearing necessary following the supporting arms preparations.

The general sequence of engineer buildup on the selected fire support base site began with a small reconnaissance team accompanying the security force and helicopter support team. The contingent grew quickly as engineers began initial work with hand and power tools, and demolitions, to carve out a landing zone capable of receiving heavy equipment, such as tractors and backhoes, for the construction of gun pits, ammunition storage facilities, a helicopter pad, a fire direction center, and other defensive positions.

The primary piece of engineer equipment used in the construction of a fire support base was the Case

450 bulldozer, a helicopter-transportable tractor procured specifically for this task. Delivered to the site in two lifts, the tractor proved invaluable in reducing both manual labor and the time required to complete the base. In addition, the tractor was used to rapidly unearth enemy supply caches.

A substantial portion of the efforts of all five Marine engineer battalions, and Army and Navy engineers as well, was expended in upgrading major lines of communication throughout I Corps. Their effort was part of the general MACV bridge and LOC restoration program which sought to create a passable road network throughout South Vietnam, both to facilitate tactical maneuver and promote economic development. The tactical advantages were evident. Not only could troops be moved more quickly, but the construction of wide, modern paved roads forced the enemy to place his mines on the shoulders or on unimproved roads. This practically eliminated mining incidents on primary roads, reducing the daily minesweeping burden of III MAF engineer units and freeing them for other tasks. Road improvements undertaken during the year cut travel time between Da Nang and Hue from six hours to two, and between Da Nang and Dong Ha to four and one-half hours. An ancillary effect was to decrease vehicle maintenance requirements. Concentrating on Routes 1, 4, and 9, Marine, Navy, and Army engineer forces had completed the upgrading of over 370 kilometers and were at work on the remaining 100 kilometers by year's end. In addition, they continued the task of bridge construction and repair, which, during a typical month, involved work on 15 spans.

Among the major engineering accomplishments during the year was the opening of the new Liberty Bridge by naval construction forces to traffic on 30 March, thereby restoring a permanent overland route into the An Hoa basin. Replacing the original 2,000-foot bridge washed away by monsoon floods in late 1967, the new 825-foot, timber-pile-supported, concrete-decked bridge not only cut travel time between Da Nang and An Hoa by half, but increased the capacity of allied forces in support of tactical and pacification operations and assisted local Vietnamese in the economic development of the industrial area. In July, Marine engineers reopened the Song Tra Bong bridge on Route 1, following its partial destruction by enemy sappers, which again provided a vital link between Chu Lai and the southern extremes of the corps tactical zone. During the same month, elements of the 1st Engineer Battalion completed the upgrading of a portion of Route 4, permitting increased access to western Quang Nam Province.

In addition to road construction and maintenance, all Marine engineer battalions regularly swept assigned segments of highway for enemy mines. Sweep teams not only employed electric mine detectors, but also purchased large quantities of ordnance from Viet-

Once cleared of trees and vegetation, a mountaintop becomes a fire support base as members of the 1st Engineer Battalion take preliminary steps to create artillery positions.

Department of Defense Photo (USMC) A371975

Marines of the 9th Engineer Battalion apply a fresh layer of asphalt to Route 1 as a part of the continuing country-wide effort to upgrade South Vietnam's primary road network.

namese civilians under the Voluntary Informant Program. During May 1969, for example, teams from the 1st Engineer Battalion swept over 1,800 kilometers of road, detecting and destroying 91 mines and boobytraps. In the month they also purchased 2,717 ordnance items, ranging from small arms ammunition to 105mm artillery rounds.[23]

While construction efforts were directed, in the main, toward upgrading and maintaining lines of communication, engineers still faced endless requirements for cantonment and fire base construction, maintenance, and rehabilitation. Except for the sixmonth reconstruction project required to return ASP-1 and other nearby damaged facilities to full operation following the 27 April fire, Marine, Navy, and Army combat engineers each month built or improved bunkers, SEA huts, showers, watch towers, and mountout boxes; provided potable water and electricity; and laid barbed wire entanglements around base perimeters. For the 1st Medical Battalion, they constructed a 200-bed hospital, dental clinic, and support facilities. For FLC, engineers completed a new maintenance complex, consisting of 25 Butler buildings with attendant support hardware. And for the 1st MAW, they constructed over 100 steel and concrete "Wonder Arch" shelters at Da Nang, Chu Lai, and Marble Mountain air facilities. Introduced during 1969 to provide maximum possible protection of aircraft from high-trajectory weapons, such as rockets and mortars, and to reduce the danger of a fire spreading from one aircraft to others, each 48-by-70 foot shelter was constructed of bolted steel sections covered with 12 inches of high-strength concrete.[24]

Engineers also constructed facilities where the Marine infantrymen could get away from the stress of combat, among them "Stack Arms," the 1st Marine Division's in-country rest center located in the 3d Amphibian Tractor Battalion cantonment just south of the Marble Mountain Air Facility. While "this program did not win the war," as Lieutenant General Ormond R. Simpson, then commanding general of the division, later noted, "it was damn important to the 'man with the rifle.'" Infantry companies were brought to the center by helicopter. During their 48-hour stay, Marines could, as General Simpson noted, take "all the showers they wanted, were supplied with health and comfort items free, got new clothing and 782 gear, if needed, swam in the sea, had beer and soft drinks, wrote letters, called home . . . got haircuts, watched movies, slept, ate the best hot food we could beg, borrow, or steal, literally, and had absolutely NO DUTY!"[25]

With the withdrawal of the 3rd Marine Division from Vietnam, Marine engineers from the 3d and 11th Battalions ceased all construction projects and began demolition of a number of installations they earlier had built. Before redeploying on 29 November, elements of the 11th Engineer Battalion completed the destruction of Vandegrift and Elliott Combat Bases and assisted the 3d Engineer Battalion in policing up Cua Viet and Dong Ha Combat Bases, prior to their transfer to ARVN and other allied units remaining in Quang Tri Province.[26]

During the year, the enemy relied, as he had done throughout the earlier years of the war, on networks of caves, tunnels, and fortifications. To destroy these fighting positions, as well as remove foliage used as concealment, Marine engineers engaged in "land-clearing" operations—the systematic destruction of selected portions of the countryside. In addition to employing organic engineer elements, III MAF organized a number of provisional land-clearing units, consisting of men and equipment from Marine force engineer battalions and the Army's 45th Engineer Group, for specific purposes.

General land-clearing operations followed an established pattern. Vietnamese provincial authorities would designate the target area, and the military unit operating within the area would furnish a company-size security force for the engineer effort. Land-clearing bulldozers would then begin scraping the assigned area section by section, clearing trees and brush and simultaneously demolishing enemy trenchlines, bunkers, and tunnels, and detonating boobytraps. Ordnance not destroyed by the initial engineering effort, as well as impenetrable tunnels and bunkers, would be demolished separately.

During 1969, III MAF land-clearing efforts concentrated on two areas—Leatherneck Square in Quang Tri Province and Go Noi Island, southeast of Da Nang. Leatherneck Square, a 450,000 square meter corridor between Gio Linh and Con Thien, bounded by Route 9 on the south, was covered by scrub growth, crisscrossed by hedgerows, and dotted by numerous enemy harbor and fighting positions. By midyear, Marines of the 11th Engineer Battalion had reduced the area to a dusty, hot piece of ground that would eventually be reclaimed by farming. To the south, in Quang Nam Province, portions of Dodge City and all of Go Noi Island, a long-time enemy stronghold, also were denuded. During 1st Marine Division Operation Pipestone Canyon, elements of the 1st, 7th, and 9th Engineer Battalions, in conjunction with Army land-clearing forces, leveled more than 8,000 acres, destroying an extensive enemy command post, 97 tunnels, 2,193 bunkers, 325 fighting holes, and 3,246 meters of trenchline.[27] As Lieutenant General Simpson noted: "We knew it was a staging point. We did clear it; there wasn't anything left." The engineers "went in there with . . . plows and actually plowed the whole damned thing up; every square foot of it."[28]

Despite restraints in manpower and materials, Marine combat engineers, working in conjunction with their Army and Navy teammates, continued to provide combat and combat service support to maneuver elements deployed throughout I Corps. Their accomplishments were many and varied, ranging from water supply to the time-consuming and hazardous task of mine sweeping. Throughout it all, Marine combat engineers found the time to assist a Vietnamese village in building a new school or repairing an antiquated water system.

Motor Transport

III MAF possessed six motor transport units at the

A 3d Engineer Battalion sweep team checks a road for mines ahead of an advancing tank. Daily road sweeps consumed a portion of the Marine engineering effort.
Department of Defense Photo (USMC) A192390

Marine Corps Historical Collection

The men of 2d Battalion, 5th Marines line up for the daily barbecue at the 1st Marine Division's in-country rest center, "Stack Arms," at China Beach south of Da Nang.

beginning of 1969. The 1st Motor Transport Battalion, reinforced in October by Company A, 5th Motor Transport Battalion, 5th Marine Division, was under the operational control of the 1st Marine Division, as was the 11th Motor Transport Battalion, a force unit. Supporting the 3d Marine Division was the 3d Motor Transport Battalion, reinforced until 23 March by a platoon of Company A, 5th Motor Transport Battalion, and the 9th Motor Transport Battalion. Force Logistic Command had operational control of the large truck company of Headquarters and Service Battalion, 1st Force Service Regiment, and the 7th Motor Transport Battalion, which supported FLSG-Bravo at Quang Tri. Both of these units supported Force Logistic Command, as well as other III MAF elements.

The motor transport battalions organic to each division consisted of a Headquarters and Service Company and three truck companies. Each truck company was equipped with thirty 2.5-ton trucks. The force transport units, 7th, 9th, and 11th, whose mission was to reinforce other elements of the MAF, each consisted of a H&S Company, three truck companies, and transportation company. The transportation company was authorized 30 tractors and 47 trailers of various sizes, while each truck company had thirty-one 5-ton trucks. The Truck Company, Force Logistic Command possessed a variety of specialized vehicles as well as a large fleet of 2.5- and 5-ton trucks.

Throughout 1969, III MAF still relied heavily on trucks to move cargo and personnel despite the ever-increasing use of helicopters. Major combat bases and the two logistic support units received most of their supplies by "Rough Rider" truck convoys. During 1969, Marine transport battalions covered 6,801,188 miles, carrying 2,416,802 passengers and 970,092 tons of freight.

Although improved roads permitted trucks to reach most major Marine positions in both western Quang Tri and Quang Nam Provinces, Marine truckers still had to contend with ambushes and mines. "On several occasions," noted Lieutenant Colonel Laurier J. Tremblay, 9th Motor Transport Battalion's commanding officer, "these convoys had to fight their way through well-established ambushes and as a result sustained many casualties in troops and equipment. During the early months of 1969, Route 9 was considered a

'Gauntlet' that our convoys were required to run through almost daily in order to provide urgently needed supplies and munitions to our combat troops operating out of Vandegrift Combat Base." Although a number of protective modifications were made to trucks, the simplest being the lining of floor boards with filled sandbags, casualties continued to mount.[29]

The year witnessed the introduction of two new vehicles into III MAF's motor transport inventory, the M116E1 marginal terrain vehicle and the M733, its armored counterpart. Designed to replace the M76 Otter of World War II vintage, the M116E1 was placed into service in April by the 11th Motor Transport Battalion to support the 1st Marine Division in the low and often inundated areas south of Da Nang. Virtually unaffected by weather, this versatile vehicle had the effect of reducing reliance on helicopter support. The armored version of the vehicle was placed into service in August as a convoy escort.[30]

The 3d and 9th Motor Transport Battalions were among the last units to redeploy with the 3d Marine Division. Needed to move the redeploying combat units and their equipment to coastal ports for embarkation, both units left Vietnam in late November. The 7th Motor Transport Battalion remained behind to assist in the relocation of Marine personnel and equipment from northern I Corps to the Da Nang area, to which it moved on 2 December.

Medical Support

Medical service support available to III MAF at the beginning of 1969, included the 1st Medical Battalion, reinforced in October by Company A, 5th Medical Battalion, which maintained the 240-bed 1st Marine Division Hospital. A similar size hospital was maintained by the 3d Medical Battalion for the 3d Marine Division. In addition the 1st Hospital Company, a force unit, operated a 100-bed treatment facility at Da Nang. Approximately 250 Navy medical officers and 2,700 hospital corpsmen were attached to the divisions, wing, FLC, and other combat support units throughout I Corps. Two Navy hospital ships, the *Sanctuary* (AH 17) and the *Repose* (AH 16), each with a capacity of 560 beds, which could be increased to 750 during an emergency, were stationed off I Corps to treat the more seriously ill and wounded. At Da Nang, the 720-bed Naval Support Activity Hospital provided most services available at a general hospital in the United States. Also available were the facilities of the

A 7th Motor Transport Battalion "Rough Rider" convoy, originating at Quang Tri, pauses at Phu Bai south of Hue before proceeding over Hai Van Pass and into Da Nang.

Department of Defense Photo (USMC) A800437

quency (UHF) channels were dedicated solely for medical evacuation communications. During the year a joint medical regulating center was established by placing a Navy and Marine regulating section with its Army counterpart at the 95th Evacuation Hospital. After helicopters picked up casualties, the flight corpsman, or a member of the helicopter crew in the absence of the corpsman, would contact the regulating center on the dedicated radio frequency and report the number of patients and the type and severity of the wounds. A center regulator would then check the status board indicating the facilities, specialties, and space available at each hospital, and direct the helicopter to the appropriate destination for treatment.[31] Specially designed litters and forest penetrators were also introduced to aid in helicopter rescue operations in jungle terrain or in combat areas too dangerous for a helicopter to land.

"The swift and orderly chain of evacuation is a many faceted thing," noted Colonel Eugene R. Brady, former commander of HMM-364, "many procedures have been adopted to shorten and strengthen the chain. The dedicated four plane package, the hot pad, the dedicated frequency . . . are but a few links in the chain. There are many other links, some small, some large. Non-essential links have been discarded." Although the process may have been evolutionary, "the dedication, motivation, and courage of those involved in tactical air medical evacuation will," Colonel Brady continued, "never change."[32]

Admissions to hospitals serving III MAF declined over the year, reflecting not only redeployments but also the slackening of combat. Of the 22,003 patients treated during 1969, 26 percent were admitted for wounds received as a direct result of combat. Illnesses, such as fevers of undetermined origin or malaria, like the year before, accounted for the majority of admissions (61 percent), while the remaining 13 percent were as a result of nonbattle injuries. Of the Marines admitted to III MAF medical facilities, 11,355 were evacuated to out-of-country installations through the Air Force's 22d Casualty Staging Facility at Da Nang for specialized treatment.

Like other support organizations, III MAF medical support facilities experienced a reduction during the latter half of 1969 as a result of redeployments. The 3d Medical Battalion, which supported the 3d Division, left Vietnam on 24 November. However, those Marine units remaining in Quang Tri Province were not without medical support. Casualties were either

Department of Defense Photo (USMC) A800568
A wounded Marine is hoisted on board a hovering Marine CH-46 helicopter. Rapid evacuation and the use of innovative techniques saved valuable time, increasing the survival rate among the seriously wounded.

95th U.S. Army Evacuation Hospital near Da Nang.

Although the medical evacuation chain and policy remained unchanged throughout 1969, improvements to shorten the time between injury and treatment continued. Hot pads specifically tailored to the dedicated two-transport, two-gunship helicopter medical evacuation package were established. This not only had the effect of reducing scramble time, but also promoted "dialogue among crews of the package, before, between, and after missions which is an important factor in teamwork." In addition, specific ultra-high-fre-

transported to Company B, 75th Support Battalion, 1st Brigade, 5th Infantry Division, or to Army or Marine facilities further south.

Communications

The corps-wide communications system which allowed Commanding General, III MAF to administer, coordinate, and direct the various commands under his control was installed, maintained, and operated by the 5th and 7th Communication Battalions.* In addition to the common functions associated with communications, installation of telephone poles, cable construction and splicing, maintenance of switching apparatus, and manning of radio relay sites, members of the battalions staffed the various Marine communications operations centers located throughout I Corps.

Centered at Da Nang, the corps-wide communications system provided III MAF with various capabilities: teletype and data, radio, and telephone operations. The III MAF teletype and data capability rested mainly with the administrative communications center at Camp Horn, although similar operations existed at the divisions, wing, and Force Logistics Command, and on down to the regimental and in some instances, battalion level. The center, staffed by officers and men of the Communications Company, 5th Communication Battalion, processed and distributed over 2,500 messages generated daily by dedicated point-to-point teletype circuits to all major subordinate units. In addition, the center maintained other dedicated circuits which provided entry into four world-wide teletype systems; to FMFPac in Hawaii, to the Navy's Naval Command Operational network in the Philippines, to CinCPac's Joint Pacific Teletype Network, and to the AUTODIN telephone network via teletype.

Instead of maintaining control over subordinate elements by voice radio communications, III MAF relied on the various teletype networks. The circuits to major units were all secure point-to-point utilizing encryption devices. In addition, the center maintained secure circuit links with the Korean Brigade at Hoi An, Army Special Forces operating in I Corps, ARVN I Corps Headquarters, and a special radio teletype net which connected major subordinate commands as well as the special landing forces and Navy ships providing gunfire support. Lastly, teletype circuits were main-

---
*On 15 April 1969, the 5th and 7th Communication Battalions were combined under the command of Lieutenant Colonel Charles L. Brady. Both battalions maintained their separate identities, but were controlled by one commanding officer and his staff.

Marine Corps Historical Collection

PFC Richard J. Wellnitz, left, of the 7th Communications Battalion, checks out the telephone line after LCpl Kenneth D. Ellis completes a wire patch.

tained to MACV and the Air Force's Task Force Alpha in Thailand.

While secure communications by radio was kept to a minimum, it was maintained as a backup to the teletype systems. III MAF did possess an unsecure command radio net with the Da Nang harbor patrol, the Navy Hospital, and hospital ships in the vicinity, but this like other unsecure radio nets was used sparingly.

The initial telephone system within I Corps Tactical Zone was tactically oriented, but as III MAF grew, larger and more complex fixed equipment was added. The final result was a combination of the tactical system, utilizing automatic dial telephone switching equipment at the division and force level, and the Defense Communication System operating fixed dial central offices. In the spring of 1969, the Air Force, under the direction of the Defense Communications Agency, inaugurated the Da Nang tandem switching center which provided intra-corps switching between all five dial central offices, stretching from Phu Bai to Chu Lai, as well as providing access to other corps tactical zones and Thailand. The system terminated in the AUTOVON switching center in Saigon, providing all users with direct dial capability throughout the world.

SUPPLYING III MAF

Logistics of Keystone Eagle and Keystone Cardinal

The redeployment of men and equipment of the 3d Marine Division posed one of the most complex logistic problems facing III MAF during the latter half of 1969. Units scheduled to be redeployed did not simply cease operations, pack up, and leave Vietnam; instead, with each withdrawal, the selected units would disengage from continuing operations. Once extricated, the departing units would exchange, if required, most of their personnel and equipment with other organizations still in combat before embarking for destinations in the Pacific or the United States. The movement was not all in one direction, for normal rotation of personnel and replacement of equipment had to continue. This flow had to be stringently regulated so as to leave III MAF at the prescribed personnel strength and Force Logistic Command with manageable materiel levels at the completion of each redeployment cycle.

In consultation with MACV, the White House and Department of Defense determined the number of troops to be withdrawn and timetable for each redeployment. MACV then apportioned the troops to be removed among the Services and requested from each component commander a list of specific units to be redeployed. CinCPac and the Joint Chiefs of Staff in turn reviewed and approved the list, determining the destination of each redeployed unit. Based on the transportation requirements provided by the separate Services, CinCPac would then prepare a schedule and timetable for the sea and air movements of men and equipment.[33]

Coordinating redeployment planning and execution for Marine Corps units was FMFPac, headquartered at Camp Smith, Hawaii. Under the command of Lieutenant General Henry W. Buse, Jr., a Naval Academy graduate and recipient of the Silver Star in World War II, FMFPac, in conjunction with III MAF, proposed specific Marine units to be redeployed. Following general guidelines established by Headquarters Marine Corps, FMFPac coordinated the movement of men and equipment from South Vietnam to other Marine Corps bases in the Pacific and the continental United States. "FMFPac was the prime coordinator," according to Major General Wilbur F. Simlik, then III MAF G-4. "FMFPac arranged the shipping—which was the controlling factor, of course. FMFPac told us which regiment, which element would be retrograded when and where."[34]

On redeployment matters, the relationship between FMFPac and III MAF was, as General Simlik later remarked, "constant and close, and personal." Buse or members of his staff made frequent visits to Da Nang to observe, consult, and to provide guidance. At the same time, a constant and friendly dialogue was maintained with CinCPac, Admiral John S. McCain, Jr., and his staff. For its part, III MAF regularly sent representatives to FMFPac and CinCPac planning and movement conferences, in addition to coordinating with MACV, the other Services, and the South Vietnamese on such matters as area responsibility, base transfers, and equipment turnovers.[35]

Redeployment plans were drafted in terms of units to be withdrawn and the total number of troops to be deducted from the authorized strength of each Service within Vietnam. For the Marine Corps, FMFPac and III MAF determined which unit, and further, which individual Marine would be removed in order to bring III MAF down to the required strength. In deciding who should redeploy and who should remain, tour equity would overshadow all other considerations. Those Marines with the fewest months remaining in their current 12-month tour would normally be selected for redeployment.

As with all other combat and support units in Vietnam, Marine units were made up of personnel with varied end-of-tour dates, and thus no unit could simply be withdrawn with its complete complement of existing personnel. Instead, for each unit selected for redeployment to Okinawa or continental United States, a process nicknamed "mixmaster" was instituted. Mixmaster involved the transfer of noneligible Marines to units remaining in Vietnam and the filling of the redeploying unit's ranks with eligible men from other Marine commands. In Keystones Eagle and Cardinal, the only major unit to undergo extensive "mixmastering" was the 3d Marines. Those Marines of RLT-3 who had served a minimum of seven months were considered eligible for return to Camp Pendleton with the unit or to normal and accelerated rotation drafts, while the remainder were transferred to other units in Vietnam, Okinawa, and Japan. Units remaining in Vietnam in turn provided a number of Marines to fill the void. Commands bound for Okinawa and Japan underwent less "mixmastering," and these units embarked with a majority of existing personnel, including those otherwise ineligible, in order to maintain the unit's integrity and combat readiness.

In implementing this complex reshuffling of manpower, each redeployment was broken down into the number of Marines of each rank, grade, and skill to be removed either by transfer to a withdrawing organization or by normal rotation. FMFPac, which held broad transfer and reassignment authority, issued strength reduction requirements and assisted, where necessary, in their implementation. Through its G-1 section, each major III MAF subordinate command then selected those Marines eligible for redeployment, arranged for the transfers, and prepared and issued the necessary orders. FMFPac, in addition, periodically adjusted the flow of replacements to III MAF to assure compliance with stated manpower ceilings, and directed special transfers of III MAF personnel to units on Okinawa or in Japan, not only to reduce numbers in Vietnam, but to rebuild other Western Pacific commands gutted during the war.

Redeploying units involved in Keystones Eagle and Cardinal began embarkation planning and preparation one to two months before their scheduled date of departure. While still conducting combat operations, equipment was inventoried and those supplies not immediately needed were disposed of or packed for shipment. Two to three weeks before embarkation, the units normally stood down and moved to secure cantonments, in the case of units of the 3d Marine Division, to Dong Ha Combat Base. There, battalions "mixmastered" their personnel, turned in supplies and excess equipment, and completed packing in preparation for shipment.

In the redeployments carried out during 1969, units leaving Vietnam carried with them their standard allowances of supplies and equipment. They, however, were to divest themselves of all rations, ammunition, fuel, and excess Southeast Asia equipment, and in the case of those units deploying to Okinawa and Japan, jungle fatigues.[36] The fatigues were one of the items that were not to be taken out of country. However, "the distribution of regular utilities had started," reported Colonel Raymond C. Damm, "but supplies were not sufficient to outfit the troops going to Japan and Okinawa. We requested authority to retain one set of jungle utilities for the movement . . . . FMFPac approved the request with the proviso that we gather them up as soon as we could issue regular utilities on Okinawa. The troops, much to the satisfaction of the troop leaders, embarked in jungle utilities."[37]

Excess equipment and supplies were turned over to Marine organizations still committed to combat or used to replenish the mount-out and mount-out augmentation (MO/MOA) stocks of the displacing forces.* Force Logistic Command acted as the conduit for redistributing these excess supplies, ensuring that those units departing Vietnam were fully prepared for expeditionary service.

All equipment and supplies accompanying units being redeployed to the United States had to meet the strict standards of cleanliness established by the United States Department of Agriculture and the Public Health Service to prevent the introduction of Asian insects and contagious diseases into the United States. Meeting these standards proved a problem, as General Simlik later noted:

> One of our most aggravating problems was that all of the gear, all of the equipment, all of the vehicles that we retrograded to the United States had to pass an agricultural inspection. So consequently they had to be spotless, absolutely spotless. And there were inspectors that were at the docks and aboard ships . . . . With vehicles that had been in combat only a few days before, this was a very difficult task to accomplish. We [therefore had to] set up all sorts of washing and scrub down stations by the docks.[38]

Packing boxes had to be constructed of termite-free wood, and all containers, vehicle bodies, and shipborne aircraft had to be sealed and treated with insecticides and rodent poisons before being loaded.

Of the total number of Marines redeploying during 1969, more than 50 percent left Vietnam by ship. The remainder departed on commercial aircraft chartered by the Military Airlift Command. In contrast, over 90 percent of all Marine equipment and cargo went by sea. Most of this cargo, as well as those surface-transported Marines, traveled by amphibious vessels provided by CinCPacFlt. During each redeployment, one of the two Seventh Fleet Special Landing Forces stood down temporarily to permit the vessels of its amphibious ready group to join the sealift. During Keystones Eagle and Cardinal, FLC squeezed 604,884 square feet of vehicle and 3,952,911 cubic feet of freight onto eastbound amphibious shipping. This

---

*Marine Corps units, as forces required to be constantly ready to be committed, maintain stocks of reserve supplies in order to support themselves during their initial period of deployment should supplies not be readily available. These stocks are divided into two 30-day blocks, the mount-out and mount-out augmentation. The mount-out block is held by the unit itself and moves with it when the unit is deployed. The augmentation block is carried by the division or regiment service support unit and is intended to supplement the primary block of supplies. Following initial Marine deployments to Vietnam in 1965, mount-out blocks were consumed and by early 1969 had to be rebuilt.

reliance on Navy ships instead of contracted vessels of the Military Sealift Transportation System (MSTS) saved the Marine Corps approximately $5,000,000 in commercial freight costs during the last half of 1969.

As the Marines left with their equipment and supplies, III MAF disposed of the vacated bases and camps. Although it possessed authority to demolish fire bases and combat positions, all major installations were first offered to the other United States Services and then to the South Vietnamese. If rejected then they were demolished. Real estate transfers, especially to South Vietnamese forces, was a complex, and often involved task. The secrecy of redeployment planning prevented III MAF and other commands from initiating discussions of base turnover with the South Vietnamese until late in each withdrawal cycle. Poorly organized and equipped to manage their own facilities, the Vietnamese made decisions slowly, and as General Simlik noted, demanded much paperwork:

> III MAF and XXIV Corps, of course, did their best to influence how the ARVN would deploy and utilize the fire bases which we occupied. But the Vietnamese were independent. There were certain fire bases which they wanted and others which they didn't, and they made up their mind with deliberate speed . . . . The fire bases and the camps which the ARVN and other units were to occupy had to be left in spotless condition—A-1; all the electrical wiring had to be exactly right, all the heads had to be functioning, all this sort of thing. And there was a formal agreement, a real estate agreement, which was to be signed by both parties and forwarded down to MACV affirming that all was in order. This almost required the services of a professional real estate negotiator. Each fire base posed its own problems, and negotiations were constant.[39]

The transfer of real estate, while at times frustrating, proved to be less of a problem than cleaning up the battlefield, as Lieutenant General William K. Jones, then Commanding General, 3d Marine Division, later noted:

> These [fire support bases] were built with huge 12 by 12 timbers. It was necessary, of course, that we completely dismantle them so that they could not be used by the enemy. This was a major problem—a major engineer problem. The ARVN were very interested in acquiring this material and I was given authority to give it to them. So they would come

The electronic equipment of the 1st Light Anti-Aircraft Missile Battalion heads out of Da Nang Harbor by ship bound for Marine Corps Base, Twentynine Palms, California.

Marine Corps Historical Collection

up and haul this bulk of material back to their camps. But, even so, why was this the big problem, was that we had to close up and police up an area that had been used by Marines for many, many years.

Everything had to be removed or buried:

> We had to remove all mines. We didn't have to remove the barbed wire, but we had to take out all the mines or give the minefield maps to the ARVN if they wanted them left in; and there weren't very many that they wanted left in, actually. So, we had to clear all that. And then, just the debris, just the cans and boxes, . . . accumulated trash we had to bury . . . . We left it absolutely clean—everything. Everything was buried and there was no trash whatsoever.[40]

The logistical effort in moving a reinforced division, in addition to an appropriate share of supporting air units, from the war zone to Okinawa, Japan, and United States bases was accomplished successfully despite the problems which arose. The mistakes and the actions taken during the Keystones Eagle and Cardinal redeployments served as useful guidelines for units involved in the increasing number of redeployments the following year.

PART VI
UNIQUE CONTRIBUTIONS

CHAPTER 16

Pacification

*The National Perspective—Pacification Planning In I Corps—Line Unit Pacification
Civic Action—The Grass Roots Campaign—Results*

The National Perspective

Long a major concern of Marines in South Vietnam, pacification, by 1969, had become the major goal of the allied country-wide strategy. Although definitions varied with time, pacification was a complex military, political, economic, and sociological process with the principal thrust of providing security for the population of South Vietnam as well as peace, prosperity, political stability, and social justice. Broad in concept, it combined a myriad of individual programs and efforts which had the following basic objectives: establishing or re-establishing local government which was responsive to the citizenry and that involved their participation; providing sustained security; destroying the enemy's infrastructure; asserting or reasserting South Vietnamese political control; involving the people in the central government; and initiating sustained economic and social growth.

In theory, a sound pacification program was inherent in successfully combating counterinsurgency. In practice, however, the program during the early years was marked by confused policies and goals, divided authority and fragmented administration, all of which permitted corruption and created little or no progress. Beginning in late 1966, major efforts were begun to create a meaningful program to deny the enemy his vital base of popular support and to coordinate security planning. Further refinements were made the following year with the combining of most American personnel engaged in pacification under one organization, Civil Operations and Revolutionary Development Support (CORDS), and placing it within the MACV command structure. Paralleling CORDS, the South Vietnamese Government created the Central Recovery Committee (CRC), first chaired by the Vice President and then by the Prime Minister. The two organizations through deputies and councils at all governing levels, coordinated, planned, and directed the pacification effort.

Following the 1968 *Tet* Offensive, during which the enemy attempted not only to inflict a major military defeat, but also to coerce the South Vietnamese people into an uprising, a comprehensive review of pacification policies and management was undertaken, resulting in the launching of a "special campaign" to seize the initiative from the enemy and expand governmental authority and control. Announced on 11 October by President Nguyen Van Thieu, the Accelerated Pacification Campaign (APC) had as its major objectives the consolidation of past achievements and the extension of government control over necessary territory and a minimum of 80 percent of the population. The main effort was to be directed at maintaining security in those hamlets rated "under GVN influence" (A, B, or C) by the Hamlet Evaluation System (HES), in order that local government and community life could flourish.* In those areas rated "contested" (D and E hamlets) efforts were to be directed toward restoring security and limited community development. As for enemy-controlled hamlets, emphasis was

---

*Instituted in 1966, the Hamlet Evaluation System arranged and analyzed information on all aspects of pacification—security, political, and socio-economic—provided by province and district advisors. The computerized system then supplied information on demand, with the most important being the placing of areas in specific categories assigned the letter grade A, B, C, D, E, or V. These security categories were defined as:

A. Hamlet has adequate security forces; infrastructure has been eliminated; public projects are underway and the economic picture is improving.

B. A Viet Cong threat exists, but security is organized and partially effective; infrastructure has been partially neutralized; and self-help and economic programs are underway.

C. Hamlet is subject to infrequent VC harassment; infrastructure members have been identified; and the population participates in some self-help programs.

D. Viet Cong activities have been reduced, but an internal enemy threat in the form of taxation and terrorism still exists. The local populace participates in some hamlet government and economic programs. The hamlet is contested but leaning toward the central government.

E. The Viet Cong are effective although some government control exists. The enemy infrastructure is intact, and government programs are nonexistent or just beginning.

V. Hamlet under Viet Cong control. No government official or advisor may enter except on military operations, and the population willingly supports the enemy.

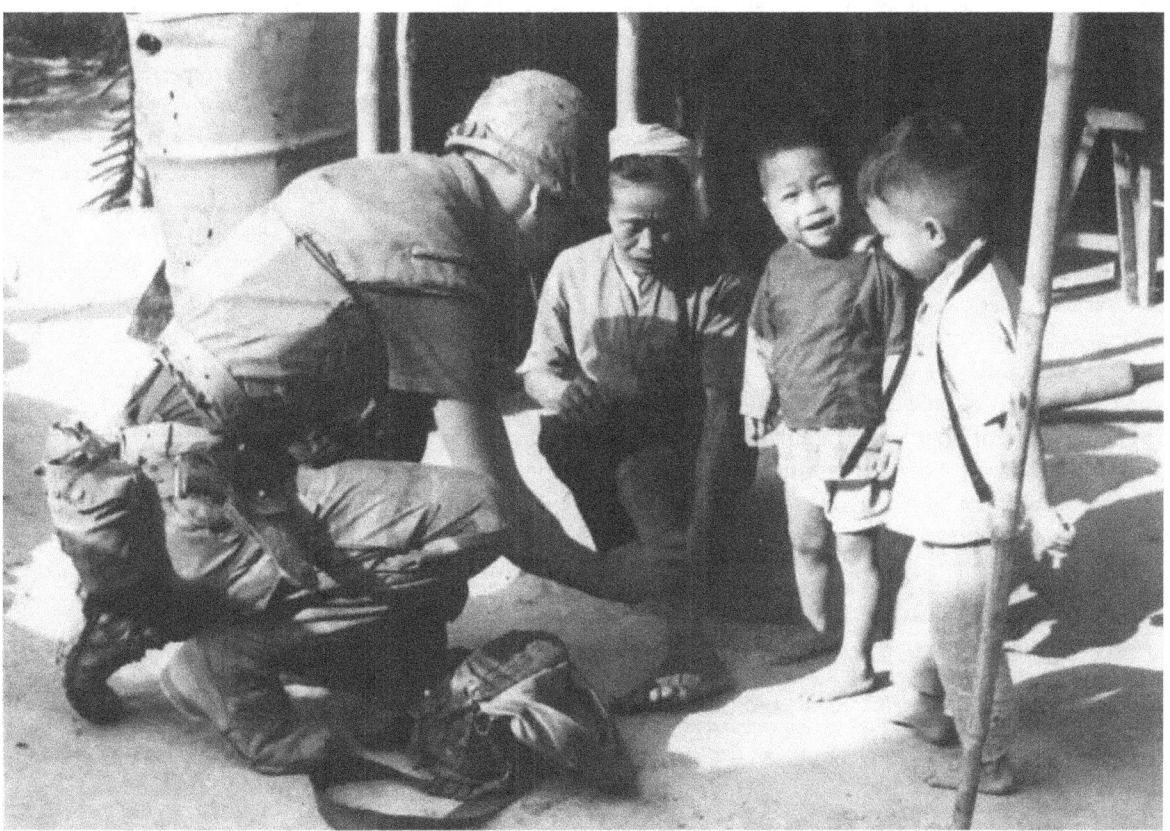
Department of Defense Photo (USMC) A371861
Navy Corpsman Donald W. Vogt, accompanying a Company L, 3d Battalion, 1st Marines patrol south of Da Nang, pauses to treat a South Vietnamese woman's injured leg.

to be placed on conducting military operations designed to disrupt enemy troop movements and destroy enemy logistical storage areas.

The primary tasks of the Accelerated Pacification Campaign were to: improve the Regional and Popular Forces; promote the anti-Viet Cong Infrastructure plan (Phoenix); reform local government; organize the people into self-defense forces; enforce economic revival measures; improve information and propaganda; implement the Chieu Hoi or "Open Arms" program; and assist in the accelerated rehabilitation and resettlement of refugees. For each task, a specific target goal was assigned: drive the enemy from populated areas; upgrade 1,000 D and E hamlets to category C; neutralize 3,000 members of the infrastructure each month; rally at least 5,000 Hoi Chanh; expand the People's Self-Defense Force (PSDF) to one million, of which 200,000 would be armed; and expand the information and propaganda campaign to exploit enemy failures and demonstrate the government's seizure of the initiative to end the war in victory.

After the various organizations and units necessary to implement the tasks were set up, the target hamlets selected, and the supporting military operations arranged, the campaign was launched on 1 November. As with all undertakings of this magnitude, problems arose, but for the most part they were overcome. An early and potentially difficult problem was that of centralized management. As the campaign progressed, it soon became apparent that the loosely organized Central Recovery Committee was ill-equipped to manage effectively a program as all-inclusive and as urgent as the APC. As a result, the permanent Central Pacification and Development Council was established, under the Prime Minister, composed of representatives of the ministries most directly involved in pacification. This new arrangement not only fostered authoritative centralized control, but assured that the momentum achieved during the initial stages of the campaign would be maintained.

Expanding upon the special 1968 plan, which was to terminate on 31 January 1969, the South Vietnamese issued the 1969 Pacification and Development Plan on 15 December. This authoritative document served not only as the foundation for the 1969 program, but was in itself a notable achievement in cooperation and coordination between the newly formed Central Pacification and Development Council, various government ministries, and MACV, therefore ensuring that the yearly pacification plan would receive widespread support throughout South Vietnam.

As a continuation and extension of the Accelerated Pacification Campaign, the essential task to be accomplished during 1969 remained the liberation of the people from the coercion and control of the enemy and to prevent his return. Underlying all pacification efforts was to be the guiding principle of "Community Spirit." As the 1969 Pacification and Development plan stressed:

> The Community Spirit Principle must originate with the people; every effort of the Government must be developed based on that principle, while carrying out any program or operation. The Community Spirit principle must work on a three-fold basis: cooperation among the people, cooperation between the people and the Government, and cooperation among Government organizations. Only then can the Government be more powerful and stable; then the people will realize that they are involved and will cooperate with the Government to defeat the common enemy.[1]

The practical goals for action were established in eight mutually supporting objectives: provide territorial security; establish local government in villages; organize People's Self-Defense Forces; increase the number of Hoi Chanh; reduce the Viet Cong Infrastructure; intensify information and propaganda efforts; stimulate the rural economy; and reduce the number of refugees.

Under territorial security, the Vietnamese Government committed itself to controlling and providing security for 90 percent of the population which lived in hamlets and villages with a Hamlet Evaluation System pacification rating of A, B, or C. Responsibility for this security involved both the Vietnamese Armed Forces (including RF and PF), Free World Military Assistance Forces, together with People's Self-Defense Force, and National Police. Each of these military and paramilitary forces would be used according to its capabilities.

As the South Vietnamese had no long tradition of nationhood, the government placed primary emphasis on unifying the village and hamlet governments with the central government, rather than attempting to win support of the state by individual loyalty. In contested hamlets and Viet Cong-controlled villages, elections were to be held, competent officials trained, and administrative organizations established, ensuring a real and durable presence of the government in rural areas.

Originally organized to obtain the commitment of as many people as possible to the government and actively involved in its defense, and to strengthen security in both rural and urban areas, the People's Self-Defense Force, the civilian home guard, had by the end of the Accelerated Pacification Campaign grown to approximately 1 million, of which nearly 200,000 were armed.* Ultimately to include all males not liable for military service and women, aged 16 and above, organized into local combat and support groups, the PSDF was potentially one of the government's most promising pacification devices. The objective of the 1969 Pacification and Development plan was to increase membership to a minimum of 2 million with 1.6 million of this number trained and 400,000 armed.

The Chieu Hoi or "Open Arms" program was considered vital to the 1969 pacification campaign. Deemed one of the most successful programs initiated, more than 90,000 Hoi Chanh, or ralliers, had returned to government control since the effort was begun in 1963, of which more than 10,000 came from enemy military units and over 4,000 from the enemy infrastructure. The 1968 Chieu Hoi program produced approximately 18,000 ralliers, with nearly 8,000 being returned during the last three months of the year. Based on these results and the desire to step up propaganda efforts, the government set a goal of receiving 20,000 Hoi Chanhs during 1969.

The anti-Viet Cong Infrastructure program, codenamed Phoenix by the Americans and Phung Hoang by the Vietnamese, had been in existence for some time. Again calling for the elimination, by death, capture, or desertion, of the enemy's entrenched infrastructure, the 1969 plan specified goals and targets. The main targets of the campaign were to be members of the National Liberation Councils and their subor-

---

*Four groups composed the People's Self-Defense Forces: the Female Support Group; the Youth Self-Defense Group; the Elders Self-Defense Group; and the Combat Group. Membership in the combat group included all males 16 and 17 years of age and ablebodied females, between the ages of 16 and 40, who joined voluntarily. Women between the ages of 16 and 50 composed the female group, while males over 51 were included in the elders group. Youth between 13 and 15 joined the youth group. Membership in the female, elder, and youth groups was voluntary, and tasks included social welfare, health activities, and morale support. (COMUSMACV msg to JCS, dtd 9Jun69 [MACV HistDocColl, Reel 56]).

dinate organizations on provincial, district, village, and hamlet levels, with particular emphasis given to areas considered contested or under temporary Communist control. For goals, the 1969 Pacification and Development plan called for the political elimination of 33,000 individuals.

Since "winning the hearts and minds of the people" was the ultimate aim of the pacification effort, a broad information and propaganda program was necessary to explain and encourage active participation and cooperation with the government in achieving the eight objectives of the 1969 campaign. In secure areas, the aim was to exploit the government's military and political successes, appeal for the people's active cooperation in destroying the enemy infrastructure, and warn against Communist attempts at terrorism, sabotage, and use of distorted propaganda calling for a coalition government. In contested areas, emphasis was to be placed on exposing Communist intentions and methods, while expounding upon the good intentions and programs of the government.

The 1969 Pacification and Development plan took careful notice of the refugee problem, stressing that the number of refugees be reduced to less than one million by resettling or returning 300,000 people to their native villages. In discussing efforts to revive the rural economy, rice production was to be encouraged, roads were to be repaired, low interest loans were to be made, farming equipment was to be available, and all unnecessary permits, taxes, and checkpoints were to be eliminated. Although committed to, but not mentioned, land reform would have to await the decision of the government as to the exact pattern a program should take.

Responsibility for achieving the eight goals was assigned to various government ministries and to military corps, provinces, and districts. Officials concerned were to draft pacification and development plans, based on the national plan, for their areas of responsibility, and to coordinate their activities with each other and with local corps and province officials.

With the 1969 pacification program well underway, the South Vietnamese Prime Minister unexpectedly announced to the 23 May meeting of the Central Pacification and Development Council that the program would be advanced to meet the 1969 goals by the end of October. This new program, termed the 1969 Accelerated Pacification Campaign, contained two objectives: the fulfillment or over-fulfillment of the original eight goals set for the 1969 campaign by 31 October, and the achievement of fully secure status (HES rating of A or B) for 50 percent of the hamlet population. Of the eight goals, only three were changed. On the subject of rendering the infrastructure ineffective, the Prime Minister proposed sentencing 5,000 VCI during the period in order to effectively remove them from the war. Acknowledging that the goal of resettling refugees could not be met, he suggested that every effort should be made to resettle as many as possible. The only goal prescribed under the objective of stimulating the rural economy related to land reform, whereby the government would dispose of excess land and initiate the purchase of additional land for distribution to farmers under the "Land to the Tiller" Act. As with the comprehensive plan, the Accelerated Pacification Campaign required the support and coordination of all appropriate agencies during the four-month program.

Pacification Planning in I Corps

In I Corps Tactical Zone, as elsewhere in South Vietnam, the 1968 Pacification and Accelerated Pacification Campaigns had achieved considerable success. Of the nearly 3 million civilians living in the five provinces, 2,200,000 people or 73.7 percent were considered to be residing in secure hamlets, with 85.7 percent under government sovereignty. The People's Self Defense Force had enrolled 225,000 members; however, the training program could indoctrinate but 98,000, with weapons available for only 30,000, far below the goal of training 128,000 and arming 48,000. Over 2,000 members of the Viet Cong Infrastructure had been arrested or killed, and almost 2,800 Hoi Chanh rallied to the government. With over 690,000 refugees comprising 25 percent of the population, I Corps had approximately 55 percent of the refugees in all of South Vietnam. Although strides were made to resettle or return as many as possible to their native villages, this area posed a grave challenge for the coming year.

Corps- and province-level pacification and development plans for the year included efforts to achieve the national goal of bringing security to 90 percent of the population, eliminating 2,600 infrastructure members, and rallying 2,500, later raised to 3,600, enemy troops. Plans also called for the substantial enlargement of the People's Self-Defense Force from 225,000 to 320,000, of which 256,000 would be trained and 64,000 would be armed, if training cadre and weapons were available in adequate numbers. Of the 509 villages in I Corps, 187 had elected councils during 1967, 194 had nonelected committees, and 128 were to elect governing bodies during the year. Thus, by the end of 1969, all Corps villages were expected to have governing bodies, 62 percent of which would be popularly elected. Although planners did not include specific numerical goals for refugee resettlement and economic development, much activity was promised in both fields.

The pacification effort in I Corps was organized to conform with the standard CORDS structure. Control of the regional CORDS effort rested with III MAF, with overall guidance administered through the Joint Staff, later renamed the Program Coordination Staff, headed by a civilian deputy for CORDS. As deputy, Mr. Charles T. Cross, replaced in May by Mr. Alexander Firfer, held Foreign Service rank equivalent to that of a major general and directed the efforts of close to 1,000 military and civilian personnel drawn from the four Armed Services, Department of Defense, Agency for International Development (AID), U.S. Information Agency (USIA), the Central Intelligence Agency, and other federal agencies. The staff controlled divisions responsible for each element of the pacification program: Government Development, Economic Development, Agriculture, Phoenix/Phung Hoang, Public Health, Refugees, Revolutionary Development, Regional Forces and Popular Forces, and Chieu Hoi.[2]

Under the control of the Deputy for CORDS were the five U.S. Army province senior advisors, each with a staff similar to that at the corps-level. The senior advisors worked closely with the province chiefs, who directed all aspects of civil government as well as commanded the territorial forces within the province. Under the five province advisors were the district senior advisors who worked directly with the local district chiefs, who in turn were responsible to the province chiefs.

Marine Corps representation on the CORDS staff during 1969 was relatively small in comparison to the size of its forces in I Corps. The highest-ranking Marine with CORDS was Colonel George C. Knapp, replaced in April by Colonel Howard A. Westphall, who served as chief of staff to the Deputy for CORDS and a member of the joint staff. In addition to Colonel Knapp, four other Marine officers held corps-level staff billets. With the redeployment of the 3d Marine Division, five additional officers, who had time to serve in-country, were added as advisors to the Revolutionary Development Cadre. Below corps-level, Marines had very little representation at the important province and district senior advisory levels.[3]

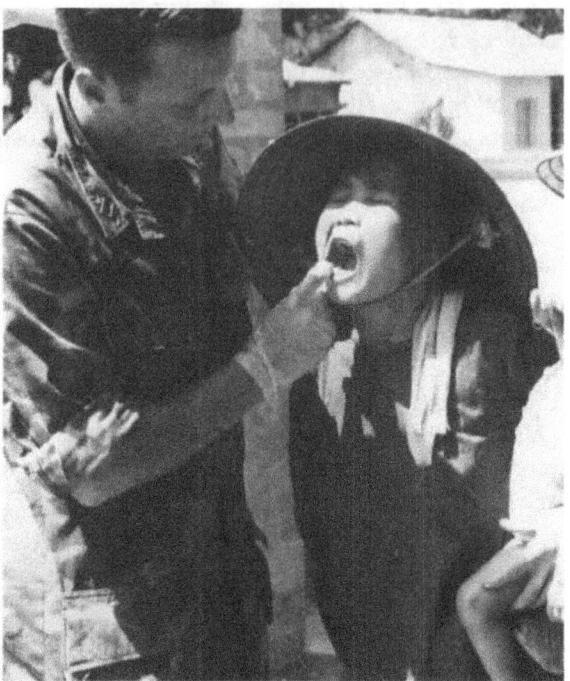

Department of Defense Photo (USMC) A371966
A Vietnamese woman has her teeth checked by Lt David W. Syrek, USN, a dentist with the 1st Dental Company, during a visit to her village as part of the 1st Marine Division Dental Civic Action Program.

III MAF and its subordinate military units maintained contact with CORDS and the provincial and district governments primarily through the G-5 or S-5 (Civic Affairs/Civic Action) staff sections, added to the headquarters staff in 1965. Responsible for pacification, psychological operations, and civic affairs, the G-5 and S-5 officers at corps-, division-, wing-, regiment-, and battalion-level attempted to fit military civic action into overall pacification planning, in addition to coordinating Marine operations in populated areas with those of local security forces and settling disputes and damage claims by local citizens against Marines. Both III MAF and the 1st Marine Division had a number of civic affairs officers during the year. At III MAF, Colonel Westphall headed the G-5 office until assuming the position of chief of staff at CORDS in April; Colonel Gilbert R. Hershey served until July; Colonel Theodore E. Metzger until September; and Colonel Clifford J. Peabody until September 1970. The 1st Marine Division G-5, Colonel Harry F. Painter, held the post until August when he was replaced by Colonel William J. Zaro and then by Lieutenant Colonel Vincent A. Albers, Jr. Colonel William E. Kerrigan headed the 3d Marine Division's G-5 section until the division departed South Vietnam in November.[4]

In addition to III MAF, ARVN, and Korean combat forces, a wide range of military and civilian agencies were involved in the pacification effort throughout I Corps. Provincial and district governments were active and relatively successful. At the beginning of the year there were about 49,800 men of the Regional and Popular Forces, organized into companies and separate platoons. Although improving in military effectiveness, they tended to be tied to static defensive positions and commanded by relatively inexperienced leaders. The People's Self-Defense Force boasted over 98,000 trained and 30,000 armed members. The corps' 11,000-man National Police Field Force and National Police, previously concentrated in the larger villages and hamlets, were beginning to move into the countryside where they relieved territorial forces of the task of maintaining public order.

Besides the police, the People's Self-Defense Forces, and territorial troops, groups of Revolutionary Development Cadre assisted the pacification effort at the hamlet-level. Organized into teams of approximately 30, recruited and trained by the central government, cadre teams worked with the local populace in organizing themselves for defense and assisting in political, economic, and social self-help programs. In order to spread the government's message throughout the corps tactical zone, Armed Propaganda Companies were kept in the field to encourage enemy desertions.

Despite this variety of organizations, the population of I Corps at the beginning of 1969 was far from secure. Of its over 2.9 million people, about 2 million resided in areas considered secure, while another 45,000 lived in areas considered contested, and the rest under Viet Cong domination. Thus, about 74 percent of the population were considered under government control. Social and economic improvement efforts left much to be desired as did proposed solutions to the resettlement of the estimated 690,000 refugees. Nevertheless, Marines throughout 1969 continued to work to strengthen and expand upon past pacification achievements.

Line Unit Pacification

"Without security your whole 1969 Pacification Campaign is down the drain," noted Colonel George C. Knapp.[5] The primary mission of Marine rifle companies and battalions during 1969 was to attack enemy military units with the aim of improving population security. Whether searching jungle-covered mountain valleys or working with Vietnamese forces in cordoning and searching villages, protecting rice harvests, or furnishing protection for government elections, the ultimate goal of Marine infantry operations was to ensure the security of the population so that normal social, economic, and political activity could be restored and allowed to flourish.

While multi-battalion attacks took place, cordon and search operations of varying sizes increased in frequency. From a single raid on a hamlet by a platoon in search of a Viet Cong Infrastructure member to a week-long search of a village complex, the tactic proved increasingly productive as the year progressed. In the larger cordons and searches, several Marine companies or battalions, working with ARVN troops, Regional and Popular Force units, the Vietnamese National Police, and allied intelligence and counterintelligence teams would move into an area, establish blocking positions, allowing no movement in or out. Vietnamese troops, aided by Marines, would then collect all the civilians at a Combined Holding and Interrogation Center (CHIC) where they would be questioned and their identities checked against lists of known or suspected Viet Cong. Searches, meanwhile, would be conducted for hidden Viet Cong and each house would be examined for concealed arms, food, and equipment.

While the searches took place, Vietnamese and Americans provided the assembled villagers with a place to sleep, food, and entertainment, which consisted of concerts, and government-oriented motion pictures, plays, and skits. Whenever possible, Marines sent in medical and dental teams to treat minor illnesses or injuries and provide instruction and advice on health. By means of these activities, the allies hoped not only to win the allegiance of the villagers, but also to increase their support of the war effort and government-sponsored pacification programs.

Although successful in weeding out the infrastructure, by the end of the year, cordon and search operations were doomed. By their very nature, these operations produced refugees. "Call them what you want," noted Major John J. Guenther, III MAF's counterintelligence officer, "people are taken out of their homes and put into a CHIC. As far as the CORDS organization is concerned, they are in the refugee category. And the word from Saigon, both U.S. and GVN, is don't generate any more refugees."[6]

During the year, Marines, aided by territorial forces, continued their effort, termed "Golden Fleece," aimed at protecting the twice-yearly rice harvest from being seized. Before the April-May and September-October harvest periods, each Marine regiment launched attacks into known enemy base and cache areas and placed patrols along infiltration routes into the rice-growing areas. During the harvest, the number of patrols and ambushes around rice paddies was likewise increased. Following the harvest, Marines assisted in guarding and transporting the rice to central storage facilities.

In March, elections were held for 128 village council and 717 hamlet chief positions throughout I Corps. Held on the four consecutive Sundays of the month, Marines cooperated with provincial and district authorities in protecting the polling places and voters from Viet Cong terrorism. While not actually guarding the polls, the Marines were deployed in the countryside to block likely enemy avenues of approach and to deny the enemy access to known mortar and rocket launching sites. Rapid reaction forces were maintained to reinforce hamlets or villages under attack. Marines were instructed to avoid populated areas unless they were under enemy attack and refrain from any activity that might be taken as an American attempt to influence the elections.

Behind the screen provided by Marine and territorial forces, the March elections were completed and were unmarred by major enemy interference. By the 23d, the last polling day, 126 village and 713 hamlet elections had been conducted, with more than 85 percent of the eligible voters participating. Fall elections for representatives to the National Assembly also experienced little enemy interference.

In addition to ferreting out the Viet Cong in cordon and search operations, securing the rice harvests, and protecting local elections, Marine combat units assisted in resettlement. Go Noi Island, a previously fertile agricultural area, inhabited by nearly 27,000 Vietnamese before the war, by 1969 was a tunneled, cave-infested Viet Cong haven. Driven out by the Viet

MajGen Raymond G. Davis, center, and Dr. Tran Lu Y, left, South Vietnamese Minister for Health, Social Welfare, and Relief, lay the cornerstone for the 120-bed, 10-building 3d Marine Division Memorial Children's Hospital complex at Quang Tri on 9 April.

Department of Defense Photo (USMC) A800546

Cong, floods, and numerous allied sweeps, most of the island's residents had joined the growing refugee population of Quang Nam Province. During Operation Pipestone Canyon, conducted between May and November, the 1st Marine Division, assisted by elements of the 51st ARVN Regiment and 2d Korean Marine Brigade, swept the island again of its NVA and VC occupiers and cleared over 8,000 acres of underbrush and treelines, at the same time destroying the enemy's extensive network of tunnels and fortifications.[7]

During the operation, the division proposed a plan for resettling Go Noi Island once it had been cleared. The plan had obvious advantages. Not only would the repopulation of the area with pro-government civilians make future Communist infiltration more difficult, but the area could provide homes and livelihoods for thousands of refugees, ultimately contributing to the economic revival of Quang Nam Province. The appropriate corps and national agencies took interest, but it was not until the end of August 1970 that the first refugees were resettled in newly constructed villages. While this was the major effort during the latter half of the year, numerous other smaller resettlement projects were carried out with Marine assistance throughout both Quang Tri and Quang Nam Provinces.[8]

During 1969, III MAF continued to support and to benefit from the Kit Carson Scout Program. Initiated by Marines in 1966 with the hiring of six former Viet Cong guerrillas as combat scouts, the program proved to be such a success that MACV extended it to all U.S. commands in Vietnam. At the beginning of the year, III MAF employed 476 of the former enemy soldiers and by the end of the year the number had grown to 597, despite the redeployment of the 3d Marine Division.

Following extensive screening, training, and indoctrination, the scouts were placed with Marine units and given a number of tasks. Scouts guided Marine patrols, participated in propaganda broadcasts, led Marines to supply and equipment caches, pointed out mines and boobytraps, and assisted in the identification of members of the Viet Cong Infrastructure.[9] In addition, many conducted training for Marine infantrymen in the enemy's use of surprise firing devices and sapper tactics. During the year, Kit Carson Scouts attached to Marine units conducted over 13,700 patrols and were credited with killing 191 enemy, apprehending 539 prisoners, and capturing 195 weapons, in addition to detecting 518 explosive devices and 143 caves, tunnels, and caches.

Civic Action

When Marines first landed in I Corps Tactical Zone in March 1965, they spontaneously undertook to assist the people among whom they were fighting by providing food, relief supplies, and medical care. Acting from a variety of motives, they not only hoped to win the friendship of the Vietnamese who in turn would provide information about the Viet Cong, but generate popular support for their own activities and those of the South Vietnamese Government. As pacification programs were developed, civic action activities contributed to them by promoting economic and social improvement, thus assisting "the government of the Republic of Vietnam in stabilizing the political situation and building respect and loyalty of the people for the legally constituted authority."[10]

The III MAF Civic Action Program by 1969 had grown from initial spontaneous acts of charity into a large-scale effort, coordinated by G-5 and S-5 staffs and integrated with the government's pacification and development plans. The program emphasized the requirement that the people, with Marine assistance, help themselves. Villagers were to identify the need, whether it be a new school, well, bridge, or dispensary. Marines would then furnish the materials, tools, and equipment, drawn from their own resources, CORDS, or from private charities; the technical know-how; and some labor. Villagers in turn would supply most of the labor and additional construction material if available. However, Marines often found themselves more heavily committed to projects than was necessary, often to the detriment of South Vietnamese efforts to assist.

In addition to community-sponsored projects, III MAF units provided individual assistance to I Corps' inhabitants with special emphasis on the large refugee population. During 1969, through the Medical Civic Action Program (MEDCAP) and Dental Civic Action Program (DENTCAP), units, in coordination with province and district medical officials, furnished over one million medical and 35,000 dental treatments and administered 100,000 immunizations. Through Project Handclasp, they distributed large amounts of food, clothing, and other essential commodities. Also, monies made available through the Marine Corps Reserve Civic Action Fund were used to purchase school and medical kits, rice, soap, and clothing through the relief agency CARE, and to support the General Walt Scholarship Fund which helped to finance the secondary and college education of selected

Vietnamese youth. Additional funds made available through a variety of other relief agencies purchased fertilizers, seeds, farm machinery, and improved strains of vegetables and livestock, enriching the economy at the village and hamlet level.[11]

The most ambitious project begun in 1969 was the 3d Marine Division Memorial Children's Hospital, built in Quang Tri City and dedicated to the memory of Marines and sailors who had lost their lives in Vietnam. The cornerstone of the 120-bed, 10-building complex was laid on 9 April and by the end of the year over $135,000 of the projected cost of $471,000 in materials had been collected. Originally, construction was to be accomplished by the 3d Engineer Battalion and the 128th Naval Mobile Construction Battalion, with Vietnamese assistance. But with redeployment of the 3d Marine Division before the hospital could be completed, remaining U.S. Army forces in Quang Tri Province assumed responsibility.

At the time construction of the permanent hospital began, a temporary facility at Dong Ha Combat Base was in operation. The 3d Medical Battalion furnished the physical plant, and, along with 19 Vietnamese nurses and 22 other civilians, undertook the task of providing the temporary hospital's medical support. By December, the complex had treated a total of 20,600 outpatients, with referrals coming from as far north as the Demilitarized Zone and as far south as Hue. When the 3d Marine Division redeployed the facility was moved to Quang Tri Combat Base and the Army's 18th Surgical Hospital, 67th Medical Group assumed the task of providing medical support.[12]

Under the administrative and operational control of Force Logistic Command, the Hoa Khanh Children's Hospital near Da Nang had grown from a small roadside dispensary into a fully equipped 120-bed pediatric facility by 1969. Built with thousands of hours of donated Marine labor and sustained by over $300,000 in annual contributions by servicemen and concerned groups and individuals in the United States, the hospital treated hundreds of children, who would have otherwise died or become permanently incapacitated from a wide variety of the simplest of childhood accidents and illnesses.[13]

While assisting in major civic action projects, individual Marines and their units continued to help Vietnamese who lived within their TAORs or near their camps and bases. Marines participated in numerous minor construction projects and provided supplies and money for local schools, religious institutions, and refugee centers. Typical of the efforts were those of Force Logistic Support Group-Bravo at Dong Ha, which in January began collecting and hauling scrap lumber and cement declared unusable for the rebuilding of approximately 200 homes and temples destroyed the year before. By May, 175 homes and two temples had been completely repaired. Marines not only shared excess material, but also their time. Three times a week, for example, members of Headquarters Battery, 12th Marines conducted English classes at the Buddhist High School, Semi-Public High School, and District Headquarters High School at Dong Ha.[14]

The effectiveness of the Marine civic action program, however, was questionable. The immediate effects were obvious: medical treatment cured illness and healed wounds; a new well provided water where there was none before; and discarded lumber built houses and schools. But the question of whether the program won support for the South Vietnamese Government and greater acceptance for the Marines among the local populace remained unanswered.

The Grass-Roots Campaign

The primary pacification mission of Marine combat units was to provide security for the local population. Much of their activity was directly or indirectly involved in keeping enemy military units from cities, villages, and hamlets, and assisting the government in eradicating the Viet Cong Infrastructure. Those Marines involved in the Combined Action Program had security at the village- and hamlet-level and the supression of local guerrillas as their exclusive mission.

The Combined Action Program originated with the Marines in 1965 when III MAF, in attempting to secure the heavily populated area around the Hue-Phu Bai Airfield, discovered a "ready-made ally" in the surrounding hamlets—the part-time soldiers of the Popular Forces, the lowest echelon of the Vietnamese Armed Forces. Minimally trained, armed, and paid, and commanded at the district-level, they could do little towards the basic mission of providing hamlet- and village-level security. From the beginning, Marines on patrol had taken members of the Popular Forces along as guides and interpreters, but with proper support and training, it was thought they could relieve regular Marines of the local defensive mission and assist in weeding out the enemy.[15] From this ad hoc effort in 1965, the Combined Action Program was to grow from seven platoons in January 1966, to 57 a year later, and to over 100 platoons deployed throughout I Corps in late 1968.

PACIFICATION

Abel Papers, Marine Corps Historical Center
Col Edward F. Danowitz, left, head of the Combined Action Program, interviews a volunteer. All CAP members were volunteers, but not all were accepted into the program.

To work with the Popular Forces, III MAF created the combined action platoon (CAP), consisting of a 15-man Marine rifle squad composed of a squad leader, M79 grenadier, Navy corpsman, and three fire teams of four men each. Together with a Popular Force platoon of approximately 35 men, the combined unit defended one village or group of hamlets. Each element of the team complemented the other. Marines provided advice, training, encouragement, and access to American medical evacuation and fire support. The Popular Forces, being local residents, provided knowledge of the area, rapport with the people, information about the enemy, and "the motivation that was inherent in the defense of one's home."[16]

Unlike conventional American and ARVN combat forces which swept through a village and then moved on, the Combined Action Platoons remained to protect the villagers from Viet Cong terrorism. As the Marines increasingly won the confidence of the people with whom they lived and worked, the platoons not only became a major source of allied intelligence, but a screen behind which the government could reestablish its authority and undertake social and economic improvements. As the platoons' successes grew so did the number of platoons, and by 1969 the program had been extended to all five provinces within I Corps. To administer and coordinate the activities of the platoons, III MAF subsequently created combined action companies and then combined action groups (CAGs).

At the beginning of 1969, four combined action groups were in operation: the 1st, under Lieutenant Colonel Earl R. Hunter, headquartered at Chu Lai, controlled 4 companies and 26 platoons scattered throughout Quang Tin and Quang Ngai Provinces; the 2d, the largest, was composed of 8 companies and 36 platoons under Lieutenant Colonel Edward L. Lewis, Jr., and worked out of Hoi An in Quang Nam Province; the 3d, under Lieutenant Colonel Robert D. Whitesell, controlled 5 companies and 31 platoons in Thua Thien Province; and the 4th, commanded by Lieutenant Colonel John E. Greenwood, was composed of 3 companies and 18 platoons operating in Quang Tri Province. Attached to each group was a mobile training team which assisted in the training of the Popular Force Platoons. The teams' function was taken over during the year by the Army's Mobile Advisory

Teams.[17] Over 1,600 Marines and 128 Navy corpsmen composed the four Combined Action Groups; these Americans worked with about 3,100 Popular Force soldiers. By year's end, the program achieved its authorized strength of 20 companies and 114 platoons.

III MAF exercised control of the four groups through the Assistant Chief of Staff, Combined Action Program, Colonel Edward F. Danowitz and his successors, Colonel Charles R. Burroughs and Colonel Theodore E. Metzger. Lieutenant General Nickerson, in consultation with General Lam, the I Corps commander, passed on every change in deployment of a Marine squad assigned to the program. To improve coordination and administration of the growing program, Nickerson late in 1969 recommended the establishment of a Combined Action Force (CAF), with its own headquarters under III MAF, as the groups, General Nickerson noted, were essentially "battalions."[18] The proposal was approved and instituted in early January 1970.

In the field, the combined action platoons operated under a complex chain of command. The Marines assigned to squads were commanded by the assistant chief of staff for the program through the groups and companies, while the Popular Forces were responsible, in theory, to their village chief, but in practice took orders from their district chief and through him from the province chief and corps commander. Generally, each combined action group headquarters was collocated at the province headquarters and provided administrative support for the companies under it, in addition to training both Marines and Popular Forces and assigning areas of operation in consultation with province chiefs and regular unit commanders. Combined action company headquarters, located with district headquarters, maneuvered the platoons in consultation with the district chief and his U.S. Army advisor, arranged for artillery and air support, evacuation of casualties, and reinforcement for platoons under its control.

The area of operation assigned to each platoon, normally a single village or group of hamlets, was mutually agreed to by the province chief, the group commander, and the commander of the regular infantry battalion operating in the area. The village or hamlets, once assigned to the platoon, became the exclusive territory of that platoon and non-CAP units were prohibited from entering the area without the permission of the district chief and combined action company commander. Within each platoon's area, the Marine squad leader and the Popular Force sergeant, neither of whom had command over the other, directed the daily operations of the platoon by consultation and agreement. The effectiveness of this system of dual command depended entirely upon the trust and respect which existed between the Marine and Popular Force leader.

Initially, Marines who joined the Combined Action Program were volunteers obtained from the two divisions. This proved to be a problem as Colonel Charles R. Burroughs noted: "we would get the man after maybe six months in-country. First thing would be R&R, then we would send him to school. We lost about a month, which left five months with the CAPs."[19] By 1969, a majority of combined action Marines were obtained directly from the United States, the remaining volunteers, those who requested transfer to the CAPs, came from other III MAF Marine units. Once personally screened to ensure adaptability to the program, the selected Marines attended the two-week Combined Action Program School at Da Nang where they received refresher training in basic infantry weapons, small unit tactics, first aid, map and compass reading, the basic techniques for requesting and controlling artillery, air strikes, and medical evacuation flights, and language. Upon graduation, the students were given a language examination and those who exhibited an aptitude for language returned to Da Nang after two to four months in the field with a platoon to receive intensive Vietnamese language instruction at the program's language school. Most training, however, was of the "on-the-job" variety: "the CAP Marine conceives of himself as a combat Marine, and therefore his classroom is the 'bush' where the VC provide the necessary training aids."[20]

Throughout 1969, the CAPs continued to perform the six basic missions assigned them: destroy the Viet Cong hamlet-village infrastructure; provide public security and help maintain law and order; protect the local governing structure; guard facilities and important lines of communications within the village and hamlet; organize local intelligence nets; and participate in civic action and psychological operations against the Viet Cong. The Marine element of the CAP had additional missions assigned: conduct training in general military subjects and leadership for Popular Forces assigned to the platoon; motivate, instill pride, patriotism, and aggressiveness in the Popular Force soldier; conduct combined day and night patrols and ambushes; conduct combined operations with other allied forces; and ensure that information

PACIFICATION

gathered was made available to nearby allied forces. Marines were to prepare the Popular Force element to assume effectively the platoon's mission upon the Marine squad's relocation to a new village where government authority was contested and where the local PF were ineffective in dealing with the enemy. "Thus, CAP Marines are engaged in a process of perpetually working themselves out of a job, a procedure which exemplifies the concept of Vietnamization."[21]

Combined action platoons accomplished their security mission by continually deploying day and night patrols and setting ambushes in and around their assigned villages. When not on patrol, the CAPs, initially, tended to be tied to fortified compounds, one of which Corporal Michael E. Gordy, platoon leader with the 4th CAG, described:

> When we first moved out here, we cleared all the trees and started laying wire. The wire around here consists of a continuous belt, this belt consists of one row of triple-strength concertina, then one row of tangle-foot, then another row of triple-strength concertina, another row of tangle-foot, another row of triple-strength concertina, another row of tangle-foot, and then a double-apron fence, and that is all the way around this compound. Now interlaced in all this wire are about 150 tripflares and there are about 40 claymores around this position . . . . We have an 81 mortar here. We have a 60 mortar. We have one M60 machine gun. In the compound at all times there is at least one M79, and of course the Marines and PFs are all equipped with M16s . . . . We are not really sweating getting overrun that much because we feel that we have a pretty tight compound here and we think our defenses are such that we could hold off probably anything up to a company until we could get some tanks here.[22]

These compounds, Marines found, not only offered the enemy lucrative targets, but weakened the security screen around the village by tying many of the platoons down to defending a fixed position.

By mid-1969, a majority of the platoons had abandoned the defensive role of the past and adopted the "Mobile CAP" concept of operations. Establishing no position more permanent than a command post at a specific location during any 12-hour period, platoons were to patrol and ambush continually among their assigned villages and hamlets without using the same routes, trails, or setting a pattern of operations. All villages and hamlets were to be checked at least once every 24 hours.[23] By doing so, they would make it impossible for the Viet Cong to feel safe anywhere in or near the protected hamlets. This tactic not only allowed the platoons to screen a larger area more effec-

Capt John D. Niotis, Commanding Officer of Combined Action Company 2-5, discusses the placement of platoons in Hoa Vang District with District Chief, Maj Mai Xuan Hau.

Department of Defense Photo (USMC) A192928

tively with the same number of men, but it kept the enemy uncertain as to the platoons' whereabouts and thus less likely to enter the protected hamlets.[24]

While security patrols and ambushes occupied a majority of their time, CAP units also participated in other types of operations and activities. They often worked with U.S., ARVN, and territorial forces in cordon and searches or helped in offensive sweeps of the villages and hamlets under their care. During Operation Bold Mariner, for example, platoons of the 1st CAG assisted Army and Marine units in sweeping the enemy-infested Batangan Peninsula. In addition to training Popular Forces so as to promote greater self-sufficiency, combined action units also provided allied forces with a substantial amount of local intelligence on such subjects as the location of heavily-used enemy trails, identity of Viet Cong Infrastructure members, and the sites of emplaced mines and boobytraps.

Away from combat and training, CAP Marines spent much of their time helping the villagers improve their daily lives. The attached Navy corpsmen held periodic sick calls where the people gathered for the treatment of minor injuries and illnesses. The corpsmen also taught personal hygiene and trained volunteers in basic first aid for service in the local dispensary. CAP riflemen distributed food, clothing, building materials, and school supplies, as well as assisted the villagers in self-help projects, as one Marine sergeant and CAP squad leader noted:

> They already had the dispensary set up, we just supplied them with necessary items. We built them two new bridges. The old bridges were rotted. The two good ones they had, someone blew them up.... So we built them new bridges so they could bring their buffalo carts across, bring their goods to the market for sale. We built, I don't know how many, buffalo pens. We got bags of cement for them, and everything, lumber, and for the church, we got them all new desks for the classrooms.[25]

Throughout 1969, the Combined Action Program continued to achieve success in its primary mission of improving local security, but the program did experience a number of problems. Disputes often arose between regular infantry units and the platoons over the requirement that line units obtain both CAP and district approval before entering the CAP area of operations. In an effort to ameliorate the situation, both formal and informal arrangements were made among the local commanders to ensure greater cooperation and coordination. At the platoon-level, difficulties remained. Of major concern was the reluctance on the part of the Popular Forces to adopt the mobile concept, preferring instead to remain in compounds or other fixed installations. This lack of mobility was a direct consequence of village pressure to keep Popular Forces as close to the village as possible in order to afford maximum personal security for the village and its officials.

Although disagreements sometimes arose that brought Marines and Popular Forces close to blows, working and social relationships were for the most part harmonious, as one platoon leader reported:

> Whatever we ate, we let them eat. Like if we got a chow supply, they'd eat right along with us. We never separated them like a lot of the CAPs I've seen. They'd tell the Foxtrots [PFs], time for chow and they'd take off for the ville . . . and eat. Well, we all ate together here, or if we wanted to go in the ville some place, one of the mama-sans, we had several of them, we had three of them we called mother, just like American mothers, and they cooked us chow and stuff . . . and we'd all eat together and play games . . . . Just a close relationship, working with them and treating them like you're treated and it helped them understand, well he's treating us just like them, there's no difference.[26]

In spite of problems, Marines and others alike, remained convinced of the success of the Combined Action Program. Among the program's ardent supporters was Mr. Alexander Firfer, I Corps Deputy for CORDS, who noted:

> Unless you had the Vietnamese governing themselves, feeling responsible for what is going on, and feeling they really had a share in decisions, instead of being told by the province chief or by the zone commander what they were going to do, it was obvious you could not get the support of the people and without the support of the people you could not beat the enemy. Within this kind of context, the CAPs played a very important role. For one thing, they were stationed out there with the people, near their villages or in their villages, helping defend those villages. Thus, in addition to the local Vietnamese military, in whom perhaps the villagers did not have great confidence, you had a group of U.S. soldiers, Marines, whom the villagers trusted and depended on. And the Marines were trained in such a way that they did more than just participate in village defense, they made friends with the people and sought ways to help them, in what I suppose you would call a "civic action way." This involved health, this involved just plain loving care, this involved small technical assistance, this involved the provision of certain commodities that the village didn't have, and this involved an organization which allowed them to call up the headquarters and say, "look my village needs so and so, please get it for me." Now with that kind of an interrelationship, the CAPs were a way of stimulating the Vietnamese hamlet residents to do something about their own defense.[27]

"You are" he continued, "fish in the sea and the sea is the population. . . . If you want the people with

Cpl Walter Rebacz and his scout dog, King, lead a CAP patrol composed of Marines and local Popular Forces out from a protected village three kilometers south of Tam Ky.

you, you had better be in touch with the people and find some way to reflect their needs, their concerns, and some how get their involvement . . . . This was the approach taken by the Marines."[28]

Operationally, 1969 was an active year for the program. Aided by the increase in size and a mobile posture, combined action platoons conducted in excess of 145,000 combat patrols and ambushes, 73 percent of which were conducted at night. Although these operations were nearly double the number executed the previous year, the overall enemy toll, 1,938 killed, 425 taken prisoner, and 932 weapons captured, was lower, reflecting the enemy's inability to penetrate, or desire to avoid, platoon-protected villages and hamlets.

Capitalizing on the success and effectiveness of the Combined Action Program, General Nickerson, in October, initiated the Infantry Company Intensive Pacification Program (ICIPP). Realizing that the Marines were about to be phased out, he felt that the concept of the combined action platoon should be continued, and thus he convinced the Army, which was to succeed the Marines in I Corps, to accept a similar program.[29] Employing the basic principles of the CAP, infantry companies, and eventually battalions, were to be assigned the primary mission of pacification; squads were to be combined with Regional or Popular Force platoons and deployed to target hamlets, selected by the province chief in close coordination with the local brigade or regimental commander. The ICIPP, however, differed from the Combined Action Program in two respects. Unlike CAP Marines, ICIPP Marines and Army infantrymen were not formally selected nor trained; they remained as members of a rifle company which had been given a special mission. In addition, the ICIPP companies remained under the operational control of its parent unit and were for the most part deployed within the regiment's or brigade's area of operations.

On 3 October, the Americal Division began ICIPP operations in Quang Ngai Province, deploying Company D, 5th Battalion, 46th Infantry in three contested Son Tinh District hamlets. Then, on 15 October, Company A, 1st Battalion, 52d Infantry was inserted into two Son Tinh hamlets, one contested and one under Viet Cong control. Initially, platoons rather than squads were deployed with encouraging results.

Participation by the 1st Marine Division began in late November with the deployment of squads from Company M, 1st Marines to three contested hamlets near Hill 55. Five additional hamlets were added in early December. Following its first complete month of ICIPP operations, the security efforts of Company M had raised the four VC-controlled and four contested hamlets to the status of five relatively secure and three contested. As the year ended, the 7th Marines selected nine hamlets for operations beginning in mid-January, and the 5th Marines started ICIPP training and initiated the selection of target hamlets in coordination with district and provincial officials.[30]

Results

Throughout South Vietnam, progress in pacification during 1969 was dramatic. Unhampered by a massive *Tet* Offensive, as in 1968, which temporarily sidetracked pacification efforts, the government made substantial gains in the reestablishment of governmental and economic structures as well as in the return of stable living conditions for both urban and rural inhabitants.

Under the three separate, but interrelated, country-wide pacification and development programs, I Corps made steady propress during 1969 in achieving most of these programs' goals. This success was largely attributable to the efforts of the government working hand-in-hand with III MAF to produce a comprehensive effort involving even the most remote communities and the lowest military echelons.

Although the overall population security posture of I Corps increased during the year from 69.3 percent to 93.6, exceeding the assigned 90 percent level, each province achieved varying degrees of security. With the shift of enemy interest in late 1968 from northern I Corps to the three southernmost provinces, Quang Tri and Thua Thien reached the highest levels. Thua Thien, the first province to indicate 100 percent of its population free from Viet Cong and NVA domination, reached this plateau at the end of June, with Quang Tri following suit three months later; however, about 9,000 persons in Thua Thien returned to Viet Cong control during December. Despite being subjected to increased enemy efforts to disrupt the various pacification programs, the three southern provinces made dramatic increases in population security. Although Quang Tin exhibited the largest increase, 57.2 to 86.7 percent, its year-end security-level rating remained the lowest of the provinces within the tactical zone. Quang Nam advanced from 62 to 92 percent, and Quang Ngai moved from 63 to 91 percent. Of a total population of 2,998,200 in I Corps, 2,805,900 inhabitants were considered secure at year-end.

The concerted drive to neutralize the Viet Cong Infrastruture was also successful. By the end of December, 5,363 members of the infrastructure, 82 percent of whom came from the three southern provinces, had been killed, captured, or had rallied, exceeding the set goal of 4,800 by more than 500. As a result of the heavy losses, NVA troops began to assume a more prominent role at the local level in an effort to create a stronger, viable organization. "This was considered by many," noted Colonel Theodore E. Metzger, Commanding Officer of the Combined Action Force, "to be an act of desperation. At the local level, it was a development productive of much resentment by the old time VC who had survived, but who were now being told what to do by aggressive, overbearing NVA regulars who were neither familiar with local problems nor with the terrain, the people, and the opposing forces."[31] Although the network had been weakened by neutralizations, the Viet Cong and NVA had replaced many of those lost during the year, leaving an estimated strength of some 19,000. The 1970 Pacification and Development Plan prescribed an even more ambitious campaign to ferret out and destroy this enemy faction.

The 1969 Chieu Hoi campaign was the highlight of the year, as an unprecedented 5,996 Hoi Chanh rallied to the government in I Corps, a dramatic increase over the 3,600 expected. Two distinct trends were reversed during the year. First, the two northernmost provinces yielded less than 10 percent of the year's total, whereas during the previous year, better than 50 percent had come from Quang Tri and Thua Thien. This reversal was caused primarily by the enemy's shift of emphasis from the northern to the southern provinces, where his soldiers and nonmilitary supporters, demoralized by personnel losses and lack of support, rallied in large numbers. The second reversal was seen in the type of defector, as more nonmilitary supporters than armed combatants switched sides, bringing with them fewer weapons when they surrendered

Although the goal of completely reestablishing popularly elected governments at the local level was not met during the year, 91 percent of I Corps' villages and 99 percent of its hamlets could boast of having elected representatives; the remainder were government-appointed officials. While the specific goal was not met, two important things did occur. First, 85 percent of the population voted, indicating the elections "meant for them something about local control, something about their involvement and their rights." Secondly, younger, more dynamic individuals replaced approximately one third of the older politicians. Thus, the elections saw participation, real campaigning, new faces, and new blood.[32] The goal of resettling and restoring to self-sufficiency all but 55,000 refugees by the end of the year, was likewise not met, although the refugee population was reduced from 619,000 to 169,000.

The effort to develop a local self-defense system showed dynamic growth in the number of citizens organized, trained, and armed during 1969. The People's Self-Defense Forces at the end of the year encompassed 548,190 members, 287,000 of whom were trained and 81,000 armed, fulfilling the stated goal in each category. Advances were also made in rejuvenating the rural economy, such as on Go Noi Island and in Leatherneck Square, but there were setbacks. Among them was the attempt to reclaim land around Phu Loc,

As part of the Infantry Company Intensive Pacification Program, a Marine instructs a member of the Popular Forces in the care and cleaning of the infantryman's M16 rifle.

Department of Defense Photo (USMC) A372497

south of Hue, and place it back into agricultural production. "There was a simple problem," the III MAF Deputy for CORDS noted, "there were land mines, there were bombs, and what was needed were some Rome Plows to just go over the field and try to explode or pull out any remaining explosives. Well, I never succeeded in convincing anyone to respond to what was proposed . . . . Putting the land back into production was giving the villagers a stake in the South Vietnamese Government."[33] In the area of psychological operations, III MAF, ARVN, and South Vietnamese Government agencies joined together in continuously providing the civilian population with information concerning government plans and policies, while degrading enemy morale through exploitation of his losses and inevitable defeat.

After five years of American involvement, the allies had erected a strong defensive screen, behind which pacification and development had taken root. Security operations had reduced Communist control of the villages and hamlets and with it the enemy's ability to draw popular support and disrupt nation-building efforts. The South Vietnamese at all levels had begun to establish elected governments and stable economies. Yet for the Marines, Army, and South Vietnamese in I Corps, much remained to be accomplished.

CHAPTER 17
Special Landing Force Operations

The Strategic Reserve — Organization and Operations — The Fleet's Contingency Force

The Strategic Reserve

The United States Seventh Fleet's amphibious arm, Amphibious Task Force 76, composed of the Amphibious Ready Group (ARG) and Special Landing Force (SLF), was established by the Commander in Chief, Pacific in July 1960 as a balanced mobile contingency force to meet strategic reserve requirements throughout the Western Pacific and Indian Ocean. From the beginning of the major United States comitment in Vietnam, the fleet's Amphibious Ready Group and its embarked Special Landing Force either augmented forces already ashore or conducted amphibious raids along the entire coast of South Vietnam, fronting the South China Sea. Since 1967, when a second force was established, their deployments, as arranged through mutual coordination between the Commander, Seventh Fleet and Commander, U.S. Military Assistance Command, Vietnam, and as made available by CinCPac through Commander in Chief, Pacific Fleet, provided for separate and alternating employments of the two forces. However, due to the heightened level of conflict in South Vietnam, notably in I Corps Tactical Zone beginning in the summer of 1967, III MAF often employed the two SLFs concurrently for operations within the zone.

By mid-1968, the Special Landing Forces were being committed ashore more often and stayed longer than originally envisioned, resulting not only in a deterioration of the fleet's strategic reserve capability, but in the Marine Corps' amphibious character in the region. Both Task Group 79 and the 9th Marine Amphibious Brigade, which directly controlled the two Marine landing forces, were "under constant and conflicting pressures concerning the employment of its combat assets," according to brigade Chief of Staff, Colonel John Lowman, Jr., "each completely justifiable from the viewpoint of the commander involved." The commonly-held view at III MAF was that "any combat Marine not ashore and fighting was not being properly utilized. Hence, the periods of OpCon ashore grew longer and longer." With the SLFs constantly ashore, the Seventh Fleet's amphibious reserve was thus unavailable to meet a sudden crisis elsewhere, and therefore "it was hard for the Navy to justify the expense of keeping under-utilized amphibious shipping hanging off the Vietnamese coast." Charged with the responsibility for operations throughout South Vietnam, constant demands were made on MACV for the use of the SLFs in areas other than I Corps, especially in the coastal region south of Saigon. "This viewpoint," noted Colonel Lowman, "had some measure of support from Seventh Fleet staff and none at all from III MAF. In fact, the easiest way to get thrown out of the III MAF compound was to even mention the subject."[1]

"The operations of the SLFs, for a long while, we were quite perturbed about," noted Colonel Clyde W. Hunter, G-3, 9th Marine Amphibious Brigade, "primarily because we thought they were being misused; that the divisions were using the SLFs improperly, actually ginning up operations just to get them ashore and then tie them down to a TAOR, or into some kind of operation, that had no connection to their mission as an SLF."[2] Although shore demands on the two landing forces diminished somewhat following *Tet* and the allied response, both forces by the beginning of 1969 had not yet fully resumed their role as forces afloat, ready to respond to any contingency throughout the Pacific Command's area of responsibility.

Some critics, both in and out of South Vietnam, continued to express the opinion that amphibious operations were a waste of time and that the Special Landing Forces should be left ashore permanently. Others saw it differently. "This is the name of the game," observed one special landing force commander, "there should be more of it. Let's face it, we are amphibious in nature, and there are only two little small units in the Marine Corps today that are active in a truly amphibious role."[3] Frustrations were evident as another remarked:

> The tenor [of operations] seems to be to go through your amphibious assault phases and as soon as you get yourself established on the beach you are chopped OPCON to the unit commander ashore, which is a pretty frustrating business.... As an SLF commander, you are somewhat of a minister without portfolio; you spend most of your time in III MAF trying to get some targeting for yourself and trying to get your troops out on board ship for necessary training and rehab[ilitation]. You play the role, so-to-speak, to get

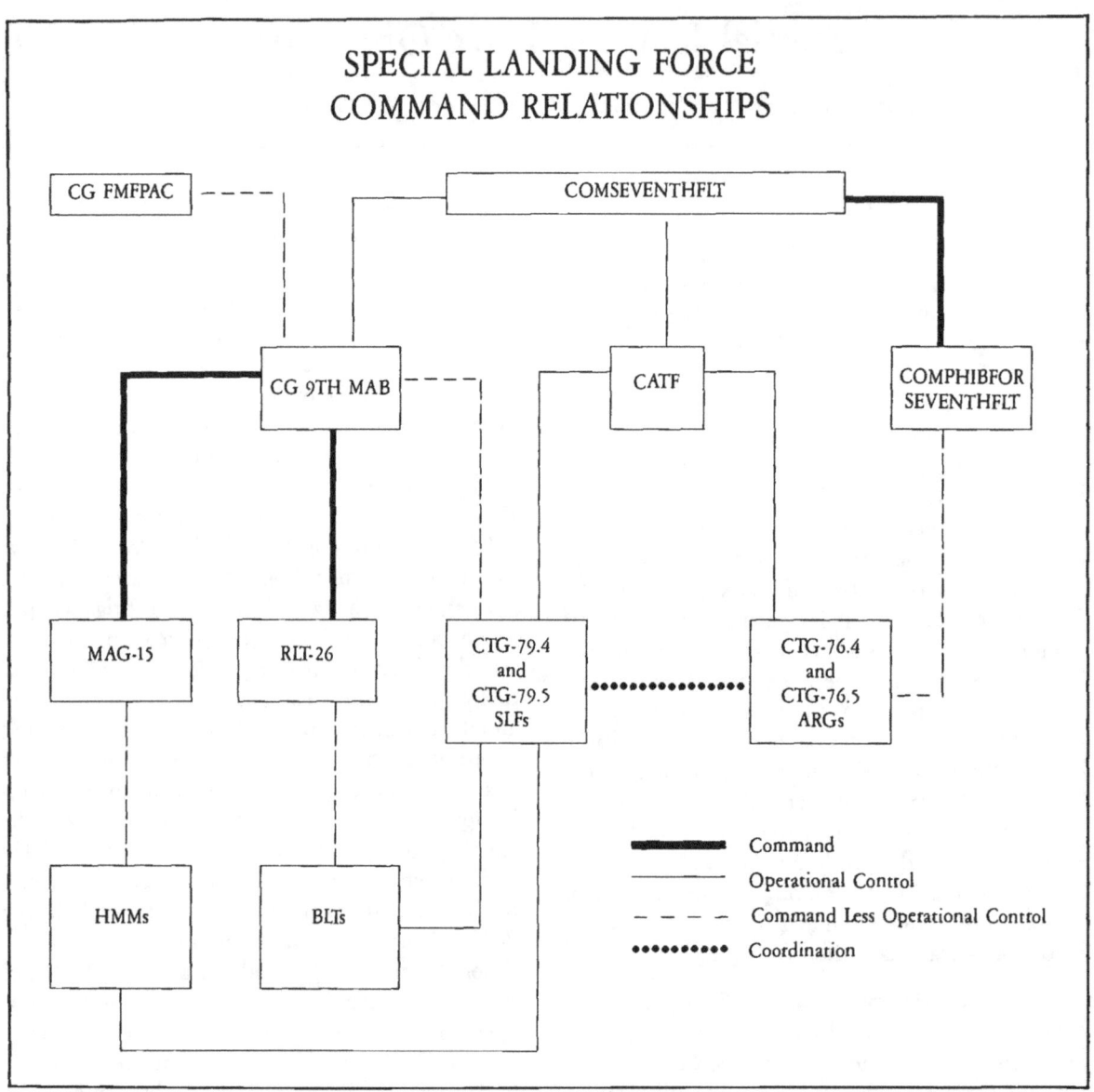

in the show yourself with your SLF, the entire SLF . . . . This SLF business is the last grasp we have on amphibious business . . . it has to be pushed. You have to target it properly and employ these BLTs in the amphibious role.[4]

The failure of some observers to realize that the United States had other commitments and responsibilities in the region, and that the two Marine landing forces could not be dedicated solely to the war in South Vietnam would be corrected in 1969.

Organization and Operations

A part of the Pacific Command reserve, the Special Landing Forces were "balanced, self-sustaining fighting units," each consisting of a Marine Battalion Landing Team and a Marine Medium Helicopter Squadron (HMM). The battalion landing team was task-organized and thus had no standard composition or size; it could vary in the number of personnel from a minimum of 1,060 to a maximum of 1,937. Typically, the team was composed of an infantry battalion with attached combat support units, ranging from artillery to reconnaissance and shore party detachments. The helicopter component was a twenty-four CH-34D, or CH-46A-equipped squadron. Also included were separate billets for the force commander and staff.

The two landing forces, Alpha and Bravo (Navy designated Task Groups 79.4 and 79.5) were under the command of the 9th Marine Amphibious Brigade, headquartered on Okinawa. While at sea, they were under the control of the Commander, Amphibious Task Force, Seventh Fleet. When in Vietnam they were

STRENGTH, ARMS, AND EQUIPMENT OF A TYPICAL SPECIAL LANDING FORCE

UNITS EMBARKED*	STRENGTH USMC OFF	ENL	USN OFF	ENL	EQUIPMENT
SLF Headquarters Detachment	10	46	0	0	68 M60 Machine Gun
					28 M20 3.5 Rocket Launcher
BLT 2/26					16 M2 Machine Gun
2d Bn, 26th Mar	37	1,160	3	61	12 M10 60mm Mortar
Mortar Battery, 1st Bn, 12th Mar	3	64	0	2	8 M20 81mm Mortar
Battery B, 1st Bn, 13th Mar	10	99	0	2	8 M40 106mm Recoilless Rifle
Platoon, Co A, 5th Amtrac Bn	1	37	0	0	6 M30 107mm Mortar
Platoon, Co A, 5th Antitank Bn	1	21	0	0	6 M101A 105 Howitzer
Platoon, Co A, 5th Tank Bn	1	28	0	0	5 M48 90mm Tank
Platoon, Co A, 5th Recon Bn	1	21	0	0	5 M50 Ontos
Platoon, Co A, 5th Engineer Bn	1	38	0	1	2 M2 Flame Thrower
Platoon, Co C, 5th Motor Transport Bn	1	31	0	0	
Platoon, Co A, 5th Shore Party Bn	1	45	0	1	36 M35 2½ Cargo Truck
Clear Platoon, Co D, 5th Medical Bn	0	5	3	20	10 LVTP-5
Det, Hq Bn, 5th MarDiv	1	8	0	0	1 LVTP-6
Det, Hq Co, 26th Mar	0	6	0	0	9 M422 1/4T Mite
Det, Communication Supt Co, 9th MAB	0	0	0	0	8 M274 1/2T Mule
Det, 15th Dental Co	0	0	1	1	5 M37 3/4T Cargo Truck
					2 M49 Tank Truck
HMM-362	55	205	1	3	2 M-54 Cargo Truck
					1 M38 1/2T Utility Truck
					1 M170 Ambulance
					(Aircraft: 24 UH-34D)
Totals	123	1,814	8	92	

*SLF Alpha, January 1969

under the operational control of III Marine Amphibious Force or its subordinate units. Prior to 1969, any reinforced infantry battalion within III MAF was liable for assignment to the Special Landing Force for a six-month tour, but under the brigade leadership of Brigadier General John E. Williams in late 1968, and with the concurrence of FMFPac and III MAF, Regimental Landing Team 26 (26th Marines, with appropriate 5th Marine Division supporting units) was reconstituted, and from it the two forces drew their battalion landing teams throughout most of 1969. Like the infantry component, any medium helicopter squadron of the 1st Marine Aircraft Wing could be assigned to the SLF, but as a result of General William's reorganization, two squadrons, HMM-164 and HMM-362, replaced in May by HMM-265, were permanently tasked to the 9th MAB for duty with the Marine landing force.[5]

When not ashore, the two SLFs were embarked on board ships of the Seventh Fleet's Amphibious Ready Groups, Alpha (Task Group 76.4) and Bravo (Task Group 76.5). Each fleet amphibious ready group consisted of an amphibious assault ship (LPH), dock landing ship (LSD), and a tank landing ship (LST). Additional ships were employed with the ARG as the situation dictated: the AP, a high-speed transport used to carry underwater demolition teams and Marine reconnaissance units, and either the amphibious transport dock (LPD), the attack transport ship (APA), or the attack cargo ship (AKA) — all employed in transporting additional supplies, troops, and landing craft.[6]

The year began with both Special Landing Forces, Alpha and Bravo, ashore. On 5 January, following the completion of Valiant Hunt, a search and clear operation begun in mid-December on Barrier Island, south of Hoi An, SLF Alpha (BLT 2/26 and HMM-362) under the command of Colonel John F. McMahon, Jr., was reembarked on board the *Okinawa* (LPH 3) and other ships of the ready group. Simultaneously, Colonel Robert R. Wilson's SLF Bravo, BLT 3/26 and HMM-164, which had replaced BLT 2/7 and HMM-165, boarded the *Tripoli* (LPH 10), *Ogden* (LPD 5), *Monticello* (LSD 35), and *Seminole* (AKA 104).

Within a week of terminating Valiant Hunt, both Special Landing Forces assembled off Quang Ngai Province in preparation for launching Operation Bold Mariner, slated to be the largest amphibious operation carried out since the Korean War. Under the command of Brigadier General Williams, in his dual role as Commanding General, 9th MAB and Commander, Task Group 79, the brigade-size Marine landing force was to join with elements of the Americal Division in an assault on the Batangan Peninsula, 18 kilometers south of Chu Lai, in an effort to destroy the enemy stronghold and reestablish South Vietnamese control.* Encompassing approximately 48 square kilometers of flat fertile lowlands and rolling hills, the peninsula harbored elements of the *38th Viet Cong Main Force Regiment*, *48th Viet Cong Local Force Battalion*, *P-31st Local Force Company*, and the *C-95th Sapper Company*. From their well-entrenched positions on the peninsula, the enemy units not only supported local village and hamlet infrastructures, but posed a continual threat to Quang Ngai City to the southwest.

The operation began on 12 January with an amphibious demonstration off Mo Duc, 40 kilometers

---

*The Batangan Peninsula was the site of Operation Piranha conducted by the 7th Marines in 1965 before being included in the 2d Korean Marine Brigade's TAOR in 1966, and later the Americal Division's area of responsibility.

VAdm William F. Bringle, right, Commander, Seventh Fleet, is introduced to Col Robert R. Wilson, commanding SLF Bravo on board the Tripoli. *Observing the introduction is BGen John E. Williams, center, Commanding General, 9th Marine Amphibious Brigade.*

Courtesy of Col Robert R. Wilson (Ret.)

The 26th Marines come ashore on the Batangan Peninsula in Quang Ngai Province, initiating Bold Mariner, a joint operation with troops of the Army's Americal Division.

south of Chu Lai, in order to mask the intended operational area. At 0700 the following morning, Lieutenant Colonel William F. Sparks' BLT 2/26 and Lieutenant Colonel J.W.P. Robertson's BLT 3/26 assaulted the northern portion of the peninsula by air and landing craft, as the Americal Division's Task Force Cooksey, composed of elements of 46th Infantry and 1st Cavalry, began a companion operation, Russell Beach, to seal off the area's southern boundary. Once ashore, the battalion landing teams pushed south and east, linking up with elements of the Army task force moving to the northeast. Within seven hours, the combined force, supported by organic artillery and guns of the battleship *New Jersey* offshore, began sweeping eastward, forcing the enemy toward the sea where avenues of escape were blocked by Navy and Coast Guard patrol boats, supported by other ships of the fleet.

Resistance was negligible as Marine, Army, and 2d ARVN Division units tightened the cordon around the peninsula. There were clashes over the next several days, consisting of brief exchanges with furtive groups of enemy or individuals attempting to flee under cover of darkness. Among the obstacles encountered were extensive networks of mines and boobytraps scattered throughout the area and an equally extensive complex of enemy earthworks, each of which had to be searched and then destroyed. In the course of clearing the mazes of tunnels, connecting trenches, caves, and shelters, numerous supply caches and training facilities were uncovered. During one such search on 19 January, Company F, 2d Battalion, 26th Marines captured 102 Vietnamese, 56 of whom were males of military age. Later interrogation revealed that they were members of the *C-95th Sapper Company* and represented the largest single enemy unit captured virtually intact up to that time.

Moving steadily eastward, the combined force encountered an ever-increasing number of civilians who eventually were evacuated to the Combined Holding and Interrogation Center, north of Quang Ngai City, where they were given food, shelter, and medical treatment, as necessary. There, U.S. forces, assisted by a platoon of National Police Field Forces, a Regional Force platoon, and three Armed Propaganda Teams, screened the detainees to determine possible affiliation with the Viet Cong. In all, the center processed more than 11,900 civilians during the month-long operation.

On 24 January, the 2d Battalion, 26th Marines completed participation in the operation and returned to its amphibious shipping offshore for rehabilitation. Two days later, Lieutenant Colonel Sparks' landing team again moved ashore, joining the 7th Marines in Operation Linn River, north of Liberty Bridge. On 7 February, operational control of the landing team was passed to the 5th Marines and for the next five days Sparks' battalion participated in Operation Taylor Common within the same operational area until backloaded on board ships of the ready group for another period of training and repair.

With the withdrawal of BLT 2/26 from the Batan-

Courtesy of Col Robert R. Wilson (Ret.)

Infantrymen of the 26th Marines force a suspected Viet Cong guerrilla from his hiding place in one of the many tunnel networks that lay beneath the enemy-infested peninsula.

gan Peninsula, operational control of Lieutenant Colonel Robertson's battalion shifted from Task Force 79 to III MAF. Working in close coordination with Army Task Force Cooksey, 3d Battalion, 26th Marines continued searching the peninsula. During the last days of the operation, the battalion observed large groups of enemy troops attempting to escape the ever-shrinking cordon. Employing air and artillery, the battalion engaged the enemy, who did not return fire although outnumbering Robertson's Marines on several occasions. On 7 February, the battalion began its withdrawal, leaving elements of the Americal Division to complete the task of searching the operational area.

Three days after completing Bold Mariner, Marines of BLT 3/26 entered Operation Taylor Common by way of a vertical envelopment, codenamed Defiant Measure. In order to allow the prepositioning of other Marine units prior to *Tet*, Robertson's battalion initially assumed responsibility for 100 kilometers of the Arizona Territory, but as the operation progressed, individual companies moved out of the operational area in search of enemy troops. On 20 March, the battalion landing team was replaced by the 2d Battalion, 5th Marines and helilifted to An Hoa Combat Base for the period of rehabilitation. Three days later, operational control of the battalion, now under the command of Lieutenant Colonel Edward W. Snelling, who had replaced Robertson on the 3d, was passed to the 7th Marines and on the 31st, 3d Battalion, 26th Marines, along with units of Colonel Robert L. Nichols' regiment and the 51st ARVN Regiment, assaulted landing zones on Charlie Ridge and in Happy Valley, initiating operation Oklahoma Hills.*

After a week of training with its amphibious ready group, the 2d Battalion, 26th Marines returned to Vietnamese waters as III MAF's mobile reserve force, liable to be committed during *Tet*. With the buildup of substantial enemy forces west of Da Nang, the battalion landing team, now commanded by Lieutenant Colonel George M. Edmondson, Jr., began Operation Eager Pursuit I on 1 March by way of an amphibious landing and helicopter assault into operational areas of the 2d Battalion, 7th Marines and 1st Battalion, 26th Marines, northwest of Da Nang. The 10-day amphibious operation was followed by Eager Pursuit II, which continued until 27 March. Under the immediate control of the 5th Marines, Edmondson's battalion, supported by elements of the 51st ARVN Regiment, swept east from Liberty Bridge, across Go Noi Island and then back west, encountering a large number of minefields and boobytraps, but only limited resistance. Following a day of rehabilitation on board ship, the battalion again moved ashore on the 28th, assuming responsibility for the combined and modified operational areas of the 2d and 3d Battalions, 7th Marines, west of Da Nang. Once firmly established in its new area, the 2d Battalion, 26th Marines was replaced on 1 April by Lieutenant Colonel George C. Kliefoth's 1st Battalion, 26th Marines as SLF Alpha's battalion landing team.

April activities of the two landing teams were routine as both were in support of operations ashore: BLT 3/26 engaged in Operation Oklahoma Hills in the mountains west of Da Nang and BLT 1/26, in search operations near the villages of Kim Lien and Quang Nam, straddling Route 1 north of Da Nang. Both helicopter squadrons, Lieutenant Colonel Richard T. Trundy's HMM-164 and Lieutenant Colonel Jack E. Schlarp's HMM-362, when not training on board ship, were rotated alternately ashore to Phu Bai Airfield, where they were placed under the control of Marine Aircraft Group 36 in support of the 3d Marine Division.

In May, the 3d Battalion, 26th Marines completed Oklahoma Hills and returned to Amphibious Ready Group Bravo for a period of rehabilitation and training on the 4th. Serving as amphibious reserve for III MAF, the BLT twice demonstrated its measure of readiness by being fully prepared to land all units within 24-hours notice and failing to do so only because of last moment cancellation of the operations. The first was to be directed against Hour Glass Island in Quang Ngai Province and the second in an area south of the Cua Viet River, west of Wunder Beach in Quang Tri. Despite preparations, both operations were cancelled within 15 hours of landing by III MAF.

Snelling's Marines remained on board ship until 10 June when they moved ashore in preparation for the relief in place of 2d Battalion, 26th Marines, which in turn began embarking on board ships of the ready group. On the 12th, Lieutenant Colonel Edmondson's Marines departed Vietnam, bound for Okinawa, marking the first time since April 1967 that a battalion landing team's rehabilitation and training cycle would take place on the island. The tempo of the war had until then precluded the movement of BLTs to Okinawa, the most desirable location for refurbishing due to the presence of the 3d Force Service Regiment.

---

*For a detailed account of BLT 3/26's participation in Operations Taylor Common and Oklahoma Hills, see Chapters 5 and 6.

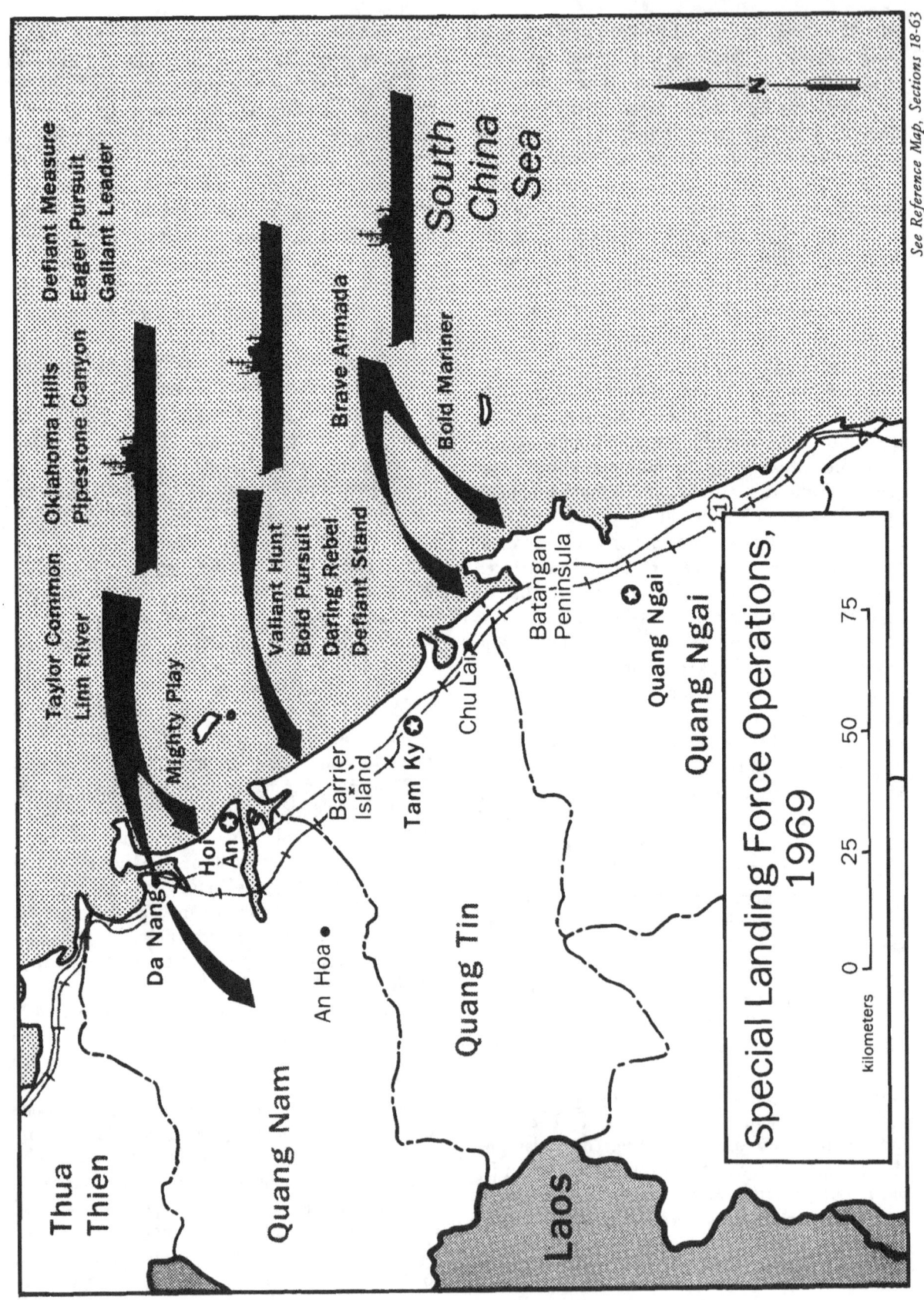

The June deployment of BLT 2/26 marked the first out-of-country rehabilitation since BLT 2/7 was refurbished at Subic Bay in June 1968. During the intervening period, three battalion landing teams were refurbished at Da Nang: 2/26 in August 1968; 3/26 in January 1969; and 1/26 in April 1969. While the Subic Bay and in-country rehabilitations were accomplished successfully, problems such as crowded port and maintenance facilities, lack of suitable training areas, and long supply lines combined to render the refurbishment less effective than under the original concept calling for deployment to Okinawa.

Following tested methods, a team from the 9th Marine Amphibious Brigade on Okinawa conducted limited inspections of the battalion's organic equipment prior to embarkation, thereby allowing sufficient lead-time for the requisitioning of repair parts and other supplies. Upon arrival, the BLT had use of all 9th MAB repair facilities, in addition to higher echelon maintenance support available from the 3d Force Service Regiment. A major contribution to the successful completion of the refurbishment was the "BLT Layette." Assembled and held by the regiment, the package contained a cross-section of supply items needed by Edmondson's Marines. Departing Okinawa on 26 June, the battalion landing team rejoined Amphibious Ready Group Bravo for movement to Subic Bay and a period of tactical training.

While the 3d Battalion and then the 2d underwent periods of training and refurbishment, Lieutenant Colonel Kliefoth's battalion participated in two major landings south of Da Nang. The first, Daring Rebel, was viewed as a complement to on-going 1st Marine Division operations designed to block the western and southwestern approaches to the Da Nang Vital Area. The amphibious objective area of the 1st Battalion, 26th Marines was to be the central portion of Barrier Island known to harbor elements of the *3d*, *36th*, and the battered *38th Viet Cong Regiments*, 32 kilome-

On the flight deck of the Tripoli, *a Marine CH-53 helicopter prepares to load elements of the 3d Battalion, 26th Marines for an air assault into western Quang Nam Province.*
Courtesy of Col Robert R. Wilson (Ret.)

A group of suspected local Viet Cong are led to a combined interrogation point by elements of the 1st Battalion, 26th Marines during the battalion's search of Barrier Island.

ters south of Da Nang, near the Quang Nam-Quang Tin provincial boundary. In conjunction with the battalion landing team, four companies of the 2d Korean Marine Brigade were to conduct search and clear operations to the northwest, while two battalions of the 51st and 54th ARVN Regiments supported the Marines with companion operation Vu Ninh 03 on the island near the Song Cau Dau, and the Americal Division conducted armored cavalry screening operations to the south and west. On Long Dong, a small island just northwest of Barrier Island, Regional and Popular forces were to provide security for a Combined Holding and Interrogation Center, operated by Vietnamese authorities, and to conduct local patrol operations. In addition, U.S. Navy and Coast Guard vessels were to conduct coastal, river, and estuary patrols, blocking enemy escape routes as well as providing coordinated naval gunfire support for the forces ashore.

Before dawn on 5 May, Amphibious Ready Group Alpha converged offshore and made preparations to land BLT 1/26, employing air strikes and naval gunfire to neutralize the landing beach and primary helicopter landing zones. At 1005, Company A, in the first wave of landing craft, moved unopposed across Red Beach to spearhead the amphibious assault. Further inland, Company C met sporadic sniper fire as its helicopters from HMM-362 entered Landing Zone Lion. Touchdown of Company D at Landing Zone Tiger was delayed an hour while air strikes completed the destruction of numerous enemy fortifications uncovered during the initial preparation of the landing zone. Once ashore, a fire support base and beach support areas were established near Red Beach as Kliefoth's Marines began search and clear operations to the northeast.

During the initial stages of the operation, as in Bold Mariner, an extensive psychological campaign was directed at the civilian population, alerting them of their impending relocation to the combined center for further screening, interrogation, classification, and eventual resettlement on the island. Aerial broadcasts, continually beamed over the entire area, instructed the civilians to move south along the beach toward the support area for transfer out of the combat zone, while leaflets amplified the instructions. The immediate effect was the relocation of over 1,300 civilians during the first two days of the operation. Ground action during the 17-day operation was limited to dislodging enemy troops and Viet Cong sympathizers from their hiding places. Throughout the endeavor, the combined force found the enemy to be extremely adept in conducting harassing attacks, planting boobytraps and concealing himself in extensive, well-prepared bunker and tunnel complexes. Despite the use of organic artillery, air strikes, and fire from the rocket-firing ship *White River* (LFR 536), and destroyers *Mullinnix* (DD 944), *Frank E. Evans* (DD 754), *Noa* (DD 841), and *Douglas H. Fox* (DD 779) on a rotating basis, these enemy fortifications only yielded their hidden caches and prisoners when thoroughly searched or probed by long metal rods.

The enemy was caught napping twice during the operation when Marine units, which had swept from the southwest to the central portion of the island, boarded helicopters and returned to their original landing zones. As Colonel William C. Doty, Jr., commander of Special Landing Force Alpha, recounted: "I felt that when the enemy saw us turn our backs and move north they would come across the river behind us. We jumped right back to the area and got them."[7]

As a result of such tactics, the combined operations netted 303 Viet Cong killed, a majority of which resulted from the actions of the two ARVN battalions; another 328 taken prisoner; and 37 tons of rice, 4 tons of salt, and 131 weapons seized. In addition, over 7,000 civilians were eventually processed through the combined center and resettled on the island under Vietnamese control. "It had taken the enemy years to set up a good infrastructure," noted Colonel Doty, "by rooting out the VCI, we've hurt the enemy's cause much more than just taking prisoners. He has to start rebuilding over again if he wants to reassert himself in this area again."[8]

The second landing came three days after completion of Daring Rebel, when Kliefoth's battalion was helilifted ashore during Gallant Leader, trucked from Hill 55 to an area just north of Liberty Bridge, and then began an easterly sweep toward Dodge City. With the 3d Battalion, 5th Marines, the 1st Battalion, 26th Marines established blocking positions along the western edge of the area while the 1st Marines and ARVN Rangers, in Operation Pipestone Canyon, attacked south towards Go Noi Island. The battalion maintained these positions until 8 June when a tactical withdrawal was conducted to ships of the ready group in preparation for yet another landing on Barrier Island.

On the morning of 27 June, Special Landing Force Alpha, employing helicopters of Lieutenant Colonel Robert L. Gray, Jr.'s HMM-265, which had replaced HMM-362 in late May, as well as amphibian tractors and assault landing craft, put BLT 1/26 once again ashore on wedge-shaped Barrier Island in Operation Bold Pursuit. Intelligence reports had indicated a rise in the number of enemy units in the Quang Tin portion of the island, apparently tasked with thwarting Vietnamese pacification efforts begun during Operation Daring Rebel in May. Enemy strength was estimated at 140 Viet Cong in main and local force units, 300 guerrillas, and elements of the *70th Main Force Battalion*, of unknown strength. The total number of enemy troops within supporting distance of the island was estimated at 1,200.

Landing at Blue Beach in the northern portion of the island, a kilometer south of the Quang Nam-Quang Tin provincial boundary, and at Landing Zones Cobra, Rattler, and Krait, Lieutenant Colonel Kliefoth's battalion began a southward purge of the island. Meanwhile, units of the Americal Division and Vietnamese Regional Forces established blocking positions on the western banks of the Song Truong Giang as a prelude to screening operations, and U.S. Navy Swift boats, augmented by Coast Guard and Vietnamese patrol craft, were stationed offshore to prevent an enemy escape by sea.

Encounters were sporadic as enemy troops again engaged in only occasional sniper fire and small-scale skirmishes, avoiding contact with the numerically superior forces of the landing team. As in Daring Rebel, Kliefoth's Marines uncovered numerous enemy fortifications and hiding places, which subsequently were destroyed by attached engineers. By the end of the 10-day operation on 6 July, 42 Viet Cong had been killed and 19 weapons seized. In addition, nine enemy troops were captured and 720 suspects detained for further interrogation and eventual classification by Vietnamese authorities.

Four days after reembarking on board shipping of the Amphibious Ready Group, BLT 1/26 assaulted into a small objective area within the 3d Battalion, 1st Marines operational area between the Song Vinh Diem and the South China Sea. Intelligence sources had placed elements of the *R-20th Local Force Battalion* and the *Q-92d Special Action Sapper Company*, in addition to scattered units of the *Q-82d* and *V-25th Local Force Battalion*, totaling more than 450 troops in the region. The presence of these major enemy units posed not only a direct threat to local allied installations guarding the southern approaches to the Da Nang Vital Area, but enhanced the possibility of rocket attacks against the Da Nang Airbase and Marble Mountain Air Facility.

Assisting Kliefoth's Marines were elements of the 2d Korean Marine Brigade positioned to the south and west; 1st Marines units to the north and northwest; and Company M, 3d Battalion, 1st Marines, directly attached to the battalion landing team. As in previous operations, U.S. Navy and Coast Guard patrol vessels were to provide screening operations along coastal and inland waterways. Also, the Vietnamese National Police were tasked with screening and classifying all civilian detainees and infrastructure suspects apprehended during the operation.

The operation, codenamed Mighty Play, began on 10 July with a helicopter assault into three inland zones, secured by Company M, 1st Marines. Since an over-the-beach assault did not take place, all logistical needs of the landing team were met by helilifts directly to units in the field or unloaded at Da Nang and trucked to the fire support base of Battery A, 1st Battalion, 13th Marines and the logistical support area established near Route 538, south of Tra Khe (1). Once ashore, each of Kliefoth's companies operated in an area adjacent to its initial landing zone, providing thorough coverage of inhabited areas and suspected enemy routes in the region. The enemy made no stand, relying instead on heavy concentrations of mines and boobytraps to disrupt search and clear operations of the landing team. As a result, contact was extremely light as Marines moved through the heavily mined terrain, engaging only isolated groups of enemy soldiers. By the close of Operation Mighty Play on 20 July, 30 enemy troops had been killed, 10 weapons seized, and over 200 enemy structures destroyed.

As the 1st Battalion, 26th Marines assumed defensive responsibility for the operational area of the 3d Battalion, 1st Marines on the termination of Mighty Play, Lieutenant Colonel Edmondson's Battalion, after undergoing a month of rehabilitation on Okinawa and training at Subic Bay in the Philippines, prepared to assault a coastal area southeast of Chu Lai in order to cordon and search a number of target hamlets for enemy forces believed to be operating within Binh Son District of Quang Ngai Province. Among the forces identified to be infesting the region were the *48th Local Force Battalion*, *T-20th*, *P-31st*, and *95th Local Force Companies*, and nearly 800 guerrillas and known members of the infrastructure. Within striking range of the objective area were elements of the *21st NVA Regiment*, *107th NVA Artillery Battalion*, and numerous local force companies, totaling more than 1,200 troops.

On 24 July, elements of the 2d Battalion, 26th Marines landed across the beach near the village complex of Le Thuy, 14 kilometers southeast of Chu Lai, while the remainder, on board helicopters of HMM-164, assaulted three inland landing zones, closing off the area. Accompanied by local Vietnamese Regional and Popular Forces, the Marines then began a methodical search for enemy troops, supplies, and fortifications during daylight hours. After dark, more than two thirds of the battalion was deployed throughout the area in ambushes, listening posts, and killer teams. However, long distance night patrols were kept to a minimum because of the heavy saturation of the area with mines, boobytraps, and other surprise firing devices. Although numerous base areas and defensive positions were discovered and destroyed, the enemy, as in previous operations, harassed or fled rather than defend positions and risk his limited formations in close engagements with the Marines.

Operation Brave Armada was terminated on 7 August with negligible results, and Lieutenant Colonel Edmondson's Marines were withdrawn by helicopter to the *Valley Forge* (LPH 8) and *Vernon County* (LST 1161). Three days later, the battalion again moved ashore, relieving the 2d Battalion, 7th Marines of its operational area, west of Da Nang. Initially headquartered at the Rock Crusher near Dai La Pass, and then on Hill 10, BLT 2/26 was given the task of defending the Da Nang Anti-Infiltration Barrier, and for the next month Edmondson's Marines covered all avenues of approach, responding to intrusions with quick reaction forces and supporting arms.

Meanwhile, to the southeast, Battalion Landing Team 1/26, now under the command of Lieutenant Colonel James C. Goodin, backloaded on board ships of Amphibious Ready Group Alpha on 8 August, following two weeks securing vital military installations and patrolling within the 3d Battalion, 1st Marines area of operations. After a month of training and equipment repair, preparations were made for yet another strike at Barrier Island. The third operation in four months targeted at this traditional coastal enemy stronghold, Defiant Stand was fated to be the last special landing force combat assault into the South Vietnamese war zone. Although the two previous operations on the island had netted close to 400 enemy troops and eradicated much of the local Viet Cong infrastructure, by July, the enemy had reinfiltrated the island, and again threatened the coastal areas of Quang Nam and Quang Tin Provinces.

SPECIAL LANDING FORCE OPERATIONS

The operation, the first to combine United States and Republic of Korea Marines in an amphibious assault during the war, was to involve two phases. The first called for the establishment of an angular block to isolate the northern end of the island, with 1st Battalion, 26th Marines holding the east-west leg and a Korean Marine battalion the other. During the second phase, maneuver elements were to attack within the cordoned area, searching out and destroying the trapped enemy.

On 7 September, the first phase of Defiant Stand began with Goodin's Marines assaulting into the central portion of Barrier Island. Despite rain and heavy cloud cover, which caused a 90-minute delay, Companies C and D, on board helicopters of HMM-265, were inserted into two landing zones along the east bank of the Song Truong Giang, while the remainder of the battalion moved ashore by landing craft. As A-4s of the 1st Marine Aircraft Wing and the guns of the destroyer *Taussig* (DD 746) covered the landing, airborne loudspeakers urged civilians to move southward to a number of predesignated safe areas. Concurrently, units of the 1st Marine Division to the north and west, Americal Division to the south and southwest, and 2d Korean Marine Brigade to the north, began local screening operations to seal off the island. Closer in, U.S. Navy, Coast Guard, and Vietnamese Navy patrol craft again covered the coastline and surrounding rivers against any enemy attempt to escape. The initial assaults of BLT 1/26 met little opposition and the Marines pushed northward, evoking scattered firefights with small bands of enemy attempting to reach river crossings and other escape routes. By the 12th, the Marine landing team had established a series of blocking positions across the north-central portion of the island, isolating the northern sector in preparation for the Korean assault.

After landing Goodin's Marines, troop and cargo ships of the Amphibious Ready Group moved up the coast and, on the 9th, embarked the 2d and 5th Battalions, 2d Korean Marine Brigade in preparation for the operation's second phase. For the next three days, the Korean Marines received amphibious assault refresher training, culminating in a landing rehearsal

Barrier Island villagers are escorted to a collection point while the 26th Marines, with Army armored cavalrymen, Korean Marines, and ARVN troops, again search the island.

Marine Corps Historical Collection

on the 11th. The following morning, the 1,100-man Korean contingent landed by helicopter and amphibious assault craft on the northern tip of the island. The initial assault was unopposed, but as the Koreans attacked south toward U.S. Marine blocking positions, they encountered increased resistance from groups of enemy trapped in the ever-closing cordon. With the enemy's escape routes barred, Korean Marines searched the caves and tunnels which honeycombed the area, accounting for most of the 293 Viet Cong killed and 121 weapons seized until both Marine contingents merged on 18 September.

With the end of Operation Defiant Stand, Goodin's Marines assumed responsibility for the operational area held by Battalion Landing Team 2/26 and, on 20 October, command was passed from the 9th MAB to the 1st Marine Division and BLT 1/26 reverted to 1st Battalion, 26th Marines. As Goodin's Marines moved ashore, the 2d Battalion, 26th Marines, configured as a BLT, went on board ships of the Amphibious Ready Group for several weeks of training, but in mid-October it too was returned to shore and on the 27th reverted to 2d Battalion, 26th Marines.

The Fleet's Contingency Force

Upon the completion of the redeployment of the 3d Marine Division (Keystone Cardinal), and the redesignation, transfer from 9th MAB to III MAF, and consolidation of the battalions of the 26th Marines, elements composing the Seventh Fleet's Special Landing Forces were to be drawn from the units of I MEF, headquartered on Okinawa. Since the Fleet's two landing forces now were to be formed from the redeployed units of the 3d Marine Division, they could no longer be introduced into Vietnam without specific authorization from the Joint Chiefs of Staff. Prevailing opinion at CinCPac was that an "enemy offensive of major proportions would have to be launched before imminent reintroduction [of the SLFs into Vietnam] would even be considered." Notwithstanding, the Special Landing Force was to be fully prepared for such a recommitment should circumstances warrant, and in recognition of such a possibility, CinCPac directed that the landing forces and amphibious ready groups maintain a 120-hour reaction posture for possible deployment to Vietnam in addition to maintaining the normal seven-day readiness posture envisioned under existing Pacific Command contingency plans.[9]

In early November, newly designated BLT 1/9 and HMM-164 embarked on board Amphibious Ready Group Bravo, followed in December by BLT 2/9 and HMM-165, which boarded ships of ARG Alpha. The pattern of SLF operations during the remainder of the year consisted of periods of normal upkeep, maintenance, and training at Subic Bay in the Philippines and periods at sea. When at sea, each landing force operated along the littoral of South Vietnam, from the Cau May Peninsula to the DMZ, remaining well outside the 12-mile limit, but constantly ready for possible recommitment to Vietnam or to any other amphibious objective in the Western Pacific.[10]

CHAPTER 18

The Advisory Effort and Other Activities

Marine Advisors and the Vietnamese Marine Corps — 1st Air and Naval Gunfire Liaison Company (ANGLICO)
U.S. Marines on the MACV Staff — Embassy Guard Marines

Marine Advisors and the Vietnamese Marine Corps

While III MAF combat and support units garnered most of the laurels during the year, over 700 Marines scattered from the Delta to the DMZ, worked behind the scenes in less noticed but equally challenging positions. These Marines provided support not only to MACV Headquarters; the American Embassy; Marine units, both Korean and American; and U.S. Army units in the field through a detachment of 1st ANGLICO, but also to elements of the Vietnamese Armed Forces. Marines attached to the 525-man United States Army Advisory Group in I Corps provided needed liaison between units of the 1st and 2d ARVN Divisions and adjacent American forces, and also coordinated the use of allied tactical and support assets. Those with the Marine Advisory Unit provided the same assistance to the Vietnamese Marine Corps.

At the beginning of 1969, the Marine Advisory Unit (MAU), commanded by Senior Marine Advisor Colonel Leroy V. Corbett and assisted by Lieutenant Colonel James T. Breckinridge, had a Marine strength of 47 officers and nine enlisted men. Attached was one Navy medical officer and one petty officer. Marines assigned to the MAU represented the full spectrum of the combat arms, and combat and service support. Advisory personnel assisted most of the Vietnamese Marine Corps (VNMC) staff sections, and normally two advisors were assigned to each Marine infantry battalion — one advisor usually remained with the battalion command group while the other assisted the forward companies.

U.S. Marine advisors supported the Vietnamese Marine Corps from its creation in October 1954 out of various Vietnamese commando companies and river patrol forces that had fought in the north. Following the Geneva Accords that split Vietnam at the 17th Parallel, these units were reorganized in the south and formed into a Vietnamese Marine infantry force. The Marine Advisory Unit, initially a division within the Navy Section of the United States Military Assistance and Advisory Group, Vietnam, acted as the link between the Vietnamese Marine Corps and the American command.

Originally formed as a component of the Vietnamese Navy, the small Vietnamese Marine Corps consisted of a landing battalion, river patrol company, river group, ranger group, and a field support group. Its main task was to conduct amphibious and riverine operations. From 1954 to 1969, the Corps expanded from a strength of 1,137 officers and men to approximately 9,300. During the same period, it grew from a single battalion to a light division, composed of six 800-man infantry battalions and five combat and combat service support units, and also achieved separate service status. With the expansion in strength, the Corps was given responsibility for conducting independent and joint ground operations with ARVN and Free World Forces, and for the conduct of riverborne operations along the coastal lowlands and throughout the Mekong Delta. As an element of the country's General Reserve Forces, battalions could be deployed to any of the four corps areas and the Capital Military District. During the 1968 *Tet* Offensive, for example, Vietnamese Marines not only assisted in the defense of Saigon, but in retaking the Hue Citadel.

Relying on U.S. Marine advisors from the beginning, the Vietnamese Marine Corps, as a result, mirrored its sister service in organization, recruitment, and training. Recruited as volunteers, with appeals similar to those used by the U.S. Marine Corps, enlistees were sent to the VNMC Training Command, located northwest of Thu Duc in III Corps, near Saigon. Accommodating about 2,000 trainees, the command provided basic recruit and advanced individual training, as well as a number of specialized courses for both officers and NCOs. Officers were appointed from the National Military Academy, the two-year infantry school for reserve officers, or the 12-week officers' course for exemplary NCOs. In addition to normal training, a select number of officers and enlisted men attended courses at Marine Corps schools in the United States and on Okinawa.

A select group of closely screened and thoroughly trained Marines, advisors viewed their mission as one of improving the expertise of the Vietnamese Marine tactical unit commander in conducting amphibious, riverine, helicopter assault, and ground operations,

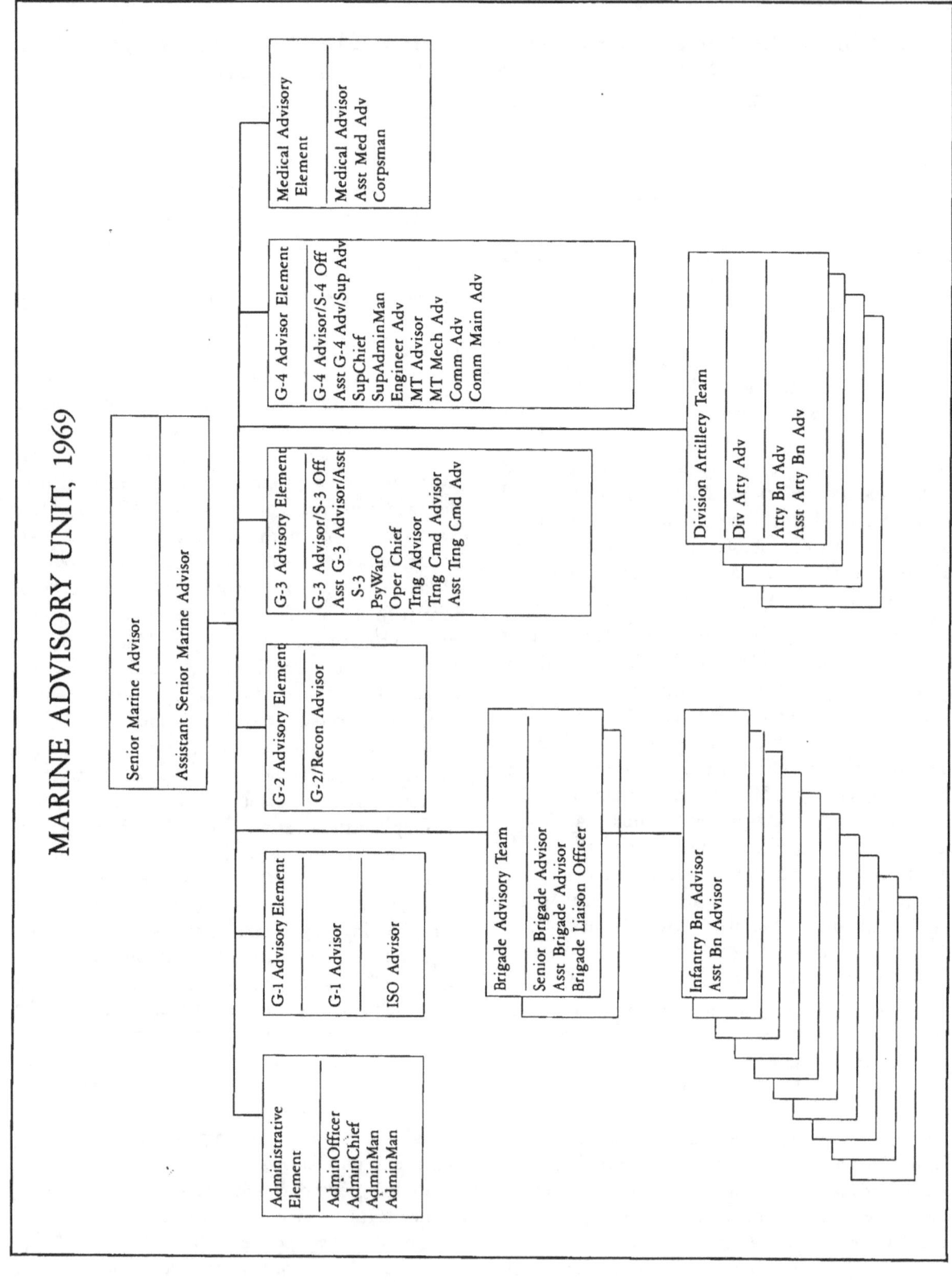

THE ADVISORY EFFORT AND OTHER ACTIVITIES

Marine Corps Historical Collection

LtGen Le Nguyen Khang, Commandant of the Vietnamese Marine Corps, continually stressed the close relationship between U.S. Marine advisors and Vietnamese Marines both on and off the battlefield.

and establishing a sound administrative and logistical organization within the VNMC.*[1] In combined operations with American forces, the advisor directed close air support and helicopter medical evacuations, and served as liaison officer between the two units. Advisors also monitored the Military Assistance Service Fund (MASF) which supported Vietnamese Marines. Drawing upon the fund, American Marine advisors furnished the VNMC with materiel and equipment not commonly available to other South Vietnamese forces.

Off the battlefield, Marine advisors worked to improve the health and well-being of Vietnamese Marines and their families, resulting not only in enhanced morale, but in unit esprit de corps. Donating many hours to civic action projects, U.S. advisors participated in projects that focused on dependent housing, upgrading of camp installations, and the establishment of health care facilities. The relationship between ad-

---

*Once selected, advisors attended either the Marine Advisors Course at Quantico, or the U.S. Army's Unit Sector Advisor Training Course at the John F. Kennedy Center, Fort Bragg, North Carolina.

...sors and Vietnamese Marines was close. They were, ...oted Vietnamese Marine Commandant, Lieutenant ...eneral Le Nguyen Khang, "our friends":

> U.S. Marine advisors never tried to command the Vietnamese Marine unit. They always stayed as a friend, they advise us, they help us, and they try to understand our problems—try to see the difficulty, and try to give us support, and try to fight things with many other agencies to give more support for the Vietnamese Marines—materially . . . . Many Marine advisors worked outside their military field, you see; they tried to go to many places, asking for many things to bring back and help the Marine dependents and Marine children . . . . But one thing, they never tried to dictate to us or to command us. Discussing—yes. Sometimes very hard discussion, but after that we remained very friendly . . . . The U.S. Marine advisors is the only one to share the food with the Vietnamese Marines in the field. They don't carry food for themselves; they don't carry the water for themselves. They shared the rice; they shared what we had in the field, together with my Marines. They do not make any distinction between the U.S. Marine Corps and the Vietnamese Marines.[2]

As units of the country's General Reserve, Vietnamese Marine battalions were liable to be committed anywhere throughout South Vietnam. Under the direct operational control of the Chairman of the Joint General Staff, General Cau Van Vien, and not General Khang, the Vietnamese Marine Corps, as a cohesive division, was used "piecemeal," according to Colonel Corbett. "Every time there is a crisis," noted the Senior Marine Advisor, "every one hollers for one or two of these Marine battalions. If things get hot in the Rung Sat Special Zone, Admiral Zumwalt wants one or two of these Marine battalions, at the same time [Major] General [Julian J.] Ewell [Commanding General, 9th U.S. Infantry Division] wants them in the Delta, at the same time III Corps insists on having them around Tay Ninh or around Bien Hoa."[3]

Operating with its U.S. Marine advisors, the VNMC continued to conduct battalion-size operations during 1969 in its assigned areas of operations. The year began slowly with the six Marine battalions operating under ARVN and American forces in III and IV Corps. But with the approach of the *Tet* holidays, activity picked up. In early February, while under the 2d Brigade, 1st Cavalry Division (Airmobile), the 3d Battalion, in searches near the Cambodian border, came upon one of the largest arms and ammunition caches of the war. Using over forty CH-47 lifts, the tons of 122mm rockets, rifles, grenades, and assorted ammunition were transferred from the elaborate enemy complex in the Parrot's Beak to the brigade support area near An Loc. Throughout the 40 days with the 2d

Brigade, the 3d Battalion conducted numerous searches, and on several occasions was called upon to reinforce heavily engaged ARVN and U.S. forces.[4]

In late February, while under the Long Bien Special Zone, near the Bien Hoa Military Complex, the 5th Battalion engaged elements of the *K.3 Battalion, 275th Regiment, 5th NVA Division* intent on attacking the town, III Corps Headquarters, and the airbase. At 0300 on the 26th, the Marines met the enemy battalion three and one half kilometers east of the airfield, near the village of Ho Nai. In fierce fighting that lasted the day, and was so close that artillery could not be used, the battalion killed over 130 enemy troops and captured 20, including the battalion commander and his executive officer. For this action, the battalion was awarded the U.S. Navy Unit Commendation.

On 1 April, the artillery element of the division was reorganized. The 1st Artillery Battalion was formed from Batteries A, B, and C; Batteries D, E, and F formed the nucleus around which a second battalion was created. A third artillery battalion would be authorized and formed in November and a seventh infantry battalion would be authorized the following month.

While elements of Brigade A continued to operate in III Corps during April and May, Brigade B's three infantry battalions conducted a series of amphibious, riverine, and reconnaissance-in-force operations under the control of the 21st ARVN Division and then U.S. Navy River Assault Squadron 15 and the Vietnamese Navy's River Assault Group. From the Nam Can Forest area of the Cau Mau Peninsula, the brigade moved into the Twin Rivers area of Chuong Thien Province of IV Corps and then into the northern U Minh Forest with moderate results. The two brigades, at the end of May, exchanged areas of operation as Brigade A moved into IV Corps and Brigade B was placed under the operational control of the Long Bien Special Zone in Bien Hoa Province.

Throughout June, July, and August, Brigade A conducted a series of reconnaissance-in-force operations in the northeastern portion of enemy Base Area 483 in Chuong Thien Province, south of Can Tho. Work-

Marine advisor 1stLt Fred H. McWaters calls for a medical evacuation helicopter. The advisors' task was not only to assist, but also to request and control allied air support.

Courtesy of Capt Joseph W. Pratte (Ret.)

THE ADVISORY EFFORT AND OTHER ACTIVITIES

Courtesy of Capt Joseph W. Pratte (Ret.)

Vietnamese Marines carry several enemy rockets captured during operations in III Corps. As a reserve force, the Marines could be committed anywhere within the country.

ing closely with territorial forces, the brigade reopened Route 12 and conducted extensive pacification operations throughout its assigned area until the end of August when it was placed in general reserve status. During the same period, Brigade B continued search and clear operations in Bien Hoa Province until the beginning of September when it was placed under Task Force 211, controlled directly by the Joint General Staff, and tasked with continuing the search of Base Area 483 and the U Minh Forest in IV Corps.*

Both brigades continued operations in their assigned areas until mid-November, when yet another exchange was made. On the 12th, Brigade A terminated its stand-by status and departed Saigon to relieve Brigade B in the U Minh Forest of IV Corps. During the relief, the command post of the brigade came under heavy enemy 82mm mortar fire. Twenty-six rounds landed with pinpoint accuracy on the CP, causing 18 casualties. Among the wounded was Captain Richard L. Porter, U.S. Marine advisor to the artillery battalion.

During the remainder of 1969, Vietnamese Marines and their advisors continued operations in both III and IV Corps, and the Rung Sat Special Zone. Unlike the rest of the year, contact was heavy as elements of both brigades encountered sizable enemy units in fortified positions, while dealing with increased sniper fire and incidents of boobytraps and mines, which took a heavy toll on Marines. Despite the losses, the division continued to meet its recruiting objective of 700 per month and by the end of the year exceeded its new authorized strength of 11,400.

Summing up his tour as Senior Marine Advisor, Colonel Corbett expressed the general feeling of all Marine advisors as to the effectiveness of the Vietnamese Marine Corps and the individual Marines who composed it:

> Some battalions are exceptionally good, one is mediocre, but most of them are very good. Depends on the officers they have with them at the time. Based on casualties, leave, and so forth, if they have the leadership there, they do the job. There is no difference in a Vietnamese Marine and a

---

*On 7 July, Colonel William M. Van Zuyen relieved Colonel Corbett and assumed command of the MAU. His assistant was now Lieutenant Colonel Tom D. Parsons, who had joined the MAU on 2 May and relieved Lieutenant Colonel James T. Breckinridge.

Marine Corps Historical Collection

Surrounded by communications equipment in the brigade's command post, ANGLICO Marines coordinate American air and naval gunfire in support of the Korean Marines.

U.S. Marine. When ably led and properly supported, he will do what he is told to do, when he is told to do it, and he will do it in a topnotch manner. I have no great concern about the Vietnamese Marine Corps' combat effectiveness. It is the support of them and the manner in which they are employed which concerns me. They are a most cost-effective unit. I would be most happy to serve with them anytime, and I have served with them. I have never felt insecure with them and I don't feel any of the advisors, other than myself, who have served with them, has ever felt for one moment that they were insecure.[5]

In essence, Colonel Corbett later noted, "if properly deployed and supported they could do the job. I believe that the events surrounding the VNMC deployment to I Corps before the downfall of everything supports my analysis of their capability in 1969."[6]

1st Air and Naval Gunfire Liaison Company (ANGLICO)

As American involvement in the Vietnam War grew and troop strength rose, a requirement for naval gunfire support developed. In response, Sub-Unit One, 1st Air and Naval Gunfire Liaison Company (ANGLICO) was activated and ordered to South Vietnam in 1965. The primary mission of ANGLICO was to support the ground elements of an amphibious force by providing the necessary control and liaison agencies that would request, direct, and control U.S. Navy support in the form of naval gunfire and Marine and naval air.

From the beginning most of the fighting in Vietnam centered on the populated coastal lowlands, and naval gunfire became a useful and flexible means of fire support. Unlike air support, naval gunfire support was available around the clock, being relatively unaffected by weather or visibility. In addition, it offered a wide variety of ordnance, from 16-inch shell fire to rockets which could rapidly saturate any point or area target.

In January 1969, ANGLICO detachments were spread throughout South Vietnam. Naval gunfire liaison and spot teams were assigned to U.S. Army, Marine, and Korean Marine units in each of the four corps tactical zones and to the U.S. Naval Advisory Group in the Rung Sat Special Zone and the 1st Australian Task Unit at Baria. ANGLICO aerial observer teams were also assigned surveillance missions of the Vung Tau Shipping Channel.[7] Commanded by Lieutenant Colonel Frederick K. Purdum, replaced in August by Lieutenant Colonel Thomas H. Simpson, Sub-Unit

One had a strength in January of 19 Marine and 13 Navy officers, and 176 Marine and two Navy enlisted men.

Within the cruiser-destroyer group of the Seventh Fleet, a designated task unit provided MACV with naval gunfire support. Composition of the unit varied as ships moved to or from differing operational commitments, but the command element remained relatively constant, either the destroyer squadron or division commander. Based on gunfire support priorities set by MACV for each of the corps tactical zones, the task unit commander published periodic ship availability reports. These reports reflected the ships assigned to each zone and period of assignment.

At least 48 hours prior to the arrival of the support ship or ships, the corps senior U.S. military commander, with the advice of the naval gunfire liaison officer, assigned the ships to specific target areas and furnished spotter team identification and necessary radio frequencies. As the ship reported on station the ANGLICO spotter supporting the designated ground combat unit briefed the ship on friendly positions, scheme of maneuver, general enemy situation, rules of engagement, navigational aids, anticipated gunfire employment, and the number and location of friendly aircraft. Throughout the operation, continual communication was maintained among the ship, the spotter, and the liaison team.

Naval gunfire support employed during 1969 varied from 40mm cannon fire of the Swift patrol boats (PCFs) and Coast Guard cutters to the 16-inch shells of the battleship *New Jersey* (BB 62). The mainstay of the fire support was the destroyer with its 5-inch guns. In shallow beach areas, particularly in I Corps, in-shore fire support ships (LFRs) equipped with 5-inch multiple rocket launchers were used to bombard close-in targets.

The highpoint of ANGLICO's employment during the year was its support of the Korean Marines during Special Landing Force Operation Defiant Stand in September. Participating in their first amphibious assault since the Korean War, the Korean Marine Brigade, with elements of the 1st Marines, assaulted Barrier Island, south of Hoi An. Planning and coordinating naval gunfire, air, and helicopter support for the Korean forces was carried out by the assigned ANGLICO support team.[8]

With the redeployment of the 3d Marine Division, ANGLICO teams took over the responsibility for naval gunfire control along the DMZ, assuming management of the installations at Alpha-1 and Alpha-2. Using the TPS-25 radar in combination with naval gunfire, ANGLICO teams were able to locate and quickly interdict enemy personnel moving within the southern half of the zone. Eighty percent of the targets that were taken under fire during darkness were fired by naval gunfire instead of artillery. The reason for this, as Lieutenant Colonel Simpson explained, was due to the unique position ANGLICO had in obtaining clearances:

> We set up a clearance station with the 1st ARVN Division Forward at Charlie-1. What I did was to put three enlisted personnel in there, and they were able to sit in there with the ARVN and as soon as the target would show up on the TPS-25 radar they would check with the ARVN to get it cleared. At the same time down at Quang Tri, we had a naval gunfire liaison officer who was clearing the target through U.S. channels. So at this time, we had the two simultaneous clearances going on. Where the artillery would go back to Quang Tri, get it cleared at Quang Tri, go back to Dong Ha, which was the CP for the 1st ARVN Division Forward, try to get it cleared, then go back down the channel, where we were getting simultaneous clearance and then we would go ahead and fire on the target.[9]

ANGLICO's strength by December had risen to 198 enlisted men and 32 officers. During the final month of the year the naval liaison teams directed 2,407 missions, firing 23,049 rounds. In addition, they controlled 107 fixed-wing and 1,716 helicopter sorties, 114 medical evacuations, and the delivery of 2,702,950 pounds of supplies.

U.S. Marines on the MACV Staff

The Marine Corps provided 77 officers and 53 enlisted men for the MACV staff in Saigon at the beginning of 1969. Another 15 officers and 12 enlisted Marines served with various MACV field components. The senior Marine officer on the staff was Brigadier General John N. McLaughlin, Deputy Assistant Chief of Staff J-3, who had relieved Brigadier General John R. Chaisson in mid-1968, and who, in turn, would be replaced by Brigadier General Samuel Jaskilka. Other Marine billets on the staff covered a broad spectrum of assignments, ranging from comptroller, to membership on specialized study groups, to duty with the public information section.

Marine participation on the MACV staff and in the various field components had a dual function. It not only helped make Marine views on important questions readily available to the staff, but allowed MACV Marines to clarify Saigon's decisions for fellow Marines in I Corps. Moreover, as General McLaughlin later noted: "I had a close relationship with General Cushman and later General Nickerson. I was not their representative at MACV, obviously, and for obvious reasons; but I think I was helpful and was as helpful as I could be. And of course I enjoyed a similar arrangement with I Field Force and II Field Force, and with the U.S. Army command down in the Delta."[10]

Participation by Marines on the MACV staff had yet another effect; it allowed them to gain a broader view of the war. "From Saigon," McLaughlin reported, "I saw that there was more to the war than I Corps or III MAF." Continuing, he noted:

> As you will recall, most of the fighting prior to *Tet* was with the large-scale NVA units that had been up in I Corps, and III MAF had borne the brunt of a lot of this. And I think there was an unspoken attitude up there that this was the war, in I Corps. Well I found that this was not the case. And of course later on when the NVA gave up, to a certain extent, their large-scale attempts to infiltrate through the DMZ, and we saw the appearance of NVA divisions that had fought up in I Corps down in the highlands in II Corps and even over in western III Corps. As the war shifted, and it did necessarily when the NVA started bringing large formations down to II and III Corps, there was less pressure from main force NVA units up in I Corps . . . . I'm not saying this as criticism of anybody. It's a natural reaction. Everybody is responsible for his own area, and naturally he's concerned with his own war.[11]

From his associations with other senior members of the staff and allied representatives, Brigadier General McLaughlin came away with the shared belief that Marines, like their Army, Navy, and Air Force counterparts, had done their job. "General Abrams . . . was appreciative of the fighting characteristics of the Marines in Vietnam," noted McLaughlin. "I would say that he treated the Marines and Marine units, Marine divisions, as well as he treated anybody in the country. I think that's about the most you can expect. I think he admired the good things we did. I think perhaps he didn't admire some of the things that we didn't do."[12]

Embassy Guard Marines

The Marines of Company E, Marine Security Guard Battalion (State Department) were assigned security guard duty at the American Embassy in Saigon throughout 1969. Led by Captain Roger M. Jaroch and then by Captain Robert P. Lacoursiere and Major Harry J. Shane, the five officers and 155 enlisted men were tasked with safeguarding classified material and protecting U.S. Embassy personnel and property, the mission performed by Marines attached to all embassies throughout the world.

Unlike 1968 when Marine guards fought off an enemy attack on the embassy during the *Tet* Offensive, 1969 was a quiet year. In July, the routine sentry duty was broken by the visit to the embassy of President and Mrs. Richard M. Nixon and Secretary of State William P. Rogers. Early the following month, General Leonard F. Chapman, Jr., Commandant of the Marine Corps, accompanied by the Sergeant Major of the Marine Corps, Joseph E. Daily, paid a visit to the Ambassador. While enroute, they were given a brief tour of the embassy, during which the Commandant took note of the number of trophies the company had won for athletic activities. For the most part, Marines at the embassy were free from terrorist activities during the year. However, embassy routine was violently interrupted on 5 March when an attempt was made on the life of Tran Van Huong, Premier of South Vietnam, 50 yards from the compound. No one on the embassy grounds was hurt in the assassination attempt. Four persons were captured and later charged in the incident.

CHAPTER 19
1969: An Overview

At the 15 January meeting of the Joints Chiefs of Staff, General Leonard F. Chapman, Jr., Commandant of the Marine Corps, reported on the situation in Vietnam as he found it during a recent inspection visit. The situation, he said, was good. He likened it to a pioneer who settles in the wilderness and begins the arduous task of cultivating a crop. In the fall, after being ravaged by Indian raids, weather, and vermin, the crop was ready for harvest. Like the pioneer, who had to decide whether to remain or move on, the time had come for America to decide. Nineteen-sixty-nine, he concluded, "would be the year of decision," as indeed it was.[1]

Sandwiched between the massive *Tet* Offensive of 1968 and the deescalation of American involvement in the war that took place during the early 1970s, 1969 marked a major change and watershed in United States policy for the Vietnam War. Following a thorough review, the Nixon Administration adopted a policy of seeking to end United States involvement either through negotiations or, failing that, turning the combat role over to the South Vietnamese. It was this decision that began the Vietnamization of the war in the summer of 1969 and that would soon greatly reduce and then end the Marine Corps' combat role in South Vietnam.

The redeployment of the 9th Marines in July began this process of disengagement and replacement. Rooted in the Marine advisory effort of the 1950s, Marine air and ground forces increased rapidly with the deployment of the first helicopter squadrons in 1962. By the beginning of 1969, III Marine Amphibious Force, encompassing Marine, Army, and Navy components, had become the largest combat unit in Marine Corps history.

Throughout this build-up, Marines on the battlefield faced two different challenges: the first from guerrillas—an enemy almost impossible to identify, who rarely stood and fought, and who would rather fade away to return at a time and place of his own choosing—and the second from disciplined NVA soldiers who sought out Marines and maneuvered to meet them in more conventional engagements. In exchanges ranging from small encounters with a few Viet Cong in a lowland hedgerow to a North Vietnamese Army battalion occupying a fortified position in triple-canopied jungle, Marine units time and again defeated the enemy—1969 was no different.

Working in close harmony with the South Vietnamese Army, III MAF and the Seventh Fleet Special Landing Forces took full advantage of the momentum achieved during 1968 to continue the unrelenting attack on the enemy's combat organization and guerrilla infrastructure. Prominent among III MAF's combat operations were those aimed at destroying the enemy's staging and assembly areas and lines of communications. In northern I Corps, the 9th Marines' Operation Dewey Canyon wreaked havoc on a major enemy command and logistic network in the Da Krong Valley, crippling the enemy's supply effort and future aggressive plans in I Corps for a year. Despite the reluctance of NVA units to engage in decisive combat within the northern two provinces, 3d Marine Division operations along the DMZ; 1st Brigade, 5th Infantry Division actions in the coastal lowlands; and 101st Airborne Division incursions into the A Shau Valley, did trigger occasional sharp exchanges, which cost the enemy heavily in both troops and equipment.

To the south, the 1st Marine and Americal Divisions conducted a series of major operations to rid Quang Nam, Quang Tin, and Quang Ngai Provinces of a substantial enemy presence directed against populated areas of Da Nang and Quang Ngai. Driving into such long-time enemy strongholds as Base Area 112, Happy Valley, Charlie Ridge, Dodge City, Go Noi Island, and the Que Son Mountains, the year-long campaign by the 1st Marine Division laid waste to a large number of enemy base camps and storage areas, denying the enemy opportunity to marshal forces for any significant offensive in Quang Nam. In the heavily populated areas of the three provinces, the two divisions' unremitting counterguerrilla effort, although undramatic, achieved steady success over the local Viet Cong Infrastructure. From the DMZ in the north to Duc Pho in the south, III MAF combat operations during the year cost the enemy over 30,000 killed or captured, a loss equivalent to nearly three divisions. Marines losses were 2,259 killed and 16,567 wounded.

Within the secure enviornment provided by III MAF, a Vietnamese farmer in the hamlet of An Ngai Tay checks his new vegetable crop with little fear that it might be confiscated.

Prominently influencing I Corps combat operations, the 1st Marine Aircraft Wing, reinforced by helicopter squadrons from the Seventh Fleet's Special Landing Force, maintained the constant air support necessary to implement and sustain III MAF's battle plan. Measured statistically, the Marine in-country air campaign encompassed 64,900 fixed-wing and 548,000 helicopter sorties, delivering over 100,000 tons of ordnance and some 895,000 troops and 115,000 tons of supplies. However, a truer measure of success was the effectiveness of the air-ground team, which was exploited to the fullest extent during the high-mobility mountain operations carried out by the 3d Marine Division early in the year—campaigns which combined the intrinsic capabilities of infantry maneuver, helicopter mobility, and coordinated air and artillery fire support to neutralize the hostile enemy threat to northern I Corps.

Complementing the combat efforts and achievements of United States forces were those of the South Vietnamese Armed Forces. As a result of the increased number of combined operations and training, and the concomitant rise in its effectiveness, the 1st ARVN Division assumed an ever-increased role in the defense of the northern five provinces of Vietnam. Upon the departure of the 3d Marine Division, General Lam's troops took over the defense of the Republic's northern boundary. Exhibiting the apparent benefits of better weapons and stronger leadership, the combat skills of Regional and Popular Force units also seemingly increased during the year, evoking new confidence among the rural citizenry whom they were tasked to defend.

Substantial progress was the hallmark of population security and Revolutionary Development plans during 1969. Unhampered by an enemy offensive as in 1968, the III MAF-supported South Vietnamese effort made substantial progress toward the reestablishment of governmental and economic conditions necessary for the return of a stable environment for both urban and rural inhabitants of the corps tactical zone.

Three separate, but mutually supporting, corps-wide pacification and development programs made headway during the year—a success largely attributable to the efforts of both South Vietnamese Government officials and III MAF working together to accomplish the programs' goals. The rise in population security, which climbed from 69 to 93 percent during the year, provided optimum conditions for civil and economic recovery. While the program to establish or reestablish popularly elected governments and officials at the hamlet- and village-level exhibited moderate gain, the campaign to reduce enemy forces through the Chieu Hoi (Open Arms) and Phoenix-Phung Hoang programs greatly exceeded expectations.

Directly related to the effectiveness of the allied military screen provided the more populated areas of the coastal plains was revolutionary development. Ranging from multi-battalion military operations to the actions of the People's Self-Defense Forces, allied and South Vietnamese forces attempted to erect a secure barrier behind which nation building and economic development could root and flourish. An integral aspect of this effort since its inception in 1965, the Combined Action Program continued to expand in 1969, reaching an authorized strength of 114 platoons in August. Its successful history of working with local forces led to the initiation in October of the Infantry Company Intensive Pacification Program, whereby infantry companies of the 1st Marine and Americal Divisions joined with territorial forces in direct support of population security.

Overall, 1969 was a year of achievement, featuring consolidation and exploitation of successes gained from combat and pacification activities alike. Despite the reduction of Marine troop strength in I Corps, the 55,000 remaining Marines would continue the full range of military and pacification tasks in the coming year. A further dwindling of the Marine presence in I Corps Tactical Zone and the transfer of most of III MAF's responsibilities to the Army's XXIV Corps would take place in 1970. Within Quang Nam Province, their primary area of responsibility, Marines would continue to develop and apply combat and counterinsurgency techniques to the fullest extent to protect Da Nang, root out enemy guerrillas and infrastructure from the countryside, and prevent enemy main forces from disrupting pacification, while encouraging Vietnamization and conducting a systematic and orderly withdrawal—a difficult task.

Notes

PART I
The Continuing War

CHAPTER 1
PLANNING THE CAMPAIGN

Unless otherwise noted, material in this chapter is derived from: Fleet Marine Force, Pacific, Operations of U.S. Marine Forces, Vietnam, January through December 1969, hereafter cited as FMFPac, MarOpsV with month and year; III MAF Command Chronology (ComdC), Jan69; and ICTZ/III MAF Combined Campaign Plan, 1969, hereafter ICTZ CombCP, 69. All documentary material cited, unless otherwise noted, is located in the Marine Corps Historical Center (MCHC), Washington, D.C.

I Corps Order of Battle

1. First Quarter Written Summary, ICTZ CombCP, 69, dtd 20Apr69.
2. Gen Robert H. Barrow intvw, 30Jan87 (OralHistColl, MCHC, Washington, D.C.), hereafter Barrow intvw, 30Jan87.
3. App. A (Order of Battle), III MAF Periodic Intelligence Report 1-69, 29Dec68-4Jan69.
4. CGIIIMAF ltr to COMUSMACV, dtd 27Jan69 (MACV Historical Document Collection, Reel 1, hereafter MACV HistDocColl, with reel number).

Strategy: A Reevaluation of Priorities

Additional sources for this section are drawn from: MilHistBr, Office of the Secretariat, General Staff, HQ, USMACV, Command History, 1968, hereafter MACV Comd Hist 1968; MilHistBr, Office of the Secretariat, General Staff, HQ, USMACV, Command History, 1969, hereafter MACV Comd Hist 1969; and JGS/USMACV Combined Campaign Plan, 1969, AB-144, 30Sep68.

5. CinCPac msg to MACV, dtd 9Jan69 (MACV HistDocColl, Reel 54).
6. Captured enemy document quoted in Gen Creighton W. Abrams msg to Adm John S. McCain, Jr., dtd 3May69 (Abrams Papers, Army Center of Military History, Washington, D.C.).
7. Gen William C. Westmoreland, Pentagon Military Briefing, 22Nov67.
8. Gen William C. Westmoreland, Speech before the Annual Meeting, Army Officers Association, Cleveland, Ohio, 18Nov68.
9. COMUSMACV msg to CGIIIMAF, et al., dtd 13Oct68.
10. Memo, MACV Commander's Conference, dtd 11Jan69 (MACV HistDocColl, Reel 11).

I Corps Planning

11. Anx A (Intelligence), ICTZ CombCP, 69, pp. 1-2.
12. Ibid., p. 4.
13. ICTZ CombCP, 69, p. 9.
14. Anx L (Neutralization of VC/NVA Base Areas), ICTZ CombCP, 69, p. 1.
15. Ibid., p. 2.
16. Ibid., p. 1.
17. Anx B (Military Support for Pacification), ICTZ CombCP, 69, p. 2.
18. ICTZ CombCP, 69, p. 6.

CHAPTER 2
MOUNTAIN WARFARE

Unless otherwise noted, material in this chapter is derived from: FMFPac MarOpsV, Jan-Feb69, and 3dMarDiv, ComdCs, Jan-Feb69.

Northern I Corps

1. MajGen Raymond G. Davis and 1stLt Harold W. Brazier, "Defeat of the 320th," *Marine Corps Gazette*, Mar69, pp. 23-30.

Off Balance

Additional sources for this section are drawn from: 3d Mar ComdCs, Jan-Feb69; TF Bravo ComdCs, Feb69; 2/3 ComdCs, Jan-Feb69; 3dTankBn ComdCs, Jan-Feb69; 1stAmtracBn ComdCs, Jan-Feb69; 4th Mar ComdCs, Jan-Feb69; 1/4 ComdCs, Jan-Feb69; 2/4 ComdCs, Jan-Feb69; 3/4 ComdCs, Jan-Feb69; 3/12 ComdCs, Jan-Feb69; 9th Mar ComdCs, Dec68-Feb69; 1/9 ComdCs, Jan-Feb69; 2/9 ComdCs, Jan-Feb69; 3/9 ComdCs, Jan-Feb69; Captain R. B. MacKenzie, "Intelligence Starts at the Top," *Marine Corps Gazette*, Jul73, pp. 40-44; and Colonel M. J. Sexton, "Sapper Attack," *Marine Corps Gazette*, Sep69, pp. 28-31.

2. Gen Raymond G. Davis intvw, 2Feb77, pp. 17-18 (OralHistColl, MCHC, Washington, D.C.), hereafter Davis intvw.
3. Barrow intvw, 30Jan87.
4. Gen Raymond G. Davis, Comments on draft ms, Aug86 (Vietnam 69 Comment File, MCHC, Washington, D.C.), hereafter Davis Comments.
5. Davis intvw, p. 20.
6. Ibid., p. 23.
7. MajGen Raymond G. Davis and Lt James L. Jones, Jr., "Employing the Recon Patrol," *Marine Corps Gazette*, May69, pp. 40-45.
8. Davis Comments.
9. Barrow intvw, 30Jan87.
10. Ibid.
11. LtCol Joseph E. Hopkins intvw, 16-18Feb69, No. 3915 (OralHistColl, MCHC, Washington, D.C.).
12. Ibid.
13. 1stLt Larry L. Eastland intvw, 16-18Feb69, No. 3915 (OralHistColl, MCHC, Washington, D.C.).
14. Capt James E. Knight, Jr. intvw, 10-12May69, No. 4091 (OralHistColl, MCHC, Washington, D.C.).

15. GySgt John E. Timmermeyer intvw, 10-12May69, No. 4091 (OralHistColl, MCHC, Washington, D.C.).
16. Capt Albert H. Hill intvw, 14-16May69, No. 4096 (OralHistColl, MCHC, Washington, D.C.).
17. BGen Joseph E. Hopkins, Comments on draft ms, 31Aug86 (Vietnam 69 Comment File, MCHC, Washington, D.C.).

From the Cua Viet, South

Additional sources for this section are drawn from: 101st Airborne Division (Airmobile) Operational Report/Lessons Learned (ORLL), Feb and May69; 1st Brigade, 5th Infantry Division (Mechanized) ORLL, Feb and May69; 1st Brigade, 5th Infantry Division (Mechanized) AAR, Napoleon Saline II and Marshall Mountain, dtd 8Apr69.

18. Davis Comments.

CHAPTER 3
THE SPRING OFFENSIVE PREEMPTED

Unless otherwise noted, material in this chapter is derived from: FMFPac, MarOpsV, Jan-Feb69; 3dMarDiv ComdCs, Jan-Feb69; 9th Mar ComdCs, Jan-Feb69; 1/9 ComdCs, Jan-Feb69; 2/9 ComdCs, Jan-Feb69; 3/9 ComdCs, Jan-Feb69; 2/12 ComdCs, Jan-Feb69; 9th Mar AAR, Opn Dewey Canyon, dtd 8Apr69, hereafter 9th Mar AAR, Opn Dewey Canyon; MajGen Robert H. Barrow, "Operation Dewey Canyon," *Marine Corps Gazette*, Nov81, pp. 84-89; and 1stLt Gordon M. Davis, "Dewey Canyon: All Weather Classic," *Marine Corps Gazette*. Jul69, pp. 32-40.

Strike into the Da Krong

1. III MAF Periodic Intelligence Report 1-69, dtd 7Jan69, pp. 1-3.
2. VMA(AW)-242 ComdC, Jan69.
3. Annex A (Order of Battle), III MAF Periodic Intelligence Report 1-69, dtd 7Jan69, pp. A5-A9.
4. 3dMarDiv msg to CG TF Hotel, dtd 14Jan69, in 3dMarDiv ComdC, Jan69.
5. CG TF Hotel msg to CO, 9th and 12th Mar, dtd 15Jan69, in ibid.
6. Barrow intvw, 30Jan87.

A Phased Operation

Additional sources for this section are drawn from: 9th Mar ComdC, Jan69.

7. Col Robert H. Barrow intvw, 8Apr69, No. 4054 (OralHistColl, MCHC, Washington, D.C.), hereafter Barrow intvw, 8Apr69.
8. Barrow intvw, 30Jan87.
9. "CO's Planning Guidance, Dawson River South-Upper Da Krong Valley," undtd, in 9th Mar ComdC, Jan69.
10. Barrow intvw, 30Jan87.
11. OpO 2-69, Operation Dawson River South, dtd 20Jan69, in ibid.; Frag Order 4-69, dtd 31Jan69, in ibid.
12. Anx H (Air) to OpO 2-69, Operation Dawson River South, dtd 20Jan69, in ibid.; Anx D (Fire Support) to OpO 2-69, Dawson River South, dtd 20Jan69, in ibid.
13. Davis Comments.
14. Anx E (Administration and Logistics) to OpO 2-69, Operation Dawson River South, dtd 20Jan69, in 9thMar ComdC, Jan69.

Phase I

Additional sources for this section are drawn from: 9th Mar ComdC, Jan69; 9th Mar AAR, Opn Dewey Canyon; and 2/12 AAR, Opn Dewey Canyon, dtd 5May69.

15. LtCol Wesley L. Fox, Comments on draft ms, 15Aug86 (Vietnam 69 Comment File, MCHC, Washington, D.C.).
16. Capt David F. Winecoff intvw, 5-9Mar69, No. 4028 (OralHistColl, MCHC, Washington, D.C.).
17. Maj Charles G. Bryan intvw, 8Mar-8Apr69, No. 4028 (OralHistColl, MCHC, Washington, D.C.).

Backyard Cleanup

Additional sources for this section are drawn from: 9th Mar ComdCs, Jan-Feb69; 9th Mar AAR, Opn Dewey Canyon; 2/9 ComdC, Feb69; 3/9 ComdCs, Jan-Feb69; 3/9 AAR, Opn Dewey Canyon, dtd 25Mar69; 2/12 AAR, Opn Dewey Canyon dtd 5May69.

18. LtCol Elliott R. Laine, Jr., intvw, 18Mar-14Apr69, No. 4063 (OralHistColl, MCHC, Washington, D.C.).
19. 2dLt Walter J. Wood intvw, 5-9Mar69, No. 4028 (OralHistColl, MCHC, Washington, D.C.).
20. Barrow intvw, 30Jan87.
21. Capt Daniel A. Hitzelberger intvw, 5-9Mar69, No. 4028 (OralHistColl, MCHC, Washington, D.C.).
22. Ibid.
23. LtCol George C. Fox intvw, 5-9Mar69, No. 4028 (OralHistColl, MCHC, Washington, D.C.).
24. Marine Air Support Squadron (MASS) 2 ComdC, Feb69.

CHAPTER 4
THE RAID INTO LAOS

Unless otherwise noted, material in this chapter is derived from: 9th Mar ComdCs, Jan-Feb69; 9th Mar AAR, Opn Dewey Canyon; 1/9 AAR, Opn Dewey Canyon, dtd 17Apr69; 2/9 ComdC, Feb69; 3/9 AAR, Opn Dewey Canyon, dtd 25Mar69; 2/12 AAR, Opn Dewey Canyon, dtd 5May69; and, MajGen Robert H. Barrow, "Operation Dewey Canyon," *Marine Corps Gazette*, Nov81, pp. 84-89; LtCol Dave Winecoff, USMC (Ret), "Night Ambush!," *Marine Corps Gazette*, Jan84, pp. 47-52..

Across the Da Krong

1. Barrow intvw, 30Jan87.

The NVA Retaliates

2. Maj Joseph B. Knotts intvw, 8Apr69, No. 4054 (OralHistColl, MCHC, Washington, D.C.).
3. 2dLt Milton J. Teixeira intvw, 18Mar-14Apr69, No. 4063 (OralHistColl, MCHC, Washington, D.C.).
4. 2/3 ComdC, Feb69.

Ambush Along 922

5. 1/9 AAR, Opn Dewey Canyon, dtd 17Apr69.
6. CGXXIV Corps msg to COMUSMACV, J-3, dtd 30Jan69, Dewey Canyon Border Incident File.

NOTES

7. COSOG, msg to MACV, J-3, dtd 31Jan69, in ibid.
8. CG3dMarDiv msg to CGXXIV Corps, dtd 3Feb69, in ibid.
9. COMUSMACV msg to CGIIIMAF, et al., dtd 12Feb69, in ibid.
10. Barrow intvw, 8Apr69.
11. Capt David F. Winecoff intvw, 5-9Mar69, No. 4028 (OralHistColl, MCHC, Washington, D.C.), hereafter Winecoff intvw.
12. Ibid.
13. CGXXIV Corps msg to CGIIIMAF, dtd 20Feb69, Dewey Canyon Border Incident File.
14. CGIIIMAF msg to COMUSMACV, dtd 20Feb69, in ibid.
15. Col George C. Fox, Comments on draft ms, 28Aug86 (Vietnam 69 Comment File, MCHC, Washington, D.C.).
16. Barrow intvw, 8Apr69.
17. Winecoff intvw.
18. Ibid.
19. Barrow intvw, 8Apr69.
20. Winecoff intvw.
21. Ibid.
22. Ibid.
23. CGXXIV Corps msg to CGIIIMAF, dtd 22Feb69, Dewey Canyon Border Incident File.
24. Ibid.
25. COMUSMACV msg to CGIIIMAF, dtd 22Feb69, in ibid.
26. CGIIIMAF msg to COMUSMACV, dtd 22Feb69, in ibid.
27. Barrow intvw, 8Apr69; 9th Mar AAR, Opn Dewey Canyon.
28. CGXXIV Corps msg to CGIIIMAF, dtd 22Feb69, Dewey Canyon Border Incident File.
29. COMUSMACV msg to CGIIIMAF, dtd 24Feb69, in ibid.
30. Ambassador Sullivan msg to COMUSMACV, dtd 1Mar69, in ibid.

Heavy Fighting

31. Capt Wesley L. Fox intvw, 19-28Apr69, No. 4086 (OralHistColl, MCHC, Washington, D.C.); LtCol Wesley L. Fox, Comments on draft ms, Aug86 (Vietnam 69 Comment File, MCHC, Washington, D.C.).
32. Ibid.
33. GySgt Russell A. Latona intvw, n.d., No 4912 (OralHistColl, MCHC, Washington, D.C.).
34. Maj Joseph B. Knotts intvw, 8Apr69, No. 4054 (OralHistColl, MCHC, Washington, D.C.).

Back Into Laos

35. Winecoff intvw.
36. Col George C. Fox, Comments on draft ms, 28Aug86 (Vietnam 69 Comment File, MCHC, Washington, D.C.).
37. Winecoff intvw.

Persistent Problems

38. Maj Charles G. Bryan intvw, 18Mar-8Apr69, No. 4028 (OralHistColl, MCHC, Washington, D.C.).
39. 9th Mar AAR, Opn Dewey Canyon, 8Apr69.

Phased Retraction

Additional sources for this section are drawn from: 9th Mar AAR, Opn Dewey Canyon, 8Apr69; 1/9 AAR, Opn Dewey Canyon, 17Apr69; 2/9 ComdC, Mar69; 3/9 AAR, Opn Dewey Canyon, 25Mar69; and 2/12 AAR, Opn Dewey Canyon, 5May69.

40. CGXXIV Corps to COMUSMACV, dtd 6Mar69, Dewey Canyon Border Incident File.

Laos: Repercussions

41. COMUSMACV msg to Ambassador Sullivan, dtd 6Mar69, in ibid.
42. "Hilltops in Laos Seized by Marines," *New York Times*, 9Mar69.
43. "Laird Foresees a Troop Cut by U.S. in Vietnam," *New York Times*, 11Mar69.
44. Ibid.
45. "Laird's Statement on U.S. Incursion Disturbs Laotians," *New York Times*, 13Mar69.
46. "Secret 1969 Foray Into Laos Reported," *New York Times*, 12Aug73; see also "Officer Began Laos Forays, Marines Say," *Washington Post*, 13Aug73.

CHAPTER 5
THE QUANG TRI BORDER AREAS

Unless otherwise noted, material in this chapter is derived from: FMFPac MarOpsV, Mar-Jun69, and 3dMarDiv ComdCs, Feb-Jun69.

No Change in Tactics

1. MajGen Raymond G. Davis intvw, 7Apr69, p. 305 (OralHistColl, MCHC, Washington, D.C.).
2. LtGen William K. Jones, Comments on draft ms, 30Jul86 (Vietnam 69 Comment File, MCHC, Washington, D.C.).
3. MajGen Raymond G. Davis FMFPac debrief, 15Apr69, p. 332 (OralHistColl, MCHC, Washington, D.C.).

The DMZ Front

Additional sources for this section are drawn from: 4th Mar ComdCs, Mar-May69; 1/4 ComdCs, Mar-May69; 2/4 ComdCs, Mar-May69; 3/4 ComdCs, Mar-May69; and 4th Mar AAR Opn Purple Martin, dtd 4Jul69.

4. 1stLt John P. Kiley intvw, 16May-13Jun69, No. 4334 (OralHistColl, MCHC, Washington, D.C.).
5. 2dLt Rick W. Prevost intvw, 16May-13Jun69, No. 4334 (OralHistColl, MCHC, Washington, D.C.).
6. Maj Raymond D. Walters intvw, 16May-13Jun69, No. 4334 (OralHistColl, MCHC, Washington, D.C.).
7. 1stLt John P. Kiley intvw, 16May-13Jun69, No. 4334 (OralHistColl, MCHC, Washington, D.C.).
8. Maj Raymond D. Walters intvw, 16May-13Jun69, No. 4334 (OralHistColl, MCHC, Washington, D.C.).
9. Maj George X. McKenna intvw, 16-18May69, No. 4094 (OralHistColl, MCHC, Washington, D.C.).

Brigade Mauls *27th*

Additional sources for this section are drawn from: 3dMarDiv ComdCs, Mar-Apr69; 1st Inf Bde, 5th Inf Div (Mech) ORLL, dtd 30May69; and 3/9 ComdCs, Mar-Apr69.

The 9th Battles the *36th*

Additional sources for this section are drawn from: 3dMarDiv ComdCs, Mar-May69; 9th Mar ComdCs, Mar-Apr69; 1/9 ComdCs, Mar-Apr69; 2/9 ComdCs, Mar-Apr69; and 3/9 ComdCs, Mar-Apr69.

The Vietnam Salient

Additional sources for this section are drawn from: 3dMarDiv ComdCs, Mar-May69; 3d Mar ComdCs, Mar-May69; 3d Mar ARR, Opn Maine Crag, dtd 2Jun69; 1/3 ComdCs, Mar-May69; 2/3 ComdCs, Mar-May69; 3/3 ComdCs, Apr-May69; and 1st Bde, 5th Inf Div (Mech) ARR, Opn Maine Crag, dtd 5May69.

10. Col Paul D. Lafond intvw, 25Jun69, No. 4335 (OralHistColl, MCHC, Washington, D.C.).
11. LtCol James J. McMonagle intvw, 16May69, No. 4124 (OralHistColl, MCHC, Washington, D.C.).
12. Ibid.
13. Ibid.
14. Col Paul D. Lafond intvw, 11May69, No. 4095 (OralHistColl, MCHC, Washington, D.C.).
15. Ibid.

Apache Snow

Additional sources for this section are drawn from: 9th Mar ComdCs, May-Jul69; 9th Mar AAR, Opn Apache Snow, dtd 20Jun69; 9th Mar AAR, Opn Cameron Falls, dtd 4Jul69; 1/9 ComdCs, May-Jul69; 2/9 ComdCs, May-Jul69; and 3/9 ComdCs, May-Jul69.

16. Col Edward F. Danowitz intvw, 9Jun69, No. 4336 (OralHistColl, MCHC, Washington, D.C.).
17. 22d Military History Detachment, "Narrative: Operation Apache Snow," n.d.
18. Ibid.
19. Col Edward F. Danowitz intvw, 6Jun69, No. 4355 (OralHistColl, MCHC, Washington, D.C.).
20. LtCol Oral R. Swigart, Jr., intvw, 11Jul69, No. 4392 (OralHistColl, MCHC, Washington, D.C.).
21. Ibid.
22. 1stLt Patrick P. Oates intvw, 11Jul69, No. 4391 (OralHistColl, MCHC, Washington, D.C.).
23. LtCol Robert L. Modjeski, Comments on draft ms, 15Sep86 (Vietnam 69 Comment File, MCHC, Washington, D.C.).

Central DMZ Battles

Additional sources for this section are drawn from: 3d Mar ComdCs, May-Jul69; 3d Mar ARR, Opn Virginia Ridge, n.d.; 1/3 ComdCs, May-Jul69; 2/3 ComdCs, May-Jul69; 3/3 ComdCs, May-Jul69; 4th Mar ComdCs, May-Jul69; 4th Mar ARR, Opn Herkimer Mountain, dtd 21Aug69; 1/4 ComdCs, May-Jul69; 2/4 ComdCs, May-Jul69; and 3/4 ComdCs, May-Jul69.

24. Maj Donald J. Myers intvw, 15Aug69, No. 4468 (OralHistColl, MCHC, Washington, D.C.).
25. Capt William J. Quigley intvw, 6Sep69, No. 4415 (OralHistColl, MCHC, Washington, D.C.).
26. Maj Charles W. Cobb intvw, 5Aug69, No. 4466 (OralHistColl, MCHC, Washington, D.C.).
27. Ibid.
28. Col William F. Goggin intvw, 4Aug69, No. 4464 (OralHistColl, MCHC, Washington, D.C.).

Eastern Quang Tri and Thua Thien

Additional sources for this section are drawn from: 101st Abn Div (AM) ORLLs, May and Aug69, and 1st Bde, 5th Inf Div (Mech) ORLL, May69.

PART II
Southern I Corps Battleground

CHAPTER 6
DESTRUCTION OF BASE AREA 112

Unless otherwise noted, material in this chapter is derived from: FMFPac MarOpsV, Jan-Mar69; III MAF ComdCs, Dec68-Mar69; and 1stMarDiv ComdCs, Jan-Mar69.

Defense of Da Nang

1. LtGen Ormond R. Simpson, Comments on draft ms, 18Aug86 (Vietnam 69 Comment File, MCHC, Washington, D.C.).
2. 1stMarDiv OpO 301-YR, dtd 9Feb69 in 1stMarDiv ComdC, Feb69.
3. Barrow intvw, 30Jan87.

Attack into 112

Additional sources for this section are drawn from: III MAF Periodic Intelligence Reports, 5Jan69-2Feb69; TF Yankee ComdCs, Dec68-Feb69; TF Yankee AAR, Opn Taylor Common, dtd 20Mar69; 3d Mar ComdCs, Jan-Feb69; 1/3 ComdCs, Jan-Feb69; 3/3 ComdCs, Jan-Feb69; 5th Mar ComdCs, Jan-Mar69; 1/5 ComdCs, Jan-Mar69; 2/5 ComdCs, Jan-Mar69; 3/5 ComdCs, Jan-Mar69; and 11th Mar ComdCs, Dec68-Mar69.

4. MACV Comd Hist, 1969.
5. LtCol John A. Dowd intvw, 17Mar69, No. 4042 (OralHistColl, MCHC, Washington, D.C.).
6. Col James B. Ord, Jr., intvw, 3Nov69, No. 4 (OralHistColl, MCHC, Washington, D.C.).
7. MajGen Ross T. Dwyer, Jr., intvw, 17Oct77, p. 35 (OralHistColl, MCHC, Washington, D.C.), hereafter Dwyer intvw; MajGen Ross T. Dwyer, Jr., Comments on draft ms, 11Sep86 (Vietnam 69 Comment File, MCHC, Washington, D.C.), hereafter Dwyer Comments.
8. Dwyer Comments.
9. Dwyer intvw, pp. 37-38.
10. Ibid., p. 40; Dwyer Comments.
11. Davis Comments.
12. Capt Roger K. Peterson intvw, Feb69, No. 4045 (OralHistColl, MCHC, Washington, D.C.).
13. Ibid.
14. LCpl Rick L. Wackle intvw, 20Feb69, No. 4011 (OralHistColl, MCHC, Washington, D.C.).
15. 1stLt Ronald E. Pruiett intvw, 19Feb69, No. 4010 (OralHistColl, MCHC, Washington, D.C.).
16. Col Harry E. Atkinson, Comments on draft ms, 24Sep86 (Vietnam 69 Comment File, MCHC, Washington, D.C.).
17. BGen Ross T. Dwyer, Jr. intvw, n.d., No. 3914 (OralHistColl, MCHC, Washington, D.C.).
18. Ibid.
19. Col Edwin H. Finlayson, Comments on draft ms, 25Nov69 (Vietnam 69 Comment File, MCHC, Washington, D.C.).

NOTES

"A Little Urban Renewal"

Additional sources for this section are drawn from: 1st Mar ComdCs, Jan-Mar69; 1/1 ComdCs, Jan-Mar69; 2/1 ComdCs, Jan-Mar69; 3/1 ComdCs, Jan-Mar69; 7th Mar ComdCs, Jan-Mar69; 2/7 ComdCs, Jan-Mar69; 3/7 ComdCs, Jan-Mar69; 2/26 ComdCs, Jan-Mar69; and 3/26 ComdCs, Jan-Mar69.

20. Capt Thomas M. Cooper intvw, 6Feb69, No. 4007 (OralHistColl, MCHC, Washington, D.C.).
21. 2dLt Wyman E. Shuler III intvw, 6Feb69, No. 4007 (OralHistColl, MCHC, Washington, D.C.).
22. LtCol Merrill L. Bartlett, Comments on draft ms, 1Sep86 (Vietnam 69 Comment File, MCHC, Washington, D.C.); Col Fred T. Fagan, Jr., Comments on draft ms, 9Jan87 (Vietnam 69 Comment File, MCHC, Washington, D.C.).
23. Capt Paul K. Van Riper, "Riot Control Agents in Offensive Operations," *Marine Corps Gazette*, Apr72, pp. 18, 22.

Americal's TAOI

Additional sources for this section are drawn from: Americal Division ORLL, dtd 10Feb69; Americal Division ORLL, dtd 10May69; and Senior Officer Debriefing Report, MajGen Charles M. Gettys, dtd 13Jun69.

CHAPTER 7
THE BATTLE FOR QUANG NAM CONTINUES

Unless otherwise noted, material in this chapter is derived from: FMFPac MarOpsV, Mar-May69, and 1stMarDiv ComdCs, Mar-May69.

Rockets Equal Operations

1. LtGen Ormond R. Simpson intvw, 25May73, p. 2 (OralHistColl, MCHC, Washington, D.C.), hereafter Simpson intvw.
2. LtGen Ormond R. Simpson intvw, 2Feb84 (OralHistColl, MCHC, Washington, D.C.).
3. Simpson intvw, pp. 3-7; LtGen Ormond R. Simpson, Comments on draft ms, 18Aug86 (Vietnam 69 Comment File, MCHC, Washington, D.C.), hereafter Simpson Comments.

Operation Oklahoma Hills

Additional sources for this section are drawn from: 7th Mar ComdCs, Mar-May69; 7th Mar AAR, Opn Oklahoma Hills, n.d.; 1/7 ComdCs, Mar-May69; 1/7 AAR, Opn Oklahoma Hills, dtd 7Jun69; 2/7 ComdCs, Mar-May69; 3/7 ComdCs, Mar-May69; 3/1 ComdCs, Apr-May69; and 3/26 ComdCs, Mar-May69.

4. 1stMarDiv, Nui-Nang-Nui-Ba Na-Charlie Ridge Special Study, dtd 1Jan-5Mar69.
5. Col Robert L. Nichols intvw, 3-5Jun69, No. 4371 (OralHistColl, MCHC, Washington, D.C.), hereafter Nichols intvw.
6. Col James B. Ord, Jr., intvw, 3Nov69, No. 4 (OralHistColl, MCHC, Washington, D.C.).
7. Ibid.
8. Capt Paul K. Van Riper intvw, 2May69, No. 4109 (OralHistColl, MCHC, Washington, D.C.).
9. Nichols intvw.
10. Ibid.
11. Ibid.
12. LtGen Robert L. Nichols, Comments on draft ms, 23Sep86 (Vietnam 69 Comment File, MCHC, Washington, D.C.).
13. Nichols intvw.
14. 7th Mar AAR, Opn Oklahoma Hills, n.d.

5th Marines and the Arizona

Additional sources for this section are drawn from: 1st Mar ComdCs, Mar-May69; 3/1 ComdCs, Mar-May69; 5th Mar ComdCs, Mar-May69; 5th Mar AAR, Opn Muskogee Meadow, dtd 5May69; 1/5 ComdCs, Mar-May69; 1/5 AAR, Opn Muskogee Meadow, dtd 26Apr69; 2/5 ComdCs, Mar-May69; 2/5 AAR, Opn Muskogee Meadow, dtd 27Apr69; 3/5 ComdCs, Mar-May69; 3/5 AAR, Opn Muskogee Meadow, dtd 23Apr69; Capt Wayne A. Babb, "The Bridge: A Study in Defense," *Marine Corps Gazette*, Jun71, pp. 16-23, hereafter Babb, "The Bridge"; and LtCol Charles K. Breslauer, "Battle of the Northern Arizona: Combined Arms at Their Best," *Marine Corps Gazette*, Jan77, pp. 47-55.

15. LtCol Richard F. Daley, Comments on draft ms, 8Sep86 (Vietnam 69 Comment File, MCHC, Washington, D.C.), hereafter Daley Comments.
16. Babb, "The Bridge," p. 21.
17. Daley Comments.
18. Col Thomas E. Bulger, Comments on draft ms, 9Sep86 (Vietnam 69 Comment File, MCHC, Washington, D.C.), hereafter Bulger Comments.
19. Col William J. Zaro, Comments on draft ms, 16Sep86 (Vietnam 69 Comment File, MCHC, Washington, D.C.), hereafter Zaro Comments.
20. 5th Mar AAR, Opn Muskogee Meadow, dtd 5May69.
21. Zaro Comments.
22. 1stLt Victor V. Ashford intvw, 3-5Jun69, No. 4319 (OralHistColl, MCHC, Washington, D.C.).
23. Ibid.
24. Zaro Comments.

Securing the Southern and Northern Approaches

Additional sources for this section are drawn from: 1st Mar ComdCs, Mar-May69; 1/1 ComdCs, Mar-May69; 2/1 ComdCs, Mar-May69; 3/1 ComdCs, Mar-May69; 26th Mar ComdCs, Mar-May69; 1/26 ComdCs, Mar-May69; 2/26 ComdCs, Mar-May69; and 3/26 ComdCs, Mar-May69.

25. Simpson intvw, pp. 27-28.
26. BGen Charles S. Robertson, Comments on draft ms, 19Aug86 (Vietnam 69 Comment File, MCHC, Washington, D.C.), hereafter Robertson Comments.
27. Simpson Comments.
28. Robertson Comments.
29. Bulger Comments.
30. Col Wendell P. C. Morgenthaler, Jr., Comments on draft ms, 2Sep86 (Vietnam 69 Comment File, MCHC, Washington, D.C.).
31. Robertson Comments.

Americal Battleground

Additional sources for this section are drawn from: Americal Division ORLL, dtd 10May69, and Americal Division ORLL, dtd 10Aug69.

32. Senior Officer Debriefing Report, MajGen Charles M. Gettys, dtd 13Jun69, p. 7.

PART III
The Third's Final Months

CHAPTER 8
REDEPLOYMENT: THE FIRST PHASE

Unless otherwise noted, material in this chapter is derived from: CinCPac, Comd Hist, 1969; MACV, Comd Hist, 1969; 3dMarDiv ComdC, Jul69; 9th Mar ComdCs, Jun-Dec69; 1/9 ComdCs, Jun-Dec69; 2/9 ComdCs, Jul-Dec69; 3/9 ComdCs, Jul-Dec69; and HMM-165 ComdCs, Jun-Dec69.

Keystone Eagle

1. MACV Talking Paper, T-Day Planning, n.d. (MACV HistDocColl, Reel 3).
2. III MAF/1st ARVN Corps, Combined Campaign Plan, 1969, AB-144, dtd 26Dec68.
3. *New York Times*, 1Jan69.
4. LtGen John N. McLaughlin, Comments on draft ms, 25Aug86 (Vietnam 69 Comment File, MCHC, Washington, D.C.).
5. U.S. President, *Public Papers of the Presidents of the United States* (Washington: Office of the *Federal Register*, National Archives and Records Service), Richard M. Nixon, 1969, pp. 215, 300, hereafter *Public Papers, Nixon, 1969*.
6. Ibid., p. 370.
7. COMUSMACV msg to CJCS, dtd 24Apr69 (Abrams Papers, Army Center of Military History).
8. CGIIIMAF msg to CGFMFPac, dtd 5Apr69, in III MAF, "Force Reduction Planning" File, dtd 4Apr-25Jul69.
9. LtGen Henry W. Buse, Jr. intvw, Jul69, No. 5022 (OralHistColl, MCHC, Washington, D.C.).
10. CGFMFPac msg to CMC, dtd 15Apr69, in FMFPac, "Force Reduction Planning" File.
11. CGFMFPac msg to CGIIIMAF, dtd 2May69, in ibid.
12. CGIIIMAF msg to CGFMFPac, dtd 7May69, in ibid.
13. CGIIIMAF msg to CGFMFPac, dtd 5Jun69, in ibid.
14. Richard M. Nixon, *The Memoirs of Richard Nixon* (New York: Grosset & Dunlap, 1978), p. 392.
15. CGIIIMAF msg to CGFMFPac, dtd 12Jun69; CGIIIMAF msg to CGFMFPac, dtd 13Jun69; CGFMFPac msg to CGIIIMAF, dtd 13Jun69, in III MAF, "Force Reduction Planning" File.

"A Turning Point"

16. LtGen William K. Jones intvw, 13Apr73, p. 57 (OralHistColl, MCHC, Washington, D.C.), hereafter Jones intvw.
17. Col Edward F. Danowitz intvw, 11Sep69, No. 4481 (OralHistColl, MCHC, Washington, D.C.).
18. III MAF Oplan 182-69, dtd 15Jun69.
19. LtGen Henry W. Buse, Jr., intvw, Jul69, No. 5022 (OralHistColl, MCHC, Washington, D.C.).

20. Ibid.
21. *Sea Tiger*, 25Jul69.
22. Col Edward F. Danowitz, Comments on draft ms, 14Aug86 (Vietnam 69 Comment File, MCHC, Washington, D.C.).
23. CGFMFPac msg to CGIIIMAF, dtd 27Jun69; CGIIIMAF msg to CG 1st MAW, dtd 27Jun69; CGIIIMAF msg to CGFMFPac, dtd 5Jul69, in III MAF, "Force Reduction Planning" File.

CHAPTER 9
"A STRANGE WAR INDEED"

Unless otherwise noted, material in this chapter is derived from: FMFPac, MarOpsV, Jul-Nov69; 3dMarDiv ComdCs, Jul-Nov69; 3d Mar ComdCs, Jun-Sep69; 1/3 ComdCs, Jun-Sep69; 2/3 ComdCs, Jun-Sep69; and 3/3 ComdCs, Jun-Sep69.

Company Patrol Operations

1. 3dMarDiv, LOI 1-69, dtd 29Jul69, p. 4, in 3dMarDiv ComdC, Jul69.
2. Col Robert H. Barrow intvw, 28Jul69, No. 4411 (OralHistColl, MCHC, Washington, D.C.), hereafter Barrow intvw, 28Jul69.

Idaho Canyon

Additional sources for this section are drawn from: 3d Mar ComdCs, Jul-Sep69, and 3d Mar AAR, Opn Idaho Canyon, n.d.

3. 1stLt Terry L. Engle intvw, 22Sep69, No. 4645 (OralHistColl, MCHC, Washington, D.C.).
4. Ibid.
5. Ibid.
6. Ibid.
7. Ibid.
8. Ibid.
9. 1stLt Richmond D. O'Neill intvw, 22Sep69, No. 4645 (OralHistColl, MCHC, Washington, D.C.).
10. 1stLt James P. Rigoulot intvw, 22Sep69, No. 4645 (OralHistColl, MCHC, Washington, D.C.), hereafter Rigoulot intvw.
11. Capt David M. Jordon intvw, 10Oct69, No. 4645 (OralHistColl, MCHC, Washington, D.C.).
12. Ibid.
13. Rigoulot intvw.

"A Significant Step"

Additional sources for this section are drawn from: 3d Mar ComdC, Sep69; 1/3 ComdC, Sep69; 2/3 ComdC, Sep69; and 3/3 ComdC, Sep69.

14. Clark Clifford, "A Vietnam Reappraisal," *Foreign Affairs*, Jul69, pp. 601-622.
15. *Public Papers, Nixon, 1969*, p. 472.
16. *New York Times*, 31Jul69; *Public Papers, Nixon, 1969*, pp. 585-586.
17. *New York Times*, 13Sep69, 15Sep69.
18. *Public Papers, Nixon, 1969*, p. 718.
19. MGen Wilbur F. Simlik intvw, 14Oct77 (OralHistColl, MCHC, Washington, D.C.), pp. 4-5, hereafter Simlik intvw.
20. Ibid.

21. Ibid.
22. Jones intvw, pp. 57-58.
23. Simlik intvw, pp. 5-6.
24. Col Raymond C. Damm, Comments on draft ms, 14Aug86 (Vietnam 69 Comment File, MCHC, Washington, D.C.).
25. Simlik intvw, p. 16.
26. Ibid., pp. 6-9.

Specter of Anarchy

27. Barrow intvw, 28Jul69.
28. 3dMarDiv memo to CGFMFPac, dtd 26May69 in CMC, WestPac Trip Report, 1969.
29. LtCol Gary D. Solis ltr to LtCol Elliott R. Laine, Jr., USMC (Ret), dtd 16Mar87.
30. Jones intvw, pp. 40, 83.
31. 3dMarDiv, Standing Operating Procedure for Apprehension of Individuals Involved in Acts of Violence Towards Members of this Command, dtd 4Jul69 in CMC, WestPac Trip Report, 1969.
32. 3dMarDiv Fact Sheet, Third Marine Division Program to Eliminate Actions of Violence, n.d., in ibid.
33. III MAF Fact Sheet, I Corps Tactical Zone Watch Committee, dtd 7Aug69, in ibid.
34. CMC to ALMAR, dtd 2Sep69 (Negro Marines, ALMAR 65 Subject File, Reference Section, MCHC, Washington, D.C.).
35. Jones intvw, pp. 83-85; Majs A. S. Painter, G. S. Pierre, and H. C. Sweet, Jr., rept, subj: Race Relations in the United States Marine Corps, dtd Jun70 (Negro Marines—Race Relations, Subject File, Reference Section, MCHC, Washington, D.C.).
36. Ibid.
37. MACV Policy Summary Sheet, Use of Marijuana by U.S. Servicemen in Vietnam, dtd 29Mar68 (MACV HistDocColl); CGIIIMAF msg to CGFMFPac, dtd 10Sep67.
38. Col Peter J. Mulroney intvw, 17Jul69, No. 4384 (OralHistColl, MCHC, Washington, D.C.), hereafter Mulroney intvw.
39. Barrow intvw, 28Jul69.
40. Mulroney intvw.
41. Ibid.

CHAPTER 10
"A DIFFICULT PHASE"

Unless otherwise noted, material in this chapter is derived from: FMFPac, MarOpsV, Jul-Nov69; 3dMarDiv ComdCs, Jul-Nov69; 4th Mar ComdCs, Jul-Dec69; 1/4 ComdCs, Jul-Dec69; 2/4 ComdCs, Jul-Dec69; and 3/4 ComdCs, Jul-Dec69.

Maintaining a Protective Barrier

1. 1st Bde, 5th Inf Div (Mech), FragO 1 to OpO 4-69 (William's Glade), dtd 14Jul69, in 1/4 ComdCs, Jul69.
2. Capt Henry W. Buse III intvw, 4Oct69, No. 4644 (OralHistColl, MCHC, Washington, D.C.).
3. Ibid.
4. SSgt William Reese intvw, 15Sep-19Oct69, No. 4516 (OralHistColl, MCHC, Washington, D.C.).
5. Maj James J. O'Meara intvw, 15Sep-19Oct69, No. 4516 (OralHistColl, MCHC, Washington, D.C.).
6. Ibid.
7. Col Gilbert R. Hershey intvw, 11Feb70, No. 4815 (OralHistColl, MCHC, Washington, D.C.).

8. 1stLt William H. Stubblefield intvw, 9Oct69, No. 4519 (OralHistColl, MCHC, Washington, D.C.).
9. Ibid.

"You Shouldered Us"

Additional sources for this section are drawn from: 4th Mar ComdCs, Sep-Dec69; 1/4 ComdCs, Sep-Dec69; 2/4 ComdCs, Sep-Dec69; 3/4 ComdCs, Sep-Dec69; and ProvMAG-39 ComdCs, Sep-Oct69.

10. 2dLt Danny G. Dennison intvw, 11Oct69, No. 4517 (OralHistColl, MCHC, Washington, D.C.).
11. Ibid.
12. *Sea Tiger*, 14Nov69.
13. LtGen William K. Jones, Comments on draft ms, 30Jul86 (Vietnam 69 Comment File, MCHC, Washington, D.C.).
14. *Public Papers, Nixon, 1969*, pp. 906-907.
15. Ibid., pp. 1026-1027.

The Brigade Takes Over

Additional sources for this section are drawn from: 101st Abn Div (AM) ORLL, Aug69; 101st Abn Div (AM) ORLL, Nov69; 101st Abn Div (AM) ORLL, Feb70; 1st Bde, 5th Inf Div (Mech) ORLL, Nov69; and 1st Bde, 5th Inf Div (Mech) ORLL, Feb70.

16. COMUSMACV msg to CGIIIMAF, *et al.*, dtd 15Jan69; CGIIIMAF msg to CGXXIV Corps, dtd 2Dec69 (MACV HistDocColl, Reel 56).

PART IV
Quang Nam: The Year's Final Battles

CHAPTER 11
GO NOI AND THE ARIZONA

Unless otherwise noted, material in this chapter is derived from: FMFPac MarOpsV, Jun-Dec69, and 1stMarDiv ComdCs, Jun-Dec69.

Vital Area Security
Pipestone Canyon: The Destruction of Go Noi Island

Additional sources for this section are drawn from: 1st Mar ComdCs, Jun-Dec69; 1/1 ComdCs, Jun-Dec69; 2/1 ComdCs, Jun-Dec69; 3/1 ComdCs, Jun-Dec69; 3/5 ComdCs, May-Jun69; BLT 1/26 ComdCs, May-Jun69; and 1st Mar AAR, Opn Pipestone Canyon, n.d.

1. Col James B. Ord, Jr. intvw, 3Nov69, No. 4 (OralHistColl, MCHC, Washington, D.C.).
2. Col Charles S. Robertson intvw, 22Jul69, No. 4400 (OralHistColl, MCHC, Washington, D.C.).
3. 1st Mar OpO 001-69 (Pipestone Canyon), dtd May69, in 1st Mar ComdC, May 69.
4. LtCol Wendell P. Morgenthaler, Jr., intvw, 8Jul69, No. 4398 (OralHistColl, MCHC, Washington, D.C.).
5. 1stLt Robert L. Leonard intvw, 25Jul69, No. 4403 (OralHistColl, MCHC, Washington, D.C.); Maj James W. Dion, Comments on

"Vietnam Anthology" ms, 12Apr78 (Vietnam 69 Comment File, MCHC, Washington, D.C.).
6. 1stLt Robert M. Wallace intvw, 22Jul69, No. 4405 (OralHistColl, MCHC, Washington, D.C.).
7. Col Wendell P. Morgenthaler, Jr., Comments on draft ms, (Vietnam 69 Comment File, MCHC, Washington, D.C.).
8. Capt Frank H. Adams intvw, 8Jul69, No. 4398 (OralHistColl, MCHC, Washington, D.C.).
9. Memo CO 2/1 to CO 5th Mar, dtd 6Aug69 in MajGen Harold G. Glasgow, Comments on draft ms, 3Sep86 (Vietnam 69 Comment File, MCHC, Washington, D.C.).
10. BGen Charles S. Robertson, Comments on draft ms, 19Aug86 (Vietnam 69 Comment File, MCHC, Washington, D.C.).

1st Marines: Protecting the Southern Flank

Additional sources for this section are drawn from: 1st Mar ComdCs, Jun-Dec69; 1/1 ComdCs, Jun-Dec69; 2/1 ComdCs, Jun-Dec69; and 3/1 ComdCs, Jun-Dec69.

11. Col Herbert L. Wilkerson intvw, 13Jul70, No. 4892 (OralHistColl, MCHC, Washington, D.C.).
12. Col Godfrey S. Delcuze, Comments on draft ms, 28Jul86 (Vietnam 69 Comment File, MCHC, Washington, D.C.).

The Arizona

Additional sources for this section are drawn from: 5thMar ComdCs, Jun-Dec69; 1/5 ComdCs, Jun-Dec69; 2/5 ComdCs, Jun-Dec69; 3/5 ComdCs, Jun-Dec69; and 5th Mar AAR, Opn Durham Peak, n.d.

13. Zaro Comments.
14. Col William E. Riley, Jr., Comments on draft ms, 3Oct86 (Vietnam 69 Comment File, MCHC, Washington, D.C.).
15. CO Comment, 5thMar ComdC, Jul69.
16. 2dLt Robert L. Lavery intvw, 9Aug69, No. 4498 (OralHistColl, MCHC, Washington, D.C.).
17. Ibid.
18. Zaro Comments.
19. Maj Gaetano Marino intvw, 9Aug69, No. 4498 (OralHistColl, MCHC, Washington, D.C.).
20. Col John M. Terry, Jr., Comments on draft ms, 2Aug86 (Vietnam 69 Comment File, MCHC, Washington, D.C.).
21. Col Noble L. Beck, Comments on draft ms, 13Nov86 (Vietnam 69 Comment File, MCHC, Washington, D.C.).
22. 5th Mar OpO 62-69, in 5th Mar ComdC, Oct69.

CHAPTER 12
DA NANG AND THE QUE SON VALLEY

Unless otherwise noted, material in this chapter is derived from: FMFPac MarOpsV, Jun-Dec69, and 1stMarDiv ComdCs, Jun-Dec69.

The 7th Marines

Additional sources for this section are drawn from: 7th Mar ComdCs, Jun-Dec69; 1/7 ComdCs, Jun-Dec69; 2/7 ComdCs, Jun-Dec69; and 3/7 ComdCs, Jun-Dec69.

1. MajGen Ormond R. Simpson memo to CGIII MAF, dtd 25Mar69 (1stMarDiv Admin File, MCHC, Washington, D.C.); III MAF Fact Sheet, Da Nang Anti-Infiltration System, dtd 2Aug69, in CMC, WestPac Trip Report, 1969.
2. 1stLt Raymond A. Hord intvw, 14Aug69, No. 4507 (OralHistColl, MCHC, Washington, D.C.).
3. Ibid.
4. Ibid.
5. Maj Peter S. Beck intvw, n.d., No. 4495 (OralHistColl, MCHC, Washington, D.C.).
6. Ibid.
7. Ibid.
8. LtCol Marvin H. Lugger intvw, n.d., No 4495 (OralHistColl, MCHC, Washington, D.C.).
9. Ibid.
10. Ibid.
11. Ibid.
12. BGen Joseph E. Hopkins, Comments on draft ms, 31Aug86 (Vietnam 69 Comment File, MCHC, Washington, D.C.).
13. LtCol Ray Kummerow, Comments on draft ms, "U.S. Marines in Vietnam, 1970-71," 25Apr83 (Vietnam 69 Comment File, MCHC, Washington, D.C.), hereafter Kummerow 70-71 Comments.
14. LCpl Jose F. Jimenez Biography (Biographical Files, Reference Section, MCHC, Washington, D.C.); 2dLt Richard L. Jaehne Award Citation (Biographical Files, Reference Section, MCHC, Washington, D.C.).
15. PFC Dennis D. Davis Biography (Biographical Files, Reference Section, MCHC, Washington, D.C.).
16. Kummerow 70-71 Comments.
17. Col Ray Kummerow, Comments on draft ms, 11Sep86 (Vietnam 69 Comment File, MCHC, Washington, D.C.).
18. Kummerow 70-71 Comments.
19. PFC Ralph E. Dias Biography (Biographical Files, Reference Section, MCHC, Washington, D.C.).
20. Kummerow 70-71 Comments.

26th Marines: Protecting the Northern Flank

Additional sources for this section are drawn from: 26th Mar ComdCs, May-Dec69; 1/26 ComdCs, Jun-Dec69; 2/26 ComdCs, Jun-Dec69; and 3/26 ComdCs, Jun-Dec69.

21. Col Ralph A. Heywood, Comments on draft ms, 11Sep86 (Vietnam 69 Comment File, MCHC, Washington, D.C.).

Quang Tin and Quang Ngai Battleground

Additional sources for this section are drawn from: Americal Division ORLL, dtd 10May69; Americal Division ORLL, dtd 10Nov69; Americal Division ORLL, dtd 10Nov69; and Americal Division ORLL, dtd 10Feb70.

22. Senior Officer Debriefing Report, MajGen Charles M. Gettys, dtd 13Jun69, p. 9.
23. Ibid., pp. 7-8.

Results

24. These figures are compiled from the monthly summaries in 1stMarDiv ComdCs, Jun-Dec69.
25. LtGen Ormond R. Simpson intvw, 8Sep81 (OralHistColl, MCHC, Washington, D.C.).

PART V
Supporting the Troops

CHAPTER 13
MARINE AIR OPERATIONS

Unless otherwise noted, material in this chapter is derived from: FMFPac MarOpsV, Jan-Dec69; 1st MAW ComdCs, Jan-Dec69; MAG-11 ComdCs, Jan-Dec69; MAG-12 ComdCs, Jan-Dec69; MAG-13 ComdCs, Jan-Dec69; MAG-15 ComdCs, Oct-Dec69; MAG-16 ComdCs, Jan-Dec69; MAG-36 ComdCs, Jan-Oct69; and ProvMAG-39 ComdCs, Jan-Oct69.

1st MAW Organization and Deployment

Additional sources for this section are drawn from: FMFPac MarOpsV, Jan-Dec69, and 1stMAW ComdCs, Jan-Dec69.

1. MACV, ComdHist, 1969, "Air Operations"; HQMC, Status of Forces, dtd 2Jan69.
2. HQMC, Status of Forces, "Distribution of Aircraft, FMFPac," dtd 9Jan69.
3. LtGen Herman Nickerson, Jr., intvw, 10Jan73 (OralHistColl, MCHC, Washington, D.C.), p. 96.
4. MajGen George S. Bowman, Jr., ltr to MajGen Keith B. McCutcheon, dtd 23Dec69 (McCutcheon Papers, 1969 Correspondence, Personal Papers Collection, MCHC, Washington, D.C.).
5. 1st MAW (Rear) ComdC, 7Nov-31Dec69.

Single Management: Relations with the Seventh Air Force

Additional sources for this section are drawn from: "Single Management" File, MCHC, Washington, D.C.

6. COMUSMACV msg to CGIIIMAF, dtd 7Mar68, in "Single Management" File.
7. Ibid.
8. Gen Leonard F. Chapman, Jr., intvw, n.d.(OralHistColl, MCHC, Washington, D.C.), pp. 70-71.
9. Ibid., pp. 71-72.
10. Ibid., p. 72.
11. MajGen Charles J. Quilter intvw, 12Jul69, No. 4362 (OralHistColl, MCHC, Washington, D.C.), hereafter Quilter intvw; Col Virgil D. Olson intvw, 11Sep69, No. 4477 (OralHistColl, MCHC, Washington, D.C.), MajGen William G. Thrash intvw, 2Jul70, No. 4850 (OralHistColl, MCHC, Washington, D.C.).
12. Quilter intvw.
13. BGen Homer S. Hill intvw, 15May69, No. 4122 (OralHistColl, MCHC, Washington, D.C.), hereafter Hill intvw.
14. Quilter intvw.

Upgrading of Aviation Assets

15. LtGen Keith B. McCutcheon, "Marine Aviation in Vietnam, 1962-1970," *Naval Review 1971* (Annapolis: U.S. Naval Institute, 1971), p. 134, hereafter McCutcheon, "Marine Aviation."

I Corps Fixed-Wing Support

16. 1stLt Earl C. Smith intvw, n.d., No. 4765 (OralHistColl, MCHC, Washington, D.C.), herafter Smith intvw.

17. Hill intvw.

The Interdiction Campaign

Additional sources for this section are drawn from: MACV Comd Hist, 1969, "Air Operations," pp. 200-223.

18. McCutcheon, "Marine Aviation," p. 142.
19. Maj Patrick J. McCarthy intvw, n.d., No. 4780 (OralHistColl, MCHC, Washington, D.C.); Smith intvw.
20. Ibid.
21. Capt Lawrence J. Karch intvw, n.d., No. 4765 (OralHistColl, MCHC, Washington, D.C.), hereafter Karch intvw.
22. 1stLt John D. Halleran intvw, n.d., No. 4782 (OralHistColl, MCHC, Washington, D.C.).
23. Karch intvw.
24. Maj James E. Buckley intvw, n.d., No. 4146 (OralHistColl, MCHC, Washington, D.C.), hereafter Buckley intvw; 1stLt Michael L. Richardson intvw, n.d., No. 4749 (OralHistColl, MCHC, Washington, D.C.).
25. Buckley intvw.
26. Quilter intvw.
27. Hill intvw.

Air Control

Additional sources for this section are drawn from: McCutcheon, "Marine Aviation," pp. 138-139.

28. Col Robert D. Slay intvw, 12Jun69, No. 4265 (OralHistColl, MCHC, Washington, D.C.).
29. Ibid.
30. Hill intvw.
31. Capt Thomas L. Hall intvw, n.d., No. 4766 (OralHistColl, MCHC, Washington, D.C.).
32. Col George C. Fox, Comments on draft ms, 28Aug69 (Vietnam 69 Comment File, MCHC, Washington, D.C.).

Helicopter Operations

Additional sources for this section are drawn from: McCutcheon, "Marine Aviation," pp. 143-154; FMFPac MarOpsV, Jan-Dec69; MAG-16 ComdCs, Jan-Dec69; MAG-36 ComdCs, Jan-Oct69; and ProvMAG-39 ComdCs, Jan-Oct69.

33. Hill intvw.
34. Ibid.
35. Ibid.

Improving Helicopter Support

36. Col Leonard L. Orr, Comments on draft ms, 4Sep69 (Vietnam 69 Comment File, MCHC, Washington, D.C.).
37. MajGen Carl A. Youngdale, HQMC Briefing, 8Aug69, No. 6010 (OralHistColl, MCHC, Washington, D.C.).
38. III MAF, Board Report for Utilization, Command and Control of Marine Corps Helicopter Assets in III MAF, 17May69.
39. Ibid.
40. Quilter intvw.
41. MajGen Carl A. Youngdale intvw, 6Mar81 (OralHistColl, MCHC, Washington, D.C.), pp. 441-442.

42. CMC ltr to all general officers, Green Letter 17-69, dtd 4Nov69.

Air Defense

Additional sources for this section are drawn from: 1st LAAM Bn ComdCs, Jan-Aug69.

Accomplishments and Costs

Additional sources for this section are drawn from: 1st MAW ComdCs, Jan-Dec69.

CHAPTER 14
ARTILLERY AND SURVEILLANCE

Unless otherwise noted, material in this section is derived from: FMFPac MarOpsV, Jan-Dec69; 1stMarDiv ComdCs, Jan-Dec69; 3dMarDiv ComdCs, Jan-Nov69; 11th Mar ComdCs, Jan-Dec69; 1/11 ComdCs, Jan-Dec69; 2/11 ComdCs, Jan-Dec69; 3/11 ComdCs, Jan-Dec69; 4/11 ComdCs, Jan-Sep69; 1/13 ComdCs, Jan-Dec69; 12th Mar ComdCs, Jan-Nov69; 1/12 ComdCs, Jan-Sep69; 2/12 ComdCs, Jan-Aug69; 3/12 ComdCs, Jan-Dec69; 4/12 ComdCs, Jan-Dec69; 1st FAG ComdCs, Jan-Jul69, Nov-Dec69; and 11th Mar, Resume of Artillery Operations, 1 December 1968 to 30 November 1969, dtd 3Dec69, in 1stMarDiv Admin File, hereafter 11th Mar, Arty Ops.

Artillery Operations

1. Col Peter J. Mulroney intvw, 17Jul69, No. 4384 (OralHistColl, MCHC, Washington, D.C.), hereafter Mulroney intvw.
2. MCDEC, Artillery Reference Data, dtd Aug70, pp. 35-45.
3. 1stMarDiv OpO 301-YR, dtd 10Dec69.
4. Mulroney intvw; Col Wallance W. Crompton, Comments on draft ms, 11Sep86, (Vietnam 69 Comment Files, MCHC, Washington, D.C.).
5. Maj Robert V. Nicoli, "Fire Support Base Development," *Marine Corps Gazette*, Sep69, pp. 38-43; MajGen Raymond G. Davis intvw, 1Jan69, (OralHistColl, MCHC, Washington, D.C.), hereafter Davis intvw.
6. Davis intvw.
7. Ibid.
8. 11th Mar ComdCs, Jan-Dec69; 11th Mar, Arty Ops.
9. Col Don D. Ezell intvw, 8Apr70, No. 4837 (OralHistColl, MCHC, Washington, D.C.), hereafter Ezell intvw.
10. Ibid.
11. Ibid.
12. Ibid; FMFPac MarOpsV, Apr70, pp. 37-39.
13. Ezell intvw.
14. Ibid.
15. Mulroney intvw.
16. 11th Mar, Arty Ops.
17. Mulroney intvw.
18. Col Joseph Sleger, Jr., Comments on draft ms, 2Oct86 (Vietnam 69 Comment File, MCHC, Washington, D.C.).

Surveillance and Reconnaissance Activities

Additional sources for this section are drawn from: 1st Recon Bn ComdCs, Jan-Dec69; 3d Recon Bn ComdCs, Jan-Nov69; 1st Force Recon Co ComdCs, Jan-Dec69; and 3d Force Recon Co ComdCs, Aug, Nov-Dec69. Extensive use was made of LCdr Ray W. Stubbe, CHC, USN, "Aarugha!, Report to Director, Historical Division, Headquarters, Marine Corps, on the History of Specialized and Force Level Reconnaissance Activities and Units of the United States Marine Corps, 1900-1974" (unpublished ms, 1981).

19. Col John S. Canton, Comments on draft ms, 3Sep86 (Vietnam 69 Comment File, MCHC, Washington, D.C.), hereafter Canton Comments.
20. FMFPac to CMC, dtd 8Dec69, III MAF Misc Msg File, Oct-Dec69.
21. Davis intwv, p. 285.
22. Ibid., pp. 285-286.
23. 1stLt Wayne E. Rollings intvw, Jun69, No. 4074 (OralHistColl, MCHC, Washington, D.C.); "Caught With His Pants On," *Sea Tiger*, 16May69.
24. Debrief Rpt, dtd 131900Apr69 in 1st For Rec Co ComdC, Apr69; "Recon Patrol Eludes 150 NVA," *Sea Tiger*, May69.
25. Ibid.
26. Debrief Rpt, dtd 050500Jun69 in 3d Recon Bn ComdC, Jun69.
27. Debrief Rpt, dtd 020533Jun69 in 3d Recon Bn ComdC, Jun69.
28. 1stMarDiv ComdC, Sep69.
29. Maj John J. Guenther intvw, 11Aug69, No. 4483 (OralHistColl, MCHC, Washington, D.C.).
30. Col Anthony J. Skotnicki intvw, 18Sep69, No. 4562 (OralHistColl, MCHC, Washington, D.C.), hereafter Skotnicki intvw.
31. 1stMarDiv ComdC, May69.
32. 1st Radio Bn ComdC, Mar69.
33. COMUSMACV msg to CinCPac, dtd 14May69 (MACV Hist-DocColl, Reel 46).
34. Canton Comments.
35. Skotnicki intvw.

CHAPTER 15
SUPPLYING III MAF

Unless otherwise noted, material in this chapter is derived from: FMFPac MarOpsV, Jan-Dec69.

Force Logistic Command

Additional sources for this section are drawn from: FLC ComdCs, Jan-Dec69; FLSG-Alpha ComdCs, Jan-Dec69; FLSG-Bravo ComdCs, Jan-Dec69; and Col James B. Soper, "A View From FMFPac of Logistics in the Western Pacific, 1965-1971," *Naval Review 1972*, pp. 224-239.

1. FLSG-Bravo ComdC, Nov69.
2. Col Frank P. DeNormandie intvw, 10Nov69, No. 4684 (OralHistColl, MCHC, Washington, D.C.).
3. 1stMarDiv ComdC, May69.
4. MajGen Wilbur F. Simlik intvw, 14Oct77 (OralHistColl, MCHC, Washington, D.C.), p. 26, hereafter Simlik intvw.
5. Col John L. Schwartz intvw, 22Oct69, No. 4564 (OralHistColl, MCHC, Washington, D.C.).
6. Col William D. Bassett, Jr., Comments on draft ms, 11Sep86 (Vietnam 69 Comment File, MCHC, Washington, D.C.).
7. FLC ComdC, Apr69.
8. Col Samuel A. Hannah intvw, 7Jul69, No. 4256 (OralHistColl, MCHC, Washington, D.C.).

NOTES

9. FLC ComdCs, Apr-May69; Col Darwin B. Pond, Jr., intvw, 22Jul69, No. 4253 (OralHistColl, MCHC, Washington, D.C.).

Naval Support Activity, Da Nang

Additional sources for this section are drawn from: III MAF/I Corps Tactical Zone Common Service Support Responsibilities File, 3Jan69-1Feb70, hereafter cited as III MAF CSS File; U.S. Naval Support Activity, Da Nang, Command History 1969, in Operational Archives Branch, NHD, hereafter USNSADN Comd Hist 1969; Cdr Frank C. Collins, Jr., USN, "Maritime Support of the Campaign in I Corps," *Naval Review 1971*, pp. 158-179, hereafter Collins, "Maritime Support"; U.S. Naval Support Activity/Facility, Da Nang, *Changes: A History*, 1970, hereafter *Changes, A History*.

10. Collins, "Maritime Support," pp. 158-159; USNSADN, Comd Hist 1969.
11. USNSADN, Comd Hist 1969.
12. LtGen Joseph M. Heiser, Jr., *Vietnam Studies: Logistic Support* (Washington: GPO, 1974), pp. 177-181.
13. Ibid., p. 184.
14. ComNavForV msg to CGIIIMAF, dtd 3Jun69, III MAF CSS File.
15. CGIIIMAF msg to ComNavForV, dtd 4Jun69, Ibid.
16. Simlik intvw, p. 17.
17. Ibid., p. 18.
18. LtGen Leo J. Dulacki intvw, 24Oct74 (OralHistCol, MCHC, Washington, D.C.), pp. 68-69; LtGen Leo J. Dulacki, Comments on draft ms, 1Aug86 (Vietnam 69 Comment File, MCHC, Washington, D.C.).
19. III MAF CSS File; Collins, "Maritime Support," p. 178; and *Changes: A History*.

Engineer Support

Additional sources for this section are drawn from: 1st Engr Bn ComdCs, Jan-Dec69; 3d Engr Bn ComdCs, Jan-Dec69; 7th Engr Bn ComdCs, Jan-Dec69; 9th Engr Bn ComdCs, Jan-Dec69; and 11th Engr Bn ComdCs, Jan-Dec69.

20. HQMC, Status of Forces, Jan69; MajGen Robert R. Ploger, *Vietnam Studies: U.S Army Engineers, 1965-1970* (Washington: GPO, 1974), pp. 148-155.
21. LtCol Adrian G. Traas, USA, Comments on draft ms, 29Aug86 (Vietnam Comment File, MCHC, Washington, D.C.).
22. Col Nicholas A. Canzona intvw, 4Mar70, No. 4796 (OralHistColl, MCHC, Washington, D.C.).
23. 1st Engr Bn ComdC, May69.
24. FMFPac MarOpsV, Dec69.
25. LtGen Ormond R. Simpson, Comments on draft ms, 18Aug69 (Vietnam 69 Comment File, MCHC, Washington, D.C.).
26. 11th Engr Bn ComdC, Sep-Nov69.
27. Land-Clearing Company (Provisional) AAR, Go Noi Island, in 7th Engr Bn ComdC, Jul69.
28. LtGen Ormond R. Simpson intvw, 25May73 (OralHistColl, MCHC, Washington, D.C.), p. 654.

Motor Transport

Additional sources for this section are drawn from: FMFPac MarOpsV, Jan-Dec69; 1st MT Bn ComdCs, Jan-Dec69; 3d MT Bn ComdCs, Jan-Dec69; 7th MT Bn ComdCs, Jan-Dec69; 9th MT Bn ComdCs, Jan-Dec69; 11th MT Bn ComdCs, Jan-Dec69; and Truck Company ComdCs, Jan-Dec69 in 1st FSR ComdCs, Jan-Dec69.

29. LtCol Laurier J. Tremblay, Comments on draft ms, 11Aug86 (Vietnam 69 Comment File, MCHC, Washington, D.C.).
30. 11th MT Bn ComdCs, Apr-Aug69.

Medical Support

Additional sources for this section are drawn from: FMFPac MarOpsV, Jan-Dec69; 1st Med Bn ComdCs, Jan-Dec69; 3d Med Bn ComdCs, Jan-Dec69; and 1st Hospital Co ComdCs, Jan-Dec69.

31. Col Eugene R. Brady, Comments on draft ms, 14Oct86 (Vietnam 69 Comment File, MCHC, Washington, D.C.); Col Eugene R. Brady, "The Thread of a Concept," *Marine Corps Gazette*, May71, pp. 35-42.
32. Ibid., p. 40, 42.

Communications

Additional sources for this section are drawn from: 5th Com Bn ComdCs, Jan-Dec69; 7th Com Bn ComdCs, Jan-Dec69; and Maj Blaine D. King, "Force Comm in Vietnam," *Marine Corps Gazette*, Feb72, pp. 35-38.

Logistics of Keystone Eagle and Keystone Cardinal

Additional sources for this section are drawn from: 3dMarDiv OpO 25-69, dtd 23Sep69, and 3dMarDiv "Lessons Learned, 3d Marine Division Redeployment, June through December 1969," dtd 5Jan70.

33. LtGen Leo J. Dulacki intvw, 24Oct74 (OralHistColl, MCHC, Washington, D.C.), pp. 66-68.
34. Simlik intvw, pp. 22-23.
35. Ibid.
36. Jones intvw, p. 57.
37. Col Raymond C. Damm, Comments on draft ms, 14Aug69 (Vietnam 69 Comment File, MCHC, Washington, D.C.).
38. Simlik intvw, p. 16.
39. Ibid., pp. 23-24
40. Jones intvw, pp. 65-66.

PART VI
Unique Contributions

CHAPTER 16
PACIFICATION

Unless otherwise noted, material in this chapter is derived from: MACV Command History, 1969; FMFPac MarOpsV, Jan-Dec69; III MAF ComdCs, Jan-Dec69; 1stMarDiv ComdCs, Jan-Dec69; and 3dMarDiv ComdCs, Jan-Dec69.

The National Perspective

Additional sources for this section are drawn from: MACV Command History, 1969; FMFPac MarOpsV, Jan-Dec69; and MACV, Hamlet Evaluation System Handbook, Jun69.

1. Republic of Vietnam, Office of the Prime Minister, Central Pacification and Development Council, "Basic Directive on the 1969 Pacification and Development Plan," p. 3 (MACV HistDocColl, Reel 56).

Pacification Planning In I Corps

Additional sources for this section are drawn from: MACV Command History, 1969; FMFPac MarOpsV, Jan-Dec69; and I Corps/III MAF Combined Campaign Plan (CCP) 1969, dtd 26Dec68.

2. Col George C. Knapp intvw, 2May69, No. 4088 (OralHistColl, MCHC, Washington, D.C.), hereafter Knapp intvw.
3. III MAF ComdCs, Jan-Dec69.
4. Ibid.; 1stMarDiv ComdCs, Jan-Dec69; and 3dMarDiv ComdCs, Jan-Nov69.

Line Unit Pacification

Additional sources for this section are drawn from: FMFPac MarOpsV, Jan-Dec69; 1stMarDiv ComdCs, Jan-Dec69; and 3dMarDiv ComdCs, Jan-Nov69.

5. Knapp intvw.
6. Maj John J. Guenther intvw, 11Aug69. No. 4483 (OralHistColl, MCHC, Washington, D.C.).
7. 1stMarDiv AAR, Opn Pipestone Canyon.
8. Ibid.
9. MACCORDS, Monthly Reports-Kit Carson Scout Program, Jan-Dec69 (MACV HistDocColl, Reel 56).

Civic Action

Additional sources for this section are drawn from: FMFPac MarOpsV, Jan-Dec69; III MAF ComdCs, Jan-Dec69; 1stMarDiv ComdCs, Jan-Dec69; and 3dMarDiv ComdCs, Jan-Nov69.

10. I Corps/III MAF CCP, 1969, p. B-3-2.
11. Ibid., p. B-3-9.
12. 3dMarDiv G-5, History of Civic Action Projects in Quang Tri During 1969, n.d.
13. FLC ComdCs, Jan-Dec69.
14. 3dMarDiv, Civil Affairs & PsyOp Newletter, Jan, Mar, May69.

The Grass Roots Campaign

Additional sources for this section are drawn from: FMFPac MarOpsV, Jan-Dec69; 1stCAG ComdCs, Jan-Dec69; 2dCAG ComdCs, Jan-Dec69; 3dCAG ComdCs, Jan-Dec69; and 4thCAG ComdCs, Jan-Dec69.

15. CAF Fact Sheet, dtd 31Mar70.
16. Ibid., p. 1.
17. 1stCAG ComdCs, Jan69; 2dCAG ComdCs, Jan69; 3dCAG ComdCs, Jan69; 4th CAG ComdCs, Jan69; and, Col Charles R. Burroughs CAP Briefing, Jun69, No. 6506 (OralHistColl, MCHC, Washington, D.C.), hereafter Burroughs briefing.
18. LtGen Herman Nickerson, Jr., intvw, 10Jan73 (OralHistCol, MCHC, Washington, D.C.), p. 103, hereafter Nickerson intvw.

19. Burroughs briefing.
20. CAF Fact Sheet, p. 2.
21. Ibid.; LtCol Earl R. Hunter, Comments on draft ms, 9Sep86, 14Oct86 (Vietnam 69 Comment File, MCHC, Washington, D.C.); Burroughs briefing.
22. Cpl Michael E. Gordy intvw, 5Mar69, No. 3913 (OralHistColl, MCHC, Washington, D.C.).
23. 4th CAG OpO, Mobilization of Combined Action Platoon 2-4-1, dtd 1Apr69 in 2d CAG ComdC, Apr69.
24. CAF Fact Sheet, Encl 7, "A Discussion of the Mobile CAP Concept."
25. Human Sciences Research, Inc., Interim Technical Report, "Marine Combined Action Capabilities: Training For Future Contingencies," Apx C, p. 61.
26. Ibid., p. 16.
27. Alexander Firfer intvw, 26Jul76, No. 6323 (OralHistColl, MCHC, Washington, D.C.), hereafter Firfer intvw.
28. Ibid
29. Ibid.; LtGen Leo J. Dulacki, Comments on draft ms, 1Aug86 (Vietnam 69 Comment File, MCHC, Washington, D.C.).
30. 1stMarDiv ComdCs, Nov-Dec69; Nickerson intvw, pp. 101-102.

Results

Additional sources for this section are drawn from: MACV Command History, 1969; FMFPac MarOpsV, 1969, Oct-Dec69; and III MAF ComdCs, Nov-Dec69.

31. Col Theodore E. Metzger, Comments on draft ms, 25Aug86 (Vietnam 69 Comment File, MCHC, Washington, D.C.)
32. Firfer intvw.
33. Ibid.

CHAPTER 17
SPECIAL LANDING FORCE OPERATIONS

Unless otherwise noted, material in this chapter is derived from: FMFPac MarOpsV, Jan-Dec69; 9th MAB ComdCs, Jan-Nov69; TF 79.4 (SLF Alpha) ComdCs, Jan-Dec69; TF 79.5 (SLF Bravo) ComdCs, Jan-Dec69; 1/26 ComdCs, Feb-Nov69; 2/26 ComdCs, Jan-Jun, Aug-Nov69; and 3/26 ComdCs, Jan-Nov69.

The Strategic Reserve

1. Col John Lowman, Jr., Comments on draft ms, 22Sep86 (Vietnam 69 Comment File, MCHC, Washington, D.C.
2. Col Clyde W. Hunter intvw, 10Jul69, No. 4363 (OralHistColl, MCHC, Washington, D.C.).
3. Col William C. Doty, Jr., intvw, 23Sep69, No. 4482 (OralHistColl, MCHC, Washington, D.C.).
4. Col Robert R. Wilson intvw, 12Jun69, No. 4263 (OralHistColl, MCHC, Washington, D.C.).

Organization and Operations

Additional sources for this section are drawn from: TF 79.4 (SLF Alpha) ComdCs, Jan-Dec69; TF 79.4 AAR, Opn Eager Pursuit; TF 79.4 AAR, Opn Daring Rebel; TF 79.4 AAR, Opn Bold Pursuit; TF 79.4 AAR, Opn Mighty Play; TF 79.4 AAR, Opn Defiant Stand; TF 79.5 (SLF Bravo) ComdCs, Jan-Dec69; TF 79.5 AAR, Opn Defi-

NOTES

ant Measure; 1/26 ComdCs, Feb-Nov69; 1/26 AAR, Opn Daring Rebel; 1/26 AAR, Opn Bold Pursuit; 1/26 AAR, Opn Mighty Play; 2/26 ComdCs, Jan-Jun, Aug-Nov69; 2/26 AAR, Opn Bold Mariner; 3/26 ComdCs, Jan-Nov69; 3/26 AAR, Opn Bold Mariner-Russell Beach; 3/26 AAR, Opn Defiant Measure-Taylor Common; HMM-164 ComdCs, Jan-Dec69; HMM-362 ComdCs, Jan-Jun69; and HMM-265 ComdCs, Jun-Nov69.

5. BGen John E. Williams intvw, 12Jun69, No. 4262 (OralHistColl, MCHC, Washington, D.C.).
6. HQMC, Final Report of Study of Special Landing Force Operations, dtd 30Mar70.
7. *Sea Tiger*, 30May69.
8. Ibid.

The Fleet's Contingency Force

Additional sources for this section are drawn from: 9th MAB ComdCs, Oct-Nov69; TF 79.4 (SLF Alpha) ComdCs, Nov-Dec69; and TF 79.5 (SLF Bravo) ComdCs, Oct-Dec69.

9. CTF 76 msg to CTG 76.4, dtd 3Dec69 in COMSEVENTHFLT Amphib Opns File, Dec69, (Operational Archives Branch, NHC, Washington, D.C.); COMSEVENTHFLT msg to CTF 76 and CTF 79, dtd 5Dec69, in ibid.
10. BGen Robert B. Carney, Jr., intvw, 21Nov69, No. 4643 (OralHistColl, MCHC, Washington,D.C.).

CHAPTER 18
THE ADVISORY EFFORT
AND OTHER ACTIVITIES

Unless otherwise noted, material in this chapter is derived from: FMFPac MarOpsV, Jan-Feb69.

Marine Advisors and the Vietnamese Marine Corps

Additional sources for this section are drawn from: Senior Marine Advisor, "Vietnamese Marine Corps/Marine Advisory Unit Historical Summary, 1954-1973," dtd 22Mar73; Senior Marine Advisor, Monthly Historical Summaries, Jan-Dec69; and Col James T. Breckinridge intvw, 2May69, No. 4060 (OralHistColl, MCHC, Washington, D.C.), and supporting documents (S908633).

1. Senior Marine Advisor, "Vietnamese Marine Corps/Marine Advisory Unit Historical Summary, 1954-1973," encl 2, pp. 1-2.
2. LtGen Le Nguyen Khang intvw, 30Sep75 (OralHistColl, MCHC, Washington, D.C.), pp. 72-73.

3. Col Leroy V. Corbett intvw, Aug69, No. 5031 (OralHistColl, MCHC, Washington, D.C.), hereafter Corbett intvw.
4. LtCol David G. Henderson, Comments on draft ms, 9Sep86 (Vietnam 69 Comment File, MCHC, Washington, D.C.).
5. Corbett intvw.
6. Col Leroy V. Corbett, Comments on draft ms, 12Sep86 (Vietnam 69 Comment File, MCHC, Washington, D.C.).

1st Air and Naval
Gunfire Liaison Company (ANGLICO)

Additional sources for this section are drawn from: Sub-Unit One, 1st ANGLICO ComdCs, Jan-Dec69; and LtCol Thomas H. Simpson intvw, 24Sep70, No. 4960 (OralHistColl, MCHC, Washington, D.C.).

7. LtCol Thomas H. Simpson intvw, 24Sep70, No. 4960 (OralHistColl, MCHC, Washington, D.C.).
8. Ibid.
9. Ibid.

U.S. Marines on the MACV Staff

Additional sources for this section are drawn from: LtGen John N. McLaughlin intvw, 18Oct78 (OralHistColl, MCHC, Washington, D.C.), pp. 16-38.

10. LtGen John N. McLaughlin intvw, 18Oct78 (OralHistColl, MCHC, Washington, D.C.), p. 25.
11. Ibid, p. 19.
12. Ibid, p. 38.

Embassy Guard Marines

Additional sources for this section are drawn from: Company E, Security Guard Battalion (Saigon) ComdCs, 1969.

CHAPTER 19
1969: AN OVERVIEW

Unless otherwise noted, material in this chapter is derived from: FMFPac MarOpsV, Jan-Dec69, and III MAF ComdCs, Jan-Dec69.

1. Memo for the Record, JCS Meeting, 15Jan69, dtd 17Jan69, Chapman Papers, MCHC.

Appendix A
Marine Command and Staff List
January-December 1969

III MAF Headquarters, 1Jan-31Dec69*

CG LtGen Robert E. Cushman, Jr.	1Jan-26Mar69
LtGen Herman Nickerson, Jr.	27Mar-31Dec69
DepCG MajGen Carl A. Youngdale	1Jan-11Jul69
MajGen George S. Bowman, Jr.	12Jul-31Dec69
DepCG Air MajGen Charles J. Quilter	1Jan-10Jul69
MajGen William G. Thrash	11Jul-31Dec69
C/S BGen George E. Dooley	1Jan-22Dec69
BGen Leo J. Dulacki	23Dec-31Dec69
DepC/S Col Michael Mosteller	1Jan-18Feb69
Col Lewis E. Poggemeyer	19Feb-27Nov69
Col Sam A. Dressin	28Nov-31Dec69
DepC/S Plans BGen Warren K. Bennett, USA	1Jan-29May69
BGen William A. Burke, USA	30May-27Nov69
Col Milton M. Cook, Jr.	28Nov-3Dec69
Col James A. Sloan	4Dec-31Dec69
G-1 Col Maurice Rose	1Jan-26Mar69
Col William J. Howatt	27Mar-20Jun69
Col George W. Callen	21Jun-21Sep69
Col Robert L. Parnell, Jr.	22Sep-31Dec69
G-2 Col Ray N. Joens	1Jan-4Feb69
Col John S. Canton	5Feb-19Dec69
Col Edward W. Dzialo	20Dec-31Dec69
G-3 BGen Carl W. Hoffman	1Jan-17Feb69
BGen Ross T. Dwyer, Jr.	18Feb-25Jun69
BGen Leo J. Dulacki	26Jun-22Dec69
BGen Thomas H. Miller, Jr.	23Dec-31Dec69
Dep G-3 Col Marion C. Dalby	1Jan-17Apr69
Col Robert H. Barrow	18Apr-19Jul69
Col Roy L. Reed	20Jul-27Nov69
Col Lewis E. Poggemeyer	28Nov-31Dec69
G-4 Col Lawrence C. Norton	1Jan-19Jul69
Col Oliver R. Davis	20Jul-2Oct69
Col Robert J. Barbour	3Oct-11Nov69
Col Wilbur F. Simlik	12Nov-31Dec69
G-5 Col Howard A. Westphall	1Jan-18Apr69
Col Gilbert R. Hershey	19Apr-27Jul69
Col Theodore E. Metzger	28Jul-20Sep69
Col Clifford J. Peabody	21Sep-31Dec69
G-6 Col Bill E. Horner	1Jan-14Sep69
Col Sam A. Dressin	15Sep-27Nov69
LtCol Richard S. Barry	28Nov-31Dec69

AC/S Combined Action Program

Col Edward F. Danowitz	1Jan-31Mar69
Col Charles R. Burroughs	1Apr-Oct69
Col Theodore E. Metzger	Oct-31Dec69

1st Combined Action Group (1st CAG)

CO LtCol Earl R. Hunter	1Jan-24Apr69
LtCol Joseph E. Hennegan	25Apr-23Oct69
LtCol David F. Seiler	24Oct-31Dec69

2d Combined Action Group (2d CAG)

CO LtCol Edward L. Lewis, Jr.	1Jan-19Oct69
LtCol Don R. Christensen	20Oct-31Dec69

3d Combined Action Group (3d CAG)

CO LtCol Robert D. Whitesell	1Jan-24Feb69
LtCol Roi E. Andrews	25Feb-24Jul69
LtCol John B. Michaud	24Jul-31Dec69

4th Combined Action Group (4th CAG)

CO LtCol John E. Greenwood	1Jan-27Feb69
LtCol Daniel J. Ford	28Feb-14Aug69
Maj Robert M. Cooper	15Aug-7Sep69
LtCol John J. Keenah	8Sep-31Dec69

5th/7th Communication Battalion, 15Apr-20Oct69*

CO LtCol Charles L. Brady	15Apr-14Sep69
Maj Donald F. Selby	15Sep-30Sep69
LtCol Dale E. Shatzer	1Oct-12Oct69
Maj Richard G. Schwarz	13Oct-20Oct69

*7th Comm Bn departed RVN on 20Oct69.

1st Marine Division

CG MajGen Ormond R. Simpson	1Jan-14Dec69
MajGen Edwin B. Wheeler	15Dec-31Dec69
ADC BGen Ross T. Dwyer, Jr.	1Jan-14Feb69
BGen Samuel Jaskilka	15Feb-15Aug69
BGen Charles S. Robertson	16Aug-31Dec69
ADC (TAD III MAF) BGen Carl W. Hoffman	1Jan-14Feb69

*Unless otherwise indicated, dates refer to the period when a unit was in Vietnam. Only permanent Marine organizations of battalion/squadron-size or larger are listed; exceptions are Task Force Bravo, Task Force Hotel, Task Force Yankee, and Force Logistic Command and its components. The following listing reflects administrative rather than operational organization.

COMMAND AND STAFF LIST

	BGen Ross T. Dwyer, Jr.	15Feb-24Jun69
	BGen Leo J. Dulacki	25Jun-25Dec69
C/S	Col Samuel A. Hannah	1Jan-7Feb69
	Col Harry E. Dickinson	8Feb-8Aug69
	Col Charles E. Walker	9Aug-31Dec69
G-1	Col George E. Lawrence	1Jan-6Sep69
	LtCol James E. Harrell	7Sep-11Dec69
	Col Robert E. Barde	12Dec-31Dec69
G-2	Col Anthony J. Skotnicki	1Jan-14Sep69
	Col Edward A. Wilcox	15Sep-31Dec69
G-3	Col Adolph G. Schwenk	1Jan-8Mar69
	Col Jo M. Van Meter	9Mar-22Mar69
	Col James B. Ord, Jr.	23Mar-31Oct69
	Col Floyd H. Waldrop	1Nov-31Dec69
G-4	Col James E. Wilson, Jr.	1Jan-12Mar69
	Col John L. Schwartz	13Mar-14Oct69
	Col Nicholas A. Canzona	15Oct-31Dec69
G-5	Col Harry F. Painter	1Jan-15Aug69
	Col William J. Zaro	16Aug-12Dec69
	LtCol Vincent A. Albers, Jr.	13Dec-31Dec69

Headquarters Battalion, 1st Marine Division

CO	Col William S. Fagan	1Jan-27Mar69
	Col Nicholas A. Canzona	28Mar-30Sep69
	Col William C. Patton	1Oct-31Dec69

Task Force Yankee, 1Jan-8Mar69*

CO	BGen Ross T. Dwyer, Jr.	1Jan-14Feb69
	BGen Samuel S. Jaskilka	15Feb-8Mar69
C/S	Col Robert L. Nichols	1Jan-16Jan69
	Col William J. Zaro	17Jan-8Mar69
G-1	Capt Richard W. Schulz	1Jan-8Mar69
G-2	LtCol John A. Dowd	1Jan-8Mar69
G-3	LtCol Raymond P. Coffman, Jr.	1Jan-8Mar69
G-4	Maj Kenneth P. Knueble	1Jan-6Mar69
	Capt Nicola M. Pereira, Jr.	7Mar-8Mar69

*Deactivated with termination of Operation Taylor Common on 8Mar69.

1st Marines

CO	Col Robert G. Lauffer	1Jan-24Feb69
	Col Charles S. Robertson	25Feb-30May69
	Col Charles E. Walker	31May-13Jun69
	Col Charles S. Robertson	14Jun-16Aug69
	Col Herbert L. Wilkerson	17Aug-31Dec69

1st Battalion, 1st Marines

CO	LtCol Alphonse A. Laporte, Jr.	1Jan-28Mar69
	LtCol Wendell P. Morgenthaler, Jr.	29Mar-8Oct69
	LtCol Godfrey S. Delcuze	9Oct-31Dec69

2d Battalion, 1st Marines

CO	LtCol John E. Poindexter	1Jan-4Feb69
	LtCol Harold G. Glasgow	5Feb-8Aug69
	LtCol William V. H. White	9Aug-31Dec69

3d Battalion, 1st Marines

	LtCol Thomas E. Bulger	1Jan-6Jul69
	LtCol Thomas P. Ganey	7Jul-31Dec69

5th Marines

CO	Col James B. Ord, Jr.	1Jan-22Mar69
	Col William J. Zaro	23Mar-16Aug69
	Col Noble L. Beck	17Aug-31Dec69

1st Battalion, 5th Marines

CO	LtCol Richard F. Daley	1Jan-26Apr69
	LtCol William E. Riley, Jr.	27Apr-30Aug69
	Maj Patrick E. O'Toole	31Aug-22Sep69
	LtCol Joseph K. Griffis, Jr.	23Sep-31Dec69

2d Battalion, 5th Marines

CO	LtCol James W. Stemple	1Jan-13Mar69
	LtCol James H. Higgins	14Mar-18Aug69
	Maj Robert E. Loehe	19Aug-25Aug69
	LtCol James T. Bowen	26Aug-31Dec69

3d Battalion, 5th Marines

CO	LtCol Harry E. Atkinson	1Jan-29Jun69
	LtCol John M. Terry, Jr.	30Jun-8Dec69
	LtCol Johan S. Gestson	9Dec-31Dec69

7th Marines

CO	Col Herbert L. Beckington	1Jan-7Feb69
	Col Robert L. Nichols	8Feb-9Jul69
	Col Gildo S. Codispoti	10Jul-31Dec69

1st Battalion, 7th Marines

CO	LtCol William F. Bethel	1Jan-22Mar69
	LtCol John A. Dowd	23Mar-13Aug69
	LtCol Frank A. Clark	14Aug-31Dec69

2d Battalion, 7th Marines

CO	LtCol Neil A. Nelson	1Jan-21Feb69
	LtCol Jan P. Vandersluis	22Feb-27Feb69
	LtCol Neil A. Nelson	28Feb-28Apr69
	LtCol Marvin H. Lugger	29Apr-28Aug69
	LtCol Joseph E. Hopkins	29Aug-21Oct69
	LtCol Arthur E. Folsom	21Oct-31Dec69

3d Battalion, 7th Marines

CO	LtCol Francis X. Quinn	1Jan-22Mar69
	LtCol James O. Allison	23Mar-17Aug69
	LtCol Ray G. Kummerow	18Aug-31Dec69

26th Marines, 7Nov-31Dec69

CO	Col Ralph A. Heywood	7Nov-12Dec69
	LtCol James E. Harrell	13Dec-31Dec69

1st Battalion, 26th Marines
CO LtCol James C. Goodin — 7Nov-31Dec69

2d Battalion, 26th Marines
CO LtCol William C. Drumright — 7Nov-31Dec69

3d Battalion, 26th Marines
CO LtCol William A. Simpson — 7Nov-26Dec69
LtCol John J. Unterkofler — 27Dec-31Dec69

11th Marines
CO Col Harry E. Dickinson — 1Jan-7Feb69
Col Samuel A. Hannah — 8Feb-2Jul69
Col Carl E. Walker — 3Jul-8Aug69
LtCol Corbin J. Johnson — 9Aug-31Aug69
Col Don D. Ezell — 1Sep-31Dec69

1st Battalion, 11th Marines
CO LtCol John A. Hamilton — 1Jan-11Mar69
LtCol Francis Andriliunas — 12Mar-21Aug69
LtCol John D. Shoup — 22Aug-31Dec69

2d Battalion, 11th Marines
CO LtCol Robert D. Jameson — 1Jan-20Apr69
LtCol Kenneth L. Smith — 21Apr-1Oct69
LtCol Vonda Weaver — 2Oct-31Dec69

3d Battalion, 11th Marines
CO LtCol Richard P. Johnson — 1Jan-28Feb69
Maj Andrew F. Bauer — 1Mar-14Mar69
LtCol Raymond B. Ingrando — 15Mar-20Oct69
LtCol Karl N. Mueller — 21Oct-31Dec69

4th Battalion, 11th Marines
CO Maj Bobby J. Ready — 1Jan-1Jun69
Maj Eric H. Wieler — 2Jun-14Jun69
LtCol John H. Strandquist — 15Jun-16Oct69
LtCol James F. Burke, Jr. — 17Oct-31Dec69

1st Field Artillery Group*
CO LtCol Raymond B. Ingrando — 1Jan-15Mar69
Maj Edward E. Johnson — 16Mar-27Mar69
1stLt Joseph H. Molen — 28Mar-13Jul69

*Reduced to cadre strength on 1Apr69 and departed RVN on 13Jul69 with RLT-9.

1st Battalion, 13th Marines, 7Nov-31Dec69
CO LtCol Donald H. Strain — 7Nov-31Dec69

1st Reconnaissance Battalion
CO LtCol Larry P. Charon — 1Jan-8Feb69
LtCol Richard D. Mickelson — 9Feb-7Oct69
LtCol John J. Grace — 8Oct-31Dec69

1st Tank Battalion
CO LtCol Maurice C. Ashley, Jr. — 1Jan-10Mar69
LtCol Dale E. Young — 11Mar-7Jul69
LtCol Robert B. March — 8Jul-8Sep69
LtCol Larry R. Butler — 9Sep-12Nov69
Maj Joseph J. Louder — 13Nov-31Dec69

1st Motor Transport Battalion
CO Maj Robert G. Reilly — 1Jan-3Jan69
LtCol Billy E. Wilson — 4Jan-30Sep69
Maj Donald C. Pease — 1Oct-1Dec69
LtCol Morris S. Shimanoff — 2Dec-31Dec69

1st Engineer Battalion
CO LtCol Donald H. Hildebrand — 1Jan-25Mar69
LtCol John F. Mader — 26Mar-31Jul69
LtCol Roland E. Smith — 31Jul-16Nov69
LtCol Walter M. Winoski — 17Nov-31Dec69

1st Shore Party Battalion
CO LtCol Donald L. Anderson — 1Jan-9Sep69
Maj John E. Duck — 10Sep-4Oct69
LtCol Richard F. Armstrong — 5Oct-31Dec69

3d Amphibian Tractor Battalion
CO LtCol Joseph E. Hennegan — 1Jan-28Feb69
Maj James W. Rahill — 1Mar-5Mar69
Maj King D. Thatenhurst, Sr. — 6Mar-12Sep69
Maj James W. Rahill — 13Sep-31Oct69
LtCol David G. Mehargue — 1Nov-31Dec69

1st Medical Battalion
CO Capt James V. Sharp, MC, USN — 1Jan-20Feb69
Capt James W. Lea, MC, USN — 21Feb-31Dec69

7th Communication Battalion, 1Jan-15Apr69*
CO LtCol Charles L. Brady — 1Jan-15Apr69

*Unit transferred to III MAF and combined with 5th Comm Bn.

11th Motor Transport Battalion
CO LtCol John A. Kinniburgh — 1Jan-12Sep69
Maj Michael J. Zachodni — 13Sep-17Sep69
LtCol William R. Kephart — 18Sep-31Dec69

7th Engineer Battalion
CO LtCol Themistocles T. Annas — 1Jan-18Aug69
LtCol William G. Bates — 19Aug-31Dec69

9th Engineer Battalion
CO LtCol Darrell U. Davidson — 1Jan-20Mar69
LtCol Billy F. Visage — 21Mar-31Aug69
LtCol Edward K. Maxwell — 1Sep-31Dec69

3d Marine Division, 1Jan-7Nov69
CG MajGen Raymond G. Davis — 1Jan-14Apr69
MajGen William K. Jones — 15Apr-6Jul69

COMMAND AND STAFF LIST

BGen Regan Fuller (Acting)	6Jul-12Jul69
MajGen William K. Jones	13Jul-7Nov69
ADC BGen Frank E. Garretson	1Jan-22Apr69
BGen Regan Fuller	23Apr-6Jul69
BGen Regan Fuller	13Jul-7Nov69
ADC BGen Robert B. Carney, Jr.	1Jan-9Jun69
C/S Col Martin J. Sexton	1Jan-29Aug69
Col Robert P. Wray	30Aug-7Nov69
G-1 Col Louis R. Daze	1Jan-26Feb69
LtCol Edward D. Gelzer, Jr.	26Feb-29Apr69
Col Marshall A. Webb, Jr.	30Apr-3Oct69
LtCol William S. Daniels	4Oct-7Nov69
G-2 Col Thomas P. O'Callaghan	1Jan-29Jun69
LtCol Charles R. Stephenson II	30Jun-7Nov69
G-3 Col Paul D. Lafond	1Jan-16Jan69
Col Francis R. Kraince	17Jan-17Jul69
Col Clarence G. Moody, Jr.	18Jul-28Aug69
Col William E. Barrineau	29Aug-7Nov69
G-4 Col Frank R. Denormandie	1Jan-7Nov69
G-5 Col William E. Kerrigan	1Jan-7Nov69

Headquarters Battalion

CO Marshall A. Webb, Jr.	1Jan-30Apr69
LtCol Stewart B. McCarty, Jr.	1May-25Aug69
Maj Robert T. Carney	26Aug-5Sep69
Maj Keith L. Christensen	6Sep-9Sep69
LtCol Charles F. King, Jr.	10Sep-7Nov69

Task Force Bravo, 1Jan-18Feb69*

CO Col Truman W. Clark	1Jan-18Feb69
XO LtCol Byron T. Chen	1Jan-18Feb69
S-1 GySgt Robert D. Smith	1Jan18Feb69
S-2 Maj George L. Shelley III	1Jan-18Feb69
S-3 Maj Harry L. Bauknight	1Jan-18Feb69
S-4 1stLt Steven L. Cox	1Jan-18Feb69

*Unit deactivated as operational control passed to 3d Marine Division on 18Feb69.

Task Force Hotel, 1Jan-8Jul69*

CO BGen Frank E. Garretson	1Jan-31Mar69
BGen Robert B. Carney, Jr.	1Apr-21May69
MGen Clifford B. Drake	21May-22May69
BGen Regan Fuller	22May-8Jul69
C/S Col Robert D. Slay	1May-6Jun69
Col Warren L. MacQuarrie	7Jun-8Jul69
G-1 Capt William K. Hoyt, Jr.	1May-15Jun69
2dLt Blaine E. Moyer	16Jun-8Jul69
G-2 Capt Robert B. Mackenzie	1May-27Jun69
Maj Larry R. Ogle	28Jun-8Jul69
G-3 LtCol George W. Smith	1May-8Jul69
G-4 Maj Donald C. Bickel	1May-8Jul69

*With the decision to withdraw the 9th Marines, TF Hotel was deactivated on 8Jul69. Names of personnel serving on staff through 30Apr69 are unavailable.

3d Marines*

CO Col Michael M. Spark	1Jan-15Jan69
Col Paul D. Lafond	16Jan-27Jun69
Col Wilbur F. Simlik	28Jun-6Oct69

*Unit departed RVN for CONUS, 6Oct69.

1st Battalion, 3d Marines*

CO LtCol Richard B. Twohey	1Jan-2Feb69
LtCol John S. Kyle	3Feb-10May69
LtCol David G. Herron	11May-21Sep69

*Unit departed RVN for CONUS, 6Oct69.

2d Battalion, 3d Marines*

CO LtCol James J. McMonagle	1Jan-2Aug69
LtCol William S. Daniels	3Aug-21Sep69

*Unit departed RVN for CONUS, 6Oct69.

3d Battalion, 3d Marines*

CO LtCol Richard C. Schulze	1Jan-19Aug69
LtCol Ernest E. Evans, Jr.	20Aug-13Sep69
LtCol David F. Seiler	14Sep-21Sep69

*Unit departed RVN for CONUS, 7Oct69.

4th Marines*

CO Col William F. Goggin	1Jan-9Aug69
Col Gilbert R. Hershey	10Aug-20Nov69

*Unit departed RVN for Okinawa, 20Nov69.

1st Battalion, 4th Marines*

CO LtCol George T. Sargent, Jr.	1Jan-21Mar69
LtCol Clair E. Willcox	22Mar-5Aug69
LtCol Joseph A. MacInnis	6Aug-22Oct69

*Unit departed RVN for Okinawa, 22Oct69.

2d Battalion, 4th Marines*

CO LtCol Joseph E. Hopkins	1Jan-6Sep69
LtCol William C. Britt	7May-6Sep69
LtCol Donald J. Garrett	7Sep-9Nov69

*Unit departed RVN for Okinawa, 9Nov69.

3d Battalion, 4th Marines*

CO LtCol William A. Donald	1Jan-10May69
Maj Raymond D. Walters	6May-10May69
LtCol James W. Wood	10May-20Nov69

*Unit departed RVN for Okinawa, 20Nov69.

9th Marines*

CO Col Robert H. Barrow	1Jan-8Apr69
Col Edward F. Danowitz	9Apr-13Aug69

*Unit departed RVN for Okinawa, 13Aug69.

1st Battalion, 9th Marines*

CO LtCol George W. Smith	1Jan-30Mar69
LtCol Thomas J. Culkin	31Mar-14Jul69

*Unit departed RVN for Okinawa, 14Jul69.

2d Battalion, 9th Marines*
CO LtCol George C. Fox	1Jan-4Mar69
Maj Patrick G. Collins (Acting)	5Mar-18Mar69
LtCol George C. Fox	19Mar-22Jun69
Maj Robert L. Modjeski	23Jun-1Aug69

Unit departed RVN for Okinawa, 1Aug69.

3d Battalion, 9th Marines*
CO LtCol Elliott R. Laine, Jr.	1Jan-16Apr69
LtCol Oral R. Swigart, Jr.	17Apr-22Jun
LtCol Donald E. Wood	23Jun-13Aug69

Unit departed RVN for Okinawa, 13Aug69.

12th Marines*
CO Col Peter J. Mulroney	1Jan-11Jul69
Col Wallace W. Crompton	12Jul-9Nov69

Unit departed RVN for Okinawa, 9Nov69.

1st Battalion, 12th Marines*
CO LtCol Ermil L. Whisman	1Jan-15Jan69
LtCol Roddey B. Moss	16Jan-7Jun69
LtCol Morgan W. West	8Jun-2Oct69

Unit departed RVN for CONUS, 2Oct69.

2d Battalion, 12th Marines*
CO LtCol Joseph R. Scoppa, Jr.	1Jan-30Mar69
LtCol Calhoun J. Killeen	31Mar-31Jul69

Unit departed RVN for Okinawa, 31Jul69.

3d Battalion, 12th Marines*
CO LtCol Eugene D. Foxworth, Jr.	1Jan-31Apr69
Maj Robert E. Gibson	1May-2Jul69
Maj Harry H. Bair	3Aug-18Aug69
LtCol David R. McMillan, Jr.	19Aug-5Nov69

Unit departed RVN for Okinawa, 5Nov69.

4th Battalion, 12th Marines*
CO LtCol Earl W. Bailey	1Jan-3May69
LtCol Joseph R. Scoppa, Jr.	4May-11Jul69
Maj Thomas L. Edwards	12Jul-31Jul69
LtCol Alfred J. Croft, Jr.	1Aug-29Sep69
Maj Harry H. Bair	30Sep-19Nov69

Unit departed RVN for Okinawa, 19Nov69.

3d Reconnaissance Battalion*
CO LtCol Aydlette H. Perry, Jr.	1Jan-29May69
LtCol Richard R. Burritt	30May-24Nov69

Unit departed RVN for Okinawa, 24Nov69.

3d Tank Battalion*
CO LtCol George E. Hayward	1Jan-31Jan69
LtCol Joseph Sleger, Jr.	1Feb-15Jul69
Maj Raymond G. Kennedy, Sr.	16Jul-16Sep69
LtCol William S. Rump	17Sep-23Oct69

Unit departed RVN for Okinawa, 23Oct69.

3d Motor Transport Battalion*
CO Maj George W. Ward	1Jan-16Feb69
Maj Joseph F. Lavin	17Feb-8Jul69
Maj Raymond S. Davis, Jr.	9Jul-20Oct69

Unit departed RVN for Okinawa, 20Oct69.

3d Engineer Battalion*
CO LtCol Walter L. Persac	1Jan-15Apr69
LtCol John R. Lilley II	16Apr-3Aug69
LtCol Raymond C. Damm	4Aug-6Sep69
LtCol James W. Medis	7Sep-23Oct69

Unit departed RVN for Okinawa, 23Oct69.

3d Shore Party Battalion*
CO Maj Edwin J. Godfrey	1Jan-7Mar69
Maj Joseph B. Knotts	8Mar-16Aug69
LtCol Eugene E. Paro, Jr.	17Aug-10Nov69

Unit departed RVN for Okinawa, 10Nov69.

1st Amphibian Tractor Battalion*
CO LtCol Walter W. Damewood, Jr.	1Jan-30Mar69
Maj David R. Stefansson	31Mar-5Jun69
Maj William A. Grubbs III	6Jun-15Jun69

Unit departed RVN for Okinawa, 15Jun69.

3d Medical Battalion*
CO Cdr Barton K. Slemmons, MC, USN	1Jan-24Jul69
Capt Jacob V. Brown, MC, USN	25Jul-24Nov69

Unit departed RVN for Okinawa, 24Nov69.

9th Motor Transport Battalion*
CO LtCol Laurier J. Tremblay	1Jan-22Oct69
Maj Larry D. Derryberry	23Oct-4Nov69

Unit departed for Okinawa, 4Nov69.

11th Engineer Battalion*
CO LtCol Robert C. Evans	1Jan-6Sep69
Maj Dale R. Thibault	7Sep-21Nov69

Unit departed RVN for Okinawa, 21Nov69.

Force Logistic Command
CO BGen James A. Feeley, Jr.	1Dec68-6Nov69
BGen Mauro J. Padalino	7Nov-31Dec69

Headquarters and Service Battalion, 1st Force Service Regiment
CO LtCol Edward Lukas	1Jan-19Aug69
LtCol John H. Miller	20Aug-1Dec69
LtCol Lewis R. Webb	2Dec-31Dec69

Supply Battalion, 1st Force Service Regiment
CO LtCol Edward G. Usher	1Jan-31May69
Col William W. Storm III	1Jun-5Nov69
Col Robert W. Calvert	6Nov-31Dec69

COMMAND AND STAFF LIST

Maintenance Battalion, 1st Force Service Regiment

CO LtCol Edward W. Critchett	1Jan-16Oct69
LtCol Edward C. Morris	17Oct-31Dec69

3d Service Battalion (Rein) /Force Logistic Support Group Alpha*

CO Col Horton E. Roeder	1Jan-13May69
LtCol William D. Bassett, Jr.	14May-18Aug69
LtCol Ward R. Reiss	19Aug-28Oct69
LtCol William J. Beer	29Oct-7Nov69

*Unit redeployed to Okinawa and replaced by Sub-Unit 1, FLSG "B" (Rear).

1st Service Battalion (Rein) /Force Logistic Support Group Bravo

CO Col Harold L. Parsons	1Jan-6Sep69
Col Donald E. Morin	7Sep-31Dec69

1st Military Police Battalion

CO LtCol James D. Bailey	1Jan-8Nov69
LtCol Speros D. Thomaidis	9Nov-31Dec69

3d Military Police Battalion

CO LtCol Willard E. Cheatham	1Jan-14Oct69
LtCol Charles Fimian	15Oct-31Dec69

5th Communication Battalion*

CO LtCol Jack D. Hines	1Jan-15Apr69

*Unit transferred to III MAF on 15Apr69 and merged with 7th Communication Battalion.

7th Motor Transport Battalion

CO Maj Jerome W. Brown	1Jan-27Aug69
Maj G. B. Tucker	28Aug-19Oct69
LtCol Richard L. Prather	20Oct-31Dec69

1st Marine Aircraft Wing

CG MajGen Charles J. Quilter	1Jan-10Jul69
MajGen William G. Thrash	11Jul-31Dec69
AWC BGen Henry W. Hise	1Jan-28Feb69
Vacant	1Mar-10Jun69
BGen William G. Johnson	11Jun-6Nov69
AWC BGen Homer S. Hill	1Jan-15May69
BGen Ralph H. Spanjer	16May-31Dec69
C/S Col Virgil D. Olson	1Jan-6Sep69
Col Robert W. Teller	7Sep-31Dec69
G-1 Col Edward A. Parnell	1Jan-4Mar69
Col Rex A. Deasy	5Mar-30Jun69
Col Grover S. Stewart, Jr.	1Jul-31Dec69
G-2 LtCol Hugh R. Bumpas, Jr.	1Jan-23Feb69
Col John J. Doherty	24Feb-11Jul69
Col Leonard L. Orr	12Jul-19Sep69
Col James R. Weaver	20Sep-31Dec69
G-3 Col Edwin H. Finlayson	1Jan-10Jun69
Col Robert L. Lamar	11Jun-31Dec69
G-4 Col Steve Furimsky, Jr.	1Jan-5Mar69
Col Norman W. Gourley	6Mar-6Aug69
LtCol Neil F. Defenbaugh	7Aug-11Aug69
LtCol Edward E. Smith	12Aug-15Aug69
Col William C. McGraw, Jr.	16Aug-31Dec69

Marine Wing Headquarters Group 1 (MWHG-1)

CO Col Thomas H. Nichols, Jr.	1Jan-26Feb69
LtCol Dennis W. Wright	27Feb-18Mar69
Col John R. Gill	19Mar-18Jul69
LtCol William Shanks, Jr.	19Jul-10Nov69
Col Laurence J. Stien	11Nov-31Dec69

Headquarters and Headquarters Squadron 18 (H&HS-18)

CO LtCol John R. Dopler	1Jan-11Jul69
Capt George P. Turner, Jr.	12Jul-3Aug69
LtCol Paul E. Shea	4Aug-5Oct69
Maj Herbert E. Hoppmeyer, Jr.	6Oct-31Dec69

Marine Air Support Squadron 2 (MASS-2)

CO Maj Edward J. Dahy III	1Jan-10Jan69
LtCol Robert A. Fuller	11Jan-5Aug69
Maj Marvin L. Crowdis	6Aug-14Aug69
Maj Ronald G. Richardson	15Aug-31Oct69
Maj Jerry D. Oden	1Nov-23Nov69

Marine Air Support Squadron 3 (MASS-3)

CO LtCol William J. Sullivan	1Jan-3Mar69
LtCol William H. Jackson, Jr.	4Mar-11Sep69
LtCol John H. Dubois	12Sep-31Dec69

Marine Air Control Squadron 4 (MACS-4)

CO LtCol Thomas M. Kauffman	1Jan-9Mar69
LtCol Edward S. John	10Mar-12Aug69
LtCol Robert E. McCamey II	13Aug-30Dec69
Maj Robert W. Molyneux, Jr.	31Dec69

Marine Wing Support Group 17 (MWSG-17)

CO Col Richard S. Rash	1Jan-5Mar69
LtCol Harry U. Carpenter	6Mar-10Aug69
Col Richard A. Savage	11Aug-31Dec69

Marine Air Control Group 18 (MACG-18)

CO Col Edward S. Fris	1Jan-16Jul69
Col Stanley G. Dunnwiddie, Jr.	17Jul-31Dec69

1st Light Anti-Aircraft Missile Battalion
(1st LAAM)*

CO LtCol John W. Drury	1Jan-7Jul69
Maj Edward L. House, Jr.	8Jul-16Aug69

Unit departed RVN for CONUS, 16Aug69.

Marine Aircraft Group 11
(MAG-11)

CO Col Robert D. Slay	1Jan-13Mar69
Col Steve Furminsky, Jr.	14Mar-12Aug69
Col John B. Heffernan	13Aug-31Dec69

Headquarters and Maintenance Squadron 11
(H&MS-11)

CO LtCol Robert M. Stowers	14May-29Aug69
LtCol Guy O. Badger	14May-29Aug69
LtCol Richard F. Hebert	30Aug-31Dec69

Marine Air Base Squadron 11
(MABS-11)

CO LtCol Preston P. Margues, Jr.	1Jan-15May69
LtCol George W. Glauser	16May-21Oct69
LtCol Paul A. Manning	22Oct-31Dec69

Marine Composite Reconnaissance Squadron 1
(VMCJ-1)

CO LtCol Bobby R. Hall	1Jan-16May69
LtCol Preston P. Marques, Jr.	17May-13Oct69
LtCol Bob W. Farley	14Oct-31Dec69

Marine All Weather Attack Squadron 225
(VMA[AW]-225)*

CO LtCol Ronald L. Townsend	5Feb-21Jun69
LtCol Donald L. Harvey	22Jun-28Nov69
Maj Peter M. Busch	29Nov-31Dec69

From MAG-14, 5Feb69.

Marine All Weather Attack Squadron 242
(VMA[AW]-242)

CO LtCol Fred C. Rilling, Jr.	1Jan-14Jan69
LtCol Adnah K. Frain	15Jan-1Jul69
LtCol Thomas L. Griffin, Jr.	2Jul-31Dec69

Marine Fighter Attack Squadron 334
(VMFA-334)*

CO LtCol James R. Sherman	1Jan-24Jan69

To MAG-13, 24Jan69.

Marine Fighter Attack Squadron 542
(VMFA-542)

CO LtCol Henry R. Vitali	1Jan-24Feb69
LtCol Ray N. Stewart	25Feb-10Aug69
LtCol Keith A. Smith	11Aug-31Dec69

Marine Aircraft Group 12

CO Col Rex A. Deasy	1Jan-28Feb69
Col Thomas H. Nichols, Jr.	1Mar-28Sep69
Col Paul B. Henley	29Sep-31Dec69

Headquarters and Maintenance Squadron 12
(H&MS-12)

CO LtCol Clifford D. Warfield	1Jan-9Apr69
LtCol John J. McCarthy	10Apr-18Sep69
LtCol Joseph J. Went	19Sep-31Dec69

Marine Air Base Squadron 12
(MABS-12)

CO Maj Lawrence Furstenberg	1Jan-30Apr69
LtCol John J. Cahill	1May-13Dec69
LtCol George J. Ertlmeier	14Dec-31Dec69

Marine Fighter Attack Squadron 121
(VMFA-121)*

CO Maj David A. Lerps	1Jan-14Feb69

Redesignated VMA(AW)-121 on 14Feb69 and assigned to 2d Marine Aircraft Wing.

Marine Fighter Attack Squadron 211
(VMFA-211)

CO LtCol John R. Waterstreet	1Jan-15Mar69
LtCol Edward T. Graham, Jr.	16Mar-5Sep69
LtCol Louis Gasparine, Jr.	6Sep-31Dec69

Marine Fighter Attack Squadron 223
(VMFA-223)

CO Maj Leonard T. Preston, Jr.	1Jan-10Apr69
LtCol Merrill S. Newbill	11Apr-27Sep69
LtCol James W. Lazzo	28Sep-31Dec69

Marine Fighter Attack Squadron 311
(VMFA-311)

CO LtCol Charles O. Hiett	1Jan-30Apr69
LtCol David A. Kelly	1May-24Nov69
Maj Arthur R. Hickle	25Nov-31Dec

Marine All Weather Attack Squadron 533
(VMA[AW]-533)*

CO LtCol Paul K. German, Jr.	1Jan-28Feb69
LtCol George H. Shutt, Jr.	1Mar-30Sep69
LtCol Frank G. Castillo, Jr.	1Oct-7Oct69

Unit departed RVN for Japan, 7Oct69.

Marine Aircraft Group 13

CO Col Norman W. Gourley	1Jan-5Mar69
Col Richard S. Rash	6Mar-14Sep69
Col Thomas E. Murphree	15Sep-31Dec69

Headquarters and Maintenance Squadron 13
(H&MS-13)

CO Maj Edgar A. House	1Jan-14Jan69
LtCol Billy M. Adrian	15Jan-13Jun69

COMMAND AND STAFF LIST

LtCol Lawrence J. Willis	14Jun-9Oct69
Maj James D. Moody	10Oct-16Nov69
LtCol Douglas L. Snead	17Nov-28Dec69
Maj Frank J. Horak, Jr.	29Dec-31Dec69

Marine Air Base Squadron 13
(MABS-13)

CO LtCol Charles V. Smillie, Jr.	1Jan-23Apr69
LtCol Ira L. Morgan, Jr.	24Apr-11Jun69
LtCol Norbert F. Schnippel, Jr.	12Jun-4Jul69
LtCol Alfred N. Drago	5Jul-5Oct69
LtCol Richard D. Revie	6Oct-31Dec69

Marine Fighter Attack Squadron 115
(VMFA-115)

CO LtCol Robert R. Norton	1Jan-1Jul69
LtCol Edwin C. Paige, Jr.	2Jul-31Dec69

Marine Fighter Attack Squadron 122
(VMFA-122)*

CO LtCol John K. Cochran	5Sep-31Dec69

*From MAG-15, 5Sep69.

Marine Fighter Attack Squadron 232
(VMFA-232)*

CO LtCol Walter P. Hutchins	21Mar-11Aug69
LtCol Ralph J. Sorensen	12Aug-7Sep69

*Unit arrived RVN from CONUS, 21Mar69; departed RVN for Japan, 7Sep69.

Marine Fighter Attack Squardon 314
(VMFA-314)

CO LtCol Frank E. Petersen, Jr.	1Jan-23Feb69
LtCol Thomas R. Morgan	24Feb-8Mar69
LtCol John W. Black	9Mar-25Jun69
LtCol Charles G. Frederick	26Jun-1Dec69
LtCol Thomas J. Kelly	2Dec-31Dec69

Marine Fighter Attack Squadron 323
(VMFA-323)*

CO LtCol Ira L. Morgan, Jr.	1Jan-25Mar69

*Unit departed RVN for CONUS, 25Mar69.

Marine Fighter Attack Squadron 334
(VMFA-334)*

CO LtCol James R. Sherman	24Jan-12Feb69
LtCol Samuel E. D'Angelo III	13Feb-1Jul69
LtCol John R. Braddon	2Jul-30Aug69

*Unit departed RVN for Japan, 30Aug69.

Marine Aircraft Group 16

CO Col Warren L. MacQuarrie	1Jan-12Mar69
LtCol Floyd K. Fulton, Jr.	13Mar-30Sep69
Col James P. Bruce	1Oct-31Dec69

Headquarters and Maintenance Squadron 16
(H&MS-16)

CO LtCol Charles W. Gobat	1Jan-25May69
LtCol James W. Laseter	26May-19Aug69
LtCol Richard A. Bancroft	20Aug-22Dec69
Maj Malcolm T. Hornsby, Jr.	23Dec-31Dec69

Marine Air Base Squadron 16
(MABS-16)

CO LtCol William Cunningham	1Jan-9May69
Maj John C. Archbold	10May-7Jun69
LtCol Joseph R. Donaldson	8Jun-30Sep69
LtCol John W. Coffman	1Oct-19Dec69
Maj Peter C. Scaglione, Jr.	20Dec-31Dec69

Marine Observation Squadron 2
(VMO-2)

CO LtCol Thomas J. Dumont	1Jan-19Mar69
LtCol Clark S. Morris	20Mar-16Jul69
LtCol Stanley A. Challgren	17Jul-31Dec69

Marine Light Helicopter Squadron 167
(HML-167)

CO LtCol Thomas F. Miller	1Jan-12Feb69
LtCol Jack W. Conard	13Feb-19Aug69
LtCol James W. Laseter	20Aug-7Nov69
LtCol John E. Weber, Jr.	8Nov-31Dec69

Marine Medium Helicopter Squadron 364
(HMM-364)

CO LtCol Merlin V. Statzer	1Jan-2Feb69
LtCol Eugene R. Brady	3Feb-22Aug69
LtCol Charles R. Dunbaugh	23Aug-31Dec69

Marine Heavy Helicopter Squadron 463
(HMH-463)

CO LtCol Roger W. Peard, Jr.	1Jan-6Mar69
LtCol Raymond M. Ryan	7Mar-31Dec69

Marine Medium Helicopter Squadron 165
(HMM-165)*

CO LtCol George L. Patrick, Jr.	1Jan-24Feb69
LtCol Thomas E. Raines	25Feb-13Aug69

*Unit departed RVN for Okinawa, 14Aug69.

Marine Medium Helicopter Squadron 263
(HMM-263)

CO LtCol Robert E. Hofstetter	1Jan-13May69
LtCol William Cunningham	14May-29Sep69
LtCol Walter R. Ledbetter, Jr.	30Sep-31Dec69

Marine Heavy Helicopter Squadron 361
(HMH-361)

CO LtCol Kermit W. Andrus	26Sep-15Dec69
LtCol Charles A. Block	16Dec-31Dec69

Marine Medium Helicopter Squadron 161
(HMM-161)

CO Maj Richard W. Carr	16Oct-14Dec69
LtCol Bennie H. Mann, Jr.	15Dec-31Dec69

Marine Medium Helicopter Squadron 262
(HMM-262)

CO Maj Donald J. Meskan	16Oct-19Dec69
LtCol Richard A. Bancroft	20Dec-31Dec69

Marine Light Helicopter Squadron 367
(HML-367)

CO LtCol Warren G. Cretney	16Oct-31Dec69

Marine Aircraft Group 36*

CO Col Bruce J. Matheson	1Jan-15May69
LtCol Herbert J. Blaha	16May-9Jul69
Col Noah C. New	10Jul-16Oct69
Col Owen V. Gallentine	17Oct-7Nov69

Unit departed RVN for Okinawa, 7Nov69.

Headquarters and Maintenance Squadron 36
(H&MS-36)*

CO LtCol James B. Bell	1Jan-12Sep69
Maj Chester L. Whipple	13Sep-23Sep69
Maj Charles A. Carey	24Sep-15Oct69
LtCol Bobby R. Wilkinson	16Oct-27Nov69
Maj Joseph F. Golden	28Nov-7Nov69

Unit departed RVN for Okinawa, 7Nov69.

Marine Air Base Squadron 36
(MABS-36)*

CO LtCol Dennis W. Wright	1Jan-9Feb69
LtCol Rondell K. Wood	10Feb-15May69
LtCol Ronald E. Nelson	16May-5Sep69
Maj Edwin W. Lockard	6Sep-23Nov69

Unit departed RVN for Okinawa, 23Nov69.

Marine Medium Helicopter Squadron 265
(HMM-265)*

CO LtCol Ralph Thuesen	1Jan-15May69
LtCol Robert L. Gray, Jr.	16May-7Jun69

Unit departed RVN for Okinawa, 7Jun69.

Marine Medium Helicopter Squadron 362
(HMM-362)*

CO LtCol Jack E. Schlarp	25May-21Aug69

To FMFLant, 21Aug69.

Marine Medium Helicopter Squadron 363
(HMM-363)*

CO LtCol Timothy J. Cronin, Jr.	1Jan-21Jan69

Unit departed RVN for CONUS, 21Jan69.

Marine Light Helicopter Squadron 367
(HML-367)*

CO LtCol Richard L. Robinson	1Jan-19Feb69
LtCol Bobby R. Wilkinson	20Feb-14Oct69
LtCol Warren G. Cretney	15Oct-16Oct69

To MAG-16, 16Oct69.

Marine Heavy Helicopter Squadron 462
(HMH-462)*

CO LtCol Ronald E. Nelson	1Jan-15May69
LtCol Rondell K. Wood	16May-13Oct69
Maj Peter F. Lottsfeldt	14Oct-20Oct69

Unit departed RVN for Okinawa, 20Oct69.

Marine Heavy Helicopter Squadron 361
(HMH-361)*

CO LtCol Kermit W. Andrus	1Aug-26Sep69

To MAG-16, 26Sep69.

Provisional Marine Aircraft Group 39
(PMAG-39)

CO Col Walter Sienko	1Jan-6Mar69
Col Edward A. Parnell	7Mar-31Jul69
Col Owen V. Gallentine*	1Aug-15Oct69

Assumed command of MAG-36 and staff merged with MAG-36.

Provisional Headquarters and Maintenance
Squadron 39 (PH&MS-39)*

CO LtCol Bobby R. Wilkinson	1Jan-18Feb69
Maj Joseph L. Felter	19Feb-11Apr69
LtCol Warren G. Cretney	12Apr-10Oct69
Maj Joseph F. Golden	11Oct-31Oct69

Unit merged with MAG-36.

Marine Medium Helicopter Squadron 161
(HMM-161)*

CO LtCol David L. Elam	1Jan-19Jul69
Maj Richard W. Carr	20Jul-15Oct69

To MAG-16, 16Oct69.

Marine Medium Helicopter Squadron 262
(HMM-262)*

CO LtCol Albert N. Allen	1Jan-23Mar69
LtCol James A. Wells, Jr.	24Mar-8Jul69
Maj Donald J. Meskan	9Jul-15Oct69

To MAG-16, 16Oct69.

Marine Observation Squadron 6
(VMO-6)*

CO Maj Hans A. Zander	1Jan-1Apr69
LtCol Billy D. Bouldin	2Apr-16Jun69
Maj Albert K. Charlton	17Jun-12Oct69

Unit departed RVN for Okinawa, 12Oct69.

COMMAND AND STAFF LIST

Marine Forces, Western Pacific

9th Marine Amphibious Brigade/Task Force 79, 1Jan-7Nov69*

CO BGen John E. Williams	1Jan-12Jun69
BGen Robert B. Carney, Jr.	13Jun-7Nov69
C/S Col John Lowman, Jr.	1Jan-22Jul69
Col John F. McMahon, Jr.	23Jul-13Sep69
Col H. Speed Wilson	14Sep-7Nov69
G-1 Maj William H. Groesbeck	1Jan-20Feb69
Capt Raymond H. Ambrose	21Feb-4Mar69
LtCol Keith L. Lynn	5Mar-28Sep69
Maj Russell E. Dolan	29Sep-7Nov69
G-2 LtCol Aubrey L. Lumpkin	1Jan-26Jan69
LtCol Conrad A. Jorgenson	27Jan-19Apr69
1stLt Everett J. Boyser, Jr.	20Apr-13Jun69
Maj Jack D. Boline	14Jun-14Oct69
2dLt Ernest E. Johnson	15Oct-19Oct69
Maj Paul B. Tubach	20Oct-7Nov69
G-3 LtCol George C. Kliefoth	1Jan-16Feb69
Col Clyde W. Hunter	17Feb-9Jul69
LtCol William M. Kull	10Jul-6Aug69
Col Clarence W. Boyd, Jr.	7Aug-12Sep69
Col Ernest R. Reid, Jr.	13Sep-7Nov69
G-4 LtCol Stewart B. McCarty, Jr.	1Jan-15Apr69
LtCol Raymond McArthur	16Apr-19Aug69
Col John H. Keith, Jr.	20Aug-7Nov69

Deactivated on 7 November 1969 and subordinate units transferred to 3d Marine Division, I Marine Expeditionary Force, and 1st Marine Aircraft Wing (Rear).

26th Marines*

CO Col Clyde W. Hunter	1Jan-13Feb69
Col Ray N. Joens	14Feb-13Jun69
Col Ralph A. Heywood	14Jun-7Nov69

To 1st Mar Div, 7Nov69.

1st Battalion, 26th Marines*

CO LtCol Charles H. Knowles	1Jan-28Feb69
LtCol George C. Kliefoth	1Mar-27Jul69
LtCol James C. Goodin	28Jul-7Nov69

To 1st Mar Div, 7Nov69.

2d Battalion, 26th Marines*

CO LtCol William F. Sparks	1Jan-27Feb69
LtCol George M. Edmondson, Jr.	28Feb-9Sep69
LtCol William C. Drumright	10Sep-7Nov69

To 1st Mar Div, 7Nov69.

3d Battalion, 26th Marines*

CO LtCol J. W. P. Robertson	1Jan-3Mar69
LtCol Edward W. Snelling	4Mar-15Sep69
LtCol William A. Simpson	15Sep-7Nov69

To 1st Mar Div, 7Nov69.

1st Battalion, 13th Marines*

CO LtCol John B. Cantieny	1Jan-27Jun69
LtCol David E. Gragan	28Jun-5Sep69
LtCol Donald H. Strain	6Sep-7Nov69

To 1stMarDiv, 7Nov69.

Special Landing Force Alpha (SLF Alpha)/CTG 79.4

CO Col John F. McMahon, Jr.	1Jan-5Apr69
Col William C. Doty, Jr.	6Apr-17Sep69
Col Clarence W. Boyd, Jr.	18Sep-7Nov69

Special Landing Force Bravo (SLF Bravo)/CTG 79.5

CO Col Robert R. Wilson	1Jan-28Feb69
Col Albert E. Coffeen	1Mar-25Jun69
LtCol Harold B. Wilson	26Jun-3Jul69
Col Albert E. Coffeen	4Jul-17Oct69
Col Clarence W. Boyd, Jr.	18Oct-7Nov69

Provisional Service Battalion/TG 79.8

CO Col William C. Doty, Jr.	1Jan-29Mar69
Maj Raymond C. Kargol	29Mar-12Apr69
Col John F. McMahon, Jr.	12Apr-22Jun69
Col John M. Keeley	23Jun-7Nov69

9th Marines

CO Col Edward F. Danowitz	13Aug-7Sep69
Col Jo M. Van Meter	8Sep-7Nov69

1st Battalion, 9th Marines

CO LtCol Thomas J. Culkin	14Jul-14Aug69
Maj Joe L. Goodwin	15Aug-5Sep69
LtCol Donald J. McAdams	6Sep-7Nov69

2d Battalion, 9th Marines

CO LtCol Robert L. Modjeski	1Aug-18Oct69
Maj Charles G. Bryan	19Oct-27Oct69
LtCol James R. Van Den Elzen	28Oct-7Nov69

3d Battalion, 9th Marines

CO LtCol Donald E. Wood	13Aug-7Nov69

2d Battalion, 12th Marines

CO LtCol Calhoun J. Killeen	1Aug-15Sep69
Maj Rodney H. Ledet	16Sep-19Oct69
LtCol Joe D. Prater	20Oct-7Nov69

1st Amphibian Tractor Battalion

CO Maj William A. Grubbs III	15Jun-30Sep69
Maj Cliff E. Delano	1Oct-7Nov69

Marine Aircraft Group 15
(MAG-15)/TG 79.3*

CO Col Clement T. Corcoran	1Jan-6May69
Col Joseph A. Mitchell	7May-7Nov69

Control passed from 9th Marine Amphibious Brigade to 1st Marine Aircraft Wing (Rear) on 7 November 1969.

Headquarters and Maintenance Squadron 15
(H&MS-15)

CO LtCol Kenneth M. Scott	1Jan-21Apr69
LtCol Conrad A. Jorgenson	22Apr-3Oct69
Maj Lloyd K. Warn	4Oct-7Nov69

Marine Air Base Squadron 15
(MABS-15)

CO LtCol Dock H. Pegues	1Jan-4Sep69
LtCol Raymond McArthur	5Sep-7Nov69

Marine Air Control Squadron 8
(MACS-8)

CO Maj Dirk C. Bierhaalder	1Jan-31Mar69
LtCol Thomas M. Kauffman	1Apr-12Sep69
LtCol George G. Long	13Sep-7Nov69

Marine Aerial Refueler Transport Squadron 152
(VMGR-152)

CO LtCol Frank R. Smoke	1Jan-31Aug69
LtCol Albert H. Manhard, Jr.	1Sep-7Nov69

Marine All Weather Attack Squadron 533
(VMA[AW]-533)

CO LtCol Frank P. Costello, Jr.	7Oct-7Nov69

Marine Fighter Attack Squadron 122
(VMFA-122)*

CO LtCol Lawrence J. Willis	1Jan-30Apr69
LtCol John K. Cochran	1May-5Sep69

To MAG-13, 5Sep69.

Marine Fighter Attack Squadron 232
(VMFA-232)

CO LtCol Ralph J. Sorensen	7Sep-7Nov69

Marine Fighter Attack Squadron 334
(VMFA-334)

CO LtCol John R. Braddon	30Aug-7Nov69

Marine Heavy Helicopter Squadron 462
(HMH-462)

CO Maj Peter F. Lottsfeldt	20Oct-7Nov69

Marine Medium Helicopter Squadron 164
(HMM-164)

CO LtCol Richard T. Trundy	1Jan-7Nov69

Marine Medium Helicopter Squadron 165
(HMM-165)

CO LtCol Thomas E. Raines	14Aug-7Nov69

Marine Medium Helicopter Squadron 265
(HMM-265)

CO LtCol Robert L. Gray, Jr.	7Jun-7Nov69

Marine Medium Helicopter Squadron 362
(HMM-362)*

CO LtCol Jack E. Schlarp	1Jan-25May69

To MAG-36, 25May69.

Marine Observation Squadron 6
(VMO-6)

CO Maj Albert K. Charlton	12Oct-7Nov69

I Marine Expeditionary Force
Task Force 79 7Nov-31Dec69

CO MGen William K. Jones	7Nov-31Dec69
C/S Col H. Speed Wilson	7Nov-16Nov69
Col Charles J. Bailey, Jr.	17Nov-31Dec69
G-1 Maj Russell E. Dolan	7Nov-31Dec69
G-2 Col Charles R. Stephenson II	7Nov-3Dec69
LtCol Joseph A. MacInnis	4Dec-31Dec69
G-3 Col Ernest R. Reid, Jr.	7Nov-15Nov69
Col H. Speed Wilson	16Nov-31Dec69
G-4 Col John H. Keith, Jr.	7Nov-31Dec69

Special Landing Force Alpha
(SLF Alpha)/CTG 79.4

CO Col Harold B. Wilson	7Nov-19Nov69
Col George G. Chambers, Jr.	20Nov-31Dec69

Battalion Landing Team 2/9

CO LtCol James R. Van Den Elzen	7Nov-31Dec69

Marine Medium Helicopter Squadron 165
(HMM-165)

CO LtCol Thomas E. Raines	7Nov-23Nov69
LtCol David H. Mitchell	24Nov-31Dec69

Special Landing Force Bravo
(SLF Bravo)/CTG 79.5

CO Col Clarence W. Boyd, Jr.	7Nov-31Dec69

Battalion Landing Team 1/9

CO LtCol Donald J. McAdams	7Nov-31Dec69

Marine Medium Helicopter Squadron 164
(HMM-164)

CO Maj Robert D. Fowner	7Nov-26Dec69
Maj Edward L. Kuykendall	27Dec-31Dec69

3d Marine Division, 7Nov-31Dec69

CG MajGen William K. Jones	7Nov-31Dec69

COMMAND AND STAFF LIST

ADC BGen Regan Fuller	7Nov-16Nov69
BGen Leonard E. Fribourg	17Nov-31Dec69
C/S Col Robert P. Wray	7Nov-31Dec69
G-1 LtCol William S. Daniels	7Nov-31Dec69
G-2 Col Charles R. Stephenson II	7Nov-8Nov69
Col Clarence G. Moody, Jr.	9Nov-31Dec69
G-3 Col William E. Barrineau	7Nov-3Dec69
Col Ernest R. Reid, Jr.	4Dec-31Dec69
G-4 Col Frank R. Denormandie	7Nov-8Nov69

Headquarters Battalion
CO LtCol Charles F. King, Jr.	7Nov-31Dec69

4th Marines
CO Col Gilbert R. Hershey	7Nov-3Dec69
Col William E. Barrineau	4Dec-31Dec69

1st Battalion, 4th Marines
CO LtCol Joseph A. MacInnis	7Nov-27Nov69
LtCol William C. Holmberg	28Nov-31Dec

2d Battalion, 4th Marines
CO LtCol Donald J. Garrett	7Nov-31Dec69

3d Battalion, 4th Marines
CO LtCol James W. Wood	7Nov-5Dec69
LtCol James P. Kehoe	6Dec-31Dec69

9th Marines
CO Col Jo M. Van Meter	7Nov-3Dec69
Col Robert J. Thomas	4Dec-31Dec69

1st Battalion, 9th Marines*
CO LtCol Donald J. McAdams	7Nov-31Dec69

OPCON To TF 79.5.

2d Battalion, 9th Marines
CO LtCol James R. Van Den Elzen	7Nov-31Dec69

3d Battalion, 9th Marines
CO LtCol Donald E. Wood	7Nov-9Dec69
Maj Billy E. Pafford	10Dec-12Dec69
LtCol Herbert M. Hart	13Dec-31Dec69

12th Marines
CO Col Wallace W. Crompton	7Nov-31Dec69

2d Battalion, 12th Marines
CO LtCol Fred W. St.Clair	7Nov-31Dec69

3d Battalion, 12th Marines
CO LtCol David R. McMillan, Jr.	7Nov-31Dec69

4th Battalion, 12th Marines
CO Maj Harry H. Bair	7Nov-31Dec69

3d Reconnaissance Battalion
CO LtCol Richard R. Burritt	7Nov-14Dec69
Maj Russell I. Kramer	15Dec-31Dec69

3d Tank Battalion
CO LtCol William S. Rump	7Nov-14Dec69
LtCol Robert W. Martin, Jr.	15Dec-31Dec69

3d Motor Transport Battalion
CO Maj Raymond S. Davis, Jr.	7Nov-31Dec69

3d Engineer Battalion
CO LtCol James W. Medis	7Nov-31Dec69

3d Shore Party Battalion
CO LtCol Eugene E. Paro, Jr.	7Nov-31Dec69

3d Medical Battalion
CO Capt Jacob V. Brown, MC, USN	7Nov-31Dec69

9th Motor Transport Battalion
CO Maj Larry D. Derryberry	7Nov-31Dec69

7th Communication Battalion
CO Maj Richard G. Schwarz	7Nov-4Dec69
Maj Albert E. Harwood	5Dec-31Dec69

1st Amphibian Tractor Battalion
CO Maj Cliff E. Delano	7Nov-14Nov69
Maj Joseph H. Alexander	15Nov-11Dec69
LtCol Allan W. Lamb	12Dec-31Dec69

1st Marine Aircraft Wing (Rear), 7Nov-31Dec69*
CO BGen William G. Johnson	7Nov-31Dec69
C/S Col Eddie E. Pearcy	7Nov-14Dec69
Col Roy L. Reed	15Dec-31Dec69
G-1 Maj Walter J. Klimek	7Nov-31Dec69
G-2 Maj Fred G. Newcomb	25Nov-31Dec69
G-3 Col Robert L. Fulton	7Nov-1Dec69
Maj James W. Pearson	2Dec-22Dec69
Col Albert R. Pytko	23Dec-31Dec69
G-4 LtCol Edward E. Smith	7Nov-17Nov69
Col Robert J. Barbour	18Nov-31Dec69
G-5 Col Leonard L. Orr	7Nov-31Dec69

Assumed MAG-36, 23Nov69.

Marine Aircraft Group 15
CO Col Joseph A. Mitchell	7Nov-14Dec69
Col Eddie E. Pearcy	15Dec-31Dec69

Headquarters and Maintenance Squadron 15 (H&MS-15)
CO Maj Lloyd K. Warn	7Nov-31Dec69

Marine Air Base Squadron 15 (MABS-15)
CO LtCol Raymond McArthur	7Nov-12Dec69
Maj Robert C. Baughman	13Dec-31Dec69

Marine Air Control Squadron 8*
(MACS-8)
CO LtCol George G. Long   7Nov-30Nov69
*Passed to MACG-18 (Rear), activated on 27Nov69.

Marine Fighter Attack Squadron 232
(VMFA-232)
CO LtCol Ralph J. Sorensen   7Nov-31Dec69

Marine Fighter Attack Squadron 334
(VMFA-334)
CO LtCol John R. Braddon   7Nov-31Dec69

Marine All Weather Attack Squadron 533
(VMA[AW]-533)
CO LtCol Frank P. Costello, Jr. 7Nov-5Dec69
   LtCol Donald L. Harvey   6Nov-31Dec69

Marine Aerial Refueler Transport Squadron 152
(VMGR-152)*
CO LtCol Albert H. Manhard, Jr. 7Nov-18Nov69
*To MAG-36, 18Nov69.

Marine Heavy Helicopter Squadron 462
(HMH-462)*
CO LtCol Peter F. Lottsfeldt   7Nov-18Nov69
*To MAG-36, 18Nov69.

Marine Medium Helicopter Squadron 164
(HMM-164)*
CO LtCol Richard T. Trundy   7Nov-18Nov69
*To MAG-36, 18Nov69.

Marine Medium Helicopter Squadron 165
(HMM-165)*
CO LtCol Thomas E. Raines   7Nov-18Nov69
*To MAG-36, 18Nov69.

Marine Observation Squadron 6
(VMO-6)*
CO LtCol Albert K. Charlton   7Nov-18Nov69
*To MAG-36, 18Nov69.

Marine Aircraft Group 36
(MAG-36), 16Nov-31Dec69
CO Col Owen V. Gallentine   16Nov-31Dec69

Headquarters and Maintenance Squadron 36
(H&MS-36), 7Nov-31Dec69
CO LtCol Bobby R. Wilkinson   7Nov-27Dec69
   Maj Joseph F. Golden   28Dec-31Dec69

Marine Air Base Squadron 36
(MABS-36), 30Nov-31Dec69
CO Maj Edwin W. Lockard   30Nov-31Dec69

Marine Heavy Helicopter Squadron 462
(HMH-462)
CO LtCol Peter F. Lottsfeldt   19Nov-31Dec69

Marine Medium Helicopter Squadron 164
(HMM-164)*
CO Maj Robert D. Fowner   19Nov-25Dec69
   Maj Edward L. Kuyendall   26Dec-31Dec69
*OPCON To TF 79.5.

Marine Medium Helicopter Squadron 165
(HMM-165)*
CO LtCol David H. Mitchell   19Nov-31Dec69
*OPCON To TF 79.4.

Marine Observation Squadron 6
(VMO-6)
CO LtCol Albert K. Charlton   19Nov-30Nov69
   Maj Jack A. Brandon   1Dec-31Dec69

Marine Aerial Refueler Transport Squadron 152
(VMGR-152)
CO LtCol Albert H. Manhard, Jr. 19Nov-31Dec69

Appendix B
Glossary of Terms and Abbreviations

A-1E—Douglas Skyraider, a propeller-driven, single-engine, attack aircraft.

A-4—Douglas Skyhawk, a single-seat, jet attack aircraft in service on board carriers of the U.S. Navy and with land-based Marine attack squadrons.

A-6A—Grumman Intruder, a twin-jet, twin-seat, attack aircraft specifically designed to deliver weapons on targets completely obscured by weather or darkness.

AAR—After Action Report.

ABCCC—Airborne Battlefield Command and Control Center, a U.S. Air Force aircraft equipped with communications, data link, and display equipment; it may be employed as an airborne command post or a communications and intelligence relay facility.

AC-47—Douglas C-47 Skytrain, twin-engine, fixed-wing transport modified with 7.62mm miniguns and used as a gunship.

AC-119—Fairchild Hiller, C-119 military transport aircraft remodified into a gunship with side-firing 7.62mm miniguns.

ADC—Assistant Division Commander.

AGC—Amphibious command ship. The current designation is LCC.

AH-1G—Bell Huey Cobra helicopter specifically designed for close air support.

AK47—Russian-designed Kalashnikov gas-operated 7.62mm automatic rifle, with an effective range of 400 meters. It was the standard rifle of the North Vietnamese Army.

AKA—Attack cargo ship, a naval ship designed to transport combat-loaded cargo in an assault landing. LKA is the current designation.

ALMAR—All Marines, a Commandant of the Marine Corps communication directed to all Marines.

ALO—Air Liaison Officer, an officer (aviator/pilot) attached to a ground unit who functions as the primary advisor to the ground commander on air operation matters.

ANGLICO—Air and Naval Gunfire Liaison Company, an organization composed of Marine and Navy personnel specially qualified for control of naval gunfire and close air support. ANGLICO personnel normally provided this service while attached to U.S. Army, Korean, and ARVN units.

AO—Air Observer, an individual whose primary mission is to observe or to take photographs from an aircraft in order to adjust artillery fire or obtain military information.

AO—Area of Operations.

AOA—Amphibious Objective Area, a defined geographical area within which is located the area or areas to be captured by the amphibious task force.

APA—Attack transport ship, a naval ship, designed for combat loading elements of a battalion landing team. LPA is the current designation.

APC—Armored Personnel Carrier.

APD—Airborne Personnel Detector.

APT—Armed Propaganda Team, a South Vietnamese pacification cadre who carried weapons in self-defense as they attempted to convince South Vietnamese villagers to remain loyal to the government.

Arc Light—The codename for B-52 bombing missions in South Vietnam.

ARG—Amphibious Ready Group.

Arty—Artillery.

ARVN—Army of the Republic of Vietnam (South Vietnam).

ASP—Ammunition Supply Point.

ASRT—Air Support Radar Team, a subordinate operational component of a tactical air control system which provides ground controlled precision flight path guidance and weapons release for attack aircraft.

B40 rocket—Communist rocket-propelled grenade.

B-52—Boeing Stratofortress, U.S. Air Force eight-engine, swept-wing, heavy jet bomber.

BA—Base Area.

Barrel Roll—Codename for air operations over Laos.

Bde—Brigade.

BGen—Brigadier General.

BLT—Battalion Landing Team.

Bn—Battalion.

Btry—Battery.

C-117D—Douglas Skytrain, a twin-engine transport aircraft. The C-117D was an improved version of the C-47, the military version of the DC-3.

C-130—Lockheed Hercules, a four-engine turboprop transport aircraft.

CACO—Combined Action Company.

CAF—Combined Action Force.

CAG—Combined Action Group.

CAP—Combined Action Platoon, see Combined Action Program.

Capt—Captain.

CCP—Combined Campaign Plan.

Cdr—Commander.

CG—Commanding General.

CH-46—Boeing Vertol Sea Knight, a twin-engine, tandem-rotor transport helicopter, designed to carry a four-man crew and 17 combat-loaded troops.

CH-47—Boeing Vertol Chinook, the Army medium-transport helicopter.

CH-53—Sikorsky Sea Stallion, a single-rotor, heavy transport helicopter powered by two shaft-turbine engines with an average payload of 12,800 pounds. Carries crew of three and 38 combat-loaded troops.

Chieu Hoi—The South Vietnamese amnesty program designed to attract Communist troops and cadre to defect to the government cause.

CICV—Combined Intelligence Center, Vietnam.

CIDG—Civilian Irregular Defense Group, South Vietnamese paramilitary force, composed largely of Montagnards, the nomadic tribesmen who populate the South Vietnamese highlands, and advised by the U.S. Army Special Forces.

CinCPac—Commander in Chief, Pacific.

CinCPacFlt—Commander in Chief, Pacific Fleet.
CIT—Counter Intelligence Team.
Claymore—A U.S. directional antipersonnel mine.
CMC—Commandant of the Marine Corps.
CMH—Center of Military History, Department of the Army.
CO—Commanding Officer.
Co—Company.
COB—Combat Operations Base.
COC—Combat Operations Center.
Col—Colonel.
Combined Action Program—A Marine pacification program which integrated a Marine infantry squad with a South Vietnamese Popular Force platoon in a Vietnamese village.
ComdC—Command Chronology.
ComdHist—Command History.
ComNavForPac—Commander, Naval Forces, Pacific.
ComNavForV—Commander, Naval Forces, Vietnam.
COMUSMACV—Commander, U.S. Military Assistance Command, Vietnam.
CORDS—Civil Operations and Revolutionary Development Support, the agency organized under MACV in May 1967 and charged with coordinating U.S.-Vietnamese pacification efforts.
COSVN—*Central Office of South Vietnam*, the nominal Communist military and political headquarters in South Vietnam.

CP—Command Post.
CPDC—Central Pacification and Development Council, the South Vietnamese government agency responsible for coordinating the pacification plan.
CRC—Control and Reporting Center, an element of the U.S. Air Force tactical air control system, subordinate to the Tactical Air Control Center, which conducted radar and warning operations.
C/S—Chief of Staff.
CTZ—Corps Tactical Zone.
CUPP—Combined Unit Pacification Program, a variation of the combined action concept and involving the integration of a Marine line company with a Popular Force or Regional Force unit.

DAIS—Da Nang Anti-Infiltration System.
DASC—Direct Air Support Center, a subordinate operational component of the Marine air control system designed for control of close air support and other direct air support operations.
D-Day—Day scheduled for the beginning of an operation.
DD—Navy destroyer.
Det—Detachment.
Div—Division.
DMZ—Demilitarized Zone separating North and South Vietnam.
DOD—Department of Defense.
DSA—District Senior Advisor.
Dtd—Dated.

EA-6A—The electronic-countermeasures version of the A-6A Intruder.
ECM—Electronic Countermeasures, a major subdivision of electronic warfare involving actions against enemy electronic equipment or to exploit the enemy's use of electromagnetic radiations from such equipment.
EF-10B—An ECM-modified version of the Navy F-3D Skyknight, a twin-engine jet night-fighter of Korean War vintage.
Engr—Engineer.

F-4B—McDonnell Phantom II, a twin-engined, two-seat, long-range, all-weather jet interceptor and attack bomber.
F-4J—McDonnell Phantom II with air-to-air capabilities.
FAC(A)—Forward Air Controller (Airborne).
FDC—Fire Direction Center.
FFV—Field Force, Vietnam I and II, U.S. Army commands in II and III Corps areas of South Vietnam.
FLC—Force Logistic Command.
FLSG—Force Logistic Support Group.
FLSU—Force Logistic Support Unit.
FMFPac—Fleet Marine Force, Pacific.
FO—Forward Observer.
Front 4—A Communist headquarters subordinate to *MR-5* and responsible for Quang Nam Province.
FSB—Fire Support Base.
FSCC—Fire Support Coordination Center, a single location involved in the coordination of all forms of fire support.
FSR—Force Service Regiment.
Fwd—Forward.
FWMF—Free World Military Force.

G—Refers to staff positions on a general staff, e.g., G-1 would refer to the staff member responsible for personnel; G-2, intelligence; G-3, operations; G-4, logistics; and G-5, civil affairs.
Gen—General.
Golden Fleece—Marine rice harvest protection operation.
Grenade Launcher, M79—U.S.-built, single-shot, breech-loaded shoulder weapon which fires 40mm projectiles and weighs approximately 6.5 pounds when loaded; it has a sustained rate of aimed fire of five-seven rounds per minute and an effective range of 375 meters.
Gun, 175mm, M107—U.S.-built, self-propelled gun which weighs 62,000 pounds and fires a 147-pound projectile to a maximum range of 32,800 meters. Maximum rate of fire is one round every two minutes.
GVN—Government of Vietnam (South Vietnam).

H&I fires—Harassing and Interdiction fires.
H&MS—Headquarters and Maintenance Squadron.
H&S Co—Headquarters and Service Company.
HAWK—A mobile, surface-to-air guided missile, designed to defend against low-flying enemy aircraft and short-range missiles.
HE—High Explosive.
HES—Hamlet Evaluation System, the computerized statistical data system used to measure pacification in the hamlets and villages of South Vietnam.
H-Hour—The specific hour an operation begins.
HMH—Marine Heavy Helicopter Squadron.
HMM—Marine Medium Helicopter Squadron.
Hoi Chanh—A Viet Cong or North Vietnamese defector under the *Chieu Hoi* amnesty program.
Howitzer, 8-inch (M55)—U.S.-built, self-propelled, heavy-artillery piece with a maximum range of 16,900 meters and a rate of fire of one round every two minutes.
Howitzer, 105mm, M101A1—U.S.-built, towed, general purpose light artillery piece with a maximum range of 11,000 meters and maximum rate of fire of four rounds per minute.
Howitzer, 155mm, M114A towed and M109 self-propelled—U.S.-built medium artillery with a maximum range of 15,080 meters and a maximum rate of fire of three rounds per minute. Marines employed both models in Vietnam. The newer and heav-

GLOSSARY

ier self-propelled M109 was largely road-bound, while the lighter, towed M114A could be moved either by truck or by helicopter.

HQ or Hq—Headquarters.

Howtar—A 4.2 (107mm) mortar tube mounted on a 75mm pack howitzer frame.

"Huey"—Popular name for UH-1 series of helicopters.

I Corps—The military and administrative subdivision which included the five northern provinces of South Vietnam.

I MAF—I Marine Amphibious Force.

I MEF—I Marine Expeditionary Force.

Intel—Intelligence.

Intvw—Interview.

IOD—Integrated Observation Device.

ITT—Interrogation/Translator Team.

JCS—Joint Chiefs of Staff (U.S.).

JGS—Joint General Staff (South Vietnamese).

KC-130—The in-flight refueling tanker configuration of the C-130 Lockheed Hercules.

KIA—Killed in Action.

Kingfisher operations—Heliborne combat patrols for quick reaction operations.

Kit Carson Scout—Viet Cong defectors recruited by Marines to serve as scouts, interpreters, and intelligence agents.

L-Hour—In planned helicopter operations, it is the specific hour the helicopters land in the landing zone.

LAAM Bn—Light Antiaircraft Missile Battalion.

LCM—Landing Craft Mechanized, designed to land tanks, trucks, and trailers directly onto the beach.

LCVP—Landing Craft, Vehicle, Personnel, a small craft with a bow ramp used to transport assault troops and light vehicles to the beach.

LKA—The current designation for an attack cargo ship. See AKA.

LOC—Lines of Communication.

LOI—Letter of Instruction.

LPD—Amphibious transport, dock, a ship designed to transport and land troops, equipment, and supplies by means of embarked landing craft, amphibious vehicles, and helicopters. It had both a submersible well deck and a helicopter landing deck.

LPH—Amphibious assault ship, a ship designed or modified to transport and land troops, equipment, and supplies by means of embarked helicopters.

LSA—Logistic Support Area.

LSD—Landing Ship, Dock, a landing ship designed to combat load, transport, and launch amphibious crafts or vehicles together with crews and embarked personnel, and to provide limited docking and repair services to small ships and crafts. It lacks the helicopter landing deck of the LPD.

LST—Landing Ship, Tank, landing ship designed to transport heavy vehicles and to land them on a beach.

Lt—Lieutenant.

LtCol—Lieutenant Colonel.

LtGen—Lieutenant General.

Ltr—Letter.

LVTP or LVP—Landing Vehicle, Tracked, Personnel, an amphibian vehicle used to land and/or transport personnel.

LZ—Landing Zone.

MAB—Marine Amphibious Brigade.

MABS—Marine Air Base Squadron.

Machine gun, .50-caliber—U.S.-built, belt-fed, recoil-operated, air-cooled automatic weapon, which weighs approximately 80 pounds without mount or ammunition; it has a sustained rate of fire of 100 rounds per minute and an effective range of 1,450 meters.

Machine gun, M60—U.S.-built, belt-fed, gas-operated, air-cooled, 7.62mm automatic weapon, which weighs approximately 20 pounds without mount or ammunition; it has a sustained rate of fire of 100 rounds per minute and an effective range of 1,000 meters.

MACS—Marine Air Control Squadron, provides and operates ground facilities for the detection and interception of hostile aircraft and for the navigational direction of friendly aircraft in the conduct of support operations.

MACV—Military Assistance Command, Vietnam.

MAF—Marine Amphibious Force.

MAG—Marine Aircraft Group.

Main Force—Refers to organized Viet Cong battalions and regiments as opposed to local guerrilla groups.

Maj—Major.

MajGen—Major General.

MarDiv—Marine Division.

Marines—Designates a Marine regiment, e.g., 3d Marines.

MASS—Marine Air Support Squadron, provides and operates facilities for the control of aircraft operating in direct support of ground forces.

MAU—Marine Advisory Unit, the Marine advisory unit under the Naval Advisory Group which administered the advisory effort to the South Vietnamese Marine Corps; not to be confused with a Marine Amphibious Unit.

MAW—Marine Aircraft Wing.

MCAS—Marine Corps Air Station.

MCO—Marine Corps Order.

MedCap—Medical Civilian Assistance Program.

MedEvac—Medical Evacuation.

MIA—Missing in Action.

MilHistBr—Military History Branch.

MO—Mount Out.

MOA—Mount Out Augmentation.

Mortar, 4.2-inch, M30—U.S.-built, rifled, muzzle-loaded, drop-fired weapon consisting of tube, base-plate and standard; weapon weighs 330 pounds and has maximum range of 4,020 meters. Rate of fire is 20 rounds per minute.

Mortar, 60mm, M19—U.S.-built, smooth-bore, muzzle-loaded weapon, which weighs 45.2 pounds when assembled; it has a maximum rate of fire of 30 rounds per minute and sustained rate of fire of 18 rounds per minute; the effective range is 2,000 meters.

Mortar, 81mm, M29—U.S.-built, smooth-bore, muzzle-loaded, which weighs approximately 115 pounds when assembled; it has a sustained rate of fire of two rounds per minute and an effective range of 2,300-3,650 meters, depending upon ammunition used.

Mortar, 82mm—Soviet-built, smooth-bore, mortar, single-shot, high angle of fire weapon which weighs approximately 123 pounds; it has a maximum rate of fire of 25 rounds per minute and a maximum range of 3,040 meters.

Mortar, 120mm—Soviet- or Chinese Communist-built, smooth bore, drop or trigger fired, mortar which weighs approximately 600 pounds; it has a maximum rate of fire of 15 rounds per minute and a maximum range of 5,700 meters.

MR-5 — political and military sector in northern South Vietnam, including all of I Corps. NVA units in *MR-5* did not report to COSVN.

Ms — Manuscript.

Msg — Message.

NAC — Northern Artillery Cantonment.
NAG — Naval Advisory Group.
NAS — Naval Air Station.
NCO — Noncommissioned Officer.
NGLO — Naval Gunfire Liaison Officer.
NLF — National Liberation Front, the political arm of the Communist-led insurgency against the South Vietnamese Government.
NMCB — Naval Mobile Construction Battalion (Seabees).
NPFF — National Police Field Force.
NSA — Naval Support Activity.
NSC — National Security Council.
NSDC — Northern Sector Defense Command.
Nui — Vietnamese word for hill or mountain.
Nung — A Vietnamese tribesman, of a separate ethnic group, probably of Chinese origin.
NVA — North Vietnamese Army, often used colloquially to refer to a North Vietnamese soldier.

O-1B — Cessna, single-engine observation aircraft.
OAB, NHD — Operational Archives Branch, Naval History Division.
Ontos — U.S.-built, lightly armored, tracked antitank vehicle armed with six coaxially-mounted 106mm recoilless rifles.
OpCon — Operational Control, the authority granted to a commander to direct forces assigned for specific missions or tasks which are usually limited by function, time, or location.
OpO — Operation Order, a directive issued by a commander to subordinate commanders for the execution of an operation.
OP — Outpost or observation point.
OPlan — Operation Plan, a plan for a single or series of connected operations to be carried out simultaneously or in succession; it is the form of directive employed by higher authority to permit subordinate commanders to prepare supporting plans and orders.
OpSum — Operational Summary.
ORLL — Operations Report/Lessons Learned.
OV-10A — North American Rockwell Bronco, twin-engine aircraft specifically designed for light armed reconnaissance missions.

PAVN — *Peoples Army of Vietnam* (North Vietnam). This acronym was dropped in favor of *NVA*.
PDC — Pacification and Development Councils.
PF — Popular Force, Vietnamese militia who were usually employed in the defense of their own communities.
Phoenix program — A covert U.S. and South Vietnamese program aimed at the eradication of the Viet Cong Infrastructure in South Vietnam.
PIIC — Photo Imagery Interpretation Center.
PRC-25 — Standard radio used by Marine ground units in Vietnam that allowed for voice communication for distances up to 25 miles.
Project Delta — A special South Vietnamese reconnaissance group consisting of South Vietnamese Special Forces troops and U.S. Army Special Forces advisors.

PRU — Provincial Reconnaissance Unit.
PSA — Province Senior Advisor.
PSDF — Peoples Self-Defense Force, a local self-defense force organized by the South Vietnamese Government after the enemy's Tet offensive in 1968.

QDSZ — Quang Da Special Zone.

R&R — Rest and Recreation.
Recoilless rifle, 106mm, M401A1 — U.S.-built, single-shot, recoilless, breech-loaded weapon which weighs 438 pounds when assembled and mounted for firing; it has a sustained rate of fire of six rounds per minute and an effective range of 1,365 meters.
Regt — Regiment.
Rein — Reinforced.
Revolutionary Development — The South Vietnamese pacification program started in 1966.
Revolutionary Development Teams — Specially trained Vietnamese political cadre who were assigned to individual hamlets and villages and conducted various pacification and civilian assistance tasks on a local level.
RF-4B — Photo-reconnaissance model of the F4B Phantom II.
RF — Regional Force, Vietnamese militia who were employed in a specific area.
Rifle, M14 — Gas-operated, magazine-fed, air-cooled, semi-automatic, 7.62mm caliber shoulder weapon, which weighs 12 pounds with a full 20-round magazine; it has a sustained rate of fire of 30 rounds per minute and an effective range of 460 meters.
Rifle, M16 — Gas-operated, magazine-fed, air-cooled, automatic, 5.56mm caliber shoulder weapon, which weighs three pounds with a 20-round magazine; it has a sustained rate of fire of 12-15 rounds per minute and an effective range of 460 meters.
RLT — Regimental Landing Team.
ROK — Republic of Korea.
Rolling Thunder — Codename for U.S. air operations over North Vietnam.
Rough Rider — Organized vehicle convoys, often escorted by helicopters and armored vehicles, using Vietnam's roads to supply Marine bases.
ROE — Rules of Engagement.
RPG — Rocket Propelled Grenade.
RVN — Republic of Vietnam (South Vietnam).
RVNAF — Republic of Vietnam Armed Forces.
RZ — Reconnaissance Zone.

S — Refers to staff positions on regimental and battalion levels. S-1 would refer to the staff member responsible for personnel; S-2, intelligence; S-3, operations; S-4, logistics; and S-5, civil affairs.
SAM — Surface to Air Missile.
SecDef — Secretary of Defense.
SecState — Secretary of State.
Seventh AF — Seventh Air Force, the major U.S. Air Force command in Vietnam.
Seventh Fleet — The U.S. fleet assigned to the Pacific.
SFD — Surprise Firing Device, a euphemism for a boobytrap.
SID — Seismic Intrusion Device, sensor used to monitor movement through ground vibrations.
SLF — Special Landing Force.
SMA — Senior Marine Advisor.

GLOSSARY

SOG—Studies and Operations Group, the cover name for the organization that carried out cross-border operations.

Song—Vietnamese for "river."

SOP—Standing Operating Procedure, set of instructions laying out standardized procedures.

Sortie—An operational flight by one aircraft.

Sparrow Hawk—A small rapid-reaction force on standby, ready for insertion by helicopter for reinforcement of units in contact with the enemy.

SSDC—Southern Sector Defense Command.

Steel Tiger—The codename for the air campaign over Laos.

Stingray—Special Marine reconnaissance missions in which small Marine reconnaissance teams call artillery and air attacks on targets of opportunity.

TAC(A)—Tactical Air Coordinator (Airborne), an officer in an airplane, who coordinates close air support.

TACC—Tactical Air Control Center, the principal air operations installation for controlling all aircraft and air-warning functions of tactical air operations.

TACP—Tactical Air Control Party, a subordinate operational component of a tactical air control system designed to provide air liaison to land forces and for the control of aircraft.

TADC—Tactical Air Direction Center, an air operations installation under the Tactical Air Control Center, which directs aircraft and aircraft warning functions of the tactical air center.

TAFDS—Tactical Airfield Fuel Dispensing System, the expeditionary storage and dispensing system of aviation fuel at tactical airfields. It uses 10,000-gallon fabric tanks to store the fuel.

TAOC—Tactical Air Operations Center, a subordinate component of the air command and control system which controls all enroute air traffic and air defense operations.

Tank, M48—U.S.-built 50.7-ton tank with a crew of four; primary armament is turret-mounted 90mm gun with one .30-caliber and one .50-caliber machine gun; has maximum road speed of 32 miles per hour and an average range of 195 miles.

TAOC—Tactical Air Operations Center, a subordinate component of the air command and control system which controls all enroute air traffic and air defense operations.

TAOI—Tactical Area of Interest.

TAOR—Tactical Area of Responsibility, a defined area of land for which responsibility is specifically assigned to the commander of the area as a measure for control of assigned forces and coordination of support.

TE—Table of Equipment.

TF—Task Force.

TG—Task Group.

TO—Table of Organization.

TO&E—Table of Organization and Equipment.

Trung-si—A South Vietnamese Popular Force sergeant.

TU—Task Unit.

UCMJ—Uniform Code of Military Justice.

UH-1E Bell "Huey"—A single-engine, light attack/observation helicopter noted for its maneuverability and firepower; carries a crew of three; it can be armed with air-to-ground rocket packs and fuselage-mounted, electrically-fired machine guns.

UH-34D—Sikorsky Sea Horse, a single-engine medium transport helicopter with a crew of three, carries eight to 12 combat soldiers, depending upon weather conditions.

USA—U.S. Army.

USAAG—U.S. Army Advisory Group.

USAF—U.S. Air Force.

USAID—U.S. Agency for International Development.

USARV—U.S. Army, Vietnam.

USASuppComDaNang—U.S. Army Support Command, Da Nang.

USIA—U.S. Information Agency.

USMC—U.S. Marine Corps.

USN—U.S. Navy.

VC—Viet Cong, a term used to refer to the Communist guerrillas in South Vietnam; a contraction of the Vietnamese phrase meaning "Vietnamese Communists."

Viet Minh—The Vietnamese contraction for Viet Nam Doc Lap Nong Minh Hoi, a Communist-led coalition of nationalist groups, which actively opposed the Japanese in World War II and the French in the first Indochina War.

VCI—Viet Cong Infrastructure.

VCLF—Viet Cong Local Force.

VMA—Marine attack squadron (in naval aviation, the "V" designates "heavier than air" as opposed to craft that are "lighter than air").

VMF(AW)—Marine Fighter Squadron (All-Weather).

VMFA—Marine Fighter Attack Squadron.

VMCJ—Marine Composite Reconnaissance Squadron.

VMGR—Marine Refueller Transport Squadron.

VMO—Marine Observation Squadron.

VNAF—Vietnamese Air Force.

VNMB—Vietnamese Marine Brigade.

VNMC—Vietnamese Marine Corps.

VNN—Vietnamese Navy.

VT—Variable timed electronic fuze for an artillery shell which causes airburst over the target area.

WestPac—Western Pacific.

WIA—Wounded in Action.

Appendix C
Chronology of Significant Events January-December 1969

1 January	South Vietnamese President Nguyen Van Thieu suggested that the ARVN was "ready to replace part of the allied forces" in 1969.
5 January	President-elect Richard M. Nixon named Ambassador Henry Cabot Lodge to succeed Ambassador W. Averell Harriman as chief U.S. negotiator at the Paris talks. He also appointed Ambassador Ellsworth Bunker to continue at his post in Saigon.
20 January	Richard M. Nixon inaugurated President of the United States.
22 January	Operation Dewey Canyon began in the Da Krong Valley of Quang Tri Province with the lift of elements of Colonel Robert H. Barrow's 9th Marines and supporting artillery from Vandegrift Combat Base into the area.
31 January	U.S. military strength in South Vietnam numbered 539,800, of which 81,000 were Marines.
16 February	Allied forces observed a 24-hour ceasefire during *Tet*. Despite the ceasefire, VC/NVA forces committed 203 truce violations, which resulted in the loss of six killed and 94 wounded in I Corps.
23 February	Communist forces launched a major offensive throughout South Vietnam, one day following the expiration of the seven-day Viet Cong proclaimed truce for *Tet*.
25 February	Fire Support Bases Neville and Russell came under heavy enemy ground and mortar attacks, resulting in the loss of 30 and the wounding of 79 Marines.
27 February	During Operation Dewey Canyon, men of the 9th Marines uncovered the largest single haul of enemy arms and ammunition in the war to date.
28 February	The 3d Marine Division ended Operations Scotland II and Kentucky. During Scotland II, more than 3,300 enemy troops were killed, while friendly casualties were 463 killed. Operation Kentucky resulted in over 3,900 enemy and 520 U.S. casualties.
2 March	Village and hamlet elections were held throughout South Vietnam. In I Corps, the percentage of the population voting ranged from 82 percent in Quang Nam Province to 92 percent in Quang Tri. The enemy made no attempt to disrupt the voting.
3 March	The Marine Corps received its first CH-53D assault helicopter. The helicopter, intended to replace the CH-53A, introduced into Vietnam in late 1966, could transport four tons of cargo or 38 combat troops.
7 March	Allied intelligence estimates of enemy strength place 40,000 NVA and between 60,000 and 70,000 VC in I Corps Tactical Zone, a majority of which were said to be in the northern provinces.
9 March	1st Marine Division Operation Taylor Common ended in Quang Nam Province. The operation, which began on 7 December 1968, accounted for close to 1,400 enemy killed and 610 captured.
16 March	The U.S. battleship *New Jersey* departed the coast of Vietnam.

CHRONOLOGY

26 March	Lieutenant General Herman Nickerson, Jr., replaced Lieutenant General Robert E. Cushman, Jr., as Commanding General, III Marine Amphibious Force.
30 March	III MAF engineers completed the construction of Liberty Bridge, which spanned the Song Thu Bon, south of Da Nang.
3 April	COMUSMACV confirmed that more Americans had been killed in Vietnam than in the Korean War. Vietnam had cost 33,641 lives since January 1961, compared to 33,629 lost in Korea.
7 April	A Joint Coordinating Council was established by CG III MAF and CG ICTZ to monitor, coordinate, and support pacification and development programs within ICTZ.
10 April	The first four AH-1G "Cobra" gunships arrived at Da Nang to begin air operations with Marine Observation Squadron 2.
15 April	Major General William K. Jones replaced Major General Raymond G. Davis as Commanding General, 3d Marine Division.
17 April	Marine firepower increased with the introduction of the first 175mm guns, scheduled to replace the 155mm guns of the 1st, 3d, and 5th 155mm Gun Batteries.
23 April	More than 250 student leaders from colleges throughout the United States made a public statement that they would refuse induction into the armed forces so long as the war continued in Vietnam.
27 April	A grass fire spread to the Navy/Marine Ammo Supply Point 1 at Da Nang, resulting in its complete destruction.
3 May	Secretary of Defense Melvin Laird said the United States could begin troop withdrawals if any of the following three basic conditions were met: agreement of mutual withdrawals; sufficient improvement of South Vietnamese forces; and a substantial reduction of VC/NVA activity in South Vietnam.
6 May	III Marine Amphibious Force, composed of the 1st and 3d Marine Divisions, 1st Marine Aircraft Wing, Force Logistic Command, and the Army's XXIV Corps, Americal Division, 101st Airborne Division (Airmobile), and 1st Brigade, 5th Infantry Division (Mechanized), began its fifth year in Vietnam.
8 May	The Vietnamese Communists issued a 10-point proposal for peace, the most important new element of which was an attempt to limit United States participation in negotiations to the subject of a unilateral withdrawal from South Vietnam.
10 May	Operation Apache Snow began in the southern Da Krong and northern A Shau Valleys and involved the 9th Marines and elements of the 101st Airborne Division. During the operation, which ended on 7 June, troops of the 101st assaulted and captured heavily fortified Dong Ap Bia, or as it later became known, "Hamburger Hill."
12 May	The VC/NVA struck throughout South Vietnam with the largest number of attacks since *Tet* 1968.
29 May	The 7th Marines multi-battalion Operation Oklahoma Hills ended. Enemy losses during the two-month operation were placed at 596, while friendly loses numbered 53 killed and 487 wounded.
8 June	President Nixon announced that 25,000 troops would be withdrawn from South Vietnam by the end of August.

14 June	Marine, Korean, and South Vietnamese troops began Operation Pipestone Canyon, south of Da Nang. Before ending in November, the enemy would lose close to 500 troops.
13 June	Secretary of Defense Laird announced that the 9th Marines, in addition to Army and Navy units, would be withdrawn beginning in mid-July.
15 June	The 1st Amphibian Tractor Battalion began deployment from Vietnam to Okinawa.
11 July	Major General Charles J. Quilter was relieved by Major General William G. Thrash as Commanding General, 1st Marine Aircraft Wing.
14 July	Battalion Landing Team 1/9 sailed from Da Nang for Okinawa on board ships of the Seventh Fleet, initiating Phase I of President Nixon's 25,000-troop withdrawal plan.
20 July	Racial riots at Camp Lejeune, North Carolina, resulted in the death of one Marine and serious injury to another.
August	The Combined Action Program reached its authorized strength of 114 platoons.
13 August	Marine Medium Helicopter Squadron 165 departed Vietnam for Okinawa under the announced 25,000-man troop reduction. The squadron was the first major unit of the 1st Marine Aircraft Wing to depart Vietnam.
14 August	The 9th Regimental Landing Team completed its redeployment from Vietnam with the departure of the 3d Battalion, 9th Marines.
18 August	The last UH-34D "Sea Horse" Squadron, Marine Medium Helicopter Squadron 362, departed Vietnam to be redesignated Marine Heavy Helicopter Squadron 362 after receiving CH-53 aircraft. The squadron was the first unit of the 1st Marine Aircraft Wing to serve in Vietnam, arriving in April 1962.
September	Three disturbances took place over alleged mistreatment of prisoners at the Camp Pendleton brig. Three guards were disciplined for using excessive force in quelling disruptive prisoners.
3 September	Marine Corps Commandant, General Leonard F. Chapman, Jr., authorized "Afro" haircuts and the use of the upraised fist as a greeting among black Marines.
3 September	North Vietnamese President Ho Chi Minh died.
16 September	President Nixon announced another troop withdrawal. Of a total reduction of 40,500, more than 18,400 would be Marines, most of whom would come from the 3d Marine Division.
21 September	Secretary of Defense Laird announced the deactivation of the 5th Marine Division at Camp Pendeton, California. The 26th Marines, still in Vietnam, would not be deactivated with the remainder of the division.
29 September	The Marine Corps announced a cutback of 20,300 in total strength. It was felt that a reduction in recruiting would reduce the size of the Corps without any rollback of temporary officer promotions or any reversion of temporary officers to enlisted status before 1 July 1970.
15 October	Throughout the United States, Vietnam Moratorium demonstrations were held.
7 November	The 9th Marine Amphibious Force was deactivated; I Marine Ex-

CHRONOLOGY

	peditionary Force was created as an amphibious ready force in the Western Pacific; and 1st Marine Aircraft Wing (Rear) was activated in Japan. CG, I MEF was to exercise operational control of the 3d Marine Division and 1st Marine Aircraft Wing (Rear).
13-15 November	Critics of the war in Vietnam demonstrated in Washington with a march from Arlington Cemetery to the Capitol.
19 November	The Nixon Administration's military draft lottery bill was passed by Congress.
20 November	Marine Air Group 36 completed its move from Phu Bai to Futema, Okinawa, where it assumed control of the helicopter and observation squadrons which had been redeployed from Vietnam.
26 November	The 5th Marine Division was deactivated and the 5th Marine Expeditionary Brigade came into existence.
1 December	The first drawing of the draft lottery was conducted; those 19-year-olds whose birthdate was 14 September and whose last name began with "J" would be the first called.
15 December	Major General Edwin B. Wheeler relieved Major General Ormond R. Simpson as Commanding General, 1st Marine Division.
15 December	With the completion of Phase II redeployment, Marine authorized strength in the Republic of Vietnam stood at 55,300.
15 December	President Nixon announced that the third round of American troop withdrawals from Vietnam was to be completed by 15 April 1970.
31 December	Marine actual strength in South Vietnam stood at 54,559 at the end of 1969.

Appendix D
Medal of Honor Citations
1969

The President of the United States in the name of The Congress takes pride in presenting the MEDAL OF HONOR posthumously to

LANCE CORPORAL RICHARD A. ANDERSON
UNITED STATES MARINE CORPS

for service as set forth in the following

CITATION

For conspicuous gallantry and intrepidity at the risk of his life above and beyond the call of duty while serving as an Assistant Team Leader with Company E, Third Reconnaissance Battalion, Third Marine Division, in connection with combat operations against an armed enemy in the Republic of Vietnam. While conducting a patrol during the early morning hours of 24 August 1969, Lance Corporal Anderson's reconnaissance team came under a heavy volume of automatic weapons and machine gun fire from a numerically superior and well-concealed enemy force. Although painfully wounded in both legs and knocked to the ground during the initial moments of the fierce fire fight, Lance Corporal Anderson assumed a prone position and continued to deliver intense suppressive fire in an attempt to repulse the attackers. Moments later he was wounded a second time by an enemy soldier who had approached to within eight feet of the team's position. Undaunted, he continued to pour a relentless stream of fire at the assaulting unit, even while a companion was treating his leg wounds. Observing an enemy grenade land between himself and the other Marine, Lance Corporal Anderson immediately rolled over and covered the lethal weapon with his body, absorbing the full effects of the detonation. By his indomitable courage, inspiring initiative, and selfless devotion to duty, Lance Corporal Anderson was instrumental in saving several Marines from serious injury or possible death. His actions were in keeping with the highest traditions of the Marine Corps and of the United States Naval Service. He gallantly gave his life in the service of his country.

The President of the United States in the name of The Congress takes pride in presenting the MEDAL OF HONOR posthumously to

PRIVATE FIRST CLASS OSCAR P. AUSTIN
UNITED STATES MARINE CORPS

for service as set forth in the following

CITATION

For conspicuous gallantry and intrepidity at the risk of his life above and beyond the call of duty while serving as an Assistant Machine Gunner with Company E, Second Battalion, Seventh Marines, First Marine Division in connection with operations against enemy forces in the Republic of Vietnam. During the early morning hours of 23 February 1969, Private First Class Austin's observation post was subjected to a fierce ground attack by a large North Vietnamese Army force supported by a heavy volume of hand grenades, satchel charges and small arms fire. Observing that one of his wounded companions had fallen unconscious in a position dangerously exposed to the hostile fire, Private First Class Austin unhesitatingly left the relative security of his fighting hole and, with complete disregard for his own safety, raced across the fire-swept terrain to assist the Marine to a covered location. As he neared the casualty, he observed an enemy grenade land nearby and, reacting instantly, leaped between the injured Marine and the lethal object, absorbing the effects of its detonation. As he ignored his painful injuries and turned to examine the wounded man, he saw a North Vietnamese Army soldier aiming a weapon at his unconscious companion. With full knowledge of the probable consequences and thinking only to protect the Marine, Private First Class Austin resolutely threw himself between the casualty and the hostile soldier and, in so doing, was mortally wounded. Private First Class Austin's indomitable courage, inspiring initiative and selfless devotion to duty upheld the highest traditions of the Marine Corps and the United States Naval Service. He gallantly gave his life for his country.

The President of the United States in the name of The Congress takes pride in presenting the MEDAL OF HONOR posthumously to

PRIVATE FIRST CLASS DANIEL D. BRUCE
UNITED STATES MARINE CORPS

for service as set forth in the following

CITATION

For conspicuous gallantry and intrepidity at the risk of his life above and beyond the call of duty while serving as a Mortar Man with Headquarters and Service Company, Third Battalion, Fifth Marines, First Marine Division, against the enemy in the Republic of Vietnam. Early on the morning of 1 March 1969, Private First Class Bruce was on watch in his night defensive position at Fire Support Base Tomahawk in Quang Nam Province when he heard movements ahead of him. An enemy explosive charge was thrown toward his position and he reacted instantly, catching the device and shouting to alert his companions. Realizing the danger to the adjacent position with its two occupants, Private First Class Bruce held the device to his body and attempted to carry it from the vicinity of the entrenched Marines. As he moved away, the charge detonated and he absorbed the full force of the explosion. Private First Class Bruce's indomitable courage, inspiring valor and selfless devotion to duty saved the lives of three of his fellow Marines and upheld the highest traditions of the Marine Corps and the United States Naval Service. He gallantly gave his life for his country.

The President of the United States in the name of The Congress takes pride in presenting the MEDAL OF HONOR posthumously to

PRIVATE FIRST CLASS BRUCE W. CARTER
UNITED STATES MARINE CORPS

for service as set forth in the following

CITATION

For conspicuous gallantry and intrepidity at the risk of his life above and beyond the call of duty while serving as Grenadier with Company H, Second Battalion, Third Marines, Third Marine Division in connection with combat operations against the enemy in the Republic of Vietnam. On 7 August 1969, Private First Class Carter's unit was maneuvering against the enemy during Operation Idaho Canyon and came under a heavy volume of fire from a numerically superior hostile force. The lead element soon became separated from the main body of the squad by a brush fire. Private First Class Carter and his fellow Marines were pinned down by vicious crossfire when, with complete disregard for his own safety, he stood in full view of the North Vietnamese Army soldiers to deliver a devastating volume of fire at their positions. The accuracy and aggressiveness of his attack caused several enemy casualties and forced the remainder of the soldiers to retreat from the immediate area. Shouting directions to the Marines around him, Private First Class Carter then commenced leading them from the path of the rapidly approaching brush fire when he observed a hostile grenade land between him and his companions. Fully aware of the probable consequences of his action but determined to protect the men following him, he unhesitatingly threw himself over the grenade, absorbing the full effects of its detonation with his own body. Private First Class Carter's indomitable courage, inspiring initiative, and selfless devotion to duty upheld the highest traditions of the Marine Corps and of the United States Naval Service. He gallantly gave his life in the service of his country.

The President of the United States in the name of The Congress takes pride in presenting the MEDAL OF HONOR posthumously to

PRIVATE FIRST CLASS RONALD L. COKER
UNITED STATES MARINE CORPS

for service as set forth in the following

CITATION

For conspicuous gallantry and intrepidity at the risk of his life above and beyond the call of duty while serving as a Rifleman with Company M, Third Battalion, Third Marines, Third Marine Division in action against enemy forces in the Republic of Vietnam. On 24 March 1969, while serving as Point Man for the Second Platoon, Private First Class Coker was leading his patrol when he encountered five enemy soldiers on a narrow jungle trail. Private First Class Coker's squad aggressively pursued them to a cave. As the squad neared the cave, it came under intense hostile fire, seriously wounding one Marine and forcing the others to take cover. Observing the wounded man lying exposed to continuous enemy fire, Private First Class Coker disregarded his own safety and moved across the fire-swept terrain toward his companion. Although wounded by enemy small arms fire, he continued to crawl across the hazardous area and skillfully threw a hand grenade into the enemy positions, suppressing the hostile fire sufficiently to enable him to reach the wounded man. As he began to drag his injured comrade towards safety, a grenade landed on the wounded Marine. Unhesitatingly, Private First Class Coker grasped it with both hands and turned away from his wounded companion, but before he could dispose of the grenade it exploded. Severely wounded, but undaunted, he refused to abandon his comrade. As he moved toward friendly lines, two more enemy grenades exploded near him, inflicting still further injuries. Concerned only for the safety of his comrade, Private First Class Coker, with supreme effort, continued to crawl and pull the wounded Marine with him. His heroic deeds inspired his fellow Marines to such aggressive action that the enemy fire was suppressed sufficiently to enable others to reach him and carry him to a relatively safe area where he succumbed to his extensive wounds. Private First Class Coker's indomitable courage, inspiring initiative and selfless devotion to duty upheld the highest traditions of the Marine Corps and of the United States Naval Service. He gallantly gave his life for his country.

The President of the United States in the name of The Congress takes pride in presenting the MEDAL OF HONOR posthumously to

LANCE CORPORAL THOMAS E. CREEK
UNITED STATES MARINE CORPS

for service as set forth in the following

CITATION

For conspicuous gallantry and intrepidity at the risk of his life above and beyond the call of duty while serving as a Rifleman with Company I, Third Battalion, Ninth Marines, Third Marine Division in action against enemy forces in the Republic of Vietnam. On 13 February 1969, Lance Corporal Creek's squad was providing security for a convoy moving to resupply the Vandegrift Combat Base when an enemy command-detonated mine destroyed one of the vehicles and halted the convoy near the Cam Lo Resettlement Village. Almost immediately, the Marines came under a heavy volume of hostile mortar fire followed by intense small arms fire from a well-concealed enemy force. As his squad deployed to engage the enemy, Lance Corporal Creek quickly moved to a fighting position and aggressively engaged in the fire fight. Observing a position from which he could more effectively deliver fire against the hostile force he completely disregarded his own safety as he fearlessly dashed across the fire-swept terrain and was seriously wounded by enemy fire. At the same time, an enemy grenade was thrown into the gully where he had fallen, landing between him and several companions. Fully realizing the inevitable results of his actions, Lance Corporal Creek rolled on the grenade and absorbed the full force of the explosion with his own body, thereby saving the lives of five of his fellow Marines. As a result of his heroic action, his men were inspired to such aggressive action that the enemy was defeated and the convoy was able to continue its vital mission. Lance Corporal Creek's indomitable courage, inspiring valor and selfless devotion to duty upheld the highest traditions of the Marine Corps and the United States Naval Service. He gallantly gave his life for his country.

The President of the United States in the name of The Congress takes pride in presenting the MEDAL OF HONOR posthumously to

PRIVATE FIRST CLASS RALPH E. DIAS
UNITED STATES MARINE CORPS

for service as set forth in the following

CITATION

For conspicuous gallantry and intrepidity at the risk of his life above and beyond the call of duty, while serving as a Rifleman with Company D, First Battalion, Seventh Marines, First Marine Division in the Republic of Vietnam on 12 November 1969. As a member of a reaction force which was pinned down by enemy fire while assisting a platoon in the same circumstance, Private First Class Dias, observing that both units were sustaining casualties, initiated an aggressive assault against an enemy machine gun bunker which was the principal source of hostile fire. Severely wounded by enemy snipers while charging across the open area, he pulled himself to the shelter of a nearby rock. Braving enemy fire for a second time, Private First Class Dias was again wounded. Unable to walk, he crawled fifteen meters to the protection of a rock located near his objective and, repeatedly exposing himself to intense hostile fire, unsuccessfully threw several hand grenades at the machine gun emplacement. Still determined to destroy the emplacement, Private First Class Dias again moved into the open and was wounded a third time by sniper fire. As he threw a last grenade which destroyed the enemy position, he was mortally wounded by another enemy round. Private First Class Dias' indomitable courage, dynamic initiative, and selfless devotion to duty upheld the highest traditions of the Marine Corps and the United States Naval Service. He gallantly gave his life for his country.

The President of the United States in the name of The Congress takes pleasure in presenting the MEDAL OF HONOR to

CAPTAIN WESLEY L. FOX
UNITED STATES MARINE CORPS

for service as set forth in the following

CITATION

For conspicuous gallantry and intrepidity at the risk of his life above and beyond the call of duty while serving as Commanding Officer of Company A, First Battalion, Ninth Marines, Third Marine Division, in action against the enemy in the northern A Shau Valley, Quang Tri Province, Republic of Vietnam, on 22 February 1969. Captain (then First Lieutenant) Fox's company came under intense fire from a large well-concealed enemy force. Captain Fox maneuvered to a position from which he could assess the situation and confer with his platoon leaders. As they departed to execute the plan he had devised, the enemy attacked and Captain Fox was wounded along with all of the other members of the command group, except the executive officer. Captain Fox continued to direct the activity of his company. Advancing through heavy enemy fire he personally neutralized one enemy position and calmly ordered an assault against the hostile emplacements. He then moved though the hazardous area coordinating aircraft support with the activities of his men. When his executive officer was mortally wounded, Captain Fox reorganized the company and directed the fire of his men as they hurled grenades against the enemy and drove the hostile forces into retreat. Wounded again in the final assault, Captain Fox refused medical attention, established a defensive posture, and supervised the preparation of casualties for medical evacuation. His indomitable courage, inspiring initiative, and unwavering devotion to duty in the face of grave personal danger inspired his Marines to such aggressive actions that they overcame all enemy resistance and destroyed a large bunker complex. Captain Fox's heroic actions reflect great credit upon himself and the Marine Corps, and uphold the highest traditions of the United States Naval Service.

The President of the United States in the name of The Congress takes pride in presenting the MEDAL OF HONOR posthumously to

PRIVATE FIRST CLASS ROBERT H. JENKINS, JR.
UNITED STATES MARINE CORPS

for service as set forth in the following

CITATION

For conspicuous gallantry and intrepidity at the risk of his life above and beyond the call of duty while serving as a Machine Gunner with Company C, Third Reconnaissance Battalion, Third Marine Division in connection with operations against enemy forces in the Republic of Vietnam. Early on the morning of 5 March 1969, Private First Class Jenkins' twelve-man reconnaissance team was occupying a defensive position at Fire Support Base Argonne south of the Demilitarized Zone. Suddenly, the Marines were assaulted by a North Vietnamese Army platoon employing mortars, automatic weapons, and hand grenades. Reacting instantly, Private First Class Jenkins and another Marine quickly moved into a two-man fighting emplacement, and as they boldly delivered accurate machine gun fire against the enemy, a North Vietnamese soldier threw a hand grenade into the friendly emplacement. Fully realizing the inevitable results of his actions, Private First Class Jenkins quickly seized his comrade, and pushing the man to the ground, he leaped on top of the Marine to shield him from the explosion. Absorbing the full impact of the detonation, Private First Class Jenkins was seriously injured and subsequently succumbed to his wounds. His courage, inspiring valor and selfless devotion to duty saved a fellow Marine from serious injury or possible death and upheld the highest traditions of the Marine Corps and the United States Naval Service. He gallantly gave his life for his country.

The President of the United States in the name of The Congress takes pride in presenting the MEDAL OF HONOR posthumously to

LANCE CORPORAL JOSE F. JIMENEZ
UNITED STATES MARINE CORPS

for service as set forth in the following

CITATION

For conspicuous gallantry and intrepidity at the risk of his life above and beyond the call of duty while serving as a Fire Team Leader with Company K, Third Battalion, Seventh Marines, First Marine Division in operations against the enemy in the Republic of Vietnam on 28 August 1969. On that date Lance Corporal Jimenez's unit came under heavy attack by North Vietnamese Army soldiers concealed in well-camouflaged emplacements. Lance Corporal Jimenez reacted by seizing the initiative and plunging forward toward the enemy positions. He personally destroyed several enemy personnel and silenced an antiaircraft weapon. Shouting encouragement to his companions, Lance Corporal Jimenez continued his aggressive forward movement. He slowly maneuvered to within ten feet of hostile soldiers who were firing automatic weapons from a trench and, in the face of vicious enemy fire, destroyed the position. Although he was by now the target of concentrated fire from hostile gunners intent upon halting his assault, Lance Corporal Jimenez continued to press forward. As he moved to attack another enemy soldier, he was mortally wounded. Lance Corporal Jimenez's indomitable courage, aggressive fighting spirit and unfaltering devotion to duty upheld the highest traditions of the Marine Corps and the United States Naval Service. He gallantly gave his life for his country.

The President of the United States in the name of The Congress takes pride in presenting the MEDAL OF HONOR posthumously to

CORPORAL WILLIAM D. MORGAN
UNITED STATES MARINE CORPS

for service as set forth in the following

CITATION

For conspicuous gallantry and intrepidity at the risk of his life above and beyond the call of duty while serving as a Squad Leader with Company H, Second Battalion, Ninth Marines, Third Marine Division in operations against the enemy in the Quang Tri Province, Republic of Vietnam. On 25 February 1969, while participating in Operation Dewey Canyon southeast of Vandegrift Combat Base, one of the squads of Corporal Morgan's platoon was temporarily pinned down and sustained several casualties while attacking a North Vietnamese Army force occupying a heavily-fortified bunker complex. Observing that two of the wounded Marines had fallen in a position dangerously exposed to the enemy fire and that all attempts to evacuate them were halted by a heavy volume of automatic weapons fire and rocket-propelled grenades, Corporal Morgan unhesitatingly maneuvered through the dense jungle undergrowth to a road that passed in front of a hostile emplacement which was the principal source of enemy fire. Fully aware of the possible consequences of his valiant action, but thinking only of the welfare of his injured companions, Corporal Morgan shouted words of encouragement to them as he initiated an aggressive assault against the hostile bunker. While charging across the open road, he was clearly visible to the hostile soldiers who turned their fire in his direction and mortally wounded him, but his diversionary tactic enabled the remainder of his squad to retrieve their casualties and overrun the North Vietnamese Army position. His heroic and determined actions saved the lives of two fellow Marines and were instrumental in the subsequent defeat of the enemy. Corporal Morgan's indomitable courage, inspiring initiative and selfless devotion to duty upheld the highest traditions of the Marine Corps and the United States Naval Service. He gallantly gave his life for his country.

The President of the United States in the name of The Congress takes pride in presenting the MEDAL OF HONOR posthumously to

LANCE CORPORAL THOMAS P. NOONAN, JR.
UNITED STATES MARINE CORPS

for service as set forth in the following

CITATION

For conspicuous gallantry and intrepidity at the risk of his life above and beyond the call of duty while serving as a Fire Team Leader with Company G, Second Battalion, Ninth Marines, Third Marine Division, in operations against the enemy in Quang Tri Province in the Republic of Vietnam. On 5 February 1969, Company G was directed to move from a position which they had been holding southeast of the Vandegrift Combat Base in A Shau Valley to an alternate location. As the Marines commenced a slow and difficult descent down the side of the hill made extremely slippery by the heavy rains, the leading element came under a heavy fire from a North Vietnamese Army unit occupying well-concealed positions in the rocky terrain. Four men were wounded, and repeated attempts to recover them failed because of the intense hostile fire. Lance Corporal Noonan moved from his position of relative security and maneuvering down the treacherous slope to a location near the injured men, took cover behind some rocks. Shouting words of encourgement to the wounded men to restore their confidence, he dashed across the hazardous terrain and commenced dragging the most seriously wounded man away from the fire-swept area. Although wounded and knocked to the ground by an enemy round, Lance Corporal Noonan recovered rapidly and resumed dragging the man toward the marginal security of a rock. He was, however, mortally wounded before he could reach his destination. His heroic actions inspired his fellow Marines to such aggressiveness that they initiated a spirited assault which forced the enemy soldiers to withdraw. Lance Corporal Noonan's indomitable courage, inspiring initiative and selfless devotion to duty upheld the highest traditions of the Marine Corps and the United States Naval Service. He gallantly gave his life for his country.

The President of the United States in the name of The Congress takes pride in presenting the MEDAL OF HONOR posthumously to

PRIVATE FIRST CLASS JIMMY W. PHIPPS
UNITED STATES MARINE CORPS

for service as set forth in the following

CITATION

For conspicuous gallantry and intrepidity at the risk of his life above and beyond the call of duty while serving as a Combat Engineer with Company B, First Engineer Battalion, First Marine Division in connection with combat operations against the enemy in the Republic of Vietnam. On 27 May 1969, Private First Class Phipps, was a member of a two-man combat engineer demolition team assigned to locate and destroy enemy artillery ordnance and concealed firing devices. After he had expended all of his explosives and blasting caps, Private First Class Phipps discovered a 175mm high explosive artillery round in a rice paddy. Suspecting that the enemy had attached the artillery round to a secondary explosive device, he warned other Marines in the area to move to covered positions and prepared to destroy the round with a hand grenade. As he was attaching the hand grenade to a stake beside the artillery round, the fuse of the enemy's secondary explosive device ignited. Realizing that his assistant and the platoon commander were both within a few meters of him and that the imminent explosion could kill all three men, Private First Class Phipps grasped the hand grenade to his chest and dived forward to cover the enemy's explosive and the artillery round with his body, thereby shielding his companions from the detonation while absorbing the full and tremendous impact with his own body. Private First Class Phipps' indomitable courage, inspiring initiative and selfless devotion to duty saved the lives of two Marines and upheld the highest traditions of the Marine Corps and the United States Naval Service. He gallantly gave his life for his country.

The President of the United States in the name of The Congress takes pride in presenting the MEDAL OF HONOR posthumously to

LANCE CORPORAL WILLIAM R. PROM
UNITED STATES MARINE CORPS

for service as set forth in the following

CITATION

For conspicuous gallantry and intrepidity at the risk of his life above and beyond the call of duty while serving as a Machine Gun Squad Leader with Company I, Third Battalion, Third Marines, Third Marine Division in action against the enemy in the Republic of Vietnam. While returning from a reconnaissance operation on 9 February 1969 during Operation Taylor Common, two platoons of Company I came under an intense automatic weapons fire and grenade attack from a well-concealed North Vietnamese Army force in fortified positions. The leading element of the platoon was isolated and several Marines were wounded. Lance Corporal Prom immediately assumed control of one of his machine guns and began to deliver return fire. Disregarding his own safety he advanced to a position from which he could more effectively deliver covering fire while first aid was administered to the wounded men. Realizing that the enemy would have to be destroyed before the injured Marines could be evacuated, Lance Corporal Prom again moved forward and delivered a heavy volume of fire with such accuracy that he was instrumental in routing the enemy, thus permitting his men to regroup and resume their march. Shortly thereafter, the platoon again came under heavy fire in which one man was critically wounded. Reacting instantly, Lance Corporal Prom moved forward to protect his injured comrade. Unable to continue his own fire because of severe wounds, he continued to advance to within a few yards of the enemy positions. There, standing in full view of the enemy, he accurately directed the fire of his support elements until he was mortally wounded. Inspired by his heroic actions, the Marines launched an assault that destroyed the enemy. Lance Corporal Prom's indomitable courage, inspiring initiative and selfless devotion to duty upheld the highest traditions of the Marine Corps and the United States Naval Service. He gallantly gave his life for his country.

The President of the United States in the name of The Congress takes pride in presenting the MEDAL OF HONOR posthumously to

LANCE CORPORAL LESTER W. WEBER
UNITED STATES MARINE CORPS

for service as set forth in the following

CITATION

For conspicuous gallantry and intrepidity at the risk of his life above and beyond the call of duty while serving as a Machine Gun Squad Leader with Company M, Third Battalion, Seventh Marines, First Marine Division, in action against the enemy in the Republic of Vietnam. On 23 February 1969, the Second Platoon of Company M was dispatched to the Bo Ban area of Hieu Duc District in Quang Nam Province to assist a squad from another platoon which had become heavily engaged with a well-entrenched enemy battalion. While moving through a rice paddy covered with tall grass Lance Corporal Weber's platoon came under heavy attack from concealed hostile soldiers. He reacted by plunging into the tall grass, successfully attacking one enemy and forcing eleven others to break contact. Upon encountering a second North Vietnamese Army soldier he overwhelmed him in fierce hand-to-hand combat. Observing two other soldiers firing upon his comrades from behind a dike, Lance Corporal Weber ignored the frenzied firing of the enemy and racing across the hazardous area, dived into their position. He neutralized the position by wrestling weapons from the hands of the two soldiers and overcoming them. Although by now the target for concentrated fire from hostile riflemen, Lance Corporal Weber remained in a dangerously exposed position to shout words of encouragement to his emboldened companions. As he moved forward to attack a fifth enemy soldier, he was mortally wounded. Lance Corporal Weber's indomitable courage, aggressive fighting spirit and unwavering devotion to duty upheld the highest traditions of the Marine Corps and the United States Naval Service. He gallantly gave his life for his country.

The President of the United States in the name of The Congress takes pride in presenting the MEDAL OF HONOR posthumously to

PRIVATE FIRST CLASS ALFRED M. WILSON
UNITED STATES MARINE CORPS

for service as set forth in the following

CITATION

For conspicuous gallantry and intrepidity at the risk of his life above and beyond the call of duty while serving as a Rifleman with Company M, Third Battalion, Ninth Marines, Third Marine Division in action against hostile forces in the Republic of Vietnam. On 3 March 1969, while returning from a reconnaissance in force mission in the vicinity of Fire Support Base Cunningham in Quang Tri Province, the First Platoon of Company M came under intense automatic weapons fire and a grenade attack from a well concealed enemy force. As the center of the column was pinned down, the leading squad moved to outflank the enemy. Private First Class Wilson, acting as Squad Leader of the rear squad, skillfully maneuvered his men to form a base of fire and act as a blocking force. In the ensuing fire fight, both his machine gunner and assistant machine gunner were seriously wounded and unable to operate their weapons. Realizing the urgent need to bring the weapon into operation again, Private First Class Wilson, followed by another Marine and with complete disregard for his own saftey, fearlessly dashed across the fire-swept terrain to recover the weapon. As they reached the machine gun, an enemy soldier stepped from behind a tree and threw a grenade toward the two Marines. Observing the grenade fall between himself and the other Marine, Private First Class Wilson, fully realizing the inevitable result of his actions, shouted to his companion and unhesitatingly threw himself on the grenade, absorbing the full force of the explosion with his own body. His heroic actions inspired his platoon members to maximum effort as they aggressively attacked and defeated the enemy. Private First Class Wilson's indomitable courage, inspiring valor and selfless devotion to duty upheld the highest traditions of the Marine Corps and the United States Naval Service. He gallantly gave his life for his country.

Appendix E
List of Reviewers

Marines

Gen Robert H. Barrow, USMC (Ret)
Gen Leonard F. Chapman, Jr., USMC (Ret)
Gen Raymond G. Davis, USMC (Ret)

LtGen Leo J. Dulacki, USMC (Ret)
LtGen William K. Jones, USMC (Ret)
LtGen John N. McLaughlin, USMC (Ret)
LtGen Thomas H. Miller, Jr., USMC (Ret)
LtGen Robert L. Nichols, USMC (Ret)
LtGen Herman Nickerson, Jr., USMC (Ret)
LtGen Adolph G. Schwenk, USMC (Ret)
LtGen Ormond R. Simpson, USMC (Ret)
LtGen Joseph J. Went, USMC

MajGen Clifford B. Drake, USMC (Ret)
MajGen Ross T. Dwyer, Jr., USMC (Ret)
MajGen Harold G. Glasgow, USMC
MajGen Norman W. Gourley, USMC (Ret)
MajGen Homer S. Hill, USMC (Ret)
MajGen Carl W. Hoffman, USMC (Ret)
MajGen Francis X. Quinn, USMC (Ret)
MajGen Herbert L. Wilkerson, USMC (Ret)
MajGen Carl A. Youngdale, USMC (Ret)

BGen Herbert J. Blaha, USMC (Ret)
BGen George E. Dooley, USMC (Ret)
BGen Frank E. Garretson, USMC (Ret)
BGen Henry W. Hise, USMC (Ret)
BGen Joseph E. Hopkins, USMC (Ret)
BGen Charles S. Robertson, USMC (Ret)

Col Harry E. Atkinson, USMC (Ret)
Col William D. Bassett, Jr., USMC (Ret)
Col Noble L. Beck, USMC (Ret)
Col Clarence W. Boyd, Jr., USMC (Ret)
Col Eugene R. Brady, USMC (Ret)
Col James T. Breckinridge, USMC (Ret)
Col William C. Britt, USMC (Ret)
Col Thomas E. Bulger, USMC (Ret)
Col Charles R. Burroughs, USMC (Ret)
Col John S. Canton, USMC (Ret)
Col Frank A. Clark, USMC (Ret)

Col Leroy V. Corbett, USMC (Ret)
Col Wallace W. Crompton, USMC (Ret)
Col Raymond C. Damm, USMC (Ret)
Col Edward F. Danowitz, USMC (Ret)
Col Louis R. Daze, USMC (Ret)
Col Frank R. DeNormandie, USMC (Ret)
Col Fred T. Fagan, Jr., USMC
Col Bob W. Farley, USMC (Ret)
Col Edwin H. Finlayson, USMC (Ret)
Col George C. Fox, USMC (Ret)
Col Owen V. Gallentine, USMC (Ret)
Col Samuel A. Hannah, USMC (Ret)
Col Paul B. Henley, USMC (Ret)
Col Gilbert R. Hershey, USMC (Ret)
Col Ralph A. Heywood, USMC (Ret)
Col William J. Howatt, USMC (Ret)
Col Ray N. Joens, USMC (Ret)
Col Ray Kummerow, USMC (Ret)
Col Elliott R. Laine, Jr., USMC (Ret)
Col Robert G Lauffer, USMC (Ret)
Col George E. Lawrence, USMC (Ret)
Col John Lowman, Jr., USMC (Ret)
Col John F. McMahon, Jr., USMC (Ret)
Col Bruce J. Matheson, USMC (Ret)
Col Theodore E. Metzger, USMC (Ret)
Col Richard D. Mickelson, USMC (Ret)
Col Wendell P. C. Morgenthaler, Jr., USMC (Ret)
Col Donald E. Morin, USMC (Ret)
Col Peter J. Mulroney, USMC (Ret)
Col Leonard L. Orr, USMC (Ret)
Col Harry F. Painter, USMC (Ret)
Col Harold L. Parsons, USMC (Ret)
Col Clifford J. Peabody, USMC (Ret)
Col Lewis E. Poggemeyer, USMC (Ret)
Col Roy L. Reed, USMC (Ret)
Col William E. Riley, Jr., USMC (Ret)
Col Horton E. Roeder, USMC (Ret)
Col Richard A. Savage, USMC (Ret)
Col John L. Schwartz, USMC (Ret)
Col William Shanks, Jr., USMC (Ret)
Col Walter Sienko, USMC (Ret)
Col Anthony J. Skotnicki, USMC (Ret)
Col Joseph Sleger, Jr., USMC (Ret)
Col Edward W. Snelling, USMC (Ret)

REVIEWERS

Col Charles R. Stephenson II, USMC (Ret)
Col William W. Storm III, USMC (Ret)
Col John M. Terry, Jr., USMC (Ret)
Col Floyd H. Waldrop, USMC (Ret)
Col Howard A. Westphall, USMC (Ret)
Col H. Speed Wilson, USMC (Ret)
Col Robert R. Wilson, USMC (Ret)
Col William J. Zaro, USMC (Ret)

LtCol Roi E. Andrews, USMC (Ret)
LtCol Merrill M. Bartlett, USMC (Ret)
LtCol William F. Bethel, USMC (Ret)
LtCol Don R. Christensen, USMC (Ret)
LtCol Richard F. Daley, USMC (Ret)
LtCol Godfrey S. Delcuze, USMC (Ret)
LtCol Robert C. Evans, USMC (Ret)
LtCol Wesley L. Fox, USMC
LtCol Donald J. Garrett, USMC (Ret)
LtCol Edward D. Gelzer, Jr., USMC (Ret)
LtCol David G. Henderson, USMC (Ret)
LtCol David G. Harron, USMC (Ret)
LtCol Earl R. Hunter, USMC (Ret)
LtCol Raymond G. Kennedy, Sr., USMC (Ret)
LtCol Charles H. Knowles, USMC (Ret)
LtCol Marvin H. Lugger, USMC (Ret)
LtCol Robert B. March, USMC (Ret)
LtCol Robert L. Modjeski, USMC (Ret)
LtCol Aydlette H. Perry, Jr., USMC (Ret)

LtCol John E. Poindexter, USMC (Ret)
LtCol Thomas E. Raines, USMC (Ret)
LtCol Ward R. Reiss, USMC (Ret)
LtCol David F. Seiler, USMC (Ret)
LtCol William F. Sparks, USMC (Ret)
LtCol Laurier J. Tremblay, USMC (Ret)

Capt Cyril L. Kammeier, USMC (Ret)
Capt Joseph W. Pratte, USMC (Ret)

Sgt Gary S. Davis, USMC (Ret)

Army

Gen Richard G. Stilwell, USA (Ret)
MajGen William A. Burke, USA (Ret)
LtCol John W. Moser, USA (Ret)
LtCol Adrian G. Traas, USA

Others

Dr. Jeffrey J. Clarke
Mr. Edward J. Marolda
Mr. Bernard C. Nalty
Ms. Barbara A. Rhenish
Dr. Ronald H. Spector
Dr. Wayne W. Thompson
Mr. Willard J. Webb

Appendix F

Distribution of Personnel Fleet Marine Force, Pacific
(Reproduction of Status of Forces, 31 January 1969)

UNIT	NOTE	ASSIGNED STRENGTH USMC	ASSIGNED STRENGTH USN	STR RPT DATE	DANANG USMC	DANANG USN	CHU LAI USMC	CHU LAI USN	PHU BAI USMC	PHU BAI USN	No I CTZ USMC	No I CTZ USN	OKINAWA USMC	OKINAWA USN	JAPAN USMC	JAPAN USN	HAWAII USMC	HAWAII USN	EASTPAC USMC	EASTPAC USN	OTHER USMC	OTHER USN
HEADQUARTERS																						
HQ, FMF, PAC																						
FMF, PAC (FWD)		74	1	24JUL68									74	1								
H&S BN, FMF, PAC	4	1673	50	15JAN69													1507	50			166	
CAMP S. D. BUTLER		810	137	15JAN69									810	137								
CASUAL		611		15JAN69									611									
HOSPITALIZED	7	1139		15JAN69									568		571							
HQ, V MEF																						
1ST CIVAFFGRP		63	7	28JAN69															63	7		
HQ, 5TH MARDIV																						
HQBN, 5TH MARDIV	4	1506	34	28JAN69															1461	34	45	
HQ, FORTRPS, FMF PAC																						
HQCO, FORTRPS	4	398	24	28JAN69															189	24	209	
HQ, 1ST MAR BRIG																						
HQCO, 1ST MAR BRIG		230	8	28JAN69													230	8				
HQ, 9TH MAB																						
HQCO, 9TH MAB		482	20	28JAN69									482	20								
HQ, III MAF																						
H&SCO, III MAF	4	993	31	28JAN69	975	31															18	
1ST CAG		436	19	28JAN69			436	19														
2D CAG	2	608	42	28JAN69	588	42															20	
3D CAG		540	28	28JAN69					540	28												
4TH CAG		302	13	28JAN69							302	13										
HQ, 1ST MAR DIV																						
HQBN, 1ST MAR DIV	4	1930	42	28JAN69	1887	42															43	
HQ, 3D MAR DIV																						
HQBN, 3D MAR DIV	4	2074	33	28JAN69							2053	33									21	
INFANTRY																						
1ST MARINES																						
HQ CO		251	8	28JAN69	251	8																
1ST BATTALION		1054	59	28JAN69	1054	59																
2D BATTALION		1046	60	28JAN69	1046	60																
3D BATTALION		1105	59	28JAN69	1105	59																
3D MARINES																						
HQ CO		217	7	28JAN69	217	7																
1ST BATTALION		1156	56	28JAN69	1156	56																
2D BATTALION		1123	61	28JAN69							1123	61										
3D BATTALION		1154	56	28JAN69	1154	56																
4TH MARINES																						
HQ CO		218	6	28JAN69							218	6										
1ST BATTALION		1158	56	28JAN69							1158	56										
2D BATTALION		1113	61	28JAN69							1113	61										
3D BATTALION		1108	59	28JAN69							1108	59										
5TH MARINES																						
HQ CO		243	7	28JAN69	243	7																
1ST BATTALION		1033	61	28JAN69	1033	61																
2D BATTALION		981	54	28JAN69	981	54																
3D BATTALION		1119	61	28JAN69	1119	61																
7TH MARINES																						
HQ CO		242	7	28JAN69	242	7																
1ST BATTALION		995	56	28JAN69	995	56																
2D BATTALION		1059	59	28JAN69	1059	59																
3D BATTALION		1018	57	28JAN69	1018	57																
9TH MARINES																						
HQ CO		214	6	28JAN69							214	6										
1ST BATTALION		1106	56	28JAN69							1106	56										
2D BATTALION		1115	56	28JAN69							1115	56										
3D BATTALION		1118	56	28JAN69							1118	56										
26TH MARINES																						
HQ CO		500	12	28JAN69	261	6							239	6								
1ST BATTALION		1571	56	28JAN69	1571	56																
2D BATTALION	1	1621	96	28JAN69															1621	96		
3D BATTALION	1	1740	75	28JAN69															1740	75		
27TH MARINES																						
HQ CO		238	6	28JAN69													238	6				
1ST BATTALION		1095	86	28JAN69													1095	86				
2D BATTALION		1129	32	28JAN69															1129	32		
3D BATTALION		1144	32	28JAN69															1144	32		
28TH MARINES																						
HQ CO		244	7	28JAN69															244	7		
1ST BATTALION		1444	43	28JAN69															1444	43		
2D BATTALION		1182	36	28JAN69															1182	36		
3D BATTALION		1235	38	28JAN69															1235	38		

DISTRIBUTION OF PERSONNEL, 31 JANUARY 1969

ARTILLERY

UNIT	ASSIGNED STRENGTH USMC	ASSIGNED STRENGTH USN	STR RPT DATE	DANANG USMC	DANANG USN
11TH MARINES					
HQ BTRY	314	11	28JAN69	314	11
1ST BATTALION	665	18	28JAN69	665	18
2D BATTALION	671	15	28JAN69	671	15
3D BATTALION	650	16	28JAN69	650	16
4TH BATTALION	557	13	28JAN69	557	13
12TH MARINES					
HQ BTRY	296	16	28JAN69	296	16
1ST BATTALION	698	21	28JAN69	698	21
2D BATTALION	658	19	28JAN69	658	19
3D BATTALION	767	18	28JAN69	767	18
4TH BATTALION	514	14	28JAN69	514	14

* UNLESS OTHERWISE NOTED, STRENGTHS AND LOCATION ARE THOSE REPORTED BY UNIT PERSONNEL STATUS REPORTS AND DO NOT REFLECT DAY-TO-DAY ADJUSTMENTS BETWEEN REPORTING PERIODS.

UNIT	NOTE	ASSIGNED STRENGTH USMC	ASSIGNED STRENGTH USN	STR RPT DATE	DANANG USMC	DANANG USN	CHU LAI USMC	CHU LAI USN	PHU BAI USMC	PHU BAI USN	No I CTZ USMC	No I CTZ USN	OKINAWA USMC	OKINAWA USN	JAPAN USMC	JAPAN USN	HAWAII USMC	HAWAII USN	EASTPAC USMC	EASTPAC USN	OTHER USMC	OTHER USN
13TH MARINES																						
HQ BTRY		310	6	28JAN69															310	6		
1ST BATTALION		292	8	28JAN69	292	8																
2D BATTALION		435	13	28JAN69															435	13		
3D BATTALION		664	16	28JAN69															664	16		
4TH BATTALION		423	11	28JAN69															423	11		
HQ BTRY, 1ST FAG		127	2	28JAN69	127	2																
HQ BTRY, 5TH FAG		122	4	28JAN69															122	4		
1ST 155MM GUN BTRY		154	3	28JAN69	154	3																
3D 155MM GUN BTRY		155	3	28JAN69	155	3																
5TH 155MM GUN BTRY		180	8	28JAN69							180	8										
7TH 155MM GUN BTRY		113	2	28JAN69															113	2		
1ST 8" HOW BTRY		188	6	28JAN69							188	6										
3D 8" HOW BTRY		220	4	28JAN69	220	4																
5TH 8" HOW BTRY		145	2	28JAN69															145	2		
1ST SEARCH LIGHT BTRY		102		28JAN69							102											
RECONNAISSANCE																						
1ST RECON BN		699	51	28JAN69	699	51																
3D RECON BN		703	51	28JAN69							703	51										
5TH RECON BN		408	13	28JAN69															408	13		
1ST FORCE RECON CO		157	9	28JAN69	157	9																
3D FORCE RECON CO		139		28JAN69							139											
5TH FORCE RECON CO		147	2	28JAN69															147	2		
ANTI-TANK																						
1ST AT BN	6																					
3D AT BN	6																					
5TH AT BN		341	10	28JAN69									54	1					287	9		
TANK																						
1ST TANK BN		773	18	28JAN69	773	18																
3D TANK BN		740	18	28JAN69							740	18										
5TH TANK BN		665	13	28JAN69															665	13		
AMTRAC																						
1ST AMTRAC BN		666	27	28JAN69							666	27										
3D AMTRAC BN		631	17	28JAN69	631	17																
5TH AMTRAC BN		672	15	28JAN69									125	5					547	10		
1ST ARM AMPHIB CO		237	6	28JAN69	237	6																
ENGINEER																						
1ST ENGR BN		702	12	28JAN69	702	12																
3D ENGR BN		744	18	28JAN69							744	18										
5TH ENGR BN		485	9	28JAN69									33	1					452	8		
7TH ENGR BN		1120	24	28JAN69	1120	24																
9TH ENGR BN		928	25	28JAN69			928	25														
11TH ENGR BN		1152	28	28JAN69							1152	28										
13TH ENGR BN		890	15	28JAN69															890	15		
1ST BRIDGE CO	5																					
3D BRIDGE CO	5																					
5TH BRIDGE CO		150	2	28JAN69															150	2		
MOTOR TRANSPORT																						
1ST MT BN		311	8	28JAN69	311	8																
3D MT BN		347	8	28JAN69							347	8										
5TH MT BN		185	7	28JAN69															185	7		
7TH MT BN		413	5	28JAN69	413	5																
9TH MT BN		416	9	28JAN69					416	9												
11TH MT BN		462	12	28JAN69	462	12																
13TH MT BN		457	8	28JAN69															457	8		
COMMUNICATION																						
1ST RADIO BN		471	2	28JAN69	383												88	2				
5TH COMM BN		718	6	28JAN69	718	6																
7TH COMM BN		692	11	28JAN69	692	11																
9TH COMM BN		619	13	28JAN69									212	3					457	10		
1ST ANGLICO	3	385	22	28JAN69													128	5			257	17
SHORE PARTY																						
1ST SP BN		453	21	28JAN69	453	21																
3D SP BN		480	22	28JAN69							480	22										
5TH SP BN		288	23	28JAN69															288	23		
MILITARY POLICE																						
1ST MP BN		673	13	28JAN69	673	13																
3D MP BN		729	14	28JAN69	729	14																
5TH MP BN		527	7	28JAN69															527	7		

SERVICE/SUPPORT

Unit	Assigned Strength USMC	USN	STR RPT DATE	DANANG USMC	USN	CHU LAI USMC	USN	PHU BAI USMC	USN	No I CTZ USMC	USN	OKINAWA USMC	USN	JAPAN USMC	USN	HAWAII USMC	USN	EASTPAC USMC	USN	OTHER USMC	USN
FLC, III MAF																					
HQ, FLC/1ST FSR																					
H&S BN	1642	58	28JAN69	1642	58																
SUPPLY BN	1958	37	28JAN69	1958	37																
7TH SEP BK FUEL CO																					
MAINT BN	1148	9	28JAN69	1148	9																
FLSG-A/3D SERV BN	1336	26	28JAN69									1336	26								
FLSG-B/1ST SERV BN	1612	19	28JAN69	1612	19																
3D FSR																					
H&S BN	1058	28	28JAN69									1058	28								
SUPPLY BN	1351	11	28JAN69									1351	11								
MAINT BN	1033		28JAN69									1033									
5TH FSR																					
H&S BN	367	22	28JAN69															367	22		
SUPPLY BN	432	18	28JAN69															432	18		
MAINT BN	555		28JAN69															555			
5TH SERVICE BN	805	15	28JAN69									805	15								
PROV SERVICE BN, 9TH MAB	764	16	28JAN69									764	16								
9TH SEP BULK FUEL CO	293		28JAN69													293					

UNIT	NOTE	ASSIGNED STRENGTH USMC	USN	STR RPT DATE	DANANG USMC	USN	CHU LAI USMC	USN	PHU BAI USMC	USN	No I CTZ USMC	USN	OKINAWA USMC	USN	JAPAN USMC	USN	HAWAII USMC	USN	EASTPAC USMC	USN	OTHER USMC	USN
MEDICAL																							
1ST MED BN		150	312	28JAN69	150	312																
3D MED BN		136	259	28JAN69			136	259														
5TH MED BN		96	157	28JAN69															96	157		
1ST HOSP CO		44	78	28JAN69	44	78																
5TH HOSP CO		30	48	28JAN69															30	48		
1ST DENTAL CO			83	28JAN69		83																
3D DENTAL CO			85	28JAN69				85														
5TH DENTAL CO			27	28JAN69																12		15
11TH DENTAL CO		3	74	28JAN69	3	74																
13TH DENTAL CO			33	28JAN69																33		
15TH DENTAL CO		3	39	28JAN69															3	39		
17TH DENTAL CO		4	57	28JAN69															4	57		
USMC		93,973			40,403		1,364		1,092		17,405		8,219		571		3,341		17,438		4,140	
USN			4,445			1,921		129		296		675		244				163		829		188
GROUND TOTAL		98,418			42,324		1,493		1,388		18,080		8,463		571		3,504		19,267		4,328	

AVIATION UNITS

Unit	Assigned Strength USMC	USN	STR RPT DATE	DANANG USMC	USN	CHU LAI USMC	USN	PHU BAI USMC	USN	No I CTZ USMC	USN	OKINAWA USMC	USN	JAPAN USMC	USN	HAWAII USMC	USN	EASTPAC USMC	USN	OTHER USMC	USN
HQ SQDN FMFPAC	61		28JAN69													61					
1ST MAW																					
MWHG-1																					
H&HS-1	726	34	28JAN69	726	34																
MWFS-1	145		28JAN69	145																	
MWCS-1	265		28JAN69	265																	
MWSG-17																					
H&MS-17	713	18	28JAN69	713	18																
WERS-17	214		28JAN69	214																	
MACG-18																					
H&HS-18	234	4	28JAN69	234	4																
MASS-2	256	2	28JAN69	256	2																
MASS-3	223	2	28JAN69					223	2												
MACS-4	372	2	28JAN69	372	2																
1ST LAAM BN	715	12	28JAN69	715	12																
MAG-11																					
H&MS-11	613		28JAN69	613																	
MABS-11	431	26	28JAN69	431	26																
VMCJ-1	354	1	28JAN69	354	1																
VMFA-542	289	1	28JAN69	289	1																
VMA(AW)-242	261	1	28JAN69	261	1																
VMA(AW)-225	328	2	28JAN69	328	2																
MAG-12																					
H&MS-12	557	1	28JAN69			557	1														
MABS-12	538	26	28JAN69			538	26														
MATCU-67	97		28JAN69			97															
VMA-121	161	1	28JAN69			161	1														
VMA-211	191	1	28JAN69			191	1														
VMA-223	180	1	28JAN69			180	1														
VMA-311	179	1	28JAN69			179	1														
VMA(AW)-533	268	1	28JAN69			268	1														
MAG-13																					
H&MS-13	490		28JAN69			490															
MABS-13	505	29	28JAN69			505	29														
VMFA-115	263	1	28JAN69			263	1														
VMFA-314	267	1	28JAN69			267	1														
VMFA-323	259	1	28JAN69			259	1														
VMFA-334	289	1	28JAN69			289	1														
MAG-16																					
H&MS-16	570		28JAN69	570																	

DISTRIBUTION OF PERSONNEL, 31 JANUARY 1969

UNIT	NOTE	ASSIGNED STRENGTH USMC	USN	STRENGTH RPT DATE	DANANG USMC	USN	CHU LAI USMC	USN	PHU BAI USMC	USN	No I CTZ USMC	USN	OKINAWA USMC	USN	JAPAN USMC	USN	HAWAII USMC	USN	EASTPAC USMC	USN	OTHER USMC	USN
MABS-16		725	27	28JAN69	725	27																
VMO-2		254	1	28JAN69	254	1																
HMM-165		206	1	28JAN69	206	1																
HML-167		148		28JAN69	148																	
HMM-364		233	1	28JAN69	233	1																
HMH-463		239	1	28JAN69	239	1																
MAG-36																						
H&MS-36		440		28JAN69			260		180													
MABS-36		520	22	28JAN69			312	22	208													
MATCU-62		66		28JAN69					66													
MATCU-68		82		28JAN69			82															
HMM-263		245		28JAN69			245															
HMM-265		221	1	28JAN69			221	1														
HMM-362		260	4	28JAN69			260	4														
HML-367		185	1	28JAN69			185	1														
HMH-462		221	1	28JAN69			221	1														
PROVMAG-39/PROV H&MS-39		485	18	28JAN69							485	18										
VMO-6		281	1	28JAN69							281	1										
HMM-161		232	1	28JAN69							232	1										
HMM-262		207	1	28JAN69							207	1										
MATCU-62, DET "A"		82		28JAN69							82											
9TH MAB																						
MAG-15																						
H&MS-15		401		28JAN69									39		362							
MABS-15		268	26	28JAN69											268	26						
MATCU-60		54		28JAN69											54							
MATCU-66		40		28JAN69									40									
MACS-8		179	1	28JAN69									179	1								
VMGR-152		468	4	28JAN69											468	4						
VMFA-122		313	1	28JAN69											313	1						
HMM-164	1	224	4	28JAN69																	224	4
1ST BRIG																						
MAG-24																						
H&MS-24		476		28JAN69													476					
MABS-24		427	23	28JAN69													427	23				
MACS-2		214		28JAN69													214					
MATCU-70		67		28JAN69													67					
VMFA-212		264		28JAN69													264					
VMFA-235		270		28JAN69													270					
3D MAW																						
MWHG-3																						
H&HS-3	4	627	9	28JAN69													608	9	19			
MWFS-3		148		28JAN69													148					
MWCS-3		220		28JAN69													220					
MCCRTG-10	8																					
H&MS-10		3		28JAN69													3					
VMFAT-101		37		28JAN69													37					
VMAT-102		33		28JAN69													33					
VMT-103		347		28JAN69													347					
MHTG-30																						
H&MS-30		299		28JAN69													299					
HMHT-301		176	1	28JAN69													176	1				
HMMT-302		250		28JAN69													250					
MAG-33																						
H&MS-33		622		28JAN69													622					
MABS-33		531	2	28JAN69													531	2				
MATCU-65		88		28JAN69													89					
VMCJ-3		341		28JAN69													341					
VMFA-214		206	1	28JAN69													206	1				
VMFA-232		306	1	28JAN69													306	1				
VMFA-531		238	1	28JAN69													238	1				
MWSG-37																						
H&MS-37		630	2	28JAN69													630	2				
WERS-37		230	77	28JAN69													230	77				
VMGR-352		399	1	28JAN69													399	1				
MACG-38																						
H&HS-38		254	3	28JAN69													254	3				
MASS-5		205		28JAN69													205					
MACS-1		272		28JAN69													272					
MACS-3		239		28JAN69													239					
MACS-7		254	2	28JAN69													254	2				
5TH LAAM BN		525	10	28JAN69													525	10				
2ND LAAM BN		253		28JAN69													253					
MAG-56																						
H&MS-56		403		28JAN69													403					
MABS-56		373	2	28JAN69													373	2				

MATCU-74	86	28JAN69								86	
HMM-163	261	28JAN69								261	
HML-267	374	5	28JAN69							374	5
HMM-363											
HMM-561	253									253	
USMC	29,494		8,291	4,467	1,786	1,741	258	1,465	1,779	9,464	243
USN	427		134	67	29	21	1	31	23	117	4
AVIATION TOTAL	29,921		8,425	4,534	1,815	1,762	259	1,496	1,802	9,581	247

RECAPITULATION OF FMFPAC PERSONNEL DISTRIBUTION

		ASSIGNED STRENGTH	DANANG	CHU LAI	PHU BAI	No I CTZ	OKINAWA	JAPAN	HAWAII	EASTPAC	OTHER
GROUND TOTAL	USMC	93,973	40,403	1,364	1,092	17,405	8,219	571	3,341	17,438	4,140
	USN	4,445	1,921	129	296	675	244		163	829	188
AVIATION TOTAL	USMC	29,494	8,291	4,467	1,786	1,741	258	1,465	1,779	9,464	243
	USN	427	134	67	29	21	1	31	23	117	4
GRAND TOTAL	USMC	123,467	48,694	5,831	2,878	19,146	8,477	2,036	5,120	26,902	4,383
	USN	4,872	2,055	196	325	696	245	31	186	946	192

NOTES:
1. FIGURES IN "OTHER" ASSIGNED TO SLF's AND ARE BLT STRENGTHS.
2. FIGURES IN "OTHER" ASSIGNED TO VARIOUS RVN LOCATIONS.
3. AT VARIOUS I CTZ LOCATIONS.
4. PERSONNEL LISTED IN "OTHER" ARE ASSIGNED TO IT, ITT, SSC, CI TEAMS, RED EYE AND NUCLEAR ORDNANCE PLATOONS.
5. STRENGTHS INCLUDED IN 7TH AND 11TH ENGINEER BATTALIONS.
6. 1ST AND 3D ANTI-TANK PERSONNEL ARE INCLUDED IN 1ST AND 3D TANK BATTALIONS STRENGTHS.
7. HOSPITALIZED AT LOCATIONS OTHER THAN OKINAWA, BUT CARRIED ON THE ROLLS OF CASUAL COMPANY, CAMP BUTLER.
8. ACTIVATED ON 1 JANUARY 1969.

Appendix G

Distribution of Personnel Fleet Marine Force, Pacific

(Reproduction of Status of Forces, 8 December 1969)

UNIT	NOTE	ASSIGNED STRENGTH USMC	ASSIGNED STRENGTH USN	STR RPT DATE	DANANG USMC	DANANG USN	CHU LAI USMC	CHU LAI USN	PHU BAI USMC	PHU BAI USN	I CTZ USMC	I CTZ USN	OKINAWA USMC	OKINAWA USN	JAPAN USMC	JAPAN USN	HAWAII USMC	HAWAII USN	EASTPAC USMC	EASTPAC USN	OTHER USMC	OTHER USN
HEADQUARTERS																						
HQ, FMF, PAC																						
FMF, PAC (FWD)	3	92	1	8MAY69													92	1				
H&S BN, FMF, PAC	3	1864	50	14MAY69													1864	50				
CAMP S. D. BUTLER		1456	124	25SEP69									1456	124								
CASUAL		423		25SEP69									423									
HOSPITALIZED	5	1168		25SEP69									1		570						527	
HQ, V MEB		1943	83	2DEC69															1943	83		
1ST CIVAFFGRP		61	3	2DEC69															61	3		
HQ, FORTRPS, FMF PAC																						
HQCO, FORTRPS		190	18	2DEC69															190	18		
HQ, 1ST MAR BRIG																						
HQCO, 1ST MAR BRIG		252	26	2DEC69													252	26				
HQ, I MEF																						
HQ 3D MARDIV																						
HQBN, 3D MARDIV		1830	79	2DEC69									1830	79								
HQ, III MAF																						
H&SCO, III MAF		1022	30	2DEC69	1022	30																
1ST CAG		509		2DEC69			509															
2D CAG		604		2DEC69	604																	
3D CAG		523		2DEC69					523													
4TH CAG		320		2DEC69							320											
HQ, 1ST MARDIV																						
HQBN, 1ST MARDIV	3	2138	47	2DEC69	2089	47															49	
INFANTRY																						
1ST MARINES																						
HQ CO		273	10	2DEC69	273	10																
1ST BATTALION		1205	58	2DEC69	1205	58																
2D BATTALION		1191	57	2DEC69	1191	57																
3D BATTALION		1202	58	2DEC69	1202	58																
3D MARINES																						
HQ CO		288	9	2DEC69															288	9		
1ST BATTALION		1456	69	2DEC69													1456	69				
2D BATTALION		1356	74	2DEC69															1356	74		
3D BATTALION		1376	86	2DEC69															1376	86		
4TH MARINES																						
HQ CO		244	5	2DEC69									244	5								
1ST BATTALION		916	56	2DEC69									915	56								
2D BATTALION		927	55	2DEC69									927	55								
3D BATTALION		1163	54	2DEC69									1163	54								
5TH MARINES																						
HQ CO		342	7	2DEC69	342	7																
1ST BATTALION		1203	57	2DEC69	1203	57																
2D BATTALION		1218	51	2DEC69	1218	51																
3D BATTALION		1202	59	2DEC69	1202	59																
7TH MARINES																						
HQ CO		283	7	2DEC69	283	7																
1ST BATTALION		1184	57	2DEC69	1184	57																
2D BATTALION		1134	58	2DEC69	1134	58																
3D BATTALION		1203	43	2DEC69	1203	43																
9TH MARINES																						
HQ CO		389	54	2DEC69									389	54								
1ST BATTALION	1	1650	82	2DEC69															1650	82		
2D BATTALION	1	1552	57	2DEC69															1552	57		
3D BATTALION		1280	55	2DEC69									1280	55								
26TH MARINES																						
HQ CO		297	6	2DEC69	297	6																
1ST BATTALION		1317	60	2DEC69	1317	60																
2D BATTALION		1302	57	2DEC69	1302	57																
3D BATTALION		1318	56	2DEC69	1318	56																
ARTILLERY																						
11TH MARINES																						
HQ BTRY		448	10	2DEC69	448	10																
1ST BATTALION		647	16	2DEC69	647	16																
2D BATTALION		638	18	2DEC69	638	18																
3D BATTALION		621	16	2DEC69	621	16																
4TH BATTALION		588	13	2DEC69	588	13																

UNIT		ASSIGNED STRENGTH		STR RPT DATE																
12TH MARINES																				
HQ BTRY		229	15	2DEC69												229	15			
1ST BATTALION		1320	19	2DEC69														1320	19	
2D BATTALION		769	17	2DEC69												769	17			
3D BATTALION		528	21	2DEC69												529	21			
4TH BATTALION		454	17	2DEC69												321	16	133	1	

* UNLESS OTHERWISE NOTED, STRENGTHS AND LOCATION ARE THOSE REPORTED BY UNIT PERSONNEL STATUS REPORTS AND DO NOT REFLECT DAY-TO-DAY ADJUSTMENTS BETWEEN REPORTING PERIODS.

UNIT	NOTE	ASSIGNED STRENGTH		STR RPT DATE	DANANG		CHU LAI		PHU BAI		No I CTZ		OKINAWA		JAPAN		HAWAII		EASTPAC		OTHER	
		USMC	USN		USMC	USN	USMC	USN	USMC	USN	USMC	USN	USMC	USN	USMC	USN	USMC	USN	USMC	USN	USMC	USN
1ST BN, 13TH MAR		758	15	2DEC69	758	15																
HQ BTRY, 1ST FAG		20		2DEC69	20																	
1ST 175MM GUN BTRY		179	3	2DEC69	179	3																
3D 175MM GUN BTRY		152	3	2DEC69	152	3																
5TH 175MM GUN BTRY		239	5	2DEC69									239	5								
1ST 8" HOW BTRY		220	5	2DEC69									220	5								
3D 8" HOW BTRY		228	4	2DEC69	228	4																
1ST SEARCH LIGHT BTRY(CADRE)																						
RECONNAISSANCE																						
1ST RECON BN		749	58	2DEC69	749	58																
3D RECON BN		501	37	2DEC69									337	28					164	9		
1ST FORCE RECON CO		145	7	2DEC69	145	7																
3D FORCE RECON CO		156	7	2DEC69							156	7										
ANTI-TANK																						
1ST AT BN	4																					
3D AT BN		154	7	2DEC69															154	7		
TANK																						
1ST TANK BN		872	20	2DEC69	872	20																
3D TANK BN		910	23	2DEC69									478	13					432	10		
AMTRAC																						
1ST AMTRAC BN		902	16	2DEC69									333	4					569	12		
3D AMTRAC BN		858	18	2DEC69	858	18																
ENGINEER																						
1ST ENGR BN		923	15	2DEC69	923	15																
3D ENGR BN		767	22	2DEC69									371	18					336	4		
7TH ENGR BN		948	24	2DEC69	948	24																
9TH ENGR BN		1051	21	2DEC69			1051	21														
11TH ENGR BN		1112	19	2DEC69									516	15					596	4		
1ST BRIDGE CO		189		2DEC69			189															
3D BRIDGE CO (-)		85	1	2DEC69															85	1		
MOTOR TRANSPORT																						
1ST MT BN		420	7	2DEC69	420	7																
3D MT BN (-)		232	12	2DEC69									144	10					88	2		
9TH MT BN		270	10	2DEC69									270	10								
11TH MT BN		517	10	2DEC69	517	10																
COMMUNICATION																						
1ST RADIO BN		364		2DEC69	297												67					
5TH COMM BN (REIN)		1060	13	2DEC69	1060	13																
7TH COMM BN (-)		427	2	2DEC69									427	2								
9TH COMM BN		491	8	2DEC69									240	2					251	6		
1ST ANGLICO		110	4	2DEC69													110	4				
SHORE PARTY																						
1ST SP BN		567	19	2DEC69	567	19																
3D SP BN		399	32	2DEC69									213	14					186	18		
MILITARY POLICE																						
1ST MP BN		671	13	2DEC69	671	13																
3D MP BN		815	12	2DEC69	815	12																
SERVICE/SUPPORT																						
FLC, III MAF																						
HQ, FLC/1ST FSR																						
H&S BN		1853	65	2DEC69	1853	65																
SUPPLY BN		1523	30	2DEC69	1523	30																
7TH SEP BK FUEL CO		150		2DEC69	160																	

DISTRIBUTION OF PERSONNEL, 8 DECEMBER 1969

UNIT	ASSIGNED STRENGTH		STR RPT DATE	DANANG		CHU LAI		PHU BAI		No I CTZ		OKINAWA		JAPAN		HAWAII		EASTPAC		OTHER	
	USMC	USN		USMC	USN	USMC	USN	USMC	USN	USMC	USN	USMC	USN	USMC	USN	USMC	USN	USMC	USN	USMC	USN
MAINT BN	1031	8	2DEC69	1031	8																
FLSG-A	617	10	2DEC69									617	10								
FLSG-B/1ST SERV BN	1707	23	2DEC69	1707	23																
3D FSR																					
H&S BN	982	32	2DEC69									982	32								
SUPPLY BN	1140	15	2DEC69									1140	15								
MAINT BN	1053		2DEC69									1053									
5TH FSR																					
H&S BN	570	18	2DEC69															570	18		
SUPPLY BN	564	19	2DEC69															564	19		
MAINT BN	792		2DEC69															792			
3D SERVICE BN	1952	49	2DEC69									1262	27					690	22		
9TH SEP BULK FUEL CO	289		2DEC69															289			

UNIT	NOTE	ASSIGNED STRENGTH		STR RPT DATE	DANANG		CHU LAI		PHU BAI		No I CTZ		OKINAWA		JAPAN		HAWAII		EASTPAC		OTHER	
		USMC	USN		USMC	USN	USMC	USN	USMC	USN	USMC	USN	USMC	USN	USMC	USN	USMC	USN	USMC	USN	USMC	USN
MEDICAL																						
1ST MED BN		203	346	2DEC69	203	346																
3D MED BN		163	276	2DEC69									99	216					64	60		
1ST HOSP CO		52	68	2DEC69	52	68																
1ST DENTAL CO			68	2DEC69		68																
3D DENTAL CO			83	2DEC69										83								
11TH DENTAL CO		4	62	2DEC69	4	62																
13TH DENTAL CO		30	30	2DEC69															30			

	USMC	USN	DANANG		CHU LAI		PHU BAI		No I CTZ		OKINAWA		JAPAN		HAWAII		EASTPAC		OTHER	
USMC	82,282		39,456		1,560		523		4,727		15,417		570		3,841		12,246		3,942			
USN		3,668		1,762		21		0		74		999		0		150		509		153		
GROUND TOTAL	85,950		41,218		1,581		523		4,801		16,416		570		3,991		12,755		4,095			

AVIATION UNITS

UNIT	ASSIGNED STRENGTH		STR RPT DATE	DANANG		CHU LAI		PHU BAI		No I CTZ		OKINAWA		JAPAN		HAWAII		EASTPAC		OTHER	
	USMC	USN		USMC	USN	USMC	USN	USMC	USN	USMC	USN	USMC	USN	USMC	USN	USMC	USN	USMC	USN	USMC	USN
HQ SQDN FMFPAC	61		2DEC69																	61		
1ST MAW																						
MWHG-1																						
H&HS-1	835	36	2DEC69	835	36																
MWFS-1	153		2DEC69	153																		
MWCS-1	304		2DEC69	304																		
MWSG-17																						
H&MS-17	710	19	2DEC69	710	19																
WERS-17	232		2DEC69	232																		
MACG-18																						
H&HS-18	251	11	2DEC69	251	11																
MASS-3	268	2	2DEC69	268	2																
MACS-4	343	4	2DEC69	343	4																
MAG-11																						
H&MS-11	641		2DEC69	641																		
MABS-11	473	23	2DEC69	473	23																
VMCJ-1	372		2DEC69	372																		
VMA(AW)-225	258	1	2DEC69	258	1																
VMA(AW)-242	266	1	2DEC69	266	1																
VMFA-542	286	1	2DEC69	286	1																
MAG-12																						
H&MS-12	447		2DEC69			447																
MABS-12	553	24	2DEC69			553	24															
MATCU-67	72		2DEC69			72																
VMA-211	171	1	2DEC69			171	1															
VMA-223	178	1	2DEC69			178	1															
VMA-311	181	1	2DEC69			181	1															
MAG-13																						
H&MS-13	501		2DEC69			501																
MABS-13	552	32	2DEC69			552	32															
VMFA-115	278	1	2DEC69			278	1															
VMFA-314	276	1	2DEC69			276	1															
VMFA-122	358		2DEC69			358																
MATCU-62	38		2DEC69			38																
MAG-16																						
H&MS-16	483		2DEC69	483																		
MABS-16	666	27	2DEC69	666	27																
MATCU-68	52		2DEC69	52																		
VMO-2	276		2DEC69	276																		
HML-167	184		2DEC69	184																		
HMA-364	222	1	2DEC69	222	1																
HMH-463	208	1	2DEC69	208	1																
HMM-263	227	1	2DEC69	227	1																
HMH-361	222	1	2DEC69	222	1																

Unit	Note	Assigned Strength USMC	Assigned Strength USN	Strength Rpt Date	DANANG USMC	DANANG USN	CHU LAI USMC	CHU LAI USN	PHU BAI USMC	PHU BAI USN	No I CTZ USMC	No I CTZ USN	OKINAWA USMC	OKINAWA USN	JAPAN USMC	JAPAN USN	HAWAII USMC	HAWAII USN	EASTPAC USMC	EASTPAC USN	OTHER USMC	OTHER USN
HMM-161		204		2DEC69	204																	
HMM-262		189	1	2DEC69	189	1																
HML-367		176	1	2DEC69	176	1																
1ST MAW (REAR)																						
MAG-15																						
H&MS-15		554		2DEC69									554									
MABS-15		429	28	2DEC69									429	28								
MATCU-60		64		2DEC69									64									
VMFA-232		277		2DEC69									277									
VMFA-334		281	1	2DEC69									281	1								
VMA(AW)-533		286		2DEC69									286									
MAG-18 (REAR)																						
H&HS-18 (REAR)																						
MACS-8		259	3	2DEC69									259	3								
MASS-2		241	2	2DEC69									241	2								
MAG-36																						
H&MS-36		445	1	2DEC69									445	1								
MABS-36		489	17	2DEC69									489	17								
MATCU-66		37		2DEC69									37									
VMGR-152		443	3	2DEC69									443	3								
HMM-165	1	295	3	2DEC69																	295	3
HMM-164	1	218	3	2DEC69																	218	3
HMH-462		234	2	2DEC69									234	2								
VMO-6		255	4	2DEC69									255	4								
1ST BRIG																						
MAG-24																						
H&MS-24		448		2DEC69													448					
MABS-24		306	21	2DEC69													306	12				
MACS-2		193		2DEC69													193					
MATCU-70		43		2DEC69													43					
VMFA-212		253		2DEC69													253					
VMFA-235		255		2DEC69													255					
3D MAW																						
MWHG-3																						
H&HS-3		668	28	2DEC69															658	28		
MWFS-3		153		2DEC69															153			
MWCS-3		231		2DEC69															231			
MCCRTG-10																						
H&MS-10		227	1	2DEC69															227	1		
VMAT-102		189		2DEC69															189			
VMT-103		199		2DEC69															199			
MHTG-30																						
H&MS-30		366	1	2DEC69															366	1		
HMT-301		172	1	2DEC69															172	1		
HMT-302		220	1	2DEC69															220	1		
MAG-33																						
H&MS-33		923	2	2DEC69															923	2		
MABS-33		419	3	2DEC69															419	3		
MATCU-65		68		2DEC69															68			
VMCJ-3		366	1	2DEC69															366	1		
VMA-214		208		2DEC69															208			
VMFA-531		309	1	2DEC69															309	1		
VMFA-323		11		2DEC69															11			
VMFAT-101		465		2DEC69															465			
MWSG-37																						
H&MS-37		635	3	2DEC69															635	3		
MWRS-37		215	1	2DEC69															215	1		
VMGR-352		358	1	2DEC69															358	1		
MACG-38																						
H&HS-38		258	3	2DEC69															258	3		
MACS-1		274		2DEC69															274			
MACS-3		268		2DEC69															268			
MACS-7		275	1	2DEC69															275	1		
1ST LAAM BN		206		2DEC69															206			
2D LAAM BN		810	10	2DEC69															810	10		
MAG-56																						
H&MS-56		449		2DEC69															449			
MABS-56		329	1	2DEC69															329	1		
MATCU-74		90		2DEC69															90			

DISTRIBUTION OF PERSONNEL, 8 DECEMBER 1969

Unit	Strength	Date									
HMM-163	322	2DEC69								322	
HML-267	513	2DEC69								513	5
HMM-265	174	2DEC69								174	
HMH-363	312	2DEC69								312	
MATCU-75	59	2DEC69								59	
USMC	29,213		7,932	4,174			1,903	2,391	1,559	10,741	513
USN	344		129	63			27	34	21	64	6
AVIATION TOTAL	29,557		8,061	4,237			1,930	2,425	1,580	10,805	519

RECAPITULATION OF FMFPAC PERSONNEL DISTRIBUTION

		ASSIGNED STRENGTH	DANANG	CHU LAI	PHU BAI	No I CTZ	OKINAWA	JAPAN	HAWAII	EASTPAC	OTHER
GROUND TOTAL	USMC	82,282	39,456	1,560	523	4,727	15,417	570	3,841	12,246	3,942
	USN	3,668	1,762	21	0	74	999	0	150	509	153
AVIATION TOTAL	USMC	29,213	7,932	4,174			1,903	2,391	1,559	10,741	513
	USN	344	129	63			27	34	21	64	6
GRAND TOTAL	USMC	111,495	47,388	5,734	523	4,727	17,320	2,961	5,400	22,987	4,455
	USN	4,012	1,891	84	0	74	1,026	34	171	573	159

NOTES:
1. FIGURES IN "OTHER" ASSIGNED TO SLF'S.
2. FIGURES IN "OTHER" ASSIGNED TO VARIOUS LOCATIONS IN RVN.
3. PERSONNEL IN "OTHER" ARE ASSIGNED TO IT, ITT, SSC, CI TEAMS, RED EYE AND NUCLEAR ORDNANCE PLATOONS.
4. STRENGTH INCLUDED IN 1ST AND 3D TANK BATTALIONS.
5. THE 597 PERSONNEL LISTED IN "OTHER" ARE HOSPITALIZED AT LOCATIONS OTHER THAN OKINAWA, BUT ARE CARRIED ON THE ROLLS OF CASUAL COMPANY, MCB, CAMP BUTLER.

Index

Key: **boldface type** = illustration; *n* = footnote; *ff* = following pages

Abrams, Gen Creighton W., USA, 3, 5, 10, 12, 41, 44-45, 47, 51, 84, 129-31, 135, 153, 265-66, 318
Accelerated Pacification Campaign, 10, 25, 77, 96, 101, 170, 172, 187, 189, 280-83
Adams, Capt Frank H., 181
Adamson, RAdm Robert E., Jr., USN, 266
Adkins, Capt Jimmie L., 190
Aerial observers, 35
Airborne Personnel Detector ("People Sniffer"), 238, 251
Aircraft types
    Bell AH-1J (Cobra), 189-90, 207, 227-28
    Bell UH-1G (Huey), **34**, 36, 55, 90, 94, 123, 143, 147, 168, 190, 207, 220, 228, 236, 238, 254
    Boeing B-52 (Stratofortress), 220, 231
    Boeing Vertol CH-46A (Sea Knight), 17, 31, 36, **37**, 55, 68, 76, 122, 133, 137, 163, 178, 183, 189, 220, 227, 237-38, 240, 244, 398
    Boeing Vertol CH-46D (Sea Knight), 96, 190, 194, 220, 227-28, 237, 298
    Boeing Vertol CH-47 (Chinook), 35, 50, **69**, 94, 313
    C-47 (Spooky), 93, 123, 147-48, 163, 166, 187, 191, 193, 250
    Cessna O-1, 220, 226, 228, 233, 235, 251
    Cessna O-1G, 220, 249, 251
    Cessna O-2, 233
    Douglas C-117D (Skytrain), 220
    Grumman A-6A (Intruder/Prowler), 27, 94, 97, 226-29, 230-31, **232**, 233, 236
    Grumman C-1A (Trader), 220
    Grumman TF-9J (Cougar), 220
    Grumman US-2B, 300
    Lockheed C-130 (Hercules), 87, 133, **136**, 198
    Lockheed KC-130F (Hercules), 36, 220, 223, 229, 234
    McDonnell-Douglas A-4E (Skyhawk), 94, 220, 226, 228-29, 231, 233, 309
    McDonnell-Douglas F-4B (Phantom II), 94, 118, 136-37, 220, **224**, 227-33, 251
    McDonnell-Douglas F-4J (Phantom II), 220, 226-28
    MIG fighter, 234
    North American OV-10A (Bronco), 123, 168, 190, 220, 223, 226, 228-30, 233, 235, 249, 251
    Sikorsky CH-53A (Sea Stallion), 35, 94, 115, 220, 227, 238, **239**
    Sikorsky CH-53D (Sea Stallion), 205, 227-28, 236-38, **305**
    Sikorsky CH-54 (Flying Crane), 50, 94
    Sikorsky UH-34D (Seahorse), 220, 228, 238, **239**
    TA-4F, 233
Air Force Commands and Units, 86, 169, 223-25, 229-35, 241-42, 251, 258, 263, 273, 318
    Seventh Air Force, 86, 223, 225, 231, 234-35, 251
    Military Airlift Command, 276
    Strategic Air Command, 220
    434th Air Division, 87
    14th Special Operations Wing, 86
    366th Tactical Fighter Wing, 2, 221
    15th Aerial Port Squadron, 86
    22d Casualty Staging Facility, 273
    Task Force Alpha, Thailand, 274
    Control and Reporting Center 241, 280-81
    Tactical Air Control Center 224
Air support radar team (ASRT), 36, 230, 235-36
Ai Yen, 103
Albers, LtCol Vincent A., Jr., 284
Alligator Lake, 193
Allison, LtCol James O., 105-106, 108, 110, 114-15, 201-202, 209
A Luoi, 68
American Embassy, Saigon, 311, 318
An Bang (2), 191
Anderson, LCpl Richard A., 358
An Hoa, 83-85, 88, 90, 92-95, 97, 103, 116-18, 120, 174, 191, 193-94, 196, 199-200, 203-204, 206, 211-12, 230, 236, 243-44, 248, 252, 254-55, 260, 268
An Hoa basin, 81, 88, 90, 116-18, 199-200, 204, 206, 248, 254, 268
An Loc, 313
Annamite Chain, 81
An Quyen, 179
An Tan, 101, 202
Antenna Valley, 101, 125, 193-94, 206, 211, 248-49, 254
An Thanh (1), 187
An Tra (1), 121, 187
An Tu (1), 121
AN/TPQ-10 radar, 51, 68
Arc Light B-52 strikes, 41, 74, 86, 130, 195, 252
Arizona Territory, 81, 84-85, 88, 91, 94, 103, 109, 111, 113-14, 116-18, 120-21, 174, 188, 190-91, 193, 196, 198-200, 202-203, 247-49, 303
Army Commands and Units
    Army Advisory Group, 2, 311
    U.S. Army Support Command, Da Nang, 2, 265-267
    1st Logistical Command, 265-66
    18th Surgical Hospital, 288
    95th U.S. Army Evacuation Hospital, 273
    I Field Force, 170, 318
    II Field Force, 318
    Provisional Corps, Vietnam, 2*n*, 16-17
    XXIV Corps, 2, 15, 17, 27, 29, 41, 44, 67-68, 78, 171, 234, 243, 250, 252, 277, 321
    XXIV Corps Artillery, 15
    1st Cavalry Division (Airmobile), 47, 301
        1st Squadron, 125, 313-14
    5th Infantry Division (Mechanized)
        1st Brigade, 2, 15, 24-25, 58, 62, 71, 73, 76, 78, 136-37, 143-45, 151, 159, 164, 166, 170, 172, 243-44, 267, 274, 319
        Company B, 75th Support Battalion, 274
    9th Infantry Division, 130-32, 313

INDEX

1st Brigade, 137
2d Brigade, 137
23d Infantry (Americal) Division, 2, 15, 17, 27, 29, 41, 44, 67-68, 78, 80, 94, 101-102, 125, 170-71, 194-95, 204, 206, 215-17, 221, 229, 234, 243, 249-50, 252, 267, 277, 294, 301, 303, 306-307, 309, 319, 321
    196th Light Infantry Brigade, 86, 88, 101, 125, 194-95, 206, 216-17
    Company A, 123d Aviation Battalion, 249
101st Airborne Division (Airmobile), 2, 15, 25-26, 29, 63, 67-68, 77-78, 136, 138, 152, 170-72, 214, 221, 229, 243-44, 257, 267, 319
    1st Brigade, 78, 171-72, 216
    2d Brigade, 171-72
    3d Brigade, 30, 38, 169, 171-72
Task Force 1/11, 60, 159, 170
Task Force Cooksey, 301, 303
Task Force Guadalcanal, 71-72
Task Force Mustang, 71
Task Force Remagen, 64, 66
Special Operations Group, 41, 44, 49-50
5th Special Forces Group, 5
    Special Forces, 83
    Special Forces Mobile Strike, 86, 88
    Delta Force, USA Special Forces, 83
1st Ranger Group, 3, 82
45th Engineer Group, 2, 267, 270
108th Field Artillery Group, 15, 29-31, 34-35, 48, 50, 64, 84, 86, 91, 94, 243-44
4th Artillery
    5th Battalion, 243-44
5th Armored Cavalry
    3d Squadron, 59-60, 77
        Troop A, 60
        Troop B, 24, 60
        Troop C, 24
11th Infantry, 125-26, 216
    1st Battalion, 59-60, 76, 142, 145, 159
        Company A, 1st Battalion, 59-60
        Company B, 1st Battalion, 59-60, 124
        Company C, 1st Battalion, 59
        Company D, 1st Battalion, 60
12th Cavalry
    4th Battalion, 77
    Troop A, 4th Squadron, 24, 60
29th Artillery Regiment
    Battery G, 249
31st Infantry
    4th Battalion, 206, 209
40th Artillery
    1st Battalion, 60, 64, 77
        Battery B, 60
44th Artillery (AWSP)
    1st Battalion, 64
46th Infantry Regiment, 216, 294, 301
    Company D, 5th Battalion, 294
52d Infantry Regiment
    Company A, 1st Battalion, 294
61st Infantry (Mechanized)
    1st Battalion, 64, 71, 76, 159
        Company B, 64, 71
        Company C, 71
77th Armor
    1st Battalion, 64, 71, 77, 142
        Company B, 71
        Company C, 64, 142
83d Artillery
    1st Battalion, 29
187th Infantry
    Company B, 3d Battalion, 68
198th Infantry Brigade, 125-26, 216
327th Infantry
    1st Battalion, 26
    2d Battalion, 26, 68
501st Infantry
    1st Battalion, 25, 26
    2d Battalion, 68
502d Infantry
    2d Battalion, 26
506th Infantry
    1st Battalion, 68
    2d Battalion, 68, 101, 125
282d Aviation Battalion, 249
59th Engineer Battalion, 24
Mobile Advisory Teams, 101, 195, 290
Army Schools
    Recondo School, 257
Arroyo, Capt Joseph V., 59-60
Ashford, 1stLt Victor V., 119
Ashley, LtCol Maurice C., Jr., 250
A Shau Valley, 15, 26-27, 63, 67-68, 78, 119, 171, 252, 257, 319
Associated Press, 51, 68
Atkinson, LtCol Harry E., 84, 87, 89, 93-94, 116, 176, 178-79, 191, 193
Austin, PFC Oscar P., 359
Australian Air Force, 229
Ayres, Mr. Drummond, Jr., 51

Babb, Capt Wayne A., 116
"Bald Eagle" reaction force, 148
Ba Long Valley, 19, 30, 60, 69, 116, 136, 160, 255
Ban Karai, 231
Bao An Dong, 179
Bao An Tay, 179
Barrier Combat Air Patrol (BARCAP), 234-35
Barrier Island, 83, 125, 209, 211-12, 217, 300, 305-309, 317
Barrow, Col Robert H., 16-19, 27-28, **29**, 35, 38, 41-45, 61, 81, 83, 94, 135, 138, 154, 157
Base Area 100, 83
Base Area 101, 13, 24-25, 27, 33, 67, 77, 136
Base Area 112, 83-86, 88-95, 103-104, 191, 193, 198, 247, 252, 319
Base Area 114, 26-27
Base Area 116, 83, 193
Base Area 117, 125, 216
Base Area 121, 13, 126
Base Area 483, 314, 315
Base Area 611, 15, 26-27, 41, 44, 50, 63, 67
Bassett, Col William D., Jr., 263
Ba Su Mountains, 125
Batangan Peninsula, 101, 125-26, 216, 217, 292, 300, 303

Baxter, Capt Harry C., Jr., 163
Beck, Col Noble L., 196, 199
Beck, Maj Peter S., 204
Beckington, Col Herbert L., 81, 95-96, 104
Belle Grove (LSD 2), 137
Ben Dau (3,) 196
Benfatti, 1stLt Raymond C., 18
Bethel, LtCol William F., 96
Bexar (LPA 237), 153, 196
Bich Bac, 186
Bich Nam (2), 121
Bien Hoa, 313-15
Binh Son District, Quang Ngai Province, 308
Bo Ban, 202
Bo Ben, 188
Bo Mung (2), 187
Boston (CAG 1), 194
Bowen, LtCol James T., 196, 199
Bowman, MajGen George S., Jr., 221
Braddon, LtCol John R., 136-37
Brady, Col Eugene R., 273
Breckinridge, LtCol James T., 311
Britt, LtCol William C., 159, 161-63
Brown, Gen George A., USAF, 223, 225
Bru tribe, 67
Bruce, PFC Daniel D., 360
Bryan, Maj Charles G., 33
Bulger, LtCol Thomas E., 110, 113-14, 122-23, 187
Burks, SgtMaj Clifford M., **121**
Burns, 1stLt James A., 145, 147
Burroughs, Col Charles R., 290
Buse, Capt Henry W., III, 56-57, 161-62
Buse, LtGen Henry W., Jr., 5, 56-57, **62**, 131, 133, 161-62, 275

Ca Ka Va, 31
Ca Lu, 20, 30-31, 49, 160-62, 165
Cambodia, 128, 313
Cam Hung Valley, 141
Cam Le (1), 123
Cam Le (2), 123
Cam Lo, 19-20, 23-24, 49, 57, 59, 61-62, 73, 75-76, 138, 143, 145, 149, 163-64, 166, 170
Cam Lo Bridge, 73
Cam Lo District Headquarters, 138, 145, 163
Cam Lo Valley, 57, 76, 163
Cam Ne, 124
Cam Vu Valley, 24
Camp Carroll, 165
Camp Courtney, 167
Camp Eagle, 15
Camp Evans, 30
Camp Horn, 234-35, 258, 274
Camp Love, 85
Camp Muir (*See* Hill 55)
Camp Red Devil (*See* Combat Bases, Dong Ha)
Can Tho, 314
Canton, Col John S., 259
Canzona, Col Nicholas A., 267
Capital Military District, 311
CARE Relief Agency, 287

Carlson, Capt Gary E., 139
Carney, BGen Robert B., Jr., 52, **171**
Carr, Maj Richard W., 168
Carter, PFC Bruce W., 361
Case 450 bulldozer, 268
Castagnetti, Capt Gene E., 192
Cau Do, 99, 182, 187
Cau Ha, 123
Cau Mau Peninsula, 310, 314
Census Grievance Teams, 189
Central Pacification and Development Council, 10, 281-83
Chaisson, BGen John R., 317
Chapman, Gen Leonard F., Jr., 67, 131, 156-57, 224-25, 318-19
Chapman, Capt Leonard F., III, 67
Charlie Ridge, 103-107, 109-11, 114, 116, 196, 199, 201, 215, 248, 252, 303, 319
Charlton, LtCol Albert K., 168
Charon, LtCol Larry P., 252
Chau Son, 95, 189
Chau Son (1), 95
Chief of Naval Operations, 265
Chieu Hoi (Open Arms) Program, 281-82, 295, 321
China Beach Public Works Compound, 264
Chu Lai, 2, 29, 94, 99, 101, 125-26, 136-37, 168, 204, 213, 216, 220, 236, 260, 264, 268-69, 274, 289, 300, 301, 308
Chuong Thien Province, 314
Circuit Rider program, 258
Citizens Council of Da Nang, 167
Civic Action Program, 287
Civil Operations and Revolutionary Development Support (CORDS), 2, 280, 284, 287, 292, 296
    Joint Staff, 284
    Program Coordination Staff, 284
Civilian Irregular Defense Forces
    Thuong Duc CIDG Camp, 106
    Civilian Irregular Defense Group (CIDG), 5, 81-82, 86, 101, 106, 138
Clark, LtCol Frank A., 204, 210-11
Cleveland (LPD 7), 168
Clifford, former Secretary of Defense Clark, 149-50
Co A Nong (Tiger Mountain), 28 (*See also* Hill 1228)
Coast Guard, 301, 306-308, 317
Cobb, Maj Charles W., 76, 99
Cobb Bridge, 99
Cochran, LtCol John K., 137
Codispoti, Col Gildo S., **202**, 204, 208, 249
Co Ka Leuye (Hill 1175), 28, 33-35
Coker, PFC Ronald L., 362
Combat Bases
    An Hoa, 84-85, 88, 92-93, 116, 118, 120, 174, 191, 193-94, 196, 230, 243-44, 252, 260
    Dong Ha, 2, 24, 77, 159, 166, 170, 221, 260, 270, 276, 288
    Elliott, 19, 22, 53, 58, 61, 73, 76, 136, 138, 141-43, 145, 147, 149, 151, 159-61, 163-66, 243, 270 (*See also* Rockpile)
    Phu Bai, 15, 252
    Quang Tri, 24, 29, 77, 135-36, 151, 154, 165-68, 170, 260, 288
    Vandegrift, 15, 18-20, 22-24, 27-31, 36-37, 47, 49-50, 52, 60-61, 64, 66, 68-72, 76, 133, 135, 138, 143, 148-49, 151-52, 154, 159-65, 172, 236, 243, 260, 270, 272
Combat Operations Bases

INDEX

Broadsword, 89
Dart, 89
Javelin, 88
Scimitar, 89
Combined Action Program, 2, 101, 189, 288-94, 321
  Combined Action Force, 290, 294
  Combined Action Groups, 189, 260, 289-92
    1st Combined Action Group, 260, 289, 292
    2d Combined Action Group, 189, 289
    3d Combined Action Group, 289
    4th Combined Action Group, 289, 291
  Combined Action Companies, 29, 198
  Combined Action Program School, 290
Combined Holding and Interrogation Center (CHIC), 285, 301, 306
Combined Unit Pacification Program (CUPP), 189
Commando Bolt Assassins, 232
Company Intensified Pacification Program (CIPP), 214, 321
Con Thien, 19, 20, 23-24, 60-61, 73, 75, 142, 145, 270
Congress of the United States, 128, 132
  Congressional Hearings on Vietnam, 51
  Congressional Medal of Honor, 36, 47, 49n, 209, 211
Corbett, Col Leroy V., 311, 313, 315-16
Costello, 2dLt Ronald W., 202
Creek, LCpl Thomas E., 363
Criminal Investigation Division, 155
Crompton, Col Wallace W., 246
Cross, Mr. Charles T., 2, 284
CS gas, 60, 73, 100, 113, 139, 187, 256
Cua Viet, 15, 23-25, 52, 58, 66, 75-76, 143, 145, 153, 159, 164, 166, 243, 264, 267, 270, 303
Cushman, LtGen Robert E., Jr., 2, 3, 6, 13, 41, 44, 156, 224, 226, 317

Dahlquist, Maj Martin J., 197
Dai La Pass, 99, 201, 204, 214, 308
Dai Loc, 101, 175, 198, 202
Daily, SgtMaj Joseph E., 318
Da Krong Valley, 19, 27, **28**, 31, 50, 55, 66-69, 78, 138, 236, 319
Dale, Maj Denver T., III, 199
Daley, LtCol Richard F., 84, 90, 116
Damewood, LtCol Walter W., Jr., 24
Damm, Col Raymond C., 153, 276
Da Nang, 2-3, 5, 7-8, 11, 13, 29, 63, 80-85, 93-94, 96-97, 99-101, 103-104, 109, 114-16, 118, 121, 124-25, 131, 133, 135, 152-53, 166-67, 174-75, 182, 187-90, 194, 201, 204, 212-15, 218, 220-21, 229-31, 234-36, 241, 243, 245, 248-50, 259-60, 263, 265-70, 273-74, 288, 303, 305-308, 319, 321
Da Nang Airfield, 167
Da Nang Anti-Infiltration System (Barrier), 201, 214, 259
Da Nang City Hall, 166
Da Nang Harbor, 153
Da Nang Vital Area, 96-97, 100, 103-104, 116, 121, 124, 174, 189, 201, 204, 214, 245, 250, 305, 307
Daniels, LtCol William S., 142-43, 145, 149
Danowitz, Col Edward F., 2, 61, 67-70, 133, 135, **289**, 290
Davis, MajGen Raymond G., 2, 16-18, 27-29, 41, 52, **53**, 86, 209, 246-47, 253
Deasy, Col Rex A., 220
Deep Water Pier, 97, 133

Delcuze, LtCol Godfrey S., 190
Demilitarized Zone, 6, 11, 15-20, 22-23, 25-26, 52, 55, 56-62, 66, 73-76, 78, 92, 138-39, 141, 143, 147, 159, 161, 163, 165-66, 170, 206, 233, 247, 252-53, 258, 288, 310-11, 319
Denial Stingray Concept, 139, 141
Dennison, 2dLt Danny G., 166
DeNormandie, Col Frank R., 261
Dental Civic Action Program, 287
Department of Defense (DOD), 275, 284
  Defense Communications Agency, 274
  Defense Communications System, 274
  Joint Chiefs of Staff, 9, 12, 130-31, 150-51, 224-25, 275, 310, 319
Dias, PFC Ralph E., 211, 364
Dickinson, Col Harry F., 243
Dien Ban, 175, 182, 186-87
Direct Air Support Control (DASC) Centers, 29, 31, 86, 224, 234-36, 240, 250
  Vandegrift, 236
  Victor, 234
Dodge City, 81, 122, 174-79, 181-88, 190, 202, 204, 248, 270, 307, 319
Donald, LtCol William A., 20, 24, 52-54, 56
Dong Den, 214
Dong Ha, 2, 13, 15, 24, 27, 50, 58, 66, 69, 77, 92, 136, 138, 145, 151-53, 159, 164, 166, 170, 221, 223, 236, 253, 258-60, 264, 268, 270, 276, 288
Dong Lien, 190
Dong Son (2), 179, 188
Dong Tiou, 163
Dooley, BGen George E., 44
Doty, Col William C., Jr., 307
Douglas H. Fox (DD 779), 307
Dowd, LtCol John A., 105, 109-11, 113-14, 202-203
Drug Use, 157-58
  heroin, 157
  marijuana, 157
Drury, LtCol John W., 241
Dubuque (LPD 8), 165, 182-83
Duc Duc District, 116-17, 198
Duc Ky, 186, 202
Duc Pho, 101, 125, 126, 217, 319
Duck Blind evaluations, 259
Duffle Bag program, 259
Dulacki, LtGen Leo J., 266
Duong Lam, 202
Duong Son (2), 185
Duyen Son, 188
Duy Xuyen District, 116-18
Dwyer, Capt Joseph M., 54
Dwyer, BGen Ross T., Jr., 84-85, **91**, 94-95

Eastland, 1stLt Larry L., 22
Edmundson, LtCol George M., 125, 212-14, 303, 305, 308
Eimco tractor, 117, 178, 204
Elephant Valley, 201, 212-13, 248
Engle, 1stLt Terry L., 141-42, 144-45, 147
Evans, LtCol Ernest E., Jr., 153, 276
Ewell, MajGen Julian J., USA, 313
Ezell, Col Don D., 97, 124, 183, 247-49

Fagan, Capt Brian J., 111-13
Fagan, Capt Fred T., Jr., 99
Feeley, BGen James A., Jr., 2, 260, **262**
Fennell, LtCol Patrick J., Jr., 258
Field Artillery Digital Automatic Computer (FADAC), 211
Finger Lakes, 196
Finlayson, Col Edwin H., 95
Fire Base Interpretation, Reconnaissance, Planning, Preparation, and Overfly (FIRPPO) Team, 87
Fire direction center (FDC), 31, 34
Fire Support Base Concept, 17, 246-47, 267
Fire Support Bases
   Alpha-1, 20, 317
   Alpha-2, 247, 317
   Alpha-4, 74-75, 138
   Alpine, 55, 61
   Angel, 159-60
   Argonne, 19, 55-57, 235
   Birmingham, 236
   Bolo, 89
   Buckskin (Hill 502), 107-109, 114
   Bullwhip, 114-15
   Cates (Hill 950), 19, 64, 69, 71, 76, 136, 152, 159-62, 164
   Charlie-1, 20, 74-75, 317
   Charlie-2, 19-20, 73-74, 138, 141-42, 144-45
   Charlie-3, 145
   Cunningham, 24, 31, 33-35, 37, 39, 41, 49-50, 238
   Cutlass, 88-89
   Dagger, 88
   Erskine, 24, 33-35, 37-39, 49, 68
   Fuller, 58, 73, 75, 138-39, 141, 145, 149, 151-52, 161, 164-66, 243
   Geiger, 18
   Greene, 56-57
   Henderson, 19, 30, 31, 69-70
   Jack, 29
   Lightning, 34, 36, 39, 68
   Longhorn, 110
   Los Banos, 244
   Mace, 87-88
   Machete (Hill 435), 90
   Marne, 87
   Maxwell (Hill 508), 88-90, 92-94
   McClintock, 67
   Mustang 105, 110-11, 113-14
   Nancy, 244
   Neville, 20, 22-23, 52, 54, 76, 243
   Passport, 19
   Pete, 73
   Pike, 87, 89
   Quantico, 71
   Rattlesnake (Hill 749), 107, 110, 114-16
   Rawhide (*See* Hill 65)
   Razor, 31, 33, 35, 37, 67-68
   Ross, 206, 209-11
   Russell, 22-23, 76, 136, 159, 162-64, 243
   Ryder, 211, 247-49
   Saber, 90
   Saigon, 64
   Sharon, 59, 244
   Shepherd, 69-71, 152, 162, 164
   Shiloh, 19, 30-31, 37
   Smith, 18
   Snapper, 18, 63-64
   Spark, 72
   Spear (Hill 558), 87-88
   Stallion, 105, 107
   Tenaru, 72
   Tomahawk, 89, 92-94
   Torch, 66
   Tun Tavern, 19, 30-31
   Turnage, 47, 49-50
   Whisman, 70, 236
Fire Support Coordination Center (FSCC), 29, 31, 50, 86, 250
Fire Support Information System, 245, 257
Firfer, Mr. Alexander, 292
Fontana, MajGen Paul J., 236
Football Island, 118, 198
Foreign Affairs, 149
Fox, LtCol George C., 18, 31, 36, 41, 45-47, 68-70, 72, 236, 307
Fox, LtCol Wesley L., 30; 1stLt, 45-46; Capt, 365
Foxtrot Ridge, 74
Foxworth, LtCol Eugene D., Jr., 53
Fraggings, 154-56, 158
Frank E. Evans (DD 754), 307

Gallentine, Col Owen V., 168
Ganey, LtCol Thomas P., 184-86
Garretson, BGen Frank E., 19, 27, 44, 52, **62**
Garrett, LtCol Donald J., 161, 163-66
General Walt Scholarship Fund, 287
Geneva Accords, 311
Gestson, LtCol Johan S., 199-200
Gettys, MajGen Charles M., USA, 2, 80, 101, 125, 215
Giang Dong, 121
Giang La, 186
Gibson, Col James M., USA, 2
Gio Linh, 24, 75, 170, 258, 270
Gio Son, 142
Glasgow, LtCol Harold G., 121-23, 177-78, 181-84, 193-95
Goggin, Col William F., 18-20, 52, 55-56, 58, 75-76, 138, 151, 159-62, 164
Golden Gate Bridge, 186
Golden, Maj Joseph F., 168
Go Noi Island, 81, 88, 90-92, 94, 97, 174-79, 181-88, 193-94, 204, 229, 247-48, 270, 286-87, 295, 303, 307, 319
Goodin, LtCol James C., 214, 308-10
Goodwin, Capt Paul B., 142, 144-45
Gordy, Cpl Michael E., 291
Gray, LtCol Robert L., Jr., 307
Green, Capt Joe B., 55
Greenwood, LtCol John E., 289
Griffis, LtCol Joseph K., Jr., 198-99
Guam, 5
Guenther, Maj John J., 285
Gulf of Tonkin, 170, 233-34

Ha Dong, 182, 185, 187
Ha Dong Bridge, 185, 187
Ha Loi, 25

INDEX

Hai Lang, 24, 170, 244
Hai Van Pass, 7, 26, 81, 103, 124, 212, 214, 223, 241, 243-44
Hall, Capt James K., 99, 166
Ham Tay (1), 196
Hamburger Hill, 68, **70**
Hamlet Evaluation System, 280, 282
Hannah, Col Samuel A., 263
Happy Valley, 103-106, 114-15, 214-15, 248, 303, 319
Harrell, Col James E., 214, **215**
Hawaii, 266, 274
Hayward, LtCol George E., 24
Helicopter Emergency Lift Pack, 48
Helicopter Utilization Review Board, 263
Helicopter Valley, 74, 138-39, 145, 149
Helton, 1stLt William C., 64, 66
Herron, 1stLt Lee R., 45, 53, 138-39, 141-42, 145, 149
Herron, LtCol David G., 73-74
Hershey, Col Gilbert R., 164-66, 284
Heywood, Col Ralph A., 212, 214
Hien Doc District, 78
Hiep Duc, 206, 210-11, 217
Hieu Duc, 188, 214
Higgins, LtCol James H., 117-18, 120, 190-91, 193-96
Hill 10, 99, 105, 114, 214, 308
Hill 22, 188, 214
Hill 37, 175, 202
Hill 41, 99, 103, 105, 214
Hill 52, 104-105, 109, 114
Hill 55 (Camp Muir), 92, 95-96, 110, 185-86, 188-89, 241, 243, 260, 262, 294, 307
Hill 65 (FSB Rawhide), 96, 105, 109, 111, 113-14, 120, 196, 198, 248-49
Hill 119, 178, 248-49
Hill 154, 147, 149
Hill 190, 212, 248
Hill 208, 59, 62
Hill 214 (See Fire Support Bases, Pike)
Hill 250, 248-49
Hill 270, 215, 248-49
Hill 327, 2, 99-100, 241
Hill 375, 87
Hill 401, 89
Hill 425, 229, 248-49
Hill 435 (FSB Machete), 90
Hill 441, 206
Hill 467, 105
Hill 471, 255
Hill 502 (See Fire Support Bases, Buckskin)
Hill 508 (See Fire Support Bases, Maxwell)
Hill 551, 88
Hill 558 (See Fire Support Bases, Spear)
Hill 575, 87
Hill 579, 211
Hill 715, 163
Hill 722, 110
Hill 728, 89
Hill 745, 108
Hill 749 (See Fire Support Bases, Rattlesnake)
Hill 785, 109, 114-15
Hill 824, 70 (See also Dong Cho Mountain)
Hill 845 (See Nui Mat Rang)
Hill 848, 195
Hill 866, 110
Hill 937, 68
Hill 943, 108
Hill 950 (See Fire Support Bases, Cates)
Hill 1044, 46
Hill 1050, 88
Hill 1062, 107-108, 110
Hill 1066, 110
Hill 1166, 107, 110, 114
Hill 1175, 34, 36 (See also Co Ka Leuye)
Hill 1224, 27, 38, 46
Hill 1228, 28, 38, 47
Hill 1235, 108, 110
Hill, BGen Homer S., 17n, 221, 225, **226**, 230, 234-38
Hise, BGen Henry W., 95
Hitzelberger, Capt Daniel A., 34-36, **36**
Hoa Khanh Children's Hospital, 288
Hoa Phat, 263
Hoa Vang, 99, 214
Ho Chi Minh, 55, 57, 147, 231-33
Ho Chi Minh Trail, 55, 57, 231-33
Hoffman, 1stLt Richard C., 147-48
Hoi An, 2, 82, 101, 174-75, 188, 202, 206, 274, 289, 300, 317
Hoi Chanh, 67, 281
Holm, Maj Robert W., 253
Ho Nai, 314
Hopkins, LtCol Joseph E., 19-20, 22, 52, 208
Hord, 1stLt Raymond A., 202-203
Horn, 1stLt James M., 61, 71, 234-35, 258, 274
Hour Glass Island, 303
House, Maj Edward L., Jr., 137, 241, 275
Hue, 3, 7, 11, 15, 25, 27, 29-30, 77, 78, 221, 223, 264, 268, 288, 296, 311
Huffman, Capt James W., Jr., 111-13, **113**
Hunter, Col Clyde W., 24, 81, 96, 139, 289
Hunter, LtCol Earl R., 297
Hunter Killer Teams, 24, 139
Huong Thuy District, 26
Huong, Premier Tran Van (of South Vietnam), 10, 15, 26, 318

Indian Ocean, 297
Infantry Company Intensive Pacification Program (ICIPP), 189, 294
Integrated Observation Device (IOD), 211, 215, 248-49, **249**, 257
Iredell County (LST 839), 133
Iron Mountain Operational Zone, 101
Iwo Jima (LPH 2), 153, 214

Jaehne, 2dLt Richard L., 209
Jaskilka, BGen Samuel, 92, 93, 116, 317
Jenkins, PFC Robert H., Jr., 366
Jimenez, LCpl Jose F., 209, 367
Joens, Col Ray N., 124, 212
Johnson, President Lyndon B., 128, 225
Jones, MajGen William K., 52, **53**, 133, 135, 138, 152, 155-56, 167, 277
Jordan, Capt David M., 149

Kansik, LCpl Frederick D., 90
Karch, Capt Laurence G., 232
Kay, Capt William M., 197
Kelley, 1stLt Edwin C., Jr., 54-55
Ken Valley, 115-16
Kerrigan, Col William E., 284
Key Hole patrols, 17
Key Quoit Deployment, 227
Khang, LtGen Le Nguyen, VNMC, 313, **313**
Khe Chua Valley, 58-60
Khe Gio Bridge, 73, 138, **139**, 141, 145, 161, 163-66
Khe Sanh, 16, 18-19, 27, 62, 64, 66, 71-72, 138, 152, 159, 160-61, 167, 223, 255, 259
Khe Sanh plateau, 18, 64, 66, 71-72, 138, 159
Kiley, 1stLt John P., 54-55
Kim Lien, 124, 303
Kit Carson Scouts, **108**, 257
Kliefoth, LtCol George C., 124, 176, 303, 305-306, 308
Knapp, Col George C., 284-85
Knight, Capt John E., Jr., 22
Knotts, Maj Joseph B., 39
Ky Hoa Island, 101
Kyle, LtCol John S., 64, 73-74

Lacoursiere, Capt Robert P., 318
Lafond, Col Paul D., **62**, 63-64, 66, 73, 90
La Huan, 186-87
La Huan (2), 187
Laine, LtCol Elliott R., Jr., 30-31, 34, 46, 154
Laird, Secretary of Defense Melvin R., 51, 129-32, **129**, 150, 169, 170, 225
Lam, LtGen Hoang Xuan, ARVN, 3, 5, **13**, 91, 133, 135, 137, 166, 167, 176, 178-79, 185-86, 202, 223, 241, 290, 320
Land-clearing operations, 24, 117, 123, 187, 270
    Equipment
        Eimco tractor, 117, 178, 204
        Rome plow (D7E tractor), 93, 117, 296
        T18 bulldozers, 117
Landing Vehicle, Tracked (LVT) 112-13, 185, 198, 214
Landing Zones
    Baldy, 205-206, 209-11, 244, 260
    Bell, 57
    Bird, 147-49
    Bison, 71
    Cardinal, 148-49, 164
    Catapult, 54-55, 76
    Champ, 73
    Champagne, 85
    Cobra, 307
    Cokawa, 71
    Cougar, 159
    Dallas, 31, 34-36, 68
    Dixie Pete, 164
    Dodge, 76
    Dry Gulch, 114
    Hawk, 64, 96, 106
    Horn, 71
    Ironsides, 73
    Junior, 73-74
    Krait, 307
    Lightning, 33
    Lion, 306
    Mack, 53-55, 57, 142, 145, 147, 149, 164
    Nancy, 77
    Owl, 96
    Pedro, 160
    Pete, 149, 164, **165**
    Rattler, 307
    Robin, 106-107
    Ross, 205, 244
    Scotch, 159
    Sharon, 58, 77
    Sierra, 54-55, 57, 76, 143, 145, 147-48, 163, 164
    Sierra North, 54-55
    Sparrow, 73, 170
    Tarawa, 67
    Tiger, 306
    Tornado, 33
    Uranus, 159
    West, 209, 217
Lang Co Bridge, 212
Lang Ha, 45
Lang Ho Valley, 76
Lang Hoan Tap, 55
Lang Vei, 19, 27, 61-64, 71-72, 255
Laos, 6, 11, 13, 15, 17-19, 26-27, 33, 35, 38, 40-41, 43, 44-45, 47-49, 51-52, 55, 57, 63, 67-68, 77, 85, 91, 103, 128, 172, 231, 234
    Prime Minister Souvanna Phouma, 45, 51
    Vientiane, 51
Laporte, LtCol Alphonse A., Jr., 122
La Tho Bac, 186
Latona, GySgt Russell A., 46
La Trap, 118
Lauffer, Col Robert G., 81, 96, **97**, 121
Lavery, 2dLt Robert A., 195
Le Son (1), 190
Le Thuy, 308
Leach, Capt Shawn W., 142
Leatherneck Square, 24, 74, 76, 78, 270, 295
Lee, BGen Dong Ho, ROKMC, 2, **13**, 171, 175
Leech Valley, 214
Lewis, LtCol Edward L., Jr., 289
Liberty Bridge, 84, 86, 93, 113, 116, **117**, 118-21, 175-76, 178, 191, 193, 196-99, 202, 243, 268, 301, 303, 307
Lien Chieu Esso Depot, 212
Logistic Support Area (LSA), 29-30, 33
Long, SgtMaj Clyde M., 167
Long Bien Special Zone, 314
Long Dong, 306
Lowman, Col John, Jr., 297
Lugger, LtCol Marvin H., 201, 204-209

M116E marginal terrain vehicle, 272
M733 armored marginal terrain vehicle, 272
MacInnis, LtCol Joseph A., 161-62, 164-65
MacQuarrie, Col Warren L., 94, 220
Magnetic Intrusion Device (MAGID), 259
Mai Guy, 89

INDEX

Mai Linh, 24, 170
Mai Loc, 24, 138, 159
Malone, 2dLt George M., 45
Manila Communique, 128
Manila Summit Conference, 128
Man Quan Peninsula, 121
Marble Mountain Air Facility, 94-95, 97, 103, 188, 220, 223, 227, 269, 307
Marfia, Maj Samuel J., 211
Marine Corps Air Facility, Futema, 223
Marine Corps Air Stations
    Cherry Point, North Carolina, 226
    El Toro, California, 153, 228
    Iwakuni, Japan, 133, 137, 223
Marine Corps Bases
    Camp Pendleton, California, 5, 153, 275
    Twentynine Palms, California, 137
Marine Corps Commands and Units
    Ground
        Headquarters Marine Corps, 136, 221, 240, 275
            Equal Opportunities Branch, 157
        Fleet Marine Force, Pacific, 5, 103, 131, 157, 240, 260, 266, 274-76, 299
            Force Logistics Command, 2, 99, 131, 153-54, 238, 260, 261-62, 264-66, 269, 271, 274-76, 288
                Truck Company, 271
                Ammunition Supply Points (ASP), 260
                      Ammunition Supply Point 1, 263, **264**, 269
                      Ammunition Supply Point 2, 264
        I Marine Expeditionary Force, 223
        III Marine Amphibious Force, 2, 5, 8, 14, 44, 82-84, 97, 103, 116, 130, 133, 137, 153-54, 156-57, 167, 174-75, 201, 204, 221, 223-24, 226, 229, 239, 251-52, 257-60, 263-68, 270, 272-77, 284-85, 287-90, 296-97, 299, 303, 310-11, 318, 319-21
            III MAF Transient Facility, 260
            Photo Imagery Interpretation Center, 252
            R&R Processing Center, 260
            Surveillance and Reconnaissance Center, 252, 259
        Special Landing Forces (SLF), 109, 228, 244, 276, 297, 299, 310, 317, 320
            Special Landing Force Alpha, 175, 212, 298, 300, 307
            Special Landing Force Bravo, 212-13, 298, 300
        Task Force Bravo, 19, 24
        Task Force Glick, 19
        Task Force Hotel, 15, 19, 24, 27, 43-44, 52, 59, 61, 63, 66, 69, 71, 136, 252-53
        Task Force Yankee, 84-86, 88-91, 101, 104, 116, 247, 252-53
            1st Force Service Regiment, 260, 271
                Headquarters Battalion, 271
        Marine Security Guard
            Company E, 318
        1st Marine Division, 2, 24, 63, 80-82, 84-86, 91, 95, 97, 100-101, 103-104, 116, 121, 126, 154, 170, 174, 201-204, 206, 213-14, 217-18, 223-24, 229, 234, 238-40, 243-44, 246, 249, 251-53, 257-58, 260, 263, 265, 267, 269, 270, 272, 284, 287, 294, 305, 310, 319, 321
            Redeployment Planning Group, 153
            1st Marine Division Schools
                Demolitions, Land Mine Warfare, and Viet Cong Boobytrap School, 267
        3d Force Service Regiment, 303, 305
        1st Force Reconnaissance Company, 84, 89, 252, 254, 257
        1st Marine Division Hospital, 272
        3d Marine Division, 5, 15-19, 27-28, 44, 52, 61, 63, 67, 69, 72, 76, 86, 95, 130-33, 137-38, 151-55, 159, 164-72, 220-21, 223-25, 229, 234, 238-40, 243-46, 249-53, 257-58, 260-61, 265, 267, 270, 272-73, 275-78, 284, 287-88, 303, 310, 320
            Headquarters Battalion, 165, 167, 271
        3d Marine Division Memorial Children's Hospital, **286**, 288
        4th Marine Division, 5
        5th Marine Division, 5, 271, 299
        5th Marine Amphibious Brigade, 153
        9th Marine Amphibious Brigade, 214, 223, 297-300, 305, 310
        Regimental Landing Team 9, 138
        Regimental Landing Team 26, 299
        1st Marines, 81, 84, 96, 99, 118, 121-24, 174, 176-78, 185, 187-91, 201-202, 240, 260, 262, 307-308, 317
            1st Battalion, 58, 122-23, 125, 138, 142, 147, 175, 177-79, 181-87, 190, 195-96
                Company A, 186
                Company B, 74, 145, 179, 186
                Company C, 179, 185-87
                Company D, 122, 178, 182-83, 186
            2d Battalion, 97, 99, 121-24, 138, 175, 177-79, 181-84, 186-87, 190, 193, 195, 313-14
                Company E, 182-83
                Company F, 97, 124, 183
                Company G, 124, 177-78, 181, 183, 186
                Company H, 123, 182, 190, 195
            3d Battalion, 99, 110, 113-14, 118, 122-23, 125, 171, 184-187, 189, 294, 307, 308
                Company I, 122, 185
                Company K, 99, 122-23, 185, 187
                Company L, 122-23, 185, 186
                Company M, 125, 185-86, 189, 294, 308
        3d Marines, 15-16, 18-19, 24, 49, 61-64, 66-67, 73-74, 78, 88, 90, 92, 95, 133, 136-39, 141-42, 148, 151-54, 161, 164, 168, 243, 263, 275
            1st Battalion, 24, 63-64, 73-75, 86-89, 92, 138-39, 141-43, 145, 149, 164, 243
                Company A, 139, 141-43
                Company B, 74, 145
                Company C, 74, 89, 139, 142
                Company D, 73, 89
            2d Battalion, 24, 39, 63-64, 66, 68, 73-75, 138, 141-43, 145, 149, 164
                Company E, 39, 64, 66, 142-43
                Company F, 64, 75, 142-43
                Company G, 39, 64, 66, 75, 142
                Company H, 64, 66, 142, 149
            3d Battalion, 24, 67, 73-75, 86-89, 92, 138, 141-42, 144-45, 147-49, 151, 164
                Company I, 142, 144-45, 147
                Company K, 75, 142, 144-45, 147
                Company L, 75, 138, 145, 147-49
                Company M, 73, 75, 144, 147, 149
        4th Marines, 16, 18-19, 23, 52-53, 57-58, 61-62, 75-76, 78, 133, 136-38, 141, 151-52, 154, 159-60, 162, 164, 165, 168, 172, 243
            1st Battalion, 19-20, 52-53, 55-58, 76, 159, 160-62, 164-66
                Company A, 56-57

Company B, 56-57, 76
Company C, 53, 56-57
Company D, 56-57, 159, 165-66
2d Battalion, 19-20, 22-23, 52, 54, 58, 76, 84, 87, 89-90, 92, 117-20, 159, 161-66, 186, 191, 193-99, 217, 303
Company E, 22, 58, 163
Company G, 23, 54, 164-66
Company H, 109, 163, 166, 211, 249
3d Battalion, 20, 22, 24, 52-58, 76, 148-49, 159, 161-64, 166-67
Company I, 54-56, 148-49, 159, 163-64, 166
Company K, 22, 54, 56, 76, 159, 163, 166
Company L, 20, 53-54, 159, 166
Company M, 24, 54-55, 159, 163-64, 166
5th Marines, 18, 81, 84, 86, 91-92, 95, 113, 116-18, 120-21, 174, 187-88, 190-91, 193, 196-97, 199-202, 243, 260, 294, 301
1st Battalion, 84, 90-91, 116-18, 120, 190, 191-93, 196-99, 203, 244
Company A, 113-14, 118, 187, 191-92, 198, 203
Company B, 118, 191
Company C, 91, 105, 111-12, 114, 192-93, 199, 202-203
Company D, 91, 118, 120, 198
2d Battalion, 84, 87, 89, 90, 92, 117-20, 186, 191, 193-99, 217, 303
Company E, 89, 117-19, 199
Company F, 118-19
Company G, 117, 119, 198
Company H, 117-20, 186, 198
3d Battalion, 24, 60, 77, 84, 87-89, 92-94, 116-19, 175-76, 178-79, 191, 193-200, 203, 307
Company I, 196-99, 203
Company K, 119, 199
Company L, 87, 92-94, 199
Company M, 92-94, 118, 178, 199
7th Marines, 81, 91, 95-96, 104-105, 113-16, 118, 125, 174, 188, 191, 196, 204, 206, 211-13, 217, 243-44, 249, 260, 294, 301, 303
1st Battalion, 91, 95-96, 105, 109-14, 117-18, 187-88, 193, 201-204, 206, 210-11
Company A, 113-14, 187, 203
Company B, 96, 105, 109, 111, 112, 113, 117, 202, 203
Company C, 91, 105, 111-12, 114, 202-203
Company D, 95, 111-13, 202-203
2d Battalion, 84-86, 88, 100, 105-109, 125, 201-202, 204-11, 213, 300, 303, 305, 308
Company E, 85, 108, 207
Company F, 85, 206-207
Company G, 85, 206-208
Company H, 85, 206-207
3d Battalion, 97, 99-100, 103, 105-10, 114-16, 188, 196, 201-203, 206, 208-11, 303
Company I, 110, 114, 211
Company K, 99, 107-108, 110, 114-15, 209
Company L, 97, 99, 107-10, 114-15, 209
Company M, 99-100, 105, 110, 114-16, 209
9th Marines, 16, 18-19, 24, 27-30, 37, 41, 44, 47-49, 51, 55, 60-63, 67-69, 73, 76, 78, 133, 135-36, 138, 141, 229, 236, 244, 319
1st Battalion, 18, 30-31, 33, 37-40, 45-46, 47, 49, 50, 61, 67-68, 71, 133, 137, 143, 147, 310

H&S Company, 45
Company A, 30-31, 39, 40, 45-46
Company C, 38, 40, 45, 71
Company D, 46, 67-68, 71
2d Battalion, 18, 31, 33-36, 38-39, 41-44, 47, 49, 61, 67-70, 72, 135, 137, 159, 236, 310
Company E, 31, 35-36, 41, 47, 61
Company F, 31, 33-35, 47, 68, 70
Company G, 31, 33-36, 38-39, 49, 61, 69-70
Company H, 31, 35, 41-44, 47, 70
3d Battalion, 18-19, 30-31, 33-35, 38-39, 46-47, 49-50, 59-60, 69-72, 76, 135, 143, 154, 159-60
Company I, 35, 50, 59-60, 72
Company K, 33-35, 38, 49, 50, 71-72, 154
Company L, 18, 30, 35, 39, 46
Company M, 33, 35, 38, 46-47
11th Marines, 81, 84, 94, 105, 174, 194, 196, 199, 215, 243-45, 247, 249-50, 256, 263
1st Battalion, 59-60, 76, 123, 142, 145, 159, 170, 176, 178, 194, 243
Battery B, 59-60, 194
Battery D, 60, 116, 123, 142
2d Battalion, 116, 194, 196, 243, 249
Battery E, 249
Battery F, 194, 196
3d Battalion, 109-10, 116, 211, 244, 249
Battery G, 110, 116
Battery H, 109, 211, 249
4th Battalion, 105, 243
Battery K, 105
12th Marines, 30, 84, 141, 147, 157, 243-44, 246-47, 249-50, 256
Headquarters Battery, 165, 288
1st Battalion, 64, 90, 141, 143, 151, 244
Battery A, 64, 143
Battery B, 124, 143
Battery C, 64, 89
2d Battalion, 18, 27, 29-31, 34-35, 39, 47, 49-50, 70, 91, 96, 125, 133, 212-14, 243-44, 300-301, 303, 305, 308, 310
Mortar Battery, 22, 31, 49-50, 248
Battery D, 30-31, 50
Battery E, 31, 47, 49-50
Battery F, 37, 49
3d Battalion, 22, 53, 55, 165, 243-44
Battery G, 22
Battery H, 22
4th Battalion, 24, 60, 77, 167, 243-44
13th Marines
1st Battalion, 97, 106, 109-10, 124-25, 175-76, 178, 184, 187, 214, 243-44, 303, 305-10
Battery A, 308
Battery C, 110
4th Battalion
Battery K, 86, 243
26th Marines, 19, 81, 96, 100, 105, 114, 116, 124-25, 174, 188, 212, 214-15, 243, 299
1st Battalion, 97, 109, 124-25, 175-76, 178, 184, 187, 214, 244, 303, 305-310
Company A, 306
Company B, 124
Company C, 306, 309

INDEX

Company D, 97, 306, 309
2d Battalion, 91, 96, 125, 212-14, 244, 300-301, 303, 305, 308, 310
Company F, 214, 301
3d Battalion, 91, 105-108, 110, 213-14, 300-301, 303, 305
Company I, 107-108
Company K, 110
Company L, 91, 107-108, 110
Company M, 110, 213
27th Marines, 122
Battalion Landing Team 2/7, 84-86, 88, 300, 305
Battalion Landing Team 1/9, 310
Battalion Landing Team 2/9, 310
Battalion Landing Team 1/26, 124-25, 214, 306
Battalion Landing Team 2/26, 91, 106, 125, 213-14, 300-301, 303, 305
Battalion Landing Team 3/26, 91, 106, 300-301, 303
1st Field Artillery Group, 243
1st Amphibious Tractor (Amtrac) Battalion, 24, 25, 77, 133
1st Engineer Battalion, 105, 114, 178, 182, 267-70
Company A, 178, 241
Company C, 105
1st Light Antiaircraft Missile (LAAM) Battalion, 133, 137, 223, 241
Headquarters Company, 241
Company A, 241
Company B, 241
Company C, 241
1st Medical Battalion, 269, 272
1st Military Police Battalion, 99, 260
Company D, 99
1st Motor Transport Battalion, 271
1st Radio Battalion, 41, 258
1st Reconnaissance Battalion, 81, 174, 252-53, 257
1st Tank Battalion, 81, 174, 250
2d Light Antiaircraft Missile (LAAM) Battalion, 223, 241
3d Amphibious Tractor (Amtrac) Battalion, 269
3d Engineer Battalion, 68, 151, 165, 267, 270, 288
Company A, 267
Company B, 151
Company C, 68
3d Medical Battalion, 151, 167, 273, 288
Company C, 151, 165
3d Military Police Battalion, 260
3d Motor Transport Battalion, 151, 165, 271-72
Company B, 151
3d Reconnaissance Battalion, 18, 22, 30, 55, 76, 151, 167, 252-56
Company A, 151
Company D, 255
3d Shore Party Battalion, 48
Company A, 151
3d Tank Battalion, 24, 62, 75, 133, 142, 165, 250
Company A, 60, 62, 75, 142
Company B, 62, 75
Company C, 133
5th Communication Battalion, 260, 274
Communication Company, 274
5th Engineer Battalion
Company A, 267, 271

5th Medical Battalion
Company A, 272
5th Motor Transport Battalion
Company A, 271
5th Tank Battalion, 96, 125-26, 216
7th Communication Battalion, 85, 114, 175, 182, 186, 198, 267, 270, 274
7th Engineer Battalion, 85, 114, 175, 182, 186, 198, 267, 270
7th Motor Transport Battalion, 260, 271-72
9th Engineer Battalion, 175, 204, 209, 260, 267, 270
9th Motor Transport Battalion, 131, 151, 167, 271-72
Company B, 151
Company C, 167
9th Provisional Service Battalion, 131
11th Engineer Battalion, 30, 84, 141, 147, 151, 157, 167, 243-44, 246-47, 249-50, 256, 267, 270
Company B, 151
11th Motor Transport Battalion, 30, 84, 141, 147, 157, 243, 244, 246-47, 249-50, 256, 271-72
1st 155mm Gun Battery, Self-Propelled, 243
1st Provisional 155mm Howitzer Battery, 31, 34, 49
1st Searchlight Battery, 22, 133, 243, 249
3d Provisional 155mm Howitzer Battery 31, 34, 50, 243
5th 175mm Gun Battery, 244
1st Air-Naval Gunfire Liaison Company, 311, 316-17
1st Armored Amphibian Company, 243
1st Bridge Company, 267
1st Hospital Company, 272
3d Bridge Company, 151, 165, 267
3d Dental Company, 167
3d Force Reconnaissance Company, 252-53, 257
Air
1st Marine Aircraft Wing, 2, 27, 29, 94, 95, 133, 154, 169, 220, 221, 223, 225-232, 234-236, 238, 240-242, 251, 257, 260, 262, 265, 269, 299, 309, 320
2d Marine Aircraft Wing, 226-27
3d Marine Aircraft Wing, 228
Marine Aircraft Groups (MAG)
MAG-11, 220, 226
MAG-12, 220-21, 260
MAG-13, 137, 168, 260
MAG-15, 136, 223
MAG-16, 94, 190, 194, 220, 223, 236, 240
MAG-18, 241
MAG-36, 29, 50, 94, 168, 220, 228, 236, 303
Provisional Marine Aircraft Group (ProvMAG), 39, 25, 29, 50, 168, 220, 236, 240
Wing Control Groups (MWCG)
MWCG-18, 221
Wing Headquarters Group (MWHG)
MWHG-12, 221
Wing Support Group (MWSG)
MWSG-17, 263
Aerial Refueler/Transport Squadrons (VMGR)
VMGR-152, 220
Air Support Squadrons (MASS)
MASS-3, 235
All-Weather Attack Squadrons (VMA[AW])
VMA(AW)-225, 226
VMA(AW)-242, 27, 220

VMA(AW)-533, 220, 223
Attack Squadrons (VMA)
   VMA-121, 226
   VMA-221, 220
   VMA-223, 220
   VMA-331, 220
Composite Squadrons (VMCJ)
   VMCJ-1, 220, 227, 233, 251
Fighter/Attack Squadrons (VMFA)
   VMFA-115, 133, 136, 220
   VMFA-122, 137
   VMFA-232, 137, 226
   VMFA-314, 220
   VMFA-323, 220, 226
   VMFA-334, 136, 220, 223
   VMFA-542, 220, 232
Headquarters and Maintenance Squadrons (H&MS)
   H&MS-11, 233
   H&MS-17, 220
   H&MS-39, 168
Heavy Helicopter Squadrons (HMH)
   HMH-361, 228, 238
   HMH-452, 220
   HMH-462, 223
   HMH-463, 238
Light Helicopter Squadrons (HML)
   HML-167, 220, 238
   HML-367, 168, 220, 223, 238
Medium Helicopter Squadrons (HMM)
   HMM-161, 36, 168, 220, 223
   HMM-162, 228
   HMM-163, 228
   HMM-164, 299-300, 303, 308, 310
   HMM-165, 96, 106, 133, 137, 220, 223, 300, 310
   HMM-262, 168, 220, 223
   HMM-265, 220, 299, 307, 309
   HMM-362, 299-300, 303, 306-307
   HMM-363, 220, 228
   HMM-364, 220, 273
Observation Squadrons (VMO)
   VMO-2, 220, 226-27, 238, 251
   VMO-3, 238
   VMO-6, 168, 220, 223, 226, 238, 251
Air Traffic Control Units (MATCU)
   MATCU-62, 168
   MATCU-66, 223
   MATCU-68, 133
Marine Corps Reserve Civic Action Fund, 287
Marine Corps Schools
   Amphibious Warfare School, 240
Matheson, Col Bruce J., 94, 220
Mau Chanh (2), 198
McAdams, Capt James M., 139, 141
McCain, Adm John S., Jr., 131, 153, 275
McClintock, SgtMaj Ted E., 67, 90
McCutcheon, MajGen Keith B., 221, 226
McKenna, Maj George X., 58
McLaughlin, BGen John N., 317-18
McMahon, Col John F., Jr., 300
McMonagle, LtCol James J., 24, 39, 64, 66, 73-74, 138

McNamara, Secretary of Defense Robert S., 258
Medical Civic Action Program (MEDCAP), 287
Mekong Delta, 83, 131, 136, 161, 311, 318
Metzger, Col Theodore E., 284, 290, 294
Midway Island, 149
MIG Continuous Airborne Alert Program (MIGCAP), 234
Milia, LtCol Carmelo P., USA, 64
Military Assistance Command, Vietnam (MACV), 2, 5, 9-12, 44-45, 51, 82, 84, 128-31, 133, 150, 157, 167, 220-21, 225-26, 231, 234, 259, 266, 268, 274-75, 277, 280, 282, 287, 297, 311, 317
   Combined Campaign Plan, 11-12, 14
   Strategic Objectives Plan, 12
   Tactical Air Support Element, 234
Military Assistance Service Fund, 313
Military Sealift Transportation System, 277
Minh Tan, 113
Mixmaster redeployment transfers, 133, 152, 275
Mo Duc, 101, 300
Mobile CAP concept of operations, 291
Mobile Concept of Operations, 16-18, 29, 52, 246, 267
Modjeski, Maj Robert L., 72, 135
Momyer, Gen William W., USAF, 223, 241
Monkey Mountain, 241
Montagnard tribe, 5
Monticello (LDS 35), 300
Morgan, Cpl William D., 47, 368
Morgenthaler, LtCol Wendell P., 123, 177-79, 182, 184, 186-87
Mortar Valley, 248
Moss, LtCol Rodney B., 90
Mountains
   Dong Cho Mountain, 71
   Dong Ha Mountain, 58, 145
   Nui Da Beo, 195
   Nui Gaing, 88
   Nui Hoat, 126
   Nui Kim Son, 188
   Nui Liet Kiem, 209
   Nui Mat Rang (Hill 845), 101, 195
   Nui Ne, 126
   Nui Oay Tre, 142
   Nui Tam Cap, 101
   Nui Tia Pong, 19, 159
Mullinex (DD 994), 105, 307
Mulroney, Col Peter J., 157, 167, 243-44, 246, 249-50
Mutter's Ridge, 61, 73-74, 138-39, 142, 145, 147-49, 164
My Hoa, 113, 119, 198
My Hoa (3), 198
My Son, 86

Nam An, 196, 202, 244
Nam An (5), 202
Nam Can Forest, 314
Nam Hoa District, 25
Nam O, 97, 125, 212, 214
Nam O Beach, 214
Nam O Bridge, 97, 212
National Front for the Liberation of South Vietnam, 12
Naval Air Stations
   Cubi Point, Philippines, 137

INDEX

Naval Regulations, 157
Navy Commands and Units, 169, 229, 231, 234-36, 241-42, 262, 288, 301, 306, 307-308, 316, 318-19
    Commander-in-Chief, Pacific (CinCPac), 9, 82-83, 130-32, 150, 230
        Joint Pacific Teletype Network, 274
    Pacific Fleet, 262, 264, 266, 276, 297
        Service Force, Pacific Fleet, 60, 73, 100, 113, 139, 187, 256, 264
        Naval Air Force, Pacific Fleet, 262
    Seventh Fleet, 244, 250-51, 276, 297, 310, 317, 319, 320
        Commander, Amphibious Task Force, 298
            Task Force 77, 234
            Task Group 76.4, 299
            Task Group 76.5, 299
            Task Group 79, 297, 298, 300
            Task Group 79.4, 298
            Task Group 79.5, 298
            Amphibious Ready Group Alpha, 297, 299, 306, 308, 310
            Amphibious Ready Group Bravo, 214, 299, 305, 310
    Commander, U.S. Naval Forces, Vietnam, 264, 265-66, 275, 297, 310
        Task Force Clearwater, 2, 15, 26, 243
        Naval Support Activity, 2, 99, 264-67, 272
            Naval Support Activity Hospital, 272
            Naval Support Facility, Da Nang, 267
        3d Naval Construction Brigade, 2, 116, 141, 161, 267-70
            128th Naval Mobile Construction Battalion, 288
        Naval Advisory Group, 316
        Naval Supply Depot, Yokosuka, 262
        River Assault Squadron 15, 314
        Patrol, Air Cushioned Vehicle, 15
Nelson, LtCol Neil A., 84-86, 88, 105-108
New Jersey (BB 62), 251, **251**, 301, 317
New Life Hamlets, 14
New Orleans (LPH 11), 214, 228
New York Times, 51
New Yorker, 51
Newport News (CA 148), 96, 105, 176
Newsweek, 51
Ngan Cau, 123
Ngan Cau (2), 123
Nghi Ha Valley, 210
Nha Trang, 257
Nhi Ha, 24
Nichols, Col Robert, 84, 104-109, 116, 201, **202**, 303
Nichols, Col Thomas H., 221
Nickerson, LtGen Herman, Jr., 6, 7, 131, 133, **134**, 135, 167, 175, 239-40, 252, 265, 290, 293, 318
Nitze, Deputy Secretary of Defense Paul, 225
Nixon, Vice President Richard M., 5; President, 128, **129**, 130, 132, **132**, 149-51, **152**, 153, 169, 170, 223, 318, 319
No Name Island, 123, 187
Nong Son, 82
Noonan, LCpl Thomas P., Jr., 36, 369
Northern Sector Defense Command, 245
North Vietnam, 17, 52, 164, 231, 233-34
    Hanoi, 170, 234
    Quang Binh Province, 147, 177
    Vinh, 26, 124, 138, 163, 234, 307
North Vietnamese Armed Forces
    District II Da Nang, 175
North Vietnamese Army, *6ff*
North Vietnamese Army Commands and Units
    4th Front Headquarters, 7, 80, 83, 194
    Military Region 5, 7, 80, 83
    7th Front, 7, 15, 138
    2d Division, 2-3, 18-20, 24, 29, 34, 49, 62, 64, 76, 80, 82-84, 101, 125, 170, 172, 175, 185, 189, 216, 223, 226-27, 241, 265, 287, 289, 301, 306, 308-309
        3d Regiment, 206
        21st Regiment, 80, 83-84, 88, 99, 308, 314
        38th Regiment, 80, 175, 300, 305
        68B Artillery (Rocket) Regiment, 80
        141st Regiment, 99-100, 103, 108, 110, 114-15
            2d Battalion, 83
                8th Company, 107
        368B Artillery (Rocket) Regiment, 80, 103, 203
            1st Battalion, 203
    3d Division, 2, 5, 15-19, 22, 24, 27-28, 30-31, 34, 44, 48-50, 52, 55, 59, 61-64, 66-69, 72-76, 78, 80, 86, 88, 90, 92, 95, 102, 130-33, 136-39, 141-42, 148-49, 151-155, 159, 161, 164-72, 191, 220-21, 223-25, 228-29, 234, 238-40, 243-46, 249-58, 260-61, 263, 265, 267, 269, 270-73, 275-78, 284, 287-89, 303, 305, 310, 320
    304th Division, 69, 71
        9th Regiment, 16, 18-19, 24, 26-30, 37, 41, 44, 47-49, 51, 55, 60-63, 67-69, 73, 76, 78, 130-33, 135-36, 138, 141, 149, 151, 162, 164, 167, 175, 204, 209, 214, 223, 229, 236, 244, 260, 267, 270-72, 297-300, 305, 310, 313, 319
            1st Battalion, 143
                1st Company, 147
            3d Battalion, 143, 162
        24th Regiment, 71, 138, 162
        57th Regiment, 69-70
    308th Division, 63, 72
        36th Regiment, 61, 72-74, 80, 122, 175, 194, 211, 305
    320th Division, 15, 17
    2d Viet Cong Regiment, 80
    3d Regiment, 80, 305

    6th Regiment, 27, 67, 125, 126, 216
    22d Regiment, 80, 273
    27th Regiment, 15, 22-23, 52, 59-61, 72-74, 122, 138, 170
        1st Battalion, 59
    29th Regiment, 68, 249
    31st Regiment, 15, 80, 103, 107-108, 116, 138, 300, 308
        18th Company, 107, 288
    65th Artillery Regiment, 27
    83d Engineer Regiment, 27
    84th Artillery (Rocket) Regiment, 15, 138, 162
        1st Battalion, 162
    90th Regiment, 191, 193, 196, 204
        8th Battalion, 203
        9th Battalion, 203
    126th Naval Sapper Regiment, 15
    138th Regiment, 15, 52
    220th Transport Regiment, 83
    246th Independent Regiment, 22-23, 52-53, 55, 57-58, 162

    3d Battalion, 162
        1st Company, 1st Battalion, 58
    270th Regiment, 15
    401st Viet Cong (Sapper) Regiment, 80
    675th Artillery Regiment, 67
    803d Regiment, 26
    812th Regiment, 15
    3d Sapper Battalion, 191
    33d Sapper Battalion, 74-75
    48th Viet Cong Local Force Battalion, 300, 308
    70th Main Force Battalion, 307
    107th Artillery Battalion, 308
    88th Field Hospital, 34
    95th Local Force Company, 273, 300-301, 308
    K3 Battalion, 275th Regiment, 5th Division, 314
    Q83d Local Force Battalion (Dai Loc), 83, 198, 199
North Vietnamese Government
    Central Office for South Vietnam, 7
    Lao Dong Party, 7
        Reunification Department, 7
Northern Artillery Cantonment, 244
Nui Loc Son Basin, 204, 206, 212
Nung tribe, 5

Oates, 1stLt Patrick P., 71-72
Observation Posts
    Eagle Eye, 214
    Reno, 214
Ogden (LPD 5), 300
Okinawa (LPH 3), 91, 300
Okinawa, Japan, 71-72, 131, 133, 135, 137, 156, 165-68, 220, 223, 260, 263, 275-76, 278, 298, 303, 305, 308, 310
O'Meara, LtCol James J., 163-64
O'Neill, 1stLt Richmond D., 147
One War Concept, 10, 12, 14
Ong Thu Slope, 88, 191
Ontos, 64, 213, 250
Operations
    Allen Brook, 174
    Apache Snow, 67-68
    Arlington Canyon, 159-64, 229
    Bold Mariner, 101, 292, 300, 303, 306
    Brave Armada, 213, 217, 308
    Bristol Boots, 77
    Butterfly, 199
    Cameron Falls, 69, 71, 236
    Clairborne Chute, 171
    Cumberland Thunder, 171
    Daring Rebel, 305, 307
    Dawson River South, 28-29
    Dawson River West, 18-19, 27-28, 30
    Defiant Measure, 91, 303
    Dewey Canyon, 24, 33-35, 38-39, 44-45, 50-51, 61, 63, 67-68, 72, 94, 135, 167, 233, 238, 247, 249, 319
    Durham Peak, 184, 187, 194-96
    Eager Pursuit I, 303
    Eager Pursuit II, 303
    Ellis Ravine, 61, 77
    Fayette Canyon, 101, 125
    Forsyth Grove, 193, 202
    Frederick Hill, 101, 125, 216-17
    Fulton Square, 170
    Gallant Leader, 307
    Geneva Park, 101, 126, 216, 217
    Georgia Tar, 159-62
    Golden Fleece (of 1966), 117, 167, 285
    Hardin Falls, 101, 125
    Herkimer Mountain, 75, 159-60
    Idaho Canyon, 138, 141-43, 145, 147, 149, 162, 164
    Iron Mountain, 101, 126, 216-17
    Iroquois Grove, 77, 160, 170
    Kentucky, 19, 23-24, 77, 171
    Kentucky Jumper, 77, 171
    Keystone Cardinal (redeployment), 164, 223, 244, 275-76, 278, 310
    Keystone Eagle (redeployment), 132-33, 136-37, 237, 244, 275-76, 278
    Kingfisher, 190, 214, 240
    Lamar Plain, 216-17
    Lancaster, 167
    Le Loi, 84
    Linn River, 91, 96, 301
    Louisiana Lee, 171
    Maine Crag, 49, 63-64, 67, 73
    Mameluke Thrust, 103
    Marshall Mountain, 24
    Massachusetts Bay, 77
    Massachusetts Striker, 63, 78
    Maui Peak, 103
    Meade River, 83-86, 174
    Mighty Play, 308
    Montana Mauler, 59-62, 77
    Montgomery Rendezvous, 78
    Muskogee Meadow, 117-18
    Nantucket Beach, 217
    Napoleon Saline, 167
    Nevada Eagle, 25-26, 77
    Norton Falls, 172, 195
    Oklahoma Hills, 105, 109-10, 114, 116-17, 122, 125, 201, 247, 303
    Pegasus, 16
    Phu Vang, 26
    Phu Vang IV, 26
    Pipestone Canyon, 175-76, 178-79, 181-82, 184, 186-88, 191, 193-94, 202, 270, 287, 307
    Platte Canyon, 26
    Prairie Fire, 41
    Purple Martin, 52, 57-58, 75-76, 235
    Republic Square, 171-72
    Richland Square, 171
    Russell Beach, 101, 125, 217, 301
    Scotland, 19-20, 23, 167
    Starlite, 16
    Taylor Common, 18, 24, 63, 84-88, 91, 94, 96, 101, 103-104, 116, 121, 175, 243, 247, 301, 303
    Todd Forest, 25
    Utah Mesa, 69, 71-72, 133, 135, 170
    Valiant Hunt, 300
    Vernon Lake II, 102, 125
    Viem Dong, 124

INDEX

Vinh Loc, 26
Virginia Ridge, 66, 73, 75, 138, 141
Vu Ninh 03, 306
Vu Ninh 05, 177
Warbonnet, 83
William's Glade, 159-60, 170
Ord, Col James B., Jr., 81, 84, 86, 93, 104, 116, 175
Oregon Operational Zone, 101, 125

Pacification, 10*ff*
    1969 Pacification and Development Plan, 10, 138, 282-83
Pagoda Valley, 211
Paige, LtCol Edwin C., Jr., 133, 136
Painter, Col Harry F., 284
Paris Peace Talks, 7, 11, 26, 41, 128, 130, 132, 169
Paul Revere (LPA 248), 133, 134, 135
Peabody, Col Clifford J., 284
Perry, LtCol Aydlette H., Jr., 253
Personnel Infra-red Intrusion Device (PIRID), 259
Philippines
    Naval Air Station, Cubi Point, 137
    Subic Bay, 305, 308, 310
Phipps, PFC Jimmy W., 370
Phoenix anti-Viet Cong infrastructure plan, 186, 281-82, 321
Phong Loc (3), 176
Phong Luc (2), 182, 185-86
Phouma, Prime Minister Souvanna (of Laos), 45, 51
Phou Nhoi Hill, 64
Phu An (1), 203
Phu An (2), 203
Phu Bai, 2, 15, 29, 67, 94, 168, 220, 223, 228, 234, 236, 252, 257, 260, 265, 274, 288, 303
Phu Bai Airfield, 220, 288, 303
Phu Lac (6), 116, 193-94, 197
Phu Loc (6), 92
Phu Loc District, 26, 78
Phu Loc Valley, 191, 193-94, 210, 229, 248
Phu Loi, 85, 88, 196
Phu Long (1), 198
Phung Hoang anti-Viet Cong infrastructure plan, 282, 321 (*See also* Phoenix)
Phu Nhuan District, 117, 121
Phu Thu District, 26
Porter, Capt Richard L., 315
Project Delta, 136, 161
Project Handclasp, 287
Prom, LCpl William R., 371
Pruiett, 1stLt Ronald E., 90
Public Health Service, 276
Purdham, LtCol Frederick K., 316

Quang Chau, 123
Quang Da Special Zone, 175
Quang Nam Province, 2-3, 7, 18, 78, 80-83, 97, 101, 122, 125, 174, 177, 182, 187, 193, 196, 204, 206, 212, 236, 244, 247, 252, 254, 257-58, 268, 270-71, 287, 289, 294, 303, 306-308, 319, 321
Quang Ngai City, 13, 80, 102, 125, 216-17, 300-301
Quang Ngai Province, 2-3, 8, 11, 13, 80, 83, 101-102, 125-26, 213, 215-17, 289, 294, 300-301, 303, 319
Quang Tin Province, 2-3, 7, 83, 101, 125, 188, 204, 206, 217, 252, 294, 306-308, 319
Quang Tri City, 13, 24, 27, 138, 253, 288
Quang Tri Province, 2-3, 7, 13, 15-17, 19, 20, 24, 27-29, 47, 52, 60-63, 66, 69, 72, 76-78, 133, 135-36, 138, 151-52, 154, 159-60, 165-68, 170, 172, 220, 223, 229, 233, 236, 244, 247, 252-53, 255, 258, 260, 267, 270-71, 273, 287-89, 294-95, 303, 317
Quan Nam, 124
Que Son District, 101, 188, 206
Que Son District Headquarters, 206
Que Son Mountains, 81-83, 86, 88, 101, 175, 178, 187, 191, 193-96, 199, 202, 204, 206, 208-11, 213, 216, 229, 244, 247-49, 319
Que Son Valley, 194, 204, 206, 208-209, 213, 249
Quigley, Capt William J., 74
Quilter, MajGen Charles J., 2, 94, 221, 221, 225, 234
Quinn, LtCol Francis X., 99, 103, 105

Racial problems, 152, 153, 156-58
    Afro haircuts, 156-57
    ALMAR 65, 156-57
    Black Power symbols, 154, 156-57
    I Corps Tactical Zone Watch Committee, 156
    Operation Freeze, 156, 159-60
Radar beacon forward air control (RABFAC), 236
Raines, LtCol Thomas E., 133, 137
Ramsey, MajGen Lloyd B., USA, 215-16
Red Beach, 260
Redd, LCpl Robert, 123
Reilly, Maj James K., 97, 175
Repose (AH 16), 272
Republic of Korea Armed Forces, 12, 14, 81-82, 175-79, 182-83, 201, 217, 221, 229, 236, 238-39, 242, 244, 250, 274, 285, 310-11, 316-17
    2d Marine Brigade, 2, 5, 82, 175, 185, 265, 287, 306, 308-309
        1st Battalion, 59-60, 76, 123, 142, 145, 159, 170, 175-76, 178, 182, 194, 243
        2d Battalion, 175, 309
        5th Battalion, 309
Revolutionary Development, 13, 14
    Revolutionary Development Cadre Teams, 189
Rigoulot, 1stLt James P., 148
Riot control agents, 60 (*See also* CS gas)
Rivers
    Song Ai Nghia, 175, 186
    Song Ba Ren, 175
    Song Bau Xau, 123
    Song Boung, 89
    Song Cai, 83, 85, 88-90
    Song Cam Lo, 149, 164, 166, 175, 193
    Song Cau Bien, 188
    Song Cau Do, 99
    Song Cau Lau, 267
    Song Chiem Son, 175, 193
    Song Cu De, 97, 213-14
    Song Cua Viet, 15, 23-25, 52, 58, 66, 75-76, 153, 164, 166, 303
    Song Da Krong, 27-28, 34, 36-38, 39, 68-69
    Song Han, 5, 166
    Song Huong (Perfume River), 15

Song Ky Lam, 91, 176, 178-79, 185-86
Song La Tho, 122, 176, 186, 190
Song Lo Dong, 214
Song Lo Tho, 175
Song Ly Ly, 206
Song Quang Tri, 60, 69
Song Rao Vinh, 138
Song Re, 102
Song Suoi Co Ca, 97, 182-83, 185, 190
Song Tam Giap, 183
Song Tan Khong, 114
Song Thach Han, 160
Song Thanh Quit, 175
Song Thu Bon, 81, 83, 85-88, 92, 95, 117-18, 174-75, 190-91, 193, 198-99, 254
Song Tra Khuc, 101, 126
Song Truoi, 26
Song Truong Giang, 307, 309
Song Tuy Loan, 99-100, 104, 201
Song Ve, 126
Song Vinh Dien, 124
Song Vu Gia, 81, 96, 103, 105, 109, 111, 113-14, 118-19, 174-75, 190-91, 193, 196, 198-99, 201, 204
Song Xe Pon, 63-64
Song Yang, 103
Song Yen, 97, 187-88, 201
Roads
  Liberty Road, 86, 99, 116, 121, 191, 193, 196-99, 201
  Route 1, 11, 17, 24, 74, 81, 123-24, 171, 175-76, 179, 182-83, 186, 188, 190, 205, 206, 212-14, 233, 258, 267-68, 303
  Route 1-D, 191
  Route 4, 95, 105, 109-11, 113-14, 175-76, 178, 182-83, 184, 186-87, 198, 201-202, 268
  Route 9, 11, 17-19, 24, 49, 61, 63-64, 71-76, 138, 141, 145, 152, 159-61, 163-65, 268, 270
  Route 12, 315
  Route 535, 205-206
  Route 536, 206
  Route 537, 191
  Route 538, 308
  Route 540 (See Liberty Road)
  Route 548, 15, 27, 46
  Route 556, 60
  Route 557, 160
  Route 558, 145
  Route 561, 19, 138, 141-42
  Route 616, 63-64, 66, 69
  Route 922, 15, 27, 28, 38, 41-48, 67-68
  Route 926, 63, 72
Robb, 1stLt John K., 215
Robertson, Col Charles S., 121-22, 124, 175-76, 178-79, 182-83, 188
Robertson, LtCol J. W. P., 91, 301, 303
Robinson, Capt Donald J., II, 185, 189
Rock Crusher, 163, 308
Rocket Valley, 159
Rockpile, 19, 49, 53, 161 (See also Elliott Combat Base)
Rogers, Secretary of State William P., 318
Rohweller, 1stLt Robert T., 154
Rollings, 1stLt Wayne E., 254, 255
Rome plow, 93, 117, 296

Romero, Capt Joseph M. A., 111-12
Rosson, LtGen William B., USA, 17, 167
Rough Rider truck convoys, 198, 271, 272
Rules of engagement, 22, 41
Rumor Valley, 214
Rung Sat Special Zone, 313, 315-16
Ruong Ruong Valley, 26, 77

Sa Huynh, 264, 267
Saigon, 3, 8, 51, 64, 87, 234-35, 274, 297, 311, 315, 317, 318
Sampson, Capt Gerald H., 145, 175, 186
Sanctuary (AH 17), 272
Sargent, LtCol George T., Jr., 19-20, 53, 55-57
Schlarp, LtCol Jack E., 303
Schulze, Col Richard C., 73-75, 88, 138, 141-42, 144-45
Schwartz, Col John L., 263
Schwenk, Col Adolph G., 122
Scoppa, LtCol Joseph, Jr., 18, 28, 39, 50
Seismic Intrusion Device (SID), 259
Seminole (AKA 104), 300
Sensor devices, 139, 258
Sexton, Col Martin J., 44
Shane, Maj Harry J., 318
Sherwood Forest, 104, 202, 214, 248
Ship types
  amphibious assault ship (LPH), 299
  amphibious transport dock (LPD), 299
  attack cargo ship (AKA), 299
  attack transport ship (APA), 299
  dock landing ship (LSD), 299
  fire support ship (LFR), 317
  tank landing ship (LST), 99
Shockey, Capt Donald K., Jr., 61
Shuler, 2dLt Wyman E., III, 96
Side looking airborne radar (SLAR), 251
Sienko, Col Walter, 220
Simlik, Col Wilbur F., 75, 138-39, 141, 143-45, 149, 151-54, 161, 164, 263, 265-66, 275-77
Simmons, Maj Roger E., 252
Simpson, MajGen Ormond R., 2, 80-81, **80**, 103-105, 121-22, 124, 174-75, 178, 182-83, 201, **212**, 218, 269-70
Simpson, LtCol Thomas H., 316-17
Simpson, LtCol William A., 215
Single Management, 223-26
Sinnott, Capt Paul J., 143
Skotnicki, Col Anthony J., 257, 259
Sleger, LtCol Joseph, 250
Smith, LtCol George W., 18, 33, 38-39, 50-51
Smith, 1stLt Earl C., 229, 232
Smith, MajGen Robert B., USA, **171**
Snelling, LtCol Edward W., 106-108, 110, 213, **215**, 303
Son Tinh District, 294
Son Yen, 123
South China Sea, 81-82, 178, 187, 220, 235, 297, 307
South Vietnamese Armed Forces, 8-9, 12, 16, 128-30, 150-51, 169, 282, 320
  Air Force, 234
    41st Tactical Wing, 3, 221
  Armed Propaganda Companies, 285

INDEX

Armed Propaganda Teams, 257, 301
Joint General Staff (JGS), 10-11, 313, 315
Army of the Republic of Vietnam Commands and Units
    1st Infantry Division, 3, 24-25, 67, 68, 77, 84-85, 88, 91-92, 94, 131, 152, 164, 170-72, 196, 211, 243-44, 257, 307, 311, 317, 320
        1st Regiment, 24-25, 138
        2d Regiment 18-20, 24, 29, 34, 36, 49, 62, 64, 71, 76, 165, 170, 172
            1st Battalion, 34, 36, 60
            2d Battalion, 20, 34, 36, 71, 165
            3d Battalion, 66, 68, 71
            4th Battalion, 62
            5th Battalion, 62
        3d Regiment, 171
            2d Battalion, 84, 87, 89, 90, 92, 117-20, 186, 191, 193-99, 217, 303
    2d Infantry Division, 3, 18-20, 24, 29, 34, 49, 62, 64, 76, 101, 125, 170, 172, 216, 301
        1st Ranger Group, 84-85, 88, 91-92, 94, 196, 307
            21st Ranger Battalion, 84, 88, 99, 314
            37th Ranger Battalion, 84, 175, 182, 194
            39th Ranger Battalion, 84, 88, 178
        1st Armored Brigade, 211
        4th Regiment, 125, 126, 216
        5th Regiment, 125, 195, 216-17
            2d Battalion, 217
        6th Regiment, 125-26, 216
        51st Infantry Regiment, 3, 82, 105, 109, 115, 178, 182-83, 188, 199, 287, 303, 306
            1st Battalion, 99, 109, 114, 175, 177, 179, 182, 210
            2d Battalion, 97, 106, 115-16, 186
            3d Battalion, 106, 123, 182, 185-86
            4th Battalion, 110, 124, 175, 177, 179, 182-83, 185
        54th Regiment, 26, 306
        62d Artillery Regiment
            1st Battalion, 34, 39, 49
        51st Reconnaissance Company, 115
        Nong Song Irregular Company, 88
    Marine Corps, 311, 313-16
        Brigade A, 314
        Brigade B, 314
        1st Artillery Battalion, 314
        3d Battalion 314
        Training Command, 311
National Military Academy, 311
National Police, 5, 12, 14, 24, 82, 123-24, 186, 189, 197, 257, 282, 285, 308
National Police Field Force, 5, 82, 186, 257, 285
Navy, 309, 311
Peoples' Self Defense Force (PSDF), 5, 11-12, 14, 189, 281-83, 285, 295, 321
Popular Forces (PF), 3, 12, 14, 24, 82, 151, 189, 213, 281, 285, 289-92, 294, 306, 308
Provincial Reconnaissance Units, 24
    Hoi An Provincial Reconnaissance Unit, 123, 177, 189, 257
    Quang Nam Provincial Reconnaissance Unit, 177
Quang Tri Provisional Rifle Company, 20
Regional Forces (RF), 3, 12, 14, 24, 26; 67, 82, 92, 123, 151, 188-89, 212, 281, 285, 294, 301, 306-308

34th Regional Force Battalion, 123
59th Regional Force Battalion, 123
Regional Force Company 1/25, 214
Regional Force Company 193, 199
Regional Force Company 369, 198
Regional Force Company 759, 189
Revolutionary Development Cadre, 257, 284-85
Special Forces, 5, 83, 236, 274
Tactical Zones
    I Corps, 2*ff*
    III Corps, 170, 311, 313-15
    IV Corps, 313-15
South Vietnamese Government Agencies
    Central Recovery Committee, 280-81
    National Assembly, 286
    National Liberation Councils, 282
Southern Sector Defense Command 250
Spanjer, BGen Ralph H., **212**, 221, 240
Spark, Col Michael M., 18, 72, 86-87, 90
Sparks, LtCol William F., 91, 301
Sparrow Hawk Reaction Force, 22, 56, 76
Stack Arms, 182, 269, **271**
Stemple, LtCol James W., 84, 92-93, 117
Stilwell, LtGen Richard G., USA, 2, **5**, 17, 41, 44-45, 67
Stingray patrols, 17, 139, 141, 254
Strike areas
    Barrel Roll, 231
    Commando Bolt, 231-32
    Commando Hunt, 232
    Steel Tiger, 231
Stubblefield, 1stLt William H., 164
Sullivan, Ambassador William H., 45, 51
Swift patrol boat (PCF), 307, 317
Swigart, LtCol Oral R., Jr., 69-71

T18 bulldozers, 117
Tactical Air Direction Center (TADC), 234-35
Tactical Air Operations Center (TAOC), 234
Tactical Logistics Group, 33
Tam Boi (Hill 1224), 27, 38, 46-47, 49, 50
Tam Ky, 80, 83, 101, 206, 215-16, 267
Tanh Hanh, 121
Tan Luu, 187
Tan My, 264
Tan Son Nhut Airbase, 87
Tay Bang An, 182
Tay Ninh, 313
Teixeira, 2dLt Milton J., 39
Terry, LtCol John M., 193-96, 198-99
Tet Offensive of 1968, 2, 7, 9, 15, 25, 28-29, 39, 91, 93, 97, 100, 103, 128, 170, 223, 239, 280, 294, 297, 303, 311, 313, 318-19
Tet, 1969, 28-29, 39, 91, 93, 97, 100, 103, 294, 303, 313
Tet, 1970, 170
Thailand, 220, 235, 274
    Nakhon Phanom, 259
Thang Binh District, 101
Thien, Col, ARVN, 175
Thieu, President Nguyen Van, 128, 130, 132, **132**, **152**, 280
Thrash, MajGen William G., **212**, 221, 225, 240

Thua Thien Province, 2-3, 7, 15, 25-26, 47, 77, 81, 171-72, 229, 252, 289, 294-95
Thu Bon (5), 198
Thuc, Col, ARVN, 183, 196, 198-99, 201
Thu Don District, 117
Thu Duc, 311
Thuong Duc, 82, 89, 103, 104, 106, 110, 114, 196, 198-99, 201-202, 248
Thuong Duc Bridge, 114
Thuong Duc Valley, 196, 198-99, 201
Tien Phuoc, 101
Tiger Mountain (Co A Nong) (*See* Hill 1228)
Timmermeyer, GySgt John E., 22
Toan, BGen Nguyen Van, ARVN, 3
Torrey, Capt Philip H., III, 192
Tortuga (LSD 26), 137
Tra Khe, 308
Tra Khe (1), 308
Tre Khe, 187
Tremblay, LtCol Laurier J., 271
Trieu Phong, 24, 170
Tripoli (LPH 10), 85, 167, 300
Trundy, LtCol Richard T., 303
Truong, MajGen Ngo Quang, ARVN, 3, 5, 307, 309
Tu Cau Bridge, 187
Tulare (LKA 112), 137
Tuy Loan, 99-100, 104, 201
Twohey, LtCol Richard B., 88-89, 91
Typhoon Diane, 145
Typhoon Tess, 182

U Minh Forest, 314-15
U.S. Government Agencies
    Agency for International Development (AID), 284
    Central Intelligence Agency (CIA), 284
    National Security Council (NSC), 128-29
    Department of Agriculture, 153, 276
    United States Information Agency (USIA), 284
Uniform Code of Military Justice, 157
United Press, 51
United States Naval Academy, 5

Valley Forge (LPH 8), 137, 308
Van Riper, Capt Paul K., 99, 100, 105
Vancouver (LPD 2), 165
Vernon County (LST 1161), 308
Viem Tay (1), 123-24, 187
Vien, Gen Cau Van, ARVN, 313
Viet Cong (VC), 6*ff*
Viet Cong Infrastructure (VCI), 5*ff*
Vietnam Salient, 19, 63, 66-67, 78
Vietnamization, 8, 150-51, 169-70, 172, 291, 319, 321
Vinh Dai Rock Crusher, 163
Voluntary Informant Program, 257, 269
Vung Tau Shipping Channel, 316

Wackle, LCpl Rick L., 88

Walker, Col Charles E., 178-79, **179**
Walt, LtGen Lewis W., 5-6, 287
Walters, Maj Raymond D., 55-56
Warner, Under Secretary of the Navy John, 153
Washburn (LKA 108), 153
Washington, D.C., 8, 128-29, 150-51
Weapons and ordnance
    AK47 assault rifle, **8**, 44, 72, 116, 142, 145, 163, 166, 177, 203
    B40 rockets, 123, 191, 193, 203
    bangalore torpedoes, 116, 255
    beehive round, 39
    boobytrap (surprise firing device), 84, 86, 121, 138, 177, 179, 181, 183, 185, 292, 301, 306
    claymore mine, 43
    flechette round, 39
    Howtar, 84
    Light Anti-tank Weapon (LAW), 203
    M79 grenade launcher, **204**, 254, 289
    M101A 105mm howitzer, 29-31, 36, 54, 84, 89, 94, 96, 107, 109, 115, 194, 201, 244
    M107 175mm self-propelled gun, 86, 88, 101, 125, 194-95, 206, 216-17
    M109A self-propelled 155mm howitzer, 29-31, 34-35, 48, 50, 64, 84, 86, 91, 94, 243-44
    M26 fragmentation grenade, 86, 154
    M42 self-propelled "Duster," 64
    M48A3 tank, 250
    M53 self-propelled 155mm gun, 244
    MK121 10,000-pound bomb (Combat trap), 87
    MK36 air-delivered mine, 231
    napalm, 88, 100, 118
    rocket-propelled grenade (RPG), 45, 54, 59-61, 66, 71, 73, 90-91, 122-23, 141, 145, 147, 149, 183, 187, 191, 193, 207
    Snakeeye bombs, 141
    surface-to-air missiles, 231
    Zuni rockets, 232
    .50-caliber antiaircraft gun, 91
    .50-caliber machine gun, 71, 91, 192, 250
    4.2-inch mortar, 29-30, 106, 160, 244
    7.62mm light machine gun, 209, 227
    12.7mm machine gun, 27, 118, 193, 209, **212**
    37mm gun, 27
    40mm antiaircraft gun, 47, 227, 317
    60mm mortar, 22, 47, 53, 72, 74, 141-42, 147, 164, 177, 187, 192-93
    75mm recoilless rifle, 75, 91, 193, 250
    81mm mortar, 22, 112, 163, 191, 193
    82mm mortar, 53, 56, 58, 90, 93, 123, 142, 164, 166, 191, 193
    85mm gun, 48, 66
    106mm recoilless rifle, 121
    122mm field gun, 19, 34, 38, 40, **43**, 47-48, 64, 66, 90-91, 97, 99, 103, 115, 160, 201, 211, 233, 249, 313
    122mm rocket, 19, 66, 90-91, 97, 99, 103, 115, 201, 211, 313
    140mm rocket, **83**, 97, 115, 201
    175mm gun, 29, 35, 48, 244, **246**, 251
Weber, LCpl Lester W., 372
West, LtCol Morgan W., 18-19, 27-28, 30, 141, 209, 217
Wester, Capt William D., 147
Westmoreland, Gen William C., USA, 9-10, 132, 223-25
Wheeler, Gen Earle, USA, **129**, **153**, 225

INDEX

Wheeler, MajGen Edwin B., **216**
Whisman, LtCol Ermil L., 69-70, 90, **91**, 236
White Elephant, 264
White River (LFR 536), 307
Whitesell, LtCol Robert D., 289
Wilkerson, Col Herbert L., 188, 190
Willcox, LtCol Clair E., 57, 159, 161*n*
Williams, BGen John E., 299-300, **300**
Wilson, PFC Alfred M., 49*n*, 373
Wilson, 2dLt Carl R., 56
Wilson, Col Robert R., 300, **300**
Winecoff, Capt David F., 31, 41-44, 47
Wood, LtCol Donald E., 135, 159, 161-63
Wood, LtCol James W., 164, 166
Wooden Elephant, 264
Worth Ridge, 104-106, 108, 114, 215
Wosmek, PFC David A., **217**

Wunder Beach, 58, 77, 303

Xuan, Mr. Nguyen, 122, 167
Xuan Tre, 122

Yang Brai, 88
Yokosuka, Japan, 262
Youngdale, MajGen Carl A., **62**, 84, 103, 239-40
Yusi, 2dLt Anthony H., 202

Zais, MajGen Melvin, USA, 2, 135
Zaro, Col William J., 117, 119-120, 190-91, 195-96, 284
Zavacki, Capt Francis, 163
Zone Interpretation, Planning, Preparation, and Overfly (ZIPPO) Team, 87
Zumwalt, VAdm Elmo R., 265-66, 313

The device reproduced on the back cover is the oldest military insignia in continuous use in the United States. It first appeared, as shown here, on Marine Corps buttons adopted in 1804. With the stars changed to five points this device has continued on Marine Corps buttons to the present day.

www.ingramcontent.com/pod-product-compliance
Lightning Source LLC
Chambersburg PA
CBHW080049190426
43201CB00035B/2149